POLITICS AND IRISH LIFE 1913–1921

POLITICS AND IRISH LIFE
1913–1921

*Provincial Experience of
War and Revolution*

DAVID FITZPATRICK

CORK UNIVERSITY PRESS

First published in Great Britain and Ireland in 1977
by Gill & Macmillan Ltd

First paperback edition 1998
published by
Cork University Press
University College
Cork
Ireland

© David Fitzpatrick 1977, 1998

All rights reserved. No part of this book may be reprinted or reproduced or utilized in any electronic, mechanical or other means, now known or hereafter invented, including photocopying and recording or otherwise without either the prior written permission of the Publishers or a licence permitting restricted copying in Ireland issued by the Irish Copyright Licensing Agency Ltd, The Irish Writers' Centre, 19 Parnell Square, Dublin 1.

British Library Cataloguing in Publication Data
A CIP catalogue record for this book is available from the British Library

ISBN 1 85918 074 0

Typeset by Seton Music Graphics, Ireland
Printed by Redwood Books, Great Britain

Contents

List of maps   vii
List of statistical tables   viii
Preface   ix
Prologue   xi
Acknowledgements   xv
Chronology   xvi

Part One
THE OLD ORDER

1   Forces of the Crown   3
    1. Before the Revolution   4
    2. Early Revolutionary Experience   7
    3. Reorganisation   16
    4. Response to Revolution   25

2   Protestants and Unionists   40
    1. Before the War   41
    2. War and Revolution   53

3   Home Rulers   72
    1. Before the War   73
    2. From War to Rising   90
    3. After the Rising   97

Part Two
THE NEW POLITICS

4   Sinn Féiners   107
    1. After the Rising   107
    2. From East Clare By-Election to General Election   122
    3. After the War   134

5   Revolutionary Administrators   138
    1. Administrative Experimentation   138
    2. Republican Courts   145
    3. Republican Local Government   154

6   Guerrilla Fighters   165
    1. After the Rising   166
    2. Guerrilla Warfare   178

7	Separatism and Social Change	192
	1. Labour and the Radical Urge	194
	2. Separatism and the Radical Urge	209
	3. Conservative Resurgence	220
	Epilogue	231
	Appendix	236
	Abbreviations	241
	Notes	242
	Bibliography	284
	Index	316

Maps

1. Co. Clare: Administrative Borders, as from 1899.   xix
   (Source: Philip's *Handy Administrative Atlas of Ireland*, London 1909.)
2. Co. Clare: Places mentioned in the text.   xx
   (Source: *Ibid.*)
3. Co. Clare: AOH and UIL, 1913–16.   84
   (Source: newspaper reports of local activity of these organisations, analysed in Appendix.)
4. Co. Clare: Irish National Volunteers, 1914–16.   87
   (Source: first newspaper reports of activity in each locality, analysed in Appendix.)
5. Co. Clare: Sinn Féin Clubs, 1917–19.   131
   (Source: *Ibid.*)
6. Co. Clare: IRA, 1921.   182
   (Source: 'Map showing operational area of 1st Western Division IRA', in Clare County Library, Ennis, presented by Colonel Tom McGrath, 2 i/c East Clare Brigade.)

Statistical Tables

1.1	Effectiveness of Law Enforcement, 1913–19	13
1.2	Enlistment of Policemen, 1913–21	22
1.3	Enlistment of Police Officers, 1920–21	22
1.4	Dismissals and Discharges of Policemen (weekly rate), 1920–21	33
1.5	Resignation of Policemen (weekly rate), 1920–21	33
1.6	Experience of Resigned Policemen, 1913–21	36
1.7	Background of Resigned Policemen, 1913–21	36
1.8	Causes of Police Resignations, 1913–21	37
3.1	Irish Recruitment, 1914–18	94
4.1	Mass Organisations, 1914–19	133
5.1	Republican Courts, 1921–22	154
5.2	Attendance at Meetings of Local Government Bodies, 1913–21	160
6.1	Background of Volunteers, 1917–19	170
6.2	Background of Volunteer Officers, 1919–21	185
6.3	IRA Engagements, 1921	187
7.1	Occupations and Industrial Status, 1926	197
7.2	Wages and Prices, 1907–21	201
7.3	Distribution of Land, 1904–20	201
7.4	ITGWU, 1916–20	203
A.1	Collocations of Various Political Organisations	237
A.2	Geographical Distributions of Various Political Organisations	238
A.3	Claremen Prominent in Politics, both Priests and Laymen	238
A.4	Subjects of Discussion at Political Meetings	239

Preface

OVER the two decades since this book first appeared, the circumstances of Irish historical research have been transformed. Students of the Irish revolution no longer work under the bewitching dome of the British Museum, in the panelled round room of the Public Record Office at Chancery Lane, or in the castellated record tower of Dublin Castle where their predecessors inhaled the decomposing powder of the state papers. Instead, they struggle with squadrons of ancestor-hunters for space and service in antiseptic search-rooms of concrete and glass, rigorously administered by trained and conscientious archivists aware that each delivery of a record reduces its lifespan. Every scholar should be grateful that the public records of both Ireland and Britain are now far better conserved, better listed, and (at least potentially, in microform) more accessible than before. The belated introduction of statutory control over Irish official archives was only part of a broader realisation that the old haphazard ways, veering unpredictably between secretiveness and negligence, could no longer meet the ever-growing demand for historical information. Yet, in the process, something of the joy and excitement of the historian's quest has been lost. Never again will a research student guiltily tip-toe along a spiral staircase in a thirteenth-century tower, scramble up a rickety ladder, and rifle through never-opened packages of uncatalogued documents concealing Ireland's untold histories.

Never again, moreover, will students of the Irish revolution be privileged to meet those who experienced it as participants, onlookers or victims. In 1972, when I began my work in Clare, the country still teemed with veteran Volunteers, Sinn Féiners, and even former Home Rule activists, who reminded me that history, for those who make it, means more than documentation. Alas, the men and women who answered or parried my questions about revolutionary Clare, and whose names appear in my acknowledgements and bibliography, are long since dead. Many of the documents and photographs that they so generously allowed me to inspect have probably disappeared, with the break-up of households and the ritual destruction of personal papers after funerals. More than that, the familial, social and religious organisation of the West of Ireland has largely collapsed over the last quarter-century, leaving only scattered remnants of the rigid system delineated by Arensberg and Kimball in the 1930s and still recognisable, if embattled, when my Australian eye first widened in rural Clare. The visitor no longer marvels at the absence of 'ordinary crime', symbolised by the convention of leaving houses and cars unlocked, at the obstinate preservation of small and 'uneconomic' family farms, often employing archaic methods and equipment, or at the punctiliousness of religious observance. For every priest, farmer, teapot or cabbage, there may now be found a reflexologist, computer analyst, espresso-maker or capiscum. Though Clare remains rightly celebrated for hospitality, this is now often dispensed by German, Dutch, American or English settlers in search of the simple life. The historian of rural Ireland, when engaged in 'fieldwork', no longer has the advantage of observing at first hand the undeniable imprint of traditional attitudes and social organisation. As 'heritage centres' multiply, the living heritage has disintegrated.

This book, then, is a product of its time. Since 1977, many private and official records relating to the revolutionary period have been released, some of which would doubtless challenge or amplify my findings. These additions must be balanced against the loss of access to personal testimony, and the destruction or closure of certain collections (occasionally through the misguided application of official regulations to private archives). Today's researcher would probably ask different questions, and might consider my integrated approach to society, economics and politics as being naïvely mechanistic. Indeed, my own approach to writing history has changed markedly, though I neither disown this book nor repudiate its analysis of Irish political logic. Its approach and conclusions have not, in my view, been discredited by the few subsequent attempts to explore local and everyday experience in the revolutionary period. Thus Peter Hart's outstanding study of Cork, though revealing that revolutionaries in that county were disproportionately townsmen rather than farmers' sons, also detects many resonances of 'my' Clare. The achievement of a comprehensive account of the Irish revolution remains as elusive as ever. Meanwhile, I hope that this book, unchanged apart from the correction of a dozen minor slips, will prove useful to new readers trying to make sense of that thrilling yet perplexing phase of Ireland's history.

David Fitzpatrick
Trinity College Dublin
October 1997

Prologue

THIS book explores Irish political behaviour during a period of extraordinary social upheaval, reaching from the passing of Home Rule through the House of Commons in 1913 to the signature of the Anglo-Irish 'Treaty' in 1921. During those nine years the conditions of Irish life were transformed by the European war and the revolutionary turmoil which followed the Armistice. Concurrently the forms and goals of Irish Nationalist politics were transformed as the dream of the Republic displaced that of Home Rule and as the construction of distinctively Irish institutions displaced the exploitation of existing British institutions. There has probably never been a time when politics—always essential to Irish life—took up so large a part of Irish energy and impinged so insistently upon Irish experience. The abruptness of social upheaval and the intensity of political activity together make this period peculiarly attractive to anatomists of the Irish political mind.

In fact, of course, 'the Irish political mind' does not exist. There are, and were, many sorts of political mind in Ireland, each the product of a particular social environment and experience of life. Ulstermen, both Nationalist and Unionist, acted according to political precepts radically different from those prevalent in Leinster, Munster and Connaught, analysis of which would require another and very different book. Even among Southern Nationalists there is no reason to assume that priests and publicans, farmers and labourers, landlords and tenants were all guided by the same rules of political behaviour, let alone the same political aims. Irish Nationalism, both before and after the 1916 Rising, was remarkably eclectic in its appeal, capable of drawing strength from social groups with sharply divergent interests and outlooks. Many of its peculiarities arose from the need to cater for disparate political minds, offering something to all without threatening the interests of any. The anatomist, therefore, must examine the experience of many groupings of politically minded Irishmen, as well as the patterns of behaviour and modes of thought common to several such groupings. This book is divided into seven chapters, each of which analyses the political contribution made by a group sharing a sense of common political involvement, and its reactions to the activities of others. Part One concerns 'The Old Order' of Irish politics—those charged with carrying out administrative directives (Crown forces), those eager to avoid transition to a native administration (Unionists), and those seeking that transition through Home Rule. Part Two concerns 'The New Politics' of those who built up the new Nationalist movement which repudiated Home Rule as its goal, who built up a new system of public administration to supplant existing institutions, and who fought a guerrilla campaign to paralyse the forces of the Crown. My last chapter examines the interplay between this new 'separatist' or 'Republican' movement and the campaigns which gathered strength concurrently to promote the sectional interests of labourers and farmers. In short, this book depicts many political minds thinking about each other, many groups, societies and institutions antagonising, influencing and imitating each other, each contributing to that extraordinary convulsion which I shall term, for want of a better name, a revolution.

The study of popular politics can only be attempted if intimate, personal records survive concerning the background, activities and associations of those involved. Questions concerning the social characteristics and status of participants, the overlapping of apparently distinct political groups, and the process by which political organisations won popular support can only be answered (if at all) by local study. Therefore much of this book concerns the history of a single county, and many crucial issues are analysed with the help of hitherto unused or unknown local sources generously shown to me by many people and institutions (see my acknowledgements and bibliography). Many other issues, however, may better be studied by reference to sources of wider range, especially those concerning the national leadership and organisation of political movements. Where local evidence has been used to suggest patterns applicable to some larger region than the locality involved, I have attempted to provide corroboration from other localities where obtainable. Where national evidence has been used to illuminate the history of localities, I have sought to relate the intentions of national leaders to the realities of local execution. Until that distant day when all surviving archives from every part of Ireland have been listed, examined and analysed, it will not be possible to write either a truly national or a truly local history. If this book should make either task seem less daunting, it will have been worth writing.

My setting is Co. Clare. Curiously, this county has been subjected to more intensive sociological and anthropological analysis than any other part of rural Ireland, although its history has remained obscure. In some respects early twentieth-century Clare was typical of rural Ireland, in some respects a caricature, in some respects unique. Geographically and demographically, it lies between Connaught and Munster, between the barren wilderness of Galway and the rich pasturage of Limerick and Tipperary. Clare is something of an island, unusually isolated from its neighbours. From Corranroo to Loop Head its border is Galway Bay and the Atlantic Ocean, from Loop Head to Whitegate it is the River Shannon (bridged at five points only) and Lough Derg, from Whitegate to Ballinruan it is rugged mountain, from Ballinruan to Corranroo it is in part the desolate Burren. Early in this century Clare's main links with the outside world were the railway and main road from Limerick to Galway, which passed through the county town of Ennis and roughly bisected the county. Even that main road, according to a roadbook of 1908, was 'poor' in the north and 'an uninteresting road, rather bumpy, taken as a whole, almost all the way' in the south. Along this road and railway, from Limerick and Cork, bumped and rattled most of Clare's supplies of wholesale goods, for secondary industry was negligible in the county. Limerick, in fact, was the mercantile capital of Clare; Ennis the agricultural capital and central market; Boston, perhaps, its spiritual capital. For the aspirations of Claremen and women dissatisfied with the monotonous life of the countryside were turned not towards

Limerick, Dublin or London, but towards the United States of America. Thus in 1911 less than 10,000 Clare-born people were living in other Irish counties, yet nearly 14,000 had emigrated (mostly to America) during the previous decade.¹ The eyes of Clare people were turned either inwards or outwards, but seldom sideways towards Dublin. Dublin, unlike Paris or London, has never dictated the social or political aspirations of great numbers of people in the provinces. It is a regrettable historiographical accident that the political history of the Irish Revolution has hitherto been focused upon Dublin, as though Dublin were the spiritual capital of Ireland. This book concerns that part of the Clare people whose eyes were turned inwards, whose hopes and dreams could only be realised in or near their own parish, at home.

Clare in the revolutionary period was remarkable only for being quintessentially 'Irish' (if to be 'Irish' is to conform to some historical caricature rather than to contemporary reality). Physical anthropologists have been attracted by the peculiar shape of its people, which seems to fit everyman's conception of the timeless peasant. In no other western county, so a Harvard team discovered in the 1930s, did women have such round heads, men such broad foreheads, broad shoulders, ruddy skins or bad teeth. Social anthropologists, also from Harvard, found in Clare a society obstinately resistant to modernising influences, densely interbred with a highly developed sense of kinship and mutual responsibility, informally governed by groups of village elders, a society tightly controlled according to traditional modes of social organisation. The casual visitor to Clare, overwhelmed by gratuitous hospitality and good cheer, might not suspect that his benefactors were the victims of a powerful and constrictive social tyranny. But the Harvard student perceived that, in Clare, 'comedy and laughter soften the sharpness of social controls. They are the velvet glove that clothes the iron hand.'²

The 1911 census confirms that Clare was in many respects an unusually homogeneous 'peasant' county. It was the county with the greatest proportion of Roman Catholics (98 per cent) and the smallest proportion of overseas-born residents (0.9 per cent). Its marriage rate was unusually low, its emigration rate unusually high. Over two-thirds of its occupied people were engaged in agriculture, and over 90 per cent lived in rural districts. Over one-third was able to speak Irish, a proportion exceeded in only four other counties; and one of the few traditional customs capable of demographic analysis, the habit of contracting marriages on or about Shrove Tuesday, was uncommonly persistent in Clare. Few of its people were illiterate, but far fewer still had experienced the disruptive impact of 'superior education'.³ The staple industry of the county was the raising of store cattle to be sent to richer pastures for fattening. The 'cyder-orchards' for which southern Clare was famous in Arthur Young's time had long since disappeared by 1913, and the proportion of agricultural land under tillage was the smallest for any county. Clare had more than its share of under-exploited grasslands, and the progress of land purchase had been abnormally slow. The median Clare peasant occupied a second-class house on a plot of land slightly larger than the national norm, but because most of the county was unusually arid, the value of his product was comparatively small. Yet for all the poverty and aridity of the countryside, its people, in the opinion of one observer in January 1914, viewed their lot with a 'placid air of contentment and resignation. . . . It would seem as though, despite all their loneliness and hardship and privation, they are as happy in their own way as the American millionaire in his automobile.'[4]

In preparing this account of the remarkable transformation of a 'placid' and contented people into a revolutionary throng, I have been helped and encouraged by several academic colleagues—especially Georgina, Sheila and Dorothy Fitzpatrick (all of whom caused the mutilation of parts of the text) and Professor Nicholas Mansergh (who suspected that this book could not be written yet gave me invaluable help in writing it). Brian Fitzpatrick passed on to me a measure of Irish blood, and an obstinate determination to write history about plain people rather than the famous or the powerful. The British Council, the Smuts Commonwealth Research Fund, Trinity College, Cambridge, and, most recently, Nuffield College, Oxford, have kindly given me means of subsistence during the years of preparation. But most of all I am grateful to those countless people of Clare who gave me so much of their time, knowledge and advice when I arrived, usually unheralded and unknown, at their doors. In my wanderings through Clare, I am happy to record, I never suffered such a rebuff as one of my precursors, the agricultural statistician Hely Dutton. 'Amongst many others,' he wrote in 1808, 'I made a personal application to Mr Young near Quin, explaining the nature of my pursuits (I was introduced to him *twice* before) and requesting information; his only answer, after hesitating some time and a vacant stare, was humph! and he very politely stepped into his coach box, and drove his family home from the church of Quin, where I had the misfortune to disturb his reveries.'[5] Once only I was refused information upon being mistaken for a British intelligence agent. I shall never forget the generosity of my helpers in and of Clare. This book is dedicated to all of them.

Acknowledgements

THE custodians of the following institutions kindly permitted me to consult, and in many cases quote from, documentary collections in their hands, full details of which may be found in the Bibliography: the Beaverbrook Library, Bodleian Library, British Museum, Clare County Council, Clare County Library, Corpus Christi College Library (Oxford), Ennis Urban District Council Museum, Imperial War Museum, Irish Valuation Office, Kerry County Library, King's College Centre for Military Archives (London), Limerick City Library, National Library of Ireland, Nuffield College Library, Plunkett Foundation for Co-operative Studies, Public Record Office and State Paper Office (Dublin), Public Record Office (London), Public Record Office of Northern Ireland, Representative Church Body Library (Dublin), St Flannan's College (Ennis), Trinity College Library (Dublin) and University College Archives Department (Dublin).

The following owners permitted me to consult and quote from documentary collections: Mr Bernard Barrett, Miss Peg Barrett, Very Rev. Dr Bourke, the late Mr Seán Burke, Mrs Tom Carroll, Mr Mark Bonham Carter, Her Majesty, Queen Elizabeth II, Rev. Éamonn Gaynor, Mr John Guthrie, Most Rev. Dr Harty, Mr Patrick Hehir, the late Anne, Lady Inchiquin, Rev. Mr Jenkins, Mr Michael Kilmartin, Dr Edward MacLysaght, Mr Seán MacNamara, the late Mr Anthony Malone, Miss Aggie Marrinan, the trustees of the late General Richard Mulcahy's papers, Mr Conor O'Callaghan-Westropp, Rev. Séamus O'Dea, the late Mr Art O'Donnell, Messrs Edward O'Loghlen and Gus O'Loghlen, Major A. J. MacG. Percival, Messrs Michael Shannon, J. C. Smedley and Robert E. Tottenham, Mrs Harriet Waldron, Mr Patrick Ward and Major C. J. Wilson.

Chronology

[This index is confined to notable events in the history of Clare, 1913–21.]

1913

October. Rapid expansion of AOH in Clare under direction of D. J. Madden, headquarters organiser.

1914

January. Elections for UDCs (in Clare: Ennis and Kilrush, plus Kilkee Town Commissioners).
17 March. First Clare branch established, Irish National Volunteers (Ennis).
June. Elections for county councils, Boards of Guardians and RDCs (in Clare: Ballyvaughan, Corofin, Ennis, Ennistymon, Killadysert, Kilrush and Scariff, plus RDCs only in Tulla and Limerick No. 2).
10 October. Clare County Board, Volunteers, avoids split after squabble between Redmondites and MacNeillites on Dublin Provisional Committee.
18 October. Clare wins All-Ireland Hurling Final.
24–25 October. First headquarters inspections of Clare National Volunteers held (postponed from previous weekend because of hurling final).

1915

April. Ernest Blythe begins organising MacNeillite Irish Volunteers, Clare.
12 July. Blythe first man in Clare to be imprisoned under DORR (for disobeying order to leave district).

1916

c. 16 April. Irish Volunteers divided into battalions in Clare in preparation for Rising.
23–24 April. No Rising in Clare.
May. One Clareman court-martialled after Rising (of 182 in all Ireland), and about 12 Claremen interned in England (of about 2,000 from all Ireland).
30 September. First court martial of a Clareman under DORR since Rising.

1917

early February. Clare Brigade, Irish Volunteers, established.
5 March. First Clare attack on policeman by Volunteers.
late March. First Clare branch of Cumann na mBan reported (Ennis).
27 May. First Clare Sinn Féin club reported (Ballycorick; others already existed but were still disorganised and did not yet seek newspaper publicity).
7 June. Willie Redmond killed in France.

11 July. De Valera's victory in East Clare by-election announced.
10 August. Four Claremen inaugurate campaign of repudiating authority of British courts and hunger-striking to attract international attention.

1918

24 February. Fatal shooting by police of Clare cattle-driver.
28 February. Clare declared Special Military Area to allow suppression of agrarian disorder. Restrictions on meetings and personal movement soon imposed.
18 March. First Clare Sinn Féiner killed by military.
2 April. *Clare Champion* closed down under DORR (reappeared 28 September).
20 April. First general meeting, County Clare Ratepayers' and Farmers' Association (Ennis).
21 April. Anti-Conscription Pledge administered in or near many churches.
25 May. First Clare branch of ITGWU formed (Newmarket-on-Fergus).
16 August. Restrictions on personal movement relaxed, but county remains Special Military Area.
7 September. Diehard 'Callers' win control of Co. Clare Unionist Club.
15 September. Ennis United Trades and Labour Council formed, upon visit of headquarters organiser, William O'Brien.
December. General election. Clare seats won unopposed by Sinn Féin candidates de Valera (East Clare) and Brian O'Higgins (West Clare).

1919

1 March. Mid-Clare Brigade established (also East and West Clare Brigades, Irish Volunteers, formed at about this time).
c. July. First court inspired by Dáil decree set up in West Clare (regularly established, 1 November).
July–August. First widespread attacks on police patrols and barracks in Clare.
4 August. First policemen killed by Clare Volunteers (no more till April 1920).
8 August. All meetings, including fairs and markets, proclaimed in Clare.
13 August. Various organisations declared illegal in Clare.
4 and 29 November. Landowners, including diehard Unionists, meet to deplore ban on fairs and markets.

1920

January. UDC elections, in which Home Rulers and other non-Sinn Féin candidates score well in Clare.
late January. General ban on Clare fairs and markets lifted.
4 April. Numerous empty police barracks destroyed, many in Clare.
14 April. First savage attack on civilian crowd by British forces in Clare.
June. RDC and county council elections, massively won by Sinn Féin.
June. First known arrests of Clare priests for seditious activities.
24 July. Clare County Council draws up scheme for breaking with British LGB, which is approved by the Dáil and formally put into effect by the council on 1 November.

22 September. First large-scale ambush by Clare Volunteers of British forces (Rineen).
November. First soldiers killed by Volunteers in Clare.

1921

4 January. Martial law inaugurated in Clare.
27 February. First admitted 'official reprisals' in Clare (Lissycasey).
May. 1st Western Division, Irish Volunteers, nominally established.
June. General election. Four Sinn Féin candidates elected unopposed for Clare (de Valera, O'Higgins, Patrick Brennan, J. J. Liddy).
June. Six 'Big Houses' (unoccupied) destroyed by Volunteers.
27 October. 1st Western Division effectively established (including all Volunteer companies in Clare and South Galway).
22 December. Clare County Council urges ratification of Anglo-Irish Treaty of 6 December.

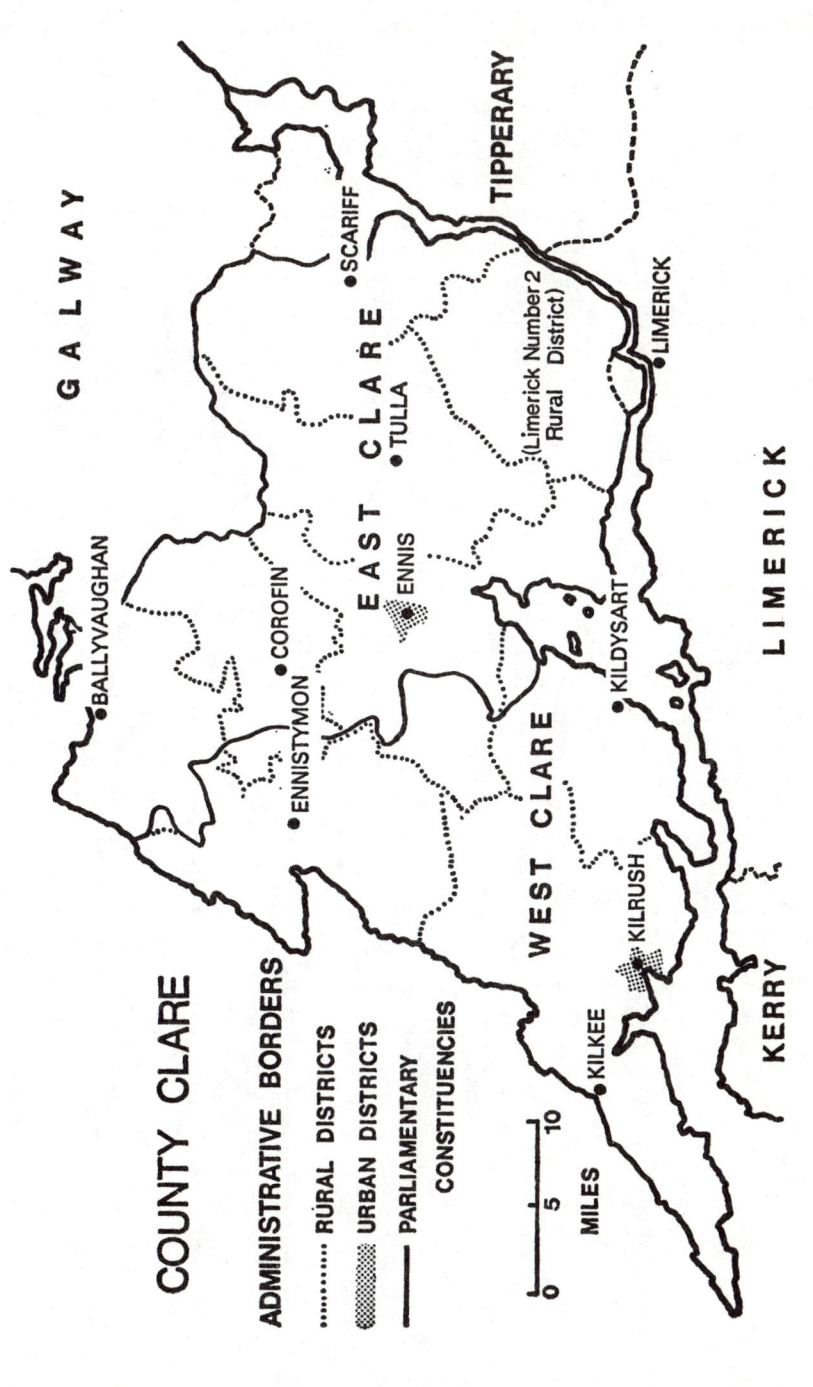

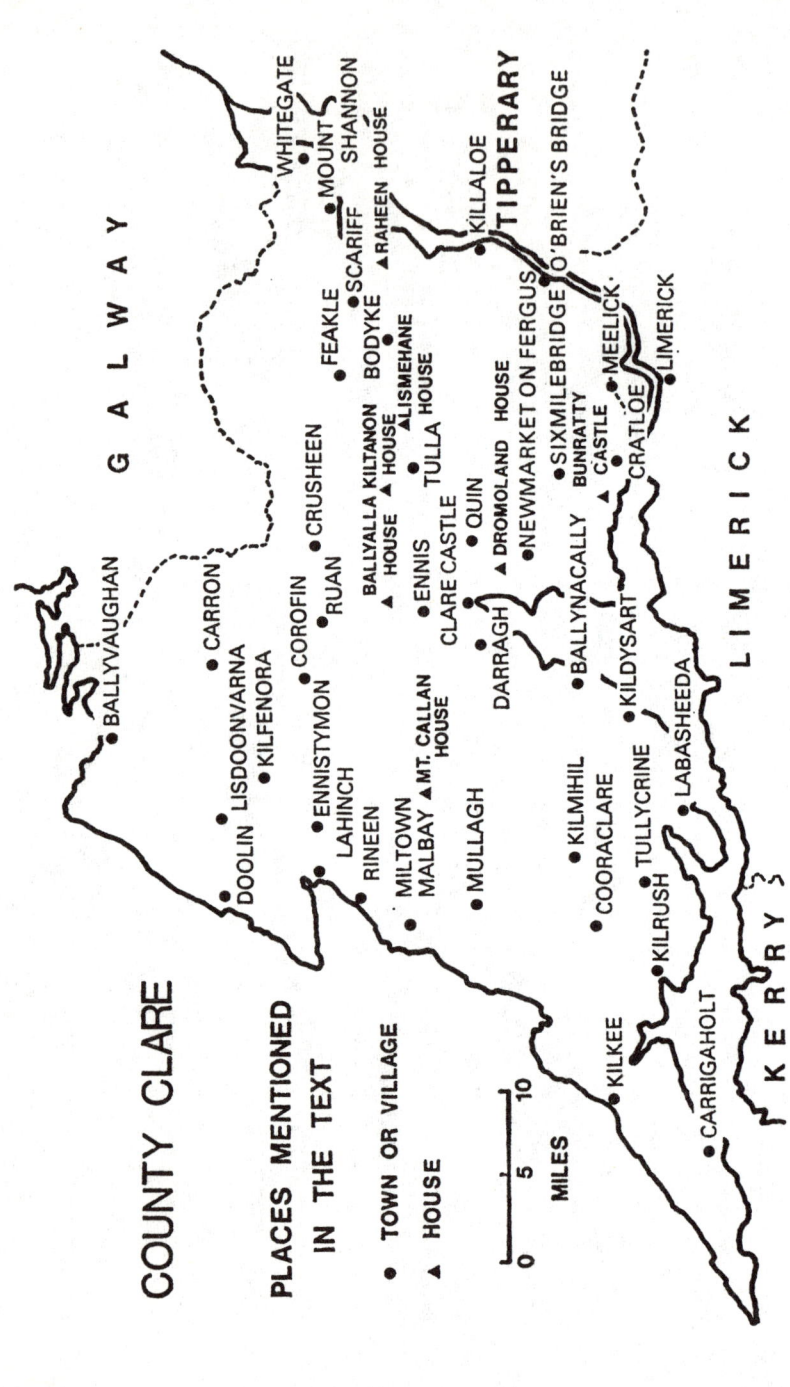

Part One
THE OLD ORDER

1

Forces of the Crown

> Blest is the sweet relief,
> Deep is the breath we draw,
> Safe is the old belief
> In justice, order and law.
>
> Calm in the wild alarm,
> Loyal, brave and true,
> Trust in the strong right arm
> Of the Guardian Man in Blue.
>
> 'JUSTIN', *Constabulary Gazette*, 27 May 1916

> That the harp of Green Erin may never be without a string while there is a gut in a 'peeler'.
>
> Spike Island prisoner, 13 October 1921[1]

NO VICTIMS of the Irish Revolution suffered keener humiliation than the police and military forces of the Crown. As the chief visible representatives of British government in the Irish provinces, policemen and soldiers were made the chief target of revolutionary abuse and revolutionary violence. Personal hatred of one's neighbour is a more potent emotion than abstract hatred of one's government; in the person of a uniformed constable or private, a 'peeler' or a 'Tommy', provincial revolutionaries found a fit object for both species of hate. In disrupting the work of the Crown forces, moreover, the revolutionaries aimed not merely to focus the angry emotions underlying nationalism, but to do practical damage to the whole system of British administration. For Dublin Castle and the British government expected their Irish soldiers and policemen to provide detailed information on the mood as well as the behaviour of the Irish people, to give the alarm as well as to arrest malefactors or suppress riots. Furthermore, Irish policemen did much of the routine administrative work entrusted to civil servants in other parts of the United Kingdom. The Crown forces were not only the most accessible manifestations of government but also its principal Irish instruments.

Policemen, and to some extent soldiers, were not merely functionaries but members of the community, not immune to the psychological power which popular movements exert upon the individual. During the Irish Revolution appalling strain was placed upon the police by an increasingly co-ordinated campaign. Their sources of information dried up; their attempts to execute government policy were thwarted; and, worst of all, their right to participate in Irish society was strenuously challenged. Unlike Protestant landlords or Irish Parliamentary Party organisers, whose predicament is the subject of the next two chapters, Crown servants could not sidestep the campaign directed at them.

Except by resignation, desertion or treachery, they could not escape responsibility for the execution of policies over which they had no control. Although their information was vital to Dublin Castle's analyses of Irish politics, their advice was frequently disregarded. The pathos which followed in the wake of the Irish Revolution is nowhere more poignantly suggested than by the story of their sufferings in revolutionary Clare.

1. BEFORE THE REVOLUTION

'Well, sir, we have very hard duty in the County of Clare. We have heard them talking of Belfast, but what about Clare, with its moonlighting and cattle-driving and every kind of things? Are there any men in Ireland working like ourselves?' 'Surely we are not going to be ground down for a lifetime in this backward and almost uncivilized place without any hope whatever of getting a transfer. . . . I have never seen a decent horse race, coursing match, football match, or athletic sports. I have had very little leave.' These querulous voices remind us that Co. Clare, with its long history of impenetrable agrarian conflict and insoluble crime and its lack of more wholesome agrarian entertainments, was not a popular posting for Irish policemen in the early years of this century. After 1907 the county was officially considered to be 'in a state of disturbance' and was supplied with an additional establishment of police, although until 1918 no soldiers were posted regularly in Clare. By the end of 1913 no less than 487 policemen had the misfortune to be serving in Clare, each with 1,618 acres and 214 people (on average) to patrol. Only Galway had a higher density of policemen to people, and only the East Riding of Cork had more police stations in a single county.[2] The reverberations of the 'Land War' were unusually persistent in Clare; and as a result the large constable with his carbine and dark green uniform was unusually prominent in the Clare community in pre-revolutionary days.

By 1914, however, Clare's black reputation was based on its past history rather than its present condition. It was true, as George McElroy (the Resident Magistrate at Ennis) reported just before the outbreak of war, that 'in cases of Family and other private disputes' Claremen sometimes reverted to direct agrarian methods—'so quick and effective'—rather than appealing to the police or the courts. There was, too (so Mathias McDonnell Bodkin, the County Court judge, believed), 'a vague, uneasy feeling in some minds that it is not wholly honourable to assist the police and the courts in the administration of the criminal law. Get rid, I beseech those who hear me, and those whom my words may reach, of this cowardly superstition.' But Clare's place of dishonour in the tables of Irish criminality was already slipping. Over the five years up to 1914 only three counties had had worse rates of indictable offences; none had exceeded its propensity to indictable drunkenness. But in 1913 Clare had only the sixth worst record of non-indictable offences, in 1914 the seventh. Still more significantly, it dropped to fourteenth and twentieth places respectively in the scale of indictable offences. In 1914 Judge Bodkin, despite his fears concerning local superstition, reflected that an Irish judge could flatter himself that his life was useful as it was pleasant. And the Resident Magistrate at Kilkee, less apprehensive than his brother at Ennis, reported that 'The people in my district except in agrarian disputes are well disposed towards the law and each other.'³ Clare was no longer remarkable for its lawlessness, and the duties of a policeman in Clare were very much the same as those of his counterparts throughout rural Ireland.

The duties of an Irish constable were not confined to detection of breaches of the law. To a greater extent than his English counterpart, the Irishman was expected to anticipate offences and criminal techniques as well as to detect them. 'Intelligent anticipation of the possible inventions of minds trained to deception, and genius to defeat them, were developed in the force to an uncanny point.' Policemen countered alibis before they were offered, just as criminals designed them before the crime. Irish constables prosecuted minor cases themselves (typical offences in Clare were said to be 'a pig wandering on the road, or a goat trespassing'). As prophets, pursuers and prosecutors, they needed to know the people of their adopted districts as intimately as a postmistress might. In this they were helped by their employment as enumerators for the census, emigration returns and agricultural statistics. It is not surprising that a section of each week's *Constabulary Gazette* comprised arithmetical tests. The arrival of a stranger, always a matter of moment in rural Ireland, was not merely to be wondered at. 'On the appearance of any suspicious stranger in any sub-district the Constabulary should not rest till they have discovered who or what he is.' A militant antagonist of the police has rightly remarked that they had 'an unrivalled knowledge of the inhabitants and a shrewd understanding of Irish character'.⁴ 'The routine work of the old RIC involved observation of human character no less exact than that expected of a novelist.

Like novelists and postmistresses, Irish policemen in 1914 felt themselves ill-rewarded for their many-faceted labours. Basic rates of pay had not increased since 1872. Since 1909 each year had seen more resignations from the RIC than its predecessor. The resignation rate was worrying rather than calamitous: 944 over the five years 1909–13, including 24 posted in Clare (of whom 14 had resigned in order to 'better their position' or join other police forces). But in 1914 the government was alarmed enough to announce that a committee of inquiry would consider the grievances of both Irish police forces. Men from all but two districts in Clare submitted memorials. Pay was, of course, the central issue, and all six memorials from Clare requested pay increases of as much as 25 per cent. But the restriction of personal freedom was almost as common a grievance. Five of the six Clare memorials complained of discrimination against married men. Although 38 per cent of RIC men were married in 1913, the practice was discouraged. Before seven years' service it was forbidden. Thereafter its enjoyment was limited to spells of no more than four consecutive hours out of barracks—if one were senior enough. Junior married constables were obliged to house their wives within the barracks, where they were condemned to the 'demoralising and repulsive practice' of sharing the only lavatory with prisoners and bachelors. Social freedom was further restricted by prohibition of policemen's wives keeping shops or taking lodgers within their husbands' counties. The tone of most complaints heard by the committee of inquiry was mournful, self-pitying, seldom belligerent. But faced with a sharp decline in the pool of acceptable candidates for recruitment, the committee agreed to recommend pay increases, while adding that this was 'not the time for considering or suggesting reforms of an unsettling character'.[5]

Despite their indignation at official maltreatment, rural policemen in 1914 retained much of their traditional self-respect—even self-importance. This was essentially a function of the degree of deference popularly accorded them and the social status assigned them by their betters. When the constable appeared at ceremonial occasions or riots splendid in his helmet, complemented sometimes by sword, boxspurs and silver crest, he could imagine that he had transcended his usually humble origins. So could County Inspector Roberts of Clare, once a school tutor, when Ethel, Lady Inchiquin and members of the Clare Sanatorium Committee presented his wife with a green leather suitcase initialled in gold, or when he himself danced with the daughters of the Big Houses at the hunt ball. Pre-war policemen touched their caps less often than other caps were touched to them, and they guarded their high position jealously. Their pay demands were often couched in terms of social status. A Limerick memorial in 1914 submitted that 'The present rate of pay is quite unable to maintain them in that degree of comfort that they consider is due to their station in life.' The sad result of government parsimony, so Constable O'Shea from Clare asserted, was to coarsen the social calibre of the force: 'I have not the slightest hesitation in saying that they [the recent recruits] are a very inferior class, and there would be no chance of their being taken into the police some years ago at all. . . . They come from labourers now, and some years ago the great majority of them were all farmers' sons.' And before long the despised labourers themselves were earning more in menial occupations than in the RIC: as the *Gazette* lamented in 1920, the constable was 'a vastly superior man to the railway porter and the agricultural labourer, and yet, behold how they have advanced!'[6]

On the eve of war Irish policemen had not yet lost pride in their high status, despite growing fears of competition from below. They had experienced nothing to shatter their self-importance. They remained fairly efficient, and the rules of conduct they had learned at depot still seemed relevant. During the early years of the European war their pride remained, but their grievance against the government intensified. Despite rapid wartime inflation, police pay rates rose only meagrely. Between 1914 and 1916 the Irish agricultural wholesale price index rose by 60 per cent, and from 1916 to 1918 by 40 per cent. In such economic conditions the statutory increases awarded in 1916 and 1918 seemed grotesquely inadequate. Junior sergeants and inspectors received increases of 10 per cent and 11 per cent respectively in 1916, and 30 per cent and 27 per cent in 1918. Junior constables were offered nothing in 1916, and 55 per cent in 1918. 'War bonuses' were awarded to all ranks just after the Easter Rising, and by December 1917 they amounted to £14 6s per annum for an unmarried RIC man—27 per cent of a junior constable's pay, and 16 per cent of a 1914 sergeant's. The consolation to be derived from war bonuses was diminished by the uncertainty of their post-war perpetuation.[7] The war, which brought prosperity to the farmer and rising real wages to the labourer, brought the Irish policeman fear of poverty and of subsiding status.

The government's wartime parsimony was made practicable by virtually freezing the RIC. Recruiting was suspended for fifteen months from mid-1915, making feasible the neglect of young constables in the 1916 statutory award. Thereafter it was allowed to fall well below pre-war rates. Retirements on pension were suspended almost simultaneously, unless for medical reasons or 'for the interests of the public service'. Only 82 retirements were approved during the next twenty-two months, 123 less than during the preceding twelve months. Early in the war, however, temporary enlistment of policemen in the army threatened seriously to deplete the force. Enlistment offered several attractions: it saved the state some ten shillings weekly for each man reduced to army pay, provided the army with men trained in the rudiments of rifle handling, and appealed to the policeman's carefully nurtured patriotism. In October 1914 the force was able to select 200 volunteers by ballot. But of these 66 subsequently withdrew, mainly, so the Inspector-General believed, 'in consequence of family pressure'. In all some 689 men and 36 officers enlisted for military service. Enlistment was limited both by police recalcitrance, fostered largely by the poor wages and conditions offered, and by official reluctance to strip the RIC of its youngest and most energetic members. In October 1915 the Inspector-General wrote that no more than 500 more policemen could be spared. Next month the Under-Secretary rejected a Recruiting Department request for the transfer of up to fourteen police officers, vaguely referring to 'existing circumstances and having regard to the state of the country under conditions which may shortly arise'. The government quietly killed enlistment from the police by declining to make the inducements to enlist more attractive. For the parsimonious mind it made good sense to banish the problem of attracting police recruits by cutting down recruiting targets and to keep up the strength of the force by rendering withdrawal still more unpalatable than staying in it. But if parsimony tended to freeze the force, it also made it older and feebler—a tendency enhanced by losses to the army. Thus the proportion of men who had served for six years or more rose from 70 per cent in 1914 to 78 per cent in 1920.[8] The giants of the RIC, none of them less than 5 ft 8 in. high and 36 in. about the chest, were beginning to totter.

2. EARLY REVOLUTIONARY EXPERIENCE

Until 1916 the self-esteem of Irish policemen was threatened more by government niggardliness than popular contempt. Even after the Easter Rising a policeman's lot, in Clare at least, was not an unduly unhappy one. As an Ulsterman sent to Clare in a mobile column early in May recorded, 'We found that the Clare people were not so slow as we Northerns believed them to be. Everywhere we met with kindness.' In Cahir's bar the visitors overheard folk-tales in Irish about a departed County Inspector. They strolled along the banks of the Fergus, clinched bargains in cattle, horses, sheep and swine 'just for the fun of the thing', played 'tug-of-war, football, handball, step-dancing in the evenings, and the usual game of nap'. A friendly local paper remarked that the men seemed to be enjoying 'an easy holiday about the town'. In Clare, after all, there had been no Easter Rising; the revolutionary new moon was clouded over.

In September, however, the County Inspector noted a turn for the worse. The resumption of police recruiting had not brought any response, and local people were now 'considerably' less friendly towards policemen than before the Rising. By December he felt that 'As a force they are regarded as enemies, and are not made welcome as in other counties.' Feeling against the police gradually intensified during 1917. In October he reported: 'The people appear to regard the police as their enemies, and have ceased all friendly intercourse with them. Shops continue to supply provisions but in many cases they would prefer that the police did not come to them.'

November 1917 brought a worrying report. Turf and potatoes at a small police post had been 'maliciously destroyed'. Next month sawmillers stopped work until the County Inspector agreed to take delivery of no further wood from the mill. The inspector was sufficiently alarmed to cite this boycott in his urgent request for reinforcement. Being an invisible but effective weapon, the boycott flourished during the subsequent months of public restrictions imposed by the military. By April 1918 most barracks were no longer supplied locally with turf, butter, eggs or milk. The policeman's position was 'not an enviable one just now'. In September it seemed less enviable still when unsympathetic magistrates fined a constable for assault and damage to a horse's reins, after he had seized a bag of turf which its owner had refused to sell him.[9]

Between 1918 and 1920 attempts to humiliate and isolate Irish policemen spread and diversified. In many districts social and sexual isolation was added to economic isolation. Grocers in one village in Clare were warned: 'Well if you want to stop bloodshed keep policemen out of your public houses.' An ex-soldier was informed by armed men that he or his family would be shot if he joined the RIC, which he did not. The husband of a servant at police barracks was instructed to 'prepare to meet his God'. Girlfriends of policemen, soldiers and coastguards were frequently subjected to a singularly vicious punishment, still in common use in Ireland: the removal of their hair. Poachers no longer guided policemen and their friends to plentiful streams on lazy afternoons, a deprivation which one keen fisherman singled out as one of those 'untold hardships' which the rise of Sinn Féin inflicted on 'that finest of Police Forces, the R.I.C.' Even at Sunday Mass policemen's creature comforts were withdrawn. In April 1920 a constable in North Tipperary reported that the pew given to the police six years earlier by a friendly colonel had been removed from the chapel: 'We were forced to kneel on the floor to-day; occasionally I could see persons looking in our direction, and laughing.' The pragmatic parish priest brushed aside police complaints, declaring that it was 'better not to mind small things'.[10]

Another instrument in the spiritual humiliation of policemen was that unworthy but insidious device, the anonymous letter. In 1918, for instance, three letters were delivered to the Inspector-General's office denouncing a sergeant posted at the west coast of Clare. He was accused of 'courting married women and when he's not doing that he has them up in his office calling them off the

Street'. A second letter added menacingly: 'This is my last report about Sergeant L— his conduct is simply dreadful wont be tolerated much longer in town or country his continually after a married woman in S— whose husband is in the navy.' Another nameless correspondent invited the Inspector-General to apply to the parish priest for further details. Astonishingly, the local inspector did so, remarking that he had confidence in the canon 'as he is one of the old stock'. But priest and police repudiated the allegations, the priest being more concerned with the lady's morals than the sergeant's. The sergeant was said to have been unusually active in pursuing Sinn Féiners, having terrorised a scout for the local Volunteer corps with a blackthorn stick. The first two letters were ascribed to this scout, brother of a notable Volunteer. The alleged author, so concerned at conduct which seemed to him a 'disgrace' to the force, by a curious irony was later to become a Republican Police officer himself. The sergeant was not transferred, but he was warned against 'indiscretions'. The campaign of innuendo had taken its toll even among his colleagues.

The intensity of the policeman's social and economic deprivation may be suggested by the case history of Doolin, a tiny fishing village near Clare's Atlantic coast. In July 1918 two men were shot and wounded after carting turf for the RIC. In November 1919 another was threatened for allowing the sergeant to take his seat in chapel. In August 1920 the village policemen were reportedly 'suffering terribly for want of food. The men have frequently to walk to the nearest village, a distance of four and a-half miles, having had nothing but a few lobsters to eat since the previous day. Provisions are said to be lying for a fortnight at the railway station before they can be obtained.' When even this means of supply was cut off, police meat and porter had to be brought in by lorry, at roughly fortnightly intervals. Yet the Doolin boycott, intense though it was, failed to satisfy one of those who organised it: 'We'd notify the people that was supplying them, but they used to be supplied just the same. . . . Begod, the people were very fond of them, some people.'[11]

That others were not fond of them is shown by a police report of July 1921. Two constables, armed but in plain clothes, had gone bathing at a beach near Doolin. On their return they were attacked, one being killed and the other 'left for dead'. They were among the last victims of the campaign of physical violence against policemen which complemented that of social ostracism after the Rising. Attacking policemen was, of course, a traditional sport in Ireland: even in peaceful 1915 a Clare railway superintendent had reported a conspiracy to shoot the District Inspector at Tulla, since 'he was worrying the people there to such an extent, and tormenting them in every way'. But after the Rising the threat of violence was realised, devastatingly, in practice, in an increasingly ruthless and co-ordinated campaign. Although no policemen were killed anywhere in Ireland between mid-1916 and early 1919, numerous unsuccessful attacks were made upon them. As early as March 1917 a constable well versed in 'the conduct of local Sinn Féiners' was wounded at Ennistymon, Co. Clare, in the head, neck and shoulders. He was again attacked and almost killed in August 1918. Also in 1917, so it is said, 'an R.I.C. man, cycling from Kilkee to Carrigaholt, was held up in the Kilfearagh district and tied to a telegraph pole'. He was released, 'almost frozen', towards morning.[12] Further armed attacks were made on Clare policemen during the agrarian unrest of early 1918, and for the first time telegraph wires were cut in order to isolate policemen from one another. Moreover, possibly for the first time in Ireland since the Rising, an attempt was made to storm a police hut. The raiding of police huts and barracks was resumed on a large scale in July and August 1919, to such an extent that a prominent Republican later wrote that 'It was really in Co. Clare that the guerilla warfare may be said to have started.' Attacks on small police patrols were now commonplace, and on 4 August 1919 two Clare policemen were killed—an event which caused 'a thrill of horror through Clare', a visit from the Inspector-General and the imposition of severe restrictions upon social life in the county. During 1920 and 1921 police casualties multiplied, as ever more ambitious ambushes were carried out against ever larger patrols. Policemen foolhardy enough to walk at large alone or in small groups were pitilessly killed, sometimes in daylight in main streets or in groceries.[13] Clare had more than its share of police deaths: 2 out of 17 in Ireland during 1919, 21 out of 168 during 1920, 14 out of 224 in 1921.[14] Begod, the people were very fond of them. . . .

Despite its intensity and diversity, the campaign against the police was only to a limited degree directed, co-ordinated and systematised. As I suggest in Chapter 6, central control of the Irish Volunteers or 'IRA' was extremely tenuous until 1920 at least. In its early stages, the persecution of the police must be ascribed to local initiative rather than central planning. *An tÓglach*, the clandestine house journal of the Irish Volunteers, contained no directives to boycott or attack policemen during 1919, restricting itself to urging Volunteers to fight those who sought to arrest or disarm them. Its posterior judgments upon unprovoked attacks on policemen were cautious and enigmatic. The disarming, binding and handcuffing of two constables in January 1919 reflected 'great credit' on those responsible, but it was 'not expedient to publish the full details of the affair'. For *An tÓglach* expediency was judged according to the interests of Volunteer headquarters, not the press censorship. The celebrated killings at Soloheadbeg were ignored until mid-February 1919, when a letter asserting that they had been done in self-defence was reproduced without editorial comment. But in April 1919 the first attempt was made to co-ordinate nationally the campaign of 'social ostracisation of people' (though not yet that of physical violence). The Sinn Féin executive, evidently upon the suggestion of the Dáil, agreed to provide its machinery for a national campaign. It only asked for definition of the term. In response the Clerk to the Dáil drafted this definition of 'social ostracisation', which is as much a description of practice in the more disturbed districts as a statement of intent:

> . . . that the Police forces [and their families (*deleted*)] must receive no social recognition from the people; that no intercourse, except such as is absolutely necessary on business is permitted with them; that they should not be saluted nor spoken to in the streets or elsewhere nor their salutes returned; that they should not be invited to nor received in private houses as friends or guests; that they be debarred from participation in games, sports, dances and all social functions

conducted by the people, that intermarriage with them be discouraged, that, in a word, the Police should be treated as persons, who having been adjudged guilty of treason to their country, are regarded as unworthy to enjoy any of the privileges or comforts which arise from cordial relations with the public. [Don't even jibe at them. (*added in another hand*)]

I know of no unambiguous central directive to kill policemen, although the approving annotations made by headquarters staff upon reports of successful attacks provided tacit encouragement to the killers. But directives issued during 1920 often left unclear the limits to approved action against policemen. In April 1920 *An tÓglach* stated that 'Information in our possession will enable us to distinguish between the criminals and those unfortunate men who joined the force without a proper appreciation of what they were doing.' Next month the Adjutant-General told a Clare commandant that prospective police recruits were 'to be made unfit for carrying out the duties of the R.I.C.' By October an angrier tone pervaded central directives to the Volunteers. The old RIC, and not the auxiliary forces sent to Ireland to assist them, were 'the real agents and instigators of the campaign of savagery' and therefore the most deserving of punishment.[15] The campaign of punishment, at first diffuse and uncontrolled, had been streamlined by deft central response to local demand until it gave the appearance of a systematic national crusade.

In personal and social terms the crusade was cruelly effective. Still more significant, from Dublin Castle's point of view, were the administrative implications of separating police from people, of making outlaws of the law-enforcers. Persecution sapped both the will and the ability of policemen to carry out their traditional duties. In 1916, at Ennis quarter sessions, Judge Bodkin had received white gloves, signifying the absence of criminal cases from the court schedule. He had commended Clare for 'progressing favourably towards perfection'. In 1920 Bodkin again received white gloves, but this time confessed that 'these do not represent the actual condition of the county'. In the meantime the police had lost the power to bring offenders before the courts. How had this come about?

The disruption of police work, like the ostracism of policemen, began quietly, trivially. During 1919 a Resident Magistrate in Louth noticed a sharp falling away in civil (though not yet criminal) cases, and a growing reluctance of those prosecuted to appear and defend themselves. Distracted by graver matters, the police showed decreasing zeal in pursuing minor offenders and enforcing decrees. The lower courts were emptied of litigants, witnesses, magistrates and policemen. The atmosphere of early 1920 is conveyed by this recollection of a Resident Magistrate in Co. Kerry:

> At one outlying sessions I arrived to dispense justice, and having taken my seat on the bench in solitude, a young man walked into court with his cap on and smoking a cigarette. I ordered him out, but on looking around I saw no one to carry out my orders! The police were not present, and all I could do was to order the fellow out. Which order was eventually obeyed! But I could do no more than adjourn the sessions, and console my wounded feelings by going to the river, where the setting of a nice fresh-run 10 lb. salmon acted as a balm.

The conduct of petty sessions was increasingly disrupted both by the reluctance of unpaid magistrates to take part and by the growth of rival Republican courts (see Chapter 5). In February 1921 the Divisional Commissioner of Police in North Munster reported that the 'only really practicable arrangement' in Clare and Limerick would be to hold courts weekly at county police headquarters, monthly at district headquarters, and not at all elsewhere—with a paid Resident Magistrate attending every sessions. But courts continued to be scheduled for remote villages where the police could not give any assistance. Between March and July 1921 one Clare RM was directed to attend 145 courts in 21 towns and villages. He managed to convene only 37 of these courts, ten others being held by other magistrates in his absence. Twenty of the 47 courts held took place in the heavily garrisoned county town. Nine courts were abandoned because travel to them was considered unsafe or impracticable, ten because the courthouses had been destroyed, another 49 because the unfortunate magistrate found no cases waiting to be heard. After the Truce the frequency of petty sessions increased only marginally. Only 50 of the 125 sessions scheduled for the months August 1921 to January 1922 were held, 64 being abandoned for lack of cases.[16]

The enforcement of decrees for overdue rent and other unrecovered property was disrupted just as effectively. Just after the Truce the Temporary County Inspector for Clare reported that the sub-sheriff had formidable difficulties to contend with: 'It is practically impossible to get any men to act as bailiff. There is no pound in the County. The roads all over the country were trenched and blocked with trees up to the time of the truce, so that if the Sheriff was found to be on the way everything seizable would be removed by the time he reached his destination.' In about March 1921—rather belatedly—he had offered the sub-sheriff 'every possible help' and had actually gone with him decree-gathering—an act 'so unexpected' that the decrees were executed! 'Had he then followed up his success I believe he would with our help and that of the military have executed a good many of the remaining Decrees, provided he was not shot by the I.R.A. in the meantime. The latter was not an unlikely contingency.' The sub-sheriff concurred, and stayed at home. He was, rather unkindly, denounced for laziness by the High Sheriff and police. But the County Court judge, moved by fellow-feeling for a much-put-upon old campaigner, recalled his fearless execution of rent decrees in the distant days of the land agitation and exonerated him.[17] The fact was that sheriff, judge and policeman were all incapable of enforcing the civil law. Internecine recriminations masked their common impotence.

The humiliation of the police was completed by their diminishing ability to secure criminal convictions, and finally to trace the criminals. Table 1.1 provides indices of the effectiveness of law enforcement from 1913 to 1919. With striking regularity, the indices of persons charged with both indictable and non-indictable offences, in both Clare and Ireland as a whole, show a steady decline in the rate at which policemen brought criminals to the courts. This trend was apparent throughout the European war, and until about 1917 may be ascribed to a marked reduction in the crime rate (a phenomenon often mentioned in police reports).[18] But between 1917 and 1919 the rate at which indictable crimes were reported

Table 1.1: Effectiveness of Law Enforcement, 1913–19

Persons proceeded against (1913 = 100)	1913	1914	1915	1916	1917	1918	1919
Indictable offences, Clare	100	131	115	80	68	82	80
Indictable offences, Ireland	100	91	83	81	74	60	59
Non-indictable offences, Clare	100	93	89	72	60	44	35
Non-indictable offences, Ireland	100	92	99	77	61	55	54
% Convicted or committed for trial							
Indictable offences, Clare	71	75	70	48	64	51	54
Indictable offences, Ireland	61	61	56	51	53	53	60
Non-indictable offences, Clare	92	93	92	90	89	89	87
Non-indictable offences, Ireland	84	83	80	81	80	79	81
Ratio of offences reported to 100 persons proceeded against							
Indictable offences, Clare	169	92	130	141	190	219	410
Indictable offences, Ireland	127	129	130	125	137	171	190

actually rose, slowly over the country as a whole but dramatically in Co. Clare. The prosecution rate continued to fall in Ireland, and remained fairly stable in Clare, only because the ratio of offences reported to offenders prosecuted rose faster than the crime rate. This ratio provides a rough guide to the efficiency of the police as enforcers of criminal law. If we assume that until 1919 the police were accurately informed as to the incidence of crime, this index may be taken to reflect several different arbiters of police efficiency: ability to identify offenders, ability to track down and arrest them, or confidence in their ability to convict an offender once charged. To what extent was police efficiency impaired in each of these respects during the revolutionary years?

Police reports up to 1919 suggest that identifying and locating of offenders were not yet major problems. In March 1919 the Inspector-General wrote that the police could still unmask malefactors by drawing on their 'complete local knowledge supplemented by confidential information', but were seldom able to force convictions. Conviction was hampered by police inability to persuade witnesses to testify, by the growing reluctance of unpaid justices to participate in court hearings, and by the old Irish custom, reinvigorated after 1916, of using jury service as a means to confound judges and prosecutors. Police doubts about the efficacy of prosecution were reinforced by disagreements between magistrates and judges. For example, Judge Bodkin, who regarded illegal drilling and unlawful assembly as 'pure "tomfoolery"—little "garsuns" in the streets playing with tin swords', spectacularly quashed a series of severe sentences imposed by lower courts. George McElroy, RM, wrote plaintively to the Chief Secretary's Office: 'Since April last [1918] an appeal has been lodged against every decision of a Crimes Court. The magistrates knew their decisions would be reversed. All the defendants knew it also and simply laugh at convictions.'[19]

No policeman, especially one responsible for prosecuting many of his captives, likes to be laid open to public ridicule and contempt by failing to get a lasting conviction. Every policeman, moreover, is to some extent a politician, who takes into account likely public reaction before taking an offender to court. As one Resident Magistrate wrote, the unusually wide discretion allowed Irish constables caused considerations of 'policy and tact' to replace the 'automatic functioning of the law' after 1919. In November 1917, for instance, Clare's County Inspector declared that arrests had been doing more harm than good since the government had accorded special treatment to Sinn Féin prisoners and released those on hunger-strike. On several occasions the RIC showed reluctance in carrying out government orders to arrest large numbers of offenders, sometimes rousing the government to wrath. Moreover, the government's violent fluctuations between coercion and conciliation puzzled and inhibited the police, making them afraid that today's convicts would be tomorrow's amnestied heroes. Late in 1920 the *Gazette* warned policemen to avoid study of the principles of official policy: 'Nothing, indeed, can be more vain or unprofitable than speculating on the outlook. The effect is upsetting, if not demoralising.'[20]

The police were however to some extent encouraged by the government's attempts to devise modes of punishment ever less susceptible to popular or judicial influence. In November 1917 the cabinet approved the convening of 'Crimes Act Statutory Courts', consisting of two Resident Magistrates unencumbered by unpaid justices, to deal with tricky offences such as illegal drilling. Seven months later the Attorney-General was empowered to transfer quarter sessions cases (in Clare Judge Bodkin's province) from Clare and elsewhere to other counties, and to appoint special juries in other criminal cases. When (as McElroy complained) even the Crimes Courts proved incapable of enforcing punishments, the still more arbitrary courts martial were frequently resorted to.[21] Imprisonment without trial of any kind became increasingly common after 1916, and legal provision for it was continually extended. But the more freely internment was practised, the more clearly had the police been rendered incapable of performing their traditional functions. Until 1919, as Table 1.1 suggests, policemen continued to obtain almost as high a ratio of convictions to prosecutions as before the Rising—at the cost of prosecuting fewer offenders. In 1920 and 1921 the problem of obtaining convictions was solved by bypassing the courts—at the cost of rendering one of the RIC's vital functions obsolete.

As the revolution intensified, still more fundamental obstacles arose to the enforcement of criminal law. The sources of police intelligence fell silent. The secrets of petty misdemeanour, common crime and revolutionary outrage were alike withheld from them. Before the Rising the police had been served by a primitive but effective system of intelligence: detectives in Dublin, Belfast, Limerick and other large towns, the RIC's 'Crime Special Branch' with men in every county and most police districts, and local policemen with their ears cocked. Vast and sometimes vivid dossiers had been compiled upon political suspects, whose movements and contacts were laboriously noted. The thoroughness of these dossiers is illustrated by a wartime description of the writer Darrell Figgis, Special War 'B' List Suspect No. 27: age 41, occupation 'none'(unkind!), height 6 ft 1 in., complexion fresh, eyes piercing grey, visage regular, nose thin, hooked, sharp, make active, hair sandy and long, beard sandy and pointed, moustache long and sandy, 'swinging gait sometimes wears volunteer dress'. By 1920, however, the police had lost touch with the currents of crime and sedition and were reliant on outdated memories of the distribution of good and evil in the days before Sinn Féin.[22] The outrages which filled local police reports in 1920 and 1921 were events which the police could neither understand nor attribute.

Police ignorance of the sources of crime and inability to capture offenders were both enhanced by the closing down of small rural outposts. Between 1913 and early 1921 only fifteen posts were established in Clare, but fifty-four were discontinued—thirty-four of them in 1920 and 1921. At first concentration of the force was a money-saving measure, opposed by the *Gazette* since it reduced the number of sergeants and therefore the rate of promotion (supporters of the scheme could only be men 'whose prospects of advancement are extremely remote'). But by September 1919 the *Gazette* considered the rate of concentration too slow in the novel conditions of physical danger:

> Why wear uniform? Why proceed on patrol according to red tape? Why continue to occupy ridiculous little arsenals in sparsely populated districts? Why pursue the old methods, now obviously clumsy and obsolete? The men who shoot the police are very clever. Of this there is no room for doubt. It would seem that the police are less clever. We doubt it, but they are denied the use of their intelligence. They are always under orders.[23]

RIC headquarters, spurred on by IRA assaults upon outlying barracks, withdrew their men to larger barracks. To discourage their return, the IRA systematically destroyed the evacuated posts: twenty-seven were burned in Clare in a single night, 3–4 April 1920. But the RIC was slow to regard their withdrawal as anything but a temporary expedient. In mid-1920 the Chief of Police wrote that 'The policy decided on is to concentrate sufficiently to ensure proper defence of barracks whilst leaving a mobile force.' Once 'transport difficulties' had been overcome, he hoped to resume 'constant patrolling of the country' in order to help 're-establish the ordinary law'. In fact the concentration of police in large barracks was still incomplete at the time of the Truce, and despite some police reluctance to venture outside barracks, the semblance of patrolling was maintained. But when Clare policemen trod the paths it was now in a dead patrol: 'They neither see nor hear anything till they return, and then his lordship—skipper in charge—will write in the Patrol Book: "Kept a sharp look-out for anything unusual." Oh! Lord such red tape.'[24] In self-protection the force drew into itself, and its 'eyes and ears', already hooded, ranged over an ever-contracting domain.

By mid-1920 the RIC was on the verge of collapse. As Sir John Anderson wrote, many of its barracks were indefensible, matters of pay and pensions were 'long overdue for settlement', the gathering of intelligence was 'entirely neglected'. The Inspector-General lived 'in daily fear of one of two things, either of wholesale resignations from the Force or of his men running amok. Either he said would mean the end of the R.I.C.' The current mood of demoralisation is epitomised by a report from the West Riding of Cork for July 1920:

> The R.I.C. hitherto have been indomitable and have carried on with fearlessness, courage, and initiative; but recent events point to the breaking-point being reached. . . . So far as the R.I.C. are concerned in this Riding, they may be considered to have ceased to function. The most they can do is to try to defend themselves and their barracks. It would seem that the time has arrived for the military to supersede the R.I.C. in this Riding.[25]

3. REORGANISATION

The Irish government's response to the castration of the police was piecemeal and tardy. At no time did it devise or execute a systematic remodelling of the organisation of law enforcement, root and branch. Yet between 1916 and 1921 that organisation was transformed by means which no systematic planner would have countenanced. Gradually policemen were turned into soldiers, soldiers into policemen, and ex-soldiers into hybrids collectively known as 'Black and Tans'. The hitherto distinct roles of soldier and policeman were fused, contorted and reassorted. The outcome aided neither the restoration of civil order nor of military peace. How was the functional transformation of the forces of the Crown brought about? How effectively did the new quasi-police forces carry out their unfamiliar functions? How smoothly did the various forces work together?

The militarisation of the RIC was a predictable response to the growing threat of physical violence against policemen. If the force were neither to be disbanded nor converted (like the Dublin Metropolitan Police) into a harmless band of unarmed traffic wardens, then it had to be rendered capable of defending itself. As the RIC, unlike the DMP, prided itself on being a 'semi-military' force, the beginnings of the path towards militarisation were smooth. It is true that not all observers thought highly of the RIC's military capacities. In 1912 the Irish government had reassessed the help which the army could expect from the RIC in times of war and had redrafted guidelines first drawn up during the Boer War. The 1912 memorandum pointed out that the force was armed only lightly, having carbines, sword-bayonets, truncheons and the odd revolver. 'Its members have only a rudimentary training in the use of firearms; and it cannot be regarded as a military force in any circumstances in the event of a hostile landing in Ireland.' At most it might be asked to watch the coastline (though even in this it could not 'always be relied on'), to patrol town water supplies, assist the military intelligence branch, and dismantle telephonic and telegraphic devices if necessary.

Under pressure of war, however, the Irish government had this unflattering assessment of the RIC's military potential modified. In February 1915 it was recognised as a military force in case of invasion, in order to release much-needed troops from passively defending the Irish coast. But the invasion never came. During wartime the RIC's military duties were confined to collecting statistics for the army, administering emergency regulations concerning the defence of the realm, food control and tillage extension, and unmasking the enemies of military recruiting.[26] War brought more arithmetic and more paper-work, but only the scent of battle.

In September 1919, however, police huts in Clare were supplied with rockets, Very pistols, shotguns and bombs, in the vain hope of rendering them proof against rebel assault. In October police patrols carried bombs with them, whereupon their assailants withdrew out of range but continued to fire upon them. By mid-1920 the RIC had become a heavily armed force without a function. By a rare stroke of imagination, police headquarters discerned a way out of this *impasse*. Within a few months, it was true, 'they would cease to function' as a police force; but they could have 'great effect' as a military force. Thenceforth the police were used increasingly as guides and fellow-fighters for the military, travelling with them in joint patrols. Their barracks became so heavily fortified that the maintenance branch found it necessary to regulate the registration of such untraditional stores as barbed wire (in huge coils, often of 30 or 112 pounds), pickets (wooden or iron), wire netting, steel plates, shell boxes and grenades (Daylight or Mills). In January 1921 the *Gazette* reflected that Irish policemen could never return to the 'easy-going quietude of what used to be'.[27] The RIC had been painfully twisted into the shape of an auxiliary army.

By this time an equally painful, equally logical, and utterly contradictory process of transformation had been undergone by the army—its politicisation. The army in Ireland had long been bound to 'aid the civil power' upon request. Sir Neville Lyttelton, army commander from 1908 to 1912, complained that his forces even then were widely 'regarded as adjuncts to the police'. But the demands made upon the army were spasmodic, the occasion usually being some riot or cattle-drive which a show of military pageantry and power was sufficient to disperse. Even under martial law in 1916 military power was displayed in Clare only sparingly, and out of a desire to impress the multitude. Some forty-eight persons were arrested immediately after the Rising, but the County Inspector admitted that some of the victims were 'only dupes—and of no importance— but had to be arrested at the time'. The bulk of the work was done by a mobile police column from Ulster and four military flying columns, whose commander found his assignment 'difficult and unpleasant'. The local police, absolved from the duty of punishing rebels who had not rebelled, reported that it was well that martial law had not been removed. The Ulstermen were greeted by 'hearty cheers from the boys stationed at Bunratty Castle'.[28] Martial law taught the Clare police how useful auxiliary policemen could be in difficult times.

Thereafter soldiers were requisitioned by the Clare police with increasing frequency. During the East Clare by-election campaign of mid-1917 the County

Inspector obtained a draft of 150 soldiers and a promise that 150 others would be hastily trained and held ready at the Curragh. Six months later, when large numbers of Irish Volunteers were drilling in defiance of the police, soldiers were marched through the county creating a 'good effect generally'. In January 1918 outbreaks of agrarian violence induced the County Inspector to call for one hundred police reinforcements, complete with bedsteads, bedding and bicycles. The Inspector-General could spare only fifty, and recommended that troops be drafted to the county to make up the deficiency. For the first time since 1916 serious discussions were held concerning the proper role of the army in suppressing civil disorder. The Inspector-General urged that soldiers, guided by the odd policeman, should take over the RIC's regular patrols during the emergency. Opposed by the army command, which believed that the mere presence of soldiers would still suffice to silence the rebellious, he excavated files concerning the use of military patrols during the Land War. The Chief Secretary evidently rejected the Inspector-General's radical suggestion, but sanctioned the dispatch of troops 'for the protection of police and others, and maintenance of public order seriously menaced by these demonstrations'. A few days later the army's role in policing the county was greatly extended by the proclamation of Clare as Ireland's first 'Special Military Area'. Although martial law had not been declared, the functions assumed by the army exceeded those of 1916. The army commandant issued thirteen proclamations during the next month, restricting entry into the county or disturbed portions of it, prohibiting meetings, and establishing 'a Censorship over Written and Printed Matter'. Curfews were imposed, fairs and markets selectively banned, pub drinking restricted and photographic apparatus outlawed from the streets. Thereafter, until the formal imposition of martial law in January 1921, these controls were applied only sporadically. But Clare remained a Special Military Area (a distinction soon conferred upon other troubled counties). The principle of energetic military interference in matters once the preserve of the police was soon firmly established. The military were no more capable than the police of reverting to their traditional functions.[29]

The more soldiers played policemen and policemen played soldiers, the more critical the shortage of manpower in both forces became. For the army, however much civil work it was required to perform, Ireland remained until mid-1920 neither a battlefield nor an occupied territory, but a training-ground. Both during and after the European war, troops training in Ireland were subject to drafting abroad at short notice. Of 111,222 soldiers stationed in Ireland in August 1918 less than 10,000 had been sent to Ireland for political reasons—and even these, should they ever obtain 'A' classification, were to become available for foreign service. Even in early 1921, when the army's role in Irish law enforcement was well established, less than 15,000 of the 50,000 troops in the country were considered capable of taking 'offensive action'—a number scarcely exceeding the establishment of the old RIC. In Clare the army maintained as many as fourteen units during the period February to June 1920. The number of troops in the county varied from 635 to 1,510, but of these only 321 to 864 were 'present and available to take the field with a mobile column'. The residue, in fluctuating proportions, were absent from their units, required for guard duties and the like, or untrained.[30] The shortage of soldiers trained either to help in police work or to do battle was a cause of great concern within the much-harassed army command.

The strength of the post-war RIC was still more inadequate than that of the Irish army. Recruitment to the force had been curtailed both by formal suspension and by government parsimony during the war years. Thereafter it was inhibited by the Republican campaign to isolate police from people. The success of this aspect of the Republican campaign should not be overstressed: during the year of intense revolution from July 1920 to June 1921 the monthly rate of recruitment within Ireland was 57, compared with 54 from 1905 to 1914, only 24 from 1915 to 1918, and 30 in 1919. But the end of the war, as we shall see, brought a vast increase in the rate of wastage from the RIC. Whereas recruitment and wastage had been fairly well balanced before the European war, in 1920–21 some 349 men left the force each month, six times the rate of Irish recruitment.[31] Had some other source of supply not been found, the strength of the RIC would have fallen by many thousands by 1921.

During 1919 both police and military authorities realised that without new sources of manpower the policing of the country could not be carried out. Each force saw the significance of demobilisation. For the police demobilisation opened up a potentially vast supply of recruits, trained as fighters and desperate for employment. The Inspector-General wrote in October 1919: 'Ever since demobilisation was ordered I have done my utmost to bring to the notice of men about to be discharged from the army, both in France, Great Britain, and this country, the possibility of their being accepted for service in the R.I. Constabulary. . . . Notwithstanding this, the response has been practically nil'—doubtless because RIC rates of pay remained absurdly low. For the Irish army demobilisation posed a threat rather than a promise. In August 1919 the Irish command warned the RIC that retrenchment made necessary by the recent signature of the Treaty of Versailles meant that 'the Garrison of Ireland will not be in a position to carry out the police duties which have devolved upon it during the War and to respond to the constant calls made on it to assist the police'. Army and police each suggested that the other should be reinforced with ex-soldiers to carry out police work: the army urged formation of special police cyclist units keeping their military equipment and organisation, the police urged the temporary re-enlisting of ex-soldiers into the Irish army. Alternatively, 'carefully selected ex-soldiers of good character, physique, and education, suitable for police service' might be induced to enter the RIC on probation—though the Inspector-General insisted that military aid would still be necessary.[32]

Eventually the government unobtrusively implemented the third plan for reform. Though in retrospect it may seem a road to chaos, the conversion of ex-soldiers into policemen subject to police organisation and control had obvious advantages. Without necessitating administrative reform, it promised both to increase the size and military capability of the RIC and to relieve unemployment. It was also the culmination of the process of militarising policemen and politicising soldiers. With feet in both camps the new recruits could serve as a bridge between the two forces, whose functions had been moving ever closer together but whose aspirations had been moving ever further apart.

Massive recruitment of ex-soldiers was made possible by the long-awaited award of pay rises. Discontented senior members of the force were to some extent placated by the awards: 104 per cent for junior sergeants, 90 per cent for junior officers, and much-improved allowances. But the raw recruit fared still better, his award being 125 per cent. The awards were recommended by a Viceregal Commission in December 1919, with prior statutory authority, paid from the beginning of 1920 with nine months' retrospective application, and given formal effect in an order by the Lord Lieutenant early in May. For the first time since 1914 employment as an Irish policeman seemed a comparatively enticing prospect—in money terms at least. As we have seen, even the Irishman, though subject to intense social pressure to shun the RIC, was not indifferent to monetary enticement. In addition to the 683 men enlisting in Ireland between July 1920 and June 1921 (8 per cent of the total intake), several hundred Irish ex-servicemen probably enlisted in Britain. But the proportion of recruits born outside Ireland rose rapidly during 1920 and 1921, from 40 per cent in the first two months of 1920 to 90 per cent before the Truce. (The corresponding proportion of ex-servicemen rose from 63 per cent to 87 per cent.) Altogether from January 1920 to its disbandment in 1922 the RIC accepted some 13,700 recruits, a number exceeding the entire strength of the force in previous years. Of these a few were enrolled as constables for service in Belfast's 'B' section, as special constables re-enlisted from the body of police pensioners, or as temporary constables attached to auxiliary units. But the vast majority, whether on temporary or unlimited contracts, were assigned to units of the old RIC. On 12 April 1920 a training depot was opened at the Curragh specifically for these hybrids from across the water. The 'Black and Tans' had come into being.[33]

As the guerrilla campaign intensified, the need to stiffen the Crown forces in Ireland still more became obvious. Former privates dispersed among innumerable police barracks, without the fatherly guidance of the officer class, could scarcely be expected to act with full military efficiency. Formation was therefore urged of an elite auxiliary force, better paid, more tightly organised and more thickly peopled with officers than the Black and Tans. On 11 May 1920 a conference of ministers asked the Secretary of State for War to draw up a scheme for a 'special Corps of Gendarmerie . . . in aid of the Royal Irish Constabulary during the emergency period'. But a War Office committee objected that such a body would be beyond the capacity of the RIC to discipline adequately, would take at least a year to raise, and would have to be paid at 'exceptional rates'. The committee urged instead formation of eight new garrison battalions consisting of 'soldiers under the Army Act' led by an unusually large establishment of officers and NCOs, to be raised in Britain, paid for and administered by the War Office. The cabinet approved, but Churchill and Lloyd George subsequently deemed it 'inadvisable' to go ahead with the plan. In July the proposal to raise a police auxiliary was revived, and on 27 July the 'Auxiliary Division' was inaugurated. It was recruited from 'ex-officers who had served in the Great War' (aided by a few hundred temporary constables as orderlies or guards) who were designated as 'Temporary Cadets in the R.I.C.' and given the status and pay of police sergeants. Between September 1920 and June 1921, 1,864 Auxiliaries were enlisted, and the total intake exceeded 2,200—considerably more than the previous establishment of sergeants in the RIC. Unlike the Black and Tans, the Auxiliaries were concentrated in about twenty virtually self-contained companies, and were never integrated into the structure of the RIC.[34] In practice subject neither to police nor to military control, the Auxiliaries blended the functions of soldiers and policemen more bizarrely even than the Black and Tans.

The militarisation of police personnel applied also to the officer corps. Of 203 men appointed officer cadets in 1920 and 1921, 139 had served in the military forces (about one-third of these had also served in the Auxiliary Division). Other inspectors had acquired military experience during temporary enlistment in the army during the European war. Furthermore the Resident Magistracy, upon which the RIC was now dependent for such civil convictions as it could obtain, was bolstered with ex-soldiers also: fourteen of the sixteen RMs appointed in 1919 and 1920 had military experience, compared with twelve of the forty-five appointed from 1900 to 1918. The militarisation of the police pyramid was capped in May 1920 by the appointment of a former general as Police Adviser to Dublin Castle, and later Chief of Police. His deputy, formerly one of the 'surfeit of Brigadier-Generals wandering about the country', was put to work organising a new intelligence staff (of 150 instead of two, as before) including many ex-officers.[35] In the course of a few months the RIC had been transformed.

The extent of this transformation may be judged from Tables 1.2 and 1.3, which analyse the RIC's intake during the revolutionary period and beforehand. In the revolutionary period both officers and men tended to be Protestant, English ex-fighters rather than Catholic, Irish-born civilians. Among the rank and file the ex-soldiers, predominantly of the urban working class, came of stock strikingly unlike that of the traditional recruit. The minority of ex-soldiers who had been farmers or clerks diminished in 1921, as the proportion of Irish ex-soldiers diminished. Even among the non-military residue, mainly Irishmen, the proportion of ex-farmers fell sharply in 1921, thus completing the process already bemoaned by Constable O'Shea in 1914. Urban Irishmen continued to join the RIC in 1921, but the sons of farmers now sought employment elsewhere.[36]

The social disparity between the old RIC and the Black and Tans engendered a sense of separateness rather than open hostility. Indeed, the more exotic the English recruit seemed, the more secure the Irish policeman's belief in his own superiority became. The policeman might no longer expect deference from the common herd, but he could at least look down upon his new colleagues—a gnarled enough yardstick of status, but better than none at all. In February 1920 the *Gazette* questioned the wisdom of seeking recruits in England, for 'an English Constable is often a craftsman of some kind, and is always ready to relinquish his job if there is a trade boom'. The paper smugly quoted the words of an English former Chief Constable who 'vastly preferred an Irishman to any man as a policeman'. Eight months later it noted the 'extraordinary' fact that Englishmen were

Table 1.2: Enlistment of Policemen, 1913–21

Constables enlisted:	Jan.–Mar. 1913	Sep.–Nov. 1916	Jan. 1920	Feb. 1920	1–7 Jan. 1921	1–11 Jul. 1921
Size of sample	178	201	205	286	217	278
% Irish-born	98	100	47	69	11	10
% Roman Catholics	86	89	40	43	11	13
% Ex-soldiers	2	—	78	53	83	87
Ex-soldiers:						
% Ex-labourers	—	—	31	20	21	39
% Ex-skilled workers	—	—	38	40	66	46
% Ex-clerks	—	—	24	27	11	14
% Ex-farmers	—	—	7	13	2	1
Others:						
% Ex-labourers	19	14	13	24	24	28
% Ex-skilled workers	7	5	13	6	39	39
% Ex-clerks	14	11	8	17	8	22
% Ex-farmers	60	70	67	53	29	11

Table 1.3: Enlistment of Police Officers, 1920–21

	Officers enlisted: 1920	1921	Serving Clare: 1913–19
Size of sample	127	76	25
% Irish-born	79	47	92
% Roman Catholics	47	34	64
% Ex-police (ranks)	44	32	36
% Ex-soldiers	62	67	—
% Over 30 at appointment	50	57	36

flocking to the RIC's London recruiting office, yet spurning their own home forces. The reason could only be that the RIC's standards for recruits had fallen far below those imposed by other forces. Certainly the new recruits were shorter and feebler than the old RIC men. According to a Resident Magistrate, some of them had other less endearing physical attributes: 'They were like a bunch of gorillas. They had india-rubber looking faces, large ears, big fat lips, and most of them had that blank, uncanny expression of the cretin.' The Auxiliaries might, as the RM observed, be 'of the Sandhurst type', an altogether stouter sort of men than the Black and Tans; but the long-suffering Irish constable strongly resented their appointment as sergeants after only six weeks' 'messing about' at depot, a title for which twenty years' unblemished service was normally required.[37]

The exotic habits of the Black and Tans sometimes made communal life uncomfortable for those obliged to share barracks with them. In Clare, for example, a Black and Tan was arrested for threatening to shoot an Irish sergeant; police in one district stole £5 from those in another; half a dozen Black and Tans threatened their own orderly sergeant in the barracks day-room and fired at another constable; and an Ennis policeman was charged with larceny after removing boots from an injured colleague in order to sell them to a civilian. Reporting the last offence, in April 1921, the County Inspector nevertheless maintained that 'co-operation between Police Military and Auxiliaries is on the whole satisfactory'. Despite a regrettable occurrence in the same month, when two Clare policemen were shot dead in a pub by Clare Auxiliaries who had been sent there by Black and Tans, the Auxiliaries at Killaloe seem to have been well received by the regular police. In November 1920 the County Inspector noted a 'wonderful change for the better in the district' since their arrival, adding that 'They are becoming acquainted with other parts of the county with good results.' The newcomers may have been wild men, but they were also fighters, and the beleaguered RIC was grateful for their protection. They were also, unalterably, strangers; as a message from Cahir, Co. Tipperary, to Cork RIC in November 1921 suggests: 'Look here there is a circular to be issued to old R.I.C. not to Tans but to pre war R.I.C. and it must be private so you must try and manage to keep its contents from the Tans and others and H[ead] constables must be kept in the dark too. Yes sir its alright.'[38] Confronted by alien comrades as well as a hostile people, the Irish policeman had shrinking reserves to fall back on.

The functional and compositional transformation of the Irish army during the revolutionary period was less spectacular than that of the police, yet almost as thorough. Already in April 1918 the cabinet had recognised the danger involved in expecting Irish soldiers to aid the civil power against their fellow-countrymen. In order to make the imposition of conscription feasible, the Secretary of State for War had been empowered 'to bring away gradually from Ireland all the Irish Reserve Battalions now in that country, and to substitute English Reserve Battalions'. After the Armistice this principle was maintained, although the large number of Irishmen serving in British regiments prevented a complete racial spring-cleaning.[39] The vast reduction in army strength which had seemed inevitable in autumn 1919 was prevented by sending in detachments of the new

Regular Army to replace the 'young soldier' battalions which had, in turn, replaced the pre-war regulars. The War Office was quick to decide that Ireland, after Britain, was the Empire's most necessary constituent, and to urge that Irish military demands be given priority over those from abroad. By early 1920 the army was committed to taking a major part in keeping the peace and pursuing and punishing the Republican warriors.

Gradually and with difficulty, the army assumed a more decisive role in Irish policing than hitherto. In January 1920 it rejoiced at 'an important change of policy' which enabled military commanders to order police inspectors 'at once' to provide police aid if required. For their part, of course, the police through the Castle were still able to instruct army commanders to provide military aid. The relative precedence of soldiers and policemen in civil affairs was further confused by the appointment of Divisional Commissioners for the RIC in March 1920. As one army commander found, their responsibilities at first seemed 'rather involved and difficult to understand'. They were expected to co-ordinate police and military activity, yet for a full year the divisions over which they presided were kept obstinately distinct from the military divisional areas. They were mostly ex-officers and held the relative rank of colonel, but were officially members of the RIC. They were eventually assigned 'full tactical control' over all branches of the RIC, but Dublin never surrendered its direct administrative control over local police units. In the martial law area the subordination of Commissioners to the military was as uncertain as their authority over the police. After vigorous army criticism of Munster police for their undisciplined conduct, the Commissioner at Cork attempted to define his duties for the enlightenment of his military superior. He was 'to be responsible to you for the maintenance of Police discipline', 'to ensure that the Police co-operate with the Military in all matters in accordance with your wishes', and (amongst other duties) 'to supervise the work of the Auxiliary Coys.' But in order to accomplish these duties he would need 'considerable increased powers' of discipline and dismissal, as well as two extra rooms, three cars and four staff members.[40]

Despite administrative tangles, the conditions of guerrilla warfare brought soldiers and policemen closer together. Their fusion of roles was symbolised in mid-1920 by the appointments of an ex-police chief as army commander and an ex-soldier as police chief. Over the next year soldiers and policemen were required to plan together, patrol together and sometimes die together. They were comrades, even though the conditions necessitating comradeship were not of their choosing, and even though the order of precedence within the Crown forces remained in dispute. But their comradeship was an unequal relationship. The police consistently encouraged military intervention which might relieve them of novel responsibilities. Thus reports from south-western districts in 1917 and 1918 consistently expressed preference for military occupation rather than civil control, courts martial rather than courts of summary jurisdiction. In 1918 and 1919 County Inspectors sent dire warnings of the effects of withdrawing troops from police work. In October 1919, when the army threatened to cut out its police functions, the Inspector-General argued that if 'these measures are carried out in their entirety the maintenance of peace and good order in Ireland may be seriously jeopardised'. Martial law elicited a somewhat tepid response from policemen perhaps jealous of their own status, but there is no reason to think the police regretted the augmentation of troops which martial law entailed. The army, on the other hand, regarded the RIC's military capabilities with scepticism and some disdain. As one army commander wrote of the old RIC before reorganisation, 'Their musketry training was almost non-existent, their fire discipline nil, and our officers had to go round their barracks to help them as much as possible in the effective use of the rifle . . . hand and rifle grenades, rockets and Verey light signals, and in the defence arrangements of their barracks.' Another officer considered that during 1920 most of the Irish policemen had given way, and that 'thereafter they were of little assistance except to act as local guides'. The Black and Tans 'were generally a very fine lot of men, and would have done well under other conditions'. The Auxiliaries, though relatively useful as fighters, suffered from division of tactical and administrative command; moreover, 'their independent status did not always make for smooth working'.[41] Indeed, smooth working was something scarcely attainable in the Irish military-police machine of the revolutionary period, a machine whose deviousness and disorderliness might have pleased Heath Robinson. How smoothly did it work when put to the test?

4. RESPONSE TO REVOLUTION

The immediate consequence of reorganisation was to put new heart into the law enforcers. First from Limerick, then Cork, then Kerry and Clare, police reports from the revolutionary south-west expressed restored optimism. In August 1920, for example, the Limerick County Inspector wrote: 'We have got rid of majority of the old useless men who were not pulling their weight against the rebels and the latter now feel that we will stand no nonsense.' Before long the inspector himself had been got rid of, but the army captain who replaced him was equally cheery in December: more information was coming in, workmen were again delivering supplies, and the police were 'now able to have a dance organized by "Black and Tans" as they are called. These have been most successful and show a good spirit returning.' But as the revolution thickened and blood continued to flow, the revival of police morale subsided. In Kerry and West Cork in particular police reports reverted to their old tone of despair. In Clare the police simply stopped reporting popular attitudes towards the force—the most eloquent of testimonies to their estrangement.[42]

The disillusionment of the new RIC followed a different course. Whereas for the Irish police reorganisation provided temporary respite from a long-drawn-out social punishment, for the newcomers it was the starting-point of a brief and exciting episode. It is likely that many of them came to Ireland with high hopes of adventure but vague notions of their duties. *The Times* drew attention to an advertisement for the Auxiliary Division obscurely classified under 'E' for 'Ex-officers' with the dry comment: 'The life is an open-air one, and will doubtless appeal to many ex-officers.' One Auxiliary recalled that the six weeks' training course did little to prepare recruits for their future activities. They were given 'a certain amount of arms and bombing practice but all very sketchy' and taught the difference between misdemeanours and felonies. A small party was sent to Macroom, Co. Cork, where they took over an empty castle and shot at game, rabbits and empty bottles. After two months they had yet to meet an armed man, having spent much of their time avoiding hoaxed ambushes. Though dimly aware that they were not ordinary policemen, the Auxiliaries passed away the time trying to break up illicit meetings and getting themselves lost on the way. Nevertheless, the County Inspector for Cork West Riding reported in October 1920 that the Macroom unit had had 'a very good effect on that district which is now about the quietest part of this County'. The Dunmanway ambush of a month later, in which at least sixteen of them were killed, seemed all the more shocking for being unexpected.[43] Experiences like this, bursting upon men who lacked proper training and mental preparation, placed intolerable strain upon the adventurers from England.

For the Irish army the experience of revolution brought neither the desolation of social estrangement nor the sudden disenchantment of a spoiled adventure, but rather the frustration of professional men thwarted. Although their estrangement from the Irish people was still more complete than that of the RIC, it was the consequence not of cruel social ostracism but of deliberate choice. In pre-revolutionary days, it is true, soldiers had been remarkably 'popular' in the Irish countryside—in demand as good customers, as eager huntsmen, and (involuntarily) as models for rebel fighters. Their popularity, accurate marksmanship and lack of local connections combined to dissuade the Republicans from launching against them a many-faceted campaign such as that which punished the RIC. Their casualties were relatively light: about 160 deaths throughout Ireland before the Truce (compared with about 400 police deaths), and nine in Clare (compared with 37).[44] Until March 1921 the officer commanding Clare, Limerick and Tipperary felt it safe to drive about Limerick unescorted. In April 1920 the Clare commander, armed only with a revolver, had attempted to break up a procession of strikers single-handed. When members of 'an angry crowd' knocked him down, the strike leaders had saved him and a bevy of women supervised by a priest had carried him to safety. Women, according to a Clare priest, never neglected the Tommy: 'British soldiers and Tans had no trouble in finding girl friends in Irish towns during the Sinn Féin war.'[45]

That soldiers sent to Ireland after the Armistice chose to shun local people rather than vice versa is suggested by a number of testimonials. A certain Major B. L. Montgomery wrote in 1923: 'I think I regarded all civilians as "shinners", and I never had any dealings with them.' A manual for trainee officers warned that 'every soldier in Ireland must realize that the most harmless looking civilian may be armed and hostile'; another asserted that 'no inhabitant or civilian employee is really to be trusted', and called upon soldiers to search for incriminating objects in such unexpected places as '(a) Removable horn on a cow; (b) In animals ears . . . ; (d) In mangolds, turnips, etc.' Soldiers at Bandon, Co. Cork, had 'no social contacts with any civilians of whatever political beliefs' and grew 'very bored'. As a brigade commandant pointed out, boredom was a common malaise among both troops and police and could have risky consequences. In Bandon, for example, it brought forth the following startling invitation:

> H.M. Army Barracks,
> Bandon, Co. Cork,
> 5th October 1920.
>
> The Bandon Detachment, British Army, herewith challenge the 1st (Bandon) Battalion, 3rd Cork Brigade, I.R.A. to a football match, to be played on the grounds of the former. The visiting team to name the first day for which no ambush or other amusement is fixed. Revolvers will not be carried, but masks may be worn if desired. Spectators to be limited to 20 on each side.
>
> To: Colonel John Hales, I.R.A.   RSVP.
> 'Uplands', Mt. Bandon.   O.C. Troops, Bandon.[46]

This challenge (whether or not a spoof) illustrates not so much the fraternal feelings of one army for another, as the frustration resulting from voluntary seclusion.

Voluntary seclusion seriously diminished the professional efficiency of soldiers in Ireland, not only by generating boredom but also by rendering the collection of intelligence almost impossible. As a Munster intelligence officer said later, it was 'fundamentally wrong' to assume that every Irishman was an enemy: one must 'distinguish the sheep from the wolves'. Army historians later lamented the inability of the secret service to penetrate the inner circles of Republicanism, and the increasing reluctance of loyal citizens to turn informer (a number of Protestant farmers near Bandon who did so were killed by the IRA). Had soldiers in Ireland spent more time chatting in public houses the flow of information would probably have increased—although its efficient processing would still have been inhibited by the profusion of intelligence services operating in competition, including two secret services, two military intelligence units, a freelance group eventually transformed into an Auxiliary company, the police Crime Special Branch, and a scattering of officers under the Divisional Commissioners who were expected to co-ordinate incoming information! The common military belief that no 'loyalists' lived in the south or west of Ireland also impeded the raising of citizen militia forces in aid of the army and police. Headquarters made no such initiative until June 1921, and only two militia forces were formed.[47] Because most Irish soldiers in 1920 and 1921 regarded the Irish as a hostile race, the solidarity of that race was scarcely put to the test.

The army's inability to obtain reliable intelligence was only one symptom of a more general military failure. In fact the army proved scarcely more efficient than the RIC in contending with guerrilla fighters. Even in conventional terms the post-war army was singularly ill-trained. Massive disbandments in 1919 robbed the army of almost all its experienced men; overseas drafts constantly removed the best of those who replaced them from Irish service; conditions within Ireland made further training on the spot 'practically impossible'. In at least one army division the 'greatest difficulty' was found in selecting suitable NCOs, and 'it may frankly be stated that the standard of efficiency of officers generally was not a high one'. Attempts to retrain soldiers in the novel techniques appropriate to civil war had only limited success. In October 1920 the 5th Division set up the first 'Guerilla Warfare Class' at the Curragh, a three-day course of lectures, mock ambushes and imitation raids. Altogether some 280 officers and NCOs and 125 police took the course, and a modified version was administered to about 500 soldiers drafted to Ireland during 1921.[48] But no three-day course could outweigh the accumulated wisdom (however cursorily passed on) of the British army, which had only lately supplanted its traditional training in medieval jousting with equally irrelevant instruction in trench warfare under international rules.

The inadequacy of the army's response to the Irish challenge was painfully apparent at the time and minutely analysed by military strategists thereafter. The official 'Record of the Rebellion' discerned numerous tactical failings, such as the possibly 'mistaken chivalry' shown to the treacherous Irish female and the excessive dispersion of military units (balancing the excessive concentration of police). But 'Apart from the tactical lessons which this particular type of guerilla warfare brought out, there are certain points in strategy, political and military, which were revealed, chiefly by their omission, but which would appear to be common to all forms of rebellion.' The army should have struck hard 'at the very beginning' and kept to one plan of campaign. Entire towns should have been taken over and barricaded. General martial law should have been quickly imposed and all appeal to civil authority prevented. Control should have been unified and 'improvised units' grafted onto existing bodies. Loyalists and moderate men should have been enlisted as 'civic guards'. Above all, the government should have announced its policy 'in clear and unequivocal terms as soon as possible'. Although the army had gradually adjusted itself to changing conditions, the revolutionaries seemed to military men to have held the initiative throughout. As one divisional commander succinctly put it, 'We were always too late.'[49]

As policemen and soldiers alike discovered their own impotence in face of the revolutionary movement, their frustration was exhibited in increasingly desperate acts. These killings and burnings came to be known collectively as 'reprisals', acts of vengeance or deterrence taking the place of the legal punishments which the Crown forces were no longer able to execute. Responsibility for reprisals was variously ascribed to Republicans masquerading in stolen official uniforms, members of an 'Anti-Sinn Féin Society' (or 'Gang', or 'League'), policemen and soldiers. Analysis of reprisals has long been clouded by uncertainty over the relative guilt of police and soldiers and of leaders and men. Although a clear verdict is still impossible, study of the official documents now available allows one to pick a path through the tangles of conflicting testimony.

General Macready, commander of the Irish army, himself admitted that four acts of reprisal resulting in a single death had been undertaken by soldiers without headquarters' permission. His own irritation at indiscipline was curiously blended with marked sympathy with the frustrated men responsible. In mid-August 1920 Macready 'issued a proclamation explaining the wickedness of reprisals'; but a month later he issued preparatory instructions for the systematic burning of houses should the revolutionaries do the same. On 27 September he wrote to the Chief Secretary that 'while retaliation cannot be defended, the effect on the rebels has been most marked'; reprisals could only be suppressed if a more effective means of punishment were devised. A form of internment was instituted and the preparatory order for systematic burnings rescinded. But a few days later Macready again urged burnings, this time in reprisal for ambushes as well as Republican arson. He regretted that the 'obvious course' of shooting hostages if murderers were not given up was probably impracticable unless a 'state of war' were declared. He again noted the atmosphere of 'cringing submission' created by reprisals, and looked forward to their regulation and control by senior officers. In the event, official reprisals were conducted only in the martial law area, from January to early June 1921. Prior warning was given and notices published in local newspapers without attempt at suppression. These seem usually to have been controlled operations rather than manifestations of intolerable frustration. When a Sinn Féin shopkeeper in Ennis lost his shop in April 1921, a grim event was suddenly turned into carnival: 'During the removal of portion of Mr Honan's goods for destruction, women and children rushed forward and secured, tea, jam, biscuits and oranges, which were distributed by members of the Crown Forces.' Military administrators expected businesslike operations, and in the case of these Ennis reprisals they asked sharply 'why so much damage was done. . . . In similar cases in your area, houses etc. have been demolished with such skill even in congested districts that no damage of any kind to other buildings have [sic] occurred.' Compensation claims for unnecessary damage were meticulously examined—and invariably rejected.[50]

Macready's admission of four unauthorised military reprisals is doubtless much understated. Many reprisals followed ambushes in which combined patrols of soldiers and policemen suffered, and it is unlikely that every soldier primly recited the regulations and stayed in barracks. As Macready forecast apprehensively on 27 September 1920, police and soldiers often gave different explanations of reprisals into which inquiries were held. After the sacking of Cork in December 1920 the report of the military court of inquiry was 'dead against the Auxiliaries and [Macready] says that the Police Officer who was a member of the Court and who did not agree with some of the findings was frightened to go against his own superior officers'. But Greenwood, uncharacteristically sceptical, thought that 'The soldiers have overdone it and proved themselves too white, the Auxiliary Company too black.' In Clare a police inquisition was held into a more modest outrage involving the shooting of cows and horses rather than men. The District Inspector satisfied himself that the culprits were soldiers, and in any case there was 'no likelihood that the men were police'.[51]

Although the number of military reprisals cannot be established, there is no doubt that the army command strongly opposed clandestine retaliation. The same cannot be asserted of the reorganised police. Ten days after General Tudor's appointment the Divisional Commissioner based in Limerick, in a report of indubitable authenticity, wrote thus: 'I have been told the new policy and plan and I am satisfied, though I doubt its ultimate success in the main particular—the stamping out of terrorism by secret murder. I still am of opinion that instant retaliation is the only course for this.' The phrasing of this statement is curious, suggesting that the new policy was not conveyed through regular police channels, and that it proposed deterrent rather than retaliatory action. This is corroborated by some accounts of the celebrated address given a few weeks later to the Listowel police by Colonel Smyth, another Divisional Commissioner. No official statement of the new policy is available, but its existence is consistent with the marked reluctance of the police authorities to condemn reprisals. Mark Sturgis, a senior Treasury official who had just been sent to Dublin to help reorganise the Irish government, expected Tudor to follow Macready's example in August 1920 by issuing a circular denouncing them; but on 4 September Sturgis wrote: 'It has not been issued yet! The number of police murders made it impossible.' Such a circular at last appeared on 28 September. It confessed that 'there are cases in which unjustifiable action has undoubtedly been taken', but sidestepped the question of police responsibility for them by referring to 'alleged acts of reprisal by police *and soldiers*' [my italics]. Such acts could not be 'countenanced', but no mention of punishments was made. In November Tudor congratulated the force upon its 'unparalleled fortitude' and gently suggested, 'for guidance' only, that policemen should not fire wildly from lorries, cut off women's hair, or commit arson or looting. Next February he sent slightly sharper instructions to the Auxiliaries' commander, admitting that 'a certain amount of indiscipline' was inevitable in 'an improvised force', but threatening 'the severest disciplinary measures' for serious offenders. The punishment of offenders was by no means encouraged by an order of 18 December 1920 that officers wishing to submit unfavourable reports upon their subordinates should have them examined and signed beforehand by those concerned! Another circular four months later omitted this stipulation without retracting it, warning that 'Failure to report at once frequently leads to prolonged investigations, subsequently, often without definite result and leaving the idea in some minds that the delay was on purpose.'[52] A rough index of the vigour with which indiscipline of all kinds was punished is the rate at which policemen were dismissed or discharged without pension or gratuity. For each month from July 1920 to December 1921 the weekly rate was as shown in Table 1.4.

Police responsibility for many 'unauthorised reprisals' cannot be doubted, and was accepted as fact, not hypothesis, by civil, military and even police administrators at Dublin Castle. In September 1920 Sturgis exclaimed: 'How the devil *can* we round up and try 50 policemen when we know that the bulk of their officers up to the top agree in principle with their action even if they prefer shooting to burning (as I do).' On reflection he added rather lamely: 'if we must have either!!' Macready, a month earlier, had been 'guilty of the human remark that if a policeman put on a mackintosh and a false beard and "reprised" on his own hook he was damn glad of it'. And an official police sheet, the *Weekly Summary*, while admitting that reprisals were 'wrong' and 'bad for the discipline of the Force', did not deny their existence: 'Police murder produces reprisals. Stop murdering policemen.' Local police reports are remarkable for what they failed to say about reprisals, and a Castle official responsible for rendering them fit for press consumption complained that they were 'on the face of them false in the main'. But one Clare report admitted that police had threatened unauthorised reprisals in one case, broadly hinting at their responsibility for others. 'Occurrences' at Lahinch, Ennistymon and Miltown Malbay after the bloody ambush at Rineen, resulting in six deaths, a score of gutted houses and 139 decrees for compensation, were ascribed by the County Inspector to an 'Anti Sinn Fein Gang'. But he greeted them with unseemly relish, noting their 'salutary effect'—for 'practically no Sinn Feiner now ever sleeps in his own house'. After another outrage, he added without comment: 'The whole able-bodied male population of Feakle fled to the hills.'[53] The RIC, once a respectable and accepted part of Irish society, had grown so isolated that the whole population seemed to them, as to the army, a hostile race. If the people could not be governed, at least they could be hounded from their houses.

The racking despair engendered by the revolutionary experience had many manifestations, ranging from reprisals against the revolutionists to defection to their camp, from self-pitying withdrawal behind barbed wire to resignation. The extent of defection and resignation in particular provides a measure not only of the spiritual resilience of the Crown forces, but also of the spiritual power of the revolutionaries. For the army, as I have suggested, revolution produced professional frustration rather than social despair, voluntary seclusion rather than involuntary ostracism. In contrast to the police, its responses to revolutionary pressure were muted. Reprisals were undertaken, but fairly infrequently. Desertion, the nearest military equivalent to resignation, was not a serious problem. During the first half of 1921, the most intense period of revolution, the weekly rate of desertion in Ireland was twelve—only 50 per cent more than the resignation rate among Auxiliaries, a force thirty times smaller. As the desertion rate remained at eleven during the Truce period we may suppose that revolutionary pressure was not one of its major determinants. Nor is there much evidence of secret defection to the Republican cause among soldiers. In November 1917 four soldiers were reported by military intelligence for participating in a welcome for released hunger-strikers at Ennis, and a leader in another welcome wore a 'Frock of a Military Pattern'. In July 1920 Macready detected 'a certain amount of sympathy with the Irish' among one or two units from Liverpool district.[54] A few soldiers in Clare are said to have sold arms to the IRA. But overall the Irish army kept both its distance from the Irish and its internal solidarity.

Among the police support for Sinn Féin was somewhat commoner. In February 1916 an anonymous 'true friend of the Empire . . . who receives the Government money' told the Under-Secretary that all but four or five policemen in Ennis were 'constantly in the company of well known Sinn Feiners . . . drinking with them in Public Houses'. The County Inspector good-humouredly replied:

> The only Constable that was ever friendly with Sinn Feiners was Constable Daly who recently joined the Navy—and his connection with them was in a boxing club, got up by some of the respectable people in the town—though it gradually lost cast and now does not exist. . . .

I have some very useless and indifferent policemen in the County, but I do not think any of them would act as alleged. The party in Ennis are all above that sort of thing.

Despite the vast expansion of Sinn Féin in the years following, Clare police reports referred to only one case of police support for the movement. While awaiting acceptance of his resignation, a constable drilled a group of Volunteers while in mufti. He was then dismissed. During the conscription controversy in the spring of 1918, according to a Republican journal, 'A great many policemen affected to identify themselves with the popular feeling on the subject, and made some impression on the trustful by their protests that in the event of conscription they would not assist in its enforcement.' But *An tÓglach* was not impressed, pointing out in September that these policemen had continued to hunt down Sinn Féiners 'with more than official zeal'.[55]

Some attempt was made by Sinn Féin to associate itself with police agitation to establish a trade union for improvement of their wretched pay and conditions. As early as 1907 Belfast police had developed the rudiments of trade union organisation, but this was severely put down. In 1916 the *Constabulary Gazette* wrote that unionisation (then being sought by members of the London Metropolitan Police) might prove 'an odious tyranny even to its own members, and men might be forced to participate in a revolt with which they do not sympathise'. Meanwhile Dublin police were showing 'organised insubordination' by joining the Ancient Order of Hibernians, hoping to use its organisation for their pay agitation. Not until December 1918 was an Irish branch of the Police and Prison Officials' Union 'openly established' in Dublin, and next month the Chief Secretary had 'no information' that any RIC man had joined. But in February 1919 it was found necessary to forbid RIC men to join the union, letters promoting its cause in the press were suppressed, and a few months later advertisements for a mass meeting in Dublin and a union journal were also withheld. According to a Sinn Féin spy in the detective division of the DMP, the Irish organiser of the union 'was bent on breaking up the force, or rendering it harmless and was financed by Collins', though 'ostensibly working to improve their pay and conditions'. In August 1919 London police held their last, unsuccessful strike. The *Gazette* was much relieved: success 'would have meant the downfall of the British Empire. . . . Heaven be thanked the Irish boys have kept their heads. Not a single individual has answered the call.' The subsequent pay settlement caused the union in Ireland to fall apart, and 'the R.I.C. turned away from Sinn Fein'.[56]

Irish police solidarity had successfully met the challenges of consensus politics and politically directed Labour organisation. The challenge of violent revolution was more formidable, and in July 1920 the County Inspector at Limerick told Macready 'in strict secrecy that the R.I.C. were now half informers to Sinn Fein and the other half prepared owing to strain to become assassins'.[57] But in Clare at least, surviving leaders of the IRA make modest claims for their success in sabotaging the RIC from within. A married constable living out of barracks helped Volunteers storm the Newmarket station, after which the sergeant in charge cut

Table 1.4: Dismissals and Discharges of Policemen (weekly rate), 1920–21[58]

	1920						1921											
	Jul.	Aug.	Sep.	Oct.	Nov.	Dec.	Jan.	Feb.	Mar.	Apr.	May	Jun.	Jul.	Aug.	Sep.	Oct.	Nov.	Dec.
RIC	1	3	5	9	5	4	6	10	13	29	15	20	16	12	12	9	18	14
RIC Auxiliary Division	n.a.	n.a.	1	2	1	1	4	11	3	6	3	7	3	1	5	4	6	3

Table 1.5: Resignation of Policemen (weekly rate), 1920–21

1920	Jan.	Feb.	Mar.	Apr.	May	Jun.	Jul.	Aug.	Sep.	Oct.	Nov.	Dec.
RIC	6	6	11	21	34	43	51	48	54	33	25	31
RIC Auxiliary Division	—	—	—	—	—	—	n.a.	n.a.	3	5	6	4
1921	Jan.	Feb.	Mar.	Apr.	May	Jun.	Jul.	Aug.	Sep.	Oct.	Nov.	Dec.
RIC	36	42	42	39	34	39	40	19	7	9	8	16
RIC Auxiliary Division	7	6	11	8	9	6	4	4	4	3	3	3

his throat but failed to die. The informer resigned and died fighting with Republicans in the Civil War. The County Inspector's own clerk worked for the Volunteers, resigned and became a Republican Police officer. He died of heart failure during an ambush in mid-1921. The Ruan barracks were taken with the help of a constable and a sergeant. The constable was 'kidnapped', decamped, joined a Volunteer flying column and was wounded. The sergeant was eventually demoted, then dismissed, then captured after the Truce trying to seize arms from Auxiliaries. But most Irish policemen had no more appetite for secret patriotism rewarded by a hero's death with the IRA than had the latter an appetite for police gold.[59] Frustrated and cheated though they might feel, policemen were less inclined to betray their comrades than to resign from the force and seek less onerous occupations.

Republican organisers were slow to realise that a concerted campaign to induce policemen to resign was more likely to break up the force than its infiltration with informers. Though encouraging resignation they were reluctant to compensate those who resigned—partly out of niggardliness, partly out of administrative incapacity, and partly out of loathing for policemen. In May 1918 the Standing Committee of Sinn Féin had been asked whether resigning constables should be compensated out of Sinn Féin or National Defence (against conscription) funds. The committee evasively replied that 'Every man who suffers in any way through the fight against conscription would be entitled to consideration from the people.' The Inspector-General perceived a 'conspiracy to corrupt the Constabulary' by urging policemen to resign rather than conscript, but ascribed it not to Sinn Féin but to 'certain priests'. Not until June 1920 did the Dáil ministry, acting on a suggestion from their absent president, ask Sinn Féin to undertake a systematic campaign. Their aim should be to 'bring about *immediately*' the resignation of all single policemen who had served for less than ten or twelve years and the retirement on pension of all who had served more than thirty years. A 'Free Men's Association' of those ineligible for pensions was to protect their interests. '*Representative* and *respectable*' delegations should openly approach the parents of younger constables and ask them to appeal to their sons to resign. Obediently Sinn Féin told its branches that resigned policemen 'should get credit for an honest intention' and that clubs should help them find employment. If there were none to be found, appeal should be made to an headquarters fund. But the Dáil subsequently allotted a mere £350 to the 'Police Employment Bureau', and its Department of Labour admitted 'rather poor results so far' in the campaign to induce employers to take on ex-policemen. Asylum boards and the ITGWU were approached for their help, and a resigned constable was authorised to travel outside Dublin to seek 'influential introductions'. But the outlook for the resigning constable was almost as bleak as for his persevering colleague. As the apostate Neligan writes, sympathetically if somewhat inaccurately, 'Sinn Féin blundered where the R.I.C. was concerned. . . . A vigorous campaign was directed at them with the object of making them resign, but no effort was made by anybody to provide alternative employment or to help them to return to civilian life. The result was that they could see nothing ahead but starvation. So literally they stuck to their guns and fought their own countrymen—to the last.'[60]

In fact a large number did not stick to their guns. As the Deputy Inspector-General wrote in August 1920:

> Resignations from the force are becoming very numerous and no body of men can be expected to support indefinitely the conditions under which the police in many places are forced to live, boycotted, ostracised, forced to commandeer their food, crowded in many instances into cramped quarters without proper light or air, every man's hand against them, in danger of their lives and subjected to the appeals of their parents and their families to induce them to leave the force and so put an end to the danger and annoyance to which continued service exposes them all.

The Castle's alarm was shown by the Law Adviser's statement on 23 July 1920 that within two months half the force outside the north-east would have resigned. His alarm was exaggerated, but about 1,590 RIC men applied to resign during 1920 and 1,428 during 1921, in addition to 82 and 292 Auxiliaries. Table 1.5 shows the weekly rate of resignations throughout 1920 and 1921. Early in 1920 the resignation rate scarcely exceeded that of 1913, one of the most troubled pre-war years (5.8), and was only double the average for the decade 1910–19 (3.1).[61] Resignations reached their peak in the late summer of 1920, but remained at a high level throughout the first half of 1921, which suggests that the reorganisation of the RIC by no means diminished the problem. What sorts of policemen resigned, and for what reasons? Without analysis of these questions, use of the resignation rate as an index of police frustration cannot be attempted.

It should not be supposed that the vast majority of those resigning from the force were disgruntled men of the old RIC. In April 1920, for example, no less than 36 of the 89 resignations came from depot; they involved Black and Tan recruits who had had no chance to experience the horrors of Irish life. In Clare less than half of those resigning in 1920 and early 1921 were of the old RIC. Throughout Ireland 32 per cent of those appointed constables in the first two months of 1920 eventually resigned, compared with less than a quarter of those recruited in early 1913 or late 1916. Even among those enlisted in 1921 a large proportion resigned in the few months available: some 19 per cent of the New Year batch and 14 per cent of those recruited just before the Truce.[62] Thus of the 4,000 police resignations of the revolutionary period only about 2,000 should be put down to the old RIC, or one Irish constable in five. Moreover, even among old RIC men inexperienced constables were more likely to resign than their seniors, as Table 1.6 suggests.

Although inexperienced constables comprised roughly the same proportion of resignations in the revolutionary period as before the war, the proportion of inexperienced constables resigning was four times greater in 1920–21. Few inexperienced constables resigned between 1913 and 1919 because few recruits were accepted during the war. Those that were accepted seem to have been either uncommonly hardy or uncommonly unemployable, for a remarkably small proportion of them resigned in 1920–21—actually a smaller proportion of the experience group concerned than had resigned in 1913. Overall, resignation

Table 1.6: Experience of Resigned Policemen, 1913–21[63]

Experience in years:	Under 2	2–5	5–10	10–14	Sample
Percentage of resignations occurring in each experience group:					
% 1913 (Ireland)	25	35	34	5	299
% 1913–19 (Clare)	10	39	39	10	31
% 1920–21 (Clare old RIC)	27	10	43	13	30
Resignations as percentage of policemen in each experience group:					
% 1913 (Ireland)	7	8	5	1	
% 1920–21 (Clare old RIC)	28	7	10	4	

Table 1.7: Background of Resigned Policemen, 1913–21[64]

Resignations:	1913–19 (Clare)	1920–21 (Clare old RIC)	1920–21 (new RIC)
Size of sample	31	30	31
% Irish-born	100	97	3
% Munster-born	52	57	3
% Roman Catholic	97	97	3
% Married	10	10	45
% Ex-soldiers	—	10	97
% Ex-labourers	7	8	59
% Ex-skilled workers	7	8	38
% Ex-clerks	20	—	3
% Ex-farmers or sons	67	84	—

from the RIC in face of revolution was considerable, but became less common as a man's experience in the force increased. This tendency was partly due to the fact that after fifteen years' service policemen qualified for a pension, a strong inducement for a fairly experienced constable to stick it out. That barrier once passed, retirement became more remunerative, and 1,247 men retired from the force from July 1920 to June 1921 (more than for the entire period 1914–19). The rate of retirement peaked between July and September 1920, actually exceeding the resignation rate in August, but dropped sharply thereafter. By the end of 1921 only 39 per cent of the force had served for ten years or more, compared with 56 per cent in 1913.⁶⁵ Like resignation, retirement was common rather than prevalent among the older members of the force.

Analysis of the social background of policemen resigning in Clare yields the information presented in Table 1.7. Comparison with Table 1.2 suggests that resigned policemen came from backgrounds typical of the Irish policemen of their generations. That Sinn Féin's campaign did not have a differential impact upon the sons of different social classes is suggested by the fairly close correlation between the first two columns, representing old RIC men resigning before and during the revolution.

Table 1.8: Causes of Police Resignations, 1913–21[66]

Causes of resignation:	1913–19 (Clare)	1920–21 (Clare old RIC)	1920–21 (new RIC)
Size of sample	31	30	31
% Conflict with RIC	42	20	—
% Family reasons	13	17	29
% Bettering one's condition	42	43	23
% Private reasons	3	13	23
% No reason given	—	7	26

What factors impelled policemen to resign? The explanations offered by those concerned must be treated with caution, but analysis of them reveals interesting results (Table 1.8). The sharp decline in the proportion of resignations caused by dissatisfaction or conflict with the force mirrors the improvements in pay and allowances effected by the Viceregal Commission of late 1919. The increasing appeal to family or private reasons suggests that Sinn Féin's campaign to press policemen to resign through members of their families may have been effective, though the prevalence of these explanations among the new RIC must be ascribed to other causes. The desire to better one's condition, often by enlistment in a colonial police force, remained a powerful incentive to resignation, though less so among the often unemployable Black and Tans. Only two resignations, both in 1919, were openly ascribed to the 'dangerous nature of duty in the R.I.C.' That simple fear was seldom a confessed motive is confirmed by the *Gazette*: 'We have had many communications referring to resignations, and we have never had one complaining of the risk.' The question remains as to how often policemen sought to better their condition, or expressed private dissatisfaction, as a result either of despair or of sympathy for the Republican cause. Quantification of the second underlying factor was attempted by Free State officials after the RIC's disbandment. They ruled that 631 of the 1,136 applicants had resigned or been dismissed 'because of their national sympathies'—a remarkably generous estimate.[67]

Generosity, however, did not characterise the treatment ultimately meted out to former policemen after the Truce by either government. Not until October 1921 did the Republican administration in Clare set up a committee to 'look after' resigned RIC men. Compensation was awarded to the two dismissed informers of the Ruan barracks, and the sergeant was given charge of the committee. A few weeks later he had been captured by his former comrades, and no more was heard of the committee. In mid-November a Clareman involved in the Listowel 'mutiny' wrote pathetically of his plight and that of two emigrated comrades whose pleas he enclosed: 'Perhaps when the Irish question is settled, you may not forget them, I am sorry for troubling you at this critical moment.' The Home Affairs ministry sent a comfortless reply. The Irish government's police compensation commission was set up in November 1922. County organisers were appointed to assist it, and Clare claimants invited to send their name, address and five shillings to Ennis Courthouse. But crippling restrictions were placed upon the granting of pensions to policemen who had lost their livelihood. No payments were made until early 1924, and applicants were refused if they had served for less than three and a half years, fought with the 'Irregulars', or refused a post in the Free State service. On Michael Collins's recommendation a number of former spies in the RIC were enrolled in the Gárda Síochána, causing much resentment among ex-IRA men; but those aged over twenty-seven were excluded, and Collins's successors declined to find employment for them. By late 1924 only 408 pensions had been granted to less than 10 per cent of those who had resigned or been dismissed during the Troubles. One disappointed applicant from Clare declared in 1925 that he had been discharged from the force after declining to testify in 1918 against six acquaintances who had taken his rifle and given him 'a cruel beating'. 'The Ministry of Finance has now refused to grant me a pension under Section 5 of the [Superannuation and Pensions] act although I claim to be the first man in Ireland to give a rifle for the cause of Irish Freedom.'[68]

To those who remained loyal to the Crown fate was in some ways still more unkind. Both army and RIC were humiliated at length during the interminable months of the Truce. The RIC, though eventually permitted to carry arms in the martial law area, was instructed to coexist with the rival Republican Police. If the latter exceeded their function of 'looking after the Irish Republican Army personnel only', the RIC man was obliged to appeal to his local liaison officer rather than to his handcuffs or hand grenade. The army, whose leaders believed that victory was just around the corner at the time of the Truce, felt 'humiliation and disappointment' at this act of betrayal, feelings quickly superseded by 'intense pleasure at the thought of a speedy and permanent departure from Ireland'. The Truce was marked by numerous open military displays on both sides, although few violent clashes were reported. The Treaty did not mark the end of British military encampment in Southern Ireland, and for some soldiers the 'intense pleasure' of July 1921 was clouded by growing gloom until General Macready left the Royal Hospital in December 1922. Meanwhile the police had been reduced to a shadow force, waiting only for the sun to go down to disappear. Before the Treaty the RIC's representative bodies had already requested the disbandment of the force rather than its division among the new Irish administrations, as provided in the Government of Ireland Act. Preliminary instructions for disbandment of all sections of the force, except the already dispersed Auxiliaries, were issued on 24 January 1922. After further delay evacuation of the force was begun at the end of March. Compensation by augmented pensions was allowed to all but temporary policemen, and disturbance allowances were paid to those forced to leave their Irish homes 'owing to molestation or danger or for any other cause whatever'. Both old and new RICs were in many cases allowed commutation of parts of their pensions to allow them to emigrate or find new employment. By December 1923, 1,206 men had been assisted in Britain and Ireland, and 1,436 assisted to emigrate—mainly to Canada, Australia and the United States.[69]

Emptying Ireland of the forces of the Crown was not accomplished without bother. When a battalion of Essexes left Cork late in 1921, one of its members climbed the rigging and blew his nose ostentatiously in a square of green, white and gold. On 31 January 1922 evacuation of police barracks was authorised, occupants being advised to leave behind their barbed wire, sandbags and steel plates for use by their successors. Next day Ennistymon barracks was grudgingly given over, after the Head Constable had publicly denounced two constables for throwing Mills bombs at school children screaming 'Up Rineen!' and 'Up the IRA!' The IRA planned to ambush the departing policemen, who fortunately took the long road to Ennis. But when Corofin barracks changed hands a week later, Volunteers and policemen exchanged gifts. A few days earlier, in its last issue, the *Gazette* had looked forward to the 'bright prospects of a new order which, we are convinced, will soon begin to beam over the land'.[70]

2
Protestants and Unionists

> Full oft in the evening's gloaming I think of the grand old race,
> And I doubt if the coming future will ever their like replace,
> Though some of them still remaining, yet many for aye are gone,
> The Stamers of old Carnelly, and the Scotts of Cahercon.
> There by the Shannon river still stands the grand old wood,
> Planted by ancient sires, where oft old Bindon stood.
> They call them still 'West Britons', such Colpoys, Lloyd and Gore,
> The Studderts of old Bunratty, and the Hickmans of Kilmore,
> The Ross's of Fortfergus, who fought in the foremost van
> Of many a British battle, and the Westropps of Fort Ann,
> Of Burtons and of Butlers the thronging memories rise;
> The Purdons of Tinneranna, and the Henns of Paradise,
> Of many a gallant soldier whose fame shall long endure,
> And with them our latest heroes, a Blood and a Vandeleur.
> Such were the Clare 'West Britons', who in days of our land's mishap,
> For a fickle and faithless people stood in the dangerous gap.
> These all loved the dear old county, its river and ocean tide
> And the poor still speak of their bounty, and mention their names with pride.
>
> RICHARD ROSS-LEWIN of Ross Hill,
> 'The Co. Clare "West Britons"' (1907)[1]

FOR the Rev. Richard Sargint Sadleir Ross-Lewin, Rector of Kilmurry in Clare and later Archdeacon of Limerick, the old Clare Ascendancy was already a nostalgic memory by the first years of the twentieth century. In his shrinking congregation Ross-Lewin saw the survivors of a generation whose church had been disestablished, land partly surrendered to former tenants and political influence broken by the democratic reform of the franchise at every level. None of that congregation could doubt that these disasters had eaten away the bases of their old social pre-eminence. Hence the elegiac, mournful tone of Ross-Lewin's verses. Sometimes a note of defiance is sounded, but his indignation is less that of an avenging son than a bereaved mother. He bewails the betrayal of that 'grand old race' which had brought civilisation to the barren west of Ireland and defended civilisation and Empire throughout the world. The 'fickle and faithless people' might equally well be the Catholic Irish and the radicalised English, whose governments of all parties had initiated the Irish disasters. But even through his most miserable verses there runs a thin vein of hope: the poor still spoke—presumably in private—of their bounty. This hope was fostered by the fact that the old Ascendancy's social prestige was too deeply impressed in the minds of their quondam dependants to wither up as soon as Westminster statutes knocked Protestants off their public pedestals. It took at least a generation to break the habits of deference and servility and the associated habits of envy and sullen hatred. The Irish Revolution, except, of course, in Ulster, occasioned the last and among the bitterest expressions of that hatred and envy and made the outward show of deference socially taboo. It merely completed the humiliation of Protestants noted by Ross-Lewin a decade earlier.

Clare Protestants experienced the Irish Revolution in intensified rather than typical form. They were both more vulnerable and more stubborn than in most other counties. The number of Protestants was minute—a mere 1,009 females and 923 males in 1911. They were scattered thinly over the county, in small clumps surrounding the sixty-odd remaining 'Big Houses'. Even in the county town they comprised only five per cent of the population, with denser concentrations in no more than three parishes. No county had so small a Protestant proportion either before or after the revolution. And that proportion was falling unusually fast—by a half in the fifty years before 1911 and a further three-quarters in the next fifty. But many of those who stayed were unusually conscious of their Irishness and unusually determined to keep their stake in Ireland as long as possible. Indeed, it would be difficult to define 'Irish' without including them. Clare, like Connaught, had escaped the Elizabethan and Cromwellian plantations by Britishers and 'Adventurers', so that its older county families were mainly descended from transplanted 'innocent papists' or the more pragmatic of the old Irish tribes. The Arthurs, Creaghs, Crowes, Macnamaras, Molonys, O'Briens (Inchiquins), O'Callaghans and O'Gormans all proudly traced their pedigrees to ancient chieftains. Before the Land Purchase Acts these families owned at least 100,000 acres, or one-seventh of the entire county.[2] Many emigrated in face of declining income and land agitation, which started late but lingered long in Clare. But those who were prepared to tolerate the impoverishment and danger entailed by staying on their properties were driven by a strong sense of birthright. The tardy start to the Land War in Clare had reflected the power rather than benevolence of the landlords, and memories of that power partly explain their reluctance to sell out to tenants. Clare Protestants had further to fall than most. Their fall, when it came, was uncommonly painful, and the consequent sense of desertion, betrayal and finally self-pity was all the more acute.

1. BEFORE THE WAR

In 1914 Protestants retained some of their old economic importance—as landlords, employers, large consumers and ratepayers, and even cottage industrialists. They were better off than Ross-Lewin suggested in one of his less elegant rhymes:

> For nothing it matters if landlords all
> Be as poor as mice, and our rents grow small,
> And crusty loyalists loudly bawl.

In fact Clare landlords had managed to keep their rents comparatively high, despite the attempts of the Land League and Gladstone's governments to reduce rents to a tolerable level. They also had more to lose by selling out than in many counties, as tenant purchasers were not prepared to pay the government higher annuities in Clare than elsewhere. The price paid to the landlord was based on the prevailing rent, the rent being reduced by an agreed amount from the prevailing sum. Clare landlords who sold directly to their tenants before the war were obliged to concede an average rent reduction of nearly 34 per cent, whereas in Ireland all told the reduction was only 28 per cent. So it is scarcely surprising that land purchase in Clare lagged well behind the general trend. In November 1914 the *Clare Champion* claimed to have it on 'very reliable authority' that more unpurchased tenants remained in Clare than in all Connaught.[3] By early 1915 only 57 per cent of the land eventually bought from Clare landlords under the British Land Acts had been surrendered, whereas for all Ireland the figure was as high as 72 per cent.[4] And considerable government pressure was needed to achieve even this slow rate of purchase—including the weapon of compulsion. Over 170 evicted tenants were reinstated before 1913 on Clare holdings commandeered from their evictors, and the Chief Secretary was eager to complete the troublesome process of coercion: 'Oh, certainly. I should be very glad to clear off the whole county.' For the Misses Butler of Castlecrine, 1908 was a bad year: 'Four "Evicted Farms" in our hands taken by Estates Commissioners to reinstate Evicted Tenants, and no young beasts bought.' Worse still, in 1909 the Congested Districts Board acquired compulsory powers over estates in its zone, which was extended to include 69 per cent of Clare. Five of the sixteen landlords compulsorily expropriated by the Board came from Clare. And Lord Inchiquin, Clare's only (fairly) resident peer, was one of only three Irish landlords to lose 'congested' holdings on his estates under compulsory powers also assumed in 1909 by the Estates Commissioners. The threat of compulsion often rendered its execution unnecessary: eight other Clare landlords accepted the Board's final offer to save the cost of fruitless legal squabbles, and about a fifth of pre-war land sales were conducted under the Board's menacing eye.[5] Reluctantly, indignantly, the landlords of Clare were induced to surrender the cornerstone of their power, but they fought harder and held out longer than in most counties.

Land purchase was a serious setback to Protestants but did not leave them economically bereft. Indeed, much of their property was untouched by the Land Acts. The acts were mainly intended to give the tenant occupier ownership of his holding, and perhaps a little more land if the holding could not give him a living. But little attempt was made to distribute untenanted or temporarily tenanted grasslands, which comprised much of the large estates, and landlords were allowed to buy back their own demesnes, parks and home farms on very favourable terms. Only one-tenth of Clare land bought up before the war was untenanted, and after independence twice as much untenanted land changed hands as under the operation of all the British Land Acts.[6] The retention of demesnes and grasslands caused the 'gentry' to retain sizeable labour forces even after the loss of their tenanted estates. Even modest households required four or five indoor servants before the war, and a moderate landowner such as Colonel George O'Callaghan-Westropp, who had surrendered to the Board's final offer, would still keep a dozen labourers, herds, coachmen and gardeners.

Henry Valentine Macnamara, 'a fine figure of a man, stocked with the old traditions, a diehard of the old régime', employed ten men in 1907 to manage his estate of five hundred tenants in North Clare. They cost him only £90 annually, since he saved wages by employing tenants part-time. Macnamara's economic paternalism extended to Ennistymon, most of which he owned. In 1907 he told a Royal Commission: 'It would be a great pity—perhaps I am prejudiced in the matter—to get rid of resident landowners, because I know in my own case that I spend in the town of Ennistymon as much rent as I get from the town of Ennistymon and out of the fields around it.' 'Industry' was almost unknown in Clare, though Florence Vere O'Brien of Ballyalla enthusiastically propagated classes in Clare embroidery, which she sold to other county ladies, keeping out of debt with profits from her other enterprise, Limerick lace. At the turn of the century Mrs Tottenham's group at Mount Callan, started by Mrs Vere O'Brien as a 'cottage industry', had specialised in 'children's frocks, beautifully smocked', and Queen Alexandra had been induced to buy some embroidery for Princess Mary.[7] But it was as landowners, however reduced, that Clare Protestants exerted most of their economic influence in the county, if not at Windsor.

Landownership was the chief determinant of the social as well as economic status of Protestants. As Macnamara told the Royal Commission, 'I think if I sold at all I would sell the whole estate and clear out. . . . Othello's occupation would be gone.' As long as a Protestant remained 'himself' he could command respect from his circle of dependants, though he often paid for this by night when daylight sycophants became 'moonlighters', knocking down walls, burning hay or digging up grass. The county was so renowned for such practices that ten of the twenty-two 'footprints of agitation' reported in a 1913 issue of the Unionist propaganda magazine *Notes from Ireland* were trodden in Clare. Even by day, displays of deference were not always followed by payment of rent. In 1914 gross arrears in the rent of Lord Inchiquin's seven hundred agricultural tenants greatly exceeded the year's collection, and on 1 November over three-quarters of his tenants were in arrears. But withholding rent no longer signified open revolt, as it had in the Land War. It was now accepted by most landlords that tenants would remain about a year behind in their payments, and on the eve of war landlords were mostly wise—and rich—enough not to evict defaulters in the peremptory manner of some of their fathers. O'Callaghan-Westropp,* son

---

*The curious career of George O'Callaghan-Westropp (1864–1944) of Lismehane, near Tulla, Co. Clare (colloquially known as O'Callaghan), gives this chapter its biographical backbone. Even without the magnificent set of letterbooks which O'Callaghan left behind him (see Bibliography, F 49), the historian of Protestantism in revolutionary Clare would be hard put to keep him off the centre of the stage. He was certainly the most incessantly active Protestant politician in the county and reacted violently and revealingly to all the major episodes of war and revolution. He followed an idiosyncratic path from extreme Unionism to non-partisan Irishism as an organiser of the Irish Farmers' Union. Although fifty when the European war began, he re-educated himself politically during the next decade, alienating almost all his fellow-Protestants in the

of the renowned originator of the Bodyke evictions and until 1912 landlord of two hundred tenants, allowed a tenant to keep his farm though by 1912 his arrears were six times his annual rental—'formerly a good and respectable tenant, now a drunkard and idler, having gone to the bad on election to district council from which he lost his seat last year'. The economic and social benefits of toleration—and enthusiasm—were reflected in increasing profits on the estate: by 1911 O'Callaghan was collecting over three times the profit averaged in his father's time. Landlord and tenant had achieved a workable *modus vivendi*. On 11 July 1914 the *Saturday Record*, still a most respectable paper, reported that

> The 'lord of the soil', the Marquess of Conyngham, has been paying a brief visit to this portion of his patrimony [Kilkee] for the past few days, and has been accorded a warm reception. Young and unassuming, he has won the hearts of everybody by his kind and generous nature, and it is hoped he will be a frequent visitor here for the future.[8]

If the report seems faintly ironical, it is because Conyngham's prestige was already in the crucible: three weeks earlier the same paper had advertised a meeting of his unpurchased tenants.

Sir Horace Plunkett asserted in *Noblesse Oblige*, a pamphlet 'addressed more especially to the resident gentry', that dispossessed landlords could effectively use their 'special advantages' to help regenerate Ireland: 'The abolition of landlordism, so far from destroying the usefulness of the Irish gentry, really gives them their first opportunity, within the memory of living men, to fulfil the true functions of an aristocracy. They have ceased to be the masters; they are no longer dealing with dependants.' But many landlords were too used to mastery, many former tenants too indignant at their old dependency, to forge new and more constructive social relationships. To Arthur Lynch, MP, the departure of the Vandeleurs signified the wiping out of 'the last traces of the foreign domination of Cromwell' in the Kilrush district: Vandeleur's dispossession was a victory for Irishness, regardless of any personal popularity he might have enjoyed when a landlord. Later in 1913 fifteen former tenants of the FitzGeralds of Carrigoran celebrated their liberation by protesting publicly against FitzGerald's denunciation of Home Rule at a Unionist meeting and praying that they would be granted Home Rule 'by our English brethren, who, like ourselves, have long laboured under the baneful influence of aristocratic government'.[9] Just as landlords in power had been accorded outward deference however

process. Yet at every critical moment the problems he faced were those common to his class, and in rebellion he never transcended his inherited social context. In his turbulent reactions to political change he revealed ingredients of personality and prejudice which, in different mixtures, were characteristic of provincial Protestants. In his violence of speech, eccentricities and slovenly habits of life—in later years he is said to have 'slobbered his food, surrounded by a pack of mangy terriers clothed in old vests to stop them scratching' (Devas, *Two Flamboyant Fathers*, p. 120)—he probably came closer to the archetypal survivor of the Ascendancy than the stiff-necked, ceremonious bores celebrated by W. B. Yeats in the 1920s. He was himself, as he termed his own heroes, a 'live man'.

contemptible their behaviour, so those who lost it tended to be forsaken however much they had to offer. Sir Horace had not reckoned with the sinister Irish habit of reducing the individual to an historical symbol and treating him accordingly.

Fortunately Protestant *amour propre* was not wholly reliant upon respect and deference being accorded them in the villages. It was succoured from other sources which enabled it to survive the breakdown of landlordism. The Protestant population of Clare was less a class than a community, largely insulated from the much larger but no more diverse community of Catholic Nationalists. Its core and *raison d'être* was, of course, the gentry, though in 1911 only 18 per cent of Protestant men described themselves as graziers or farmers (some of them small). Serving their interests were Protestant domestic servants, shopkeepers, engineers and surveyors, clergymen and civil servants (in descending order of number). A fair sprinkling of policemen, military and naval men recalled a less sedate tradition of Irish Protestantism. The occupational distribution of Protestants reflected the special patterns of demand for services prevalent among the gentry, who dealt wherever possible with their co-religionists. Although less than one man in fifty was a Protestant, the minority was heavily represented in business and the professions. More than a third of bankers, engineers and surveyors were Protestant, and a quarter of the lawyers. Disproportionately many gardeners, gamekeepers and bailiffs were also Protestant. Indeed, non-Catholics had their own world within the world of Co. Clare.

Within this world the gentry were able to enjoy the respect they were losing outside, and the servants in the 'Big House' could consider themselves a cut above their Catholic equivalents. The more the gentry's economic power shrank, the more important the comforting sense of status became. 'Upon class depended status and any fun that was going,' recalls a general's daughter of the years just before the war. 'The sense of loyal superiority was recognized and cherished down to the Protestant charwoman, copying her letters, whose scorn for her Roman Catholic opposite would be uninhibited.' To the newly purchased farmer every country gentleman might seem to embody 'aristocratic government', but among Protestants his status was rigidly graded according to his income and antecedents. General Parsons's daughter discerned four distinct 'top social rows' in about 1910: titled lieutenants, High Sheriffs and Knights of St Patrick, whose sons would join the Guards, 10th Hussars or navy: their sons, lesser peers, baronets and 'solvent country gentry' (Green Jackets or Highland regiments); 'less solvent country gentry' (Indian army or cheaper Irish); and professional men and substantial tradesmen, who could usually afford more expensive regiments than their social superiors. The incentives to unite against a common social threat never dulled the Protestant sense of social hierarchy. When the Irish Unionist Alliance split in 1918, O'Callaghan dismissed the victorious Clare diehards with these words of scorn: 'One of our new delegates is a Gardener, another a bailiff, and three are women!!'[10]

But communities cannot live by hierarchical sense alone. Common activities and services are also needed. In Clare Protestants had the annual hunt ball, where doctors, solicitors and police inspectors danced with the wives and daughters of landed gentlemen, and the still more egalitarian spring rook shoots, where, so it is said, anyone down to the poacher was welcome if he had a gun. Protestants did their best to maintain such self-perpetuating community services as schools and medical practices. Lady FitzGerald, with occasional help from church collections and the odd 'teaparty for coal', kept a small school near her village, Lahinch. When Protestant doctors were not readily available, men like O'Callaghan were prepared to search far afield to avoid dependence on the local man:

> There is a few miles away a most worthy dispensary practicioner, but he has only the regular practice of that sort, i.e. amongst farmers villagers and labourers, and from my observation, in spite of my personal regard for him, I think him very rusty, and we only call him in for want of anyone else in dire emergency.

For Protestants with business in the county town, the Clare County Club provided a meeting and eating place. It was necessarily more eclectic than the most exclusive clubs in Cork or Dublin, where several clubs catered for pedigrees of varying purity. A young Catholic Nationalist, Edward Lysaght (later MacLysaght), won admission to the Clare County Club when nominated by his shooting friend H. V. Macnamara. But when during the war he not only brought two uniformed Volunteers to tea, but invited the execrated Colonel Maurice Moore to stay as a 'temporary member', the collective indignation of the clubbers burst forth and Moore's name was 'formally expunged' from the visitors' book. Thereafter his host decided he could no longer afford six guineas a year 'for the privilege of occasionally visiting a certain humble apartment or shall we say of consulting a railway guide'.[11]

The institution which did most to foster community sense among Protestants was the Church of Ireland. Having escaped the pre-Restoration Munster plantations, Clare had a non-Catholic community unusually free from denominational divisions.[12] Like the community as a whole, the Church had corporate vitality enough to survive the snuffing out of its national influence. Ross-Lewin felt that many a parson's life would be justified, despite his 'scant and niggardly pay',

> If one precious soul he may help to gain.
> A soul that without his efforts were lost,
> A soul that was purchased at terrible cost.

What the Church lacked in missionary zeal it made up in tenacity when its own members threatened to apostatise. The father of a girl who had been converted (in England!) to Catholicism, despite her training in 'good broad Protestant views', admitted that in their parish 'the sense of decay or want of vitality is terrible, and I suppose unbearable to the young and sensitive'. But to leave the Church, however enfeebled, was to repudiate one's membership of the Protestant community:

> If she persists she passes out of our life, for I must protect my younger children from such influence within their home, and by reason of the bitter shame she

will put on her mother and myself, and these are as nothing to the scandal which will be caused in these parts by a child of mine deserting her Church.

'God help you child,' he wrote to his daughter, 'who are ready to believe a Roman Catholic against a Protestant.' Church attendances fell as the old Ascendancy emigrated or became extinct, not because the survivors lost interest in the Church. Indeed, the more it shrank the more dutifully its adherents struggled to preserve it. In October 1893 fifty Ennistymon worshippers, on average, contributed 11s 8d to each Sunday morning's collection. In 1913 only thirty donors managed 8s 4d, and two years later twenty-two contributed a triumphant 12s 11d.[13] The Church's pride and moral strength were tested in 1918 when detachments of Presbyterian soldiers arrived in the county. Far from embracing his fellow-Protestants as comrades in the struggle against Rome, the Bishop of Killaloe outlawed combined services in the Tulla church—despite the absence of a Presbyterian chapel and the inability of the brigade chaplain to visit each unit more than once monthly. O'Callaghan protested to the Primate of All Ireland, pointing out that Presbyterians who had joined Episcopalian services had helped 'in improving our music and contributing liberally to our offertory. . . . It would be deplorable in the face of the R.C. domination if we Protestants had to sort ourselves out into separate congregations.'

For all its troubles, the Church retained a slightly ridiculous institutional arrogance which repeatedly brought its administrators under fire, particularly from the pertinacious O'Callaghan. In March 1913 he noted a 'marked cleavage between Clergy and Laity' over the election of a new bishop, though those were times 'when Churchmen should close up'. Two years later he publicly deplored the failure of clergy to pray for an end to excessive rain despite the fact that last year's prayers, reluctantly and tardily ordered by the Bishop of Killaloe, had been 'answered by three glorious weeks which saved us from ruinous loss, though much irreparable harm had been done'. In view of the latter, O'Callaghan had diverted his favours from parochial assessment to war charities. By 1918 a special weather prayer was being offered in Tulla unfailingly every Sunday—but without regard for the changing state of the weather. To O'Callaghan the Church's meteorological failures signified not only carelessness of its duty but its social isolation from the Protestant farming community.[14] But for all their exasperation with the Church's spinelessness and remoteness, Clare Protestants could not repudiate it without abnegating their own community membership and the sense of status that went with it. This very few were prepared to do. O'Callaghan remained a church politician, not a rebel.

In pre-revolutionary Ireland a man's political creed, like his religion and land, were more often inherited than freely chosen. Rejection of Unionism by a Protestant was socially as suicidal as that of Nationalism by a Catholic. When almost all one's peers professed the same creed it was possible to claim to have 'no politics'. Lady Inchiquin recalled: 'I don't think any of the bigger families had anything to do with politics.' Her father-in-law's family 'never discussed politics because it might have been heard down below'. How could one discuss politics when, like Miss Parsons in Cork, one had 'never met a Nationalist and only about three English liberals'? Unionists held sway over a number of public offices of no importance which gave their holders ceremonial opportunities to expound their philosophy to the faithful few. The Grand Juries, which had supervised some important aspects of local administration until 1898, continued to gather at the solemn openings of assizes and gravely receive the apocalyptic addresses of the judges. County and Deputy Lieutenants were still appointed, but assigned only decorative functions. When O'Callaghan was offered the High Shrievalty of Clare in 1919 he went to great pains, though without avail, to discover the meaning of the fiat that he should 'take charge and custody of County Clare'. He inquired 'what they mean by the words quoted, and what my powers and responsibilities are. . . . It really looks as if Dublin Castle had forgotten what the Duties of High Sheriffs are.' The only influential public office in which provincial Protestants retained something of their old ascendancy was the Commission of the Peace: at the end of 1911 62 per cent of Irish justices and 50 per cent of Clare justices were non-Catholics. But even in this office their influence was being gradually eroded, for only 34 per cent of those appointed in 1912 and 1913 were Protestants, and in Clare only one out of ten.

By 1914 Irish Unionists, except in Ulster, Britain and the cities, had lost almost all political influence. A few paternalist landlords such as Macnamara retained membership of the local Boards of Guardians after the extension of the franchise in 1898. But only two Unionists in all Munster are reputed to have survived the 1906 county council elections. Occasionally politically frustrated landlords would strike back: as late as 1914 a Kerry Fitzgerald sought rent decrees against 21 of his 74 tenants, supposedly in reprisal for their failure to support his candidacy to the County Council. Other Unionists kept a foot in the back door of local government. In 1914 the Clare county surveyor, half his assistants and the council secretary were Protestants. Protestant ladies sponsored a district nurse in Ennis and dominated a County Council committee on the dispensary and sanatorium scheme. But, as Standish James O'Grady infelicitously put it, the Irish aristocracy had already surrendered most of its power 'to a hungry, greedy, and anarchic *canaille*'.[15]

Politically adept Protestants, of course, shunned appeal to O'Grady's rancorous adjectives. Having lost their political influence in Southern Ireland, they sought support among more congenial audiences elsewhere rather than striking heroic, Yeatsian postures among irredeemable opponents. Very few followed the Protestant tradition of supporting and attempting to remould according to their own vision the separatist movement—those who did were usually, like Maud Gonne and Constance Gore-Booth, women, always more prone to escape conventional shackles than their brothers. Even to espouse the Home Rule cause was considered foulest treachery. Florence Vere O'Brien promoted the interests of her Nationalist friends by whispering into influential ears 'on the sofa in the vestibule' at Ballyalla; but she baulked at organising a local meeting for Anna Louise Strong, the young Home Ruler later notable in very different contexts. However, to demonstrate her 'sympathy with Lady Aberdeen's persistent energy—in spite of everything' Mrs Vere O'Brien dispatched a party of her Clare embroiderers to Dublin, evidently to coincide with an Aberdeen–Strong enterprise. O'Callaghan, a Unionist though equally broadminded, was still more sensible to the susceptibilities of his fellow-Protestants, most of whom despised the Lord Lieutenant and Lady Aberdeen, with their utterly undignified liking for Canadian polkas, Kodak cameras, the Hill of Tara, etc., etc. When asked by the IUA to help arrange a visit to Ennis by Warrington students of the Irish question, O'Callaghan suggested that a prominent Nationalist, P. J. Linnane, should be among those invited to receive them. But he should see the visitors, alone, only between 6.30 and 7.15, before supper interval, after which the Unionist spokesmen should have their chance—'some of ours would not sit in the room with him'. Other broad-minded Protestants supported supposedly apolitical regeneration movements like the Gaelic League. The founder of the Carrigaholt Irish College represented the League on the Irish Guild of the Church of Ireland, which produced a Gaelic hymnal and a magazine called the *Gaelic Churchman*. Indeed, the Bishop of Killaloe himself was the guild's president until 1918, when he resigned over the rescinding of an earlier affirmation of loyalty to the King. But attempts to bridge the social gulf between Catholics and Protestants met sullen mistrust on both sides. A pre-war Ratepayers' Association in which Nationalists and Unionists joined forces 'in a common and worthy cause' provoked Nationalist opposition as a plot to subvert Home Rule.[16] In 1914 there seemed no prospect of breaking down the mutually damaging polarisation—social, economic and political—of the two communities. Their wretched insulation against each other, which has formed the backdrop of so many sectarian battles in Ireland, was becoming more, not less complete as Protestants lost popular respect.

'I do not seek to alter the political faith of a single Home Ruler.' Thus O'Callaghan, announcing the revival in 1911 of the County Clare Unionist Club. Like the Church, the Southern Unionist movement lacked missionary spirit. Its aim was to whip up active support for the cause among dormant sympathisers in Ulster and, even more, in Britain. When the earlier threats of Home Rule had transformed Unionism from a set of basic assumptions to a fighting creed, an 'Irish Loyal and Patriotic Union' had been formed to fight the Nationalists in Irish elections. But Unionists quickly found they could muster far stronger parliamentary support outside Southern Ireland than within it. The IUA, which succeeded the ILPU in 1891, and the Unionist clubs, founded in 1893 both in North and South, soon became propagandist rather than electoral organisations. When the general election in December 1910 gave Irish Nationalists the whip-hand, making certain the early introduction of a third Home Rule Bill, lapsed Unionist branches were quickly resuscitated. Clare's was the first Southern club to reorganise, and soon claimed about 120 attending members. The Alliance had no branch in Clare, but its executive included at least four Claremen by 1913.[17] Although Inchiquin presided over the club, its most active members were O'Callaghan and Macnamara, who made frequent forays into Ulster and beyond to publicise the isolation and vulnerability of Southern Protestants. Strong talk became easier the further one went from Clare, as their mission in September 1911 to Holywood, Co. Down, showed. The visitors denounced cases of outrages against themselves and their friends, and were reported to have ascribed the outrages to Catholic bigotry. Local Protestants fearing further maltreatment in reprisal hurriedly informed local newspapers that many of their best friends were Catholics. Six members of the club committee, including O'Callaghan's landlord friend R. J. Stacpoole, publicly repudiated the Holywood speeches as reported, causing great rancour among Unionists. O'Callaghan feared a 'permanent political and social split amongst the Clare Unionists' unless the repudiations were justified or withdrawn; the six had feared a general boycott against Protestants unless the repudiations were publicised. Neither boycott nor permanent split occurred. When Clare Unionists did split in 1918 O'Callaghan counted three of the six among his firmest supporters. The clear lesson of the Holywood fiasco was that Clare Protestants were too weak to risk offending their neighbours. Throughout 1912 Clare Unionists confined themselves to generalised expostulations among friends, and never met 'a case of hostility or insult to any Unionist meetings'. As long as the papers reported their meetings, they could not entirely escape contumely. In 1913 one correspondent jeered: 'You are as burlesque as the Sinn Feiners of some years ago.' A Belfast paper in January 1914 noticed O'Callaghan and Macnamara once more issuing 'like rats from their holes, on missions of defamation all over Ulster against the people of Co. Clare'. But on the whole Unionists behaved circumspectly in public. One Nationalist meeting was 'surprised and horrified' by one Unionist's attack on the Leaders of the Irish Race, but added that the culprit had 'felt sorry' two days later, when 'he wished to throw oil on the troubled waters by inviting the neighbouring children, what he never did before, to a little entertainment at his residence at Clifden'.[18]

The basic prejudices and assumptions underlying the Unionist creed were quite inconsistent with the straightforward attachment to Britain and dislike for Ireland ascribed them by Nationalist rhetoricians. Jostling with devotion to the British Empire, which had allegedly been 'won by Irish soldiers / Of the grand old fighting breed', was an almost hysterical hatred for modern Britain. In early 1913 O'Callaghan instructed his solicitors not to invest his funds

> in British Railways, British Industrials, or any Indian stock or enterprise. . . . In view of my probable early departure with my family to settle in a foreign country, of the possibility of my death in the Ulster War, and of the national break-up which I regard as inevitable in the near future, you will appreciate why I don't want a host of trust funds when the house of cards falls.

This apocalyptic fear was not simply an expression of anti-Liberalism. 'We loath Unionist Governments (with their petting and pampering of our enemies and snubs to ourselves) only a few degrees less than Radicals and Nationalists from whom we expect no better.' For some Unionists their party at Westminster had been discredited by Wyndham's 1903 Land Act and Sir Antony MacDonnell's Devolution scheming. Ross-Lewin, that charmingly naïve exponent of naked prejudice, felt that their fathers would never have 'crossed o'er the sounding sea / To a land that was ruled by Sir Antony'. But as the Home Rule Bill struggled through stage after stage, Southern Protestants of all persuasions increasingly feared that 'Radicals and Nationalists' and perhaps their own party as well were engaged in a plot to drive them back across the 'sounding sea', out of Ireland. As Robert Vere O'Brien lay dying, his wife 'could make out that he was speaking once about the "Irish people" and "Asquith", but everything seemed to be penetrated with a sense of overpowering oppression and helplessness, and I heard him say, at different times "I am tired", "we must stick on to the end"—and "I am overburdened"—as indeed he has been for most of his life.'[19]

Odder even than Unionist anglophobia was a streak of admiration for 'Fenianism'. When O'Callaghan discovered that a kinsman in America had been 'one of the old Independent Fenian Party', he wrote to him:

> 'Ireland a Nation' was a fine manly sentiment, and something to live for and die for if need be, and I dare say you would be surprised at how often I have been cheered for saying as much on Ulster platforms, where I have not hesitated to describe my self as a Nationalist. The present so called Nationalists are only trafficking upon a fine old name as their acceptance of the present Home Rule Bill shows. It is enough to make Parnell turn in his grave. . . . The Ulstermen, as I know from talking intimately with them, can understand a Fenian all right, but they cannot stomach a Moonlighter or a Cattle-driver, or the sort of fraud who is always gassing about his nationality and always on the look out to turn it into cash.

In Edinburgh he rejected claims that Home Rule was unanimously demanded by Nationalists, arguing that two-thirds of the nation were either strong theoretical Nationalists or of the 'old enthusiastic Fenian Party', both enemies of government by 'Tammany on Liffey'.[20] To the old soldier the separatists, with their single-mindedness and penchant for dramatic, violent expression, seemed 'live men'; to the old politician they seemed much-needed possible allies against the immediate threat. Soldiers exchanged glimpses of recognition across the chasm, but during the revolution they hardly ever jumped.

What could save Southern Unionists if Home Rule were established? The provision of a Senate, to be nominated in the first place by Lord Aberdeen, gave cold comfort. O'Callaghan sent the Duke of Bedford eight copies of a book denouncing Home Rule, with a stirring covering note: 'With us South and West Irish Unionists it is truly now "Save our Souls". Home Rule for us means the poor mercy of a quick if cruel death, or the long agony of servitude.' The Clare Unionist Club called for an adequate military garrison to defend HM's loyal subjects against expected attacks. O'Callaghan sketched out 'Notes on the Defence of Irish Country Houses'. Unless civil war or an insurrection broke out, mass assaults were not expected; but Protestants should prepare for raids by gangs of perhaps fifty land-hungry Nationalists. 'Doubtful' persons should be excluded from country houses, piano-tuners searched, friends asked to hide in the shrubberies before dawn and 'stalk the snipers'. The host at that Clifden children's party summed up the fears felt by many Unionists as to their fate under a Home Rule parliament: 'It will be ruinous to Ireland, dangerous to Great Britain, and destructive of the unity of the Empire, and . . . will inevitably make omnipotent in the country a system of graft and jobbery, for the sole benefit of professional politicians.'[21] Unionists in the last years of peace were struggling desperately to secure their future as a respected group in Irish society. Their increasing political isolation and awareness of the falsity of their friends diminished their effectiveness in political lobbies but strengthened their determination to gesture on, unanimously, to the last.

As long as Southern Unionists were able to merge their struggle with that of the Protestant majority in Ulster, they did not lose heart or hope. In the Ulster Volunteers they saw a body which shared their own ferocity and contempt for modern Britain and which manifestly terrorised the government as they could not. Carson made clear that the Ulster Volunteers were intended to defend Ulster Protestants against Englishmen, not Irishmen: 'Our quarrel is with the Government alone, and we desire that the religious and political views of our opponents should be everywhere respected.' Of course, the Ulster movement had elements of love as well as hatred for Britain. As one Southern Unionist explains, his 'sympathies and reason were entirely on the side of Ulster. I was British first and Irish afterwards, and make no apology for my sentiments.' The ambivalence in Ulster's attitude towards English ways was neatly pointed out by Kipling:

> What answer from the North?
> One Law, one Land, one Throne.
> If England drive us forth
> We shall not fall alone.

In other words, Kipling preferred either one land or none to two. But it became ever clearer that Ulstermen were prepared to sacrifice not only England but Southern Ireland in their zeal to preserve their own power—three lands might also be better than two. In September 1913 O'Callaghan reported that some Clare Unionists were 'much alarmed' at rumoured attempts to hold a conference on Home Rule—'the party will not stand further wobbling'. Next month he denounced the *Irish Times*, 'always posing' as Unionism's mouthpiece, for its 'sneers' at Ulster. But by March 1914 he was pressing the IUA to consider the danger of compromising the cause by excluding Ulster from an agreed Home Rule 'settlement'. He did not yet accuse Ulstermen of urging such a betrayal—Englishmen, first government, then opposition, were to blame. Later that month he was busy urging Dublin Unionist bodies not to betray the Ulstermen as Churchill began to flex his flabby muscles. At meetings of the Landowners' Convention and IUA executives he had 'almost enough fighting to satisfy me, with fools who would not be saved from suicide'. He reached Belfast on 19 March and dined with members of the Provisional Government with a revolver in his dinner-jacket pocket—'I was glad I was armed and had not even to cadge on Ulster for a cartridge.' But if the South, at least O'Callaghan, stood by Ulster, Ulster soon deserted the South. By late April

> While Ulster is regarded for the moment as a valuable political asset in the British Party Game, we others are looked on as disreputable poor relations, and will be thrown aside at the first convenient opportunity; Ulster is now fighting

for her own hand (I don't blame her), and Bonar Law never troubles to remember us Southerns.

O'Callaghan became thoroughly disenchanted with Ulstermen as allies. Their indifference was exhibited in the cool rejection of his request for parties of Ulster workmen to help out beleaguered Southerners—free of charge. Each of his public appearances after 1911, he noticed, had cost him a servant or a farmhand, so that by May 1914 he had himself to work as 'a common labourer'.[22] Despite repeated appeals for help, he was still doing so after the war. Friendless, powerless, deserted by every faction in the Union, Southern Unionists began to lose their nerve. Few changed their political creed, but many, including O'Callaghan, lost interest in propagating it.

2. WAR AND REVOLUTION

Then came European war. The *Irish Times* sighed with relief:

> We believe that the people of these kingdoms are to-day more cheerful than they have been at any time since the war cloud began to gather over Europe. . . . In this hour of trial the Irish nation has 'found itself' at last. Unionist and Nationalist have ranged themselves together against the invader of their common liberties.

Indeed, not all Protestants joyfully embraced yesterday's enemies and betrayers on 4 August. Canon Hannay, who later became an army chaplain in France, noted the 'curious detachment' with which Southern Unionists greeted the war, despite the quick dispatch of their sons to the front: 'They had seen many dawns of brighter days and many new eras of union among Irishmen for the good of their common country. They were aware that dawns and new eras generally end in little crops of knighthoods to be gathered by the men who repeat with most conviction the catchwords of the moment.' In Clare Florence Vere O'Brien had noted the absence of 'any burning personal interest' in the prelude to war, and O'Callaghan felt on 6 August that there was 'far too much gush, emotion, and hysteria just now'. Unionist disgust with the government increased when Home Rule, and its suspension, were at last enacted in September. This was a 'flagrant breach of faith', which took 'advantage of the patriotism of the Unionist Party'. Said the *Irish Times*: 'The Unionists have been tricked and deceived, but for the moment they are powerless. At any other time the most extreme protest would have been natural and justifiable.' Nevertheless, the paper rightly predicted that Home Rule would never become operative.[23] Gradually Unionists recognised that not only they but also the government were prepared to lay aside cherished principles in the pursuit of national unity.

The rather cautious social optimism of August 1914 was manifested in Protestant approaches towards the Irish National Volunteers. Already in early June the Volunteers had seemed to the *Irish Times* a restraining force among Irishmen, representing 'a cause, not a party'. Even if the Irish Party managed to capture the organisation, it would have to pay the price of accepting 'the first article of their creed'—resolute opposition to partition. Soon an 'Irish Volunteer' wrote to the editor that Protestants and Unionists should join up and 'renounce these wretched party politics with all their works and pomps'. A few Unionists did so, but the new *Irish Times* dream of a non-partisan party of violent men of peace did not appeal at first to the down-to-earth Protestants of Clare. O'Callaghan thought the *Irish Times* arguments 'stupid even for it' and pointed out that local Volunteers had recently burnt Carson's effigy on the Tuamgraney rectory gate. 'So much for "Toleration", and the National Volunteers having no enmity to Carson and Ulster.'[24] Florence Vere O'Brien expressed affectionate distress at her son's request that she allow Volunteers, among whom he was becoming 'quite a leader', to drill on her island in the Shannon. But she admitted that 'If we are to have volunteers at all, the better trained in all good and soldierly ways they are—and by the right people— the better for all of us.' Unionist interest in the Volunteers increased when John Redmond, just after the outbreak of war, committed the force which by now he ostensibly controlled to the defence of Ireland in case of invasion. O'Callaghan, though privately sceptical of Redmond's motives, appealed to Clare retired officers to 'fall into line', provided their neighbours wanted their help and the government wanted the Volunteers' help. An eager Protestant wrote: 'Now that the Volunteers of Ireland, both Protestant and Catholic, have come together, all religious controversy should be given over for ever. My greatest friends have always been Roman Catholic clergymen.' About a dozen ex-officers expressed willingness to train Volunteers, and three of them met the County Board at an Ennis hotel. The entry of Unionists to the force was accepted in principle, though O'Callaghan found the tone of the meeting unjustifiably 'shy and suspicious'. Negotiations foundered when the County Board insisted that ex-officers join the ranks and submit to election to office, in O'Callaghan's view an 'unspeakably silly' proposal. A second meeting convinced him that the 'good keen chaps' were 'overloaded with politicians, theorists and other varieties of unpractical windbags'. Apart from his father's former land agent, who later became a Sinn Féiner, it seems that the only gentry to join the force formally were the successive county Inspecting Officers.

But soon Unionist interest in the Volunteers cooled. Volunteers were afraid of being sucked into the Regular Army, the government was afraid to assign them home defence duties, Protestants and Catholics mistrusted each other. Moreover, the Volunteer split late in September left two stark options for Unionists: to join the active Sinn Féin faction, who did not want them, or the moribund majority, now assimilated into the hated Irish Party machine. Afterwards O'Callaghan sympathised with the 'many idealist nationalists, who had never touched party intrigue' and had been 'disgusted at becoming a wheel in the Party Machine', but as a loyalist he could not join them.[25] As far as the Volunteers were concerned, the war emergency generated nothing but conciliatory gestures.

In other fields Protestants were more successful in escaping their pre-war social isolation. Enough Catholics were recruited even in Clare to justify the belief that war's demands had transcended class and religious affiliations. For their part, Protestants ostentatiously set aside old enmities. The select vestry at

Kilrush decided to raise a flag on the church tower in 'honour' of the radical Lord Lieutenant's recruiting tour. O'Callaghan asked the Catholic Bishop Fogarty to use his 'great influence in steadying the people' when police instructions in case of coastal invasion led to popular panic. *Notes from Ireland* was delighted to see Nationalists and Unionists on the same platforms, though it could not refrain from deploring the 'chronic disposition and constant eagerness' of such Irish Party chiefs as Dillon to exploit the 'present situation' in the interests of Home Rule alone. Behind the scenes, of course, factionalism was, as always, rife. In 1916 the recruiting drive in Clare was divided between the Lord Lieutenant's organisation, which enlisted the help of Nationalist local government bodies, and the more traditionalist War Office. O'Callaghan, who supported the Wimborne faction, complained that 'the whole thing is evidently a mass of intrigue'. But at least on the surface war had allowed many Protestants to escape their choking social isolation. Although war had generated little enthusiasm or interest, it had served to postpone the dreaded resolution of most of the vexed social and political disputes which had menaced the last years of peace. Romantic Ross-Lewin 'indulged in the hope', remarkably like Pádraic Pearse's, that Irishmen would draw together, 'having cemented with their blood a new brotherhood of Irishmen all the world over, imbued with new thoughts and new inspirations'. But hard-headed O'Callaghan knew that war would provide at best temporary relief for Protestants: many Nationalists were 'anxiously waiting for the end of the war for our expulsion'.[26] Protestants made hay while the sun shone—and got excellent prices for it.

Many Protestants made not hay but clay. Virtually every county family sent all its able-bodied sons to fight, leaving a lop-sided community at home overstocked with women, the very young and very old. By late 1917 O'Callaghan had lost five cousins killed and nine wounded. Those who had to stay home often found their servants more prone to volunteer than most other classes, and found it harder than ever to attract replacements for them. Over-fifty-year-olds like O'Callaghan anxiously waited to be 'called out at any moment'. Even in February 1915 he thought himself 'almost certain' to be recalled to military duty next May. By mid-year no less than twenty-nine members of the IUA executive committee had been mobilised, though O'Callaghan was still at Lismehane trying to swallow his chagrin. Like many old officers, he campaigned vigorously on the home front. Unavailingly he urged the resurrection of his old Clare Militia, though this should be done at first on the quiet lest he seem to be 'making a job for myself'. Ross-Lewin and his brother devoted their literary talents to the composition of recruiting verses for the *Saturday Record* as well as the diehard Dublin *Daily Express*. At Dromoland Castle in 1916 the children of Kilnasoolagh were doubtless astonished at the contents of the scroll flung down by Father Christmas at their annual treat:

> Have courage!
> To those who nobly fight
>   Victory and peace shall come.
> But shirkers shall have naught
>   But misery as their doom.

For some Protestants recruiting zeal was tempered by the belief that military service should be made compulsory in wartime. O'Callaghan ascribed much of the recalcitrance among 'the better stamp of labourers and farmers' sons' to 'the cruel unfairness of "voluntary" recruiting by badgering'. Universal service, with exemptions for those in truly essential jobs, would be juster and, he felt, more popular; it would also put an end to 'fancy employments such as drapers' assistants whose work could be done by girls, and surplus or partially employed home workers'. The IUA later advocated the extension of the Military Service Act to Ireland on the ground that Irish divisions would otherwise have to be restocked by Britishers.

But universal service never came, so Unionists missed the challenge of helping to enforce it—luckily for them. Protestant women were kept busy organising the seven war charities established in Clare. By the late summer of 1918 Clare had contributed over £6,600, most of it from a score or so of prominent families. Clare prisoners of war, 110 of them, did particularly well out of the largesse of those at home, receiving 5,897 parcels of food, 102 of tobacco and 17 of clothing, 156 pairs of socks, seven mufflers and two footballs. When they arrived home in January 1919 'plentiful tea' and concerts greeted them, though work was harder to find.[27] In other words, the gentry of Clare managed to express their approval of the war effort in ways almost indistinguishable from those followed in the quietest, loyalist village in the British Isles. The fact that the brave show was presented against a backdrop of mounting hostility towards the war effort, the Empire and the gentry themselves, lends an air of unreality to the wartime behaviour of Clare Protestants. Just as the Nationalist visionaries pursued their revolution with scant regard for the world war, so the loyalists knitted their mufflers with scant regard for the developing revolution.[28]

Still, April 1916 did not pass unnoticed. Fortuitously, Messrs Browne & Nolan had dispatched twenty-two bound volumes of newspapers to Lismehane in early April, which O'Callaghan found 'such a convenient means of making windows bullet proof that I have not yet unpacked them [24 July], nor do I propose doing so until more quiet times come'. To most Protestants, though not O'Callaghan, the Rising came as a surprise, and its aftermath shattered many of the illusions which the sense of wartime unity had fostered. Even diehards had laid aside in August 1914 their pre-war grievances against the Asquith government, the Irish Party and the selfish Ulster Unionists. But the sequel to the Rising reinvigorated the old fears and generated new ones. Maxwell's military executions met with widespread approbation from Unionists, including the Church of Ireland Archbishop of Dublin, the *Irish Times* and Colonel O'Callaghan. But the government's subsequent efforts to pacify the angry Irish by presenting a revised set of Home Rule proposals, from which the six north-eastern counties would probably be exempted, alarmed Southern Unionists more than the Rising. On 27 June Lloyd George received an indignant deputation of Unionists from the other twenty-six counties which denounced both partition and the surrender to Nationalists of government in the South. The

Irish Times agreed, though admitting 'that they must accept the inevitable—when it becomes inevitable'. O'Callaghan deplored the announcement that the IUA's executive would so much as meet to discuss the proposals—they must not admit 'that this swindle is capable of amendment or safeguard'. He felt keenly that Ulster and the government had again betrayed Southern Unionists: 'I know the Irish Unionists are abandoned. I was a Unionist, I am a Protestant.' But he predicted a further and still more sinister consequence of this panic-driven breach of the 'Party Truce'. All the credit for Home Rule would go to the rebels, and what he now considered the 'steadying influence of John Redmond and the Catholic Bishops' would be swept away. The squashing of Lloyd George's proposals did not restore confidence in the way Ireland was governed. In November O'Callaghan was still writing: 'Far worse than the Rebellion was the Government muddling after it.'[29] These reactions illustrate two important lessons many Southern Unionists had learnt since 1914. First, that in critical times it was necessary for them to move out of their self-protective shell and co-operate with such untouchables as Redmond and the bishops. Second, that once out of the shell they could not maintain the old façade of unity of interest with Unionist parties in Britain and Ulster. But many preferred the old shell, despite the receding tide, to pragmatism.

The history of Southern Unionism from 1917 to 1919 was one of division. As it became clear that the two evils of Home Rule and partition could not both be averted indefinitely, dissension arose as to which cause could better be sacrificed for the sake of the other. Lloyd George's 1916 proposals had alarmed both factions by attempting to impose both evils. But the division among Unionists was made clear in 1917, when Lord Midleton, chairman of the IUA, proposed to the Irish Convention that an all-Ireland parliament be set up with limited fiscal powers, including control of internal taxation and excise. Unionist acquiescence to these 'Home Rule' proposals would be the price of freedom from partition. The Ulsterites, intent on keeping all Nationalist fingers out of the six counties pie, rejected the proposals, splitting the Convention and the IUA. Calls by Lord Monteagle and Sir Horace Plunkett for Dominion status for a united Ireland got equally short shrift from government and Ulstermen alike. After a long struggle the diehard opponents of Home Rule won control of the IUA, and the Midletonites seceded to form their own Unionist Anti-Partition League. Thereafter the supporters of APL attempted with varying acuity to judge the pragmatic course for a Southern Protestant wishing to remain an Irishman, while those of the IUA took an increasingly sour and negative view of the Irish problem in general. For many of the diehards, commonly known as 'Callers', the social lowering entailed by the course of reconciliation was simply too cruel to bear: as the Archbishop of Dublin wrote to his brother Canterbury of his Roman Catholic counterparts, 'All these prelates are peasants.'[30]

In Clare the effect of division was to renew interest in Unionist organisation before killing it again. The Clare Unionist Club was dormant in early 1916: although its members had 'not weakened in their faith', according to Lord Inchiquin, it had not met since war began. Although the club could no longer hope to attract the large pre-war attendances, the threat of schism and end of the 'Party Truce' attracted many old schemers back to the game. Inchiquin lost the presidency after suggesting that the club be allowed to lapse since only Macnamara and O'Callaghan took 'any interest in it'. But the diehards, led by Macnamara, took enough interest in it to wrest control from O'Callaghan and the 'quiet folk', who were 'afraid to attend'. O'Callaghan unsuccessfully urged Midleton to help him form a rival organisation, enclosing a list of twenty prominent Unionists who might oppose Macnamara's faction: 'I am sorry, but we must take off the gloves or be pulled down in the general ruin by these Ulster-inspired fanatics.' But as the excitement of schism receded it became increasingly clear that pragmatists stood to gain little by battling on within Unionist ranks. By January 1919 O'Callaghan detected five conflicting factions within the movement. 'What a muddle!! And all the time Sinn Fein goes steadily on its way, knowing its own mind and heeding no one.' In fact, over a year earlier he had declared his intention to work for Ireland regardless of the policies and politics of the Unionist Party:

> My personal loyalty to the King remains. Subject to that alone I hope in such years as remain to me to do some work for Ireland. Not being a spaniel I owe no further allegiance to Great Britain and its factions.[31]

Thereafter O'Callaghan threw himself into whatever movement seemed least likely to fall under the thumb of any of the discredited parties, whether Unionist or Nationalist, and most likely to redirect Irish energies towards reconstruction rather than revolution.

Why did men like O'Callaghan choose to cast in their lot with Ireland, despite the difficulty and discomfort of doing so, rather than to sell out and emigrate to more secure and peaceful places? Clearly pride, nostalgia and a sense of communal responsibility for one's beleaguered neighbours played a part in such decisions, as did wartime restrictions on travel. But for landowners, still the backbone of the Protestant community, war generated a still more powerful incentive to stay home at peace with one's neighbours—an agricultural boom, with its promise of rising income. Prices for almost all agricultural produce, both crops and stock, rose consistently from 1915 to 1920 in response to the dislocation of world trade. By 1920, the peak year, prices had roughly trebled since 1913. Thus the lesson of each war year for the Irish farmer was that still better circumstances awaited the man who held his ground. Not until the third quarter of 1921, Truce time, did prices begin to fall overall. The entire Irish Revolution was conducted in an atmosphere of agricultural euphoria. The large producer, so often a Protestant, stood to gain more from the prices boom than the semi-subsistence farmer, and was all the less likely to give up his stake in the soil willingly. Protestants who had struggled grimly to maintain a respectable livelihood before the war suddenly found their income rising. The Misses Butler of Castlecrine reaped almost three times their pre-war annual gross profit during the years 1915–21, yet bought less than half as many cattle annually. Before the war their proceeds had exceeded outlay by a mere 51 per cent; during the boom the margin increased to 187 per cent. The net deficit on Lord Inchiquin's large estate fell from £5,918 in 1914–15 to £4,301 in 1917–18, though it then rose again because of mounting arrears of rent from his tenants.[32] Even where the effects of government restrictions and revolutionary disruption outweighed the advantages of the boom period the promise remained that, if only political conditions returned to normal, a golden future awaited the farmer. But these negative influences also did much to determine the political behaviour of farmers, particularly those most severely punished by market restrictions and revolutionary hostility—the Protestant graziers and landlords. The resultant antagonism between the promise of prosperity and the reality of agricultural disruption was a major factor in the fragmentation of the Protestant community in the revolutionary years.

Farmers of all creeds shared indignation against the government's attempts to control Irish agriculture in order to help British consumers. But for the Protestants the discovery of a cause common to all farmers had far-reaching social effects. To combat pernicious restrictions, farmers had to organise and fight together, whatever their social or religious status. Even more than the recruiting campaign, the farmers' movement transcended class barriers and helped break down Protestant insularity. As usual, O'Callaghan was among the first Protestants to fling himself into battle. Within a few weeks of the promulgation of the first order to increase the proportion of arable under tillage, he had interviewed the Chief Secretary and sent him a detailed list of constructive criticisms, which got lost in the post. At this early stage he was, in principle, 'strongly in favour of the Tillage scheme' and hoped the authorities would be 'very peremptory' in enforcing it. But when the government ordered a further general extension of tillage for 1918 with no concessions to virtuous pre-1916 tillers, as well as imposing maximum prices on meat and minimum wages for agricultural labourers, O'Callaghan wrote indignantly to the secretary of the Landowners' Convention that 'the cumulative effect of these will make farming impossible in a great part of Ireland'. He urged the convention to send a deputation to Lloyd George. More tillage meant less hay, and for owners of livestock this could prove disastrous. O'Callaghan lost several animals allegedly through starvation in 1918 and 1919, and none of his two-hundred-odd stock were marketable in April of either year because of hunger: they were 'too thin and weak'.[33]

In April 1918 local papers reported the first general meeting of the County Clare Ratepayers' and Farmers' Association (CFA), in which O'Callaghan was a leading light. Colonel Tottenham, one of the leading diehards, was a founding member. R. J. Stacpoole, his old antagonist from Holywood days, was chairman. But the association bridged more gulfs than those between Unionist factions. From the first Nationalists appeared on its platforms. Early on the association did encounter difficulty in forming parish branches, perhaps because its leaders were still distrusted politically, but this did not stop O'Callaghan, on its behalf, swamping the Castle with letters of remonstrance and advice, resolutions and deputations. In 1919 attempts were made by some Nationalists to establish rival organisations of unimpeachable political purity. The editor of the *Clare Champion* launched a Farmers' Association in May, and in October a meeting was held of Co. Clare farmers and Ennis traders, only to be repudiated by Sinn Féiners, prominent at the May meeting, as an Irish Party stunt. But while party men and Sinn Féiners squabbled, O'Callaghan's movement was catching on. O'Callaghan, aware of the difficulty of his position, preferred not to address a meeting at Kilkishen in July:

> It would be ruinous to the movement if ignorant or malicious persons persuaded the farmers that it was being captured by either Unionists or Landlords. . . . Unhappily in Clare we live in an atmosphere of distrust and suspicion from which other counties have long since escaped, and until we also escape out of this poisonous swamp we can never make a united and manly stand for the public good.

But by sheer will-power and energy O'Callaghan managed to build the CFA into a formidable machine, of which he became chairman early in 1921. Signs of militancy among the lower orders caused Stacpoole and Inchiquin to resign from it, but O'Callaghan regretted their action, while praising the Irish Farmers' Union for admitting landlords—unlike its English counterpart. Such was the strength of the Irish Farmers' Union by 1921 that O'Callaghan now hoped it might be the long-sought vehicle for regenerating Irish life without regard for political affiliations. The *Clare Champion* reproved him for attempting to direct Irish energies away from politics, but expressed measured approval for his efforts: 'In normal conditions, Ireland would request, even demand, the services of such men.'[34]

War had driven the government to unpopular measures to satisfy home demand for food, and even after the war the temptation to keep on managing the markets proved irresistible. But revolution provoked punitive measures against farmers which antagonised an even wider range of Protestants than tillage, price, export and wage regulations had done. From February 1918 markets and fairs in various districts in Clare were banned in response to violent local incidents. But in August 1919 the ban was extended to the entire county, the Chief Secretary stipulating in October that 'So long as the community do not assist the Government in tracing the outrages and bringing the culprits to justice the general prohibition must remain.' Thus quietly unco-operative districts were to be punished as harshly as those in open insurrection. The CFA immediately voiced its protest, as did 'certain residents in the parish of Tulla and County of Clare' (that is, O'Callaghan). Advice came too from the High Sheriff of the county—also O'Callaghan. Soon, however, even the diehards became alarmed enough to summon a meeting of protest for 'important local people'. O'Callaghan ridiculed this announcement: 'They will be promptly reported by the police as a handful of back number landlords scared about their rents! For O'Loghlen, you [Stacpoole], and I, to try this after our official failure to get justice is like coming down from rifles to bows and arrows.' In the event Protestants held two protest meetings in November, and in at least one of them diehards and pragmatists combined to denounce 'undeserved penalties on the innocent' which tended 'to increase the risk of crime and outrages by the discontented or criminal'. Both Houses would hear of it should their protests pass unheeded. The reversion to Unionist unity was temporary, for soon the restrictions were relaxed, though spasmodically reapplied up to the Truce.[35] But the fight against the ban had brought more Protestants into common cause with Catholics than, perhaps, any episode since the Union.

If the government's restrictions on agriculture tended to bring Protestant and Catholic, landlord and tenant, together, its restrictions on land purchase tended to sunder them. In 1915, at the Treasury's insistence, the Congested Districts Board suspended acquisition of estates, thus freezing landownership in two-thirds of Clare. The allocation of lands previously acquired proceeded slowly, and in March 1916 the sale of one-third of these estates in Clare had not been completed. The Estates Commissioners continued to supervise direct sales from landlords to tenants in other areas, but wartime uncertainties reduced the exchange value of the stock with which vendors were paid, increasing their reluctance to sell. Although wartime land purchase was rather brisker in Clare than elsewhere, only 14 per cent of all the land sold up under the British Land Acts was surrendered between 1914 and 1920. In March 1920 the expropriation of Clare landlords was less than half complete. Significantly, the acquisition of untenanted land was even worse hit in these years than that of tenanted land. Before the war 13 per cent of land sold by owners under the 1903 and 1909 Land Acts had been untenanted, but in the years 1915–20 that proportion was a mere 4 per cent.[36] The curtailment of land purchase during the years of war and revolution had two major consequences for landowners. The impracticability of selling out encouraged landlords to make the most of the agricultural boom and helped stem the Protestant exodus which had greeted the Land Acts before 1914. But the frustration engendered in tenant occupiers and landless men, whose expectations of owning and extending their own field or plot had never been so high as in 1914, gave rise to increasingly bitter and desperate attempts to wrest the land from landlords by extra-legal means. Landlords kept their stake in the county, but at the cost of provoking more open hostility than at any time since 1903.

Such hostility was, of course, a long-standing tradition in the Irish countryside. But once Wyndham's Act had conceded the principle of ownership by occupiers, the complex machinery of agrarian agitation was mainly diverted to negotiating terms as generous as possible to the buyer. The modern function of 'moonlighting' was to make a landlord's life just unpleasant enough to persuade him to seek terms, while the parish priest pulled strings in the Congested Districts Board and the United Irish League prepared dossiers for parliamentary questioners. But the machinery could not cope with a situation in which the facilities for land purchase were withdrawn. The obsolescence of the old machinery was recognised by one writer to the *Champion* as early as January 1915: 'There is neither organisation, nor attempt at organisation, in the county.' Not surprisingly moonlighting—not to mention sunlighting—came back into its own—first as an expression of individual frustration, later as a calculated stratagem. In the four years *after* he sold out to his tenants O'Callaghan claimed to have suffered no less than five hundred outrages, including 'Digging up Grass Lands by night, injuries to Harvesting Machines, attempt to wreck a motor car, throwing down a gate, throwing down coping stones of walls, and stoning meadows'.[37] All this was typical of life in Co. Clare—as was the RIC's persistent failure to detect a single offender.

But after 1917 the frustrations of land-hungry men began to assume more organised form, potentially far more dangerous to the landowner. Soaring food prices encouraged the poor to seek land to till, but the tillage regulations forced tillage on those who did not want it and compensated them by guaranteeing still higher prices. In January 1917 came the first signs of a movement to divide and plough the grazing ranches of Clare, using the regulations as a 'lever'. Unpurchased tenants on three estates were reported to have marked off portions of ranches which they believed should be tilled. By the end of the year cattle-driving and 'ploughing' of grazing lands were commonplace. The police ascribed this to the suspension of land purchase and predicted a renewal of 'agitation for the sale and division of grass farms'. Soon afterwards Macnamara was forced to till twenty-five acres of his own land, and the local council called on him to let out those parcels which had been 'ploughed and striped' to the 'uneconomic holders' of the district. Before the imposition of military rule in February 1918 temporarily suppressed it, the agitation had shown itself to be tightly enough co-ordinated to strike terror into the hearts of many Protestants (and many Catholic Nationalists as well). The Armistice brought a resumption of land purchase by government bodies and the promise of further legislation to allow its speedy completion. But the resumption was half-hearted, the legislation not forthcoming, and the police increasingly incapable of suppressing agitation. Countrymen were encouraged to take the law, and the land, into their own hands. On 23 April 1920 Captain R. F. Hibbert, a retired cavalry officer who had married into land in East Clare and had managed to win membership both of the IUA executive and the Scariff RDC, expected the worst:

> Our tenants, having previously refused to purchase their holdings, decided to do so just before the war. So far as I can see, they will now adopt the attitude that if they wait a little longer, they will get their lands free.

In fact a vigorous campaign was already under way to induce landlords to surrender their lands—not without compensation, but usually at prices determined by unofficial arbitration in which tenants and landless men had the whip-hand. After mid-year the movement to grab land lost momentum, but the fear of its resumption remained. Moreover, sporadic incidents persisted, often pitting small grazier against large grazier rather than tiller against stock farmer (as in 1917). In December 1920 one of Macnamara's farms was let out by 'the IRA' to favoured graziers, whom the police surprisingly managed to evict. Next July local farmers distributed their stock over 4,000 of his acres, but he did not bother even to call for action. For the battle had been lost.[38]

So hazardous did the life of large landowners become in the revolutionary years that some of them became as eager to complete the sale of their tenanted lands, if not their leased-out grazing lands, as their tenants had once been to buy. But by May 1920 land stock had plummeted to £475 in the thousand, compensation which no landlord could afford to accept. Post-war attempts to put through practical provisions for land purchase created little interest at Westminster. When Major O'Neill introduced the subject in mid-1919 the House had broken up for lack of a quorum in the middle of his speech. Nearly a year later Bonar Law promised a measure while the Government of Ireland Bill was being considered. But further procrastination ensured that no Land Purchase Act was ever assented.[39] O'Callaghan and the Irish Farmers' Union lobbied hard but fruitlessly: at a time (May 1921) when Irish farmers were 'very nervous' he felt 'the early introduction of the Land Purchase Bill would do much to close down a source of grave unrest'. So clearly did he perceive the damage being done to both landlords and tenants by the government's inaction that he publicly condoned a controversial branch resolution asking landlords to cease suing for rent until tenants had met with them and sought an amicable settlement—though privately he advised the IFU county organiser to pursue the resolution no further. It was over this resolution that Inchiquin and Stacpoole, still partly dependent on rents from their tenants, resigned from the CFA. Inchiquin, indeed, had cause for alarm over rent arrears: from a typical £11,333 in November 1919 these rose to £12,633 in 1920, £17,499 in 1921 and £24,549 in 1922. Even O'Callaghan, broad-minded and tenant-free though he was, could not escape punishment from land-hungry locals. In December 1921 he heard that Volunteers 'had divided my farm between them' and had forbidden him to put 'one of my very most respectable labourers into my gate lodge'. The young bloods were out of hand indeed.[40] No large farmer, whether landlord or grazier, Catholic or Protestant, could feel secure from the growing indignation of the poor or envious. It was little solace that the government was as much to blame as the landowners.

The abnormal economic conditions of wartime and revolution posed social problems for rich Protestants in another field—that of employment. One of the bases of their social prestige had been the dependence on them of a large body of deferential servants and labourers. Wartime recruitment not only robbed them of many of their trustiest employees, but also caused the entire labour force to shrink rapidly—especially in Ulster and England where many west of Ireland Protestants sought their labour. Employers responded to the scarcity not by offering higher wages, which would have eaten into their profits, but by reducing their establishments. Before the war O'Callaghan had expected the steady reduction of his labourers to cause the early closure of his farm; after 1914 they did not return, but his complaints grew fainter as he reaped the benefits of working himself to the bone to eke the best out of the boom. Wages rose much more slowly than the cost of living, and by early 1915 prices were beginning to tell on the poor. Some Protestants wondered if the poor should not be allowed a slice of the cake. George McElroy, RM, not himself a substantial employer, could not attend Mrs Hickman's meeting to help relieve the poor of their distress, but wrote:

The poor are with us always, but our sympathy with them is dormant until war comes, then they need them to defend their homes, their trade, and their wealth. Why should distress be allowed in Clare at present? They speak of war and hard times, but the fact is that there was never more money than now.

But charity did not begin in the pay packet. O'Callaghan and the CFA campaigned strenuously against the modest minimum wage guaranteed agricultural labourers late in 1917—which for Clare exceeded the minimum customary in 1914 by only three-quarters, though food prices had doubled in the interim. O'Callaghan suggested a minimum 16s weekly, just 4s 3d above the 1914 wage. The Vere O'Briens managed to spend less on their household of servants in 1916 than the previous year.[41] By economising and cutting down their labour forces rather than sacrificing profits for higher wages, Protestants diminished their own importance and status in the economic system.

Worse was to come. The end of the war flooded Ireland with ex-servicemen seeking work, but brought no relief from rising prices. To prevent employers lowering wages still further in response to the sudden influx of labour, workers joined unions and strikes proliferated. Employers tended to blame the government for the growth of their powerful new enemy. A Cork auctioneer accused the Chief Secretary of allowing the existence of unions 'for the one purpose of driving Protestants and other loyal Men out of the south so that Sinn Fein may run rampant'. O'Callaghan felt the labour conflict was made 'inevitable' by the government's regulations, which put 'the farmer at the labourer's mercy, while the labourer is at liberty to defy the Government Regulations against strikes and knows it well'. It was easier to denounce government than unions, especially after the IFU affiliated to the ILPTUC. Pragmatic employers tried to live in peace with the unions. It is said that members of the Inchiquins' hundred-man workforce guarded Dromoland Castle from midnight to 6 a.m. after learning that Volunteers had imported petrol from Dublin to burn it down. Until 1921 the benevolence necessary to inspire such devotion did not empty too many Protestant pockets. But agricultural recession, accompanied by increasingly effective labour organisation and consequent 'softening' on the government's part, threatened to impoverish many employers. On 31 May Florence Vere O'Brien wondered how she should respond to the increase of 2s weekly ordered by the Agricultural Wages Board: 'Of course the natural advice when people are over-spending in wages is to dismiss some of their men—but this is not so easy as it sounds.' The Tottenhams of Mount Callan, who paid wages of £770 annually in 1919–20, discovered this in November 1921 after dismissing two herds and reducing wages by 2s 6d weekly. All but two workmen went on strike. Next day Colonel Tottenham tersely recorded in his rainfall book: 'Bridge on avenue and up rd smashed. . . . [*Illegible*] Burnt Plantation blocked. Branch cut near well. . . . Motor tampered with and our 2 Maids withdrawn.' Of the servants only the cook stayed. Soon Godmother IRA intervened and decided in Tottenham's favour. Within eight months he 'was able to reduce wages without any difficulty'.[42] But the growth of the union and the impoverishment of farmers had badly tarnished the paternalist image of the landed employer.

It should now be clear that the abnormalities of the wartime economy did not have a uniform or consistent impact on the conditions under which Clare Protestants lived. The agricultural boom and the suspension of land purchase encouraged landlords to keep their stake in the county; but the frustration of those excluded from the benefits of the boom and from purchasing holdings engendered new acrimony and revived old grievances. Were mounting profits, or the promise of them, worth the discomfort involved in acquiring them? Differing judgments on this question helped to widen the gulf between the demoralised traditionalists and the pragmatists, prepared to sacrifice ease and comfort in order to get their slice of cake, whatever the icing. After 1918 revolution made the Protestant dilemma still more acute. Hostility to the old Ascendancy took increasingly violent form. Cattle-driving was joined by arms raiding, house- and church-burning, and armed attacks on Protestant parties. It is difficult to disentangle the economic, political and military strands in this campaign of violence, for the same assailant was often Volunteer, Sinn Féiner and uneconomic holder or landless younger son. But it is certain that the separatist movement gave guns and organisation to those with agrarian grievances, and that Protestants were increasingly linked by separatists with their prime political and military targets—police, army and government. The revolution gave bite to the agrarian struggle and drew much of its own vitality from it. The Protestants were targets of both campaigns, and their function as symbolic enemies was to justify the fusion (never complete) of the two revolutionary strands in Irish history.

Already in 1918 many Protestants believed that agrarian agitation had taken on a revolutionary, political character. Amidst the February cattle-driving O'Callaghan wrote:

> Violence and defiance of the common law have taken the place of industry, and the most improbable people now welcome naked revolution as a welcome release from the stupidities and incompetence of the British Government. Conditions here are far more dangerous than during the Rebellion of 1916. I remember well the country in 1879–1882. It is far worse now.

A week later Captain Hibbert of Woodpark told the Chief Secretary of 'the unspeakable state of terrorism and intimidation now general', and deplored the government's feebleness in protecting property. He had experienced repeated trouble from land agitators before the war, but his troubles in 1918 took on an ominously political colour. After he declined to sign a Republican 'plebbysite' his gates were decorated with the words 'TO HELL WITH HIBBERT', and he expected worse treatment presently. At this time Volunteers, desperately short of weapons, were forcing or cajoling many owners to surrender their shotguns or rifles, though they preferred to approach malleable farmers or soldiers on furlough rather than the gentry, with their servants and Yale locks. By late 1919 these sources of supply were exhausted. Shotguns, rifles and a telescope were taken from Mount Callan after Volunteers had knocked down and knelt on the elder Colonel Tottenham, who is said by one raider to have 'put up a fierce resistance'. A maid fainted, giving another raider a 'terrible job to raise her'.

Over the next fifteen months the house was twice raided when the Tottenhams were at church, though the booty was of less military value—in the second case a watch, two daggers, a compass, £5 and a pair of gaiters. On 6 January 1920 O'Callaghan fired on raiders at Lismehane, shattering a stained glass window but missing the Volunteers. The raiders also missed O'Callaghan, 'did no mischief, and even expressed regret for having to do what they did'. On the same night Captain Hibbert routed his raiders with a repeating rifle, and shortly afterwards his herdsman, who wished to join the RIC, escaped the vigilance of fifteen armed and masked men by hiding under a bed. Hibbert was convinced that many who had suffered in such ways were 'afraid to report what has occurred to the authorities, lest worse should befall them'. Attempts were also made to disarm groups of Protestants in the open. Four Volunteers were ordered in November 1919 to disarm a Vere O'Brien shooting party, but 'mishandled the job'. Next month H. V. Macnamara and another shooting party were ambushed at Shessamore. Macnamara was wounded after crying: 'No, No! No surrender.' No arms were secured but a motor car, an overcoat and several pairs of shoes suffered.[43]

In later attacks it appears that land-hunger and arms-hunger were no longer the sole motives behind attacks on Protestants. In May 1921 a tennis party was attacked at Roslevan, home of Lord Inchiquin's brother. Volunteers secured six guns and two motor cars, though 'one had to be destroyed by fire as its mechanism was new to all the mechanics in our force'. But the officer who suggested the attack was inspired by higher motives than greed for matériel:

> Even in the absence of enemy Officers, the party would be composed of the county aristocracy who are certainly associates of the enemy. In short, all this class in my opinion, must be made to realise that the country is at war, and that therefore amusement like Tennis cannot be indulged in by them while the ordinary people are denied the right of even attending fairs and markets.

Even less did military motives lead to the burning of Protestant churches in at least three Clare villages. Police ascribed the firing of one in July 1920 to a desire 'to introduce religious strife into the present unrest'. But they noted that local Sinn Féiners helped douse the blaze. Overall, Clare Volunteer leaders did their best to suppress anti-Protestant bigotry, unlike their Cork counterparts, who destroyed so many Big Houses that 'our only fear was that, as time went on, there would be no more Loyalists' homes to destroy'. It is true that six Big Houses in Clare were burnt down just before the Truce as a regular Volunteer operation, of which the Chief of Staff 'fully approved'. But the houses were unoccupied, and the Volunteers appear to have feared that the military or police would commandeer them for barracks. Just before Captain Hibbert left Ireland he had written: 'The state of the country is such that I and my family have to leave and shut up the house. I have little doubt that when we are gone, and there is a caretaker in charge of the house, it will be broken into and destroyed.' On 13 June 1921 Woodpark was razed. But if actions like this were inspired by tactical rather than sectarian motives, Volunteer officers often proved unable to contain the vengeful fury of their rank and file in the villages and countryside, obsessed with ancestral grievances. From 1919 onwards Protestants had good reason to complain that their property and lives were no longer secure—though none was in fact murdered in Clare. To many of them emigration seemed the only tolerable course, despite the financial loss that hasty evacuation entailed. For those who remained, the psychological pressure was terrible. After the Mount Callan raid Colonel Tottenham was so shaken that he had to employ a young Scot to help with farm and home, where he had acted as his own steward since the 1890s.[44] Even Colonel O'Callaghan broke down under a variety of burdens in 1920, but after a year's battling against illness and his doctors he returned to the fray undaunted, still manager of his own farm.

It should not be supposed that life became uninterrupted nightmare for Protestants. Shafts of sunlight occasionally lit even the west of Ireland, as in mid-1918 when country gentlemen in Kerry found locals 'touching their hats to them as of old'. During 1919 a record number of Masonic lodges were warranted under the Grand Lodge of Ireland. Late in 1920 the Church of Ireland at last decided to guarantee its struggling clergymen a minimum stipend. At Carrigoran Lady FitzGerald strode undaunted through the first months of revolution:

> I am too busy to live!!—getting new servants into my ways.... Really housecoming is no joke until the wheels begin to turn smoothly. However, I *have* captured servants—quite an event in England. I *do* miss our motor-car on lovely days like this when we could run up and see you for the day. How refreshing to read of these arrests—it looks as if Lord French were going to *act*. William is rather run down and there is *so* much to be done that we grudge the time spent here. Things looked so serious that we felt it was our duty to come home and stand by B—.

But war and revolution certainly brought irritations—as well as disasters. At the Kilrush select vestry in September 1919, so we are told, 'A lamp for lighting the church—there being no gas in the town—was examined, and a trial ordered to be made of its lighting powers.' At Mount Callan in November Colonel Tottenham 'lighted stove, but so little coke can only have it short time in afternoon. 1st part fine but cold. 2nd part wet and cold. More frosty nights than I can remember this time of year.' The Inchiquins' visitors' book was signed by twenty-four guests in 1913 but only two in 1921, the disparity being explained by the sorrowful inscription: 'No shoot. No guns allowed.' When their gamekeeper and wood-ranger proved in court that trees had been cut down and walls damaged at Dromoland, Judge Bodkin supposed that 'Your position as head gamekeeper is rather a sinecure now. There is no shooting? WITNESS: Oh, there is *(laughter)*. HIS HONOR: I mean shooting of birds.' And as life in the country houses became drearier, so escape from it became more difficult. Raids disrupted the post, telegraph wires were cut, bridges blown up and roads trenched by Volunteers. With travel so hazardous it is not surprising that the Studderts took 'the loss of their Motor Car very philosophically', though Florence Vere O'Brien judged it a 'serious deprivation'.[45] Clare Protestants needed all their good humour to avoid sinking into sullen depression.

Such was the crucible in which the political attitudes of Protestants were formed during the revolutionary period. They were threatened economically, socially and physically, and all but the tough and energetic tended to emigrate or fall back on old prejudices spiced with righteous indignation. The toughest and most energetic of all, O'Callaghan, felt that the weaker brethren should be

> given the option of being expropriated by the State and given safe conduct out of Ireland, if they so elect, before the Government of Ireland Act comes into force. This is due to people who have been betrayed. Those who elect to remain in Ireland would then do so at their own risk and have no grievance, which would be a relief to the new Irish Government.

The suggestion was not adopted, and as the revolution intensified a growing wail came forth from the diehard residue. True to their belief that Irishmen could still live peacefully under the Union, if only properly administered by the right people, the diehards threw all the blame for revolution on the government, not the rebels. In August 1919 the editor of *Notes from Ireland* dismissed talk of Irish self-government: 'Of course it is all obvious nonsense. The leopard cannot change its spots. The cold truth is this: Ireland is not fit for self-government, and was never less fit than it is to-day.' A Munster correspondent claimed in the spring of 1920 that Unionists who had been wobbling over the Home Rule proposals were 'now thoroughly ashamed of their temporary falling-away'. Ten months later he heard the 'stroke of midnight', but still hoped that 'the strong arms and true hearts of the British soldiers' might save Protestants from doom. This hope faded with the signature of the Truce in July 1921: 'The Munster lamb is eaten first. The English ewe's turn will come quickly, unless some shepherd with courage is found.' Military intelligence reported that North Munster loyalists viewed the August peace proposals 'with horror', and had decided to 'clear out of the country' if they were implemented. The Treaty was the final stroke in their humiliation (or so it seemed until the Civil War burned down still more of their houses): 'Loyal Munster men see only years of trouble ahead—years with no light behind. The retribution for the victims of cowardice and betrayal is truly terrible.'[46]

Fortunately the crucible brought forth precious metal as well as slag. Many Protestant pragmatists struggled through the revolution and thereby benefited Ireland, if not themselves. They shared the sense of betrayal which obsessed the intransigents, and O'Callaghan summed up British policy as manifested in the Government of Ireland Bill in the sentence 'All the damned Irish will kill each other and a good thing if they do.' When soldiers began to give the 'damned Irish' a helping hand in this enterprise through the medium of 'unauthorised reprisals', the indignation of old officers like O'Callaghan and Maurice Moore knew no bounds. The Crown forces were 'running wild', lamented O'Callaghan, and the shame of their behaviour 'just breaks my heart. . . . *Our men*, that is the shame of it, were recruiting for Sinn Fein by their crimes and creating bitterness which is the main cause of a difficulty in making a permanent settlement.' Some of this bitterness was vented on O'Callaghan himself when in January

1921 fires were lit in his hay-barn and cattle-shed. On the gamekeeper's door he found a notice in blue pencil:

> Notice to O'Callaghan Westropp [sic], commonly known as Mouse Trap. Our society has its eye on you. You are a double dealer and a twister. One more of your ruddy speeches or letters and you are doomed. There is no fool like an old fool, so beware. Be wise.
>
> Anti-Sinn Fein Gang.[47]

Needless to say speeches and letters continued to pour forth. Rather than give way to despair in face of criminal behaviour from the government and its agents, men like O'Callaghan concluded that Irishmen, not Englishmen, must be given the task of rescuing the country.

O'Callaghan's political reorientation did not stop short of public sympathy with the rebels. We have already noted the empathy felt by the old soldier for the 'Fenians', with their honesty, simplicity of heart and ingenuity of mind. Even the diehard Macnamara had told a Unionist organiser in January 1916: 'Sinn Feiners increasing. I would prefer a Sinn Feiner to a Redmondite, because he is an open enemy.' His own son later 'sided against his father, Ireland for the Irish with the Sinn Fein', and after Macnamara's injury in the Shessamore ambush, his son's house at Doolin was allegedly burned in reprisal. At the height of the 1918 agrarian troubles Florence Vere O'Brien wrote that many people 'do honestly prefer to be on the extreme side' and lamented 'the want of picturesqueness in the steady-going Nationalists', which womanly words her devout sister read 'with sighs and smiles all mixed up'. This empathy allowed an independent man like O'Callaghan to accept Sinn Féin as a possible instrument for reinvigorating Ireland much more easily and quickly than any brand of Westminster politicians, transfixed by the memory of Biggar and Parnell, was able to do. His reactions to the 1917 East Clare election campaign illustrate the speed with which his political reorientation occurred. On 19 June he mused:

> Poor Willie Redmond, a live man if ever there was one, has been killed fighting against the Germans, and now a man called de Valera, who fought for the Germans in the Irish Rebellion last year, is in a fair way of succeeding Willie as Member for East Clare! It does not make us prouder of our County does it?

But six days later, after hearing de Valera and Mac Néill speak, he had 'never heard a cause pleaded with more transparent honesty and loftier patriotism. . . . No National Convention can be complete and authoritative without such as they.' He abstained from the poll, but just after it he wrote to the *Irish Times*, which had expressed surprise and foreboding at the result, claiming that the Sinn Féin gospel preached in the campaign was 'essentially National and non-party, and it was wholly free from incitements to class or religious hatred'. De Valera, he now felt, had a 'very similar personality' to Willie Redmond's: 'May not we Irish Irish hope that so great a fire may light us on the road to nobler things, rather than consume the land we all love in a senseless conflagration?' He contrasted this pure fire with 'the villainous "Nationalist" Party Machine with its Tammany methods, class-hatreds, and intolerance, which soured Irish life, corrupted Parliament, and hustled King Edward into his Grave'.

Indignant Irish Party men accused O'Callaghan of wearing 'party spectacles' and of devising a diabolical plot to split the Nationalist ranks, which one writer hoped would nevertheless unite in 'one solid phalanx, thus defeating the subtlety of such scribes as this gentleman'. O'Callaghan soon perceived, with regret, signs of such a phalanx developing: by October 1918 he was certain that Sinn Féin had been forced to pay a 'dividend' to those who had voted for de Valera, 'and the ordinary currency in which those dividends are paid has always been land'. A year later he lamented the duplication by the violent wing of Sinn Féin of 'the practices of the extremists who conferred thirty years of autocratic power on the Nationalist Party'. But he never gave up hope that the pure fire would eventually consume the dirty, Irish Party-like elements in the revolutionary movement. On the other hand, he did not echo the rather sentimental accounts of a Sinn Féin utopia administered by benevolent Volunteer traffic wardens which some Unionist converts were putting about. Probably he understood the men of the flying columns better than the Republican bureaucrats who so sedulously sought to reproduce the paraphernalia of British administration in the nascent Republic. He would certainly have understood one young RM, son of the head of the Local Government Board: 'I often felt in those days that had I been a single man with nobody to think of but myself, I might have chucked up the sponge, taken up a gun, and gone out into the streets.'[48]

But O'Callaghan and his kind, like good soldiers, did not desert the King to join his enemies, however detestable their own generals might seem. Instead they continued to press the Southern Protestant case on a heedless government, and increasingly they applied pressure in separatist lobbies as well. The Irish Dominion League, including many former Unionists, sought a generous peace to restore prosperity and deplored the viciously repressive policies of Lloyd George's administration in 1920–21. An Irish Peace Conference with similar aims was held in Dublin. Groups of businessmen and large farmers were dispatched to England to ensure that the government would protect their interests when peace terms were ultimately agreed. The *Irish Times* strongly supported the pragmatists: 'Neither tears nor cheers will help them in this grave crisis of their fortunes. They must be up and doing. They must take prompt and concerted action for the protection of their political and economic interests.'

O'Callaghan, of course, had fingers in several of these pies. He fought hard to keep out the Canadian invaders who threatened in 1921 to undercut the price of Irish store cattle (the staple of the Clare economy) and represented Irish farmers at the London inquiry. He accepted office in the abortive Southern Ireland Senate of June 1921. But, as a leading figure in the Irish Farmers' Union, he came into ever-closer contact with William T. Cosgrave, Minister for Local Government, and other leaders of the alternative administration. Although he declined to associate himself with such a Republican propaganda stunt as the American Committee for Relief of Distress in Ireland, he helped Figgis's inquiry into Irish industries and resources with notes on milk production and agricultural co-operation as well as personal discussions. After the Truce was agreed he kept close contact with Cosgrave during the crisis which arose in Clare when impoverished farmers threatened to stop paying rates—thus endangering not only the structure of local government but also, he feared, the very fate of the peace negotiations. After Cosgrave had called on the Dáil to ratify the Articles of Agreement for a Treaty, O'Callaghan begged him 'to accept the hearty congratulations of an old non-party Royalist, who in a humble way tries also to be a good Irishman'. A year later Cosgrave recognised his services by offering him nomination to the Free State Senate as a 'minority' representative. But O'Callaghan declined, replying proudly: 'Since my stand against the unauthorised reprisals of 1920–21, I have been loathed by the "Die-Hards", and I am suspect among the Unionists and Landlords. The only people I could represent are the Farmers, and they are a Majority, not a Minority.'[49] His dream of the regeneration of Ireland by a non-partisan farmers' movement was not fulfilled, but we leave him energetic, optimistic and inimitable, with twenty years of wayward enthusiasms still lying before him.

For most of those Protestants who survived the turmoil of revolution and the subsequent civil war, life in Clare under the new regime was quiet, peaceful and dull. Here and there an old retainer may still be found who remembers their previous social eminence, but, particularly in the west, the material basis of that eminence has long since disappeared. The compulsory purchase of 188 Clare estates under the 1923 Land Act deprived such families as the Inchiquins, Macnamaras and Stacpooles of their remaining agricultural tenants. A notice of auction for a Cork demesne of Lord Listowel's signified the social change which had overtaken the country since the days when gentlemen dealt with gentlemen: 'Will be sold in lots of 150 to 200 acres each, to suit Hunting and Racing men, Cattle Shippers, Dairy and Tillage Farmers and others.' And others. . . . Lady Inchiquin mused gloomily on the growing dreariness of life:

> [19 February 1924] . . . I went in my chair round the lake with Lucius and Helga. Planted Fritillaries. Read Just So Stories.
> [20 February] Garden in morning. In aft. went in my chair to see the cutting outside McGraths. [*Illegible*] Still depressed.

In mid-1922 young Republicans had taken over Ennistymon House, now empty of Macnamaras, where they poached the salmon and drank the wine in the cellars. A year later, after thirty-one years at Mount Callan, Colonel Tottenham moved out.

> Many of the old neighbours came to wish me 'Farewell'—one said 'Sure! you came among us, and we made you our own', and another said, 'Sure! you were our Father'. I like to leave it at that, hoping there may be even a *grain* of truth in it.[50]

3

Home Rulers

The intellectual interest of the people is politics—if politics can be called intellectual. And even politics are not popular except in the form of speeches.
GEORGE A. BIRMINGHAM (1919)[1]

In this case, as in all others, the Irish people will be guided entirely by the advice and counsel of Mr John E. Redmond; in him they have, and must have, implicit and absolute confidence and trust.
Clare Champion, 22 May 1915

THE workings of the Irish political mind in the decade before independence can only be understood by the student of that strange phenomenon, the Home Rule movement. Policemen compiled dossiers about it, Protestant Unionists indignantly denounced it, Sinn Féiners in the end overwhelmed it. The promise, or threat, of Home Rule was the driving force behind every substantial faction in Irish politics from 1870 to 1916. Thereafter the movement was weak enough to fall apart in the course of a few months when Sinn Féin raised its challenge, yet strong enough to impose much of its own character (for better or worse) upon the organisation which conquered it. The political party which headed the campaign for Home Rule was an oddity at Westminster. Whereas most MPs of other parties represented only the strongest of several electoral factions in their constituencies, most Irish members could fairly claim to represent almost their whole electorate. In the last general election before the European war (December 1910) every predominantly Catholic constituency in Ireland elected Home Rulers. Two-thirds of John Redmond's seventy-odd supporters were elected unopposed. Two-thirds of the remainder were opposed not by Unionists but by independent Home Rulers (usually William O'Brien's fellow-mavericks), who themselves won a handful of seats. At local government elections the supremacy of Home Rulers was equally unchallenged. Catholic Ireland was virtually a one-party nation by 1914. Yet this triumphant party formally existed only at Westminster! It had no provincial branches, no rank-and-file party members, no formal party hierarchy through which the aspirant politician could chart his course to local or national political office. Instead he was obliged to grope his way through a maze of disparate, competitive pressure groups, all professing loyalty to the party yet in no way bound to it by any formal organisational links. By what system of informal links, checks and balances was the virtual unanimity of Nationalist Ireland maintained? Why did the party seem all things to all men, and why did all political men find it necessary to praise the party? Who were the most influential political men in the Irish provinces, and what form did their praise take?

1. BEFORE THE WAR

The chief spokesmen for the Home Rule cause were, of course, the members of parliament. Their involvement in local affairs outside election campaigns varied considerably. As F. S. L. Lyons has shown, 'the party was big enough to find room for both types—the local man and the full-time politician'. Over the two decades before 1910 the proportion of members with local ties had steadily increased. Among members of the first parliament of 1910, 60 per cent had been born in the region of their constituencies, 55 per cent were resident there, and only 28 per cent were neither residents nor natives. About one-third were either farmers or local merchants, and the number of farmers had been rising steadily (at the expense of doctors and big businessmen). By 1914 the proportion resident in their constituencies had dropped slightly to 47 per cent.[2] Even so, far more members had close connections with their provincial supporters than in the days before the reunification of the party under Redmond.

In Clare, however, both members after 1910 were absentees, virtually without local affiliations. Their visits to Clare were infrequent, ceremonial happenings, in which speeches were delivered, deputations received and complaints against British misgovernment collected for question time in the Commons. Their remoteness from local affairs was underlined by oddities of their background and experience. Willie Redmond in East Clare was a barrister born in Liverpool, reared in Wexford and living in Wicklow, married to an Australian and, most significantly, brother to John Redmond himself. In Clare he seems to have been universally admired, particularly after his heroic death in the European war. He was given a large funeral at a time (1917) when the party was falling apart, with Hibernians, National Volunteers, Land and Labour men, bandsmen, National Foresters, hurlers, O'Connell clubmen and Oddfellows in the procession. Yet, after twenty-six years as the local member, he had so little penetrated the network of local loyalties that his memorial fund gathered only thirteen subscriptions from the county—0.5 per cent of the number received overall, most of them from Wexford. Arthur Lynch in West Clare was a still more bizarre choice for local member. He was Australian-born of a Scots mother and Clare-Galwegian father, resident alternately in Paris and London. He was a man of much experience and unsurpassed *amour propre* in many capacities—as athlete, poet, novelist, linguist, critic, mathematician, psychologist, philosopher, crime reporter and prophet. During his imprisonment after leading an Irish Brigade in support of the Boers, Lynch (like another member for Co. Clare two decades later) whiled away empty hours with Hamilton's *Quaternions*. He was surely slightly mad, and his intellectual triumphs passed largely unacknowledged. Alfred Harmsworth thought him 'a very able journalist' but 'a most unpractical person otherwise'.[3] The speeches and exploits both of Lynch and Redmond were widely reported in Clare newspapers, and whenever the party inaugurated a new policy their comments were solicited and discussed. But they were exotic rather than familiar figures. The day-to-day direction of the Home Rule movement in Clare was left to other hands.

The busiest provincial advocates of Home Rule were members of the numerous and active local government bodies. The 1898 reform of Irish local government had divided all the important administrative tasks amongst a complex array of fairly democratically elected boards and councils. Clare had two urban district councils (with municipal functions), one body of Town Commissioners, a county council (responsible for maintenance of roads, collection of rates, and other essential services), nine rural district councils (mainly concerned with sanitation and public health) and seven Boards of Guardians of Poor Law unions (responsible for upkeep of the workhouses and hospitals). In 1914 at least 365 Claremen (including two women) were elected to local bodies. All parliamentary electors (just over half the adult male population), as well as all similarly qualified women (mainly householders or those occupying property valued at ten pounds or more), were entitled to vote. Popular interest in local elections is indicated by the high turn-out in 1914 elections for which figures are available: 85 per cent in contested wards of the Ennis UDC, 84 per cent in four wards of the Clare County Council, 82 per cent in contested wards of the Ennis Board of Guardians.[4] Proceedings of most of these bodies were extensively reported in the local press, and the reports were minutely scrutinised and analysed by editors and their correspondents alike. For most Home Rulers, election to a local body was the peak of their ambition; and public advocacy of Home Rule was a prerequisite for election to local bodies. The extension of the local franchise in 1898 ensured that local, like national, politics became the preserve of those supporting the Irish Parliamentary Party.

Among those who held or sought local political office, publicans and shopkeepers were probably the dominant group. In the towns at least, shopkeepers tended to have more time and opportunity to scheme, campaign and attend meetings than most farmers or labourers. They were the first to hear local gossip, and the best able to spread it. Moreover, the 'gombeen grocer', still a familiar figure in the pre-war western village, had the advantage of holding a section of the electorate in his debt. Unlike his indebted customers, he had ample ready cash to contribute with appropriate flourishes to Nationalist funds. His advantages were seldom counterbalanced by deep-rooted separation from the electorally decisive farming class. Even in Ennis, so Arensberg and Kimball found, only about one shopkeeper in ten had inherited his shop, from a townsman. In the rural parishes most shopkeepers ran farms as well as shops. That the primacy of shopkeepers in the Nationalist movement was a truism of pre-war life is suggested by the very casualness of newspaper references to them. Upon the opening of a branch of the Hibernians in Ennistymon, the *Champion* reported: 'On Thursday in the middle of the noon day the Nationalists of Ennistymon closed their shops to come and open what will, without any doubt, become one of the most powerful Divisions in Clare.' And when a monster meeting in aid of evicted tenants was advertised, attendance was solicited not only from farmers and labourers, but from shopkeepers: 'Come, shop keepers of the Banner County, you, whose prompt and generous response to the National appeals mainly supplied the sinews of war for the past 30 years.' However much other Irishmen might distrust the canny grocer, they simply could not do without his help if they were to pay for the winning of freedom. As 'Paddy the Cope', the advocate of economic co-operation, once said, 'One enemy at a time. . . . Of the two we have, we consider the English by far the worse. Whenever the Gombeen man is fighting the English, we are with him in that fight, but as soon as we are rid of you [the English], we will tackle him, and believe me, he will not last seven years, don't mind seven hundred.'[5]

The principles of Home Rule were not disseminated by politicians alone. There was another group still better informed as to the social fabric, more prestigious and more widely trusted, because it neither sought political office nor had children to solicit jobs for. The Catholic priests, when they chose to offer their services, were usually welcomed both as teachers and organisers. Mass was the only weekly occasion when large numbers of countrymen came together, so that the vast majority of public meetings were held on Sundays outside the chapel doors. No fund-raising could hope to succeed without the blessing and, preferably, contribution of a priest. Moreover, the priests, and to a smaller extent the schoolteachers, carried with them the mystique which a wider education generates among unschooled people (a mystique more pervasive, however, in chapel or schoolroom than in kitchen or bar). Their rhetoric tended to carry more weight than the same words spoken by a shopkeeper. Their contribution to the Home Rule movement was often and fulsomely recognised in the press. One priest, after his promotion to Administrator of another parish, was told by the branch of the United Irish League which he had chaired: 'When you first came to this parish and assumed command of our branch of the National Organisation, your patriotism and political teachings had the magical effect of doubling the roll of our membership, and the branch immediately became a bulwark of justice, and a deterrent to harsh measures towards our people.' And a neighbouring branch celebrated its recruitment of a curate as chairman in these terms: 'Now that a typical Irish Soggart [priest] stands the helm, with the exception of a few irregularities, which, we are sure, need only be referred to to be rectified, we can confidently say that all goes well with the National Organisation in this parish.'[6]

Clerical enthusiasm for the Irish Parliamentary Party and its policies was not universal. Patrick O'Farrell informs us that the Church's enthusiasm cooled, at least temporarily, when enactment of Home Rule ceased to seem certain after Gladstone's failures. The popular religious revival of the turn of the century, he argues, had 'its real temperamental links with the emerging cultural rebels, not with the Home Rule movement'. But in Clare at least, priests were more inclined publicly to support the Home Rule cause, during the period 1913–16, than the revival of the Irish language. At least forty-two priests, about one-third of those stationed in Clare during those years, patronised Home Rule meetings. But only nineteen are known to have associated themselves with the Gaelic League before 1917, and of these seven were associated also with the Home Rule movement. It may be supposed that many other priests supported Home

Rule without getting notice in the press. Very few priests publicly opposed Irish Party causes before the Rising: one lonely O'Brienite, two opponents of military recruiting, two supporters of the 'Sinn Féin' section of the Irish Volunteers.[7]

The active support of a large minority of priests greatly facilitated the organisation of Nationalism. The tacit support of the majority made effective organisation a practical possibility in the first place. Yet, crucial though their organisational role was, the power of priests in initiating rather than merely co-ordinating patterns of political behaviour was closely circumscribed. As one Clare priest admitted to an English trade union deputation in 1914, 'if he wanted to influence his people in politics they would take no notice of him'. And when a parish priest declared that 'there was not a decent man in the [United Irish] League' at Feakle, his former parish, he was publicly reprimanded by twelve angry natives. The bishop was asked to inhibit him 'from still interfering and meddling in our temporal concerns'.[8] Had he still preached at Feakle there would have been no public admonition, but the same factional resentments would probably have simmered beneath the surface of things. Priests were expected to be adjutants, not generals.

In disseminating the doctrines of Home Rule the co-operation of the county newspapers was crucial. The countryman might hear the local shopkeeper orating, he might even listen to his priest sermonising upon the wrongs of Ireland. But if he was to relate their arguments to a world wider than his parish, if local politics was to appear merely a facet of a far greater, truly national movement, he had to be reminded that the same arguments were being presented, week by week, in every part of the country. This reminder was ceaselessly forthcoming from the numerous weekly papers which circulated in the provinces. British military intelligence treated these papers with due respect: 'Owing to the fact that the standard of education is very low, the Press has great influence in the country Districts, the views of the people being drawn from the local paper, the Priest and the National Schoolmaster.' Today more than half the adults of rural Ireland are believed to read morning dailies from the larger cities, but 80 per cent still read their provincial paper. In 1914, however, dailies did not circulate widely in country districts. As the IRA organiser Ernie O'Malley recalled, 'The house that took in a daily paper would be the teacher's—the Master's, Mr So-and-so, or the Big House; mostly the people were content with the *Weekly Freeman*, or the weekly local papers from the nearest big town.'[9] To understand the manner in which the Home Rule movement impinged on the lives of rural Irishmen, we must study the character and contents of those small, poorly printed, yet remarkably vital weeklies.

In 1914 Clare had four newspapers (today it has one). The *Kilrush Herald and Kilkee Gazette* was a miserable sheet put together by a retired schoolmaster and his son. Two of its four pages were printed in England; the other two consisted of advertisements and reports of local courts and local government meetings. But the *Clare Champion* and the *Saturday Record* (which also appeared in two parts twice weekly under the misnomer *Clare Journal*) were far more serious publications. They were wholly set up in Clare, though they carried syndicated columns of 'Home Rule Notes', 'Hibernian Notes' and other Irish Party news, as well as extracts from Dublin and occasionally British newspapers. The *Champion* claimed the largest circulation of any paper in Clare: 'We are prepared to pay £10 into any local charity if this statement can be shown to be incorrect.'[10]

Both *Champion* and *Record* offered extensive coverage of Clare affairs, and in half a dozen successive issues reference would often be made to events in almost every parish in the county. About one-third of each issue was devoted to advertisements (of which about one-quarter, in the *Champion*'s case, were inserted by public bodies). Of the news reports the majority, at least before the European war, related to Clare. The remainder was almost exclusively concerned with Irish affairs. Yet the horizons of both papers stretched well beyond county boundaries. In the period 1913–21 about one-third of commercial advertisements in the *Champion* issued from outside Clare, and one-quarter of those in the *Record*. The *Champion*'s leading articles were still less tied to county concerns. From 1913 to 1916, 41 per cent of them concerned aspects of the national struggle, 13 per cent the administration of Ireland, 12 per cent world affairs and only 14 per cent specifically local issues.[11] County newspapers gave Irish countrymen a window on the outside world—small, cracked and faulty though it often was.

The tone of pre-war newspaper commentaries, and of the political speeches they reported, was reverent and loyal rather than critical or curious. Week after week the reader was confronted with the prescribed chants and prescribed responses of the Home Rule antiphon, to which constant repetition lent an eerie resonance comparable to that of the liturgy in a great cathedral. When confidence was expressed in John Redmond's labours, it was almost always 'unbounded', 'implicit' or 'unwavering'. Strong opinions were often expressed, but they were invariably those expressed by the Leaders of the Irish Race a short time earlier. Landlords were greedy, policemen were 'almost utterly useless and inefficient', secular philanthropists were 'wretched proselytisers' eager 'to snatch the little children from the folds of the Holy Catholic Church'—in the opinion of the *Champion* and of the whole great movement for which it was spokesman.[12]

Public disagreements among Home Rulers were frequent and vigorous, but the terms of argument were narrow. One Home Ruler might defame another's motives or question his fidelity to Nationalist principles. But to question those principles, to analyse for oneself the grounds of Nationalism, was rare indeed. Disputants did not pit one creed against another. Instead they competed for recognition as the most faithful among the faithful. Such competitions did not read well in cold print, as this example (from the Kilrush Urban District Council in 1915) suggests:

> MR GREENE: I will not take it from you. No matter what you say you will not make me stay away. I am entitled to come here for two years, and I will!
> MR CARMODY: You are a good Home Ruler.
> MR GREENE: I am better than you.
> MR CARMODY (*sarcastically*): You have proved it.
> The Chairman appealed for order.

The necessity of resurrection was universally agreed, but the geography of the Home Ruled paradise was not discussed. As the moment of enactment approached, thinking men worried increasingly about public indifference to the shape of the future. In 1911 Erskine Childers prefaced *The Framework of Home Rule* thus: 'We are face to face no longer with a highly speculative, but with a vividly practical problem. . . . Unfortunately, after eighteen years the problem remains almost exactly where it was. There are no detailed proposals of an authoritative character in existence.' Next year Tom Kettle took heart from the hope that introduction of Home Rule would stimulate the fundamental social discussion which had not preceded it. Home Rule, he speculated, would provide 'the theatre in which other ideas that move men find an arena for their conflict. . . . In order to get rid of politics in Ireland, you must give Ireland Home Rule.'[13] During the next three years, with the bill 'to amend the provision for the Government of Ireland' under minute scrutiny at Westminster, Irish Party leaders spent more of their time totting up the arithmetic of Home Rule and discussing the proper division of functions between the Irish and imperial parliaments. But their new political curiosity did not infect the provinces.

Incuriosity, indeed, was one of the foundations of organised Nationalism in Ireland. The Home Rule movement, even more than most political movements, embodied many disparate traditions which always threatened fissure. It embraced farmers and labourers, Protestants and Catholics, city and country, elements which could be expected, under Home Rule, to find their interests mutually at odds. It invited all of them to crowd under the one umbrella as long as the sky seemed threatening, and encouraged them to restrict discussion to generalities about the 'national cause' to which no interest group could take exception. Vague slogans could win acceptance from a far more diverse army than any well-formed, and therefore controversial, programme of future action could have done. 'Ireland a Nation' was a slogan equally acceptable to friends and enemies of Britain, each of whom could assign what meaning they chose to the phrase. Willie Redmond spoke for Britain's friends in 1913:

> Thirty years have seen the grievances of Ireland removed one by one, and to-day sees the representatives of Ireland in the face of the outstretched hand of friendship from Great Britain no longer bitter, but ready and willing on the basis of the Home Rule Bill to enter the future on terms of friendship and goodwill for all time with the people of England, Scotland, and Wales, and the whole Empire.

Yet in the same year Redmond's loyal supporters in Clare struck a very different note in advertising the annual commemoration of the Manchester Martyrs:

> Walking up the rugged steps to the scaffold, surrounded by English soldiers and police, yelled at and groaned by a depraved and infuriated English mob, their thoughts still turned to their suffering country. . . . Nationalists of Clare, assemble in Ennis in your thousands on Sunday next and do honour to the memory of the men who risked all—even life itself—to free our country from the rule of the tyrant and oppressor.[14]

The voices of reason and of racial hatred commingled in the Nationalist chorus, but both were subdued. The latent disharmony between them was suppressed in the interest of national unanimity.

The strength of the Home Rule movement is shown by the fact that for a decade and a half, from 1900 to 1916, the disparate and potentially antagonistic forces of organised Nationalism were kept in a state of delicate equilibrium. We have observed the outward manifestations of unanimity—the monopoly of local and national political office by loyal supporters of John Redmond and his party; the unremitting advocacy of Home Rule by the most influential community spokesmen, priests, shopkeepers and newspapers; the tacit acceptance by most Home Rulers of the need to avoid searching discussion of political principles, which always threatened to inflame one section of Nationalists against another. But to understand how unanimity was achieved and maintained, we must examine more closely the character of the disparate interest groups, and their relationship to each other and to the party itself.

The diversity and sheer density of active social and political organisations in the provinces is suggested by analysis of Clare newspaper reports over the four years from 1913 to 1916. No less than eighty-two villages in that county of 100,000 people had active branches of some sort of political or social organisation (United Irish League, Ancient Order of Hibernians, Volunteers, Gaelic League, Labour societies, ratepayers' associations or co-operative societies). Twenty-six villages had two such organisations, twelve had three, five had four, four had five and three had six (out of seven possible). The organisational structure of the rural parish was further complicated by other societies on the periphery of politics and social agitation: race committees, fife and drum bands, sporting clubs affiliated to the ostentatiously Nationalist Gaelic Athletic Association. During those four years rural Clare alone produced more than 749 persons (about one of every thirty adult males in the county) who found it desirable to solicit, or were prominent enough to receive, public notice of their association with Nationalist causes.[15] What gave vitality to these dense clusters of village societies, and in what fashion were they attached to the Home Rule movement?

In their most innocent aspect the parochial societies often combined the roles of village college, amateur dramatic society and women's institute. They offered lectures, dances, concerts or simply meeting places for those who could not afford more extravagant amusements. The Gaelic League and the Ancient Order of Hibernians were particularly active in organising concerts and dances. Nationalist demonstrations of all sorts offered forums not only for speech-making, but also marching, holding flaming tar-barrels aloft, waving flags and banging drums. Thus participation in Nationalist societies gave country youths an outlet for their otherwise largely thwarted craving for social distraction. Sometimes politics was an alternative to pub drinking, sometimes the occasion for it. In either case, politics was an integral part of social life.

The parochial organisations not only brought people together, but (more significantly) set them apart. Each society attempted to protect the interests of a particular section of the community (even the Gaelic League, though primarily a pedagogical body, took an active part in the recurrent battles over the payment and conditions of employment of the National Teachers who conducted the League's Irish classes). The sectional interests of many societies are suggested by their names: Town Tenants' Association, Evicted Tenants' Committees, Land and Labour Association, Trade and Labour Association. But the two most widespread and influential organisations of all bore curiously bland titles: the United Irish League and the Ancient Order of Hibernians. Unrestricted by explicit names, both organisations had subtly changed their sectional character in the decade before 1913 until they had become (like the Irish Party itself) amorphous, eclectic bodies admirably constituted to follow the tortuous paths of consensus politics.

The UIL, like the Land League before it, had been established to defend the interests of the tenant farmer. At the turn of the century it gave organised expression to the deep-rooted agrarian grievances resultant from rack-renting and tenant-evicting and led the campaign to enable agricultural tenants to purchase their holdings. The passing of Land Purchase Acts in 1903 and 1909 marked partial success for this campaign and deprived the League of some of its impetus. Nevertheless, at the beginning of 1913 the UIL still had more than 1,200 parochial branches with 130,000 members. During that year the branches collected nearly £12,000, only £500 less than the average for the nine preceding years. The strength of the UIL in Clare (with fifty branches, over 3,000 members and £270 collected in 1913) might be ascribed to the unusually slow and limited implementation of the Land Purchase Acts in the county. Yet in such counties as Cork and Limerick, where land purchase was far further advanced by 1913, the League was at least as strong as in Clare. What characteristics allowed the League to outlive the grievances which had brought it into being?

The UIL's elixir of life was its members' discovery that a massive, co-ordinated national organisation could influence other political sectors than the law regarding land tenure. The political broadening of the UIL began in 1900, when the Irish Party found it necessary to recognise its status as the official Home Rule organisation. Parnell's ideal of a self-perpetuating, virtually autonomous parliamentary army nominated by sham conventions manipulated by headquarters bosses had been thoroughly discredited by 1900. The price of centralism had been persistent dissension among rival manipulators, leading to the creation of at least two rival centres and to a growing indifference to Home Rule among the powerless rank and file. To restore unity and enthusiasm, the party had turned over selection of parliamentary candidates to locally convened conventions subject only to observation by a provincial officer of the UIL, who was to speak only if spoken to. Although many organisations (Trades and Labour bodies, Hibernians, Gaelic Athletes, National Foresters, even national literary societies, as well as the churches and local authorities) were invited to nominate representatives to these conventions, they were at first dominated by the UIL. In most constituencies the League was more densely organised than any of its competitors. Since representation was proportionate to the number of branches, the UIL normally held the largest bloc of votes. The winds of decentralisation do not seem to have dissipated in a flutter of wastepaper constitutions. Although party leaders exercised discreet pressure in favour of certain candidates, their advice was occasionally disregarded. The nomination of Arthur Lynch in West Clare in 1909 was achieved despite discouragement by John Redmond and headquarters' support for a less unpredictable candidate. Although the short notice given of the second general election of 1910 allowed the party to dispense with local conventions 'in view of the extraordinary and unprecedented nature of the emergency', there was no reason to suppose that the party had reverted in the long run to the old discredited centralism.[16] Between elections the parliamentary leaders were accountable, if at all, only to the expertly packed National Directory of the UIL. But if the National Directory was flooded with parliamentarians, the party itself was periodically subject to flooding by provincial League nominees. The UIL's influence in national politics, together with its decisive role in elections for local bodies, ensured that it rapidly outgrew its agrarian roots in the early years of the century.

The range of the UIL's interests is suggested by press reports of resolutions and speeches at 204 Clare meetings between 1913 and 1916 (147 of them reported in 1913). No less than seventy-eight of these meetings found it necessary to publicise their loyalty to the Home Rule cause, while fifty-eight discussed agrarian matters—a fair measure of the relative weight of the two sectors in the League's provincial operation. Forty-seven meetings offered their condolences for departed friends, fourteen denounced aspects of British administration, nine gave support to other Nationalist organisations, and eight dissociated themselves from criminal outrages. The extent to which League branches were themselves responsible for such outrages is more difficult to assess. Certainly, the alleviation of agrarian conditions by government legislation had not eliminated the old rural feuds over boundaries, bog rights and ancient evictions for which Clare in particular was notorious. Colonel O'Callaghan-Westropp discerned 'mysterious local influences', stronger than the Irish Party, which secretly controlled life in rural Clare as late as 1915. Even in 1921 a Clareman whose cowhouse and fence had been demolished could explain to quarter sessions that these acts were the result not of revolutionary conditions but of a dispute over ownership of a plot which 'is going on for 23 years—since I first bought it'. Occasional press reports suggest that UIL branches sometimes became tools of factions in such disputes as these. In October 1913 a member of the League's East Clare executive armed himself with a sixteen-pound sledge-hammer, broke down the door of an evicted tenant's cottage, reinstated her, and barricaded themselves and the cottage against attack by the landlord (neatly reversing the landlords' techniques of twenty years earlier). The League's old weapon, the boycott, was brandished in nearby Co. Limerick as late as May 1915, when an MP called upon another League regional executive not to allow a rack-renting land agent 'to put a four-footed beast in any fair, market, race-course or hunting field in Ireland'.[17] The RIC continued to treat the UIL officially as a dangerous and seditious organisation, but the number of outrages ascribed to it during and after 1913 was negligible. By then the League was, above all, a launching-pad into Home Rule politics.

The Ancient Order of Hibernians had experienced a parallel transformation in the last pre-war decade. During the nineteenth century it had acquired a sinister reputation as the Roman Catholic counterpart of the Orange Order. Then, as they still do today in border regions with populations of mixed denominations, the 'Hibs' or 'Ribbonmen' had self-consciously protected the interests of the Catholic community against supposed Protestant threats. In 1904, however, most of the warring bands of Hibernians were united under the presidency of Joseph Devlin, who proceeded to remould the character of the organisation. By 1913 the AOH was a direct competitor of the UIL's as principal launching-pad for political office in Nationalist Ireland. Its branches had spread extensively in the South, where even the most eager sectarian would have been hard put to discern a Protestant menace. Its main communal function was to administer sickness and unemployment benefits for its working members under the National Insurance Act of 1911. Its insurance section was limited to healthy male Catholic Nationalists aged between sixteen and seventy, but auxiliary sections catered for 'friendly or honorary members', juveniles, ladies and professional, commercial and government-employed men who wished to get on better together. In 1913 police observers in Clare and Kerry ascribed the rapid growth of Hibernian divisions to the approval of the AOH as a benefit society. But early in 1914 the Clare County Inspector became suspicious. In February the AOH was spreading 'apparently as a benefit society, but in reality as a power in the county'. In March he noted that no less than thirteen divisions had been formed in the previous twelve months: 'Consequently they must be regarded as Secret Societies with some other object in view—of which no information can so far be obtained.'[18]

That object seems to have been nothing more mysterious than the supplanting of the UIL as the party's most active provincial organ. In March 1914 West Cork police reported that the Hibernians had 'practically absorbed the functions of the various branches of the U.I. League, though they still, when it suits them make use of the latter's name'. Because of its secretive and sectarian origins, the Hibernian revival met with strong opposition both from Protestant Home Rulers and certain church leaders disturbed by the zeal of the laity. But at least after 1913 the Church in Clare was publicly associated as much with the AOH as with the UIL. Eight Clare priests (six of them parish priests) patronised Hibernian meetings, whereas nine (including four parish priests) supported the League.[19] At least twelve Hibernian meetings in Clare from 1913 onwards returned the compliment by singing the Church's praises. Otherwise the subjects discussed by Hibernian meetings followed the pattern of League proceedings. Of 266 meetings reported (132 of them in 1914), no less than ninety-three offered condolence for the dead. Thirty-three meetings expressed support for Home Rule or the Irish Party, ten for other Nationalist organisations. Twenty meetings offered entertainment or instruction to members, seventeen denounced aspects of British administration, and thirteen denounced criminal outrages. The revived AOH was almost a carbon copy of the UIL; and as the one shrank, the other spread.[20]

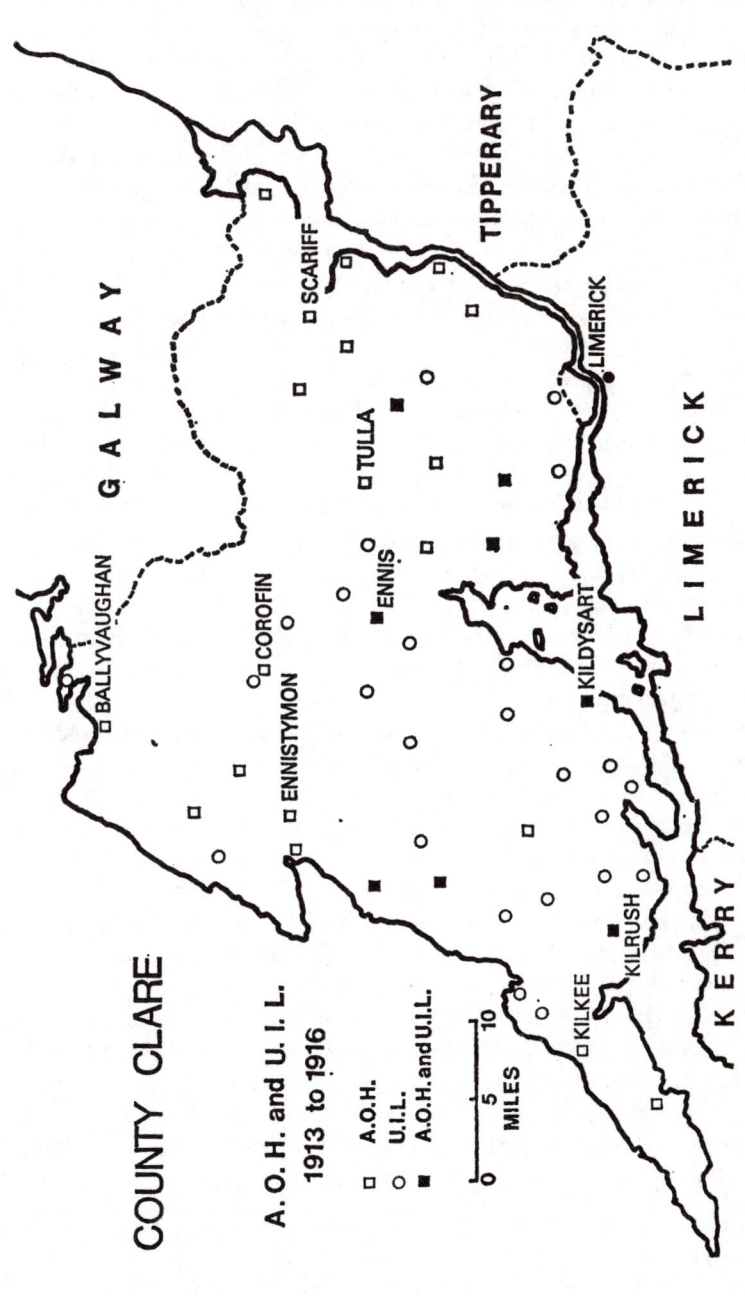

Newspaper reports testify to the ceaseless struggle for power both within and between the networks of local organisations. Without prior support from one of these organisations, few men could hope for election to local government bodies (with all the benefits for oneself, one's friends and relatives that election promised). Without representatives in government, no parochial pressure group could effectively protect its group interests. As the official 'national organisation', the UIL had a head start on its rivals and disdained to campaign for its candidates in so crude a form as publishing resolutions in the county press. But the Hibernians' intervention in local politics was foreshadowed just before the urban district council elections of January 1914 by the syndicated 'Hibernian Notes': 'While up to the present the Order has rarely taken an official part in such elections, the members as a body were always found supporting the candidates who stood for the Nationalist ticket.' By 1914 the contents of that ticket were vigorously debated by many societies. Organised ratepayers in Clare were expected to 'stand to the back of every independent and fearless County and District Councillor' in the struggle against Labour's extravagant demands. When an official of the Gaelic Athletic Association lost his post with the Clare County Council, the secretary to the County Board called for his reinstatement in menacing terms: 'It would be well if the Gaels called upon their representatives on the County Council and impressed it on their memory.'[21] Almost every councillor or Guardian was 'representative' of some organised faction or other, which urged him to be 'independent' only to the extent of opposing the claims of rival factions. From 1913 onwards seventeen meetings of the Clare AOH publicly supported or congratulated candidates for office (or employment) in local government, as did five meetings each of the ratepayers' associations and the Land and Labour Association. And we may assume that after Sunday Mass other local societies urged the claims of countless other aspirant politicians in every parish in the county.

Aspirant politicians needed organised support as much as sectional organisations needed representatives in politics. Drawing upon their cardinal affiliations with clan and neighbourhood, local politicians built up their own village empires in mutual competition, and periodically waged vigorous colonial wars. Some Clare Home Rulers achieved note in as many as half a dozen parochial societies, and 15 per cent of all those examined were associated with two or more causes after 1913. One letter to the *Record*, more explicit than most, bares the logic which guided the practice of parochial politics. The clerk of the Ennistymon Union, a publican, the man (as an admirer put it), 'who is at the head of everything good in the town, the man who has the prayers and blessings of the poor', had been challenged by a rival faction in the Town Tenants' Association. He wrote indignantly:

> I will give Mr H—— and the little clan at his back an opportunity of proving how popular they are in Ennistymon. If they put down £10 in the hands of the committee I will put down £20, and if I don't beat the whole lot of them together by 5 to 1 in the Town Tenants' Association, the National Volunteers, the A.O.H., the Band Committee, and the Race Committee, I will forfeit my £20,

and if I win I will hand the £30 to the poor of the town, or to the Belgian [Refugees'] Fund.[22]

At every discussion of communal affairs, whether concerned with tenancies, horses, musical instruments or Belgians, one imagines Clerk Griffy at the bar, pouring out the rounds and counting the numbers. One recalls George Birmingham's remark: 'The intellectual interest of the people is politics.'

In 1914 the Home Rule movement held a well-established place in Irish communal life, which it seemed likely to vacate only when Home Rule was achieved. Those with political ambitions in Southern Ireland generally accepted that speeches on any subject of public interest which omitted professions of loyalty to the leaders of the Home Rule struggle were wasted breath. Groups wishing to protect their own interests accepted that success was possible only within the Home Rule machine: to aid a section of the people, a society had first to subjugate itself to the interests of the whole people. The members of the Irish Parliamentary Party, once so self-sufficient and irresponsible, were by now merely the spokesmen for a seething mass of Home Rulers in every parish. If the communicants could not take the host without the priest's consecration, neither could the priest keep up the church without the help of communicants. The vitality of the Home Rule organisation depended on maintaining the delicate balance between centre and provincial supporters. Not only must Home Rule seem the only conceivable creed for an ambitious Irishman to profess, but any temptation which threatened to divert communal energies away from politics must be overcome. The almost mechanical reaction of Home Rule organisers when confronted by an energetic popular movement claiming to be without politics was to infiltrate it, reorganise it and add it to the cluster of party auxiliaries. 'Irish Ireland' movements like the Gaelic League and the Gaelic Athletic Association, which had once threatened to divert communal energy from the public house to the schoolroom and playing field, had been to a large extent drawn into the machine. The ideals of 'Irish Ireland' were subtly incorporated into the Home Rule dream, just as the ideals of the tenant farmer had been ever since the 'New Departure' of 1879. Canon Hannay ('George Birmingham') noted with dismay the growing influence of the party in the Gaelic League: 'I thought then [1905] that it was setting the people . . . free from the twin tyrannies which are crushing our lives out—the tyranny of the priest and the tyranny of the political boss. . . . But I find of late [1907] that some of its members are becoming cowardly and trucking to priests and politicians.'[23] When the Irish National Volunteers seized the national imagination in 1914 the party rose to the challenge in its accustomed way. The history of its takeover illustrates the techniques of the party vampire at its most incisive, and deserves detailed description.

* * *

The Irish National Volunteers were an unofficial civilian army, the Nationalist answer to the militant Ulster Volunteers, which they closely resembled in organisation. But no simple definition can do justice either to the richness or to the amorphousness of the new force. The hopes it engendered were great—and vague. At first it was widely expected to restore the manly martial virtues which Irishmen were believed to have possessed in the past. Volunteering, so one Clare organiser predicted, would create young men 'trained and disciplined in physical culture, better men, and healthier than they were to-day (hear, hear)'. In June 1914 Edward Lysaght (later MacLysaght), a young enthusiast for all things Irish, living in East Clare, was half excited, half sceptical: 'They are in fact either actuated by pure patriotism: or else the movement is a mere transient flame kindled by curiosity and fed by sheepism, usually the curse of Ireland, which will die out when the novelty is no longer in it.' But later in the same diary entry he affirmed that 'In six months the whole spirit of the young men of Ireland has changed.'[24]

The new martial spirit was remarkable in that it promised to suffuse all sections of the population, whatever their politics and background. We have already observed the eagerness with which many Protestant Unionists offered their services to the force. And no longer, according to the *Champion* in June 1914, did the returned soldier or sailor walk 'the lanes of his district musing to himself on the scenes of battle in other lands, he is the hero of his parish, the beloved of its manhood'. For old soldiers were indispensable at drilling classes. The 'Irish Irelanders', hitherto mainly on the periphery of politics, threw themselves wholeheartedly into the new movement. At its inaugural meeting one Clare corps was offered 'the willing services of the Kilkee senior and junior football teams under the Irish Volunteer Flag'. Volunteering, of course, took second place to games: later in 1914 the first county inspection had to be postponed for a week as it would have clashed with the All-Ireland Hurling Final in Dublin (which Clare unprecedently won). The Gaelic Leaguers were, perhaps, more earnest champions of the force. The Volunteers' Inspector-General, Colonel Maurice Moore, later recalled his first forays into the provinces thus: 'Who, sir, were the men who helped me in every town? . . . In every case the Gaelic Leaguers carried the torches, showing the way to the timid and the hesitating; they did the practical work of the Volunteers, and history will award them the credit.' In July 1914 Alice Stopford Green celebrated, prematurely, the emancipation of Irish corporate enterprise from the chains of party politics:

> We find among them [the Volunteers] not only the men who have so long supported Home Rule at the polls, but the young men of the athletic associations—as daring a race as exists in the world—the farmers' sons, the clerks from the towns, the sons of professional men, the Gaelic Leaguers, the rising world of Ireland which is without votes and not enrolled therefore in the lists of the United Irish League.[25]

By 6 May 1914 the Volunteers numbered some 27,000, of whom 800 had joined seven branches in Clare. Already some provincial Nationalist societies had associated themselves with the Volunteers on their own initiative. Late in April nine Hibernian divisions had linked with the Ennis (Brian Boru) Volunteers, each carrying his own 'artistically fashioned wooden gun', and several other corps, to celebrate nine hundred years of regress since Clontarf. As early as 14 November 1913 (eleven days before the public inauguration of the force at the

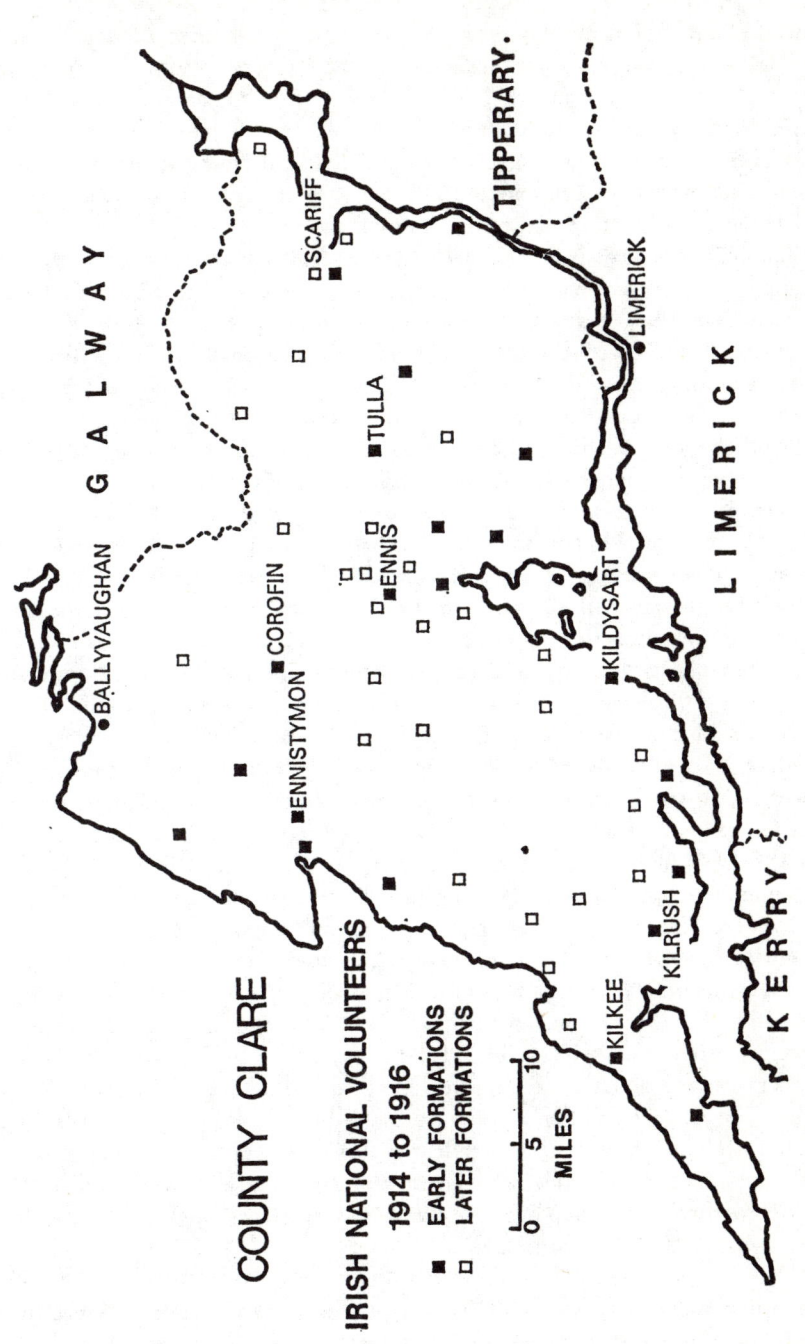

Dublin Rotunda) the West Limerick UIL executive, in the presence of its MP, had urged formation of a Volunteer force 'to resist Sir E. Carson and the weak-kneed Liberals'. But five weeks later in East Limerick another MP had warned the UIL executive to await 'orders from their leaders' before committing themselves to the movement. These orders were slow to come. The Irish Party regarded the Volunteers with mistrust, fearing their independence and vitality. But even without party support they multiplied alarmingly, and at last the party's vampiric urge prevailed. On 9 May 1914 the national secretary of the AOH instructed local organisers to draft Hibernians into the Volunteers. 'If the Volunteers have already been organized in your Parish or District you should co-operate in the movement. If on the other hand no company exists you should at once establish a company.' His aim was to ensure that the Volunteers act 'in perfect harmony with the other national organisations in Ireland' after the enactment of Home Rule. Hibernian halls should be made available for drilling, Hibernian funds for paying instructors. The Volunteers' Provisional Committee's first official intimation that the Irish Party was prepared to support the force was an approving letter from William Redmond, MP for East Clare.[26]

The party's change of tactics accelerated the growth of the Volunteers. On 17 May Lahinch Hibernians resolved to establish a corps. A week later the Hibernian vice-president at Mullagh, already a force to be reckoned with in the Gaelic League and UIL, urged formation of a local corps to 'relieve the dull monotony of rural life' (to which he himself had contributed liberally). In Corofin the AOH division was first to contribute to the Volunteer fund, slipping in £5 before those outside the Order had their chance at Sunday collection. Then two days after chairing a Hibernian meeting the curate at Tuamgraney invited Edward Lysaght to attend a Volunteer procession and address the subsequent meeting, at which two resolutions were to be put: 'one expressing delight at passing of Home Rule Bill [third session, third reading in the Commons] and another of Confidence in the Irish Parliamentary Party'. By 1 June 1914, when the members for Clare came to Ennis to address a united monster meeting of Volunteers, Hibernians, United Irish Leaguers and Labourites, Clare had at least twenty-three Volunteer companies with 1,600 members. As Willie Redmond told the meeting, 'The Volunteer movement had been taken up in every part of Ireland by the most respectable people in the country. It had won the admiration and support of high and low, of the clergy as well as the laity.' He offered his services as a private, and his wife's as a conferrer of colours upon the Brian Boru Corps. His brother's dramatic takeover of the national Provisional Committee on 15 June merely reflected the *fait accompli* in the countryside. Next month the police Inspector-General reported that 'The Governing Council, as well as the membership of the Force, is now overwhelmingly in accord with the policy of Mr John Redmond.'[27]

Under the influence of 'the most respectable people in the country', the Volunteer movement was quickly assimilated into the network of Nationalist societies. We cannot now determine how many respectable men, priests or laymen, joined the movement as agents of the Irish Party machine, and how many out of frustration at the narrowness of Irish communal life. We may surmise that the politicians outnumbered the men, such as Edward Lysaght, of independent vision. Newspaper reports suggest that a fair proportion of Volunteer leaders were also prominent in the overtly political organisations. Of the twenty-two known Volunteer priests in Clare, two were associated with the Hibernians and three with the UIL. Of the 311 lay leaders of the Volunteers identified, twenty-five were also prominent Hibernians and twenty-one United Irish Leaguers.[28] Among the Volunteer rank and file, the proportion of Leaguers and Hibernians was certainly much higher. But it was the leaders, more than the men, who set the tone of the three organisations—and made certain that a single tone was common to all of them.

The influence of the Bishop of Killaloe, Dr Michael Fogarty, facilitated the blending of the political and military movements in his diocese. Described later by John Redmond as 'one of the most able and broadminded Irish Catholic Bishops, and a man who has always been a strong supporter of the Irish Party', Dr Fogarty played an active part in ensuring that the vast majority of Clare Volunteers stayed loyal to Redmond when the Provisional Committee split late in 1914. Just before the county inspection of October 1914 he warned Willie Redmond that defections would reduce the turn-out. But 'MacNamara and *nearly* all in Ennis are *now* right and will be there,' he added. The bishop had enjoyed his recent visit to Redmond's home in Co. Wicklow. He promised to 'speak to the priests at the Conferences about the Volunteers'. He also invited Redmond and party, including Colonel Moore, to dine at his palace. When Moore expressed disinclination to accept Dr Fogarty's invitation, Redmond protested that it 'certainly will not help the movement if we administer what would really be a slight to one who is our best friend'. Moore reluctantly agreed to come, but resolved to leave the palace 'at 8 o'c latest'.[29] In Ireland politicians are unwise to refuse the hospitality or despise the power of bishops.

Within their narrower domains Irish shopkeepers wielded almost as powerful an influence as Irish bishops. They were quick to perceive that volunteering was capable of raising not only the community's moral tone but also its consumption of retail goods. At the height of the movement the *Champion* carried this advertisement: 'War declared! Volunteer Corps can have a complete Outfit of Bandoliers, Belts, Haversacks, Water Bottles, all guaranteed Irish Manufacture. "Shamrock Brand" on clasp of Buckle. Price List on Application.' Another draper capped this by offering puttees, tweeds, and caps. Alas, higher retail consumption sometimes lowered moral tone, as one curate complained to Colonel Moore in April 1915:

> Volunteer Companies in some places have been broken up and in other places seriously injured through the self interest of publicans. They have managed in many places to get themselves appointed Commanders and then have the drilling carried on at the back or front of their premises. I know of one case where the publican—a very prominent man in the County—marched the men from the drilling ground through the village and gave them the 'dismiss' in front of his premises—needless to say there is no volunteer Company in that parish now

and it was not the split broke it up either. . . . 'Bung' [?] has captured and controlled the Gaelic Athletic Association for his own benefit. Will he be allowed to do the same thing with the Volunteers? He is very patriotic, but in many cases his patriotism is in his pocket.[30]

The comparison between the Volunteers and GAA may be extended. Both organisations were heavily patronised by politicians, both were considered important elements in the Nationalist movement. But they remained on the outskirts of politics, giving vitality to the Home Rule dream but seldom lobbying in the political interest of particular Home Rulers. The Volunteers' Provisional Committee had forbidden the use of Volunteer companies as political pressure groups: 'Irish Volunteers acting as such, shall not take part in any political movement, or participate in any Local Government or Parliamentary Election, or in any demonstration of a sectional or political character.' The phrase 'as such' was frequently stretched in practice, and the rather derogatory term 'sectional or political character' was compressed to exclude Home Rule demonstrations of the more eclectic variety. But the Clare press reported no resolutions in favour of political candidates from National Volunteer meetings. And when the Ennis commander, himself an urban district councillor, had the temerity to seek co-option to the County Council in his capacity as a Volunteer, he received only two votes and came last of six candidates. The Volunteers never became a power in local politics, yet they conformed increasingly to the conventions and style of those societies which had power. Wordy resolutions of the familiar sort began to appear in the Clare press in mid-1914, usually issuing from 'committees' of popular and influential supporters (not to be confused with the staffs of 'officers' and 'instructors' who led the practical work of drilling and marching). Twenty of the 218 reported meetings declared their support for the Home Rule cause, and three for the activities of other Nationalist societies. Ten meetings denounced aspects of British administration, and twelve passed resolutions of condolence.[31] By August 1914, when the Volunteers in Clare had reached their peak membership of 5,200 divided into over sixty companies,[32] the force was no longer a miracle. Already it had become a familiar, unremarkable feature of the Irish political landscape.

2. FROM WAR TO RISING

The life of an Irish patriot had seldom seemed so tranquil or assured as in the summer of 1914. At home the Irish Party's political supremacy was unchallenged in most parts of the country. The energy and vitality of 'Irish Irelanders' and Volunteers had been made to serve the party, not to threaten it. At Westminster intransigent Unionists were still snarling, but seemed to have abandoned hope of saving more than a quarter of Ireland from Home Rule. The Irish Party's triumphant summer was capped by Britain's intervention in the European war. John Redmond's prompt declaration that the 'armed Nationalist Catholics in the South' would take part in the home defence of Ireland met with general approval, both at Westminster and at home. On the same day (3 August) Redmond told the Volunteers' Provisional Committee to make no statements on policy, as any divergence from his assurances to the Commons 'would split the country and be fatal to the Home Rule Cause. . . . As things stand now, our position has been improved enormously by the foreign complications.' The party's few opponents were disheartened. It 'immediately became apparent' to a young rebel poet in Kerry that Redmond's statement 'really represented the views of the majority of the Irish people. . . . Our dream castles toppled about us with a crash.' An immediate consequence of the outbreak of war, the withdrawal of the order prohibiting importation into Ireland of military arms, parts and explosives, pleased all factions in the Volunteers. More triumphs were soon to come. On 12 September Willie Redmond wrote to a friend: 'The Bill will be on Statute Book *Tuesday* or *Wednesday*: a Bill to suspend operation for a year may also pass. . . . The Volunteer men [?] have to be put on a secure footing and *cranks* must be *faced*.' Royal assent to Home Rule was duly given on 18 September. Two days later John Redmond felt strong enough, amidst the expected chorus of national gratitude, to inform the Wicklow Volunteers, and through them 'Young Ireland', that it was their 'duty' to defend freedom—whether at home or abroad. The subsequent split in the Volunteer organisation, which he may well have expected, rid the party of the troublesome conspiratorial part of the Provisional Committee at the cost of only 7 per cent of the national membership.[33] The party's control over its most vital auxiliary, and its authority in the country, seemed complete.

But the very events which marked the party's triumph were also the sources of its subsequent petrification. The withdrawal of the arms proclamation, for instance, raised high hopes among provincial Volunteers (long subject to ridicule as soldiers without weapons). Yet despite the illegal running of guns before the war and legal importation thereafter, only a trickle of arms reached the west. Organisers in Clare grew frantic. P. J. MacNamara, secretary to the County Board, wrote on 1 September to Robert Barton at Volunteer headquarters: 'What steps are to be taken to equip the Clare Volunteers with arms. What portion of the American Aid are they to receive, and when shall they receive same. What provisions are made to defray Expenses of Co Board.' No reply came. Four days later the county convention expressed 'great indignation' at Dublin's silence, and 'made insistent demands for rifles'. When Colonel Moore's representative implored delegates to 'avoid Politics', his remarks 'were not received sympathetically'. MacNamara then turned to Willie Redmond for help: 'If you can do anything in this line for us, we would be obliged for without the rifles, the people are getting sick of the whole idea.' On 7 October a company instructor attributed the recent drop in attendance to 'the absence of Rifles and the monotony of the Drill'. Eventually a few rifles arrived, but never enough. In January 1916 (when Clare's 2,718 remaining National Volunteers were reported by the County Inspector, RIC, to have only 192 rifles between them) a Miltown Malbay man wrote despondently to the *Champion*:

> The volunteer movement, at all events, looked bright, and as time rolled on a collection was made to provide arms, etc., for the members. They got part of the etc., but no arms. The remainder of the collection, which I learn was about £40, now rests quietly in the National Bank. I heard mutterings—I did, many.[34]

Another promise which at first provoked applause, then mutterings, and at last resentment, was Redmond's pledge that party and Volunteers would support Britain in the European war. It soon became clear that while most Irishmen professed to approve of others fighting, they preferred not to participate in person. The war-fever which swept middle-aged England in August 1914, and the consequent communal and family pressure on young men to join up, scarcely affected Ireland outside Ulster. Leading articles in the *Clare Champion* suggest the cool, businesslike reaction of Nationalist Ireland to the emergency. On 8 August the *Champion* felt that 'The wisdom or unwisdom of her final action [the declaration of war] can only be tested by time and result.' Three weeks later the editor called upon Britain to withdraw her army from Ireland, leaving the Irish to defend their own shores as Redmond had suggested. Ireland didn't want her seat of government moved from London to Berlin, but she had 'no quarrel with the German people'. All in all, 'The Irish Press, and unfortunately, too large a section of the Irish people, are badly in need of a cold douche at the present moment—something to steady the nerves and clear the vision and restore the powers of reason.' When Redmond announced on 20 September that Ireland had a quarrel with the German people after all, the *Champion*, like most of its readers, tactfully desisted from immediate comment or reaction. Like other provincial papers it extended its coverage of European affairs: twenty of its sixty leading articles during 1915 related to the outside world, and about one-third of its news reports concerned the war. Yet despite the editor's sister-in-law's participation in Queen Alexandra's Royal Army Nursing Corps, he was finding the war 'a little wearisome' by July 1915.[35] The loyalty of the press to the party did not waver under the stress of the recruiting campaign, but the enthusiasm feeding that loyalty gradually diminished.

The *Champion*'s waning enthusiasm for the war effort, to which the Irish Party leaders were irrevocably committed, accurately reflected the mood of the country. The suggestion that the Volunteers should be recognised by the government as a territorial militia was well received, for members of a recognised militia would be not only supplied with weapons but exempted from overseas service. As Sir Bryan Mahon, Kitchener's observer in Ireland, reported soon after the declaration of war, 'In many places I became friendly with the leaders of the Volunteers, and often inspected the men. Some of these were drilling by night; and all were enthusiastic about the Great War. . . . *All* the Volunteers should be recognised, or else none of them.' In the end none were, since Volunteer and Hibernian administrators could not induce the War Office both to take responsibility for the force and to perpetuate their own day-to-day control over it.[36] The War Office's decision not only made Irish recruiting immeasurably more difficult, but badly dented the party's prestige. Redmond's speech of 20 September alarmed more Volunteers than it inspired. Several county police reports for September 1914 noted a decline in Volunteer enthusiasm, which they ascribed to the calling up of the reservists who had instructed most companies and to fear that the Volunteers as a body would be incorporated into the Regular Army. The number of National Volunteers who joined up as individuals was relatively small. Apart from the 7,331 National Volunteer reservists mobilised in August 1914 (41 per cent of all the reservists in Ireland), only about 18,000 (one-tenth of the force and less than one-quarter of those recruited outside Dublin) had joined the colours by the end of 1915. Only in the last quarter of 1914, when 48 per cent of all Irish recruits were National Volunteers, did much of the force appear to share the party's desire to aid Britain in the war. In Clare the National Volunteers were even less eager to join the army than in the country as a whole. By the end of 1915 only about 300 had done so, about 6 per cent of the county force at its peak.[37]

The rate at which Irishmen were recruited for the armed forces varied according to region, as is shown by Table 3.1. From section (A) of the table, we may induce that the four counties of the south-west (Clare, Cork, Kerry and Limerick) did not share the war-fever which infected Ulster in 1914, when as many recruits were forthcoming as in 1915 and 1916 together. Not until 1915 did recruiting in the south-west reach its peak, but thereafter the rate declined fairly uniformly over the country until 1918. Section (B) shows that Clare contributed far less than its fair share of recruits in 1914, rather less in 1915 but only a trifle less in 1916 (a trend roughly followed by the four south-western counties as a whole). Up to the middle of August 1915, Clare contributed only 324 reservists and 519 army recruits from its population of more than 100,000. Of the recruits more than half joined up in Ennis and Kilrush, the two major towns.[38] Despite extensive use of Nationalist slogans such as 'God Save Ireland' in recruiting propaganda, and despite the establishment under government patronage of an 'Advisory Committee on [Recruiting] Publicity' which was officially expected to be 'practically an outpost of the National Parliamentary Party', Nationalist Ireland declined to respond to the exhortations of its leaders. Influential Home Rulers in the provinces (including at least eleven priests in West Clare alone) gave their blessing to the recruiting campaign, but their loyal efforts were thwarted by the mood of the people.[39]

But of all those deceptive Irish Party triumphs of 1914, that which did most in the long run to petrify the Nationalist movement was the enactment of Home Rule. The act itself made the party's slogans redundant; its suspension left the party without a programme of action; the promise of its future amendment at Ulster's insistence raised new fears of betrayal. Royal assent was greeted with the customary expressions of gratitude to the Irish Party and its wise leaders. The *Champion*'s view was that 'This week closes the last chapter in the history of our struggle for Home Rule, and opens up the first in [the] history of our emancipation.' The editor did not mention the Suspension Act. For P. J. MacNamara of the National Volunteers, enactment effected what 'we and our fathers and forefathers before them have heard from their Childhood', and he thanked God that Willie Redmond at least had been spared to see such a glorious achievement. But no crowds larger than three hundred celebrated it in Clare, and the police inspectors had heard 'no comments made and you never hear any person speaking of it'.[40] Indifference, the recurrent cancer of Irish Nationalism, spread swiftly, unobtrusively, through every organ of the Irish Party.

Table 3.1: Irish Recruitment, 1914–18

(A) Number of recruits, 1914 = 100

	Clare	4 Counties	Ulster	Ireland
Recruits, 1914	100	100	100	100
Recruits, 1915	344	162	72	105
Recruits, 1916	208 (est.)	88	28	43
Recruits, 1917	n.a.	65	22	32
Recruits, 1918	n.a.	41	20	24
(B) Irish total = 100				
Recruits, 1914	0.3	9	60	100
Recruits, 1915	1.1	13	41	100
Recruits, 1916	1.6 (est.)	18	38	100
Recruits, 1917	n.a.	18	42	100
Recruits, 1918	n.a.	15	49	100
Army Reservists mobilised, 1914	1.8	15	53	100
Available for military service, 1914	1.8	17	38	100
Population, 1911	2.4	18	36	100

As each month of war made the eventual partition of Ireland with the party's acquiescence seem more certain, local Home Rulers began to betray novel doubts as to the infallibility of their leaders' judgment. A turning point in the party's history came in May 1915, when it gave its qualified support to the new coalition government (which included several intransigent Unionists). Thereafter the taboo which hitherto had forbidden criticism of party policy within the Nationalist movement gradually lost its power. On 3 June 1915 Bishop Fogarty wrote bitterly to John Redmond: 'Home Rule is dead and buried and Ireland is without a national Party or National Press. . . . May God guard you Sincerely yours. . . .' Far from taking offence, Redmond forwarded the letter to Asquith as evidence of the mood among 'intelligent men' in Ireland as well as the 'unthinking crowd'. Explicit criticism of the party began to be heard in the public bodies. In August 1915 a Clare county councillor said he was still Redmond's follower, but that 'the so-called Liberal Government had completely fooled him and the Irish Party'. In November a Kilrush Guardian reportedly said: 'I consider Redmond no better than a traitor. But if the Irish Public Bodies did their duty, the Irish representatives would act differently.' The suggestion that local bosses might seize the political initiative from national bosses was premature, so he explained to the *Champion* that his 'meaning' had not been to denounce Redmond. But he repeated that his expectations had been disappointed.⁴¹ In the months before the Rising provincial Nationalists did not dramatically repudiate party or cause. But they did begin to examine their leaders critically, and their minds were filled with dangerous notions.

The chain of command in the Home Rule movement was weakening. Ironically, one symptom of this process in Clare was a series of articles expressing more emphatically than ever before the *Champion*'s fidelity to the party leaders. The intention of these articles, however, was to debase the authority of West Clare's own representative in the party, Arthur Lynch. His idiosyncratic behaviour had earned him not only ridicule but the hatred of many sections of the Nationalist movement. His declaration in February 1914 that he would support the Empire should war break out had infuriated the conspiratorial separatists led from America by John Devoy (whom Lynch had tried to outshine after his escapade with the Boers). The *Champion*, still vaunting its oldfashioned hatred of the Saxon foe, supported Devoy and carried a lively correspondence upon the pros and cons of 'the gallant Colonel'. When the other Clare newspapers took Lynch's part, the contest of opinions became a contest for circulation. The *Champion* pointed out triumphantly that the *Journal*, Lynch's main forum, was also 'the paper which used to publish Mr H. V. Macnamara's election addresses and which goes into ecstasies over the promotion of a peeler, and sends a special reporter to the meetings of the Clare Unionists'.⁴² The revision of the party's policy towards the Empire after the outbreak of war deflated the *Champion*'s campaign for the moment. But Lynch's solemn warning early in 1915 that the party was being tricked 'into the acceptance of the Unionist programme', and his subsequent denunciation of the party's support for the coalition government, allowed the *Champion* to reprimand him for disloyalty, while expressing its own 'full confidence in Mr Redmond to deal with any situation, no matter how critical, which has arisen or may arise'. Then in the autumn of 1915 Lynch published his remarkable book *Ireland: Vital Hour*, which included a balanced and diverting account of the role of the Church in Irish politics. The *Champion*, edited by a leading Hibernian organiser, gave forth no less than eleven indignant leading articles and several 'reviews' of the book over the subsequent five months. The priest who had nominated Lynch as the party's candidate for West Clare wrote to the *Champion* to express 'deep regret for having assisted to foist on the sterling Nationalists of West Clare the glorifier of Cromwell and Queen Elizabeth, of Luther, and Pitt, and Castlereagh; and the vilifier of the Catholic Church, the Pope and the immortal Daniel O'Connell'.⁴³ What was significant in the Lynch affair was not its exposure of latent hostilities between Lynch and his party superiors, or between Lynch and his fellow-politicians in Clare. Rather, it was the openness with which all parties denounced each other, and their refusal to defer to the tactical judgment of their seniors. The frankness of the dispute signified the moral deterioration of the Home Rule movement and the disturbance of the delicate organisational balance which had been achieved before the war.

As the authority of the party weakened, so the vitality of its auxiliary organisations dissipated. The decline of the United Irish League had already begun in 1914. On 12 January 1915 its general secretary reported that a 'considerable number of branches' had not paid their affiliation fees in 1914, which he ascribed to the outbreak of war and the fact that 'in order to give an opportunity for the better organisation of the National Volunteers, the work of organisation in connection with the United Irish League was not pressed during the year'. But next May, when the Volunteers had become moribund, League organisers in East Clare admitted that only four branches were still affiliated—one-ninth of the peak figure. Sporadic attempts were made to revive the League, but according to the police Inspector-General in August 1915, these were 'not very successful'. The party took 'little interest in the League at present, except in places where it can be used for local agitation'. Clare press reports suggest the extent of the League's decline: 147 meetings were reported in 1913, forty-four in 1914, ten in 1915, and one in 1916 before the Rising. The Ancient Order of Hibernians, though its main function of dispensing insurance benefits was unaffected by wartime conditions, also became less active: 132 meetings were reported in 1914, fifty-seven in 1915, and eighteen before Easter in 1916.[44]

The decline of the third great Nationalist organisation in Clare, the National Volunteers, is more fully documented. Clare newspapers again trace the shape of its decline: 132 meetings in 1914, sixty-five in 1915, and eighteen in early 1916. Already in October 1914, just after Mac Néill's faction in the Provisional Committee had broken with Redmond's faction, the Clare Inspector of Volunteers, Edward Lysaght, noted that 'The men are falling away and whole companies have lapsed rather than disbanded.' In January 1915 Secretary MacNamara reported that the 'general state' of the Volunteer movement in Clare was '*simply rotten*'. In the same month Lysaght organised a fairly successful training camp at his home, Raheen, but lost interest in the force thereafter. Organisation of the force in Clare was taken over by John Bianconi—great-nephew of the Liberator, grandson of the entrepreneur of the Bianconi car, but a man who confessed that he had 'very seldom been to the east of the line from Limerick to Ennis'. In successfully urging his promotion to the rank of colonel, a headquarters inspector wrote to Colonel Moore: 'There are certain drawbacks to making a Col. of Mr B. (1) He is rather deaf and weighs about 22 stone. I attach his photograph as I think this is all I can see against the man. . . .' Bianconi repeatedly complained that people no longer listened to local leaders, 'even our friends among the priests'. An outsider, he felt, 'would have more weight with the slackers than any local speaker'. But outsiders, like weapons and *raisons d'être*, were in short supply, and the Volunteers continued to crumble. On 16 March 1916 Bianconi wrote: 'Will my present uniform do or should I wear staff tabs? Our County Committee is defunct. I hope some steps will be taken to revive it shortly. Is there any badge I could wear on my cap?' Headquarters suggested a green band with an Irish harp on green silk, but had no suggestions as to how the county organisation might be revived. The once virile Volunteer movement had become ridiculous. At the Ennis Volunteer carnival in August

1915, 'different from any yet held', the flower of Ireland's young manhood was invited to test its skills in the Boot Race, Donkey Race, 3-Leg Race, Tilting the Bucket, Mop Fighting Competition and Sack Race. The third largest prize was offered for the thirteenth item on the programme: 'Best Drilled Section Irish National Volunteers'.[45]

By Easter 1916 the marvellous machinery of the Home Rule movement was almost silent. For nearly two years the machines had had nothing to produce. Party managers looked forward impatiently to the end of the war, when production of a new range of goods could, belatedly, start. A ballad of the time catches the futility of Home Rule politics in the period of waiting:

> We've Home Rule now the Statute Book adorning
>   It's there to be seen by every mother's son
> We brush the cobwebs off it every morning
>   For the Constitutional Movement must go on.[46]

3. AFTER THE RISING

But the war did not end in time—instead came the Rising. To John Redmond it seemed above all an attempt to destroy the Irish Party. 'The attempt to torpedo Home Rule and the Irish Party has failed,' he cabled to American supporters. 'Though the hand of Germany was in the whole thing, it was not so much sympathy for Germany as hatred of Home Rule and of us which was at the bottom of the movement. It was even more an attempt to hit us than to hit England.' Whatever its motive, the Rising did indeed hit the party harder than England. By appearing to acquiesce in certain retributive acts carried out under martial law after the Rising, the party irrevocably separated itself from the new spirit of Irish Nationalism which took the Easter martyrs for its founding fathers. A few Irish Party MPs expressed fellow-feeling with the rebels but received little thanks. Arthur Lynch 'could not withhold his admiration for the extraordinary courage, and devotion, of the young leaders. Whatever politicians may say of their wisdom or judgment, he added, they will inevitably take their place in the gallery of Irish heroes and martyrs beside Robert Emmet and Wolfe Tone.' In parliament he called for a general amnesty and 'free play and free scope' for the new spirit in Ireland, 'no matter how far it will lead Ireland on the way to nationality'. But when he pleaded for Arthur Griffith's release from prison, Griffith publicly snubbed him. The old enemies of the party had, in effect, grabbed the apostolic succession, and they showed no inclination to allow their predecessors to creep back into the Holy City as cardinals. Willie Redmond was among the first to admit that the party was obsolete: 'He pressed upon his brother that we should all retire, saying plainly that we had been too long in possession, and should hand over the task of representing Ireland at Westminster to younger men.'[47]

John Redmond ignored his brother's advice, but young men began to take over the task of representing Ireland willy-nilly (though they eschewed Westminster). Already at the end of May 1916 the Kerry County Inspector of

Police thought the party 'might have some difficulty in retaining some of the seats' if a general election were held. After an unofficial Redmondite had won West Cork the party lost four successive by-elections in 1917. The most disheartening poll was that to replace Willie Redmond in East Clare in July 1917. Party spies had reported the exceptional local influence of the Home Rule candidate, Patrick Lynch, KC (unrelated to the member for West Clare). The assistant secretary of the United Irish League gleefully quoted the words of a Sinn Féiner: 'We cannot touch Ennis and Lynch is a strong candidate—he has defended one half of the murderers in Clare and is related to the other half.' One League organiser telephoned the Chief Secretary's Office to ask for petrol supplies, then severely restricted: 'His [Patrick Lynch's] party have 40 motor cars, but no petrol. They would want 300 gallons. . . . They will win the election if they get the petrol, and will lose it if they don't.' They got 400 gallons 'from somewhere' but lost the election. Lynch's defeat appalled party managers, though at the start of the campaign they had resolved not to 'identify ourselves publicly with the contest although we are privately in favour of the candidature of Mr Lynch'.

Early in 1918 the party attempted to associate itself with the new political spirit by linking forces with Sinn Féin in the campaign against conscription and by withdrawing its remaining members from Westminster. In March Arthur Lynch had made his own attempt to regain the patriotic initiative by inviting Dillon, Devlin, William O'Brien, Healy and 'the romantic, and I will say the heroic, figure of Mr de Valera' to join him in 'one general national movement'. But once the threat of conscription receded the uneasy truce with Sinn Féin broke up, the party returned to Westminster, another by-election was lost and Arthur Lynch immersed himself in a fruitless attempt to recruit a new Irish Brigade (this time to fight for the Allies).[48] By 7 August 1918 John Dillon, the party's new leader, expected to win only ten seats at the December general election. In fact he won six.[49] Challenged by an alternative body of Nationalists, the Irish Parliamentary Party had lost the vitality to fight back.

The decline of the Home Rule organisations in the provinces was still more precipitous than that of the party itself. If these organisations were already moribund before the Rising, they died after it. In November 1916 the Ennis Manchester Martyrs demonstration had to be abandoned when only eleven Hibernians turned up. A year later the Clare police reported that the growth of Sinn Féin clubs was 'killing the A.O.H.' Local papers carried no reports of Hibernian activities after September 1917 except from Kilrush, where weekly Hibernian dances were still held late in 1919. No meeting of the United Irish League was reported in Clare after June 1916, though the League was clearly active in the by-election campaign a year later. The last published evidence of League activity in Clare is a letter to the *Record* from a Kilrush urban district councillor and League organiser, referring to a collection for the party's general election fund in 1918. The writer broke with precedent by publishing no list of subscribers, merely noting that 'Comparatively speaking the collection was a record one. In common with the subscribers I feel that within a very short time the methods and policy of the Irish Party will be fully and amply vindicated.' The National Volunteers did not outlive the League or the Order. They became the special target for popular contumely immediately after the Rising when several companies in Clare offered the police their help 'in quelling disorder, if necessary'. Thereafter the major concern of National Volunteer organisers was to dispose of their remaining arms for payment, rather than losing them by government confiscation or Sinn Féin raiding. Attempts to keep the force alive by encouraging its members to defy the government's ban on drilling caused John Redmond to split the organisation again in 1917, but hardly anyone but Colonel Moore cared. By December 1917 Clare police knew of only seven surviving branches, all of them inactive.[50]

But the spirit of the constitutional movement did not die with the body. However inexorable the decay of the party and its auxiliaries might appear, the individual's decision to repudiate the political convictions with which he had grown up was seldom easily made. It need not surprise us that many of the converts from constitutionalism to Sinn Féin carried their old political habits and assumptions with them. They were more often lost sheep than sheep in wolves' clothing. To conclude this chapter we shall trace the political wanderings of some of these lost creatures whose instincts called them back to constitutionalism but whose common sense urged conversion.

No spokesmen for popular opinion were more cruelly troubled by the changing mood of politics than the newspaper editors. Those editors who failed to gauge those changes of mood lost their readers; those who reflected the changes too faithfully risked losing their presses under the punitive provisions of the Defence of the Realm Act. Moreover, too vigorous a repudiation of one's former leading articles might alienate one's more critical readers as much as dogged persistence in yesterday's opinions. Dogged persistence in the party's line nearly ruined the *Freeman's Journal* after the Rising, before it passed into more pragmatic hands. In October 1916 a Cork newsagent warned Redmond that the *Freeman* was selling only eighty copies in the city to the *Independent*'s 1,500 (a fact which he ascribed to the 'taproom logic' of the latter). The taproom logic of most provincial newspapers sometimes drew wry smiles even from police observers. In November 1918 the Kerry County Inspector remarked that the three Tralee newspapers were 'rapidly becoming Sinn Fein' for fear that their circulation 'would cease', though two of their proprietors (all of them constitutionalists) had officer sons in the army. Nine months later all three papers were 'sufficiently Sinn Fein to suit the needs of their readers'.[51]

In Clare the persistent rivalry of *Champion* and *Record* was manifested in their divergent response to the new movement. The *Record* did its best to avoid political comment, but at least until 1919 its sympathies were unmistakably with the Irish Party. The Easter rebels were 'brave, but misguided young Irish dupes and tools' who should be spared punishment but whose acts would 'ever make Irishmen blush for shame'. Patrick Lynch, KC, came from 'a good old Clare stock' and stood 'for the constitutional methods which won so much for the Ireland of to-day'. His campaign was afforded greater prominence than de

Valera's, though the paper avoided explicit support for his candidature. John Redmond's death in March 1918 was 'a tragic blow to the Irish people', all the sadder since 'he was within sight of the Promised Land'. The *Champion* did not desert the party for a year after the Rising. Immediately afterwards it congratulated Clare for 'its magnificent and unanimous loyalty to Mr Redmond', though it was 'not for us to sit in judgment'. By mid-November 1916, however, the *Champion* felt that no group of Nationalists, parliamentarians, Sinn Féiners or Irish Nation Leaguers could 'claim a monopoly of patriotism'. It unambiguously supported de Valera for East Clare, but directed its attacks not at the Irish Party in general but at Lynch himself, one of a family long at loggerheads with the *Champion*. Parnell, in the editor's opinion, would have disapproved 'of all those attempts to push the Irish Party into the position of sponsors for Mr Lynch'. As late as October 1918 the *Champion* welcomed hints that the party might even then adopt and act upon the slogan 'self-determination'. Only after the electoral rout of the party did the paper finally repudiate it. In April 1919 the editor offered a veiled apologia for his changing opinions:

> Every Irish Nationalist wants Sovereign Independence, and if any of us ever agreed to accept less, it was simply that we were in the grip of a powerful country, and had only to make the best bargain we could. For half a century we bargained with the Ministry—and got nothing. The war has given us an opportunity we never had before.[52]

Nothing illustrates the mentality of Irish newspaper editors more vividly than their dealings with the press censor. Military censorship was established in Ireland on 1 June 1916 and transferred to civilian authority in November 1916. It outlived its British counterpart, remaining in force until August 1919. Its aim was to keep track of seditious or disloyal matter published even in the most obscure provincial papers, and to persuade editors not to publish copy which might lead to the suppression of their papers under DORA.[53] The *Record* was always, as its proprietor explained in April 1917, 'very particular' to follow the censor's instructions, but it became increasingly disturbed by the *Champion*'s habit of publishing articles which the censor had disapproved. The *Record*'s scrupulousness was not well rewarded, and in May 1917 its sister paper was discontinued 'owing to paper scarcity and war conditions'. The *Champion*, however, captured the belligerent mood of the nation in its dealings with the censor, and its suppression was under frequent discussion from November 1917. The editor defiantly told the censor that 'If the authorities have made up their minds to suppress the Champion nothing that I can do can save it.' On 2 April 1918 policemen and soldiers seized parts of the *Champion*'s machinery. After the reissue of the paper in September 1918 the editor, much chastened, took care to answer the censor's queries promptly and politely, and by October 1919 Clare police were noting the 'singularly moderate' tone of the local press. As the *Champion* moderated its tone in order to avoid further suppression, the *Record* became increasingly indignant in its criticism of government actions in order to build up its circulation. By August 1919 the press censor considered that the *Record*, as well as the *Champion*, was among the forty-five provincial newspapers showing 'Sinn Fein Tendencies'. Of the fifty-nine papers still supporting the Irish Party only the *Kilrush Herald* was published in Clare.[54] If the amount of advertising carried by each paper be a fair guide, the *Champion* won its revolutionary obstacle race with the *Record* by a short head.[55]

For local politicians the process of political conversion was at least as painful as for newspaper editors. By training and inclination, few councillors or Guardians were attracted to Sinn Féin's radical doctrines, beckoning them into dangerous and unfamiliar territory. But as the electorate moved towards Sinn Féin, most politicians moved with it. Elections for local bodies were not in fact held until 1920, but since they had been postponed in 1917, 1918 and 1919 politicians were kept in painful suspense throughout the period of Sinn Féin's growth, awaiting judgment.

In the major towns in Clare the Irish Party retained control over local politics until 1920 at least. The towns were never so susceptible to political infections as the countryside, where communal pressure invariably enforced a remarkable uniformity of loyalties and opinions. The growing concentration of police and military in the towns hampered not only revolutionary violence but also Republican propaganda. Moreover, during 1918 and 1919 two largely urban groups found their political interests increasingly at odds with Sinn Féin's: the working class and the largely unemployed soldiers home from the war. Though many labourers and ex-soldiers joined the Sinn Féin movement or Irish Volunteers, others preferred to dissociate themselves from a movement which insisted that social reform be set aside until freedom had been won. In 1917 political divisions appeared in the Clare Labour movement. As P. J. MacNamara, president of the United Labourers' Association (once a militia man and secretary to the County Board of the National Volunteers) put it, 'Political differences took place in the Ennis organisation at the recent election [July 1917]. There were two distinct bodies. Things came to a climax, and . . . [I advised] that politics should not be debated in the room of the Society. That arrangement was now [January 1918] being observed.' In September 1918 William O'Brien, ITGWU organiser and a strong opponent of the Irish Party, organised a United Trades Council in Ennis with delegates from twenty-three groups. One of his first appointments was with MacNamara; and it was the old-fashioned United Labourers' Association (with nearly a third of the votes), not the ITGWU, which continued to dominate the Ennis Labour movement.[56] Old-fashioned politicians on the Ennis Urban District Council saw their chance to make an expedient alliance with the organised workers and jobless men. In return for their electoral support, the politicians offered support for many of Labour's demands (which were frequently opposed by the representatives of Sinn Féin). Championship of the Labour cause by provincial Home Rulers was novel, yet in keeping with the vampiric tradition.

Sinn Féin's relative weakness in the towns, together with the Irish Party's exploitation of the Labour movement, allowed Clare opponents of Sinn Féin to defy the national trend at the urban district council elections of January 1920. In Kilrush the weakness of Sinn Féin was such that the twelve council seats were divided between seven sitting Home Rulers and five Labour men, who were able to fight each other bitterly without taking account of Sinn Féin's opinions. In Ennis, however, the new council was shared by six Sinn Féiners and six Home Rulers—four Trades Council (TLC) representatives, one independent Labourite and one Comrade of the Great War. Three of the 'Labour' men had belonged to the old council, and two of them had long histories of involvement in the Home Rule movement but short ones in the Labour movement. The new chairman made the allegiance of his faction clear: 'The town of Ennis had there and then proclaimed that it was still true and loyal to the teachings of Parnell, Davitt, Redmond, and Dillon.' The defeated Sinn Féin leader fumed: 'De Valera is thundering at the gates! He has not been kept out of the Co. Clare! He is there—paramount.' But it took a squalid legal battle involving the disqualification of two councillors to eject the chairman. Until common horror at British misgovernment induced Sinn Féiners, Labour organisers and even the ejected chairman to set aside their political differences, the old party clung tenaciously to its power in the county town of Clare.[57]

Outside the towns, however, the party had long since ceased to be a power in local politics. Bewilderment had been the commonest response to the Rising and its aftermath. The reflex of obedience to party directives was not easily conquered. When the party's handling of the post-Rising Home Rule negotiations was discussed late in the summer of 1916, one Ennis Guardian, still leader-struck in his disillusionment, exclaimed that 'It was John Redmond's fault; everything was his fault.' But the Board of Guardians, by four votes to two, praised the party for its 'political sagacity'. Ennistymon decided likewise, though not without some constructive criticism of the party leadership:

MR MALONE: Where will you get another leader like John Redmond?
MR MOLONEY: Parnell!!
MR MALONE: Oh, but he is dead.

Only in Corofin did councillors denounce the party's acceptance of proposals involving partition, resolving that it had 'no mandate to accept these conditions, and in doing so misrepresent and betray the trust reposed in them by the Irish people'. In the spring of 1917, when Count Plunkett convened an anti-Redmondite conference at the Mansion House, most councils in Clare marked their invitations 'read' (that is, ignored). Throughout Ireland at least sixty-eight local bodies accepted their invitations, whereas 209 rejected or ignored them. But the only Clare delegates were those from Corofin and Ennis. The Ennis Guardians at a small meeting had rejected the invitation, one speaker expressing horror at 'such self-assertiveness' and another feeling that if the party were in trouble, then was the time to help them out of it. But the decision was reversed at a second meeting by 23 votes to 13, after alleged intimidation and an acrimonious debate.[58]

After de Valera's by-election victory, most councillors sensibly stopped declaring their loyalty to the Irish Party. In September 1917 Ennistymon Rural District Council, by a small majority, called upon Arthur Lynch to resign his seat. The proposer said sternly: 'The country must fall into line. Let the opinion of the country be taken. He no longer represents our views.' But the distribution of power within the councils did not change with the slogans. Councillors fell into line behind different standards but the same bosses. The Sinn Féin organisation was unable to displace the chairman of any rural district council or Board of Guardians at the annual elections of officers in 1918 and 1919. In at least two cases in 1919 Sinn Féin conventions tried unsuccessfully to induce outgoing chairmen to resign their honorary magistracies in return for Sinn Féin's endorsement, then could not prevent their re-election. Political labels were debased. One outgoing chairman accused the priest who had headed the Sinn Féin convention which had endorsed his opponent (a revolutionary who had been local UIL secretary from the age of fifteen) of being a Redmondite! The incumbent won on his own casting vote. In mid-1918, it is true, the County Council did accede to a Sinn Féin club's demand that it elect a new chairman and vice-chairman, choosing men 'who possessed strong Sinn Féin views'. Yet after much acrimonious debate upon this demand, the council did nothing more radical than unanimously re-electing the incumbent vice-chairman! A new chairman was indeed elected; but, as his proponent put it, 'he intended no insult to their present Chairman, when he referred to Sinn Fein, because as a matter of fact, there was not a bit of difference in the principles and policy they were following'. Both office-holders were established men of influence, both former presidents of Hibernian divisions who had lately been converted to Sinn Féin.[59] It is clear that this reshuffle, whatever its true genesis, had little to do with the clash of political philosophies, of constitutionalism and separatism. By 1920 most influential local politicians had repudiated the old party, but they had by no means submitted themselves to the direction and discipline of its successor.

At last, in mid-1920, Sinn Féin succeeded in removing almost all the old bosses from public office, and in replacing them with humbler councillors, more passionately involved in the new politics and less prominently connected with the old. County rural elections had been postponed repeatedly since 1917, largely for fear that Sinn Féin would sweep the constitutionalists out of office; but in June 1920 the elections took place, with an electorate vastly enlarged and therefore released from its old domination by publicans and men of substance. Sinn Féin was able to win control of virtually every county council, rural district council and Board of Guardians outside Ulster for its own endorsed candidates. In Clare Sinn Féin gave its endorsement to scarcely any of the old bosses who had paid lip-service to its cause, and they were driven out of public life.[60] Many had painfully sacrificed their old party allegiance in order to preserve their status in the councils, only to find that they had lost their status in the county.

What did the Home Rule movement bequeath to Sinn Féin and the revolutionaries? It left them a certain number of politician-converts, important in the formative period of Sinn Féin but less influential as the revolution developed. Far more significant was the bequest of style, method and manipulative sophistication brought to the new movement by those countless thousands of minor organisers who abandoned Home Rule for self-determination not out of canny opportunism but out of 'sheepism'—or conviction. But most significantly of all, the Irish Party handed on the popular obsessions which had once given life to its own political organisation, obsessions to which the party had managed to give political expression. How would Sinn Féin cope with the disparate and often conflicting traditions which demanded political embodiment? With traditions as diverse as agrarian agitation, the Labour struggle, and the defence of the Catholic community against outsiders? How much freedom would the party's successors have to mould their revolution as they wished, or according to any coherent programme? How tightly would they be bound by those ancient passions which had once driven political curiosity out of the minds of Home Rulers?

Part Two

THE NEW POLITICS

4

Sinn Féiners

> O wise men, riddle me this: what if the dream come true?
> What if the dream come true? and if millions unborn shall dwell
> In the house that I shaped in my heart, the noble house of my thought?
> PADRAIC PEARSE, 'The Fool' (1915)

1. AFTER THE RISING

IN ITS beginnings, the new mass movement which swept Ireland after 1916 showed few signs of revolutionary planning or even of stylistic novelty. It was the sane creature of that conjunction of visionary outcasts, the Easter Rising. Experience of the Rising and what followed it taught countless Irishmen to hate the Irish Parliamentary Party; yet in building up an alternative party the principles they applied were not Ceannt's or MacDermott's but Devlin's and O'Brien's. The extent to which the new 'Sinn Féin' imitated the enemy's methods need not surprise us. In many parts of Ireland its organisers were familiar with no other political model. With astonishing ease, Sinn Féin beat the Irish Party at its own game. Only then did the defects of the model become apparent. To keep their cause alive Sinn Féiners had to challenge new opponents to new games. Knowing that its second opponent, the British government, held the initiative, Sinn Féin played black with enormous flair and ingenuity. But its game was necessarily defensive and was planned no more than a couple of moves ahead. In December 1921 it drew white at last, and not surprisingly showed a pitiable inability to plan the social transformation which so many Irishmen had casually supposed would follow political victory. The resourcefulness of the hard-pressed revolutionary gave place once more to imitation—this time of the methods and institutions of the government so lately dispossessed. As Seán O'Faoláin has written, 'Our leaders after 1916 were not thinkers. They played their revolution by ear. They were almost to a man gallant, idealistic, untutored, inexperienced and unworldly. . . . The policy of Sinn Féin had always been since its foundation that simple formula: Freedom first; other things after.'[1]

The new movement offered an alternative slogan to 'Home Rule'—'self-determination'. The old wine was decanted into new bottles, but drinkers were warned not to uncork them until years in the cellar had given the wine character and refinement. The reasoning behind that terminological revolution was simple: Irishmen must cease to trust the British government because it had returned in wartime to the old mode of coercion and exploitation; the Irish Party because it had become the government's spaniel; the Home Rule slogan because it had been devised by the Irish Party. As Fr Patrick Gaynor, the young inspector of schools for the Diocese of Killaloe, said in mid-1917, 'Why have we adopted a new battlecry if our beliefs are the old unchanging beliefs?

... Because the sacred word "Nation" has been corrupted to destroy the old idea of nationhood ... because British hirelings have profaned our symbols—the shamrock, Harp and Green Flag—to destroy their old-time significance.' The case against the party was stated more explicitly by Fr James Clancy, an older Clare priest whose O'Brienite past gave extra venom to his adjectives. 'Parliamentarianism', he claimed, was 'treasonable to our national demand, destructive of Irish national energy, and useless, or worse than useless, for the attainment of the end which all national movements in this country have in view'. And of John Dillon: 'We find him in 1916 closeted with Birrell and Nathan in Dublin Castle, plotting against the men who in Easter Week saved the soul of Ireland.'[2] Betrayal is the theme of countless attacks on the party—betrayal allegedly manifest in Redmond's willingness to compromise over partition, his acceptance of coalition ministries including Ulster Unionists and his scathing condemnations of the Rising as a device to destroy the Nationalist movement. But if the country sensed betrayal in September 1914 or May 1915, it did not put its indignation into words, publicly and in unison, until mid-1916. Why did the Rising, despite its military futility and chaotic organisation, dramatically succeed in changing the national mood just as its crazy yet crafty leaders had envisaged?

Augustine Birrell, the disgraced Chief Secretary, marvelled at the change which the Rising brought about in Irish assumptions as to what was practical in politics. His own aim had been 'to make any other solution [than Home Rule] of the problem *impossible*. ... In my wildest moments I never contemplated the possibility of what actually happened.' His failure, as he told an unsympathetic Royal Commission, had allowed old hatreds to find a new popular forum: 'The spirit of what to-day is called Sinn Feinism is mainly composed of the old hatred and distrust of the British connection, always noticeable in all classes and in all places, varying in degree and finding different ways of expression, but always there.' But the revolutionary impact of the Rising on Irish politics cannot simply be explained by latent hatred of Britain, or for that matter by admiration for the brave rebels and indignation at their long-drawn-out punishment. States of mind may be the context in which revolutionary decisions are made; they may provide the vocabulary of revolution; but for the genesis of those decisions one must turn from state of mind to rational calculation. An impulse of homely logic governs every grand gesture which stirs popular imagination and induces people to repudiate their former allegiance. MacDonagh's bony thumb, one surmises, was caked with chalk from the blackboard. The effect of the Rising was to convince most Irishmen that Redmond's logic was obsolete. His guiding principle throughout the European war had been to barter Irish support of the war effort for the assurance of post-war Home Rule. But the party's attempts to speed up recruiting had been hampered by the inflexible War Office; and the threat of compulsory military service, which until 1918 seemed likely to be enforced without regard for any political contract, intensified as the forces ran short of men. The repression after the Rising convincingly pointed out the limits to British goodwill, and the frustration of Lloyd George's constitutional endeavours suggested the crippling restrictions which Unionists would impose on any future scheme of self-government by British grace. Still more damaging to the Irish Party line was the fact that these negotiations had been undertaken in wartime, despite the suspensions of the Home Rule Act which Redmond had accepted as part of the bargain. In September police reported widespread assertions 'that one week of physical force did more for the cause of Ireland than a quarter of a century of Constitutional agitation'.[3] For the boys at the crossroads who wished to stay there, Redmond's broken contract gave place to a far more comfortable principle—that freedom could be wrung out of the British more easily by defiance than by co-operation. The government's conduct after the Rising provided a rational justification of the old animosity, and so allowed the renewed expression of that animosity in public life. Hatred gave Sinn Féin a rhetorical power which the party had chosen to abnegate; reason gave men the incentive to channel hatred into action, and to organise a new political machine to co-ordinate action.

The subtle process by which imagination is set free is difficult for an historian to reassemble after nearly sixty years. Fortunately, however, the diaries of one prominent political observer from Co. Clare have survived under the careful guard of their author, and their uncorrected pages provide glimpses of the impact of the Rising on a thoughtful outsider. On 25 April 1916 Edward Lysaght (later MacLysaght), whom we have already met as an employer, County Club man and National Volunteer organiser, with his house-guest and fellow-advocate of co-operation, 'AE', caught the Dublin train at Nenagh, Co. Tipperary. They knew nothing of the commotion in the capital except that the Irish Volunteers were said to have gone out against the British Empire, which in response had sent a warship to Dublin. At Ballybrophy station the train was halted, and the two men returned to Lysaght's home, Raheen on Lough Derg. Next day Lysaght was already mulling over his assumptions about Irish politics. His previous line all along had been this:

> The dream of an independent Irish nation is impracticable; let us therefore make ourselves spiritually independent by development of our individual national entity from within, by co-operation for our economics, by the Gaelic League for our culture. Let us make sure of the meagre act of justice we have obtained from England by helping her in the European war. . . . Patriotism for the British Empire, imperial feeling, is and has always been to me impossible. . . . Redmond, of course, should have made a bargain with England: Irish rights for Irish assistance. Redmond's attitude now will be interesting. . . . Ireland itself is I think vaguely stirred; there is no real excitement in the country but a feeling of sympathy with the rebels as I suppose they will be called; sympathy, that is, with the cause they are fighting for—the complete independence of Ireland—and respect for fellow countrymen ready to sacrifice their lives, without any sympathy with the time and methods they have chosen.

Three days later his judgment was still confused, warped by disparate loyalties: 'My speculations have led to nothing. I don't want the English and I don't want the Germans. Maybe I am crying for the moon.' The Rising was still a distant, puzzling, though fascinating event—a Dublin miracle, imperfectly reported, and only sporadically imitated in the provinces by minor demonstrations in Cork, Galway and Wexford, but not Clare. The reactions of the two poets at Raheen were strikingly akin. AE, in a poem he wisely omitted from his last collected edition, told the dead Pearse that his (Pearse's) dream had left him (AE) 'numb and cold' until death allowed the poet to refashion 'in burnished gold / The images of those who died'. Lysaght's verse, which was suppressed not by its author but by the press censor, depicted the Irish farmer's transition from political alienation through shock to rebirth:

> Till came the sudden bolt that left us numb
> We felt no more than strangers at a wake.

In both verses rebirth is ascribed not to the act of rebellion but to the suffering which followed under General Maxwell's direction. His policy of arresting and often deporting journalists, Sinn Féiners and Irish Volunteers, regardless of whether or not they had taken part in the Rising, affected not only Dublin but every part of the country. By 11 May Lysaght was indignant enough to 'unhesitatingly affirm the moral right to exercise physical force in certain circumstances of unparalleled tyranny or opportunity—even as a desperate if hopeless protest. It is immaterial now whether such circumstances can be said to have arisen; my purpose is with our future not the past.' Soon afterwards he wrote that the Rising had made him 'regard England as a dangerous alien, similar to Germany, less thorough, more hypocritical'. An entry for 27 June shows, more eloquently than his verse, the extent to which his response to the Rising had risen from reason into passion:

> After several years of hard work here in Clare, of indifference almost, certainly of unrealized, sub conscious and groping feeling, I began to find a passion arising in me which combined the fervour of love and the strength and faith of religion. Love, religion and patriotism are closely akin. Love and patriotism lead us and have I suppose led me into extreme and unconsidered acts but the basis of them is pure. Unfortunately my ideas on this subject will not flow tonight. AE is talking fluently in the next room—the Upanishads, underworld or heaven world, ancient Irish gods. . . .⁴

AE's fey talk was not so strange to the new political spirit as one might suppose. The proclamation of an Irish Republic in 1916 was first a revelation, then the object of a curious cult. Only after several months of undirected veneration of the martyrs were serious attempts made to reorganise Irish political life so that the proclamation could be given practical effect. Country policemen, mainly immune to the spiritual infection of the country, were puzzled by the post-Rising mood. At the end of May the Clare County Inspector wrote that since the Rising the county had been 'very quiet, no drills or meetings', yet feared it would 'take very little to cause it to break out again—in perhaps a more widespread form'. Groping to reconcile the evident sympathy with the rebel cause with the continued absence of an organised Sinn Féin movement, the police spoke of 'an undercurrent of unrest', more menacing than the most efficiently organised political faction. A year after the Rising Sinn Féin's vitality in Clare was still a mystery: it had not 'shown any life—it is not dead'. Police unease arose from their observation of the extraordinary martyrolatry of those months. By the end of July 1916 some 7,000 Irishmen had been seen wearing badges either in memory or expectation of the Republic. Next month the Clare County Inspector noted that fewer badges were to be seen but that the county was being plastered with 'expressions written up on walls etc.' During February 1917 twenty Republican flags were hoisted on trees, schoolhouses and telegraph wires in the county. And three months later all three symbols of disaffection— badges, flags and seditious remarks—were again in fashion. Many Requiem Masses were held in memory of the rebels. Postcard likenesses of the victims joined Emmet, Mitchel and the Blessed Virgin over countless cottage hearths. A few months after the Rising 'Editor's Gossip' in the *Irish Book Lover* noted that the market price of Thomas MacDonagh's book of verses had risen from 2s to 25s.[5] The symbols of the Easter martyrdom were being forged, in fact, into the iconography of a new political movement.

But if the objects of the cult were new, the mode of worship was not. Pearse was venerated just as a hundred dead heroes had been venerated, from Brian Boru to the Manchester Martyrs, from O'Connell to Parnell. In case any Irishman had forgotten the rhetoric of seven hundred years of national struggle as transmitted through the primary schools, magazines such as the *Catholic Bulletin* spelt out the historical parallels with tireless enthusiasm. Even W. B. Yeats, never a friend of the *Bulletin*, wrote a play, *The Dreaming of the Bones*, in which an escaped Easter rebel, sheltering in the shadow of the abbey at Corcomroe in Clare, communes with the spirits of Irish antiquity entombed beneath the abbey. The language of Sinn Féin as a cult rather than a party was the immemorial language of Irish Nationalism, extended and updated.[6]

Had the rhetoric of Sinn Féin brought to mind nothing but the rhetoric of the *Catholic Bulletin* and the old Irish Party and the National Schools, Sinn Féin would have been a poor dry thing. Fortunately for itself, it had another, richer tradition to draw upon—that of 'Irish Ireland', which the Gaelic Leaguers and Gaelic Athletes had set about recreating in the last years of the nineteenth century. Irish historians have rightly stressed the crucial influence of these societies upon the spirit of the revolution. In December 1920 Daniel Corkery wrote in *Studies*:

> Indeed it was the Gaelic League, although a strictly non-political body, rather than the remaining tradition of Fenianism that accounts for Ireland being so overwhelmingly committed to Republicanism to-day. This it brought about unwittingly. It trained up a body of young men as free from the passion of party politics as they were alive to the sense of continuity of the Irish tradition, the continuity of the Irish struggle, Ireland against England.

In a famous address in 1892 Douglas Hyde had ironically admitted 'the risk of encouraging national aspirations' by his programme for 'de-anglicising Ireland', although in later years Hyde's programme seemed apolitical to the point of inanity: 'My one and only request to the people of Clare is this—talk Irish to the children and all will be right.' But many Gaelic League organisers considered the spiritual and political struggles one, and in July 1915 they caused Hyde to resign the presidency by inducing the Árd-Fheis to resolve that the League 'devote itself to realising the ideal of a free Gaelic-speaking Ireland'. Many Gaelic League organisers, most of whom were National Teachers, felt that one way to de-anglicise Ireland was to avoid fighting England's wars for her. On the very day that Redmond pledged his Volunteers to fight wherever the firing line might be, the League's chief organiser in Clare told a *feis* at Doonbeg: 'We are not at war with anyone and we have enough to do to fight our own battles, so my advice to you is to let England fight hers.' A few weeks later the County Inspector reported that 'The Sinn Fein movement [sic] is encouraged and spread nearly altogether by National School teachers,' and after the Rising Mr McElroy, RM, indignantly wrote to the Chief Secretary: 'There is not a loyal N.S. Teacher in Clare that I know.' In some districts priests and teachers allowed the MacNeillite Irish Volunteers to use Gaelic League premises, intended for Irish instruction and placid amusements, as drill halls. In March 1916 'Brian Boru', an Ennistymon Gaelic Leaguer, found it necessary to reaffirm the League's independence from politics:

> There are at present two parties of Irishmen in nearly every town in Clare— Sinn Féiners and Redmondites. The Redmondites believe that every man who is willing to do a man's part in assisting the Gaelic League is a Sinn Féiner. Every man is welcome into the Gaelic League, let him be a Sinn Féiner, Redmondite, Catholic, or Protestant—every man is welcome so long as he is willing to help our mother tongue.

And what the League and GAA had to offer the politicians they offered indiscriminately to Sinn Féiners and Redmondites alike: zest for Ireland, tangible rather than rhetorical reminders of Irish nationality, Irish reels, sets, jigs, a few words of Irish, aggressively un-English games. Prejudice was inculcated into Gaels by means more memorable than newspaper editorials: for example, the founders of the O'Curry Irish College at Carrigaholt set up 'a Court of Justice for trying offences against the law of Ireland, such as using foreign manufacture, or speaking English within the precincts of the College, or perhaps having your name in English on the collar of your dog'. The influence of the 'Irish Ireland' movement on those who became Sinn Féiners after the Rising cannot be done justice by counting the number of local organisers of the League or GAA (in brief, 'Gaels') who later shone in Sinn Féin: of 913 secular separatist leaders in rural Clare a mere 17 are known to have been top Gaels from 1913 to 1916, and only 8 of 73 separatist priests. By way of contrast, 24 of 749 lay Irish Party bosses and 13 of 46 Irish Party priests also achieved notice as Gaels.[7] It was not experienced leaders that the Gaelic movement bequeathed to Sinn Féin, but zestful followers. For the sources of Sinn Féin's style and technique of political organisation, we must look elsewhere.

At first sight one might suppose that the organisers of post-Rising Sinn Féin were able to build on a robust tradition of anti-Redmondite, anti-recruiting, anti-British agitation. On 28 November 1914 the Irish government found it necessary to threaten suppression of certain 'seditious' newspapers under the Defence of the Realm Regulations. The new Under-Secretary, more alarmed by them than his chief, wrote to John Dillon: 'Their cleverly worded and insidiously scattered papers spread all over the country, and in the distribution of leaflets they [the loose assortment of factions colloquially labelled 'Sinn Féin'] and their American allies have the field practically to themselves.' But a Castle document giving the weekly circulation of 'certain publications' in September 1915 shows how sparsely they had spread in Co. Clare: thirty-one copies of the *Irish Volunteer* and seven of *The Spark* (both figures roughly median for all the Irish counties), nine of *Nationality*, three of *The Hibernian* and none whatever of the *Workers' Republic*.[8] To buy papers like these was to set oneself in a class apart; and this, it seems, almost no Clareman or woman was prepared to do. In 1904 the very name 'Sinn Féin' had been suggested to Arthur Griffith by a Clarewoman. But a decade later Sinn Féin still had only one branch in Clare, in the tiny village of Carron, isolated in the most desolate reaches of the Burren country. The RIC treated it with exaggerated respect, for until the war it was the only known centre of disloyalty in the county. In January 1913 its 'mischievous activity' was still flourishing, inspired by Tomás Ó Lochlainn, an early member of Sinn Féin's National Council and a lonely distributor of those much-feared seditious newspapers. Two years later the club had forty members, all of them herds, who 'meet after chapel on Sundays and talk over matters in the chapel yard'. What they talked about may be guessed from a manifesto which Ó Lochlainn had published in 1902 in the hope of winning local office. After a ritual promise to keep the rates down he couched his appeal in national rather than parochial terms: 'If you respect pretended Nationalists who on all possible occasions crawl before the Saxon tyrant—vote for my opponents. Some people believe that grazier gold and South African plunder will prevail; teach them by your votes that Patriotism and Justice will triumph.' But more important to Ó Lochlainn than any sectional struggle was the pure cause of nationality, and the purity of its epitome, the Carron Sinn Féin Society. To rant against particular graziers was to join in common cause with the detested United Irish League. Thus in March 1913, after discussing a proposal that graziers be called upon to surrender their ranches, 'The meeting decided that any ranchman who was still ignorant as to what his duty was with respect to his country and his neighbours was a person of denser intellect than that of an ordinary bullock, and that appeals to the better nature of such animals were quite useless.' At later meetings the club declined, in case asked, to act as agrarian arbitrators, and resolved, at Ó Lochlainn's urging, 'not to stultify themselves' by addressing appeals to government boards, but to stop speaking and start acting—though always 'well within the Law of God'. Carron Sinn Féin kept its purity, but at the cost of seeming in retrospect harmless and rather absurd. After the Rising a District Inspector recounted the history of the club since the outbreak of war:

> In the autumn and winter of 1914 the members became Irish Volunteers, and had frequent drillings, without arms, or uniform, until July 1915 when they ceased.

About twelve of them had three practices with a miniature rifle. They took no part in the Easter Week rebellion, but they surrendered their shotguns under the Proclamation. Of course they voted to a man for De Valera.'

If Clare was deficient in the Sinn Féin tradition of non-violent national self-regeneration, it was equally deficient in the Fenian tradition of conspiracy and apocalyptic planning. In neighbouring Limerick City the old Fenian John Daly could attract 180 rebels to a 'cinematograph performance' on St Stephen's Day 1914, which was rumoured to have ended with the singing of the German imperial anthem. So strong was opposition to the Irish Party in that region that according to Michael Brennan, a precocious initiate of the Irish Republican Brotherhood from nearby Meelick Cross, Co. Clare, he and his friends were able quietly to dominate the original Provisional Committee of the Irish National Volunteers in Limerick. From Co. Galway to the north came periodic solemn warnings from the police about a secret, oath-bound society founded by Dublin Invincibles which was blamed in July 1916 for 'most of the agrarian crime and unrest in Galway and was at the back of the recent rebellion'. But Clare itself, despite its glorious memories of the assault on Kilbaha coastguard station in '67, was so far outside the mainstream of Fenianism by 1915 that Éamonn Ceannt, born in Galway and a leading organiser for the conspiratorial part of the Irish Volunteers, could list 211 names in his pocket book of contacts without mentioning a Clareman. Accounts differ as to which Claremen were sworn into the Brotherhood, though most survivors agree that several active organisers of Clare's eleven anti-Redmondite Irish Volunteer corps were among them. According to Diarmuid Lynch, who appears to have been 'Divisional Centre for Munster' after 1911, Clare had only two IRB Circles, one of them unofficial, and a few small groups in the years when it was his duty to inspect and supervise their activities. The unofficial Circle revolved about none other than Tomás Ó Lochlainn—in his capacity as an Ennistymon lodger rather than a native of Carron, and as a conspirator rather than a passive resister. Lynch remembered that Ó Lochlainn was 'very secretive in all his talk and actions' and 'held the strange idea of keeping his men apart from any official contacts'. He was delighted by 'the old man's spirit' in 1915, when Lynch, Ó Lochlainn and a young policeman on leave were staying together in an Ennistymon hotel. Lynch shared his bedroom with a few rifles which the Irish Volunteers had just bought from the Redmondites. Next morning he found that Ó Lochlainn had spent the night guarding his door in case of surprise attack by the enemy. When the Rising came Ó Lochlainn had to be restrained from rising all alone by his landlady, priest and fellow-lodger (the Irish teacher Éamonn Waldron, whom, it is said, he never spoke to again). His pride was salved by subsequent deportation to Wakefield Jail. Just before his death from influenza in 1918 he wrote a delightfully transparent conspiratorial letter which illustrates his lovable and ungrown-up character:

Seán a Chara
  Bully-Beef is sold at Roughan's in tins at 1/6 each. The tin would I think contain 12 oz. and ought to be enough for 2 men. It is also sold at 1/11 a lb.

without any cover or for 11/- a 6 lb. tin. It's almost useless for a picnic except in the small tin (1/6). If the Committee intends to invest in matter they should send for a small order by the first confidential member who has a car in town and if they approved of sample they could instruct Mr Roughan to have all they would require.

do Chara
T. Ó Lochlainn

The Committee I mean is of course the Anti-Conscription Committee.[10]

If future revolutionaries could expect little hard-headed, practical help from the romantic Ó Lochlainn, they could expect even less from most of his fellow-Fenians in Clare, who had mainly become cautious, law-abiding, respectable men, reluctant to associate with rebels under fifty. The reinvigoration of the IRB's Supreme Council had not, it seems, inspired imitation in the west. Ernest Blythe, himself a sworn Brother who organised the Irish Volunteers in Clare and other counties in 1915, was advised by Seán MacDermott to ask help from three Fenian cobblers in Ennis. After Blythe had explained his mission the eldest cobbler took him to a window through which an RIC man could be seen. 'Do you see that man over there, and do you think it's fair to bring such a man watching this house? I would be very glad if you would clear off immediately.' When the Volunteers were reorganised after the Rising their leaders, in Clare at least, had little use for the IRB men. Michael Brennan was a sworn Brother at fifteen but a sceptic at twenty: 'In Clare they were the conspirator type and didn't want to fight at all. Our fellows wanted to get out in the open and fight. They just pushed the old I.R.B. men aside.'[11] The organised remnants of previous separatist movements had little to teach the post-Rising generation, either as politicians or fighting-men. In provincial Ireland there was only one political school which mattered—and that was the Home Rule movement.

In May 1918 an advertisement appeared in the *Saturday Record*: '3 years old, by Commander, dam by the famous Old Warrior . . . having some of the best of Shire blood and qualities must get well. He has good, flat bone, and good, true action, and is a big, bony colt with good feather. . . . Owner not responsible for accidents to mares or foals sent to these sires, but every care will be taken of them.' The horse's name was Sinn Féin Warrior. Except for a slight anachronism, one might suppose that the advertiser had in mind an allegory of the Irish Revolution—rebel fathered by Home Rule boss (Commander) and mothered by one who had the blood of national tradition in her veins (daughter of Old Warrior). For in that coupling of the power and technique of the old boss with the spirit of the Rising and the Gaelic League, we find the sources of Sinn Féin's early triumphs of mass organisation, its persistent vitality, and its genetic intellectual limitations. We have already touched upon the frequency with which party bosses became separatist bosses when fashions changed: 12 per cent of Hibernian leaders, 13 per cent of United Irish Leaguers, and 23 per cent of Redmondite Volunteer chiefs in rural Clare. Among 913 prominent rural separatists 55 had been local councillors before 1920, 54 Irish Party organisers and 72 Redmondite Volunteers. By contrast, a mere 41 Claremen publicly showed separatist leanings before the Rising. Thus over the whole period 1913–21 there was a thick strand of continuity in political leadership, doubtless much stronger in the provinces than among the national leaders, far more of whom were drawn from the conspiratorial groups which had planned the Rising. It was natural that men of local 'influence' and 'popularity' should play a large part in organising any new movement which aimed at building up a vast following in the shortest possible time. And in Clare, as we have seen, such men were almost exclusively former stalwarts of the Irish Party. After the Rising shopkeepers still had cash and dependent customers as in the party's halcyon days, local councillors still had favours to distribute to those who treated them with respect. Such considerations governed Bertie Hunt's response to a request from Count Plunkett that he organise a Liberty Club in Corofin. Hunt himself had been interned in 1916, but was a councillor and well versed in the techniques of local politics:

> I have interviewed some influential local people with reference to the matters mentioned. Rev Fr S— C.C. and Rev Fr H— C.C. both of Corofin are whole heartedly in favour of your policy and have authorized me to say so. Mr P. S— also an influential local merchant is of the same opinion. The Chairman Corofin D.C. and 7 or 8 members I can speak for are prepared to join a Sinn Féin organization. As a matter of fact we can command a majority of this body.[12]

For many prominent Sinn Féiners the old assumptions about which people mattered stayed as firm as though the Rising had never occurred, as though the labourers and shop-boys of Dublin had never wrought havoc upon their masters' property.

But it was not the shopkeepers but the priests who did most to ensure the continuity of the Nationalist tradition of organisation. At least seventy-three priests, about half of all those working in Clare between 1917 and 1921, publicly associated themselves with the separatist cause, and almost no parish was forced to reorganise without the help of one curate at least. Curates were more inclined than their seniors to support the new movement, but the Rising did not produce a simple division between turbulent curates and traditionalist parish priests. Indeed, sixteen of the latter are known to have advocated self-determination, of whom seven had been associated with the Irish Party organisations and another two with the National Volunteers. Among the fifty-seven separatist curates more than a fifth had had previous experience as political organisers: six as Irish Party men and eight as National Volunteers. Only five priests, three of them curates, had turned against the party publicly before the Rising, including the desperate Fr Charlie Culligan, who had told the first meeting of the Clare County Board of the Irish Volunteers in January 1916:

> . . . if they could not get long-distance rifles to get shot guns, that shot guns were very useful in the hands of Irishmen. . . . If they could not get shot guns they should get revolvers and if they could not get revolvers they should get pikes, that any blacksmith could make them, and that if they could not get pikes that every man had a hatchet or a slasher in his house.

But a large proportion of milder curates, of the generation which had passed through Maynooth in the early years of the century, had learned the techniques of Sinn Féin politics at Maynooth itself by passively resisting the stern rule of its famous President, Dr Daniel Mannix. Many students, incensed at his prohibition of smoking and other simple vices, refused to clap at prize distributions and refused to offer friendly welcomes to distinguished episcopal visitors. According to one of them, their protest gradually changed from defiance of a particular tyrant to a depersonalised, self-conscious exercise in Sinn Féin methods of combat. Other priests were attracted to Sinn Féin by their experience of defying the ruling order in other contexts. One of these, the lonely O'Brienite Fr James Clancy, was to become first president of Sinn Féin's West Clare executive. He had derided both wings of the Volunteers in March 1916, denounced the Cork Sinn Féiners in July for being 'very busy making terms for themselves and handing in their arms, while the fight for an Irish Republic was actually on', but more than any of these he had loathed the Irish Parliamentary Party. Like his mentor, Fr Clancy backed Sinn Féin only when it seemed capable of destroying the party: as he freely admitted in November 1917, 'it was not until the East Clare Election he finally made up his mind to embrace the Sinn Fein policy'. It may be apposite to quote his jibe at the party's candidate for East Clare, a former Crown prosecutor in Kerry: 'A mere change of garment does not mean a change of character.'[13]

The majority of Sinn Féin priests, however, did not support the new cause because of long-nurtured revolutionism or out of rancour, but with motives at least as mixed as their parishioners'. Significantly, they were often drawn into Sinn Féin at the urging of uninfluential enthusiasts rather than rushing into the vanguard to assume command. The enthusiasts needed their support to impart that aura of responsibility and trustworthiness without which no parochial society, whatever its politics, could win a mass following. Thus one of Count Plunkett's correspondents wished he would contact two East Clare curates who were 'on the right side' about forming Liberty Clubs, though in the meantime he promised to do his 'best to spread the light'. But the Church had responded to the turbulent politics of late 1916 warily enough. Dr Fogarty, Bishop of Killaloe, had hoped in mid-May that the spirits of the dead rebels would 'rest for the present in peace in the silence of eternity'. Although this phrase implied that it might become expedient thereafter to haul them back out of eternity, the bishop 'advised his priests to exercise discretion and to refrain from comment on the rebellion, and set them an example in this respect'. But gradually rumours reached the Castle of Cork Capuchins laughing at and enjoying their pupils' indulgence 'in seditious songs and rebel cries'; of the President of St Flannan's College telling Co. Clare that it should be ashamed at not having joined the Rising; of a Kilkenny curate who 'sang the seditious ballad "Who fears to speak of Easter Week", and in response to an encore repeated the offence'. General Maxwell attempted to extend the area of his martial powers to the Holy See, suggesting that the Pope might 'be induced . . . to prevent Priests from mixing themselves up with matters political, seditious or unconnected with their spiritual position'. By early 1917 the police Inspector-General was thoroughly alarmed: 'practically all' the clergy, especially the younger ones, 'showed open sympathy with, or approval of, the action taken by the rebels'.[14]

Many students of the Church, from George Birmingham and J. P. Mahaffy to John A. Murphy, have concluded that the priests had ceased to lead the people. As Mahaffy wrote in October 1916, 'They are only watching the trend of public opinion among the masses, and either putting themselves forward as leaders or carefully avoiding to stem the rising tide.' But Patrick O'Farrell has uncovered many clerical motives for adhering to Sinn Féin apart from canny adulation of success: disgust with the Irish Party, fear of socialism, fellow-feeling for the rebels with their grandiose dreams, gratitude to them for adopting the terminology if not the principles of the Gospels, and so perhaps spurring on the current revival of interest in religion. There is also evidence that anxiety to glean the fullest advantage from the prosperity of the time made some priests more than usually eager to maintain close accord with their parishioners in late 1916. In November Fr J. Glynn, PP, told his bishop that he wished to repair one of his churches: 'For some time we have been preparing the ground as best we could. The people are in an expectant mood and we must not miss our tide lest we might be told later, when agricultural prices get lower, that our opportunity had gone.' Architects had reported in 1915 that the main roof was sagging, various tiles loose and broken, the roof of the sacristy 'quite beyond repair', the gable barges defective, the pipes too small, the wooden doors and windows irreparably decayed, and the plastering 'loose, damp and discoloured'. In July 1917 he was among the fairly few parish priests to found a local Sinn Féin club, at the first meeting of which he promised the co-operation of the clergy. Fr Glynn and his parish worked together in perfect harmony and when the bishop visited the parish in 1917 he noted that no less than £900 had been subscribed by the people of an unusually arid district.[15] Priests in leaking churches simply could not afford to fight unpopular causes, and because the churches built in the wake of Emancipation were far past their half lives, many of them leaked. It was a happy coincidence that the Rising excited many of the priests as much as their parishioners. Their function in the movement inspired by the Rising was as trustees of good faith, leaders dutifully following the mass will. Apart from the odd parish priest who foresaw 'red ruin and revolution' if de Valera reigned, and the odd bishop who attempted to curb his more turbulent curates, the Irish clergy tactfully gave Sinn Féin free rein. In October 1917 one curate recalled, to the disgust of the police sergeant present, that 'the priests on Retreat at Ennis College during the election could only pray for Mr de Valera's success and for an Irish Republic'. The atmosphere of those retreats, which played an important role in determining the group attitudes of the priesthood of a diocese, is suggested by the unseemly relish with which another curate home from a slightly later retreat celebrated Ireland's spiritual liberation:

> Only a very short time ago we all had to take off our hats to the landlords when we met them, we almost had to take them off [to] the old peelers, the degraded old peelers but thank God we need not take them off to-day to the bloody old peelers. We have our own Sinn Fein army who are as solid as rock.[16]

That Sinn Féin army owed much, both in the composition and function of its leadership, to the Home Rule model. But its greatest debt of all was for its overriding organisational principle—the desire to unite all Irishmen under one banner. The wonderful sense of oneness which pervaded Irish politics in the years after the Rising long remained in the memories of those who lived through them. As Edward MacLysaght (formerly Lysaght) recalls, 'There was a unity of purpose actuating us which is unique in Irish history. In that period there were no informers and no potential Quislings. In those parts of the country where English influence was strong there were of course not a few whose sympathies were with the enemy, but I doubt if there were a dozen such in East Clare.' Until mid-1917, as we have seen, solidarity was expressed mainly in the observation of solemn rituals in memory of the Easter martyrs. Sinn Féin was more a mood than an organisation, a repudiation of the old political Nationalism more than a promise to replace it. But as the new mood spread, and more and more men of influence turned against the Irish Party, the manipulative, political instincts of Irishmen asserted themselves with ever increasing urgency. Each successive parliamentary by-election, from West Cork to East Clare, was fought by anti-Redmondite candidates with more and more clearly defined programmes of opposition. The emotive rhetoric of Easter Week gradually gave place to the cool demand that Irishmen should pledge their loyalty and energy to a new political order.

The two styles were combined by Éamon de Valera, who although nominated for East Clare as a hero of Easter Week, showed a keener political sense than Count Plunkett had done in North Roscommon by behaving as if he were the leader of a political party with clear aims—to withdraw from Westminster and put its claims before the expected Peace Conference. Certainly, his supporters did not disdain to use Rising rhetoric: a Limerick Sinn Féin propaganda sheet calling itself 'the smallest paper in the world' wrote that '*The issue* is clear—a brave Soldier of Ireland, representing all that is best and purest in the land today and standing for the principles of the Martyred Dead of Easter Week, on one side, and a place-hunting ex-Crown Prosecutor who stands in the name of the National Imperial Party on the other.' But a collection of campaign leaflets preserved by William O'Brien suggests that de Valera's campaign organisers, mainly ex-internees from outside Clare, relied surprisingly little on defamatory smears against Patrick Lynch. Balancing such leaflets as *Dalcassians! Do You Want a Hero to Represent You?* and *Lynchites Belying the Bishop of Limerick* are others suggesting that Sinn Féin at last had opinions to express on specific political issues: *Is Conscription Coming?*, *How the English Parliament Taxes Ireland*, *Parnell's Policy*, *The Bogus Convention* and *Peace and Prosperity or Red Ruin*. To broadcast the Sinn Féin message an elaborate campaign machinery was put together, including corps of armed Volunteers to frighten off pugnacious Redmondites, which were felt by the County Inspector to constitute 'a great source of danger to the Peace', and groups of local canvassers, one of whom proudly recalls that not one vote was missing from his district, though 'people didn't rightly know what it meant at that time'. These hastily assembled groups formed the nuclei of the

Sinn Féin clubs and Irish Volunteer companies which were formally established with appropriate protocol after the election. Immense significance was attached by press, police and politicians to de Valera's surprisingly large majority. The Under-Secretary felt it 'not unlikely that Ennis may become the Centre of Sinn Fein activities. Valera is said to be taking a house there: and it is possible that it may become the centre of a rival Government.' But de Valera stayed in Dublin, and Ennis remained a political backwater, for Sinn Féin was rapidly transforming itself into a political mass organisation not only in Clare but in many other counties. By the end of June, ten days before the poll in East Clare, Cork had six Sinn Féin clubs, Limerick twenty-two, and Ireland overall 166.[17] The businesslike spirit of the East Clare campaign was a symptom rather than the cause of the national drive towards practical organisation for the achievement of political power.

In the provinces, then, Sinn Féin's first year was a reckless rush towards unity, first spiritual, then practical. How is this picture to be reconciled with that of Dublin after the Rising, with its petty bickering and faction-fighting? A glance at one proselytising weekly, the *Irish Nation*, reveals furious denunciations of the Irish Party, the Irish Nation League, the O'Brienites, the Pimians and the Griffithists, but curiously few suggestions for the national betterment except repeal of the Act of Union, to which end an entirely uninfluential Repeal League was launched. The struggle for domination of metropolitan politics was less the clash of policies or ideologies than the jousting of a few forceful individuals eager to win acceptance as leader of the Irish nation, the great man to supplant John Redmond and carry on his tradition of command from the clouds. In these months small men, their superiors safely incarcerated, could sense greatness; poets could believe themselves politicians. Herbert Pim, home early from his internment, 'felt sure that it would be a simple matter to make use of this misdirected sympathy [for the Easter martyrs] to lead the public unconsciously into adopting the policy for which the name Sinn Fein really stood', and he modestly accepted responsibility for reviving the Sinn Féin movement. The Irish Nation League, *alias* Anti-Exclusion League, *alias* Anti-Partition League, attracted influential Southern bosses such as Stephen O'Mara of Limerick as well as Ulster Nationalists disgusted with the Irish Party's conciliatory gestures towards Craig and Carson, and dreamed of uniting 'all our fellow-countrymen on the same platform for the purpose of reviving all things Irish'. Count Plunkett, having secured election at North Roscommon as the father of his rebel sons, became convinced that he had been chosen for command, and launched his own Liberty League in competition with both Sinn Féin and the INL. Political life, particularly in Dublin and Cork, was further complicated in December 1916 and June 1917 by the arrival home of interned physical-force men, but these were usually content to take over key posts quietly without joining the undignified dash for personal supremacy. But in the provinces no interest was taken in these drawing-room or saloon-bar squabbles. As Michael Laffan has shown, parochial organisers showed a delightful insensitivity to the nomenclature used by Plunkett in his campaign to out-organise Sinn Féin in April and May 1917. An Ennis woman promised him she would join one of her local clubs: 'The clubs here do not bear the name of Liberty Clubs but have the same object.' One of those who had organised them wrote: 'Unless you wanted to get me killed by the young men of this County I could not attempt to establish a branch of any Club here except *Sinn Fein*. They are all anxious that you should be President, but Sinn Fein must not die at any cost. . . . P.S. I am the oldest member of the Ennis R.D. Council and B. of Guardians I am the worst educated man in the lot, as well as being the worst speaker and after all I have to do the hard work.' Altogether one Liberty Club, no INL branches and at least sixty-eight Sinn Féin clubs were established in Clare. At last the various aspirant gods in Dublin accepted their obsolescence and agreed to place de Valera at the head of both the civil and military organisations at the conventions of Sinn Féin and the Volunteers in October 1917. The Clare County Council, reapplying a familiar slogan, saluted the 'chosen leader of the Irish Race'. The leader replied that 'it was easily the proudest day in his life'.[18] The fact that de Valera's formal assumption of leadership did not take place till nearly a month later didn't matter in the least. God was in his heaven, de Valera was in Clare, all was right with the world.

In almost every aspect the parochial organisation of Sinn Féin resembled its Home Rule model. Already in August 1916 a Cork policeman had noted the superficiality of some of the changes in political style: 'An excursion, for instance, which before would be called either a "Molly" or "All-for-Ireland" excursion, is now a "Sinn Fein" one, or else not known by any political name at all.' On 11 July 1917 eleven Ennistymon publicans raised the tricolour, as they had been accustomed to raise the green flag; and doubtless by their increased custom they more than recouped the few shillings they subsequently lost in fines. Sinn Féin branches, like those of the UIL or AOH, normally met after Mass and passed strong resolutions—but then, as the wise George Birmingham wrote, 'Resolutions are well understood in Ireland, and the passing of them is recognised as a harmless way of placating troublesome enthusiasts.' Familiar themes recur in newspaper reports of Sinn Féin resolutions: condolences were offered by no less than 101 of 449 meetings analysed, 50 meetings discussed the raising or disposing of funds, 25 protested at arrests or prison sentences, 19 supported candidates for local jobs, and 11 raised their voices in praise of the Church. Torchlight processions, marches with tuneless bands, bonfires and the like continued as before, though de Valera, with his drab repetitive but cunningly over-qualified style of speech, set a new vogue which, to the sorrow of many connoisseurs, has ever since largely shut the old theatrical style out of Irish political life. Like the UIL, the provincial Sinn Féin machine was used to collect national campaign money (supplemented, as in Irish Party days, by vast subscriptions from Irish-Americans). By June 1918, apart from the huge sum raised for wounded heroes of Easter Week and their dependants, branches had sent over £20,000 to headquarters, spending over £11,000 locally and having nearly as much in balance. Branches took on the character of social clubs: concerts and lectures were given, tracts issued listing approved reading from *Cuchulainn, the*

Hound of Ulster to Griffith's *Meagher of the Sword*. All men aged between fourteen and ninety were invited to join up. Lady supporters were tactfully advised to channel their energy into the fast-growing Cumann na mBan, though for the time being their subscriptions would be gladly received. Late in 1917 Scariff Sinn Féin awakened from its post-electoral 'dull sleep', and the *Champion* reported:

> Any night you do not hear the whack of the billiard balls, or the occasional merry peals of laughter or shouts at the expense of some awkward player . . . you are certain to hear the steady determined movements of the Volunteers (who drill not less than twice a week) punctuated now and again by the steady orders and reprimands of our redoubtable commandant.

But Republicanism had its duties as well as pleasures. Already in June 1917 branches were told that 'the first thing to be done' was to win every possible public office for Sinn Féin. Every occasion should be used for propaganda: 'agricultural shows, race meetings, fairs, big country auctions'.[19] Sinn Féin was above all a political machine; but like its Home Rule model it was many-faceted, offering its members a way of life whereby they could set aside individuality in the quest for a mysterious treasure which one did not talk about.

Like the Home Rule movement it superseded, young Sinn Féin was more concerned with national unity than national planning. When campaigning in East Clare de Valera took care to solicit votes from all factions, whatever their constitutional views, if any. In one much-quoted speech he said: 'We want an Irish Republic because if Ireland had her freedom, it is, I believe, the most likely form of government. But if the Irish people wanted to have another form of government, so long as it was an Irish government, I would not put in a word against it.' The Republic, like the Nation Once Again, was a vessel into which each man could pour his own dream. After glumly reporting the outcome of the East Clare by-election, the County Inspector observed: 'The prevailing impression seems to be that after the establishment of the Irish Republic people will be able to do exactly as they please.' In its early months Sinn Féin was a 'movement' only as a patch of oil-slick moves, spreading outwards to encompass every body in its vicinity; but as a whole it was amorphous and directionless. In November 1917 Edward Lysaght wrote to Sir Horace Plunkett: 'My belief is that, with the exception of a few young hot-heads, the people generally are a little afraid of themselves and their new movement, not knowing whither it will lead them yet having, as they believe, no alternative.'[20] Only when its adolescence was far advanced did Sinn Féin seriously ask itself: Why do I exist?

2. FROM EAST CLARE BY-ELECTION TO GENERAL ELECTION

In the eighteen months between de Valera's election for East Clare and the general election of December 1918 Sinn Féin reached maturity. It was guided by one clear aim: to displace the Irish Party as the acknowledged representative of Nationalist opinion. It built up, to this end, a massive, unified electoral machine, designed along sound traditional lines. Its tacticians relied on three simple principles: to get as much publicity as possible, to whip up hatred of Britain by exploiting her clumsy errors of government, and to discredit the Irish Party. These principles were in practice intertwined: the party was discredited by coupling its interests with those of the government, publicity achieved by goading the government into overreaction. Sinn Féin's moral force was exerted in every parish by the homophonic chorus of its massive following, and its organisers fought stubbornly all attempts to refine or whittle down its membership. Sinn Féin had learned its Home Rule lessons well.

With astonishing obtuseness the government played into the hands of Sinn Féin. By doggedly trying to restore the Irish Party's prestige, it seemed to confirm Sinn Féin's allegations that Redmond and Dillon had sold their souls to the Saxon. The Irish Convention of 1917–18, like Lloyd George's Home Rule proposals of 1916, was offered to the Irish Party as a lifeline; but the party grabbed it too eagerly, caught up its limbs in the slack and drowned. Sinn Féin managed to suggest that the Convention was a sordid scheme devised by Redmond and Lloyd George to hoodwink the nation, without repudiating in advance any settlement it might recommend. Like abstention from Westminster, abstention from Regent House was a gesture of purity rather than constitutional intransigence. Sinn Féin had many valuable sympathisers, in fact, who hoped not for a Republic but for some form of Home Rule without Party Rule. In July 1916 independent-minded men such as AE, Sir Horace Plunkett and Edward Lysaght had considered summoning 'a conference of unofficial folk to consider the Home Rule question'. Ten months later Lysaght felt inclined at first report to back the government's proposals for Home Rule with a consultative council to bridge the gulf between the six counties and the twenty-six counties:

> If I confirm my present view that these proposals should be accepted subject to fiscal autonomy being agreed to, and if they are wrecked by Nationalist Ireland I shall feel inclined to abjure all politics. Alas! politics are not sectional matters in Ireland whereas in other countries, if displeased with one party one can vote for the other or another. Whatever blunders Nationalist Ireland makes I could not vote Unionist or feel Unionist.
> (*Note:* Dr MacLysaght points out that by the term 'Nationalist Ireland' in this passage, dated 15 May 1917, he was referring to such Nationalists as were then organised—at that time still predominantly Redmondites.)

When, a few weeks later, the Convention was assembled to formulate constitutional proposals along these lines, Sinn Féin's twin desires for purity and unanimity were reconciled by a curious stratagem. Sinn Féin declined to send official delegates, but kept in close touch with two independent participants, AE and Lysaght, who in practice expounded the Sinn Féin mood to an apprehensive audience. Lysaght was evidently endorsed by Sinn Féin leaders as 'their unofficial representative', though certainly he did not wish to be regarded as such by the Chief Secretary. As a man with 'more or less Sinn Féin ideas' he dined and talked with Mac Néill and de Valera and was found useful as an informant by Sinn Féin and the members of the Convention alike. In his only speech, drawn up with the advice, which he regarded 'as instructions', of an informal committee including Eóin Mac Néill, Lysaght warned the Convention: 'If the Convention fails it will require revolution and bloodshed to arrive at the inevitable result: Irish freedom. . . . Sinn Féin is not, now at least (*it may soon be too late*), is not intransigent.' By January 1918 Lysaght was convinced that the Convention would not agree on any acceptable set of proposals, and announced his resignation. Dr Fogarty approved: the Convention's forthcoming deputation to Lloyd George might well 'agree to one of his funny "treaties"'. For AE, who resigned a few weeks later, the Convention's failure released him to 'go back to my own work of cooperation writing and painting. Ireland is going to descend into Hell and I won't help it in that direction.'[21] But Lysaght's resignation was a statement not of renunciation of all politics but of closer commitment to Sinn Féin. He emerged certain that the chance of a successful outcome had been lost not, as he had feared in May, by Nationalist wrecking, but by government meddling. The hollower the government's promises of a tolerant settlement seemed, the less inclined were thoughtful Nationalists to quibble with the more doctrinaire elements in the Republican programme.

If the Dublin leaders showed ingenuity in exploiting the government's constitutional endeavours, their provincial followers showed even more in exploiting the government's clumsy instruments of coercion. By the sporadic exercise of ill-directed *force majeure*, by interference in public assemblies, arrests, trials and imprisonments, the Castle made heroes out of nobodies and provoked savage indignation among countless families which had previously supported the new movement, if at all, only out of herd instinct. The mistakes of 1916 were repeated again and again. When the government threatened to learn from its mistakes, alert rebels cajoled it into reverting to them. During the East Clare campaign, which was, disturbingly, undisturbed by police interference, a Clare Volunteer leader devised a cunning plan to set the Castle snorting. Michael Brennan recalls:

> During the election my brother, Paddy, had worked out a completely new policy which I'm afraid he didn't submit to G.H.Q. for approval. He was pretty certain it wouldn't be approved, but on the other hand, he thought if it worked, G.H.Q. would accept it and issue it as their own policy. (This was in fact what happened a few weeks later.)

Paddy Brennan suggested drilling illegally, preferably in the presence of policemen, which 'would stimulate interest as the British would have to treat it as a challenge and take action against us'; pleading guilty to all charges and refusing to recognise the authority of the courts, thus winning publicity and cutting legal costs; and going on hunger-strikes to win the status of 'political prisoners', though 'none of us knew what political prisoner status meant'.[22] The plan was dramatically effected late in July 1917 when, after urgent requests for their courts martial from the military and police authorities, the three Brennan brothers were arrested after repeatedly wearing uniforms, drilling and pledging Volunteers and haranguing them with strong speeches. Scores of others followed their example, and the police responded gratifyingly by arresting all the drill-masters who could attract their attention. In September 1917 even military intelligence seemed concerned by the arrest of such 'youthful nobodies' as Thomas Keane of Ennis. As the Under-Secretary commented, 'The boy Keane is a bit of a humourist. He joined the Army, and had to be discharged because of his youth. He is, I am told, likely to join up again when he is 18. Meanwhile he likes drilling the boys and girls, boasting of his prowess as a rebel and getting his picture in the papers.' The boy Keane ended up a Senator. Meanwhile the Brennans and a number of others, mostly Claremen, had duly denied the power of the courts to try them and had gone on hunger-strike in a series of jails. Hunger-striking gave new dignity to the concept of imprisonment, which had been debased somewhat by the evident enjoyment derived by many post-Rising internees from their overseas holidays. A Cork man had written in January 1917: 'Now any common or garden fellow with a smell of Sinn Féin can get to Frongoch free of charge, but I can tell you it takes a fairly smart chap to keep out of Frongoch.... Give my best wishes to Thomas and Terence and I hope they will deserve jail again soon.' Hunger-striking renewed the thrill of discomfort and danger, the more so when Thomas Ashe died in the Mater Hospital after being forcibly fed. The new attitude was expressed by a young Clare drill instructor in November: 'Don't be afraid of the Peelers. All you have to do, if you are sent to Mountjoy, is go on "Hunger Strike".' The police were flabbergasted: 'The law is openly defied, and everything points to a time in the near future when it will be set aside in favour of laws made by the Sinn Fein Convention in Dublin.... Sinn Fein is the law of the land.'[23]

The government's attempts to draw up a firm, consistent yet unprovocative policy towards illegal drilling and hunger-striking did little to comfort the police and prison administrators. On 2 November 1917 the Chief Secretary decided that prominent leaders should not be arrested without government consultation 'unless it is necessitated by a sudden armed rising in Ireland'; but 'any body of men engaged in drilling or marching in military formation as a military exercise' was to be dispersed by the police (with military help if needed) and its 'ringleaders' arrested and prosecuted. The Inspector-General drily accepted the impracticability of arresting the leaders 'who are inciting the people to these illegal acts', but successfully argued that attempts to disperse Volunteer parties would expose the troops and police to ridicule, since the sound of a peeler's tread was detectable at a great distance. On 10 November the Chief Secretary agreed that police should disperse drillings only if they were present in sufficient force (which they hardly ever were), call for military help only if confronted by uncontrollable riot or disorder, and otherwise confine themselves to sending the military authorities annotated lists of those involved in drilling (more useful to social historians than generals).[24] As a result the drillers themselves were able to determine when and by whom they should be arrested. In the prisons where they had been brought together the former hunger-strikers by now held virtually undisputed sway. Ashe's death had caused the government to abandon forcible feeding, and the prisoners were able to bully the governors into granting them privileges of which the suffragettes had never dreamed. By 11 October Michael Brennan was writing thus:

> We are more or less all right now here and although we still have a few grievances left on the whole we are having a good time. It's heaven compared with what it was before the strike. We are all together from 6.30 a.m. to 9.30 p.m. and can sing, whistle, talk, or do anything else we like. The food is good and we have plenty of smoking and reading.

Life grew monotonous, the more so when Brennan's request for a concertina was indignantly refused ('musical instruments are obviously out of place in prison'). In September 1917 and March 1918 special regulations were issued specifying 'ameliorations for various prisoners', and in August the General Prisons Board recognised privately the scope of that concession: 'The ameliorations are applicable only to prisoners who are in the popular phrase "political prisoners".' The government's limp capitulation, while holding it up to universal ridicule, rendered Patrick Brennan's master plan obsolete. Since almost nobody any longer felt savage indignation at the government's handling of the illegal drillers, the Irish Volunteers decided to keep out of jail, however comfortable, and conserve both men and energy for work at home. In December 1917 military intelligence reported a decline in illegal drilling in Southern District: 'Information has reached me that it is getting less easy than it was to get men to turn out for drill parades and route marches. This is partly due to the wintry weather, but mainly to another cause, namely that route marching has been wearing out their boots, and boots nowadays are very expensive to replace.' In April 1918 the Volunteers were formally ordered to stop drilling in public and devote themselves instead to struggling against a threat more serious than any prison regulation: conscription.[25]

By the spring of 1918 much of Ireland, and Co. Clare in particular, had become virtually ungovernable. Timid and inept though Duke's administration seems, his vacillations illustrate, grotesquely enough, a dilemma of policy which would surely have ensnared the wisest Chief Secretary. Britain's first need in wartime, made still more urgent by Germany's spring offensive, was for men to stock the trenches. But these Ireland would not provide, whether ruled openly by a Sinn Féin assembly in College Green, or covertly by a committee in the Mansion House. Britain's few allies in her desperate drive for recruits had become lepers in the vision of most Irishmen. With the percipience of an able lawyer expounding a hopeless brief, Duke told the Commons on 14 March 1918: 'I do not take the view that you can make valuable political changes by force of arms. I do not think you can cure Bolshevism by Czarism.' But because Sinn Féin lawlessness had made life 'impossible in Clare for decent people', he stuck by his decision to apply force of arms and military rule in the county. Military rule certainly caused the suspension of illegal drilling, which had briefly revived in association with the outbreak of agrarian crime which had threatened the livelihood of decent people. But it also united Clare against British rule as never before. Soldiers were rude and inconsiderate; military permit books were cumbersome to fill out and each one cost a shilling to renew; vast numbers of once inconspicuous farm boys were arrested according to the familiar pattern; a teacher of Irish died after a soldier's bayonet thrust.[26]

But in April the renewed threat of Irish conscription made even military restrictions seem an insignificant burden by comparison. Representatives of all Nationalist groups and the Church agreed to co-ordinate their campaign of resistance. Some Sinn Féin leaders evidently opposed joint action with the Irish Party in case the purity and supremacy of their own organisation should be impaired; but in the event it was their former antagonists, not they, who were sucked dry. Hardly a voice was raised against the campaign, and Sinn Féin became more respectable day by day. The Church gave full support to the administration of the Anti-Conscription Pledge and Fund and relished its political reinvigoration. Demonstrations of unity were necessarily curtailed in Clare, where 'the holding of or taking part in meetings, assemblies or processions in public places' had been prohibited on 1 March. But Dr Fogarty invited his congregation to take the pledge inside the cathedral, after a Mass of Intercession. The canon at Tulla expressed satisfaction at the effects of the crisis on the Church:

> Sometimes in the past they had heard the cry even in Ireland—'no priests in politics.' It was well for them that there were Bishops in politics last Thursday! Well for them that there were priests in politics for the past few years of stress and turmoil; and it was to be hoped that one result of the happy turn of events would be that such silly parrot cries would be heard no more, and that the shibboleths of Freemasonry would be left to work their ruin in other lands.

The 'happy turn of events', indeed! More than cringing fear, however prevalent this was, it was an intensified sense of national unity, joy in solidarity, which gained public expression during the crisis. Opinions differed as to what should be done if enforcement were in fact attempted. Fr Gaynor, by disposition a mild and scholarly priest, argued that 'If an attempt is made to conscript us—if guns are forced into our hands—the fit resting place for an Irish bullet is in an English heart.' Village blacksmiths were set to work fashioning pikes since guns were hard to come by. Offaly Sinn Féin discussed tactics and 'decided to meet the menace of conscription by passive resistance and (pointing to the sack) they sent me in for a bag of bombs'. Edward Lysaght favoured a more conventional sort of passive resistance, to be reinforced by a boycott of all those involved in imposing conscription, 'or even perhaps of those openly in favour of the measure'.[27] Recruits rushed not into the army but into Sinn Féin and the Volunteers. Between the end of March and the end of May the national membership of Sinn Féin rose, according to RIC figures, by 29 per cent. This rise was not uniform across the country, and seems to have been greater in those areas where Sinn Féin was less securely established. In Clare, where Sinn Féin was unusually widespread by March 1918, police figures show virtually no rise during the crisis, but this might be explained by the prohibition of meetings, which deprived the police of their main source of information.[28] The qualified suspension of the conscription threat in May did little to reduce tension, and any such effect was far outweighed by the resumption of internment and the replacement of the Irish executive, which signalled an intensification of government bullying and bluster now unmitigated even by Duke's inefficacious percipience. Not until the Armistice ended the conscription threat did the almost euphoric sense of solidarity show signs of weakening. Meanwhile, government desperation and wrongheadedness sent Ireland lurching uncomprehendingly towards revolution.

While it lasted Sinn Féin's unity was magnificent and all-embracing. It wished to represent everybody and everything Irish. Anyone was welcome who would denounce the Irish Party or the government, or pay others to denounce them. On New Year's Day 1918 a leading Sinn Féin priest in West Clare reprimanded a branch which had refused to accept the subscription offered by a magistrate who had been denied membership. 'I would take money from anyone,' declared the curate ingenuously. 'We took and got money from people in Kilrush who were not Sinn Feiners, and who would do anything they could against us.' If, as one survivor recalls, Kilrush 'was not a great Sinn Féin town' and 'did not fall into line', its recalcitrant inhabitants could at least be pressed and bullied for their money. Without doubt, unity was reinforced by communal pressure, and the police took comfort from the belief that 'People who are not in reality Sinn Feiners must show sympathy with the movement, otherwise they could not live in peace among their neighbours.' One example of the herd's vengeance on a black sheep reached quarter sessions in October 1917. The band committee of the De Valera Guards, once known as the Newmarket-on-Fergus Brass and Reed Band, successfully sued a former bandsman who had supported Patrick Lynch and held on to his two clarinets. Lawyers engaged in a sharp discussion:

L: I want to know why he should be expelled because he was not a Sinn Feiner?
R (plaintiff): He would not fall into line with the rest of the band. . . .
L: When the band was started was it non-political?
R: No, it was always a political band. . . .
L: Would it have played at a meeting of Mr Redmond's?
K (plaintiff's counsel): I object, and an answer was not pressed.

But such cases of communal vengeance seem to have been rare. So strong and diverse was Sinn Féin's appeal that intimidation was seldom necessary. In a manner recalling the vampirism of the old party, Sinn Féin organisers lined up a battery of subsidiary interest groups in the 'national cause'. The diversity of that battery is suggested by a suppressed interim programme for the proposed celebration of de Valera's escape from Lincoln Jail early in 1919. Processional places were assigned, in order of precedence, to the Irish Volunteers, Irish Citizen Army, Fianna Éireann, Cumann na mBan, Fianna Girls, Sinn Féin, trades bodies, women's societies, university students, GAA, National Foresters and Evicted Tenants' Association, not to mention a tantalising 'etc.' Sinn Féin organisers, like their Irish Party predecessors, often diversified their social involvement in what might seem the old imperialist manner. Thus 18 per cent of prominent separatists in rural Clare are known to have promoted several causes (apart from any previous participation in the Home Rule movement), compared with 15 per cent of Irish Party men, *mutatis mutandis*.[29]

But in some vital respects the relationship between the political organisation and its peripheral interest groups had changed since Irish Party days. The party, like Sinn Féin, had set out to capture key posts in the local and national organisations of the Gaelic League and GAA; but it had never attempted to transform Irish classes and football matches into extramural sessions of the United Irish League. The party preferred to fatten its prey before draining it. Sinn Féin, on the other hand, tended to treat the 'Irish Ireland' bodies as a convenient mask of boyish innocence behind which the calculating features of the politician could hide. Certainly, many Sinn Féin policy-makers believed that an Irish education would make their followers more reliable Nationalists. As Fr O'Kennedy, treasurer of the East Clare Election Fund, wrote in October 1917:

> A Sinn Fein Club ought to be more than a meeting place for the manufacture of resolutions—it ought to be a school for national thought. Hence there ought to be at least once a week a class in Irish history. . . . If there is a branch of the Gaelic League in the parish, it will look after the language and, of course, all true Sinn Feiners will be members. If there is no branch, it becomes the duty of the club to take up the language.

But that menacing phrase 'all true Sinn Feiners' threatened to ossify that enthusiasm for the language which O'Kennedy imagined he was promoting. His edict, and others like it throughout the country, were widely interpreted as a call for compulsory Irish classes, so that attendance rather than enthusiasm became the test of a good Irishman. (Ireland has learned slowly from the mistakes of her revolution.) One Sinn Féin club resolved 'that we request all members of this Club to attend the local Gaelic League class; that the teacher record the attendance of these pupils, and, that at the close of the session those who have not made a fairly average attendance be expelled from the club'. True Gaels became indignant: 'Some doff their caps to the movement in respectful recognition and in patriotic guise; but, it is questionable whether such reverential action is prompted by pure undiluted patriotism or by base political trimming. . . . It would be certainly unwise to adopt the contrary attitude.' The League, which had been declining slowly in Co. Clare before the Rising, suddenly mushroomed. In the last quarter of 1917 alone meetings were reported from twenty parishes. Many more leading separatists achieved note as Gaels after the Rising than before: in Clare seventeen priests and thirty laymen, compared with eight priests and seventeen laymen beforehand.[30] From spring 1917 onwards the RIC believed that the Gaelic League was becoming an adjunct of Sinn Féin. This was recognised by the government in its coupling of Sinn Féin and the League as 'dangerous' organisations in July 1918, and in its joint suppression of them in Clare in August 1919 and throughout Ireland three months later.

The connections between Sinn Féin and the GAA, which escaped outright suppression, were rather different. Just after the Rising an alarmed policeman had written from Galway: 'The G.A.A. is under the control of the extreme members of this Secret Society [allegedly created by the Dublin Invincibles] and in this way the young men of the County are reached and influenced.' Later in 1916 the Castle decided to disallow allocation of special excursion trains for football and hurling matches, believing that such matches gave 'occasion for collecting together and exciting the disloyal youth'; and in April 1921 the police were still adamant: 'As everything is adapted if possible to serve the purposes of the I.R.A. there is little doubt that excursion facilities would be made use of by the murder gang. Sunday is at present a favourite day for murder. The state of the country is not yet fit for increased railway facilities.' In July 1918 the Castle reluctantly agreed to the more far-reaching police demand that a nominal ban should be placed on all unauthorised meetings. But police were told privately that it was 'not intended to interfere with village or local gatherings for sports or games', and that permits should be required only for political meetings and those 'where there are both sports and speeches, which are to be held *out of doors, and are advertised either by poster or in the Press*, at which a considerable number may be expected to congregate'. Absurdly, these qualifications were not made public and, incited by the provocative behaviour of some policemen, the GAA was able to gain considerable prestige by defying the supposed ban and indefinitely suspending those unfortunates who played in matches for which government permits had been secured. If rebel permeation of the GAA was not complete before July 1918, the government's assumption that it was, and its clumsy attempts to do something about it, ensured that it became so thereafter. Even so, the GAA never became as subservient as the Gaelic League to the political organisation. No attempt was made to drive every Sinn Féiner into a football team; rather, football teams tended to establish Sinn Féin clubs. The convention which nominated de Valera for East Clare in June 1917 was in fact summoned by a meeting of the GAA's County Board which reconstituted itself after hearing of Willie Redmond's death in France—although the candidate favoured by that meeting was not de Valera.[31] As Michael Brennan points out, Sinn Féin made use of matches rather than organising them, although, of course, the organising committees themselves consisted largely of Sinn Féiners. Gaelic games were more useful to the politicians as spectator than participant occasions. Political schemers and recruiters could mingle unnoticed among the cheering factions, protected from police molestation by the crowd, its emotions heightened by combat on the field. Sinn Féin may have suffocated the Gaelic League, but its relationship with the GAA was vital and mutually profitable.

Sinn Féin's education in Irish Party methods, together with its growing realisation that the interests of pupil and teacher differed crucially, are most clearly illustrated by its handling of the agrarian crisis of 1917–18. The shortage of food in that terrible war winter had caused both the government and the hungry to take extreme measures to maintain food supplies. The government ordered increases, more severe than those of 1916–17, in the proportion of arable devoted to tillage—a policy unthinkable before 1914 but one which left vast tracts of grazing land uncultivated. The hungry, especially in Clare and Connaught, drove the cattle off the ranches and attempted to parcel out allotments to landless men and 'uneconomic holders'.[32] A movement which arose from the frustration of the land-hungry and the food-hungry was taken over by Sinn Féin and the Volunteers in standard Irish Party style. It is true that in December 1917 the RIC's Inspector-General had 'no evidence that the Sinn

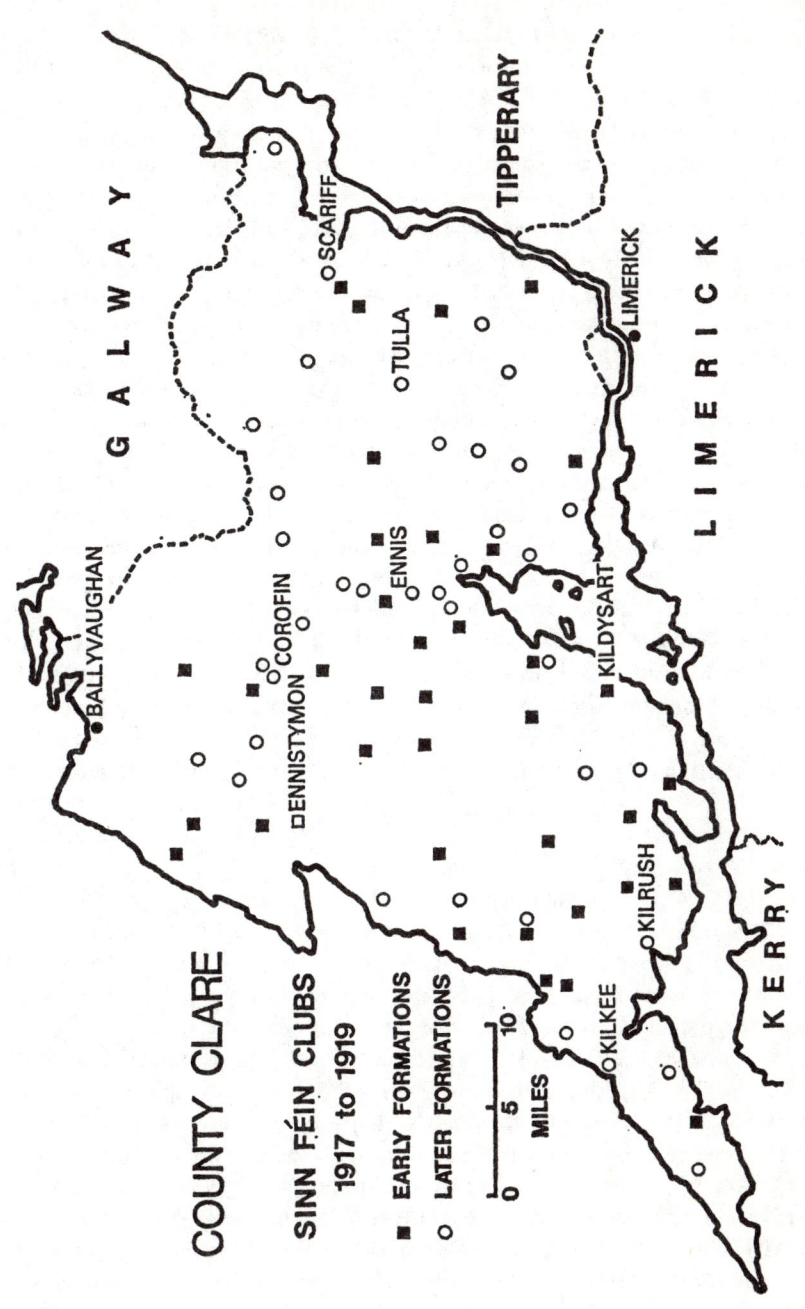

Fein movement is officially identified with land agitation'. But at local level the identification was unmistakable. According to Michael Brennan, 'There was much agrarian discontent in Clare and we decided to "Cash in" on this. Cattle drives became very popular and all over the county Volunteers took part in them as organised units.' But if the agrarian struggle provided a new source of zest and vitality for the rebels, it also threatened to split the movement into warring social factions. The police heard rumours that Sinn Féiners feared that their participation in the struggle might provoke hostility from 'extensive farmers and shopkeepers who are frequently interested in grazing'. Rather unconvincingly, Fr O'Kennedy denied in March 1918 that the cattle-drivers were being directed by Sinn Féin: 'Make no mistake about it: this is a spontaneous outburst of the whole people. Most of them are in politics with Sinn Fein. This is inevitable, because nearly everyone in Clare is, to-day, a Sinn Feiner.' But he noted with alarm that cattle-drives were being directed not only against the hated landlords, but against 'comparatively small farms' and 'non-ranches'— against, in other words, good Catholic Nationalists. 'It is a pity to mix up Sinn Fein in the land question. . . . Of necessity, questions of the land, food, industries turn up—but, all are of secondary importance, and none must obscure our objective.' Sinn Féin unity seemed to be slipping away; it could not be retained unless the earthy but class-oriented slogans of agrarian agitation were displaced by the lofty slogans of self-determination. On 23 February the Standing Committee of Sinn Féin decided that no branch should 'organise or conduct a cattle drive' without reference to its divisional executive; and in East Clare, after hearing Fr O'Kennedy's strictures, the executive added the proviso that individual members of Sinn Féin should not take action without reference to their branch. On 2 March Volunteer headquarters evidently sent out similar instructions, but their application in West Clare was somewhat less severe than Sinn Féin's in East Clare: 'Volunteers should not be allowed to take part in cattle-drives as Irish Volunteers. No prominent officer should be seen at cattle-drives.'[33] But whatever practical interpretation was given to the orders, the lesson of Sinn Féin's public repudiation of the agrarian struggle as it had been conducted hitherto was clear. Sinn Féin was determined that it should not be held responsible for any sectional agitation (however invigorating) which threatened the interests of potential advocates of Sinn Féin policies. Sinn Féin's desire for universal support was stronger than its thirst for blood.

By the end of 1918 Sinn Féin seemed almost to have achieved universal support. The formation of clubs was still proceeding, but slowly, for in most counties almost every parish already had at least one club. On 31 December 1918 there were, according, to police reports, 1,354 clubs with 112,080 known members. If Sinn Féin's own statistics are to be believed, the number of clubs was nearer 1,750; but in any case it far exceeded the number of Catholic territorial parishes and benefices in the country (1,113). It is interesting to compare the number of Sinn Féiners per thousand of the population in 1911 with the proportion for other mass organisations in the Irish past (Table 4.1). Whereas in Ireland overall the Irish Party's largest organisations had been larger than

Sinn Féin, in most counties of Munster Sinn Féin was larger than the party. The more rural the region, the stronger Sinn Féin tended to be: thus Connaught had 47 Sinn Féiners per thousand, Munster 38, Leinster 21 and Ulster only 16 (this figure being dragged down by the hostility of the Unionist majority). Sinn Féin organisation proceeded unevenly: by the end of 1917 it had achieved only 48 per cent of its peak membership in Ulster and 51 per cent in Connaught, but 61 per cent in Munster and 62 per cent in Leinster. In Co. Clare its development was unusually rapid, and was substantially complete when military restrictions were applied in March 1918, although the last branch was not reported until January 1919.[34]

Table 4.1: Mass Organisations, 1914–19

	Sinn Féin (31 Dec. 1919)	Irish National Volunteers (23 Sep. 1914)	UIL (31 Mar. 1914)
Ireland	27	42	31
Clare	49	49	25
Cork	34	26	19
Kerry	41	28	11
Limerick	33	58	17

But what of the allegiance of the 973 Irishmen per thousand who did not become members of Sinn Féin clubs? The obvious measure of this, to which great significance used, perhaps uncritically, to be ascribed, was Sinn Féin's sweeping electoral victory in December 1918. Sinn Féin secured 47 per cent of the popular vote and 59 per cent of the seats in contested constituencies, and twenty-six further seats in districts where it was considered unchallengeable. Two of these districts were East and West Clare, where de Valera and Brian O'Higgins were returned unopposed. Like their Irish Party predecessors, neither candidate was a Clareman—de Valera being a Spanish-American born in the United States and resident in Dublin, and O'Higgins an Irish teacher and sugary poet, later creator of Ireland's most hideous Christmas cards, born in Meath and secretary of the Carrigaholt Irish College only since February 1917. Both men were originally nominated at the urging of Sinn Féin headquarters, and local pressure groups had to be pressed to drop their support for local candidates.[35] The relationship between parochial organisations and national headquarters had changed radically since Irish Party days. The party had allowed its local organisations to select its own future members, but in return exacted a blind and stultifying obedience to its directives on policy and tactics. Sinn Féin headquarters ensured that its own men won parliamentary selection, but in many aspects of policy and tactics it could do no more than authorise what parochial followers had initiated. National unity had become a dynamic thing.

3. AFTER THE WAR

At its moment of triumph Sinn Féin could claim to have largely wriggled out of the mould it had inherited from the old Irish Party. The old sycophancy had disappeared, as Lysaght reflected in early 1918:

> In East Clare the day of passing resolutions of confidence in politicians is almost gone. The people, while they respect the men they have elected to the head of their movements, are trusting in themselves to act. No longer are the actions which forward the popular cause the work of a few wilder spirits controlled from a political headquarters: the whole countryside, with the exception of police, parsons, graziers and a few shopkeepers, are heart and soul in the work which is going forward in Clare.
> (*Note:* Dr MacLysaght remarks that he did not intend in this passage to imply that no policemen, parsons or graziers favoured the 'popular cause' in Clare.)

But critical observers perceived flaws in the great new movement. In order to preserve unanimity, its leaders had deliberately avoided committing themselves to long-term political programmes. Instead, they had expressed faith that by holding firm and solid they would shame Britain into granting Ireland freedom, or else the allies at the forthcoming Peace Conference into forcing her to do so. 'Sinn Fein Notes', deleted by the press censor in September 1918, spelt out this simple creed:

> Under the Sinn Fein policy the Government's only alternative to withdrawing altogether from Ireland is to jail all the Irish people. It is merely a question of holding out. . . . It would take then all the powers of the English propaganda department to convince the world that the very negation of government is 'Government by the consent of the governed'.

Still Edward Lysaght could not overcome his scruples. On 25 January 1919, four days after the convocation of Dáil Éireann, he felt little faith in that *deus ex machina*, 'the rambling old Peace Conference', could not feel the confidence of the Republican leaders in the outcome of their struggle and, in short, found it hard to say that he was 'a Sinn Féiner absolutely'.[36]

The late winter of 1918–19 was a time of aimlessness, half-understood misgivings, a many-faceted uneasiness reminiscent of the summer which had preceded the war just ended. Labour was rampant; the influenza epidemic was at its height; February days were unseasonably fine, December excessively wet. W. B. Yeats, restlessly moving from house to house in Dublin, felt that some revelation was surely at hand. Fr O'Kennedy thought he had isolated the cause of the national malaise:

> Set your face sternly against 'Pitch and Toss', as it demoralised the whole county last summer and autumn. It caters for one of the worst elements in man's composition—viz, his cupidity. If it is allowed to continue, it will beget a whole host of evils. It will disorganise society, and the sacredness of the Sunday will be polluted by brawls over the toss of a coin. . . . If the evil grows it will stunt the

physical and moral career of many a decent young fellow. In Clare it is the principal obstacle to a genuine national revival.

Sinn Féin itself seemed to be losing momentum. Police noted 'signs of apathy' in Clare. The Árd-Chomhairle was informed that 'The Clubs seem at present to be resting on the Victory secured at the General Election.' By July Fr O'Kennedy was seriously worried. 'It was only the young men who had any idea of what Republicanism was, but he thought they were not at all as active in Clare as they ought to be. It really looked very like as if what John Dillon said some months ago—that Clare was tamed—was true.' A few days later the Dáil ministry found it necessary to lend Sinn Féin, on request, £400 'for organisation'.[37] What was going wrong?

The answer probably is that the Armistice and its immediate sequel were gradually eroding the assumptions on which dynamic mass unity had been built. The electoral extinction of the Irish Parliamentary Party removed the first object of Sinn Féin hatred and left it without an organised opposition to joust with. The Armistice removed the most emotive cause common to almost all Irishmen: the struggle to avoid conscription. As Michael Brennan observes, 'The end of the war and the removal of the anti-conscription stimulus had taken much of the "kick" out of the Volunteers, and it was difficult to hold them together. On paper we had large numbers, but it was unusual if more than 25% of these reported for any parade. In many places no organised unit remained and all I could contact were two or three individuals.' But the conscription crisis left Sinn Féin an unwelcome bequest after its life-giving power had dissipated. Many contemporaries believed that men who had joined it out of 'funk' stayed in it thereafter out of canny calculation. The historian P. S. O'Hegarty considered that the election victory of December was in fact a victory for bosses:

> We did not realise it at the time, but what had happened was not that Sinn Féin had captured Ireland, but that the politicians in Ireland and those who make them, all the elements which had sniffed at Sinn Féin and libelled it, which had upheld corruption and jobbery, had realised that Sinn Féin was going to win, and had come over to it *en masse*.... In their hearts they remained still corrupt, still just politicians.[38]

For a man of peace writing in 1924 recent Republicanism seemed much dirtier, old Sinn Féin much purer, than they seem today. From the very start Sinn Féin was crucially influenced by the men and methods of the old Home Rule organisations which O'Hegarty so heartily loathed. Nevertheless, the increasing tendency of young men to leave their Sinn Féin club for the Volunteers, and the consequent enfeebling of the clubs, gave old bosses more opportunity than hitherto to use the clubs as they had once used the largely middle-aged Home Rule organisations.

But perhaps as dangerous to Sinn Féin solidarity as the crafty bosses who slipped into line behind its banner were the shiploads of potential line-breakers who came home from the war over the winter. Some returned soldiers, eager to bring the thrills of Flanders to their home fields, joined the more violent groups in the Volunteer movement. But many others viewed the Republican movement with ignorance and suspicion, hated its supporters for having kept out of the war and envied them their settled jobs (now so hard to find). Both the ITGWU and the ex-servicemen's self-protective organisations showed the desire to raise an independent voice, to avoid annexation by any political party.[39] There are many reports from Munster police of riots and bad blood involving Republicans and ex-soldiers. In Clare a schoolhouse was set on fire and the newly appointed teacher sprayed with three hundred pellets because, though the son of the previous teacher, he was an ex-soldier. The loneliness of the returned soldier, and the divisive consequences of his homecoming, are illustrated by a case which reached Ennis petty sessions in January 1919. A father complained that his ex-soldier son had broken one of his windows and 'put the blessed candle all around the floor' after a squabble over the money to be paid by the son for his keep. The son explained to a sympathetic RM that 'The cause of this row is that my father and the rest of them are Sinn Feiners, and since I came home they are always going on to me for joining the army.' The magistrate banished him from his father's house and added: 'Go and get married Thomas and have a home of your own.'[40]

Peace not only brought threats to Sinn Féin solidarity from within and without, but challenges to the simple political creed which de Valera had put forward in the hope of alienating no possible supporter by speaking too explicitly. As early as May 1917 a prominent Clare rebel had poured scorn on the notion, advocated by Count Plunkett as well as de Valera, that Ireland's fate should be handed over to the Peace Conference. He sent Plunkett £1 despite his muddleheadedness, but wrote that Ireland would 'only make itself ridiculous by presenting itself before an assembly that will refuse to listen to it'. The Peace Conference would never attempt what it could not hope to enforce: 'Neither abstention from Westminster nor pressure at Westminster, nor an attempt to enter the Peace Congress nor actual pressure of Irish delegates at that Congress can do anything whatever to establish the complete independence of Ireland.' This unpopular view was gradually confirmed. As President Wilson failed to make any but the most generalised noises of sympathy for the Irish cause, faith in his intervention slowly weakened. In December 1918 the Clare County Inspector reported that some Sinn Féiners felt that Wilson spent 'too much time in the atmosphere of Buckingham Palace'. Next month speakers at an Ennis meeting steeled their audience against possible disillusionment: 'Peace Conference, or no Peace Conference, we will never lie down.' 'If they failed at the Peace Conference the struggle would go on. Times were changed. The political outlook of the world was changing.' In April hopes in Clare were high, but in May the Allies delivered the draft of a treaty which ignored Ireland's claims.[41] Who then was to grant Ireland her freedom? Britain's conduct in Ireland since the Armistice clearly showed that she had no thought of offering a quick settlement or reverting to peacetime styles of administration; not a single victorious ally had raised the Irish question at Paris. It seemed the Irish would have to win freedom on their own, and that entailed revolution.

The history of that revolution is one of experiment, improvisation, self-discovery. The prohibition of Sinn Féin late in 1919 made the continuation of an open mass movement of traditional mould physically unfeasible, but the flaws in the policy which sought unanimity above all else were already all too apparent. In place of that vast and cumbersome machinery, a revolutionary elite developed, a clandestine fighting force which bore little resemblance in its composition or mode of operation to the old Irish Volunteers. The failure of the *deus ex machina* philosophy generated an extraordinary attempt to put Griffith's principles into effect and establish a *de facto* Republic within the shell of British rule. Nominally directing that attempt was the Dáil, many of whose members were old Sinn Féiners who had outgrown their trousers. Yet the rump of Sinn Féin headquarters struggled on, unaware that it had become obsolete. The Árd-Fheis's reaction to the proclamation of October 1919 was to waive individual membership fees but raise branch affiliation fees to £3. Not surprisingly, affiliations dropped sharply. Elaborate instructions for the year 1920–21 were sent out to beleaguered branch secretaries, now under constant threat of arrest, asking them to arrange Irish and history classes, lectures and library facilities, and to pay special attention to such problems as re-afforestation. The provincial organisation fell to pieces. On 9 January 1921 the Dáil ministry laconically resolved: '3. Home Affairs (*b*) Sinn Féin Organisation. A. G. to get after.' After the Truce Sinn Féin headquarters had, however, survived intact enough to behave with aggressive self-importance and to launch an appeal for £10,000 to restore their national network.[42] Long afterwards various versions of Sinn Féin lingered on, fighting tenaciously for control of the money collected yet never spent. But Sinn Féin had ceased to function as a mass organisation (except perhaps at election time) long before the Truce. The pursuit of national independence had passed into other, and bolder, hands.

5

Revolutionary Administrators

> I note in your letter you want 'Rinso' to be sent to you. Why on earth don't you ask for 'Washo'? Do you want the Shinners on your house for not supporting Home manufactures? . . . For peace sake we will send you some Washo. I believe it is not quite so good as Rinso, but one would do anything these times for a quiet existence.
>
> From a letter to an internee at Rath, June 1921

1. ADMINISTRATIVE EXPERIMENTATION

FOR policemen, Protestants and Irish Party men the Irish Revolution was a phenomenon, the half-understood agent of social or personal crisis, always an external influence over which they had little control. Even for many Sinn Féiners, who had repudiated Irish Party catch-cries without finally discarding Irish Party style or technique, it was an unexpected, unhoped-for aberration, an insane and unnecessary adventure. But for some thousands of Irishmen in 1920 and 1921 revolution was not external, but a vital part of their life and love, vital as the air they breathed. Thousands who saved hay in the sunlight sought to save Ireland by moonlight. For them revolution was exhilarating, a 'heartening experience', for Seán O'Faolain at least something in which 'all animal passion was sublimated'.[1] Fifty years later the inquirer still finds among survivors a curious nostalgia for the Troubled Times which is also nostalgia for lost adolescence. Revolution offered them a route of escape from the inhibiting ambience of parish and extended family. They went 'on the run' not only from the police but from their childhood. Robbery, murder and arson, outrageous crimes in the light of day, were transformed under moonlight into 'stunts'—wild, chivalrous and heroic. How so many Irishmen managed to break out of traditional social impediments, how the national struggle was diverted from mass indignation towards guerrilla warfare, how, in short, Irish politics was turned upside down, we shall try to explain in the following chapters. But other, darker questions lurk in the background, questions which have caused many survivors of the revolution to wonder if it was all worthwhile. What abiding inhibitions or imaginative failures caused the triumphant revolutionaries to imitate in their new state almost all the defects of the state they had struggled to destroy? Why did Irish politics, upside down in 1921, end up firmly on its feet by 1924? Had Ireland abandoned Rinso only to redesign Washo according to the Rinso formula?

During 1920 and 1921 both the revolutionaries and the government and its armed forces (henceforth referred to more concisely as 'the enemy') acted with a degree of violence and desperation inconceivable in pre-war years. Both sides realised that too great a separation of their actions from those of their predecessors might discredit them in Irish minds, always conscious of historical tradition and precedent. Therefore publicists of both sides portrayed the revolution as a defence of established constitution against wrecking. To the members of the First Dáil English rule had always been 'based upon force and fraud and maintained by military occupation against the declared will of the people', whereas the Irish Republic had been 'proclaimed' in Easter 1916.[2] Castle propagandists, hastily recruited to counter this insidious message, replied that the Dáil, for all its clever pretences of legitimacy, was in fact a mere front for gangs of murderers whose aim was to terrify the Irish people into disobedience and disloyalty. If these gangs could be destroyed, the people would revert to its natural preference for law and order, which only the Castle could restore. Common to both arguments was a dual misconception: underestimation of one's opponent's popular support, and overconfidence in one's own. Tragically, these misconceptions governed not only the propaganda but the conduct of the revolutionary war. In their pursuit of order the government forces spread disorder more effectively than any bandit campaign could have done, by burning houses, disrupting local government and abandoning the routine civic functions of the police. In their pursuit of native self-reliance the revolutionaries threw together a national army and national system of justice and local administration, but central direction of local units was so tenuous that civil war was needed to assert control after independence. The effect of the Anglo-Irish War was to largely discredit the claims of both pretenders to legitimate government. Out of all the wastage of revolution only one campaign may escape the censure of history, what the publicists called 'the constructive work of Dáil Éireann'. Nowhere was the gulf wider between revolutionary myth and reality, yet nowhere was so much ingenuity and energy applied to the tackling of practical problems.

On 21 January 1919 the successful Sinn Féin candidates who were not in prison constituted themselves as an Irish parliament, and ten weeks later appointment was sanctioned of a regular 'ministry', consisting of seven secretaries and two heads of departments proposed by the President, de Valera. To many publicists the creation of Dáil and ministry conferred legitimacy on the Republic. 'There was nothing revolutionary in the Dail [wrote Mrs Green] except that it transferred from the English to the Irish the control of the daily life and the destinies of the people of this island.' Quiet assumption of political authority without violent revolution had long been a dream of the more ingenious Nationalist constitution-makers. The governing aim of the original Sinn Féin programme had been to bypass the existing administration and convene a national assembly, which would transform the national polity by fostering a series of social contracts within the Irish nation alone. Eóin Mac Néill, just after the outbreak of war, had hoped that the Irish Party leaders might 'constitute a kind of unrecognized national cabinet, claiming no technical powers of government, but exercising every possible power through and over the existing executive system, and outside of it'. After the Rising Sinn Féin had espoused a scheme closer in spirit to Mac Néill's informal cabinet than Griffith's elaborately conceived assembly. At the suggestion of the Ennis (de Valera) Sinn Féin Club, unanimously endorsed by the executive, the Sinn Féin convention of October 1917 had approved the setting up of 'clearly defined departments' in at least eleven sectors, including foreign affairs, social reform and food control.[3] But the holders of 'portfolios' sanctioned only by a political party, however popular, could not claim to be members of a legitimate government. Only after the lop-sided general election did the Dáil break the choker of its partisan origins by claiming legitimacy. Combining Griffith's pomposity with Mac Néill's opportunism, Republican constitutionalists erected an imitation House of Commons to govern the nation.

Until early 1920 national self-help, however familiar an ideal, was attempted only feebly and sporadically in practice. Sinn Féin's administrative experiment was acknowledged as a failure even by Darrell Figgis, honorary secretary, who later wrote that most department heads had no time to attend to their duties and left the tasks of administration to the honorary secretaries. Nevertheless, Sinn Féin gave provincial Republicans one taste of the administrative problems which threatened to choke them in the revolutionary months. Late in 1917 the shortage of food in Ireland became so acute that the government attempted to restrict both prices and exports of certain products. But enforcement of marketing regulations was hampered by its inability to construct an effective system of local control outside the cities, and by constant bickering between the Ministry of Food and the Irish Food Control Committee. Sinn Féin saw its chance both to humiliate the government and to bring its own activities out of mere politics into the everyday concerns of the people. It called on parochial Sinn Féin clubs and clergymen to carry out the local supervision of food supplies of which the government had proven itself incapable. By February 1918 food committees (not exclusively contrived by Sinn Féin) had been convened in a dozen counties and attempts had been made, with patchy success, to establish the existing stock of foods and to prevent their exportation.[4] Markets selling cheap turf and potatoes to 'the working class' had been reported from six counties; the Thursday market in Ennis was already, as the *Champion* put it, 'a feature of town life'. In Kilrush, however, the innovation was not welcomed. The priest-chairman of the town's Sinn Féin club pointedly reminded members that the St Vincent de Paul Society was already keeping the poor in potatoes. Other West Clare organisers urged the district councils to underwrite a disaster fund to augment winter stocks, but the Ennistymon RDC prudently advised them 'to do as is done in the Districts around here—to get the farmers to bring in food and fuel for the use of the poor, and to get subscriptions from those who wish to pay' (evidently a rare species in the south-west). Republicans soon learned that even good works with good propaganda value might alienate one class of likely allies while benefiting another. As Fr Gaynor, who put forward the Ennis market scheme, remarked later:

> This incursion into the economic field had a disconcerting result; the low charge in the Sinn Féin market brought prices down in the shops and a few staunch Sinn Féiners who depended chiefly on sale of farm produce were made bankrupt and had to be subsidised for a time out of the funds.

Republicans were discovering that unanimity was more easily maintained by Nationalist movements with vague, eclectic slogans than by informal governments with social consciences. Once the coming of spring and martial law had closed their potato markets, Clare Sinn Féiners only once more ventured into the market-place. In October 1919 illegal cattle fairs were organised throughout the county, but police intervention kept most dealers away, so that prices were low and farmers dissatisfied.[5] Economic reform, like economic revolution, proved difficult to administer and socially divisive. Sinn Féin's experiments taught future Republican administrators more about their limitations than their capabilities.

The creation of the Dáil heralded a directive as well as benevolent intervention by the Republic in the practical affairs of people. From the start the two sectors which seemed to promise most prestige for the Dáil administration were local government and justice. Local government was now largely in the hands of men who claimed to support self-determination; justice was administered by the police and magistrates with increasing inefficiency as the campaign of boycotting and intimidation took its toll. The Dáil appointed secretaries for both sectors, and schemes for Republican intervention were discussed. But the Local Government Committee, which first met on 23 July 1919, could do little more than devise programmes for future candidates and propaganda campaigns. For until the elections of 1920 the local boards and councils largely consisted of recent converts from Redmondism who were not prepared to change their political habits, however deftly they might change their coats. The setting up of a Republican legal machinery at first seemed more practicable than the exploitation of the existing but obstinate local government apparatus. This course was recommended to the Dáil by the Sinn Féin executive as early as February 1919. In April the question of voluntary arbitration courts was raised in private session, in June their establishment was decreed, and in August a rough scheme providing for petty, district and superior courts was agreed. The notion of referring local disputes to unofficial arbitrators rather than regular courts was not new: long before the revolution they had existed both in Arthur Griffith's imagination and Land League reality. After the Rising courts were reported from several counties. Late in January 1919 Arthur Griffith wrote from Gloucester Prison that courts were said to have been formed in Kilkenny and Cavan: 'The idea should be copied and the courts carefully constituted.' In Clare, too, a former magistrate offered himself as an arbitrator, provided litigants would undertake to accept his decisions, just after his dismissal by the Lord Chancellor (he had combined Sinn Féin with his magisterial office and had fined a policeman 2s 6d for assaulting a Sinn Féin colleague on the night the East Clare poll was announced). Yet despite these promising precedents, even Republican propagandists admitted that the Dáil's decree was promptly applied only in one constituency—West Clare. As Arthur Griffith confessed to the Dáil in private session on 27 October 1919, elaboration of the courts scheme had 'met with difficulties'. 'Although so little is yet known in the country about this institution, there are cases coming in from time to time.'[6]

Throughout 1919 the Republican administrators were largely concerned with stating lofty intentions rather than executing decrees. The Dáil had no apparatus behind it, and even its moral leadership of the Republican movement was not easily established. Provincial Republicans were puzzled as to whether their allegiance was due to the Dáil, Sinn Féin, the Volunteers or even the IRB. An instructive conflict of loyalty emerged in April 1919 when the East Clare executive of Sinn Féin discussed a dispute over payment of rates:

> FR O'KENNEDY: ...To avoid future trouble I propose that we [Sinn Féin] set up an 'Arbitration Court' which will deal with such disputes in the future.
> MR HUNT: I beg to second that; in the Volunteers we have directions in this matter.
> FR CROWE: I think the whole question should be referred to the Dail before we take action.

The formal separation of the Republican organisations into military, electoral and administrative sectors was never fully realised, and the longer traditions and greater immediacy of the first two restricted the Dáil's status at home, whatever its prestige abroad. The Dáil, moreover, worked on a tiny budget in its early months. The ministry itself deliberated upon such modest requests as 'Local Government Department. Application of Munster for £10 petty cash' (granted, 19 December 1919). Although some £250,000 had been collected for the Anti-Conscription Fund in 1918, less than £18,000 apparently reached the Dáil after the menace had ended. Defence, propaganda and official stipends had first call on what income there was, and the ministry could ill afford the cost of appointing regional organisers to carry out its schemes. De Valera himself admitted the partial impotence of the Republican administration in April 1919: 'They had the occupation of the foreigner in their country, and while that state of affairs existed, they could not put fully into force their desires and their wishes as far as their social programme was concerned.' It is difficult to contradict Desmond Ryan's judgment that many of the Dáil's most grandiose organs were 'solemn pretences' with 'a large spicing of humbug'.[7] The government of the Republic seemed more impressive and substantial the further away from Ireland one observed it.

Yet in the course of a few months the Republican administration was transformed. By the summer and autumn of 1920 it could be seen functioning not merely in the Mansion House at infrequent intervals, or nightly in the bars of certain grimy hotels on the 'north side' of Dublin, or in the pages of the *Irish Bulletin*, but in the streets of almost every town and village in Munster and many elsewhere. In February 1921 Lloyd George recalled the state of Ireland six months earlier, with characteristic emphasis: 'The Irish Republican Organisation had all the symbols, and they had all the realities of a Government.... Sinn Fein courts were held openly, attended by litigants, jurors and advocates, and their decisions were respected.... Sinn Fein soldiers patrolled the country.... The Sinn Fein police patrolled the towns.'[8] Acting President Arthur Griffith reported the administration's work to the Dáil in less highly coloured terms, yet briskly conveyed his confidence in the Republic's ability to adjudicate civil and criminal cases, raise loans with which the landless might buy divided grazing lands and carry out a host of other social functions.

Although the foreigner still occupied the country, de Valera's pessimism of April 1919 seemed suddenly out of date. Almost despite itself, the ministry found itself supervising the translation of yesterday's solemn pretences into today's hectic reality. How did this come about, and how sound were the foundations of the *de facto* Republic?

On the surface this change might seem easily explained. By mid-1920 the revolutionaries had not only wrecked much of the existing administrative apparatus but secured enough income to attempt its reconstruction, however rough and ready, under the Dáil's auspices. The Volunteers' wrecking campaign, at least in the first half of 1920, was selective enough to leave the administrators with the manageable task of taking over and redecorating a damaged building rather than raising a new one out of the rubble. With co-ordinated precision the police were driven out of their village barracks, which were burned by the hundred to prevent reoccupation. Yet such law-enforcers as the coastguards, who posed no threat to revolutionaries, were mostly left unmolested in their isolated stations. Even the dislocation of the official courts and local government machinery, as we shall see, was tempered by toleration of many cogs which performed tricky jobs without clashing with the Republican programme. Nevertheless, one should not exaggerate the orderliness of the wrecking campaign—the easiest and most enjoyable part of the revolution. For military reasons roads were trenched and mails raided despite the inability of the Republic to provide alternative postal or transport services. For doctrinaire reasons boycotts were imposed on importation of various goods both from Britain and Ulster, despite the backwardness of Southern Ireland as a source of manufactured goods. As one West Clare arsonist put it, 'it was easy for linen to burn'; but it was more difficult for the South, practically empty of flax, to cover patriotic beds with patriotic sheets.

In other sectors Republican planners misjudged their ability to reimpose order after the deluge. In June 1920, for instance, Michael Collins proposed that all Republicans, except publicans, public servants and various classes of businessmen highly susceptible to enemy distraint or seizure, should be encouraged to send their income tax payments to the Dáil instead of the Department of Inland Revenue. He hoped thus to augment the Dáil's income by perhaps £500,000 annually, and later on to divert 'certain classes of Land Annuities' as well. In mid-September the Secretary for Local Government suggested, and the Dáil agreed, that Collins's Finance Department should consider using these payments to maintain the Republican apparatus of local government. The withholding of taxes and annuities had, of course, a strong material appeal: in late 1919 local bodies in Clare had threatened to support the non-payment of rents, rates and annuities unless market restrictions were ended, and in April 1920 scores of tax offices and the documents in them had been burned by Volunteers. But eventually the Dáil backed down from its ambitious programme. Farmers and men of substance feared seizure of their land or assets if they refused annuities or taxes, and those who did not showed no eagerness to send them to the Dáil instead. In December 1920 Collins admitted that 'Owing to many causes the matter of Income Tax has somewhat lain in abeyance, but it is not by any means dropped, and our hopes are still high about it.'[9] Inland Revenue reports suggest that the impact of the tax boycott was fairly small: the amount of income tax received in Ireland as a percentage of tax assessed fell from 99 per cent in 1919–20 to 86 per cent in 1920–21 and 77 per cent in 1921–22 (compared with 94, 96 and 96 per cent for the entire United Kingdom). As for land annuities, in June 1920 the House of Commons was told that they had 'hitherto been met with great regularity', and in August Collins told the Dáil that 'it would not be good business to withhold' many of the payments and that further action should be delayed.[10] In 1920–21 there seem to have been no deductions at all from Clare grants-in-aid to cover unpaid annuities. Only after 1921, when agricultural demand sank and wartime prosperity ended at last, were threats translated into practice. And this campaign was not only undertaken without the Dáil's urging, but it was actually directed against the Irish Free State, not against Britain.[11]

Despite its failure to secure taxes or annuities, the Dáil swelled its revenue hugely during 1920. Money, so scant in 1919, poured in from the (American) Friends of Irish Freedom and Self-Determination Funds, from the Dáil loans both internal and external. From May 1920 to June 1921 the Dáil's home account received just over £500,000, and at the latter date a sum almost as large remained untapped in its foreign account, as well as £250,000 in balance at home. Expenditure on social administration was lower than one might expect: over £200,000 was used to underwrite an institution never formally recognised by the Dáil (the National Land Bank Ltd, which bought up a small number of farms for division amongst landless men and uneconomic holders, and attempted to attract 'Irish Ireland' investors despite the jeers of the Minister for Finance); and of £100,000 set aside for loans to bankrupt local authorities, only 10 per cent had been disbursed by August 1921. Only £180,700, even less than the amount estimated, was in fact spent on all the departments of the Dáil between May 1920 and June 1921—and of this almost half was devoted to 'defence' or mainly propagandist activities. Even so, expenditure on social administration was of a scale undreamed of in 1919: over £6,600 on labour, £7,300 on local government, £12,600 on 'home affairs' (including the court system).[12] The Dáil was thus able to employ a certain number of provincial inspectors and organisers and Dublin staffs to co-ordinate administrative effort. The notion of setting up a Republican administration, however skeletal, no longer seemed absurd by mid-1920, though the Dáil was still too poor to envisage major administrative initiatives requiring minute supervision. The Dáil could hope to act as a national liaison office if not a fully-fledged civil service.

But the genesis of the Republican social administration cannot simply be explained in terms of the opportunities created by the wrecking campaign and the Dáil's increasing ability to pay the cost of exploiting them. If the Republican leaders were to make the most of their chances, they would have to possess both the vision to discern opportunities and the will to exploit them. Several factors impaired their vision and sapped their will. Ever since 1916 Sinn Féin, in defiance of its name and tradition, had relied on outside intervention to win freedom for Ireland: American pressure on its wartime ally, the goodwill of the Peace Conference, the influence of Britain's trading partners, and, when all these had been proven ineffective, the sympathy and indignation of Britishers at their government's misdoings. Throughout 1919 the Dáil had devoted itself almost exclusively to impressing journalists, American investigators and international 'opinion', and it was hard for the publicist to turn his attention from the lecture hall to the office or courtroom. Why bother creating a Republic if your audience was already convinced that one existed? Moreover, reconstruction, however natural an outcome of wrecking it may seem in retrospect, was not its main motive. The men who shot policemen did not dream of becoming imitation policemen themselves. To ensure that they did so required not only a fertile imagination on the planners' part, but also the courage to work against the prevailing revolutionary mood—violent, iconoclastic, individualist. The Dáil's constructive enthusiasm was further dampened by the great difficulty of maintaining even the simplest administrative apparatus in occupied Dublin where clandestine offices were continually raided, papers destroyed and officials arrested. Such hazards, and the scarcity of men and women with the spirit to play out the game, help explain the sizeable excess of the Dáil's income over its expenditure. Yet despite enemy harassment, revolutionary iconoclasm and the propagandist tradition, the reluctant Dáil was induced by influences still more powerful than these to assume the responsibilities of a government as well as a press bureau. To establish how this came about, how the will was bent to the way, let us examine the two schemes which most impinged upon the lives of ordinary Irishmen—those for legal administration and local government. What limitations restricted these social experiments, and how successful were they if judged according to their stated aims?

2. REPUBLICAN COURTS

The first Republican experiment to gain widespread notice abroad was the setting up of the 'Dáil Courts'. The most unlikely people wrote in praise of them: a Liberal peer felt they were 'dispensing even-handed justice between man and man', a friend of Walter Long's (like the peer a Limerickman) found that 'Sinn Fein rules the County [Limerick]—and rules it admirably', even a former Castle information officer lamented the absence of 'the judicial humorist' but confessed that Republican justice was 'feared as much as it is loved'.[13] Yet the most likely people, the Dáil ministers, were at first sceptical and cautious with regard to the courts which, in the spring of 1920, were springing up by local initiative in many parishes in the west of Ireland. The new courts might superficially resemble the largely imaginary arbitration courts decreed by the Dáil in 1919, but in function they were more often instruments of factional coercion than preservers of neighbourliness. Even the rules of the West Clare parish and district courts, much praised for their exact application of the Dáil's decree of August 1919 and used as a model for the revised scheme of June

1920, provided for mandatory judgments as well as the voluntary arbitration envisaged by the Dáil decree. 'Guards' were to be appointed 'to preserve the peace', fines imposed for breaches of licensing regulations. In the early spring of 1920 Brian O'Higgins reported that 'the Volunteers have cooperated with the Comhairle Ceanntair' of Sinn Féin in administering justice in West Clare—hardly an appropriate collaboration for a voluntary tribunal. The character of that co-operation is suggested by a case reported to Kilrush quarter sessions in January 1920. Sinn Féin organisers had urged a plaintiff to transfer his suit from the October sessions to the Sinn Féin court, but he had refused and won his case. His refusal was punished by shots fired outside his house, a notice on the chapel gates signed by the 'Competent Military Authority', and a boycott by shopkeepers and tradesmen. The more ineffective the enemy court system became, the more eagerly local factions sought to pursue their own interests, using where possible the Sinn Féin courts to legitimise their actions. During the spring of 1920 numerous reports reached the Dáil from Munster and Connaught of agrarian outrages, often carried out in the Republic's name but with a different and much older tradition behind them. Land-hungry labourers and smallholders, frustrated by the slowing down of land purchase since 1915 but encouraged by the inability of police or soldiers to prevent land seizure, resumed the campaign of cattle-driving and ranch-dividing which had so alarmed Republican leaders two years earlier. The political connotations of these acts were evidently variable:

> A drive was prepared in the Kilbride locality, with a tricolour in readiness to lead the advance, but the aggrieved man declared he would appeal to Dail Eireann; so the White and Orange were torn off the rag and the job was done in the name of the A.O.H.

Nevertheless, as a Clare correspondent of *The Times* pointed out on 2 May 1920, cattle-driving was an essential component of the system of enforcing 'arbitration court' decisions. In preparation for the previous day, when most of the county's grasslands were parcelled out to eleven-month leaseholders, parish courts had been busy fixing purchase prices (some fair, some not) while parish committees ensured that owners accepted the courts' rulings by driving their cattle with increasing abandon, demolishing gates and walls, sending threatening letters and digging graves. As the journalist said, 'The large and small holders suffer together.' The Dáil ministry was alarmed both by the divisive effects of the campaign and its evident inability to supervise the local courts involved in it. The Secretary for Home Affairs (Austin Stack) complained that most cases put before the courts were not in fact directed against large holders but against small farmers by the families of allegedly evicted tenants. Such a campaign threatened 'to divert the attention of the people from the national struggle', and the enemy was probably at the bottom of it. Art O'Connor, Substitute Minister for Agriculture, later attributed the land trouble not only to the impotence of the enemy but to that of the Republic—the land-hungry westerners knew that 'Even if it [the Dáil] objected, it too would be powerless to touch them till they had gained their ends.'[14] If the Dáil were to restore order, not only to rural life but to Republican justice, it would have to devise and enforce a far more centralised, less elastic court system than that which had mushroomed from the publicists' careless spawn.

The growing disorder in the provinces alarmed the Dáil but did not at first inspire it. Art O'Connor later admitted that 'For a little while it seemed to shrink from its duty as one shrinks from the fulfilment of an unexpected joy.' When (on 30 January 1920) the Dáil ministry discussed the establishment of mandatory civil and criminal courts to supplant the 'enemy tribunals', Austin Stack commented: 'I cannot see how this could be successfully carried out for the moment.' Instead, the ministry devised a subtle plan. By decreeing the setting up of national arbitration courts modelled on those working already in West Clare, the ministry appeared to be drawing the courts under a national scheme which elaborated rather than superseded the decree of August 1919. Yet the choice of model implicitly condoned the unauthorised practice of compulsion. The ministry submitted to a *fait accompli* but kept its propagandist tradition intact. On 13 May it approved the scheme for parish and district courts, but decided 'to concentrate on one or two counties'; on 10 June it directed 'A.S. [Austin Stack] to organise in any counties where he thinks it advisable'. Characteristically, it tried to impose order and logic on an opportunist policy by adding: 'Dislocation of Enemy Courts. Resignation of Bailiffs, Process Servers. Wait till our own Courts are ready.' In fact, of course, dislocation had preceded establishment of local courts, which had in turn preceded the decreeing of their 'own' Dáil Courts; but the looking-glass logic of the publicist insisted that the flow of events should be reversed for the edification of the world at large. But the Dáil was now showing as much pragmatic energy at home as sophistry abroad. Having embraced reality it proceeded to remould it. Within four days of the ministry's approving the new scheme, Kevin O'Shiel was hearing agrarian cases in Co. Mayo as a Special Judicial Commissioner accountable directly to the ministry. In the next three months he rushed about Connaught and other troubled parts taking over major cases from the 'arbitration courts', so often the tool of parochial factions. After a conference on 29 May of TDs, Volunteer leaders and Sinn Féiners from Connaught, North Longford and West Clare, O'Connor decided that the land-hungry should not be starved but fed a more balanced diet. The division of demesnes and 'ranches' was not discouraged, but the hearing of 'eviction' claims was forbidden without licence from Stack. By early June the *Champion* reported that 'Sinn Fein Land Courts' in Ennis had heard more than twenty-five cases from North [Mid-]Clare, and that those making 'frivolous and unjust claims' were now being severely dealt with. But the courts were acquiring 'nearly all the big ranches in Clare' and would divide them up 'in a very short time'. On 26 June the ministry approved proposals for a Land Commission to institutionalise Kevin O'Shiel, and in revised form these were ratified by the Dáil in mid-September. Meanwhile the polite fiction of 'voluntary arbitration' was quietly forgotten. In late June mandatory courts of justice and equity were decreed, and the ministry empowered to establish criminal courts when it wished. Two months later the parish and district courts were formally accorded both civil and criminal jurisdiction, and cumbersomely capped with circuit, supreme and high courts for good measure.[15] At first nervously, then energetically, then with rejuvenated propagandist glee, the Republican leaders responded to the provincial challenge.

By the late summer of 1920 the Dáil appeared to have constructed a parody of the traditional legal system. Careful attempts had been made to simulate its style and structure, both to impress British opinion and help lawyers and litigants to accustom themselves to the new ways. Some participants were evidently awed by the juridical paraphernalia—as one Dublin defendant allegedly exclaimed, 'But here you are. Judges, Court, lawyer and all. By the Lord! the Shinners mean business. I'll pay, that's all. Let me down as easy as you can.'[16] At first, their professional livelihood being threatened by the collapse of the traditional courts, most lawyers willingly participated in their successors. But after the autumn of 1920 increasing government interference cramped the Republic's legal style and frightened the lawyers. After a raid in November on the East Clare District Court the four solicitors present were threatened with court martial if they attended again. They did not. Dignity as well as expertise became harder to maintain when courts had to be held in 'creameries, farmhouses, outhouses, barns and any place with four walls and a roof which could be made serviceable'. In such contexts the elaborate decrees and rules churned out by the ministry seemed out of place. In fact they were more carefully studied by foreign journalists than justices or counsel. As Kevin O'Shiel writes of the decree establishing the Land Commission:

> It was much too complicated for the times and conditions it was destined to meet. I did not see it till some time after it had been enacted, nor, as far as I know, did any of my colleagues. Our Minister, Art O'Connor, kept it very much to himself. . . . Few, if any, lawyers saw the decree (it was not in print).

It appeared to have been copied by a non-lawyer from the law incorporating the enemy Land Commission, and was enacted, like most Dáil decrees, 'largely for much-needed propaganda purposes'. But even the rules and forms of the parish and district courts, which O'Shiel himself had helped draft, contributed little to their practical conduct. On 23 August 1921 an East Clare brehon (justice) wrote to the Minister for Home Affairs:

> Brehons for the most part are amateurs in the way of the law. They pick up many things from experience. In matters of procedure and detail they require the help of an expert authority to guide them. This can best be rendered by a set of rules touching these points.

The ministry posted him a copy of its *Judiciary. Rules and Forms* next day. It was dated 1920! Many justices would probably not have read them even if available. In the tradition of the old RMs, their common sense usually exceeded their legal acumen. When a North Clareman complained that a neighbour's donkey had trespassed and eaten his cabbages, all parties agreed that in recompense the plaintiff should be allowed to graze his own ass among the defendant's cabbages.[17]

Republican justice imitated Somerville and Ross in practice just as it imitated the statute and common law of England in theory.

These incongruities of theory with practice illustrate the overall weakness of central direction. Despite elaborate provisions for appeal from their decisions, local courts retained much of their original independence throughout the revolutionary period. Higher courts were costly, dangerous and difficult to operate, and the Dáil's inability to build up an adequate inspecting staff before the Truce left it impotent in the face of non-co-operation from the parish clerks. Even on paper no attempt was made to control or sanction the appointment of parish justices. In August 1919 the Dáil had ruled that they should be 'elected locally on adult suffrage' in each chapel area, all clergymen and resigned magistrates being justices *ex officio*. In June 1920 the ministry accepted for the time being a more workable but equally uncontrolled mode of appointment, by a 'Confce. of Local Bodies and reps. of Trade Unions, Sinn Féin, Volunteers and Clergy. Women eligible.' But, as Stack explained, the new instructions were to be applied with discretion. In Clare and Galway, for instance, the arbitrators had been

> appointed by the Comhairlí Ceanntair of Sinn Féin, and so, cannot, strictly speaking, call themselves Dáil Éireann Courts. I have not however ordered new elections in Galway and Clare owing to the success of the Courts so far, and with the permission of the Ministry intend to allow them to work until Arbitrators be elected by popular vote about the end of the present year.

In fact new elections were held in West Clare a month later, though only in those parishes where the incumbents had not been elected by ballot. But whatever the mode of their appointment, the justices inevitably represented the dominant factions in their districts, and were susceptible to parochial pressures. Justices were often priests or older, inactive Sinn Féiners of 'standing', but the registrars who supervised the working of the courts were almost always active Volunteers.[18] The composition of the courts mirrored the distribution of local power.

Even more significant than the susceptibilities of justices was the role of local Volunteer companies in detecting offenders and executing judgments. Once again the ministry was obliged to accept and ratify, rather than alter, the existing state of affairs. On 19 June 1920 the Adjutant-General announced that the Volunteers would 'place at the services of the Dáil' company police forces recruited from the ranks and subject to 'the control and direction' of their military superiors. They were ordered to ignore personal and partisan squabbles and actions 'not definitely criminal or disturbing to the community'. Orders issued in November sought to make the police co-ordinators of the legal and military systems rather than being, as before, Volunteers doing odd jobs: the police should 'be quite detached from the Army', might include non-Volunteers and were bound to see that court orders were carried out. But in practice the police remained soldiers first and court servants second. As late as December 1921, only a few weeks before the disbandment of the company police, the brigade police officer in East Clare reported: 'The Police in the Brigade area are quite a distinct organisation from the Army. This Officer allows his men to attend Army parades when off duty.'[19] The decisions of the courts could be enforced only as impartially as the disposition of the local Volunteers allowed.

In many parts of Ireland both Republican justices and Volunteer police were embroiled in parochial faction-fighting to a staggering degree. Fr Patrick Gaynor, curate at Mullagh in 1920, has left a remarkable account of judicial proceedings in his neighbourhood. His fellow-curate (Fr Mick McKenna) and he had antagonised those with agrarian ambitions by suppressing cattle-drives and opposing the claims of certain influential 'evicted tenants'. But the West Clare District Court judged differently, wrongly awarding an acre of long-disputed bog to a Cooraclare Volunteer and exonerating a hero who left the RIC in 1920 and proceeded to persecute his uncle, occupier of a disputed property, by breaking his windows, driving out his aged tenant and throwing manure into his drains. As local Volunteer commandant, Fr McKenna dismissed the court which, though duly elected according to the Dáil's instructions, allegedly included a county councillor with an 'itching palm' and a future TD 'who was amenable to influence'. He induced an *ad hoc* tribunal of Volunteer brigade officers, Sinn Féin leaders and justices of the reformed District Court to reverse the bog decision, and had the ex-policeman imprisoned by a battalion court martial on Mutton Island. Whereupon the brigade chief of police gave authority for an expedition of Cooraclare Volunteers into Mullagh to eject the vindicated uncle! Eventually Fr Gaynor appointed himself acting police chief and induced another *ad hoc* tribunal to order ejectment of the ejectors. He did the job himself with the help of three men, a rifle and a most unpriest-like death-threat. The uncle eventually paid the trouble-maker about £100 to emigrate to the USA and leave him in peace.[20] It will be observed that neither priests, policemen nor Volunteers showed great respect for the Dáil Courts as constituted, though all shared a robust faith in the efficacy of *force majeure*. The Republican courts in practice were utterly unlike the solemn, orderly, disciplined tribunals so effectively publicised by the Dáil. Judged by its own pretensions, the Dáil's legal system was a sham.

But judged by its effectiveness in keeping disorderly conduct among neighbours within traditional bounds, the system was not a sham. Despite gloatings by Lloyd George and the *Weekly Summary* in February 1921, the enemy's attempts to raid and disrupt the courts were only partly successful. As Kevin O'Shiel writes of the land courts, 'They survived the most violent attacks and carried on, and their order[s] were executed, even during the darkest period, though not, understandably, without sustaining a considerable drop in their achievements.' In East Clare the District Court sat in every month from its foundation until the Truce, except in December 1920 when its books were lost in a raid. In the last six terrible months of revolution it had seven official and 'several private sittings', and special reference was made to the Dáil concerning the success of the court system there. In West Clare the District Registrar reported early in June 1921 that regular sittings were continuing, though only three parish clerks had sent him reports. As Kevin O'Higgins commented, 'The main thing is that the Courts are working and have been working all the time.' Nevertheless, many courts did collapse under the stress of revolution: in Ennistymon and Kilkee, sizeable towns which retained enemy garrisons throughout, sittings were suspended in September 1920. In May 1921 Austin Stack had to acknowledge widespread dislocation, but noted that justices and registrars were now 'bestirring themselves in many places'. 'There is abundant evidence that given a fair opportunity the Courts of the Republic will be functioning in most parts of the country soon again.'[21]

'All my records were captured by the enemy some time before the Truce.' The Minister for Home Affairs's misfortune is also the historian's. Nevertheless, post-Truce attempts to remedy the deficiency allow one to sketch the character and range of work done by the revolutionary courts. The work-load for most parish justices seems to have been fairly light: the five West Clare parish courts for which pre-Truce data have survived heard 21 cases before September 1920, 14 from about May to September 1920, 21 before April 1921, 37 between April and September 1921, and 6 in July 1921 alone. The District Court heard 88 cases between 6 May 1920 and 11 July 1921, of which 18 were appeals from parish court decisions, 18 claims for payments due, 19 for possession and 8 for damage done. Seven questions of land title were considered but only one criminal case. Some of the thorniest sectors of law were sensibly left to the exclusive consideration of the enemy courts—including, it seems, dog licences, probate and workers' compensation. Others, such as licensing regulations, were dealt with only sporadically by the Dáil Courts. Responsibility was assumed sometimes by one administration, sometimes the other, or both, or neither. In August 1920 the president of the Ennis Parish Court asked a licensee: 'Do you recognise this court?' The defendant replied: 'I do, but I will have to recognise the British Court at the Licensing Sessions next October, or have myself and my family thrown out in the streets. . . . Suppose the Imperial Police come around while the Sinn Fein Police are in my house, and the Imperial Police catch the Sinn Fein Police, where will the publican be then?' Similar dilemmas confronted many litigants, who tended to appeal to the administration more likely to favour their claims. One prominent West Clare grazier, victim of repeated cattle-drives between 1919 and 1921, at first 'showed some inclination to go before some other tribunal that they don't know anything about', according to George McElroy, RM, but repented and obtained mild convictions in the official courts. Later the Republican Police took the job of protecting him over from the RIC, only to be betrayed to the latter by his enemies. At last in May 1921 the West Clare District Registrar reported that the cattle-drivers 'were now prepared to submit the case to the Republican Courts. I believe they have knocked off K—— their former Leader.'[22]

Even more obstructive to Republican justice than enemy interference or competition for litigants was the great difficulty of adequately punishing offenders. Neither Volunteers nor Republican Police had the facilities or the leisure to keep prisoners for long terms. When the police were inaugurated in June 1920 they were told for the time being to hold offenders only until the following Sunday, when they should be 'publicly paraded after the principal Mass'. In later months a few were 'kept on islands or in boggy and remote parts', but most were merely taken out of their parishes and dumped on the roadside. Even these mild punishments were often effective: after Kevin O'Shiel's first land judgment, the unsuccessful claimants had 'stamped out of the hall in an arrogant temper' and jeered at the Dáil's authority in fairs and markets, whereupon the ministry had them arrested. Their womenfolk immediately resumed forcible occupation of the disputed property, but, as the parish priest shrewdly predicted, they caved in after a week. The men were released, peace restored, and only the priest suffered by losing many of his parishioners' dues. The Dáil Courts relied heavily on the goodwill of litigants and communal pressure to make their decisions effective. The outcome of cases heard in West Clare suggests the small scale of the Republic's legal deterrent. Of seventy-three cases between May 1920 and July 1921 for which district court decisions were recorded, three were settled out of court and thirty-six dismissed. Four appeals were upheld, at least in part, four decrees for possession were granted and twenty-six decrees for money or damages. Of the seven cases heard in Kilkee during September 1920, two were adjourned (indefinitely, as it happened), one passed on to the District Court, one settled out of court, two settled by awards of 5s costs for trespass, and the other by a decree for 2s costs together with a promise to keep the peace, leave Kilkee within a week and pay the cost of damage done to the battered and assaulted victim. It is astonishing that in many areas the requisite co-operation was forthcoming to allow the courts to perform their modest functions—provided, of course, that justices did not probe too inquisitively into the interminable clan feuds which had defied all legal interventions for generations past. As a Kerryman recalls, 'Generally all parties were inveigled into shaking hands as they smoked the pipe of peace and drank my mother's tea.'[23]

Thus the Dáil Courts maintained the semblance of traditional justice in difficult times, though their success was circumscribed by weakness of central direction, undue influence of local faction, feebleness of punitive powers and disruption by the enemy. Remarkably, they (or some of them) survived. But what of that much larger claim of the Dáil publicists, that the courts averted social anarchy and brought economic revolution under a rule? Could it be that the spring land agitation of 1920 died down in May as much because the year's leaseholds had been agreed on 1 May as because of Kevin O'Shiel's activities after 17 May? That the absence of similar agitation next spring was largely due to the flooding of the country with soldiers and extra police, which made public assemblies such as cattle-drives impracticable?[24] Were the Republican courts instruments of social control, as their organisers claimed, or mirrors of social reality with all its seething antagonisms, as I have suggested? A glance at the performance of the courts after the Truce indicates an answer to this question.

The immediate effect of the Truce upon the Republican courts was to increase, revive and strengthen them. The RIC was instructed to get all possible information about them 'without direct interference', but they were not to be suppressed by force. Other orders admitted that many varieties of 'Sinn Féin courts' breached the Truce, but forbade police intervention without Dublin's sanction. Nevertheless, cases were reported of frustrated RIC officers threatening to disperse courts as 'political meetings', and the Dáil ministry advised registrars and justices to hold their courts regularly but in out-of-the-way places, and not to 'invite too much publicity'. Central organisation was improved, inspectors sent to the provinces, regular reports solicited from registrars. As Austin Stack wrote:

> All went well until the enemy organised his ruthless campaign against them [the parish and district courts] and as this campaign has been partially successful, it is our duty now, to counteract his success by a 'Big Push' to bring them to the wonderful state of efficiency to which they had arrived last Autumn.

By February 1922 courts were functioning in thirteen of nineteen parishes in West Clare and eighteen of thirty-two in East Clare, though some parish clerks were still recalcitrant in submitting reports of their proceedings. The extent to which Dáil Courts responded to the ministry's call to reorganise and to report their proceedings to Dublin is indicated by Table 5.1.[25] By the time of the Treaty the court system, in West Clare at least, was once again both active and widespread, and under closer central supervision than in its heyday, the autumn of 1920. If anarchy was to be quelled, the Republican courts were as well placed to quell it as they had ever been. Now, moreover, the Republicans had the field virtually to themselves. Soldiers and RIC men were inactive and demoralised, and were no longer a threat to cattle-drivers; petty sessions and other official courts, though to some extent revived, devoted their hearings to trivial and uncontroversial cases. But social discontent, increased by agricultural recession, revived. Rent-strikes, cattle-drives, strikes by agricultural labourers, all indicated the renewed truculence of the landless. Even more than in 1919 and 1920, sections of the Volunteers were identified with social protest, and the Dáil Courts, still dependent on Volunteer aid to enforce their decisions, seem to have made little attempt to resist it. On occasion, it is true, Dáil arbitrators with Volunteer help managed to settle strikes to the employers' advantage. But increasingly the suppression of social unrest passed out of the hands of justices into those of armed factions. More and more obviously the courts became the tools of those factions, but whereas in earlier times they had served a vital purpose in legitimising the partisan interests they served, by early 1922 Irishmen had witnessed too much violence and destruction to set much store by legitimacy or legal decorum.[26]

In their last year of existence the limitations of the Dáil Courts were revealed with increasing clarity. Their impotence in face of the social turmoil of late 1921 and 1922 suggests that their role in subduing that of spring 1920 was small. When all the hypocrisy cloaking Republican justice is stripped away, all that remains is a history of ingenious expedients undertaken within a very narrow range of human activity, and scarcely touching the great social problems which surfaced during the revolution. Yet however limited their influence, the courts did bring the Republic to some extent into the daily lives of Irishmen,

Table 5.1: Republican Courts, 1921–22

	Up to Sep. 1921	Oct. 1921	Nov. 1921	Dec. 1921	Jan. 1922	Feb. 1922
East Clare:						
Parish courts reporting	4	2	4	6	13	4
Cases heard	37	5	10	21	47	21
West Clare:						
Parish courts reporting	8	9	8	10	11	6
Cases heard	196	68	41	99	68	58

whatever their politics. And it may be that one five-shilling decree for trespass in a remote western parish was worth a dozen Declarations of Independence.

3. REPUBLICAN LOCAL GOVERNMENT

The most adventurous of all the Dáil's experiments in civil administration was its takeover and transformation of local government. The local administrators, unlike the court organisers and officials of the ministry, entered revolution with a valuable inheritance—an existing apparatus needing not dislocation but adaptation. But the possibility of adapting to revolutionary purposes the old fabric of Boards of Guardians, county, urban district and rural district councils (with their attendant boards and advisory committees) was by no means self-evident. As in so many aspects of revolution, it was local enterprise, not central planning, which governed the conduct of this experiment. As in the case of the Dáil Courts, propagandist gestures were gradually transformed into revolutionary acts, against the better judgment of the propagandists.

The men who were to conduct the takeover were the representatives elected on the Sinn Féin ticket in 1920. The imperial cabinet having rejected advice that all candidates for public office should be required to declare their allegiance to the Crown, the Dáil ministry imposed an alternative declaration on its candidates: 'I recognise the Republic established by the will and vote of the Irish People as the legitimate Government of Ireland.' Care was taken to ensure that the new councillors were not mere lip-servants of the separatist cause, as most of their predecessors had by this time become. In February 1919 Sinn Féin's central executive had ruled that district candidates should be selected by local Sinn Féin clubs, subject to the executive's ratification. They should form joint conventions with club delegates, chaired by headquarters representatives, to select county council candidates. The East Clare executive had drawn up a similar scheme a few weeks earlier, excluding district candidates (*per se*) from the county council conventions, but allowing Volunteer corps to send delegates instead of Sinn Féin clubs. Opportunists were disappointed by the restriction of the franchise to those who had joined clubs before 22 January 1919. In West Clare, however, one club launched a membership drive on the basis that only club members would be able to influence the choice of local councillors! In a few districts Sinn Féin's new, thoroughly vetted candidates boasted background and qualifications curiously like those of the despised changelings they were intended to sweep aside. Thus for Kilrush UDC three candidates were put forward:

> Three outstanding men, men of great family connections, business men and men that would be worthy of any public board. There was Jack Dwyer, Jack Lynch (a draper in Moore Street), and Josie Kett. Jack Dwyer was a publican and general grocer. None of the three of them was elected.

But in most parts candidates were both less traditional and more successful. Many of them were Volunteer officers and ex-prisoners—in the new Ennistymon RDC these comprised at least twelve of the twenty-three members. From this class most of the office-bearers were drawn, following the Dáil's nicely weighted instruction that they 'should be most carefully selected, due regard being paid to National principle, ability and knowledge of local administration'. But the salaried officials could not so easily be replaced by able but untrained men of principle. However black their political backgrounds, they mostly kept their posts and maintained the *gravitas* of local administration as best they could. Early in 1921 a Dáil inspector reported that at least half the district clerks in Clare were former Irish Party men, yet all had proved satisfactory. One was 'doing his work as he is instructed,' another 'Ex-party but now O'K', a third 'a Quondam Party-man . . . also a *Publican*, his house being a favourite resort for Black and Tans etc., but the man is alright and is doing good work'. With this incongruous mixture of canny old clerks and untried boy-soldier-administrators, Irish local government entered its most exotic period. The new chairman of the Clare County Council was none other than Michael Brennan, the most feared fighting-man in the county, though for the time being without formal office in the Volunteers. He addressed the new council's first meeting rather nervously:

> I do not know what kind of a fist I will make of this chair, as I do not think I was made for a Co. Councillor (*laughter*). I do my best, being a soldier, and will continue to do my best. . . . I will do my best to represent the County in the battlefield.[27]

Republican local government began with a series of prearranged gestures. On 1 June, while elections still proceeded, the Dáil's Local Government Department had instructed the new councils to pass resolutions of allegiance to 'the authority of Dáil Éireann as the duly elected Government of the Irish People', copies of which (in Irish and English) were to be transmitted in advance to foreign governments. Many councils printed and illuminated presentation copies, sometimes sealing them with wax before sending them to the Dáil. Also by prior arrangement the county councils resolved at their first meetings to refuse to levy extra rates to meet criminal and malicious injuries decrees, and to withhold all financial information from the enemy Local Government Board.[28] But these brave gestures could not disguise the fact that the Dáil leaders had only the haziest plans for future action. Indeed, the circular of 1 June counselled 'no drastic action' relating to the Board's authority until further notice. Before the elections the sabotage of local administration had been considered as often as its adaptation. In February 1919 a Sinn Féin committee on local government had considered only two alternative programmes for county council candidates: continuing work under the Local Government Acts, or ignoring the Board's supervision and promoting independent schemes. But early in 1919 Austin Brennan had unsuccessfully urged East Clare Sinn Féin to ask all local bodies simply to resign till the Republican prisoners were freed (a course already adopted by the Killarney Guardians). On 25 March 1920 the Dáil ministry had actually laid down a 'General Policy. 1. Resignations of Sinn Féin members should be obtained,' though in the event they were not. The difficulty of reconciling defiance of the Board with maintenance of local government—clearly the most desirable course—seemed immense. In mid-May 1920 Kevin O'Higgins passed on to the ministry some gloomy opinions culled from a conference of experts. He 'could not recommend' taking a course which would deprive local bodies of government grants, and thought it better 'to place the responsibility of withholding these large sums upon the enemy rather than to cut them off by our own deliberate act'. In the meantime the councils should pledge their allegiance and hope for the best. On 2 June, just after his department had advised councils not to levy extra rates, O'Higgins drew comfort from his belief that confrontation over the matter could be delayed until April 1921 when the rates were due to be struck. An 'immediate' breach with the Board should still be avoided. Instead the Dáil should explore the possibility of maintaining local government without grants, 'manoeuvre the enemy' into taking responsibility or, if unfeasible, simultaneously cease to function at the last practicable moment. O'Higgins, though regretting the ministry's prevarications, was begging time for his own advisers. The Republican leaders, quick to gesture but slow to plan, nevertheless expressed irritation at the same attributes among local councillors. 'Stop Councils from passing foolish resolutions,' snapped the ministry on 17 July. And a few weeks later the department was uneasy:

> It has been reported to the Department that some Councils are willing to obey instructions re political matters but that outside of this, they should have free scope. There would be little use in having a Department of Local Government unless the general business of the Local Authorities were under supervision.[29]

But if the Dáil were to exert effective supervision, it would have to devise a detailed, coherent plan of campaign—and this it had still not done.

It was the enemy Board which, albeit rather unwillingly, took the initiative early in August. Its vice-president had at first justifiably maintained that the chorus of disobedient council resolutions was as shrill and shallow as usual. Encouraged by the uninterrupted stream of correspondence from the councils, he expected them to cave in when the time of application came for essential Treasury advances (which could not legally be accepted without the Board's sanction). He changed his policy only after Bonar Law had undertaken, without consulting him, to withhold all government grants and advances to councils failing to undertake *in advance* to submit their accounts for audit and obey the Board's rules and orders. At the end of July the Board passed on the government's 'specific instructions' to the councils in such terms that no council could make the required assurances without abjectly recanting its brave resolutions of a few weeks earlier.[30] In popular eyes the enemy had assumed responsibility for the withdrawal of local government moneys. So challenged, almost every council defied or evaded the Board's demands. By 1 September the only bodies which had complied were two county councils, twelve urban councils and twenty-one district bodies (all but half a dozen of them from the six north-eastern counties). A total of 160 bodies had marked the letter 'read' or decided to make no order, twenty-eight were to reconsider it later, twenty had burned, destroyed or demonstratively ignored it, six had asked the Dáil for instructions, twenty-one had explicitly refused to submit their accounts, and no less than 220 (including over two-thirds of the county councils and even that unrepentantly anti-Republican body, the Kilrush UDC) had not considered it at all. The Board was now obliged to take action against almost all the local authorities of Ireland. By January 1921 only fifteen rural bodies in the twenty-six southern counties were considered worthy to receive their grants, and of these only six (almost all in border regions) seem to have had direct payment authorised by the Lord Lieutenant. Even these, of course, were faced with still savager deprivations than their disloyal fellows should the government apply the threatened levy on the rates in their districts. As the Minister for Local Government told the Dáil in May 1921:

> The 'grants' as a dazzling bribe to surrender have lost their efficacy, for, though it took some time to sink in it seems now to be well understood that the million and a half in 'grants' is available for local authorities on condition of their paying approximately ten times that sum on foot of Decrees for 'Criminal and Malicious' Injuries. . . . The grim logic of a fact of this kind is undoubtedly an asset.[31]

The reluctant Board had been forced by the government to threaten its enemies less potently than its friends, which naturally caused its enemies to multiply.

Once the enemy's initiative had brought forward the day of financial reckoning from April 1921 to August 1920 the Dáil was at last induced to draw up a coherent plan of independent administration. On 29 June the Dáil had set up a new Commission of Enquiry into Local Government, with the proviso that local councils should not initiate radical changes in procedure until it reported not later than 1 September (a proviso which provoked strong opposition in the Dáil). But some councils were growing frustrated—one had already 'started the clean cut and opened the fight' by amending its rates independently. Then on 24 July, at a meeting where no minutes were taken and no officials were present, the Clare County Council had concocted its own scheme for transferring the bulk of local administration to the Dáil's effective supervision. All rates collected were to be lodged not with the previous treasurer, a bank, but with three secret trustees; the money was to be lodged by a bonded 'paymaster', also responsible for its distribution as wages; the rate-collectors were to be offered reappointment by the Republic on resigning their service with the Board. If the government withheld the largest grant to local authorities, that which relieved the rates on agricultural holdings, each tenant was to deduct from his rent or annuity an amount equal to the relief denied him and hand it to the County Council instead of the landlord. Thus government and landlords were to bear the cost of restoring the council's revenue. On 6 August, spurred on by local pressure and the Board's belligerent circular of the 4th, the Dáil's Commission of Enquiry recommended that the Clare scheme 'be applied not only to that County but also to others similarly situated', subject to approval by a financial sub-committee. Councils were to '*formally cease* all further connection with the English Local Government Board' at a date to be fixed. Four days later 'all public bodies in Ireland' were accordingly sent confidential instructions for reorganising their finances pending the 'clean cut'—including the attractive suggestion that all credit should be exhausted immediately to avoid its seizure. The Clare County Council formally approved its own suggestions on 26 August and heralded the coming austerity by forbidding the supply of coal to any county administrative offices except its own. Once the Commission had presented its final report on 17 September, including detailed proposals for economies, the Republic was poised for 'The Clean break—The Local Government Department to function on the lines of the Custom House.'[32]

As in other sectors of revolutionary administration, the break was not in fact as clean as the planners envisaged. The enemy Department of Agriculture was eager to maintain its prosaic functions and avoid collision with the Republicans, who responded by blurring the break and reaching a sensible compromise. The plan to divert land annuities to county councils or Dáil was quietly dropped, as we have seen, and a breach with the old department's main auxiliaries, the Irish Land Commission and the CDB, was averted. Closure of some, perhaps all, of the county committees of agriculture (bodies elected by the county councils) was urged by the Local Government Commission. At first Art O'Connor, believing that their position would become 'intolerable' once the councils had broken away, urged that the Dáil should take over and maintain rather than close them. But on 11 December the Dáil ministry ruled that the committees 'be allowed to submit to Audit if they ask for instructions', and on 20 January 1921 O'Connor confessed that he was 'rather glad' his advice had been ignored, as large enemy grants were still coming in.[33] In practice, despite Kevin O'Higgins's prim censure of the inconsistency of such a course, local administrators happily accepted whatever money the enemy offered. Early in 1921, for example, Michael Brennan was approached by his reputedly Unionist county surveyor with 'an extraordinary proposal':

> He said he had a friend in the Treasury in London and if I would permit him, he thought he could get a grant from the British for the relief of unemployment amongst their ex-soldiers. He would have to use this grant on road work but he promised not to interfere with our obstructions. He added that as practically all the ex-soldiers were Volunteers, the British would in effect be financing us and relieving the Council of a heavy strain. . . . I thought it a fantastic idea, but I gave him the necessary permission. He returned with about £50,000.

The practical success of Republican local administration depended ultimately on the intelligence and vigour of local men, not on the directives issued by the Dáil. The department tried to exercise a 'strict supervision' over the councils, but without complete success. Just before the Truce Cosgrave, Minister for Local Government, reported that twenty inspectors were now employed, yet confessed that 'One of the worst results of the almost complete disappearance of the Sinn Féin Organisation is that there is no local authority or organisation to control the action or censure the inaction of those who were put forward as public representatives on Boards and Councils.'[34] Let us examine how the representatives in Co. Clare, thrown heavily upon their own ingenuity, fared.

The most obvious problem facing them was how to get together. Military duties, the blockage of roads and the vigilance of the enemy made travelling to council meetings increasingly inconvenient, laborious and dangerous for many representatives. After raids on several local government offices in November and on a meeting of the County Council itself on 14 December, councillors decided to meet secretly in future so that the incriminating documents they had managed to hide on the latter occasion could be brandished and discussed without inhibition. Not surprisingly attendances were often low. In mid-November Michael Brennan complained to the *Champion* that turn-outs at the latest meetings of three important county committees had been 6 out of 16, 4 of 18 and 2 of 30. He added ominously: 'As there seems to be no use in appealing to their sense of public duty in most cases, I now appeal to the ratepayers to bring pressure on them to attend and look after the County business.' In April 1921 a Dáil inspector complained that Ennistymon meetings, like those in Kilrush, were 'very poorly attended . . . and often fall through for want of a quorum. Except that the military occupies part of the building there seems little reason for such laxity.' Like its enemy counterpart, the Dáil administration made stiff demands on its servants. Neither was altogether successful, as is shown by Table 5.2.[35] The County Council's attendance at general meetings was remarkably high during the revolutionary period, and the Ennistymon Guardians' no lower than usual. But the finance committee, which played the largest part in making Republican local government work, could rely on the consistent participation of only a few devotees. The council's general meetings, less essential but more widely publicised, were conducted after an uncertain beginning with increasing panache. The first of its four clandestine meetings was held in a cowhouse outside Ennis, with three boxes for furniture, on which sat the chairman, the assistant secretary and the council records. The other participants sat on bundles of hay, most of them with 'their rifles across their knees'. Michael Brennan was most displeased by the press report, which made the meeting seem 'most undignified and frivolous'. He pointed out: 'When a meeting is held under such al fresco circumstances decorum is only a very secondary consideration, and as everybody there was intent on getting certain business done and nothing else, very little attention was given to such petty details as what their remarks would look like in print.' The council's *coup de théâtre* came next February, when Knoppogue Castle was occupied in Lord Dunboyne's absence. This time not only was the meeting reported, but the names of those present were published. A leading Volunteer staff officer congratulated the organisers upon their striking gesture, which had ended with a delectable exchange by letter of civilities between Dunboyne and his uninvited guests, but the Local Government Department's inspector was not amused. It was 'simply a piece of deliberate tomfoolery. . . . Whatever the motives impelling those responsible may have been the result has been to put all the essential and working members of the Council on the run, and to put 2 also in jail.' He totted up the resultant disposition of the thirty-one councillors: thirteen on the run, two interned and one jailed before Knoppogue, another two jailed and six put to flight afterwards, seven still free to run the county. Yet significantly it was not these seven unmarked men but eight of those who were on the run who composed the council's next meeting.[36] Despite disapproval of Dáil functionaries and pursuit by enemy forces, the sturdiest of the Republican councillors kept on the job.

Table 5.2: Attendance at Meetings of Local Government Bodies, 1913–21

Average attendance	Clare Co. Co.	Co. Co. Finance Cttee	Ennistymon Guardians
1913–Jun. 1920	22 of 31	not counted	11 of 40
Jun.–Dec. 1920	21	12 of 31	7 of 23
Jan.–Jul. 1921	16	5	7
Jul.–Dec. 1921	24	10	10
Members attending at least half meetings held between Jun. 1920 and Jul. 1921	23	5	4

Their most exacting task was to stop the councils being bankrupted. Of the county councils' revenue in 1918–19 some four-fifths comprised locally collected rates, one-sixth grants from the Local Taxation (Ireland) Account and the remainder (in Clare nearly 5 per cent) other imperial payments. Local Taxation grants were rather more vital to the rural boards and councils, but the urban councils relied on rates for over 95 per cent of their income. Thus even if the government were to freeze the entire Local Taxation Account and withhold other grants, Irish local government might reasonably hope to survive, provided it succeeded in collecting and appropriating rates payments and economised in sectors normally financed from the withdrawn grants. But rapid inflation and Labour's increasing success in winning wage increases constantly threatened the management of local administration, however fully funded. Moreover, the fear that the enemy would find some means to levy the criminal injury decrees, 'by hook or crook', caused one county councillor to write despondently to the *Champion* in March 1921: 'Under those circumstances might it not have been just as well not to have levied any rate at all.'[37]

Nevertheless, the rates were levied. The Republic's first simple design to re-employ the old rate-collectors and repudiate the status as treasurers of the respectable banks was soon challenged by the Board. On 11 November the Board warned collectors of their liability for all moneys lodged with 'unauthorised persons'. They were given three options: to resign on a retiring allowance; to lodge the rates in their personal accounts until the banks were restored as treasurers; or to be dismissed without pension if they accepted instructions from disobedient councils. The Dáil responded in kind. Disobedience to council instructions would lead to dismissal, but pensions might be paid to men who resigned their posts without impeding the Republican administration. Pensions, it was shrewdly explained, were payable not out of enemy grants but rates. Pension-conscious collectors were thus placed in a distressing quandary, worsened by the current scarcity of alternative jobs. Not knowing which persecutor would prevail, many collectors retreated into canny inactivity. The Minister for Local Government admitted after the Truce that collection had come 'very near the point of closing down but they never actually reached that point'. Ratepayers as well as collectors feared that both administrations would hold them liable, and suggestions were made in the Dáil that the Republic should abandon local government altogether and call for a rate strike.[38]

Instead the Clare County Council decided to take the offensive. Volunteers raided the recalcitrant collectors' homes early in February, seized the rate books and removed £8,013 in cash. Of nearly £108,000 warranted for the half-year ending 31 March 1921 a mere £882 had been lodged with the council's trustees. Though the old collectors were not immediately dismissed, their functions were taken over by the Volunteers and Republican Police—a procedure later followed in many other counties. A Dáil inspector commented: 'I don't know whether the Clare Scheme of Collection has had sanction of defence or not, but I think it is as well not [to] interfere now as the collection is a success.' In fact the success was partial, since £26,000 was still outstanding early in September 1921. In Mid-Clare as many as six of the fourteen Volunteer collectors had failed to deposit two-fifths of their warrant as late as 28 February 1922. Brennan attempted to explain the delay by this revealing argument: 'The Truce prevented the Army taking the necessary action to enforce the closing of the collection, hence the present situation.' Still more serious was the unmistakable failure of the collection of the first moiety for 1921–22. At Knoppogue Brennan warned that 'If any large number of ratepayers by delay or refusal to pay rates, render it impossible to maintain local services, the Council must disclaim responsibility.' Before long his worst fears were realised. Extensive recalcitrance by citizens faced both with rates raised by nearly a quarter and with agricultural recession led to fiscal chaos after the Truce. Not a penny had been collected by 3 September—an 'extremely serious state of affairs' in

William T. Cosgrave's opinion. Only after the council, the ministry and Colonel O'Callaghan-Westropp's powerful Clare Farmers' Association had compromised on 12 November did collection begin in earnest, never to be completed. The depositing of the rates was further inhibited by a sinister feud among the Volunteers charged with collecting them. The Mid-Clare collectors were sanctioned by the council only after threats that any others preferred to them would be shot, and peace between the brigades was only restored, for the time being, on 28 October. It was widely believed that a large part of the rates collected in Mid-Clare was never deposited with the council.[39] All in all, the financial state of local government, particularly in Clare, grew steadily worse during 1921, despite occasional interventions from the Dáil to pay outstandingly outstanding salaries in emergency.[40] To what extent did fiscal catastrophe disrupt routine administration during the revolutionary period?

Under the circumstances described it may seem odd that a serious attempt was made not only to conserve the rudiments of administration but to innovate and reform. One of the few unambiguous aspirations of the 'Democratic Programme' of January 1919 had been to abolish 'the present odious, degrading and foreign Poor Law System, substituting therefor a sympathetic native scheme for the care of the Nation's aged and infirm'. This aspiration was echoed by the Dáil's Local Government Commission in September 1920, though its motive was less respect for the aged and infirm than the belief that £50,000 annually could be saved by 'abolition and amalgamation of workhouses'. On 18 October a county conference chaired by P. J. O'Loghlen of Ballyvaughan approved amalgamation in principle, and early in 1920 a committee of inquiry started drawing up a scheme. This was drafted by June 1921, mainly by Fr Patrick Gaynor. Two of the seven workhouses were to be closed, another converted into a sanatorium and parts of four reconstituted as 'district hospitals'. The aged and infirm, chronic sufferers, sane epileptics and harmless lunatics were to be thrown together into a 'central home' in Ennis. Outdoor relief would be elevated into 'home assistance', with higher payments in cash instead of kind to be given to adults as well as children. When the report was discussed by the council immediately after the Truce it became clear that the proposals were more revolutionary than one might have supposed. The council hoped to dismiss without compensation the most influential and respectable of its employees— those with 'hundreds of pounds per year and plenty of land, etc.' As with several other county schemes previously put forward, furious objections were raised from many quarters—the County Council's solicitor, the District Clerks' Association, the Board of Guardians of one of the unions which was to lose its workhouse and attached sinecures yet pay higher rates towards the general good. (Its chairman, who eventually resigned in protest from the County Council and warned that loyalty to the Dáil had its limits, was P. J. O'Loghlen himself.) Worse still, the Dáil department refused to sanction the proposed dismissals, drawing forth another spirited response from Michael Brennan: 'Now with all due respect to Dail Eireann we will request our representatives [including Patrick Brennan] to get the people at present responsible for the working of that department removed from office, and get men in their stead who know how to do their work.' By 18 October the scheme had been revised and provisionally accepted, the provision being that the whole matter would be reviewed over the next year.[41] Amidst a flurry of dissension the thriftful initiatives of individual councils were gradually absorbed into the national consolidation and reduction of local government carried out in 1922 and after.

If revolutionary thrift stimulated imaginative planning, it also upset familiar routine. Yet in Clare the normal functions of the Boards of Guardians and RDCs were maintained to a surprising extent, as analysis of the Ennistymon bodies suggests. In October 1918 military occupation of the workhouse and institution had caused a premature and involuntary amalgamation of the union with its neighbours: lunatics, idiots, fit unemployed and unbedridden aged and infirm people were ejected. But in the infirmary the Guardians managed to keep a fairly constant number of patients from early 1919 to late 1921, and after August 1920 the distribution of outdoor relief actually increased. Prosaic civic functions such as street-cleaning suffered more. In October 1920 the medical officer protested 'that cows should not be allowed to be milked in the Lanes and Streets of Ennistymon. The Square at Ennistymon and Main St are not kept clean.' Despite RDC orders that cows be persuaded to change their habits, the town grew ever filthier, until after the Truce public collections were made to pay for a definitive clean-up. The vital operations of sanitary sub-officers were somewhat curtailed: from 1913 to mid-1920 they inspected on average 84 houses, yards and other premises each week, but in the second half of 1920 and the first of 1921 the average dropped to 49 and 64 respectively. Collection of rents for the cottages provided by the council for labourers also declined. During the revolutionary period the two rent-collectors lodged only 53 per cent and 42 per cent of the rents on time, whereas each had managed 71 per cent in the previous eighteen months. The ministry, appalled at this record, urged the council not to 'allow any of the tenants to take advantage of the existing conditions to evade their liabilities'. One old collector was understandably confused as to what authority was criticising his efforts:

> I wish to remind you that I was often before the Board ten or eleven years ago and will go there again if required so please let me know the date you intend bringing the case before the Board [sic]. . . . The quarterly collection nearly failed me owing not to be able to get a hired car to go on the roads in account of the danger of meeting with the Crown Forces, and trenches on the roads, its not so easy as you seem to imagine, its just enough for me to risk it quarterly.

Even after the Truce collections remained poor, and the same unfortunate collector was again denounced in the last quarter of 1921, at the end of which twenty-three of his seventy-three tenants were in arrears. But the orderly-minded Dubliners, had they known more about the traditional chaos of provincial administration, might have been less harsh. In March 1915 for example, 26 per cent of Ennistymon cottagers had been in arrears, and still more elsewhere (54 per cent over all Clare, 40 per cent over all Ireland). Arrears were consistently, but only moderately, higher during the revolution than in earlier years.⁴² With deteriorating efficiency, most officers of rural district bodies struggled through.

Preservation of the public roads, the major task of the county councils, was far trickier. Their maintenance was the object of most government grants and loans to the councils, and the withdrawal of these grants threatened disaster. On 1 November 1920 the Clare County Council decided to postpone all improvement schemes and purchase of plant and machinery, to patch lesser roads instead of sheeting them, to freeze the supply of flagged footpaths and to allow roads 'used almost exclusively by enemy forces' to fall into disrepair. Next month the county surveyor complained that quarrying had been undermined by the ban on explosives, contractors were 'more than usually behind' in their work, and the crusts of many roads were being seriously damaged by 'the very heavy military traffic'. The Direct Labour Scheme, under which most county roads were now built rather than by contract, was 'working as well as can be expected under very adverse circumstances'. By 28 February 1921, however, lack of money had forced the dismissal of all county road workers, and soon their supervisors too were suspended. Only the county surveyor and his staff still drew their pay—their main function now being to distribute unemployment benefits! Meanwhile unpaid contractors were growing restive. On 2 April the finance committee gave first priority to paying them out of the rates, even before district bodies had received their share. Then, a month later, enough rates had been collected to allow the resumption of quarrying (with less than a quarter of the workforce of November 1920), and of road work (with about half the old staff of overseers). Ambitious estimates were approved, by which expenditure on the roads was actually to exceed the unfulfilled estimates for 1920–21. But the Volunteers, in particular the chairman of the County Council, continued to trench the roads, and the enemy to break them up with its Crossley tenders. As the County Inspector remarked at the end of May, road obstruction was 'likely to ruin the tourist season this Summer'.⁴³ After the Truce tourism may have increased, but the financial mess persisted and restoration of the roads was slow to begin.

Yet, until the Civil War, the administrative chaos which had seemed just around the corner throughout the revolution did not take over. Civic services, however truncated, were maintained to a surprising degree. Brennan's administration precariously survived in a social no-man's-land, avoiding the ever more menacing salvos both of organised Labour, fighting to raise wages and maintain employment, and of the organised farmers and ratepayers, fighting to keep down rates and restrict wages and employment. Somehow, Brennan was able to win the respect of such unlikely figures as the old Unionist O'Callaghan-Westropp and the old Home Ruler and Labour leader, P. J. MacNamara.⁴⁴ The task of maintaining civic services and civic peace during the revolutionary years was daunting, but the raw Republican administrators tackled their task with dogged optimism and a contempt for lop-sided balance sheets which would have shocked their predecessors. Their successors can only marvel.

6

Guerrilla Fighters

> We, who seven years ago
> Talked of honour and of truth,
> Shriek with pleasure if we show
> The weasel's twist, the weasel's tooth.
> W. B. YEATS, 'Nineteen Hundred and Nineteen' (1921)

CONFUSIONS of name often betray confusions of identity. We have already touched upon the carelessness with which the terms 'Sinn Féin' and 'Dáil Éireann' were applied, in common usage, to county councils, courts and cattle-drives which owed little or nothing to their eponyms. Labels like these lost their traditional connotations, being attached instead to a loose, diverse assortment of objects which (for some reason) people wished to lump together. Sometimes, as in Home Rule days, a political label was used to confer respectability upon some factional enterprise badly in need of it. Sometimes, as in the months after the Easter Rising, misuse of an old label saved people the trouble of learning a new word to describe a new situation. Almost always, misuse of political terms reflected political reality more faithfully than their proper, historically authenticated use. The naming of the military arm of the revolution was no exception. Until 1922 it was called the 'Irish Volunteers', or 'Óglaigh na hÉireann', both in its constitution and in the military orders issued by its leaders. The official name asserted the continuity of its development from the bodies established in November 1913 and October 1914 (both of which had the same name in Irish), not to speak of their ancestor of the 1770s and 1780s. But because many of its members wished to carry on the very different tradition of Pádraic Pearse's 'Irish Republican Army' of April 1916, the latter term (less redolent but more resonant) gained increasing currency within the organisation. To their enemies the militant patriots were neither Volunteers nor IRA men, but 'Sinn Féiners'—a reasonable extension of the term, since in the provinces the two bodies were virtually identical in composition. Only in late 1920 did police reports begin regularly to echo Republican usage by referring to the exploits of the 'IRA', and by that time Sinn Féin was no longer an active or influential organisation. The revolutionary army had many names in common usage, and each expressed a facet of its essential character. In names and nature, it was a hybrid.

Above all, the relationship between the military and administrative arms of revolution, between 'Dáil Éireann' and the 'IRA', may be illuminated by the study of names. Civilian leaders in the Dáil used peculiar circumlocutions to describe the military. To de Valera, always a master of circumlocution, they were 'the voluntary military forces which are the foundation of the National Army'—a definition nicely blending reality and aspiration, November 1913 and April 1916. In August 1919 Cathal Brugha, Minister for Defence, formulated a similar definition, though his tongue was more obviously forked than de Valera's. He 'regarded the Irish Volunteers as a standing Army', and stated 'that as such they should be subject to the Government'. But the Volunteers were slow to subject themselves to the Republican government's authority, and the Dáil was slow to take responsibility for the actions of the Volunteers. Neither party was eager to formalise its bonds with the other, even to the extent of publicly renaming the Volunteers as the IRA. In the autumn of 1919 Volunteer representatives are said to have accepted Brugha's demand (backed by a large majority in the Dáil) that all members of the force should take an oath or affirmation of allegiance to the Dáil. But several brigades opposed the proposal: one urged that Volunteers should withdraw their allegiance if the Dáil 'demand or accept less than an Irish Republic', another if 'decreed by General Convention of the Irish Volunteers'. At last, in about March 1920, a ballot of brigade delegates rejected these riders, and four months later orders were issued to complete administration of the oath (or affirmation) by 31 August. But the majority of delegates still clung to their old label, with its independent connotations. They defeated a motion to rename their organisation with an Irish version of 'IRA'. The Dáil, for its part, was still more dilatory in admitting, or asserting, its responsibility for military actions. No doubt it was inhibited by the growing division between its Minister for Defence （*primus inter pares* in the general executive of the Volunteers) and the Volunteers' headquarters staff (which by 1921 had taken over practical direction of the force from the executive). Finally, in March 1921, the Dáil authorised de Valera to take 'full responsibility for all the operations of their Army'. Brugha was absent with influenza. On 30 March, after a year of unacknowledged guerrilla warfare, de Valera made a public statement in accordance with the Dáil's resolution.[1] Only the retention of the official name of the army suggested that the union of civil and administrative bodies might still be incomplete, that the army might not yet be the instrument of the government of the Republic.

The purpose of this chapter is to establish whether or not the Volunteers of 1919 can properly be described as 'a standing Army', and to what extent changes in the character of the organisation over the next two years justified the increasing currency of the term 'IRA'. Dáil declarations and Volunteer constitutional amendments alone cannot provide answers to these questions. It is also necessary to examine how the organisation worked in practice: the accountability of its local units to their headquarters; their relationship to the civil arms of the Republican movement; their ability to function, when required, as military units. For real soldiers do not merely swear allegiance to governments. They also obey their superior officers and know how to shoot.

1. AFTER THE RISING

The Irish Volunteers of 1919 had many of the strengths and the weaknesses of the pre-Rising bodies which had given them their name. Judged as a mass organisation of the traditional sort, densely organised in almost every rural parish, they were strong. In 1917 and 1918 the first aim of Volunteer organisers had been to enlist as many members as possible in the shortest possible time. This ideal was expressed by de Valera just after his election for East Clare:

> All Irishmen between the ages of 18 and 45 should join the Irish Volunteers; those under 18 should join the Fianna (Irish Boy Scouts) to be subsequently drafted into the Irish Volunteers. Men over 45 should join the political club; and the women the Cumann na mBan where they would be trained in first aid to assist the men as they did in Easter Week.

Voluntary service was never in fact universal, but it was remarkably extensive. By about March 1919 Mid-Clare, an area covering rather less than one-third of the county by population, had no less than thirty-one Volunteer companies with at least two officers already appointed, and four others still being organised. Roughly the same number of Sinn Féin clubs existed in the district. The size of these companies may be guessed from police reports. Although the RIC had long since lost track of those companies which chose to drill secretly, the Volunteers' policy during 1917–18 of selective open drilling enabled them to analyse the size and composition of a fair sample of Volunteer corps. Groups of eighty men or more were observed drilling in ten districts in Clare during the last two months of 1917, showing that many companies at this time were close to their nominal strength (120 men). In January 1918 the average size of the 27 Clare companies known to the police was 74, nearly twice that of the eleven companies of MacNeillite Volunteers reported in April 1916 (40). Throughout Munster similar increases in company size were reported over the same period: from 40 to 68 in Limerick, 58 to 92 in Kerry, 42 to 72 in Cork. After the Armistice the parade strength of many companies dropped sharply, but appears to have been restored roughly to its previous level by a vigorous organising campaign early in 1919.[2]

The parochial organisation of the boys' and women's auxiliary bodies was more spasmodic. In mid-1918 the Inspector-General reported that the Cumann na mBan appeared to be training 'Green Cross' nurses to tend the expected victims of conscription, though he suspected that 'the movement is possibly largely spectacular'. In Clare only nine branches with at most 339 members were reported by the police, but meetings of Republican women in as many as twenty-two villages are recorded in Clare newspapers during the two years after March 1917.[3] During the winter of 1917–18 policemen came upon young boys drilling illegally in seven districts in Clare. Usually they drilled with groups of older men, but in two villages they conducted their own practices, in groups of 35 and 37. Probably policemen seldom bothered chasing small bands of unaccompanied children in order to analyse their curious games. They seem to have noticed none of the four *sluaghta* (troops) which were formally established in the Ennistymon region before April 1918, with original rolls of 16, 20, 24 and 25 boys. In fact the Fianna Éireann, unlike the Republican women, suffered the indignity of not being declared either dangerous or illegal under the wide-ranging proclamations of 1918 and 1919. Their self-respect was constantly threatened, moreover, by the common practice—followed even by de Valera—of calling them 'Boy Scouts', a 'gross error'; as a notice published in the *Champion* protested, 'One might as well describe the Irish Volunteers as "Tommies", as dub the Fianna Eireann as "Boy Scouts".'⁴

As in pre-Rising days, the military movement was drawn eclectically from all sections of the youngish, male, Catholic community (with a sprinkling of sisters and very young brothers in the auxiliary forces). The only major change in the social composition of the Volunteer force since 1914 was the disappearance of certain kinds of traditional 'leaders'. The bellicosity and disloyalty of the new movement frightened off most of the Protestants, priests and shopkeepers who had associated themselves with the Volunteers in 1914. Moreover, their public participation was no longer encouraged. The old company committees of elderly, influential citizens were not reconstituted, and control of the companies was exercised unashamedly by young men, by drillers rather than fund-raisers. The influential citizens were consigned instead to the Sinn Féin clubs. The appointment of drill instructors and company officers seems to have aroused relatively little political interest in the parishes. Even before the Rising a MacNeillite Volunteer could justifiably write to the *Champion*: 'The Irish Volunteers do not give a rotten potato who leads or doesn't lead.' Company rank was a commodity freely dispensed among those with military skills or simply enthusiasm enough to spend their weekends bicycling about the parishes in search of recruits. When a parish produced more enthusiasts than company offices, the amoebic principle of dividing up into several companies was usually adopted. Indeed, few surviving organisers can remember the procedure by which they were appointed officers. In effect, they appointed themselves. Since headquarters exerted virtually no influence over parochial appointments, there was little reason to follow the official procedure (whereby the full company on parade was to elect its captain and two lieutenants, and the captain in council was to appoint squad and section commanders, if any).⁵

The young men who organised and drilled the Volunteer companies of 1917–19 were by no means typical of the force as a whole. As in 1914, immense respect was accorded the relatively few people who knew how to clean a rifle and march in a straight line. Just as most pre-war companies had been trained by army reservists, so most post-Rising companies were helped by army deserters, soldiers on leave, or demobs. In June 1918 Edward Lysaght noted the attention paid to 'British' soldiers home on furlough: 'Boys of military age, even prominent members of Sinn Féin clubs, do not boycott natives of their parish home on leave but foregather with them and listen with interest to their stories of modern warfare.' When demobilisation began, the Chief Secretary warned the war cabinet of the possible dangers involved in not finding jobs for the returning soldiers: 'In the present state of unrest it would be highly dangerous to have a large number of men standing about idle. . . . It is of the highest importance that everything should be done to let it be known that those who have done their duty are receiving proper assistance.' But parish and family pressure, together with the government's inability to provide the 'proper assistance', encouraged many old soldiers to react wildly to the strange conditions in which they suddenly found themselves. Some, as we have seen, allied themselves with the remaining adherents of the old Irish Parliamentary Party in the urban district councils, in the hope of improving their conditions of life by corporate action outside the serried ranks of Sinn Féin. Others became extreme Republicans, in the hope that the Republic would be kinder to them than the Castle had been. By the end of 1919 Colonel O'Callaghan-Westropp was convinced that the 'great mass' of demobs had been so disgusted by the government's errors that they were 'ready to throw in their lot with the Republicans where they have not done so already'.[6] The number who did so is difficult to determine, but in Clare at least many of the most efficient and reckless IRA fighting-men received their training in the Allied armies during the European war.

Apart from military training, several personal and social factors influenced the composition of the officer class of the revived Volunteers. The leaders, more than the men, tended to be in their twenties—neither young enough to be despised as mere adolescents, nor old enough to have lost their physical vigour or bachelorhood. A larger proportion of the leaders were men employed in the villages, where they were more readily available for consultation than farmers' boys, often isolated in inaccessible cottages. These distinctions are strikingly illustrated by statistics drawn from police reports and census returns (see Table 6.1). The officer class is represented by three categories with heavily overlapping membership, and the rank and file by those listed by the police as taking part in open drills during the winter of 1917–18. Further analysis of the background of the officers of the third category (those appointed in North Clare before about March 1919) suggests that many of them inherited attributes likely to win them social prestige in the countryside (always acutely conscious of fine gradations despite, perhaps because of, its apparent social homogeneity). No less than 65 per cent of those analysed were the eldest sons at home in 1911, though the average officer household had 3.5 sons. Moreover, a quarter of those officers with families on the land in 1911 came from the largest property in their townland—a region normally shared by a dozen or more occupiers—and a similar proportion came from sizeable farms of more than fifty statute acres. Thus a large proportion of the early Volunteer officers were men of social stature, if not necessarily political influence—prospective heads of families, likely inheritors of strong farms. Many of those who helped organise the post-Rising Volunteers might reasonably be termed 'natural leaders' of the younger part of their parish, men of the sort who captained football teams and attracted clusters at crossroads. They were probably of similar stock to those who became officers (though not committee men) in the 1914 Volunteers.

Up to 1919 the military organisation was strong in the parishes, but weak in its national direction. Like so many Irish political bodies, it was strongly resistant to interference from headquarters and deeply immersed from the first in parochial traditions and parochial loyalties. Reinvigoration of the movement after the military fiasco of Easter 1916 had been achieved not by men of national prominence, but by those obscure and provincial enough to be released early from their internment. In many cases their first instinct on returning home was to repair rather than initiate, to bring together whatever remained of their old

Table 6.1: Background of Volunteers, 1917–19[7]

	Sample	Age: % under 20	% 20–29	over 30	Sample	Occupation: % in shops or trades	% labour	farming
Officers 1	69	4	67	29	67	27	13	57
Officers 2	124	7	70	24	n.a.	n.a.	n.a.	n.a.
Officers 3	36	3	75	22	38	24	5	71
Rank and file	120	11	47	43	118	9	13	74

companies and await inspiration. When Art O'Donnell, a West Clare organiser, left Frongoch late in July 1916 he received no instructions from his superiors in the IRB or the Volunteers. But he and a few comrades set out, 'on our own', to revive their lapsed companies and recruit new members. They made no attempt to form new companies, get arms or demonstrate in public. In October an allegedly 'reliable source' told the police that the Volunteers were to be reorganised as an 'Irish Republican Army', that the old County Boards might be abolished and that the possibility was being discussed of swearing every Volunteer into the IRB. But next month the Inspector-General reported that this reorganisation seemed to have made little progress, for no County Inspector had referred to it. In fact it was probably not until November that Cathal Brugha and a temporary executive first attempted to re-establish contact between headquarters and the provinces. In Clare the first signs of reorganisation at county rather than parish level came in February 1917. A county brigade was established, consisting of eight battalions mainly led by members of the three families which were to dominate the revolution in Clare—the O'Donnells of Tullycrine, the Barretts of Darragh and the Brennans of Meelick Cross. But the erection of this imposing hierarchy probably drew forth as many knowing winks as respectful salutes. Observant Irishmen would not have forgotten the ludicrous schemes of May 1914, when the old soldiers of the Irish National Volunteers had divided their toy soldiers into elaborately supervised companies and battalions; or seven months later, when Pádraic Pearse had dreamed of squads, sections, centurion companies, battalions, brigades, pioneers, signallers, buglers, ambulancers, even courts martial.[8] In early 1917, as in 1914, the Volunteer executive manifestly had neither the resources nor the prestige to exercise close, hierarchical discipline over provincial Volunteers. The only vital unit of organisation was the company.

On 22 May 1917 the temporary executive issued a revealing instruction, which not only emphasised its own functional limitations but hinted at a factor tending to increase them. Volunteers were asked to accept orders only from 'their own Executive' and not to devote 'too much time or energy to any movement except their own'; yet headquarters found itself unable to offer in return any help in training or arming them, tasks for which each county was held responsible. During much of 1917, indeed, the Volunteer executive was engrossed as much in a futile competition with its rival, the IRB executive, as in improving its liaison with the provincial companies. The Volunteers pledged their members to 'implicitly obey' their superior officers; the IRB revised their constitution to provide for the expulsion of members joining any other oath-bound body. But judging from the acerbic recollections of several Clare organisers about the plottings of the IRB (of which they had formerly been active members), these Dublin faction-fights were treated with as much disdain locally as the squabbles of Liberty Leaguers, Sinn Féiners and Irish Nation Leaguers in the political sector. The apparent reconciliation of the two factions achieved at the Volunteer convention of November 1917, like the almost simultaneous assertion of solidarity at the Sinn Féin convention, merely emphasised the irrelevance of Dublin deviousness to the sturdy Republicanism of the provinces.[9] Local men took the lead in reorganisation. Headquarters, like a snappy and incontinent dog, waddled behind.

During 1918 and 1919, however, headquarters began to show greater adeptness at directing and supervising the Volunteers. They began to offer more and demand less. During the spring of 1918 the growing threat of conscription encouraged both headquarters and local units to seek a more effective liaison in case the Volunteers should have to resist the conscriptors by physical force. Early in March a businesslike headquarters staff, with Dick Mulcahy as Chief of Staff, took over effective administration of the force from the unwieldy, faction-ridden National Executive. Still more elaborate army hierarchies were devised, but now attempts were made to give substance to the dreams. Late in July the Chief Secretary was appalled to discover, after reading documents captured from arrested Volunteer leaders, that 'there was a complete military system existing in the South and West of Ireland—a military system which soldiers tell me was worked out with very considerable skill and knowledge, going from headquarters down to divisions and brigades and from regiments down to platoons'. During 1919 headquarters sent out organisers, including the desperate Ernie O'Malley, to put these plans into effect and give local men some notion of the rudiments of military organisation.[10] The hierarchical structure seemed no longer ludicrous, but merely incomplete.

The working partnership between headquarters and the provincial units was not achieved without some painful confrontations. Many local commanders continued to improvise and plan without consulting Dublin, as the Brennans had done with such dramatic effect in 1917 with their programme of open drilling and hunger-striking. In March 1918 Volunteers in West Cork infuriated Brugha by raiding a police barracks for carbines without seeking the National Executive's permission. Eleven months later the 3rd Tipperary Brigade, which had just inaugurated the campaign of ambushing and murdering policemen (again without instructions) at Soloheadbeg, proclaimed South Tipperary a 'military area' and threatened to kill all soldiers and policemen still there after a certain date. The brigade ignored Dublin's refusal to sanction its initiative, and Dublin found itself powerless to enforce its decision. The fragmentation of the Volunteers into fiercely independent armed bands, contemptuous of central direction, was always on the cards. Even in Ennis a small independent company was formed, which Dick Mulcahy's brother joined in February 1919, believing that it had headquarters' sanction. Significantly, a month passed before he learned from his sister, a nun, that an alternative official company existed.[11]

The manner in which headquarters learned to avert destructive confrontations is illustrated by its dealings with the Volunteers in Clare. Late in 1918 it decided to divide Volunteers in the county into three brigades instead of one. But in November Michael Collins wrote to Austin Stack:

> We are having a good deal of trouble with Clare. Will likely work it out harmoniously in the end. The matter arose on our suggestion of division of the Clare Brigade into three. At first [Patrick] Brennan was taking it alright and in fact Dick M[ulcahy] and I had agreed with him on the actual areas but in the course of a few days afterwards when we met him with some of his Bn Commandants he and [H. J.] Hunt wanted to foist a Divisional Staff before any such division of Brigades was carried through. Now I believe Brennan has the hell of a grievance against me but that won't make me expire. He has resigned and from the Ex. too.

Now this tripartite division was no mere Dublin whim. Headquarters, we may reasonably surmise, had realised that a single brigade was too small to contain three such ambitious families as the Barretts, Brennans and O'Donnells, and had therefore decided to give them one each. Its acceptance of the realities of local power was shown in the selection of commandant to replace Patrick Brennan in Clare, and later East Clare: first his brother Austin, then his brother Michael, who would, like Patrick, have preferred to reinforce Brennan supremacy in the county by erecting a divisional staff over the new brigades. Headquarters offered each influential family just enough to carry the day. Soon Michael Brennan, Frank Barrett and Art O'Donnell were installed as commandants in East, Mid- and West Clare respectively. 'After that', as one company captain recalled, 'there was a rapid improvement in the Volunteer movement in our district.'[12]

The few records which survive suggest that collaboration between Dublin and Clare grew increasingly intimate in the months after reorganisation. During July and August Michael Collins was able to offer Frank Barrett, in Mid-Clare, something more than friendly advice. Collins could make available grenades at 6s 6d or 7s each, and Barrett expressed 'the most profound confidence' in a mysterious Collins scheme 'respecting shops in Manchester and London'. At Collins's request, Barrett had a man from Meath 'connected up' as a company captain in his area, though he could not recommend still higher distinctions for a man from Offaly. On 26 August he sent Collins £16, said he was going on holidays soon (leaving his brother Joe in command) and hoped to visit Collins in Dublin.[13]

But collaboration was always restricted by the inability of headquarters to provide provincial brigades with arms more effective than hand grenades, coupled with its misgivings about provincial ploys for securing them at home. Once again, Michael Brennan's sense of initiative brought him in conflict with Dublin. In the late summer of 1919 he secretly arranged a 'general onslaught on the R.I.C. all over the Brigade for one night', but news of the scheme reached Mulcahy two days before the chosen night. Brennan accepted Mulcahy's countermand, but not his argument 'that the people had to be educated and led gently into open war and what I proposed doing might scare them off'. A few months later he raided the Limerick post office in order to get old-age pension money with which much-needed revolvers could be bought on the black market. He enraged the Dublin Brigade by 'spoiling the market' by offering high prices, and was again berated by Mulcahy for forcing the pace. But once again headquarters acted shrewdly, knowing its limitations. Michael Brennan was dismissed as commandant, but replaced by his brother Austin! His brigade was permitted to keep the stolen money and buy its revolvers after all. Some brigade officers wished to break away from Dublin's control, as another brigade had done, but Michael persuaded them to keep their side of a canny bargain.[14]

By the end of 1919 Volunteer headquarters had struck a fairly acceptable bargain with its provincial followers. Headquarters provided advice, instruction, a little equipment and a welcome sense of national togetherness. In return provincial units accepted the dismissal and appointment of commandants, provided the families of local influence were not seriously inconvenienced; and to some extent they modified their military activities to accord with headquarters' preferences. One necessary condition for describing the force as a 'standing army' was thus fulfilled: the Volunteers could justifiably claim to be a body standing upright rather than a mass of legs without a head. But in what sense did the Volunteers become 'subject to the Government', as Cathal Brugha thought a standing army should be? Did the history of the military–political relationship up to 1919 suggest that the Volunteers were an organisation likely to subject itself to a political authority? Or were the Volunteers likely to obey the Dáil only if the Dáil happened to be in accord with the Volunteers?

In the cities the military and political sectors of the Republican movement were clearly differentiated. Their relationship may be analysed in terms of the collision and collaboration of two distinct bodies, the Volunteers and Sinn Féin. Collisions were common. According to an honorary secretary of Sinn Féin, 'A keen rivalry in fact existed between the two organizations, many of the Volunteers despising the political movement, planning always to bring it to subservience.' In Cork City the Sinn Féin chairman complained bitterly to his diary at the success of MacCurtain's 'advanced' (Volunteer) faction in securing most of the plum Sinn Féin offices for themselves. But the advanced men's failure to win control of the Sinn Féin National Executive in October 1917 cheered him considerably: 'Our relations with Óglaigh are altogether better now and the position of our Executive [in Cork] is improved and strengthened and will be more so in a very short time when new elected Executive is formed. There is the inevitable "split" in Cumann na mBan, however.' The advanced men, on the other hand, became increasingly irritated at their inability to overwhelm the Sinn Féin organisation, with its archaic programme and obdurate adherence to the principle of passive resistance. In August 1918 Collins complained to Austin Stack: 'The Sinn Féin organisation lacks direction at the present moment.' Four months later Sinn Féin's Standing Committee was fighting hard to preserve its influence over the conduct of the Nationalist movement: 'It was the opinion of the meeting that while the taking of drastic action should be left to the Volunteers, there should be no action taken without reference to both Executives.' In May 1919 Collins deplored the moral-force men's success in excluding from the Standing Committee those who believed in 'the utility of fighting', and feared that 'official SF' was 'inclined to be even less militant and even more political theoretical' than before. On further reflection he added: 'There is I suppose the effect or tendency of all Revolutionary movements to divide themselves up into their component parts.'[15] The moral was clear: if the politicians would not accept revolution, the revolutionaries would have to bypass the politicians.

In the countryside the military–political dialogue took a different form. It was not so much a conflict of two organisations as a debate within the individual. Each parish might have its Sinn Féin club and Volunteer company, but in the early days of Republicanism membership of the two bodies was, as often as not, identical. Both were the product of the national mood after the Rising—undisciplined defiance. Outside the cities, as we have argued before, there was no widespread tradition either of passive resistance or of revolutionary conspiracy (traditions which in Dublin and Cork played vital parts in determining the distinct characteristics of Sinn Féin and the Volunteers respectively). Executives might debate the proper division of responsibility, but to parochial enthusiasts there was only one movement. During 1917 organisers repeatedly confused the functions of the two bodies at parish level. Austin Stack and Fionán Lynch in Kerry called on youths to join Sinn Féin clubs in order to receive military instruction. Even Eóin Mac Néill said: 'Every man should join a Sinn Féin Club and be a soldier and be prepared to act as a soldier.' Often clubs simply reformed into companies after meetings. Even where the two bodies were separate entities, each served the interests of the other. The clubs taught the Volunteers new slogans and prepared them mentally for the coming onslaught against the Saxon foe. The companies taught Sinn Féiners how to protect themselves against Irish Party thugs, and how to impress journalists with their discipline and good cheer.[16]

From the first, provincial Volunteers regarded Sinn Féin, like the Gaelic League, as useful in the role of teacher or servant, but in no sense an independent or competitive organisation. Ernie O'Malley has pinpointed the general attitude, though his particular reference is to his own company in Dublin: 'The men had little use for anyone who was not of the physical force belief. Gaelic Leaguers and members of Sinn Féin Clubs who did not belong to the Volunteers were sneered at. Most of the men had joined Sinn Féin and the Gaelic League.' In October 1917 the Clare prisoners at Mountjoy made their sense of organisational priorities clear. They published in the press an imperious recommendation that the Volunteer commandant, Patrick Brennan, should be appointed county representative on Sinn Féin's Árd-Chomhairle, emphasising the political supremacy of the Volunteers by attaching military ranks to their signatures. When the governing bodies of Sinn Féin and the Volunteers moved apart in 1918 and 1919, provincial Sinn Féin was doomed. Survivors recall that when life got 'too hot' the active Volunteers simply dropped out of their Sinn Féin clubs, leaving a few older, married men behind to uphold the doctrine of passive resistance. As one arrested Volunteer said at the end of 1918: 'I am not a member of the Sinn Fein organisation.... It is too constitutional. I believe there is nothing to be gained except by the pike.'[17] Scarcely any provincial Nationalist would have cared to argue with him.

Had the leaders of Dáil Éireann emulated those officers of Sinn Féin who actively opposed the policy of violent revolution, it is likely that they too would have been treated with contempt in the provinces. But they did not. Many of them were active Volunteers themselves. Almost all owed their election to the support of local Republican conventions strongly imbued with the violent ideals of Easter 1916. The Standing Committee of Sinn Féin, though it retained the power to sanction or refuse every local nomination, in practice interfered with the local choice only if several constituencies nominated the same candidate. The chance of conflict between the Volunteers and the Dáil ministry was reduced by the appointment of Michael Collins as Minister for Finance, the most vital post in the government. Unnecessary discussion by the Dáil of the manner in which the army was run was avoided. Whereas other departments submitted estimates and accounts to the Dáil and outlined their programmes, the Ministry of Defence was allocated one million dollars out of money raised in America and left to spend it when and how it wished.[18] By refraining from futile attempts to control or direct the military organisation, the Dáil was able to avoid a battle which it would almost certainly have lost. The Volunteers may have served the Dáil, but in so doing they served their own interests.

Clearly, the Irish Volunteers were rather a peculiar standing army in 1919. Local chiefs tolerated national chiefs—as long as they (local chiefs) were not unduly interfered with. The national chiefs tolerated their political counterparts—as long as they (national chiefs) were not unduly interfered with. All parties shared that keen instinct for maintaining the *status quo ante* which has coloured so many facets of modern Irish history. But before final judgment can be given upon the use of the phrase 'standing army', we must establish whether or not the Volunteers were an army at all. Did they have a programme of military action, or the weapons to carry out such a programme, or the know-how to make use of any such weapons?

The key-stone of the Volunteer programme was the promise of fighting the British. Without this promise, however long deferred, Irishmen could scarcely have been persuaded to resume the familiar and time-consuming routines of drilling, route-marching and sloping wooden guns. But the ignominious military failure of the Easter Rising had taught them that military programmes need something more than key-stones. The promise of a fight, without a careful strategy for winning it, was no longer attractive. In May 1916 General Maxwell accurately surmised 'that recent events have proved to the extremists that rebellion without ample arms and organisation cannot succeed'. Rational men such as Eóin Mac Néill and Bulmer Hobson had, of course, been saying this to the visionaries for years past. Pearse and his comrades, with visionary shrewdness, had perceived that only a bloody demonstration, however ill-conducted, could win over national support for the separatist ideal. But having attracted this support, even the visionaries (if any were still living) could have seen little sense in repeating the military errors of the Rising. In fact the hard-headed men who reorganised the Volunteers remembered with horror the callous and feeble attempts of Pearse's group to draw provincial Volunteers into a fight they could not win. The headquarters instructions which reached Michael Brennan a few days before Easter Sunday 1916 had been 'so vague as to be incomprehensible'. The Clare Brigade, at that time equipped with one service rifle, two revolvers, two or three .22 rifles and thirty shotguns, was to collect all the arms it needed from the shipment expected in Kerry. If this plan failed, the brigade was to 'capture' arms—presumably by raiding police barracks with shotguns. Brennan's main military task was to cut the half-dozen roads leading from Clare to Limerick. 'I couldn't even learn in which direction I was supposed to face— whether I was to prevent people getting in or getting out.' Was Clare to establish a Republican *enclave*, or was it to tempt the enemy into its lair and so relieve the pressure on Dublin? Nobody knew. Nevertheless, the Clare leaders had dutifully mobilised their little companies and awaited the call to action. After a rainy miserable weekend spent receiving countermands, nods and winks, they were told by the Limerick Provisional Committee of the Volunteers to call it off. Brennan tried to enter Galway to see if Liam Mellows had risen, but could not get in. He tried to enter Limerick to raise a force large enough to force entry into Galway, and was arrested. The Rising in Clare was over.[19] He, like many others, concluded not that the enemy forces were impregnable, but that the next rebellion should be guided by a more responsible, strategical sense.

After the Rising Volunteer organisers spoke in cautious tones. In May 1917 the temporary executive promised that they would 'not issue an order to take the field until they consider that the force is in a position to wage war on the enemy with a reasonable hope of success'. Before the East Clare by-election de Valera, too, felt that revolution would be justifiable 'under present circumstances' only if there were 'a good chance of success'. But his election evidently convinced him that circumstances had changed somewhat: 'This victory would show to the world that if Irishmen had only the ghost of a chance they would fight for the independence of Ireland and for an Irish Republic (*loud cheers*).' When the threat of conscription was revived in the spring of 1918, the 'ghost of a chance' almost revived with it. According to the propagandist Robert Brennan, 'The Volunteers in general were hoping that the British would go ahead with their conscription plans. They would have cheerfully faced a fight in which they would have the backing of the Irish people.' Rumours reached Brennan's ear that Collins and the conspirators were planning a Rising whatever the enemy's course of action. Brennan passed the news on to de Valera, who allegedly had a 'showdown' with Collins. But whatever its secret hopes, the face of Volunteer headquarters remained calm. Assistant Chief of Staff Mulcahy, sick with lumbago, received the staff in his bedroom. They decided to continue the prevailing policy of avoiding arrest, defending their arms but not provoking disorder.[20]

Improvement of their internal organisation remained their first priority. Unless their hand was forced by government belligerence or the collapse of Sinn Féin's political campaign, they were not prepared to risk revolution. Some hoped, some feared that these conditions would soon arise, but none dared take the initiative as long as they did not.

Remembering 1916, even the most sanguine conspirators were inhibited by their desperate lack of weaponry. The legal sources of arms had been progressively closed up during the European war. Using his ever-widening powers under the Defence of the Realm Acts, the Irish Competent Military Authority had banned the unauthorised sale, manufacture and importation of heavier firearms, ammunition and explosives in December 1914, of .22 miniature rifles and shotguns in November and December 1915, and of military parts in March 1916. Three months later he forbade the carrying of most sorts of weapons. Then in February 1918 he outlawed the 'carrying, having or keeping of Firearms' in Clare and two other districts (an order which applied to the entire country by October 1918). All these orders except the last seem to have been largely effective, and the acquisition of arms, even on the black market, was already difficult to arrange in Easter 1916. To make matters worse, a great many weapons were surrendered to the police immediately after the Rising, even by MacNeillite Volunteers. Of the 1,887 rifles believed by the RIC to have been in their hands on 31 March 1916 (outside the capital), only 902 remained eleven months later. Of these, twenty-four, according to police reports, belonged to Irish Volunteers in Co. Clare.[21] The recollections of surviving Clare Volunteers suggest that few, if any, rifles were kept without the knowledge of the RIC. During the 1918 conscription crisis many gunless companies took to arming themselves with pikes, more redolent of ancient Irish battles than the wooden rifles preferred by pre-war Volunteers. In one district pike-shafts were commissioned from the village blacksmith upon the surety of 'a very successful dance', and some laborious exercises took place. But pikes could not win the Republic. If more effective weapons were to be obtained, Volunteers would have either to import them illegally, or steal, capture or buy them on the sly. In wartime the secret ferrying of arms from American friends was unfeasible. Only a few soldiers home on furlough were prepared to barter away their rifles to Sinn Féiners. Shotguns, however, were easier to steal or buy (of the ten arms 'raids' conducted in Clare during March 1918, nine are said to have been conducted with the approval of their owners). By the end of 1918, 311 civilians had reported arms raids to the police throughout the country, and during 1919 another 191 raids were reported.[22] But without rifles the Volunteers could not pretend to be a real army. And how were unarmed Volunteers to set about disarming the policemen and soldiers who alone could replenish their supply of serviceable weapons?

Revolutionary planning was further inhibited by the difficulty of giving Volunteers a sound military training. Without rifles, they could not practise marksmanship; without enough expert instructors, they could not learn the theory of marksmanship; without a clear programme of action, even the best instructor could only guess at which form of instruction his men should be given. Yet without arms and trained men, how could the strategists devise a clear programme of action? In the early months of the Volunteer revival, it is true, this vicious circle did not trouble the strategists. Their aim was not so much to develop an army as to attract publicity. This they did with great aplomb. In October 1917, for instance, de Valera was welcomed in Kilrush by contingents of Volunteers, Cumann na mBan and Fianna Éireann from fifteen West Clare villages. All the men carried 'dummy rifles, hurleys or sticks', and one of them even had a genuine Lee-Enfield. They were accompanied by 150 cavalry, sporting Sinn Féin rosettes. De Valera examined his bodyguard of sixfooters and crooned: 'What could not a nation do with such men?' But in mid-1918, when the provocative policy of selective open drilling had been dropped, it became necessary to devise a form of drill with military point rather than dramatic point. The familiar patterns of close-order drilling, forming fours and sloping arms were all very well when the route-marchers could be dismissed in a public house, and when policemen stood about taking notes and villagers applauded. But in isolated fields in the late evening the same manoeuvres seemed all dull work and no glory. In 1919 the organiser Ernie O'Malley tried both to relieve the monotony and increase the aptness of training by substituting battalion field manoeuvres for company drill. As one of his students recalled, he 'told us to lie down, take cover and all that'. But O'Malley found it 'a difficult task' to revive enthusiasm for training among the Clare Volunteers: 'All day they worked hard at their farms or in the towns; when evening came there was an added task.'[23] Moreover, what was the point of training when one had nobody to impress, and (for the time being) nobody to fight?

Thus in 1919 the Irish Volunteers were singularly ill-prepared for revolution. Warlike talk kept their spirits up, arms raids provided diversion, drilling sessions kept them in close contact with each other; yet these activities served merely to preserve the organisation of the Volunteers, not to transform them into an army. For that transformation to be brought about, the familiar principles upon which the Volunteers had built their organisation would have to be abandoned. Miraculously, that is precisely what happened.

2. GUERRILLA WARFARE

'The Irish Volunteers, the Dáil, had drifted into a guerilla war, without conscious impulse. It just happened.' P. S. O'Hegarty's striking summary is a fairer analysis of the origins of the revolution than those which stress the foresight and manipulative skill of Collins, Mulcahy and the headquarters staff. In the drift towards guerrilla warfare, headquarters followed helplessly some distance behind its more adventurous provincial followers, unable either to catch up or to stop the drift. Its helplessness is illustrated by many articles in its journal, *An tÓglach*. Ernest Blythe's celebrated article 'Ruthless Warfare', held by some to have pointed out the strategy of the future as early as October 1918, specifically advocated fighting 'with utter ruthlessness and ferocity' only if conscription were imposed, which it was not. Certainly the journal hinted broadly at a wider application by republishing it just after the Armistice, but it was significantly slow to propose specific measures whereby Volunteers could demonstrate their ruthlessness. As shown in Chapter 1, it greeted the news of the first killings of policemen in January 1919 with singular caution and ambivalence—even though, as a clandestine journal, its candour was not constrained by the supervision of the press censor. In February 1919 it urged Volunteers to continue the 'state of war by every means at our disposal and in the most drastic actions', regardless of the ending of the conscription threat. But Volunteer officers, though asked to 'contemplate the possibilities of offensive as well as defensive action', were instructed to leave the choice of specific sorts of offensive action to the ministry. Advice from the ministry was seldom forthcoming. In March *An tÓglach* speculated that the Volunteers might not always be '"in the trenches". We may not be there for long.' In April 'The spirit of the Volunteers should be that of a hound straining at the leash.' In December it might 'not be very long before we are able to make a fresh "big push", and register a fresh advance'. A year had passed, yet *An tÓglach*'s incitements to offensive action were still phrased in the conditional mood. Only in February 1920 did its incitements emerge from the conditional into the indicative: 'To-day the Army of the Republic is certainly out of the trenches with a vengeance. . . . Volunteers must push on the War of Independence with ever-growing energy and enthusiasm.' Yet even then the actions which it so enthusiastically condoned had been committed without its prior advocacy. Small wonder that a few months later the journal was obliged to remind readers that 'G.H.Q. is not working in the dark.'[24] The great mass of provincial Volunteers had drifted imperturbably towards revolution, oblivious to the whistlings of their leaders, governed by the logic of local experience.

What factors governed the direction of the drift? For O'Hegarty, ardent devotee of passive resistance, the transition to violent revolution was the deplorable outcome of a double misjudgment: overreaction by the Volunteers to overreaction by the government to the actions of the Volunteers. In some cases (as Michael Brennan's account suggests) the actions of the more ingenious Volunteers were probably calculated to inspire government overreaction, since they realised that only by provoking government blunders could they hope to win passionate popular backing. But however clear some Republican minds may have been, the confusion of the Castle and cabinet was pitiably apparent in their attempts to suppress 'sedition' and 'disloyalty' among the Irish. We have already outlined the government's ceaseless vacillation between punitive severity, which not only failed to reduce disaffection but actually inflamed it by stimulating the Irishman's acute sense of indignation, and cautious conciliation, which bred contempt for government without bringing peace.[25] The government's growing though spasmodic severity was largely responsible for transforming the Volunteers into a force capable of focusing indignation into systematic military resistance. In the course of protecting themselves the Volunteers, willy-nilly, changed their shape and character.

The more the government hounded the Volunteers, the more like revolutionary soldiers they became. By driving them from their homes, it helped create a class of full-time rebels who could only hope to return to normal life, to their jobs and families, after British rule had been ended. By the spring of 1918 most Volunteers were convinced that a free man could do more for the cause of Irish freedom than a popular hero in jail. The rate of arrests for offences threatening the defence of the realm dropped sharply thereafter: 67 Claremen were imprisoned in the first third of 1918, but only 22 during the rest of that year. For 1919 the number of committals dropped to 14. In January 1919 Michael Brennan, free at last, met his old friend Seán Treacy from Tipperary:

> We came to one definite conclusion—that we had had more than enough of prison and that we were not going back there again. Next time an attempt was made to arrest us we would fight and consequently we would always be armed in future. Seán pointed out that this was in effect a declaration of war on the British Empire and he laughingly suggested an examination of our financial resources. The examination disclosed that I had 1s. 6d. and he had 4d.

Going 'on the run' to avoid arrest became commonplace. In May 1918 a Mid-Clare officer expressed shock at the arrest of a careless friend: 'If Poor J. J. only took advice from others and myself he'd never risk going into his own house, extremely dark nights such as last night.'[26]

But not every Volunteer could afford to take to the hills or leave his own house in order to fight the British Empire. As long as there were cows to milk, hay to save, and women to order about, the vast majority of Volunteers would have to remain part-timers, on the plains. Only a small minority could afford to become revolutionaries. During 1920 this minority became increasingly detached from the great body of enrolled Volunteers. Their detachment was recognised by the increasing currency of the terms 'flying column' and 'active service unit', terms borrowed from British military jargon. Formation of these units in each brigade area is said to have been recommended by headquarters in late August 1920 and ordered a month later. But in the preceding months small groups of wanted men had been coagulating and moving about together in several counties, without formal organisation or direction. In East Clare, according to Michael Brennan, 'No instruction of any sort to form a Flying Column ever reached us and in fact we ourselves did not consciously organise a column. It was a purely spontaneous development which arose directly from the prevailing conditions.' Early in 1920 the three or four most wanted men in East Clare were still wandering about on the run individually. But as the enemy multiplied and stepped up its pursuit, they began to band together, both for safety and for company. From mid-year Brennan had the sense of being part of a regular group, though not for another six months did the group become relatively stable, with twenty or thirty members at any given time. In other parts of Clare the columns were evidently slower to develop. In West Clare the column seems to have been formed in response to headquarters instructions. One man from each company was sent to a training camp at Tullycrine, where lectures were given on the 'rudiments' of column tactics and practices with miniature rifles were arranged. But the nascent column was shattered by an enemy raid. Although no trainees were captured, the alarmed brigade staff suspended training and temporarily disbanded the column. In Mid-Clare the brigade column was 'reorganised' on 6 January 1921, by which time there were thirty men prowling about the district, sometimes eluding, sometimes seeking out an elusive enemy. The brigade had no 'officer training school' of the sort inaugurated at Tullycrine, but on 29 April the commandant promised: 'I will at once go to work with a view to establishing a school.'[27] Headquarters issued increasingly sophisticated instructions for regimenting and training the columns, but their success arose not from Dublin blueprints but from the common interest of groups of fugitives in learning how to defend themselves effectively. This they learned by painful experience.

These small, embattled columns were far better suited to fighting a war than the vast, cumbersome Volunteer organisation out of which they had emerged. They had virtually all the rifles in their brigades, time enough for training, the incentive to develop military skills, and little chance to get bored with being revolutionaries. Separated from their home parishes, the column men were freed from the inhibiting influences of family, friends and priests. The dead weight of the Irish organisational tradition no longer threatened to crush them. Their obsession was to preserve themselves, not, as in the past, to preserve their organisation. They developed their own rules of life, scrounging from compliant farmers but living frugally. I know of only two cases of a column man seducing a compliant farmer's daughter. Even drink was approached with more than military discipline. In East Clare Michael Brennan's initial 'flat prohibition' failed, but his column submitted to a subtler form of tyranny: each man was allowed just two glasses, while the vice-commandant stood by and paid the bills. The petty cash book of the Active Service Unit, 5th Battalion, Mid-Clare Brigade, covering six weeks in mid-1921, tells a tale of exemplary self-denial: fourteen payments for cigarettes, four for shoes, soles and socks, two for clothing, one each for razors and 'Rangoon Oil'. Only one entry, for 23 June 1921, suggests relaxation: 'Refreshments 18.0.' With dedication and self-discipline the column men made themselves into formidable antagonists for the soldiers and policemen. They matured as fighting-men surprisingly fast. As Shaw Desmond wrote in 1923, 'What the leaders of the I.R.A. relied upon was the curious fact which the Great War had shown: that a first-class soldier able to hold his own with the flower of Continental troops, could be made within six months.'[28]

As the columns grew stronger, the parish companies grew weaker. Some fossilised, others changed their function. Often the company officers joined the local battalion or brigade column, only occasionally calling out their men to act as guides, scouts or sentries when the column decided to engage the enemy in the company district. Men might also be asked to trench or block roads, cut wires and perform other routine tasks of dislocation. Parades probably continued in many districts, but increasing enemy activity made them hazardous. Records of one company in Mid-Clare show that at least 14 parades were held between 8 February and 26 June 1920 (before the consolidation of the columns), with an average attendance of only 16 (ranging between 23 and 10). The effective strength of the company had shrunk to a fraction of its roll (72 in July 1921, for

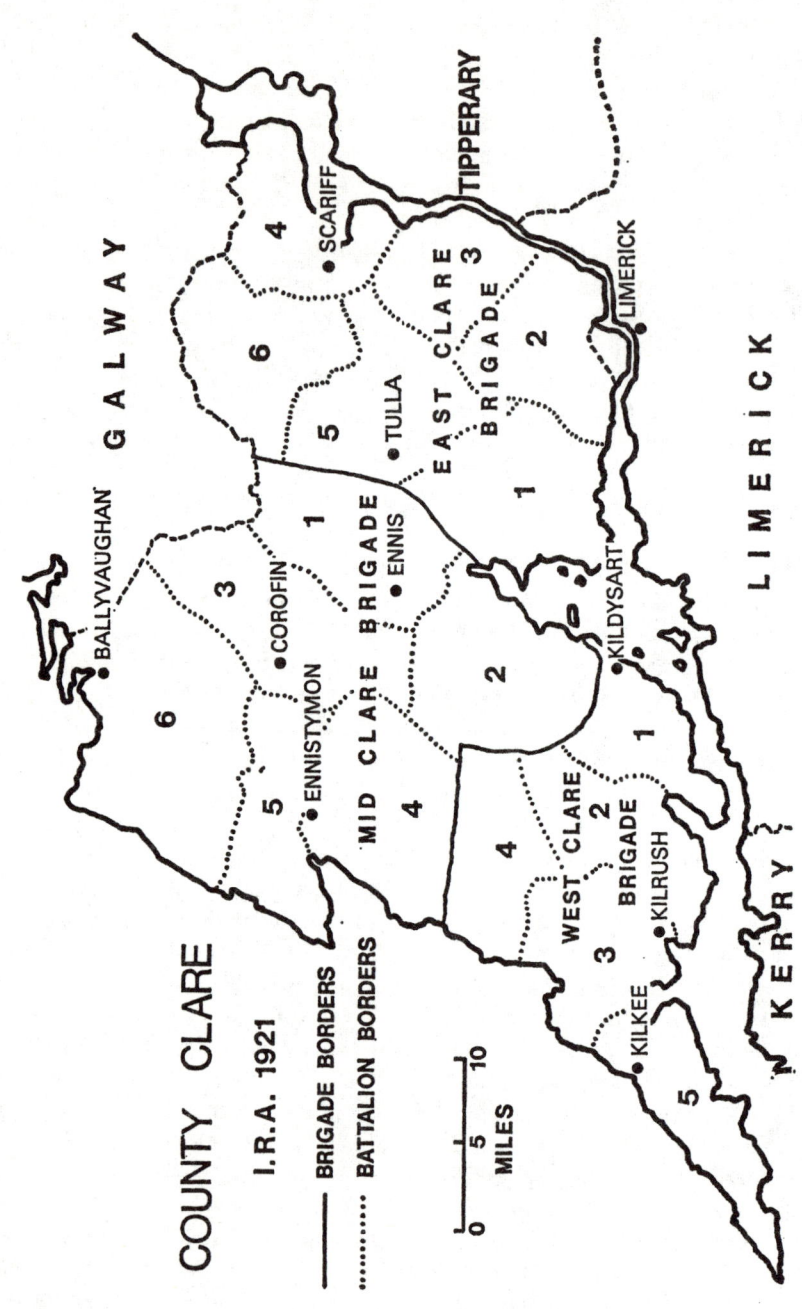

the ears of the Department of Pensions; 42 in May 1921, of whom 30 were considered 'reliable'; 52 in June 1921, according to the brigade roll book, not for the department's ears; 42 in about 1918, according to the company roll book). In the whole Mid-Clare Brigade area 974 men were considered reliable, according to the brigade book, on 1 May 1921—rather less than half the number which the Department of Pensions was told were active members of the IRA at the time of the Truce. The effect of enemy harassment was not merely to separate the fighting-men from the part-timers, but to separate the faithful part-time drillers from the drop-outs. It was also to separate town and country. Only in the countryside, or in the wilderness of the largest cities, could revolutionaries hope to elude their stubborn pursuers. In middle-sized towns such as Kilrush the condition of the Volunteers became pitiable:

> Although we were few we were very active and very effective in many ways. Actually we had no military activity. There was military in the workhouse. There were British marines over in Cappa. The Black and Tans were down here in Toler Street. And we were helpless if you like as a military organisation. We were meeting regularly though. The company would meet regularly below in the wood.

Ennis, the county town, was even more heavily populated with enemies. When Frank Barrett reported that on 31 March 1921 his men had gone to every village in Mid-Clare which had an 'enemy station' in the hope of finding enemies to attack, he had to add cryptically: 'For special reasons Ennis was not visited.' The few revolutionary engagements which took place in the towns were almost always the work of roving column men, who solicited little help from the townsmen. When an Ennis man did try to attack a police sergeant in April 1921, his performance demonstrated the unfitness of the townsman for guerrilla warfare. According to Frank Barrett, 'Our man took hold of his Sergts bicycle and followed for 30 yds. The revolver missed 6 times—hard luck.'[29]

As the complexion of the Volunteers changed, that of the boys' and women's auxiliaries changed also. There was more need for efficient signalling and first aid, less for parish meetings and pretty uniforms. Instead of passing resolutions, mothers and sisters served the cause by bringing out tea, griddle-bread, butter and bandages to the ambushers. Their methods of administering first aid were rough but effective. Republican women in the village of Lahinch were instructed to cleanse wounds 'by washing. If not possible scrape out dirt with scissors.' At another lecture they learned to 'inject Saline Solution if suffering from Shock through loss of blood. Rest and heat (hot water bottles etc) a cup of tea or coffee.' Formal organisation virtually collapsed. Two months after the Truce, meetings of the brigade councils of the Volunteers were told that only six branches of the Cumann na mBan were still organised in East Clare, two in Mid-Clare and none in West Clare. But elsewhere informal groups of women were active. As the Mid-Clare staff was told, 'Though unorganised in other areas they help the Army in the nature of cooking, clothing, and raising money.'[30]

The Fianna organisation suffered very much the same fate. Early in 1921 the Fianna was formally 'recognized as one of the units at the disposal of the

Republican Government'. Local organisers were placed directly under the command of Volunteer brigade commandants, and told to set up Fianna *sluaghta* (troops) in each company area. These *sluaghta* were to be trained by Volunteer section leaders until boys were ready to take them over. At eighteen years of age members of the Fianna were to be promoted to the Volunteers, unless needed to train the *sluaghta*. But these plans proved too ambitious. Most schoolboys could not be expected to play an active part in a bloody revolution. One young Republican from Mid-Clare has left an account of the critical change in character of his Fianna *sluagh* after the first local ambush. The captain 'addressed us for most of an hour and finished up by stating that it was too dangerous taking so many young boys together as the Tans might surprise us and shoot us down, so he was about to disband the slu for the time being anyway'. He then called aside the most frequent and punctual paraders, and offered them the choice of leaving the movement or reporting 'to the nearest Vol. we knew' for further instructions. Enthusiastic boys gave valuable help to the Volunteers, but increasingly as individuals rather than tightly organised *sluaghta*. They ran messages, signalled the approach of enemies, ran under policemen's feet where a grown man might have run into a pair of handcuffs. Very few were promoted to the Volunteers before the Civil War, probably because the tasks assigned them had always appealed more to small boys than self-important adolescents. By about August 1921, when a national survey was conducted of Fianna organisation, there were only two properly constituted *sluaghta*, with forty-four members, in East Clare, three in Mid-Clare (one of them being reorganised) and three in West Clare, with about thirty members.[31] The conditions of guerrilla warfare gave forth an increasingly informal army of revolutionaries: scouts without uniforms, nurses without green blouses, column men without caps.

What sorts of men comprised the new revolutionary elite, and how did they differ from the leaders of the 1917–19 Volunteer force? To answer this question we have examined two classes of Volunteer leaders in the Mid-Clare district. As representatives of the pre-revolutionary leadership we have taken those men with company, brigade or battalion rank as at March 1919. As representatives of those who came into prominence in the thick of revolution we have chosen men achieving these ranks between March 1919 and June 1921, provided that they still held office at the latter date. The turnover of officers was very high, because of arrests, dismissals, resignations, deaths, the collapse of certain companies, and possibly also the introduction of new procedures for the appointment of officers. Of 108 officers in the Mid-Clare Brigade in about March 1919, only 42 still held any ranking post in June 1921. It is true that a few of the new officers were not column men—some were merely stand-bys for more active men who had dropped their ranks when they went on the run. But most officers were at least intermittently column men, though many column men were not officers. Since no reliable list of regular column men can be drawn up, I have preferred to base my analysis on the authentic officer lists which have been miraculously preserved. Table 6.2 compares certain characteristics of the two groups. Though based on fairly small samples, these figures suggest that the

Table 6.2: Background of Volunteer Officers, 1919–21

	Pre-revolutionaries	Revolutionaries
Sample	38	31
Age as at	Mar. 1919	Jun. 1921
% under 20	3	23
% 20–29	75	61
% over 30	22	16
% eldest sons	65	38
% from farming households with largest holding in townland	25	10
Father's occupation:		
% farmers	71	65
% labourers	5	26
% in shops or trades	24	9
Size of parent's farm (if any):		
% under 20 acres	43	41
% 20–50 acres	32	45
% over 50 acres	24	13

revolutionary movement to some extent escaped from the 'natural leaders' of parish youth who had assumed command of the provincial Volunteers in 1917–19, just as the 1917–19 movement had escaped from the publicans and politicians of pre-war days. More of the new officers were youths rather than young men, sons of labourers rather than of shopkeepers, from medium-sized rather than large holdings. Fewer, too, were eldest sons—perhaps because eldest sons, as their fathers' actual or future legatees, were under greater family pressure to work at home rather than run off on column work. The new breed of officer was someone very like the representative young rural Irishman. For almost the first time in Irish history, revolutionary leadership had passed into the hands of men without any discernible social peculiarities or distinctions. As one battalion commandant told me (himself a labourer's son and according to Eóin O'Duffy 'the best Batt. Officer in the Brigade'), the Irish Revolution was one in which the boy might give orders to the boss.[32]

The character of the revolutionary war was largely determined by the peculiar circumstances of the life of a column man. The motive for almost every violent engagement can, indeed, be traced to one driving, self-preservative obsession: to get arms, and to use them to get more arms. This aim proved so difficult to realise that the revolutionaries were never able to bring about the widespread misery and chaos which one associates with more recent guerrilla campaigns. Despite wild newspaper stories of immense consignments of American arms, the number of weapons in Co. Clare was remarkably small. Even after the Truce, at the end of September 1921, there were only 158 rifles in the county in IRA hands: 73 in the east, 71 in Mid-Clare and 14 in the west. Of these 12 were miniatures, others not in service order, and all seriously short of ammunition. An additional 372 shotguns and 178 revolvers and automatics completed the armament of the Clare IRA. The arms cache of one company on the west coast was two shotguns, of which one was 'no good'. As the lieutenant recalled, 'Some of them big fellas that had them, they were against the organisation—which everyone of them was, though they were living well-to-do.'[33]

The desperate shortage of arms drove the column men to ever more ingenious expedients in order to get them. The old routine of raiding 'big fellas'—and even small and middling fellas—for shotguns continued throughout the revolution. In the four quarters of 1920 police throughout the country reported 204, 159, 2,307 and 132 raids against civilians, a much higher rate than in 1918 or 1919. But of far greater importance were the increasingly violent attempts to disarm soldiers and police. During 1918 and 1919 sporadic attempts were made to disarm individual policemen on patrol, with enough success to encourage men like Michael Brennan to try taking whole barracks by stealth or storm. Despite Dublin's interference with his plans for simultaneous raids upon all barracks in East Clare, Brennan took part in several attacks on police huts in July and August 1919. Bombs, service rifles and revolvers were used, and despite the failure of the attacks, Piaras Béaslaí considered them a turning-point in revolutionary history: 'It was really in Co. Clare that the guerilla warfare may be said to have started.' In response to these initiatives, as already explained, the police greatly strengthened their defences, whereupon the revolutionaries strengthened their attacks. As late as October 1920 thirty Volunteers, helped by a police informer, managed to take a barracks in Mid-Clare, winning fourteen sets of rifles, revolvers, bicycles and bayonets, 1,400 rounds of .303 ammunition and other priceless armaments. But as the barracks grew less and less vulnerable, the column men were forced to ambush heavily armed enemy parties in order to swell their arms cache. Considering the violence of many of these ambushes, one is amazed at the meagreness not only of their military yield but also of the military outlay involved. The dramatic Rineen ambush of September 1920 was mounted with eight rifles (one inoperative) and sixty rounds of ammunition. Six enemies were killed, but only five rifles and a thousand rounds were captured! During the entire year ending April 1921 Michael Brennan's very active column spent only 2,850 rounds, of which 600 were evidently captured by the enemy.[34]

If wars were won and lost by fighting, the Irish war, like most others, should have been ruled a draw by repetition of moves. Each side parried the other but could make no decisive thrust. The military futility of the revolution may be judged from figures in Table 6.3, showing the military activity in the Mid-Clare Brigade area early in 1921, the blackest period of all. As fast as the roads were cut they were cleared, and cut again—often by the same people under different direction. Interminably, the columns lay in wait beside empty roads; interminably, the Crown forces ransacked or raided houses empty of column men. Between November 1920 and June 1921 Mid-Clare Volunteers set at least 144 traps for the enemy, but on 130 occasions they failed to get so much as a clear sight of their quarry. Only seven times did they draw blood. Neither side could glean enough accurate intelligence about the other to lay its traps effectively. Both sides were virtually impregnable. Volunteers still raided the mails (on twenty-six days between March and June 1921 in Mid-Clare) and cut telegraph wires (on nine days), but all important official messages were now dispatched by Crossley tender. Deaths were comparatively sparse. In Clare about thirty-seven policemen, nine soldiers and six Volunteers were killed as a result of engagements during the entire pre-Truce period. Six Volunteers were killed accidentally, five civilians shot for informing and thirty others killed by government forces in reprisals or as a result of breaching extraordinary military restrictions.[35] Except perhaps in Cork, the Irish Revolution had come to an uneasy military standstill by mid-1921. If the military madness of 1916 had awakened Nationalist Ireland, the military madness of 1920–21 left her tired yet incapable of sleep.

Table 6.3: IRA Engagements, 1921

No. of days when:	Roads cut by IRA	Roads cleared by Crown forces	Attacks planned against Crown forces	Attacks made against Crown forces
April 1921	4	6	14	3
May 1921	14	13	11	4
June 1921	16	11	22	2

Both headquarters and the provincial brigades showed signs of frustration and puzzlement early in 1921. After examining the brigade diary from which my figures for military activity in April 1921 were calculated, Dick Mulcahy (Chief of Staff) wrote to Frank Barrett:

> To me they indicate the absence of practically any military intelligence or technique. On the Volunteer side it shows constant watching for the Enemy in a district in which there is almost daily activity on the part of the latter, yet contact with the Enemy is only established on three days in the month. . . . It would be a disastrous thing if at a time when there is so much real development practically throughout the whole country if there should be found in the heart of Clare anything like stagnation or inefficiency with the resultant discontent.

Probably Mulcahy had been deceived. Other more inefficient brigades may well have been less frank in their diary reports. Barrett replied that there was no fear of demoralisation, as the men 'feel and know exactly the position in which they have placed the enemy'. Having driven the enemy into a corner, he could think of no new way of luring it out. Only a few weeks earlier (on 4 April 1921) he had issued a remarkable set of instructions to his brigade council:

(a) attack the enemy everywhere at all times.
(b) to make every effort to destroy himself, his agents, his transport, and his communications and supplies everywhere.
(c) armed or unarmed; on duty or off duty he is not to be allowed escape.
(d) in no stronghold, in no post, in no street or road is he to pass unchallenged.[36]

The results of the campaign which followed, conscientiously executed though it was, were negligible. Headquarters, drunk with its own propaganda, was asking for what was impossible.

By this time headquarters' supervision of provincial brigades was probably closer and more systematic than ever before (however wrong-headed some of its advice may have been). Inspectors, strategists and statisticians multiplied. Copies of the training magazine, An tÓglach, were widely distributed: Frank Barrett put in a regular order for 200 copies for his brigade in mid-1920. Occasionally headquarters even provided a little ammunition: 500 rounds reached Michael Brennan's column before April 1921. In order to tighten central control, Dublin began early in 1921 to cap the already top-heavy army hierarchy by establishing divisions, covering about two counties each. Their commandants, carefully chosen from among Dick Mulcahy's closest associates, were warned to tread carefully: 'It is important to develop initiative amongst subordinate Officers. Hence your work is rather to direct action than to undertake it.'[37] At first glance one might suppose that the Volunteers were being steadily consolidated into a centralised and disciplined, if not very effective, national army.

But in the moonlit world of the flying columns, central authority and the national interest cut far more shadowy figures than appreciative students of the Mulcahy Papers might suppose. The more fugitive, isolated and self-dependent the columns became, the harder it was for any outsider to influence their conduct, however high his rank. Analysis of the revolutionary army in Clare suggests that each knot of fighters guarded its territory, secrets and rifles with fierce jealousy against any intruder. Examples from all three brigade areas in Clare should suggest the intensity of the local and personal rivalries which bedevilled the Irish revolutionary movement long before Truce, Treaty or Civil War:

(1) A battalion commandant was sent into a neighbouring district to help arrange an ambush. He was ordered out by the local commandant. He proceeded with the ambush without local help, but the attack was unsuccessful.

(2) A commandant recently installed by a headquarters' inspector arranged with a neighbouring commandant that the latter should attack a military patrol if it entered his territory. The patrol came, but no Volunteers were there to destroy it.

(3) One brigade column 'did not at any time go west of K——. A Free Republic on the best Central American lines functioned here from the end of 1920.'

(4) 'Some wanted men decided to move into some more active areas' after a planned engagement in a quiet district had been called off by the local brigade commandant.

(5) A battalion commandant and his staff quarrelled with their brigade officers, left the area to join another brigade column, and left their battalion 'unorganised for 1½ years'.

The reader need not be surprised that Michael Brennan, commandant-elect of the 1st Western Division, was unable to take up his full command before the Truce. As he wrote later, 'There had been a certain amount of friction for years between the staff of the Mid-Clare Brigade and East Clare, and I was directed that for the present I was not to assume command over the Mid-Clare Brigade.'[38] In the very months that the Dublin publicists were trumpeting most boldly the theme of Republican unity in face of the Terror, the Irish Republican Army was divided and fragmented to an astonishing degree.

Nevertheless, until the Truce the IRA managed to present to the outside world a fairly united front. Despite their internal rivalries and military frustrations, many Volunteers played a noteworthy part in the constructive and conservative work of the revolution. They not only policed courts and manned local government bodies, but also collected money and promoted 'Irish Ireland' causes. When the prospectus of the Dáil's internal loan was being printed Michael Collins was told by Terence MacSwiney of Cork: 'Our reliance is almost entirely on Volunteers for distribution of literature and canvassing.' Early in 1920 the Mid-Clare Brigade urged the proposed Volunteer convention to bind the force not only 'to support goods produced and manufactured in Ireland, but also to encourage the support of such goods amongst all classes of the community and to discourage by every means in their power, the importation to and sale and purchase of all foreign goods in Ireland'.[39] Volunteers in the countryside pursued revolution almost as much by persuasion as by firing guns.

But no constructive programme can coexist in perfect harmony with a programme of destruction. Sometimes it was simple blood-lust which struck discord in the revolutionary movement, the lust which one hunger-striker set down in May 1920: 'Had we more men like James Ledden [of Limerick] we would now have our Republic but personally I would be sorry if I did enjoy it without a fight.' But it was not the motives, but the consequences of guerrilla warfare which did most damage to the constructive programme—the ever more terrible social disruption wrought by each side in its effort to protect itself against the other. As Fr Gaynor put it, 'I can say from experience that those who had the task of helping Dáil Éireann to function in the civil administration of the country were hampered by the "war of freedom" because it gave free scope to British terrorism.' In fact it was the Republicans as much as the British who hampered civil administration. The massive disruption of mails, for example, may have helped military intelligence, but it also made life less pleasant for civilians. In the four quarters of 1920 mails throughout Ireland were raided 20, 77, 487 and 425 times, nearly half of them in Munster. A total of 376 raids occurred in the first quarter of 1921, and no fewer than 1,179 in the second. As a result of the 89 raids in Co. Clare between May and December 1920, of which 49 involved mail cars, at least sixteen mail-car services had to be suspended. As a Post Office official explained to the Under-Secretary, such stoppages had serious results, involving 'in addition to the stoppage of the usual Postal, Money Order and Savings Bank &c. facilities, the cessation of payments of Old Age Pensions, Army and Navy allowances and National School Teachers' Warrants'. Even more inconvenient was the destruction of road surfaces. As Michael Brennan told the Chief of Staff on 29 April 1921, this was essential if the columns were to be saved from encirclement. A few weeks later the brigade adjutant in West Clare reported: 'The breaking of roads and bridges have been effectively systematised. Enemy repairs of same [are] rendered ineffective as soon as his back is turned.' Attempts were made to trench the roads so that donkeys and carts but not Crossley tenders could pass, but the farmer's life was vastly complicated. Frank Barrett in Mid-Clare admitted: 'Of course people have to travel considerably longer distances and at much trouble and disadvantage both to themselves and their means of transport. However, as far as I can ascertain they see the matter in the proper light and accept the consequences in a grand spirit.' One who did not was Colonel O'Callaghan-Westropp, who had written a few days earlier (30 March 1921): 'We have no regular posts now, in consequence of raids on mails, and no telegrams as the wires are down; most of the bridges have been blown up, and the roads are a horror!' Loyal men despaired. In May 1921 the County Inspector, RIC, reported: 'Now that they [the Volunteers] realise they cannot get control of the country, [they intend] to wreck it to such an extent that it will not be capable of paying its way as an Imperial unit.'[40]

By mid-1921 the IRA had reached an *impasse*. Despite its vast improvement as a fighting force since the days of close-order drilling after Sunday Mass, it was too poorly armed to have much hope of dislodging the enemy from his heavily fortified strongholds. Despite the growing organisational energy of headquarters, the flying columns had become little more than fragmented bands of armed men intent on defending themselves against all outsiders. Despite Volunteer co-operation in the tasks of Republican administration, military necessity was tearing that administration to pieces. But the opposing forces, and the government behind them, had also reached an *impasse*. On 11 July 1921 both sides acknowledged defeat by agreeing to a Truce.

In the year which followed the Truce the underlying weaknesses of the IRA's organisation were gradually revealed. On the surface the administration of the force was polished and improved in the first months of peace. The number of active Volunteers multiplied the instant fighting finished. By September, according to the County Inspector of police, it was 'exceptional to find a young man who does not belong to the "I.R.A."'. The brigade council in Mid-Clare defeated a motion to admit no further Volunteers after 12 July, and by the end of November 2,000 men were enrolled in the brigade, of whom 1,879 turned out on parade to welcome President de Valera. Six months earlier scarcely half as many men had been considered reliable Volunteers, and less than 1,500 men of all degrees of reliability had been on the brigade rolls. Branches of the Cumann na mBan and Fianna Éireann multiplied.[41] Inspectors buzzed about underdeveloped and rebellious battalion areas, reshaping companies, replacing officers and setting up special services. Attempts were made in September 1921 to put the IRA on a 'regular basis'. In the provinces the Volunteers ruled with increasing disdain for all unmilitary authorities. On 21 November Patrick Brennan reproved Frank Barrett for having 'insinuated that until such time as peace comes the Volunteers are to be masters of the situation'. He urged civilians to report complaints about Volunteer conduct to the 'civil authority', but had to add that they should contact the Home Office, Mansion House Dublin, 'if they do not know who the civil authorities are'. A few weeks earlier Barretts and Brennans had at last been reconciled to coexistence in a division commanded by Michael Brennan. But the unity and discipline of the post-Truce Volunteers were fragile. On the first day of the Truce Michael Brennan had denounced the noisy new patriots:

> 'Get a good brick,' said the Chairman [of the County Council], with a characteristic touch of humour, 'and hit on the head anybody who is trying to cause disturbance, especially the people who kept behind the door and under the bed while the war was on. . . . If hostilities are resumed I will call on all those flag-waggers to make good their boasts and come with me.'[42]

In the succeeding months ill-feeling increased between the fighters and the flag-waggers. Moreover, serious disputes continually came between the various factions of fighters, despite their apparent absorption into a single division. But the unsavoury history of the renaming of those factions as Republicans and Free Staters, of the elevation of territorial jealousy into high-minded principle, and of the civil war which pitted column against column, must await examination by some other student of Chaos.

7

Separatism and Social Change

Parnell came down the road, he said to a cheering man:
Ireland shall get her freedom, and you still break stone.

W. B. YEATS, 'Parnell' (1938)

IF revolutions are what happen to wheels, then Ireland underwent revolution between 1916 and 1922. In the tumultuous years after the Easter Rising its major social and political institutions were turned upside down, only to revert to full circle upon the establishment of the Irish Free State. Sinn Féin displaced the Irish Parliamentary Party as the mouthpiece of Irish Nationalist aspirations; Dáil Éireann displaced the imperial parliament as the chief forum for Nationalist debate; Republican courts superseded the traditional judicial system in many of its functions; local government bodies transferred their allegiance from the Castle's Local Government Board to the Dáil's Local Government Department. Yet once the revolutionaries had completed the revendication of three-quarters of their country, those satisfied with the terms of the Treaty proceeded ostentatiously to imitate the institutions which they had worked so conscientiously to overturn. The local authorities were amalgamated and placed under central control as stringent as any exercised by Sir Henry Robinson's board; the courts were dissolved and replaced by a system almost indistinguishable from its pre-revolutionary predecessor; the Dáil was supplied with standing orders and the rudiments of an opposition on the Westminster model. Sinn Féin fragmented and collapsed, and even the Irish Republican Army, the most effective instrument of the revolution, achieved respectability when much of it was transformed into the Irish army. After the Treaty the search for respectability displaced revolutionary enthusiasm; imitation drove out imagination; the solemn trappings of familiar institutions enveloped and began to stifle the iconoclasts.

During the next half-century (except in six counties conveniently stowed away in the north-eastern corner) traditionalism and respectability consolidated their triumph. Despite the disorder created by the Civil War of 1922–23 and sporadic terrorism thereafter, successive Irish governments were remarkably successful in restricting social and institutional change. It is scarcely surprising that many half-stifled iconoclasts looked back upon the revolutionary period as one when chances of radical change had been created, only to be squandered. Surely the Republican rank and file, fired by unprecedented enthusiasm, had been edging towards social revolution, only to be hauled back to respectability by the conservatism or cowardice of their leaders? The iconoclasts' interpretation was shared by many men of substance, astonished by the Free State's skill in quelling what seemed to them social anarchy redolent of Bolshevism, delighted and surprised by their own unexpected retention of power and property. Grateful men of substance and frustrated revolutionaries alike believed that the revolutionary experience had generated a strong popular impulse towards radical social change. If this were so, then the Irish struggle might properly be counted among the second rank of social revolutions, the glorious failures (or providential abortions). In conclusion we shall analyse the grounds of this belief, and the extent to which pre-Treaty Republicanism influenced, and was influenced by, any popular impulse towards radical change.

Our analysis of the Republican movement has already pointed out certain flaws in the argument that this movement contained a thwarted drive towards social revolution. Even in the wildest days of revolution the iconoclastic spirit was considerably weaker than the *Irish Bulletin* and the nostalgic Nationalist historians suggest. The revolutionary institutions retained much in common with the traditional institutions of Irish Nationalism and British administration which they supplanted. Sinn Féin inherited much of the style and character of the Irish Parliamentary Party and its auxiliaries, being a loosely organised mass movement seeking support from a national consensus. The IRA was constructed with the help of British army manuals and instructors, and entered its guerrilla campaign with the improbable burden of an order of battle almost indistinguishable from its opponent's. Even before the Truce, the clandestine courts and councils of the Republic attempted with comical solemnity to reproduce the familiar rituals of their British counterparts. Dáil Éireann, from its very first meeting, deliberately gave the impression of being an imitation House of Commons. The separatist movement absorbed not only much of the panoply of the old order, but also clerks and officials who had served the rival administration, and organisers and publicists who had learned their Nationalism in the Home Rule movement. Far from breaking violently with tradition, the post-Rising separatists put their political education to good use and showed little inclination to experiment with novel institutional forms. The administrative reorganisation which followed the Treaty merely pointed out in plain language a traditionalism and underlying respect for the familiar which the Republican institutions had never lost. Those institutions had not been designed by iconoclasts but by ingenious copyists, and were singularly ill-suited to carrying out programmes of radical reform.

Furthermore, the informal conduct of Republicanism was in many respects as familiar and unradical as the form of its institutions. It is true that the respectable façades of many institutions concealed wild and utterly improper goings-on: solemn courts became the tools of local factions, rates were scrupulously collected only to pay for arms and ammunition rather than the mending of roads, Volunteer officers (knowing the fragility of the IRA's hierarchical structure) paid scant respect to the wishes of their 'superiors' in the 'order of battle'. But even in these clandestine improprieties continuity with Irish tradition may in many cases be discerned. The factions which exploited the courts, grabbed the rates and dominated Volunteer companies resembled to a remarkable degree the factions which had once burned haystacks, boycotted shopkeepers or landlords and dominated local politics under the Home Rule banner. Ultimately it was the alignment of local factions, not the form of Nationalist institutions, which determined what influence (if any) social radicalism would exert upon the separatist movement.

Radical separatist leaders were no more capable of creating social revolution than traditionalist leaders were capable of suppressing it, unless they could command massive support at local level. Study of the Irish Revolution at local level provides us with a sensitive instrument for measuring the power of Irish social radicalism, for the revolutionaries were the prisoners, not the manipulators, of the society in which they lived.

The Republican movement itself provided the forum for many of those countless factional disputes over land-ownership and occupation which merely carried on the patterns of pre-revolutionary rural social life. Familiar patterns inevitably imprinted themselves upon every institution purporting to serve the interests of every social section, whether those institutions were Republican, Home Rule or instruments of government. Unfamiliar patterns of social agitation, on the other hand, could not hope to imprint themselves upon existing institutions unless independent organisations were created to give them public expression. Social radicals, unlike agrarian faction-fighters, had publicly to demonstrate their corporate power before they could hope to wield social influence. If we define 'social radicals' as those seeking to alter the status and degree of respect popularly accorded a particular section of society, then the radical's task is nothing less than to revise the underlying assumptions of communal life. During the revolutionary period only one social section attempted this task—Labour. The post-Rising Labour movement was radical because, far from begging governments or men of property to raise the labourer's status in the traditional fashion, by granting him land, it arrogantly asserted that the landless worker, as chief producer of the nation's wealth, was a superior person in his own right. Whereas the would-be peasant proprietor sought no more than legal recognition (in the form of ownership) of his already high social status (secured by his occupation of land), the modern Labour agitator sought to raise his social standing by compelling employers to grant him higher wages and more comfortable conditions of life. The rise of Labour provoked an equally novel response among those whose interests and sense of self-importance it threatened most—the farming class. Farmers, first swollen by unaccustomed wartime prosperity, then menaced by post-war recession and by the mounting demands of men without property, organised themselves in defensive alliance to protect their wealth and social status. Their growing sense of class solidarity was manifested in the remarkable spread of the Irish Farmers' Union, just as Labour's class sense was manifested in the spread of the Irish Transport and General Workers' Union and the Trades and Labour Councils. Thus two unfamiliar strands of social struggle were woven into the revolutionary fabric, embodying Labour's radical urge and the farmer's conservative resurgence, confronting each other and impinging upon organised Republicanism. Let us first examine Labour's radical urge, its aims and its impact.

1. LABOUR AND THE RADICAL URGE

Before the European war the social aspirations of the provincial Irish labourer were modest enough. On 31 December 1912 five hundred Clare people followed the band of the United Labourers' Association to St Flannan's Cathedral, Ennis, to the strains of 'Adeste Fideles' and 'A Nation Once Again'. The *Clare Champion* found it 'a truly edifying sight to witness the poor labourers—God's poor—after their hard day's toil outside the House of their Lord thanking Him for the many blessings He had bestowed on them during the old year, and praying for a continuation of His guidance and help.' True, the Lord's help was not always forthcoming, and a year later an Ennis Labour leader invited his audience to count not their blessings but their privations. While 'every one' of 'the working classes of people' (except in Ennis, Shalee and Kilnamona) were 'doing their best to elevate their position in life, to have a comfortable home, motor cars to drive around in, and a lounge to rest on while reading their papers, and have all the luxury that Providence can bestow on them', Ennis labourers were condemned 'to stay in the mire trying to eke out a living out of a wage that is hardly able to keep us alive, and those people fatten and grow rich out of our labour'. In his indignation the speaker revealed a certain confusion of mind, for the very aspirations which he found so deplorable among 'those people' at the end of his sentence were those which, at the beginning, he had ascribed to 'every one' of his fellow-workers. Disgust at the rich man's fatness was blended with the envious desire to grow fat in one's turn. The meeting ended quietly with another performance of 'A Nation Once Again', but on this occasion, doubtless in response to the Almighty's discrimination against the labourers of Ennis, Shalee and Kilnamona in His bestowal of lounges and newspapers, the band desisted from 'Adeste Fideles'. These two reports epitomise the mood of pre-war provincial Labour, never defiant, never proud, alternating between pleadings for a fair deal and gratitude when it was offered. Before the war a fair deal cost the employer little, since the labourer's expectations were low, and paternalist employers with intensely loyal and grateful labour forces were not uncommon. When, for instance, the benevolent nurseryman Edward Lysaght returned with his new wife to Raheen, he was presented by his twenty-seven employees with both a teapot and a coffeepot, and informed that he was 'an ideal Christian master. You have treated those under you kindly and justly and you have come to their aid like an indulgent father in their trials and troubles.'[1]

The labourer's relationship with government was no less subordinate. He was disfranchised, with few public spokesmen, and dependent on goodwill. From a great height the Department of Agriculture beamed down, bestowing frugal and improving benefits upon the farm labourer: seeds and plants, shrubs and trees, at wholesale prices, carriage free; domestic economy classes where his 'wife and daughter can learn how to cook and use the vegetables and to preserve the fruit they have learned to grow' with the departmental instructor's help; ploughing matches, hedging, ditching, rick-making competitions; and, above all, clean cottages at low rents, often set in half-acre plots where labourer could play farmer. 'In contemplating', wrote a departmental pamphleteer, 'this paternal system, and the country labourer in the midst of it, living his wholesome open-air life, his varied, developed life, one thinks of the contrast with the worker in the typical city tenement, with his soulless toil and sordid surroundings, to whom even personal cleanliness is often almost impossible because of the squalor that overwhelms him.' The government's benevolence was skilfully directed, whetting the labourer's appetite for land by bestowing half-acre plots upon him, sharpening his envy of the larger land-holder, blunting any aspirations he might have after higher wages or recognition as an independent being. These tendencies were enhanced by provisions in the Land Purchase Acts allowing for the distribution of untenanted lands among such groups as estate employees and the descendants of 'evicted tenants', many of them labourers. It is true that the government's promises were only slowly and partially fulfilled. By the end of March 1915 only 45,592 labourers' cottages had been provided throughout Ireland, 1,100 of them in Clare, catering for about one-quarter of the agricultural outdoor labour force. Distribution of untenanted holdings among the landless was still more sluggish: by 1915 some 9,000 acres of untenanted land had been distributed in Clare under the Land Purchase Acts, 4 per cent of all land distributed, and of these parcels more than one-third had been consolidated with the holdings of former tenant occupiers. Only 205 parcels remained to benefit migrants from congested districts, victims of eviction and employees.[2] But the government's sloth in satisfying the labourer's hunger for land, far from inducing the labourer to change his appetite, merely sharpened it and increased his envy of the farmer with his parlour and the tenant occupier with his hopes of ownership. The juxtaposition of a smiling government and a scowling Treasury helped channel the rural worker's energy towards improving his social status according to that traditional determinant, the possession of land.

The Irish labourer's yearning to possess land was the natural consequence of his experience as member of a relatively small, despised class in a society dominated by self-employed farmers who neither needed hired help nor respected those who provided it. Table 7.1 suggests the paucity of employees in the Irish occupied population, particularly in the largely rural, agricultural western counties. Demographically, as well as geographically, Clare nestled between Connaught and Munster, with over two-thirds of her occupied population engaged in agriculture, and only one-third either employed or unemployed. Well over half the total were self-employed or relatives assisting them. Agricultural labourers comprised a fairly large part of the body of manual workers, but a fairly small part of the agricultural population. Just under half of Clare's manual workers in 1926 were employed in agriculture, or just over one-quarter of all employees— a higher proportion than for Munster or Connaught overall, but considerably lower than that which seems to have prevailed in 1911, when many of Clare's large estates remained intact and in need of hired labour. But the proportion of employees in the agricultural population of Clare was only 13 per cent in 1926 (compared with 19 per cent for the entire Irish Free State), and rather more than a quarter in 1911. Most Irish farms were too small and poor to provide work even for their occupiers' families, let alone hired helpers—in 1911 only 11 per cent of Clare agricultural holdings were valued at more than £30 annually (compared with 16 per cent over the entire country).[3] These oddities of Irish rural demography had two major consequences for the Irish Labour movement. The predominance of agricultural labourers among manual workers ensured that no

Table 7.1: Occupations and Industrial Status, 1926

% Occupied population (1926):	Connaught	Clare	Munster	Leinster	Ulster	Irish Free State	Ireland
Occupied in agriculture	77	68	52	34	n.a.	52	n.a.
Employers	4	5	8	6	8	6	7
Self-employed	38	31	20	15	16	23	19
Assisting relatives	36	31	21	11	67	21	67
Employees	20	29	45	61		44	
Out of work	2	4	7	8	10	6	8

Labour movement could make headway in the countryside without tailoring its programme to the demands of farm workers. The comparative unimportance of the latter in the agricultural population discouraged sentiments of pride and self-importance and encouraged sentiments of envy and inferiority to the landed classes. Isolated in small clumps on large estates, bound to their employers by loyalty as well as conventional rights and duties, the agricultural workers of rural Ireland offered a formidable challenge to any Labour organisation which hoped to create a united front of the working class, unbroken by vying loyalties or disparate occupations.

The development of a class-conscious Labour movement in rural Ireland was further inhibited by the absence of a clear distinction between small farmer and labourer. Those designated in official statistics as 'assisting relatives', many of them ageing 'boys' waiting impatiently to inherit farms, were in effect unpaid labourers compensated by free upkeep and future promise of advancement to the status of farmer. Many of them, especially from Connaught, supplemented their livelihood by spending spells over the water as 'migratory labourers', further blurring their sense of class affiliation. 'Agricultural holders' often doubled as occasional labourers on larger estates, performed laborious customary duties for their landlords (if any), and provided unpaid mutual services for each other at critical moments in the farming year. Many labourers crept into the legion of smallholders by keeping a cow on their half-acre of government-subsidised garden. The confusion of roles of labourer and small farmer was epitomised in the usage of that deceptive term, 'evicted tenants'. In the rhetoric of Home Rule the evicted tenant was normally portrayed as a poor labourer who had been toppled from his high station as a farmer by the cruelty of his landlord. On occasion, however, the connotations of eviction were stretched to include the whole history of the Gael's dispossession by the Sassenach, so that every labourer could be deemed the victim of eviction. In April 1913, for example, an Ennistymon Labour organisation called upon the government 'to acknowledge the claims of the agricultural labourers, who are tenants of labourers' cottages, in the distribution of untenanted land, as we consider that there is no body of Nationalists in any part of Ireland more worthy of the land from which their forefathers were evicted in bygone days'. A certain hypocrisy coloured the glib equation of labourer and evicted tenant, for out of about 160 Clare claimants for the status of evicted tenants known to the police in 1906, only 44 were landless labourers, herds or servants. Ten were publicans or shopkeepers, 31 were in 'good' or 'very good' circumstances, and as many as 51 were occupying farms.[4] But the equation of labourer and eviction victim, however specious, allowed rich men to share in the pity showered upon those degraded by loss of their land and status, and allowed labourers to be absolved from the contempt normally accorded to persons without land. The rhetoric of Home Rule, like the paternalism of the government and the peculiarities of Irish rural demography, encouraged the labourer to aspire after land rather than higher wages or proletarian power.

For these reasons the rural Labour movement before the European war was dominated by organisations harnessing together the ambitions of labourer and small farmer. The Land and Labour Association, with eleven Clare branches reported between 1913 and 1916, was the strongest of these organisations, being active in local politics and firmly committed to the many-faceted Home Rule movement. Remnants of Davitt's Trade and Labour Union, and an indigenous Labourers' and Farmers' Association, also voiced the proprietal yearnings of Clare labourers. Organisations primarily concerned with bettering working conditions were, by comparison, insignificant. Local trade and craft unions seldom won notice in the press. The lack of extensive secondary industry in rural Ireland discouraged the formation of large groups of organised workers in the towns, and those which existed (such as the Ennis United Labourers' Association and certain associations of shop assistants) seldom extended beyond a single town.[5] The demographic limitations to Labour organisation in the modern British pattern are suggested by analysis of the 1926 census for Clare. Of some 10,000 non-agricultural employees or unemployed, only 834 worked in transport and communications, 1,240 in secondary industry, and 2,426 in building and construction. But 1,209 were professional workers, 1,554 clerks, shop assistants and government servants, and 2,144 domestics—none of them groups commonly associated with aggressive Labour organisation. Not surprisingly, pre-war Clare had no central Trades and Labour Council, and demands for 'One Big Union', loud in Dublin and Belfast, were seldom heard. Attempts to establish a branch of the militant Irish Transport and General Workers' Union in nearby Limerick 'completely failed' in July 1914. Until 1918, indeed, rural Ireland proved indifferent to the ITGWU's exhortations. Only five provincial branches sent delegates to its first conference of delegates in May 1915, all from major towns, and when an organiser ventured into Kerry later that year his meetings were not very successful, 'many appear[ing] not to trust him'. The Dublin labour troubles of 1913–14 had few reverberations in the west, apart from a solitary 'echo of the strike epidemic' in Kilrush, where dockers declined to unload coal without a 25 per cent pay rise. The coal was quickly discharged by others. In July 1914 the lonely voice of 'Progress' asked in the *Champion*: 'Is it not time that a general Workers' Union was established for the Banner County with headquarters at Ennis to include such different occupations as farm labourers, road workers, carriers, milk and factory workers, masons, dock labourers, hotel porters, and domestic servants; besides the different grades of shop assistants, etc.?' But his dream was to establish a union on 'truly democratic lines, with due regard to Christian principles. This will ensure that no extremists will boss the Union for their own selfish ends.'[6] The spirit of Clare's most 'progressive' proposal for Labour organisation was far from the spirit of those extremist bosses, Larkin and Connolly. Workers' power was scarcely so much as a dream in pre-war Clare.

* * *

During the European war workers' power at last began to fascinate a growing number of provincial Irish dreamers, though the instruments for realising it were still puny and primitive at the time of the Armistice. Wartime economic conditions encouraged more ambitious Labour organisation than before by increasing the importance of labourers in the rural economy, by raising without satisfying their expectations of prosperity. Economic expectations were raised by two factors: the growing wealth of employers, particularly agriculturists and shopkeepers profiting from inflation of agricultural prices, and the growing demand for labour in Ireland resulting from recruitment of Irish labourers for British munitions factories and the armed forces. Employers had more to offer, and fewer to choose from. In June 1912 the Clare county surveyor had reported that he had found 'no difficulty in getting workmen. I regret to say the difficulty is in the opposite direction.' Massive unemployment in the provinces had been avoided only by massive emigration, amounting to 13 per 1,000 annually between 1901 and 1911 in Clare, and just under 8 per 1,000 for all Ireland. The wartime naval blockade reduced emigration to a trickle, at less than 1 per 1,000 both in Clare and Ireland in 1917 and 1918, thus increasing the population of Ireland by some 110,000 before the end of the war, and that of Clare by about 5,000. But for Ireland as a whole this increase was outweighed by military recruitment alone (150,000); and for Clare, which contributed about 1,500 men to the armed forces, the effects of recruitment and stopping emigration upon the labour force were fairly evenly balanced. Taking into account the loss of Irish labourers to munitions factories, and the extra demand for agricultural labour resulting from the extension of tillage after 1915, we need not be surprised that labour was frequently said to be scarce during the war period. Firms found difficulty in replacing employees who had joined the forces: by February 1915, when 13 per cent of workers in 567 Irish firms had joined up, the pre-war male labour force had shrunk by nearly 9 per cent. As shown in Chapter 2, several agricultural employers in Clare also found difficulty in making up their labour losses, and official reports both in 1914 and 1915 stressed Clare's shortage of farm workers.[7] At last the provincial labourer was in a position to bargain strongly for higher wages and better conditions—provided that he had organisations to press his claims.

But wartime Labour failed to take advantage of Ireland's growing wealth and shrinking labour pool. Throughout the war period, as for many years beforehand, Irish real wages remained fairly stable. Table 7.2 contrasts changes in minimum wages for Clare agricultural labourers—those most likely to have benefited from the wartime agricultural boom—with price changes for those agricultural products which provided the basis for the labourer's diet. In March 1916 the police Inspector-General remarked that farmers, though flourishing, did 'not however appear disposed to share increased profits with their labourers'. In Chapter 2 we discussed the reluctance of several large agricultural employers in Clare to pay even the modest minimum wages laid down by the Agricultural Wages Board in November 1917 (from which the indices for wages in the fourth column of Table 7.2 have been culled). Employers like Edward Lysaght, who tripled wages paid to his poorest labourers over the decade before 1919, far exceeding the board's requirements, were probably rare. For town workers, whose employers did not always benefit from the agricultural boom, life during the European war was still gloomier. Thus weekly wages paid to road workers by local councils (hard hit by wartime re-trenchment, rising costs and ratepayers' niggardliness) rose still more slowly than agricultural wages. Under 'Direct Labour' schemes inaugurated in 1913, 1916 and 1919 they were paid 12, 14 and 20–22 shillings respectively, receiving an overall rise of only 67 per cent in poorer districts and 83 per cent in richer ones.[8] Few Irish manual workers did well out of the war.

Table 7.2: Wages and Prices, 1907–21[9]

1913 = 100	1907	1913	1915	1918	1919	1920	1921
Wages:							
Ordinary farm labourers	90	100	130	200	235	300	320
Labourers with board and lodging	91	100	109	205	n.a.	273	282
Prices:							
Wheat	108	100	156	227	227	286	206
Potatoes	103	100	104	146	197	266	162
Butter	95	100	132	230	273	310	200
Pork	79	100	116	240	247	294	202

The failure of Irish Labour to form combinations capable of exploiting the abnormal economic conditions of wartime was due in part to the persistent appeal of the old Land and Labour agitation with its lack of concern with the mundane matter of wages. War brought a sharp reduction in the rate at which estates were purchased, but did not impede the distribution of the many estates

Table 7.3: Distribution of Land, 1904–20

	[Annual average 1904–14 = 100]						[thousand acres] Total
Year ended 30 March:	1915	1916	1917	1918	1919	1920	1904–14
Clare:							
Land distributed	88	77	253	158	86	163	144
Untenanted land distributed	115	84	331	341	206	141	8.2
Ireland:							
Land distributed	69	57	58	58	59	70	5,339
Untenanted land distributed	62	170	190	168	174	112	198

which had been purchased but not resold beforehand. The incomplete statistics presented in Table 7.3 suggest that untenanted lands were actually distributed at a faster rate during the war period than during the pre-war decade. The partial suspension of purchase by government organs engendered frustration among potential labourer-occupiers as well as tenants; but the increasing rate at which untenanted lands were distributed during wartime, largely due to the Congested District Board's operations, helped sharpen the labourer's expectations of impropriation. In Clare the period of most intensive distribution of congested lands, about one-fifth of which were untenanted, was 1916–18. During 1917 one branch of the Land and Labour Association was reorganised and a second established, Trade and Labour Union activity was reported, and meetings of labourers claiming their share in land distribution were held in at least two villages. Another LLA branch was set up in 1918, and meetings of the organisation were noted in the Clare press as late as 1920. At the end of 1918 the LLA's benefit society still had nearly 8,000 members insured in Ireland, five-sixths of its membership five years earlier and more than half the number insured with the ITGWU. Throughout the war years Clare's traditional Labour organisations remained influential. The Easter Rising, led jointly by members of the IRB and the ITGWU, changed provincial Labour still less utterly than provincial Nationalism. Whereas many prominent Home Rulers found it necessary to change their affiliation from Redmond to de Valera during 1917, many traditionalist Labour leaders continued to organise under their old banners until the Armistice at least. Not until July 1919 did the police Inspector-General report that the ITGWU had absorbed both LLA and TLU, as Sinn Féin had once absorbed the United Irish League.[10]

The first clear sign in Clare of Labour's determination to compel employers to share out their wartime spoils among workers came only in September 1918, when William O'Brien of the ITGWU and Trades Union Congress convened the

Ennis United Trades and Labour Council in the hope of promoting Labour's industrial and political organisation throughout the county. Twenty-three bodies with 1,085 members were represented at the council's first meeting, ranging from the coopers of Ennis (all five of them) to Paddy MacNamara's United Labourers' Association (300 members). No branch of the ITGWU existed in Ennis until February 1919, and despite O'Brien's role in initiating the council, it was dominated throughout the revolutionary period by MacNamara and his men. The ULA, like the Land and Labour bodies, proved powerful enough to retain both its old leaders and its old name despite changing political fashion. But unlike the LLA and TLU, which remained indifferent to changing Labour fashion also, the United Labourers retained their power by changing their manner and methods. Doubtless spurred on by the successes of massive strike action in Britain and the multiplication of ITGWU branches in Ireland, the canny leaders of the ULA transferred their faith from God, the dispenser of incalculable benefits to the humble labourer, to Solidarity and the Strike, the agents of calculable benefits to the audacious labourer's pay packet. Immediately after the council's first meeting, at which MacNamara acted as secretary, William O'Brien addressed the United Labourers 'on the advantages of solidarity and the evils of industrial sectionalism'. At the council's first meeting for 1919 its permanent secretary admitted that Clare still had far to go before it could claim to have been blessed with a modern Labour movement: 'Although the principles of trade unionism may be said to be innate in most of the working people of Clare, yet the application of these principles to the requirements of everyday life was not generally understood.'[11] Just as the war was ending, Clare Labour set about exploiting the favourable economic conditions which the return of peace already threatened to put to an end.

Labour's new spirit was still more clearly evident in the rapid development of the Irish Transport and General Workers' Union during 1918 and 1919. Whereas the Trades Councils sought to facilitate joint action by diverse Labour organisations, many of them long established in local politics, the ITGWU sought to bring together into a single body workers from every county and every sector of industry. The ITGWU, by radical reorganisation of workers, attempted to achieve on a national front what the Trades Councils, by co-ordination of existing organisations, sought at county level. Thus the growth of the ITGWU, tabulated from various sources in Table 7.4, provides a measure of the Irish worker's determination to break with the past not merely in terms of his aspirations, but also his institutional affiliation. Despite inconsistencies in statistics, it is clear that by mid-1919 the ITGWU had successfully transformed itself from a small body of urban militants to a mass organisation bearing comparison with bodies such as Sinn Féin. At its peak the union included some 21 Irishmen in every thousand (19 in Clare), compared with Sinn Féin's peak figure of 27 (49 in Clare). But its growth was less uniform by region than Sinn Féin's. Of the 501 branches reported by the RIC in December 1920, 211 were in Leinster and 205 in Munster, with only 57 and 28 in Connaught and Ulster respectively. Within Co. Clare, moreover, its spread was equally irregular. Of the 22 Clare branches reported in the files of the union, the RIC and the local press, nine were in Mid-Clare, nine in the east and

Table 7.4: ITGWU, 1916–20[12]

	Ireland						Clare			
	Apr. 1916	Dec. 1917	Dec. 1918	May 1919	Dec. 1919	Dec. 1920	Dec. 1918	May 1919	Dec. 1919	Dec. 1920
Branches:										
Reported by RIC	n.a.	n.a.	239	415	488	501	7	13	13	16
Reported by ITGWU	9	51	210	n.a.	433	n.a.	6	n.a.	14	8
Registered at head office	5	32	215	n.a.	429	558	3	7	7	16
Sending remittances	n.a.	n.a.	235	n.a.	386	480	3	n.a.	7	13
Members (thousand):										
Reported by RIC	n.a.	n.a.	48	65	79	83	0.57	1.3	1.3	1.9
Reported by ITGWU	5	25	68	n.a.	103	n.a.	n.a.	n.a.	n.a.	n.a.

only four in the west. In the east the ITGWU's sway was scarcely challenged by other Labour bodies after the Rising, of which meetings were reported in only two villages. In the centre the union competed vigorously with its rivals, which held meetings in five ITGWU villages and four others. In the west other Labour bodies existed in nine villages, including all four where the union had managed to get a foothold.[13] The ITGWU never swept the country as Sinn Féin had done, for traditional Labour bodies, as already shown, retained far more vitality during the revolutionary period than traditional Nationalist bodies.

As in local politics, it is not always easy to determine whether the ITGWU was colonising Clare, or the old order of Clare colonising the ITGWU. To some extent the union's new spirit was tempered by its desire to win over every worker, however old-fashioned his social aspirations, and by the desire of entrenched Labour organisers to take over and tame the union's branches. Thus in Newmarket-on-Fergus, where Clare's first ITGWU branch was registered in May 1918, the first president was the same man who had headed the Trade and Labour Union and its successors, the Direct Labour Association and the District Cottiers' Association—with each change of wind the same boss appeared under a different banner. In Kilrush, however, the union's branch seems to have avoided covert conquest by its rivals. In October 1918 the union held a 'conference' with the powerful Direct Labour Association of road workers; five months later the union demanded that its members alone should be appointed gangers; and before November 1919 the Direct Labour Association had become a section of the union. The ambivalent relationship of Labour's old and new orders is epitomised by the history of the local Trades Councils and their parent body, the Irish Labour Party and Trades Union Congress. Every year between 1918 and 1922 ITGWU leaders held either one or two of the Congress's four top posts; and from December 1917 to March 1919 Labour's weekly newspaper was published by the 'Irish Labour Press', a body controlled in August 1918 by eight men, of whom two were members of the union's executive, two of the Congress's executive, and two of both. The Ennis Trades Council at first reflected its parent's close bonds with the union: both its secretary and assistant secretary of 1918 were later to become secretaries of the ITGWU branch. But by 1921 ITGWU men were no longer prominent in the Trades Council's leadership, and general meetings of the union's Clare branches were being summoned independently to discuss Labour's political and industrial policies. In Dublin ITGWU and Congress remained in harness together, partly because union delegates as well as Trades Council delegates were entitled to vote at Congress elections. But in the provinces unions and Trades Councils drifted apart, as the inherent antagonism between the 'One Big Union' and the many medium-sized councils of small unions became apparent. After an open split between the Dublin Trades Council and the ITGWU in June 1919, O'Shannon wrote in the *Voice of Labour*:

> The question arises whether such a form of organisation has not outlived its day. Effective local action by labour forces is no longer possible through a federation of trade union branches. Direct workshop representation on workers' committees

for each industry is what the present circumstances call for, and a reactionary Trades Council is but an obstacle to their formation.[14]

If the union were to retain its radical urge, it would have to avoid absorption into local alliances of traditional Labour organisations.

The power of traditional Labour to resist the encroachments of the ITGWU varied not only according to geography but industrial sector. The union placed no limitations upon the occupations of its recruits, and already in mid-1918 the transport workers who had given the union its original name were outnumbered fourfold by general workers. Over the next eighteen months membership doubled and diversified further. The proportion of transport workers fell from 20 to 15 per cent, while that of clerical workers and shop assistants, hitherto negligible, rose sharply. Even domestic servants, 326 of them, were induced to join up. But the most significant change was in the agricultural sector. In June 1918 less than 10,000 agricultural workers were paid-up members; in January 1920 the number had increased to nearly 40,000, including 959 small farmers. From 1913 at least the union had sporadically attempted to enlist farm workers, but the persistent appeal of the old-fashioned agitation for land for labourers proved a formidable impediment to the union's expansion. In May 1918 the Labour newspaper declared:

> The agricultural labourers the country over are awake to their needs and their duties. . . . The dry bones of the old land and labour organisations are stirring and sedulous efforts are being made by J.P.'s and D.C.'s to keep these moribund organisations on safe lines and to preserve the souls of the rural workers from that form of mammon worship which demands hard cash for honest work.

But many agricultural labourers were not yet awake to their 'duties', and when the *Voice of Labour* declaimed in August 1919 that 'the Land War (1919 campaign) is over', it could only cite victories in the rich grazing counties of Kildare, Tipperary and Meath, with their great commercial farms and large labour forces. In the less commercialised, more custom-bound counties of the west, the wages movement was slow to seize the imagination of farm workers. In Kerry the police first reported ITGWU agricultural activity in spring 1919, when labourers were said to be roving the county removing non-union workers from their farms. In Cork suspected ITGWU labourers tried in January 1920 to break up a farmers' dance, but were driven off by a barrage of 'porter bottles and stones'. By September, however, Cork organisers had learned more panache, having staged a six-day strike policed by 'Red Guards' in one district, and having won weekly wage rates in ten regions which varied between 43s and 57s 6d, far more than the statutory minimum.[15]

In Clare the ITGWU was unusually slow to win support in the countryside. Its early successes were mostly among town workers: flour workers, bakers, drapers, shop assistants. It is notable that among the most militant trade unionists in Clare in 1918 and 1919 were white-collar workers such as shop assistants, asylum assistants and law clerks, who used the strike weapon to great advantage without, in many cases, transferring their allegiance from their old combinations to the ITGWU. Between June 1918 and September 1920 at least twenty-eight Clare pay disputes reached the press, of which seventeen involved the ITGWU. Liberty Hall paid out £211 to three Clare branches in support of strikes during 1919, £482 to seven branches in 1920, and £93 to six branches in 1921. But the two major towns, Ennis and Kilrush, accounted for twenty-four of the twenty-eight reported pay disputes, and £500 of the Liberty Hall strike money.[16] Domestic servants could be induced to strike in Kilrush, but in the countryside farm workers remained obdurately hostile to the programme of class warfare. Though the County Inspector reported as early as January 1919 that farmers were growing worried by the ITGWU's successes in other sectors, the first ITGWU-directed pay demand by agricultural workers was not reported until August 1920. When a doctor in Kildysart dared declare to the Trade and Labour Union in March 1919 that farmers and shopkeepers were the 'natural enemies of labour', and 'advised all labourers to strike out at once for an improvement in their conditions of labour', he was howled down. The secretary replied that workers had too many holidays already without strikes, and that 'farmers and labourers and shopkeepers were living as befits Irishmen and Catholics, in absolute and complete agreement and harmony with one another'. The ITGWU had recently adjourned its attempt to set up a branch at Kildysart, and its formation was delayed until May 1920. Edward Lysaght's experience at Raheen illustrates the limits to the rural labourer's militancy when met by a benevolent employer. When an ITGWU branch was formed in February 1919 he felt 'no antagonism towards it, rather a sense of being bustled which is disturbing'; but he resented suggestions that his recent wage rise had been given out of fear of the union. By April he was being threatened with strike action over employment of non-union labour, as well as being pressed by further wage demands. Though 'not disposed' to fight his workers, he was much depressed by demands which he could not afford to satisfy. Suddenly he fell ill with influenza and left for Dublin to recuperate. There he learned 'that they wouldn't think of going on strike and I in the state I was', and returned home to receive an address in Irish framed in oak, the work of ITGWU craftsmen. As he told the Raheen Club, 'they understood one another pretty well'. But for employers who ruled their labourers not with generosity and understanding but with the arrogance born of ancestral habit, even Clare was becoming an uncomfortable county by mid-1920. In July a landowner who had refused to dismiss two non-union farm boys was shot and wounded by disguised men, responding in kind. In October the *Watchword of Labour* reported victory in the battle 'against lords, ladies and non-titled agriculturists' in Newmarket district. Captain Jack Casey and his pickets starved out a farmer who had been rash enough to accept food from Black and Tans; one lord surrendered after being deprived of food and liquid for three days; another, it was darkly hinted, would be the target of 'bigger struggles yet to come'.[17] Labour had at last become a force in the countryside.

Labour's remarkable invigoration between 1918 and 1920, like its curious lethargy between 1914 and 1917, bore no simple relation to the changing economic prospects of the labourer. In its report for 1918 the ITGWU claimed: 'The economic conditions created by the War combined with the growth of a more self-reliant spirit in the country to stimulate a general zeal for Trade Unionism, of which the Irish Transport and General Workers' Union got full advantage.' But, as already shown, 'zeal for Trade Unionism' was negligible outside the cities early in the European war, when agricultural prosperity was growing fastest and the labour pool shrinking most dramatically. By early 1919, when trade unionism was spreading faster than ever before, wartime economic conditions were already giving place to the chaos of peacetime. The war's end brought the fear, though not yet the fact, of agricultural recession, and with it still greater reluctance among employers to share their profits among workmen. It also brought home tens of thousands of demobilised Irish soldiers, many of them former labourers, virtually all demanding work. The ITGWU alone had contributed 5,000 members to the forces by March 1917, equal to its entire strength a year earlier. By April 1920 the Ennis United Labourers included four hundred ex-servicemen, one hundred more than their total membership in September 1918. Demobilisation, which took over a year to accomplish, beginning in January 1919, threatened the job security of workers already employed and, as James Connolly had warned in January 1916, also threatened to force down wages as scarcity of labour gave place to glut.[18] Why, then, was 1919 to be remembered as Irish Labour's most triumphant year?

Labour's vitality in 1919 may partly be ascribed to the impetus built up during the previous year, when the benefits of working-class solidarity had first become apparent, just as its lethargy hitherto owed much to long-practised habits of deference, respectability and humility. It may also be, as the ITGWU report suggested, that the 'more self-reliant spirit' of the post-Rising period had helped workers to break their bad old habits—though the student of Sinn Féin might well suggest that its characteristic spirit was not self-reliance but the desire to change one's unquestioning allegiance from one party to another, while the student of Labour might wonder why workers showed so little self-reliance in 1917, that most passionate and enthusiastic of all the revolutionary years. A further partial explanation for Labour's vitality in 1919, like its revivification in late 1921, may be the worker's perception of the growing threat to his well-being posed by the expected recession, a threat more likely to urge him towards self-defensive action than the promise of improving his well-being which accompanied the agricultural boom. But one significant impulse towards Labour's post-war enthusiasm came from the very source which placed Labour in gravest economic peril—demobilisation. The veterans swelled Labour's ranks with a vast body of angry men, unused to the mild manners of civilian life, unpractised in the habits of deference, determined to wrest a livelihood out of the shopkeepers and strong farmers who had done so well out of the continental blood-letting. At first established workers displayed understandable ambivalence towards the wild men from the trenches. During spring 1919 ex-servicemen were given precedence in an ITGWU procession at Kilrush, but Sinn Féin workers at Bandon, Co. Cork, spurned a similar procession because veterans had joined the band. In April

1919 'Spartacist' warned the *Voice of Labour* that the 'master-class' was busy enlisting veterans into their fellowship, the Comrades of the Great War. Rather than 'abandon or cold-shoulder' their potential allies, thus driving them into the arms of loyalists, Irish Party men and policemen, Labour should actively solicit their support. The persistent mistrust felt by many Republicans towards ex-servicemen, discussed in Chapter 4, sometimes led to dissension within provincial Labour; but perceptive Republicans who were also Labour leaders, such as the journalist Cathal O'Shannon, saw that the ex-serviceman's anger and experience could be far more valuable to the Labour movement than his old-fashioned politics was dangerous. As O'Shannon wrote in October 1920:

> We hope that in all the Trade Unions which ex-service men have joined since coming back to work, steps are being taken to make use of the military knowledge and military discipline acquired by many of our workers during the Great War. These two extremely useful acquisitions are needed not only in the Little War [for] the Irish Republic, but in the war for the Workers' Republic.[19]

Labour needed the ex-soldier's support, far more acutely than did Sinn Féin or even the IRA; and in receiving his support it gained not only an access of energy but also a strong incentive to retain an independent political stance, free from the shackles of the Sinn Féin consensus.

In the months after the Armistice Irish Labour achieved a degree of social influence in rural Ireland unthinkable before the war, and showed an enthusiasm which struck terror into the hearts of every respectable citizen, whatever his political affiliation. The police grew alarmed: by January 1919 the ITGWU was 'very active' in West Cork; by February it was striking vigorously and demanding a fifty-four-hour week in East Cork; by March it was making 'strong headway' in Clare. In Clare the union was winning wage increases of a scale undreamed of before 1918: 33 to 45 per cent for trained domestics in Kilrush; 50 to 125 per cent for shop assistants in Ennis; 75 per cent for boatmen on the Shannon. By the end of 1920, despite frenzied protests by ratepayers, council road workers throughout Clare were receiving from £1 15s to £2 8s weekly, compared with 12s in 1913. The psychological supremacy of organised Labour was recognised in November 1919 by the Ennis Urban District Council's chairman when confronted by a similar demand from town road workers:

> Of course if we refused this demand, eventually the Labourers' Association would get the better of us by resorting to a strike. We have got on very well during our term of office, and now that it is drawing to a close it would not be very appropriate to cause turmoil and confusion in the town.

Even the farm labourer was beginning to revel in the power of united Labour, though his loyalty to benevolent employers had not dissipated, nor had his thirst for land been extinguished—as the agrarian agitation in the spring of 1920 clearly showed. But for the first time the sense of pride and power in being a worker, a producer, now vied with the labourer's traditional sense of inferiority to the land-holder. Yet in late 1920 and early 1921 the growing violence of the revolutionaries, the undiscriminating severity of the Crown forces, and the consequent social and economic disruption, together with the impoverishment of employers struck down by the sudden onslaught of agricultural recession, combined to halt Labour's crusade. In the second quarter of 1920 oats reached their peak prices; barley in the third; store cattle, pigs and potatoes in the fourth; fat cattle in the first quarter of 1921. Despite government attempts to provide work for ex-servicemen, Irish unemployment rose rapidly, from 58,000 at the end of 1920 to 84,000 a month later and 113,000 by the end of 1921. In November 1920 a general demand by Kilrush workers was 'in process of formulation in this centre, but the members have wisely decided to defer action until the outlook is more promising'. In its report for the year 1920 the ITGWU proudly cited 1,191 pay demands which it had sanctioned, covering 59,070 union members, who had benefited on average by 8s weekly. Although some might not realise it, these victories constituted 'the capturing of so many outposts along the highroad to Economic Freedom'. But the 'vast majority' of these successes had been achieved before September 1920, when the British 'Terrorist Campaign' had begun to choose 'the Union as a special target for its malignity'.[20] Despite the resumption of Labour activity amidst the economic gloom of the Truce period, Irish Labour never entirely recovered the impetus it lost during the months of revolution. For the revolution not only interrupted the industrial crusade, but also, by gradual degrees, stifled Labour's independent voice and independent vitality. Let us examine Labour's efforts to remain distinct from the mainstream of Republican politics, and the process whereby Labour and the Republican movement were sucked together.

2. SEPARATISM AND THE RADICAL URGE

The growing industrial power of organised Labour after the Rising engendered two great political aspirations in its leaders. Firstly, they sought means by which to impress their industrial demands upon political institutions with a part in the running of the economy, upon parliament, government boards and local authorities. Secondly, excited by the energy and influence of their movement, some began to dream of social revolution as an enticing short cut to workers' power over the conduct of industry. These disparate aspirations were bound to bring Labour's leaders intermittently into conflict not only with each other but also with established political movements. The desire for social revolution was as foreign to the priests, shopkeepers and farmers of Sinn Féin as was the desire for an independent Labour political lobby to the ratepayers and electors of the Home Rule movement. Both political movements, nevertheless, were eager to harness and exploit the energy of Labour's rank and file, and were therefore cautious in fulminating against her leaders. Labour and the Irish Party were able to work in close accord because in the party's heyday the socialist dream was confined to a small clique of citymen and because provincial Labour, not yet enfranchised, was content to lobby through the party's agency. But Sinn Féin, confronted by Labour's growing militancy and consciousness of its own strength, had at the same time less to offer and more to fear.

James Connolly had written in January 1916: 'The Labour movement is like no other movement. Its strength lies in being like no other movement. It is never so strong as when it stands alone.' Urban Labour's desire to stand alone had been fostered by the antagonism of Irish Party, Sinn Féin and the Church alike to the struggles of 1913–14. Among some leaders, including Connolly, reckless insurrection had seemed the appropriate culmination of Labour's alienation from popular politics; but among those who led the Trades Union Congress, alienation had engendered caution and the desire to avoid involvement in political disputes for fear of splitting the movement. The case of the men of caution was at first strengthened by the Easter fiasco, and Thomas Johnson, the chairman of the August 1916 Congress, declared that trade unionists were 'of varied minds on matters of historical and political development and consequently this is not a place to enter into a discussion of the right or the wrong, the folly and the wisdom of the revolt'. The affairs of the shattered ITGWU were temporarily taken over by the Congress, and for the time being Labour confined itself to industrial organisation. But during 1917 and 1918, encouraged by the rapid spread of Trades Councils and ITGWU branches, by Sinn Féin's success in marshalling popular enthusiasm behind a novel banner, even by the Bolshevik seizure of power in Russia, Labour's most cautious leaders gradually fell victim to political optimism. In February 1918 the prudent Thomas Johnson, Congress treasurer, spelt out the lesson of the Bolshevik revolution: 'It means that as society is based upon labour Labour shall rule.' In his remarkable article, 'If the Bolsheviks Came to Ireland', Johnson wrote:

> The Soviets—the councils of workmen, of peasants and of soldiers—who are now in power in Russia, have their Irish equivalents in the trades councils, the agricultural co-operative societies, and—dare we say it?—the local groups of the Irish Republican army. An Irish counterpart of the Russian revolution would mean that these three sections, co-operating, would take control of the industrial, agricultural and social activities of the nation.[21]

The language of the Bolshevik revolution was to linger on in Irish Labour circles for many years, tirelessly reiterated by Cathal O'Shannon, communist editor of Labour newspapers. It would lend rare glamour to strikes and sit-ins which, had they been reported in more familiar terms, would have been recognised by contemporaries and subsequent historians as skilfully conducted but ideologically primitive expedients for inducing particular employers to raise wages and shorten hours by practicable margins.[22] But glimpses of the Red Flag thrilled those glutted with green, and Johnson's and O'Shannon's excited analogies reflected the buoyant optimism of the time more vividly than any well-considered programme of action could have done.

The first practical expression of Labour's political optimism was its intervention in the campaign against conscription in April 1918. For one contemporary, Labour's collaboration on the Mansion House Conference with representatives of Sinn Féin and both Home Rule factions signified its political coming of age: 'Even Socialism no longer speaks in affrighting accents. Thus crossing the Sinn Féin agitation, disturbing and to some extent confusing it, is this new movement for social betterment.' Labour, like Sinn Féin, was able to transform the personal fear aroused by the conscription proposals into the desire to become part of a wide-ranging defensive combination: the political and economic struggles were harnessed together. Like Sinn Féin, Labour could only promise to 'resist to the uttermost', without going into details; but to show its determination Congress called a general strike on 23 April, and Mayday processions a week later. On Mayday 7,000 Limerick trade unionists resolved not only to resist conscription but 'to induce every unorganised worker to become a Trades Unionist', sending fraternal greetings to Russian comrades into the bargain. Labour's initial fear of conscription was more acute than that of any other class, since labourers were least likely to win exemption as vital contributors to the war effort at home. Moreover, its fears were unusually persistent, as the government's subsequent suspensions of conscription were regarded as incitements to employers to impose 'industrial conscription' by easing workers out of their jobs into the forces. By midsummer the Labour paper was openly criticising the Mansion House Conference for its apparent complacency in believing that the crisis was past, and its consequent lethargy in organising resistance at local level. If Sinn Féin used the crisis to make the Irish Party's protests seem a tame echo of its own orotundities, Labour used it to announce its own existence as a political voice independent of all parties. Its success was later admitted even by a Sinn Féin polemicist, who declared that 'Irish Labour was the most effective force in defeating Conscription'.[23]

Heady with success, Labour rushed into the 1918 election campaign. On 31 August the *Voice of Labour* called for immediate selection of Labour candidates for sanction by Congress's National Executive, to prevent other parties from stealing the Labour vote: 'Beware of the cloven hoof, whether it be wrapped in Orange or in Green. Red is Labour's colour.' Despite Sinn Féin attempts to avoid electoral confrontation with Labour, the National Executive decided early in September to put forward 'a number of Labour candidates as an independent political party', to prepare for 'full representation of Labour in a future Irish Parliament'. As in the conscription struggle, Labour was determined to be heard but had little to say. It was 'of little use to lay down any detailed programme of reform' until the war had ended and self-determination had been won. Labour's leaders had made their daring gesture: 'The rest remains with the local and union leaders and the rank and file. Up till this they have not failed. We do not think they will fail now.'[24]

Provincial response revealed that Labour's leaders had rushed almost as far ahead of their followers as Connolly had done in 1916. Trades Councils and ITGWU branches were multiplying, but they were incapable of organising slick election campaigns in opposition to Sinn Féin's highly tuned election committees. In Ennis, for example, the Trades Council, with its twin duties of undertaking 'the industrial and political organisation of the county', was convened only five days before the executive drew up its directives for local action! The *Voice of Labour*, at first so full of faith, reported only two rural constituencies where Labour candidatures were so much as mooted. Even in the towns the impulse to select candidates soon fizzled out. The Waterford Trades Council at first 'heartily endorsed' the executive's programme, but later called for a plebiscite on participation. No candidate was offered, and no further preparations were reported. The Cork nomination conference was adjourned, and Wexford decided that time was too short to allow an effective campaign. Serious preparations were confined to Dublin, but organisers were able neither to arrange an electoral pact with Sinn Féin, nor to persuade Dublin labourers to oppose Sinn Féin. Flustered, Congress endorsed the executive's disputed decision to withdraw its few remaining candidates, muttering about the necessity for maintaining a united front for self-determination now that peace was approaching. In fact, as the Congress president later confessed, Labour withdrew because it could not win—anywhere. Labour shamefacedly put the heady past behind it, just in time, and changed its name from the Irish Trades Union Congress and Labour Party to the Irish Labour Party and Trades Union Congress. It has been argued that Labour, in failing to accept Sinn Féin's pact proposals in Dublin, had failed to recognise 'a political weapon that might be captured by a vigorous Labour leadership and shaped into a socialist sword'.[25] But the election in Dublin of a tiny group of Labourites by grace of Sinn Féin would surely have retarded, not assisted, Labour's growth as an independent political force in the provinces. Urban Labour unbacked by a powerful provincial organisation would have been a very junior partner in any national alliance. Labour's abortive entry into the campaign was the product of euphoria, its withdrawal a belated reassertion of calculation and common sense which averted a fiasco potentially as damaging as Connolly's Easter abnegation of his life's work.

After its withdrawal Labour quickly became the organisational menace to Sinn Féin which it had not been beforehand. For Sinn Féin, with the Irish Party defeated, the conscription struggle over, hopes of American intercession fading, and no clear plan for future action yet formulated, early 1919 brought aimlessness and torpor. But for Labour it brought more vigorous growth than ever before, and a revived sense of energy and purpose. The ITGWU in the provinces, though concerned for the time being with industrial rather than political matters, showed a keen disinclination to being swallowed up by the drowsy Republican leviathan. Clare police reported in February 1919 that union leaders were urging workers 'to look after their own interests and not mind Sinn Fein or other political parties'. In Limerick labour troubles had 'rather overshadowed' Sinn Féin of late. Four months later the union in Clare was still 'trying to keep clear of politics', despite its members being Sinn Féiners. To avoid assimilation into Sinn Féin, the union began to imitate its antagonist. According to the union's report for 1919, each branch should make itself far more than 'a mere protection and benefit society'. It should encourage music-making and study; establish a library 'so that every member may have an opportunity of becoming acquainted with the writings of James Connolly and other great social thinkers'; even set up 'co-operative distributive stores', out of which a national Workers' Food Committee, capable of grappling with the food problem, could eventually develop.[26] Bands, leaflets and food committees had long been part of Sinn Féin's organisational armoury. By building up a rival armoury Labour challenged Sinn Féin's domination of local politics. By eschewing 'politics' it became a political force.

In the municipal elections of January 1920 the effectiveness of Labour's growing participation in local affairs was put to the test. Even before 1914, when Congress had first added the title 'Labour Party' to its name, Irish Labour had set about seeking its independent representation upon public boards. But little practical effort had been made to implement this resolution, since Labour had no machinery for selecting, vetting or campaigning for its candidates. In 1914 Ennis Labour had scored a minor sensation by winning two of sixteen seats on the Urban District Council and three of twelve seats on the town section of the Board of Guardians. The successful candidates were all members of the United Labourers' Association. But when one of them was proposed for co-option to the County Council on the ground that Labour had stood loyally beside Nationalism during the Land War, he received only three votes from the ungrateful assembled Nationalists. When the next elections took place six years later, however, Labour's challenge was immeasurably stronger. The extension of the franchise to persons without property, the introduction of proportional representation, the reiterated postponement of the elections, all helped Labour take advantage of its growing organisational power. Serious preparation began in 1918. When William O'Brien convened the Ennis Trades Council in September he stressed 'the necessity of organising as a political party of labour, so as to man the public boards with labour representatives. It was to their interests to dominate these boards.' In February 1919 Sinn Féin was informed that Labour was determined to have its own local councillors; next month the ITGWU president told organisers that all Labour candidates must be nominees and active members of unions affiliated to the Irish Labour Party (including his own), 'pledged to act and vote' with their party. In September Congress approved an ambitious programme for co-ordinated social reform through the agency of the local boards; in October a conference of Trades Councils forbade trade unions to give their names to unaccredited candidates and urged every local Trades Council to convene a nomination conference. Labour aimed at nothing less than 'increasing the power of the Local Councils, where the workers can obtain actual control over matters affecting their daily lives, and resisting the authority of the Central Government in matters of local concern'.[27] By fragmenting the processes of political decision-making Labour hoped to make full use of its own rather unevenly distributed local influence.

Labour made a fine statistical showing, winning 18 per cent of first preferences and 21 per cent of contested seats, its successes being fairly evenly distributed among the four provinces. Incomplete returns in the *Watchword of Labour*, covering two-thirds of all municipal towns, show that pledged and accredited Labour Party candidates won majorities in at least six councils, and more than one seat in three in twenty-nine others. Except in Cork and Dublin there is no evidence of conflict between Trades Councils and ITGWU branches in nominating candidates, and at least 143 of the *Watchword*'s 330 accredited Labourites were members of the union. In addition, at least sixteen councillors, though trade unionists, were elected as independents, many of them having refused the pledge. The Labour Party was unable to prevent at least 46 trade unionists from being elected as Sinn Féiners (eleven of them ITGWU men), eleven as Home Rulers, seven as political

Unionists and one as a returned soldier. Overall, however, Labour's first attempt to create a political party with an independent voice in town politics was remarkably successful. Labour representatives allied themselves with whichever factions offered them most. In Ennis, as described in Chapter 3, the four Trades Council nominees and one independent Labourite allied themselves with a Comrade of the Great War, under the Home Rule banner, to oppose the six Sinn Féiners. In Kilrush five accredited ITGWU men opposed seven Home Rulers without showing enthusiasm for unrepresented Republicanism. Sinn Féin and official Labour are also known to have formed rival alliances in Dalkey, where Labourites, political Unionists and Home Rulers opposed Sinn Féin, and Ballinasloe, where Sinn Féin and the Ratepayers' Association opposed Labour.[28] In January 1920 Irish Labour seemed set fair upon a course of constructive and independent political activity.

Labour's persistent determination to remain politically independent of the Republican movement is only in part accountable to disagreements over political aim, just as Republican eagerness to curtail Labour's political independence did not entail acceptance of Labour's social programme. In one sense the interplay of Labour and Sinn Féin was a muted battle for territory, with Labour jealously guarding her organisations and Sinn Féin seeking means to assimilate Labour's vitality into herself as the Home Rule movement had once done. In January 1919 the Sinn Féin polemicist 'Lector' expressed the impatience of the thirsty vampire:

> There can be no doubt that Labour's retirement from the electoral contest was a very noble and friendly action. But what are our Labour allies going to do now? Are they going to keep sulking or pouting apart? The Labour rank and file are with us; but the organisations as such, as well as the leaders, are holding mysteriously aloof.

There was no mystery: Labour's organisations remained aloof in order to remain alive. Many labourers might be Republicans, but their organisers were seldom Republican organisers. In rural Clare, for example, only sixteen of 913 separatists are known to have doubled as Labour organisers. Only in the larger cities was Labour occasionally strong enough to play vampire, as perhaps in Limerick where Transport Union Hall provided the headquarters for the IRA's Mid-Limerick Brigade. Overall Labour's organisational spirit was self-preservative rather than imperialist, as the editor of *Old Ireland* made clear in November 1919: 'No one desires that there should be any merging of the two movements. Each movement has its fixed programme and the greatest harmony can be brought about by each respecting the individual rights of the other and working side by side for the objects common to both.'[29]

But what objects were common to both? The editor cited 'the smashing of the capitalist and imperialist tyranny', without pointing out that the conjunction of these two adjectives would have displeased many Republican capitalists. Both Sinn Féin and Labour leaders urged 'self-determination', but Labour was no less vague than Sinn Féin in defining the term. Vagueness of political programme was essential to both organisations if they were to satisfy the divergent opinions of their members. In Labour's case vagueness was fostered by the desire to win the support of Ulster workers, and to take advantage of the material benefits obtainable from the 'capitalist and imperialist tyranny'. By far the densest concentrations of industrial workers lived in Ulster, yet Sinn Féin made little headway in the province and eventually squandered even that by ridiculous gestures of hostility, culminating in the 'Belfast boycott', equally damaging to merchants and workers. Labour sedulously though rather unsuccessfully solicited Ulster support for its national organisations, and tried to avoid treading on loyalist toes. Just before the Easter Rising the *Workers' Republic* published a striking advertisement for the ITGWU:

> UP THE RED HAND! The Transport Union Badge this year is the Arms of Munster, but the Red Hand of Ulster is dear to us because of what we suffered for the right to wear it. Therefore it is the Badge we have adopted for OUR UNEQUALLED 2/6 SHIRTS, Made by our own Members in our own Work Rooms.

Later Labour papers often lamented the sluggishness of ITGWU and Labour Party organisation in Ulster: in August 1918, for example, the *Voice of Labour* inquired: 'Have the men and women of the North a word to say? Are they willing to become consciously and definitely Labour and not merely Unionist or Home Rule or Sinn Féin?'[30] Labour could only hope to win support from Ulster Unionists if their concept of 'self-determination' were broad enough to embrace self-determination for Ulster.

Labour's hostility to the British tyrant was further tempered by the advantages to be gained by accepting its gifts, offered in its paternalist disguise. However desirable self-government might be, in the interim the British government had more material benefits to offer Irish workers than the almost penniless rival administration. Sinn Féin could signify its self-reliance by abstaining from Westminster; but how could Labour rely on Sinn Féin to provide cottages and gardens for its rural workers, advances for land purchase, nationwide price controls and agricultural wage minima, national health insurance or the 'out-of-work donation'? Should Labour alienate the unemployed by boycotting the dole, or ex-servicemen by denying them their pensions, preferential medical treatment, precedence at labour exchanges, aid in re-establishing themselves in their former occupations, loans, reconstruction schemes, grants for apprenticeship and education, grants of farming land and cottages? Labour might protest at the government's niggardliness in applying the dole to Ireland or assessing wage minima; but as long as benefits, however flawed, were forthcoming, Labour's leaders continued to press for their improvement, and to avoid unambiguously 'seditious' statements which might provoke the government into banning their organisations and silencing their lobbies. Even the Republican county councils were later to alternate their public gestures of self-reliance with tactful acceptance of British government handouts (see Chapter 5), and in this they were motivated in part by fear of Labour's reactions if they bit the hand that fed.[31] Sinn Féin did not disdain to eat the crumbs from the hated master's table; but Labour, lacking alternative provision, tempered its hatred in the hope that crumbs might be made into meals.

If Labour's interest in winning Ulster support and British benefactions tempered its Republicanism, Sinn Féin's interest in winning over all Nationalists to Republicanism tempered its enthusiasm for social change. In a period of revolutionary turmoil the issue of political priorities was crucially important to both movements. The issue of ultimate political aims, of the desirability of socialism or a society of contented peasant proprietors reciting bardic poems to each other, was far less important: de Valera could use the language of Bolshevism as fluently as Cathal O'Shannon, without committing Sinn Féin to even the mildest reformism pending independence. At the end of 1917, in its first issue as Labour's official journal, *Irish Opinion* warned against Hibernian and Sinn Féin attempts to court 'the favour of Labour' with specious expressions of sympathy. De Valera in particular was rebuked for calling upon Labour to postpone its social programme until liberation. Labour, declared the editor, would 'claim our share of our patrimony when and where opportunity offers'. In the spring of 1918 the paper carried an interesting debate on ultimate goals which gradually crept back to the issue of priorities. Taking for his text the pamphlet *The 'Faith and Morals' of Sinn Féin* by Fr Gaynor of the Killaloe diocese, a Labour writer ridiculed Sinn Féin's claims to being sole true custodians of the Easter tradition and argued that Sinn Féin visualised 'the same old tyrannical round of wage-slavery' as before. Gaynor replied that Sinn Féin's tactics were as yet 'vague and unformed', its doctrines elastic enough 'to satisfy a Marxian Socialist'—or a Catholic archbishop. Its interests could not be at odds with Labour's, since they were still undefined. Next week the pugnacious 'Lector' stepped in, dismissed the talk about ultimate aims as dishonest and irrelevant, and declared that Sinn Féin was concerned with the interests of the whole nation, not its constituent parts, being 'therefore compatible with different programmes of internal administration'. Labour should postpone its social demands until independence, when Sinn Féin's great alliance would inevitably break up.[32] Labour sought tangible benefits for the workers whenever and however they could be obtained; Sinn Féin sought to avoid alienating men of properly by supporting reforms which threatened their interests.

The formation of the rival Republican administration transformed the debate over priorities from theory to practice. Ever pragmatic, Labour's leaders lobbied the nascent alternative government as they lobbied the British government, eagerly accepting what it had to offer but soberly criticising its failings. At first the Labour paper was suspicious of Sinn Féin's administrative experiments, fearing a further encroachment upon Labour's territory. Thus *Irish Opinion* was 'pleased' that Ennis Sinn Féin had organised a potato market for the poor early in 1918, 'but we cannot commend the method. . . . Why did the club itself undertake the work? Was it not possible to start a distributive co-operative society for the people of Ennis? Is the object political or economic?' By January 1919, however, Labour was sufficiently self-confident of its own organisational strength to regard the formation of Dáil Éireann as a promise rather than a threat, despite the absence of Labour representatives. The *Voice of Labour* was content to allow the Dáil to devote its first attention to making 'impossible all government other than that of the Irish people and nation', but stressed that the Dáil was not bound by the December mandate to seek 'any particular constitution, or any special form of Republic, Soviet, Federal, Centralised, or Capitalist'. Labour's hopes of influence were raised by the Dáil's immediate acceptance of the 'Democratic Programme', largely composed by Labour officials, though watered down by Seán T. O'Kelly. In April Aodh de Blacam wrote in *New Ireland* that Labourites should 'help the Dail, with counsel and practical aid, to bring about something like the Soviet scheme in the organisation of the country. Let the trades unions and the local societies take control into their own hands of what lies in their hands, and they will find the Dail ready enough to reorganise and co-ordinate their powers.' But de Blacam's hopes that Republicanism might be 'reinforced with all the energy of a social enthusiasm' were already obsolescent, for military anti-British enthusiasm was proving a more effective stimulant. On the very day that de Blacam's article appeared de Valera announced the postponement of much of the Democratic Programme, claiming that 'he had never made any promise to Labour, because, while the enemy was within their gates, the immediate question was to get possession of their country'. A week later 'Lector' ridiculed de Blacam's sanguine vision of a Soviet social system co-ordinated by a beaming Dáil:

> Can any sane man really advocate the handing over of, say, Limerick or Cork to the local Trades Council? . . . Anyone who knows anything of the inner state of Irish Labour must realise how uneducated and narrow-minded and incompetent the workers are as yet. . . . They cannot run a small co-operative store, they cannot control their stevedores or foremen, they cannot be induced to read social literature . . . and even on the fundamental question of Irish Independence they are hopelessly divided.[33]

As guerrilla warfare spread and intensified, Republicanism climbed out of its post-election trough, and Labour's bargaining power within Republican circles diminished.

During the next two years organised Labour appeared as a suppliant rather than an initiator before the Republican administration. This change was not unaccompanied by signs of resentment on Labour's part. During 1919 the official Labour paper repeatedly denounced the candle-maker Charles Burgess (otherwise Cathal Brugha, Minister for Defence) for dismissing a shop-steward allegedly in reprisal for an ITGWU wage claim: 'The moral is that the S.F. employer is just an employer in relation to his workers, and the nature of the capitalist is the same under the green, white, and gold, as under the red, white, and blue.' But, for reasons which are mysterious, a few weeks after spelling out the moral the *Watchword* offered a grovelling apology and retraction. The agrarian trouble of early 1920 brought fresh signs of resentment towards the Dáil administration on the part of provincial Labour. In January 1920 Kerry's County Inspector of police surmised that friction between farmers and labourers might 'be all for the general good and will be to the disadvantage of Sinn Fein'. The ITGWU, though primarily concerned with wages and conditions of work, strongly supported the widespread agitation among labourers to receive parcels of conacre from the unexploited 'ranchlands' of the west. On Mayday 1920 a correspondent of the *Watchword*'s wrote that if Sinn Féin property-holders would not agree to a 'fair divide' of ranchlands, 'then the workers of this country will understand that as far as they are concerned there has been no real change in the attitude of the property holding patriots towards them since Connolly's time, and that until their own unaided efforts free them this island must remain for them what it has been for centuries—an island of chains and collars!' On that same day *An tÓglach* referred to 'drastic steps' being taken by the IRA against land-grabbers; within a few weeks, as described in Chapter 5, the Dáil had firmly condemned the wholesale redistribution of grazing lands under local duress and instructed its courts to reject claims for land put forward by 'evicted tenants', still a euphemism for land-hungry labourers and others. By the end of June Clare police considered the ITGWU 'probably the most violent and least controllable party in the Community' and thought a split with Sinn Féin possible 'at any moment'.[34]

By mid-1920, however, Labour's resentment at Sinn Féin's increasingly obvious social conservatism was outweighed by the factors drawing the two movements together. Labour had more to gain by submitting wage disputes to the Dáil's local 'conciliation boards', and land disputes to the Dáil's district or parish courts, than by spurning the Republican administration and confronting the farmer or employer naked in an unequal contest.[35] Provincial Labour's increasingly suppliant posture before the Republican administrators became clearly evident in June 1920, when Labour performed miserably in the county and rural district elections. The *Watchword* in April 1920 had considered it 'the duty of Irish Labour, then, pending the Great Social Change, to attempt to dislodge the Irish Farmers' Union from its place of vantage on the Administrative Councils'; but in rural districts Labour's potential vote was far smaller than in the towns, and its actual vote was still further decreased by IRA intimidation against prospective non-Sinn Féin candidates. 'Republican Labour', normally tolerated by Sinn Féin, is said to have won only 5.8 per cent of the total votes. Clare newspapers identified as Labourites only two Republican Labour county councillors (both ITGWU men, elected unopposed), and one lonely Republican Labour rural district councillor in Ennistymon. The *Watchword* warned the few successful Labour candidates to 'beware of getting swallowed up by the majority'; but one of the Clare County Council's two Labour members immediately became chairman of the powerful finance committee, where he proved so scrupulous in imposing economies upon council expenditure that one union branch disowned him and called, in vain, for his resignation. Labour's tiny contingents could not hope to implement their elaborate programme of exploitation and reform of local government, and were henceforth content to plead with their Sinn Féin colleagues for amelioration of the crueller effects of administrative retrenchment. Except for a brief moment in April 1921, when the Labour Party's National Executive called upon 'all loyal citizens' to give 'practical effect' to the principles of the 1919 Democratic Programme, Labour's political activity, like its industrial organisation, faded almost to nothing during the last year of the War of Independence.[36]

The silencing of Labour's individual political voice was brought about not merely by Sinn Féin's growing administrative strength, but by Labour's increasing suffering at the hands of the British government and forces. As the social disruption of the country intensified, the application of British welfare measures became increasingly sporadic, and Labour's desire to keep a foot in both administrations diminished accordingly. This process was hastened by the failure of the Crown forces to recognise fine distinctions between Republican and Labour leaders and organisations. Often unable to trace Republicans 'on the run', they pounced gratefully upon trade union officials, tied to their homes by industrial duties. A Clare military commander rushed out of the County Club brandishing a revolver to break up a procession of several hundred trade unionists who had enraged him by marching in fours. A gathering of labourers and their families in Miltown Malbay was fired upon that same night, causing three deaths. In Ennistymon the ITGWU secretary was killed and his house fired in wild reprisals after the Rineen ambush, in which he had taken no part. The campaign against the ITGWU culminated in the arrest of four senior officials and seizure of property at Liberty Hall in November 1920.[37] Common suffering as well as self-interest drove Labour into the arms of the Republicans.

The growing unity of the two movements is exemplified in the co-ordination of strike action and Republican protest during the revolutionary period. In the winter of 1919–20 motor-drivers went on strike in protest at government restrictions upon the issue of driving permits, a strike which in the Inspector-General's view was 'promoted and fomented' jointly by Sinn Féin and the ITGWU and 'could not be regarded as an industrial dispute'. In April 1920 the ITGWU called a one-day general strike against the continued imprisonment of hunger-strikers. Then between May and December 1920 increasing numbers of Irish members of the National Union of Railwaymen (without London's sanction), and other unions, refused to run trains carrying armed forces or military stores, causing the closure of many lines. The *Watchword* was unenthusiastic about the strike, which threatened the jobs of many workers outside the railways; but according to the Limerick County Inspector, the effect of the consequent unemployment and poverty was to drive Labour 'slowly but surely' towards Sinn Féin. In Clare at least two IRA companies and three Sinn Féin clubs openly contributed to the Railwaymen's Fund, and the bonds between Labour and Republicanism tightened. Clare Labour meetings grew increasingly loud in denouncing British misdoings, condemning one outrage and four policies in 1919, and four policies and eight outrages in 1920. By July 1920 the *Watchword* was finding it 'more and more difficult to disentangle political from industrial objects'; by December, in its last issue, it was thundering: 'True Soldiers of Ireland, we will stand to pray, every face to the foe, enregistering a common vow—to fight and win, or to fight and die—but to fight on to *the end*.' Only when the Truce put a halt to the bloodshed did Labour attempt to piece together the shattered remnants of its old independence of spirit. O'Shannon said defiantly that Labour was 'not tied to the tail of Dáil Éireann, or to the tail of the Irish Republican Army, because we might at any moment have to fight them and get as clear of them as we had of the British Army'.[38] But try as it might, Labour in Ireland was never to recover the organisational power and social influence which it achieved in 1919.

3. CONSERVATIVE RESURGENCE

If Labour and its radical urge were tamed by Republicanism during the final year of intense guerrilla warfare, Republicanism itself had been tamed by the men of substance almost from the start. Like the Home Rule movement which it so closely resembled, Sinn Féin was heavily dependent upon shopkeepers, employers and large farmers for its income, and the Republican county councils for their rates. Without income Sinn Féin could not organise; without rates the councils could not administer. An armed, masked Volunteer could, of course, intimidate the odd man of substance into paying over his donation or rates out of fear rather than sympathy; but systematic intimidation might have alienated a substantial and articulate group of Irishmen from the Republican cause, thus breaching the underlying principle of consensus Nationalism. Sinn Féin could not prevent its adherents from killing each other, driving cattle or seizing bogs; but it was determined to keep every faction of Catholic, Nationalist Irishmen marching with or against one another under the same banner. Throughout this study attention has been drawn to episodes in which the Republican movement associated itself with sectional grievances in its quest for vitality, only to stamp ostentatiously upon them at a certain point in response to indignant protests from those men of substance whose interests were threatened. Early in 1918 provincial Sinn Féiners, both labourers and small farmers, openly fought to break up the great grazing farms of the west—perhaps to increase food production, perhaps to secure land for themselves. Organisers encouraged their participation until early spring, when auction day for eleven-month leases was approaching, bringing with it likely confrontation between Republican lessee graziers and landless Republican cattle-drivers. Volunteer and Sinn Féin headquarters, backed up by their provincial underlings, then forbade open participation of their organisations in agrarian agitation. The pattern was repeated in early 1920, though on this occasion, the agitation being far more violent and widespread than in 1918, Republican administrators wisely refrained from attempting to squash agitation until Mayday, the first date for auction of temporary lettings. In neither case should Republican leaders be held responsible for the subsequent lessening of agitation: in 1918, in Clare at least, the imposition of military restrictions five days after Sinn Féin's first directive was almost certainly the more effective measure; in 1920 agitation had no focus once the auction of lettings had been completed.[39] The lesson of Sinn Féin's involvement in agrarian agitation is not that Republican leaders were capable of controlling their followers, but that they found it necessary at critical moments to reassure men of property that they were with them in spirit.

In its reactions to the agrarian disputes of 1918 and 1920 the Republican leadership was guided not by the arguments of organised lobbies but by its canny understanding of the mood and aspirations of the rich and poor members of its own organisations. After the Rising the moribund United Irish League was not replaced by any comparable body representing the interests of small farmers, nor did graziers and lessees formally combine to protect their grasslands from the hungry and the land-hungry.[40] But organised Labour's radical campaign for higher wages, better conditions and recognition of trade unions provoked a novel response among those whose interests were threatened—militant organisation among ratepayers. The debate over land-division was carried on within the Sinn Féin clubs and Volunteer companies as it had once been carried on within the United Irish League; the novel debate over the social and economic status of the worker was carried on by organised lobbies outside the Republican movement (at least until the final months of violent guerrilla warfare before the Truce). Let us trace the growth of organisation among ratepayers and its interaction with Republican institutions. To what extent was the ratepayers' lobby responsible for inducing Republicanism to tame Labour's social radicalism, and to what extent was Labour-taming a natural function of the party of national consensus?

Even before the Rising organisation among ratepayers and employers was not unknown. Notoriously, the Bantry-born contractor W. M. Murphy induced 404 employers in 1913 to pledge themselves to exclude members of the ITGWU and dismiss all workers who dared resist 'the instructions of those placed over them'. In Clare, where no such threat existed, meetings of shopkeepers and traders showed their solidarity in such grave matters as the suppression of Christmas boxes for their customers. One meeting resolved 'that in future the absurd practice be tetotally [sic] abolished, the traders interested unanimously agreeing, should any infringement of the decision arrived at be brought home to any trader, the culprit agrees to pay £10'. Indignant householders forgathered a month later to announce that they placed no value upon Christmas boxes or the 'long bottles' inside them. Several branches of a 'Ratepayers' Protective Association' were formed in Clare during 1913, aiming 'to take an intelligent interest in the expenditure of the money which you pay as rates, and to criticise and call public attention to any extravagance or mismanagement in the expenditure of rates'. According to one supporter, the association's natural antagonists were those inciters of public extravagance, the associations of Ratecollectors, Direct Labour and Land and Labour. It is not surprising that in ten of the thirteen Clare villages with RPA branches between 1913 and 1916, Labour meetings were also reported. But the pre-Rising ratepayers' organisations were local government pressure groups rather than standard-bearers in the class war, doubtless because Clare Labour was far too respectful and polite to make a credible antagonist. Only one ratepayers' meeting publicly denounced a Labour proposal. A second pompously called for good relations between employers and workers, and a third called upon labourers to join the association.[41] In no sense was the pre-Rising ratepayers' movement a sign of conservative resurgence in response to a radical Labour challenge.

After the Rising, however, the growing bellicosity of the small men inspired the men of property to reconsider the degree to which their social pre-eminence was secure. Combinations multiplied of farmers, the vast majority of provincial ratepayers, concerned with issues far broader than the regulation of local government expenditure. Already in March 1917 the *Irish Farmer and Stockowner* had received 'so many applications' from the provinces for advice on setting up local associations that it published a set of rules based on those of the Dublin Farmers' Association. Non-political and non-sectarian, they should aim not only to negotiate with local authorities but also to enter 'any agreement or arrangement for the union of interests' of farmers and other groups which might seem desirable. The Dublin Farmers' Association provided a room and a secretary for the 'Irish Farmers' Union', which set about organising a network of provincial associations at both county and district level. Thirteen associations had been affiliated by July 1917, 22 by October, 28 by February 1918, 37 by April, and 50 by October. Among the earliest affiliates was the old Limerick and Clare Farmers' Association, which was joined in February 1918 by the County Clare Ratepayers' and Farmers' Association (CFA) (in which Colonel O'Callaghan-Westropp was to play so prominent a part), a direct descendant of the pre-Rising RPA. Before long the county association began organising local branches, with help from a headquarters official in mid-1919. The organiser planned to inaugurate no less than fourteen village branches in just over a fortnight, but at least five advertised meetings collapsed and the county executive was unable even to ascertain the names of the branches established. O'Callaghan, upset by this temporary reverse, blamed several malign influences: the organiser's premature withdrawal, the 'premature winding up' of the old RPA and consequent friction between old and new officials, the foolish attempt to organise at harvest-time, and the restrictions imposed upon meetings by the military. From February 1920 the CFA had its own organising secretary, but he complained that 'unfortunately the farmers of Clare are the worst organised section in the country at present', at the end of a year which had seen the IFU's membership grow from 5,000 to 60,000.[42] Only after the Truce did the CFA surpass the forty branches which O'Callaghan had deemed its quota in October 1919. Newspaper reports suggest the CFA's uneven rate of growth: in 1918, one branch was formed, in 1919, 6, in 1920, 25, in the first half of 1921, 4, in the second half, 17.[43] Yet with 36 branches formed before the Truce the CFA was by no means insignificant in the revolutionary period, however dissatisfied its organisers might be with their efforts.

As the associations' branches spread through the villages, they became more representative of Irish farmers as a class and less the preserve of paternalist landowners and large employers. From the start the associations had invited farmers of all incomes to submit themselves for election, charging them according to the size of their rateable valuation. But a large proportion of the IFU's public spokesmen were former or present landowners, Unionists and landlords of the sort who comprised the Irish Landowners' Convention. O'Callaghan-Westropp, as shown in Chapter 2, emerged from this sort of political education to become a crusading county president at a time when the small farmer's voice was growing louder and louder in the counsels of the CFA. Despite the frequent assertions of Labour papers that the IFU was nothing but a front for the Irish Unionist Alliance and Irish Landowners' Convention, it is likely that many former landlords entered the movement, like O'Callaghan, to escape from their past rather than to recapture their stranglehold over the unruly lower classes. O'Callaghan recognised the danger of the former Ascendancy playing too prominent a role in the movement, but in August 1921 he triumphantly declared: 'Our people are giving the Lie to the absurd idea that the small farmer does not believe in the Union [IFU].' The Irish Farmers' Union was careful to avoid involvement in agrarian disputes which threatened to put the interests of small and large farmers at odds. Only once in Clare did the county association become embroiled in such a dispute, that concerning payment of rents by tenants to landlords. Late in 1919 unsuccessful attempts had been made to induce tenants to withhold their rents until military restrictions upon fairs and markets had been removed. Early in 1921, when military restrictions had been coupled with the beginnings of agricultural recession, a more successful campaign was inaugurated—encouraged partly by tenants' increasing inability to pay, partly by process-servers' and sheriffs' increasing inability to enforce writs. Certain village branches of the CFA expressed antagonism to the demands made by landlords, and the county executive called upon landlords in January 1921 to stay their writs until a conference had been arranged under the association's sponsorship. The executive's conciliatory proposals were fairly well received by tenant farmers, but they antagonised several prominent landowners with posts in the association, who resigned in protest. O'Callaghan, however, criticised their divisive action, publicly supported the association's rent policy, and pointedly commended the toleration showed by the farmers who had just elected him president.[44] The CFA at least managed to broaden its class support without driving out all its richest members.

The interests of organised Labour were potentially antagonistic to those of both sections of the farmers' movement, the ratepaying small farmer and the large farmer with his agricultural labourers. But as long as rural Labour organisation remained backward, organised farmers sensibly played down the latent disparity of interests of the two classes. In 1918 at least one district association resolved to admit labourers, delighting the *Irish Farmer,* which remarked that the branch was becoming 'as it were an unofficial District Wages Board' to help prevent industrial strife in agriculture. In March 1918 the journal remarked, rather patronisingly, that so far there was 'very little movement among farm labourers towards organisation into trade unions', a regrettable fact which would impede the functioning of the Agricultural Wages Board. Although the workers and not their masters 'must see to that work themselves', the *Irish Farmer* proffered a few hints: part-time labourers might be allowed into farmers' associations at reduced fee; full-timers near large towns should join their local ITGWU branch; but elsewhere (could any reader help with information?) the Land and Labour Association might 'be to them of greater use'. The *Irish Farmer* continued to assure peace-loving farmers that joining their local association was in no way 'a threat to their employees. This impression is altogether wrong. The Association is a purely defensive organisation, and does not aim in any sense at curtailing the reasonable demands of the labourer.'[45] But during 1919 and 1920 the demands of the labourer were voiced with ever greater urgency and power by the ITGWU and the Trades Councils. By the spring of 1919 the IFU and ITGWU were already locked in vigorous conflict over wages and conditions in Meath and Kildare. Organised farmers were no longer in a position to treat farm workers with condescension. Two choices remained to them: to fight, or to negotiate.

Advocates of battle and compromise alike agreed that before the IFU could blunt Labour's power it would have to imitate Labour's organisation. As one farmer wrote to the *Irish Farmer* (now the IFU's official organ) in April 1920, 'Labour is showing them what combination can do, and unless they speed up, Labour will be in the saddle and ride them to a standstill.' A year later another contributor quoted with approval Burke's dictum that 'When bad men combine good men must associate.' The IFU, like the ITGWU, sought to establish a closed shop within its own industrial sector. In May 1919 the IFU had decided not to affiliate itself with the Central Employers' Federation, and a year later registered itself as a trade union. Blacklegs were vigorously denounced: Fermoy farmers solemnly pledged themselves to withhold their labour, horses, bulls and boars from 'any farmer who up to the end of this month [May 1920] remains outside the Irish Farmers' Union in this parish'; and after the Truce the CFA, in true trade union fashion, deemed every recalcitrant farmer in the county either a selfish sponger or 'the enemy of his industry and class'.[46] Alarmed yet encouraged by Labour's organisational successes, farmers' organisers sought to deal with Labour's challenge on Labour's own terms.

The more successfully the IFU built up its closed shop, the more respectfully it was treated by Labour. In May 1919 the Limerick and Clare Farmers' Association, after some debate, urged the IFU to appoint a standing committee to negotiate with the ITGWU. During 1919 and 1920 numerous wage agreements were signed by the two bodies, most of them in the richer counties of Leinster with their large farm workforces. The ITGWU valued the efficiency with which the IFU induced its members to observe wage agreements, and in at least one case it urged unorganised farmers to join up, 'as the Farmers' Union are out for the protection of our members as well as their own'. But the IFU's deliberate emulation of Labour's organisational principles was not designed solely to strengthen its hand in negotiation. Between March and May 1920, the same months in which the IFU transformed itself into a trade union, prominent farmers' leaders discussed the formation of a 'Farmers' Freedom Force' dedicated to the suppression of strikes, socialism and Bolshevism, 'capable of meeting force by force, where the action of the existing governments is either undesirable, unavailable, or unexercised'.[47] Just as the ITGWU had its 'Red Guards' organising and protecting striking farm workers, so the IFU toyed with the formation of a 'White Guard' to protect employers and intimidate strikers.

The advocates of the Farmers' Freedom Force, from Wexford and Kilkenny, made no bones about their militancy: 'Physical force only counted; and it was physical force which lay behind arguments which secured them a hearing. An ignorant man with a stick could chop more logic than a thousand professors (*applause*).' Every IFU branch was to have its branch force, with 'a first line' consisting of not less than one IFU member in ten, available for 'muster' at short notice. The tasks of the Force were not clearly defined, but it was to be 'a national bulwark against Labour Socialism and Bolshevism', ready to organise labour, transport and distribution of produce, to provide pickets and 'protection' for them if necessary, and to arrange dances and 'social fêtes' to get the women in.

The delicate matter of weapons was not discussed in print, but the use of military terminology (in keeping with the spirit of those times) left no doubt in readers' minds as to the means by which 'protection' would be afforded.[48]

Modish though these militant proposals seemed in 1920, they roused little enthusiasm in the provinces. The IFU's general secretary, aware of the movement's organisational deficiencies in many parts of the country, warned the National Executive against taking 'hasty and ill-considered steps'. Local branches and county executives were invited to comment upon the proposals, and of the twenty-three resolutions reported in the *Irish Farmer* only two were in favour of formation of such a force in their own regions, and rather grudgingly at that. Two Connaught branches approved in principle but considered the proposals impracticable, five branches thought the time unripe, and three disapproved for reasons not revealed. But objection to the scheme was raised as often on strategic as on organisational grounds. Six branches urged the IFU to try out the Republic's new arbitration courts, or otherwise seek to resolve labour problems by peaceful means rather than confrontation. The CFA considered 'the present time inopportune for the raising of such a force', and simultaneously resolved that each branch should appoint a member to the local arbitration court if necessary. On 24 June the IFU National Executive shelved the scheme.[49] Thereafter the farmers' movement confined itself to ever more urgent warnings regarding the iniquity of Labour's goals and methods, combined with ever more determined attempts to negotiate and compromise with the devil.

A striking aspect of the programme of this abortive Force was its reference to 'the action of the existing governments'. The *Watchword of Labour* dismissed this as a ploy intended 'to fool' Republican farmers into believing that the Force and the IFU were not, after all, instruments of the Irish Unionist Alliance and Dublin Castle. The *Farmers' Gazette*, less alert, carelessly omitted the plural. Yet the Force's attempt to avoid identification with either rival administration was characteristic of the IFU's determination to avoid involvement in 'politics' and to apply pressure to all political factions, whatever their colour. The IFU's abhorrence of 'politics' was still greater than Labour's, but arose from similar arguments and fears. Like Labour, it wished to encompass Ulster Unionists as well as Home Rulers and Sinn Féiners; like Labour, it failed to breach what was before 1921 still an unmarked border. Hoping to induce the Ulster and Mid-Ulster Farmers' Unions to amalgamate with his own in mid-1919, one IFU representative tried rather too hard to please:

> He was a landlord still (although he had sold out a great deal); he was a Protestant, a Freemason, and a representative of the Protestants of Wexford for the Union, a President of a Co-operative Society, and a member of the Farmers' Union. He thought that was proof enough that the Irish Farmers' Union did not consider politics.

Neither Nationalist nor Ulster Unionist fears were allayed, the Ulster bodies remained autonomous, and some months later Ulster's fears were enhanced by reports of IFU branches singing 'A Nation Once Again'—long after most Nationalists had replaced their old favourite with 'Who Fears to Speak?'[50]

Within Southern Ireland, however, the IFU was able to hold a non-partisan stance amidst the warring factions. The *Farmers' Gazette* stressed in June 1919 that 'There must be no tinge, or even a suspicion of a tinge, of anything which savours of politics in it; farming is an industry, a branch of business, and that solely; those engaged in it may be of widely different political schools of thought.' At the height of its popularity in Clare the CFA was headed by a former Unionist, with a Redmondite as deputy, and a horde of Republicans as rank and file. Just after the Truce its vice-president addressed the Clare County Council, in particular its chairman, Michael Brennan:

> . . . as the representative of those great and wonderful boys that went down fighting for their country and their God. I could say a lot of things, but the Farmers' Union is non-political and my mouth is closed. I respect you all, and I like the boys, and the boys are with me (*laughter*). I may say that I was always a Redmondite up to the last ditch, but still the boys liked me.[51]

The boys might laugh, but Thomas Falvey remained vice-president, Redmondite or not.

The farmers' movement carried its abhorrence of politics further than Labour's by shunning participation in all political assemblies, largely because its electoral capabilities were still more meagre than Labour's. In July 1917 the IFU was urged to impose a pledge upon farmers standing in local elections, but decided at its first general meeting that this was 'a bit premature'. It had recently been rash enough to seek representation at the Irish Convention, only to be rebuffed. Fifteen months later the IFU council was asked to appoint, after Labour's model, a parliamentary committee, but after several objections had been raised the chairman closed the meeting, declaring that 'he would not allow politics here'. Whereas the old Clare Ratepayers' Association had evidently won representation in local government and had kept checks on its representatives' voting records, its more cautious and politically diverse successors put up no candidates either for the 1920 local or 1918 general elections. In January 1921 the Chief Secretary alarmed the IFU by remarking that the union would doubtless seek representation in the Southern Ireland parliament, a suggestion hastily repudiated by the National Executive (which at O'Callaghan-Westropp's urging reiterated its rule that 'no political or sectarian discussion shall be raised, or resolution proposed, at any annual congress or meeting of the Union or National Executive'). Only after the signature of the Treaty did the *Irish Farmer* find that there seemed 'to be no sufficient reason for further abstinence from organised interest in political questions' and that opinion was 'rapidly crystallising' in favour of the formation of a farmers' party. O'Callaghan lamented this tendency: 'Our Union is being steadily dragged into politics, and into faction fighting which is worse. Our only safety lies in Parnell's policy at Westminster; *ally yourself with no party but wring what you can out of both.*'[52]

In accordance with this principle the IFU had spent much of its energy resisting administrative interference with the agricultural economy, from whichever administration it stemmed. Whereas Labour did its best to cajole both administrations into increasing their economic intervention in the worker's interest, the farmers' movement consistently resisted the extension of state controls. In the British case farmers were threatened both by regulatory and punitive measures. We have already portrayed O'Callaghan-Westropp's mounting rage at the imposition of government controls between 1917 and 1921, in opposition to which he became among the best-known IFU spokesmen: wage minima, price maxima, compulsory extension of tillage, export restrictions for Irish store cattle (Clare's staple product). Government controls were deplored by nine of the CFA's forty-four meetings reported in Clare before the Truce, and seven of its fifty-eight meetings during the Truce. The only subjects of discussion of comparable concern were labour matters (seven meetings before the Truce, none thereafter), local administration (seven and twenty-two), land purchase (three and three) and government punitive measures (three and none). The IFU leadership interpreted tillage controls as the first step 'towards nationalisation of the land' and each new measure of economic regulation as a further encroachment upon the farmer's right to own and exploit his property. By November 1920 the *Irish Farmer* had detected 'organised and powerfully directed efforts towards the creation of an artificial famine', part of a 'deep diplomatic move' to advance British foreign policy at the Irish farmer's expense. Three months later Thomas Falvey from Clare showed no more tender a regard for the government and its instruments than his ex-Unionist superior O'Callaghan-Westropp (no lover of 'Bonar Law turned Bolshevic'): 'The Department of Agriculture and Liberty Hall were evil enough in themselves without working in combination. It was about time they took the devil by the throat and threatened that they would finally choke him.'[53]

Imposition of punitive economic measures further enraged the IFU and increased its determination to be heard both at the Castle and beyond. Between 1918 and 1921 fairs and markets were repeatedly banned in districts where Crown forces had been subjected to outrage. The IFU (see Chapter 2) joined landowners, Unionists, Sinn Féin and local government bodies in denouncing these punishments, which dislocated agricultural distribution and imperilled the prosperity of the farmer (particularly the grazier). Small farmers dependent upon the sale of animal products were harder hit by the destruction of creameries in 'reprisal' for atrocities which had nothing to do with milch cows and little to do with their owners. Between April 1920 and January 1921 alone forty-one co-operative creameries were attacked, and in May 1921 the County Inspector for East Cork noted with satisfaction that military closures of creameries in response to IRA road-blocks were having 'excellent effect'. As the *Irish Farmer* remarked just after the Truce, 'As a class the agriculturists bore the brunt of all the penalties which the exigencies of the situation forced upon the populace'—the burning of haggards 'on an extensive scale', banning of fairs and markets, destruction of creameries and dairies, cutting of roads and disruption of railways. But farmers' indignation at unmerited punishments and their principled condemnation of state encroachments into the private sector did not extinguish their desire to extract from the British administration what benefits it had to offer. In March 1921, for example, an IFU branch 'respectfully urged' the Department of Agriculture (otherwise that devil in league with Liberty Hall) to consider the completion of land purchase and the regrettable exclusion of Ireland from the new Agriculture Bill with its minimum price provisions.[54] Principle might urge that state intervention in land sales and agricultural prices threatened the rights of property, but pragmatism whispered that if state intervention were profitable to the farmer, state intervention should be encouraged.

Organised farmers treated the rival Republican administration with the same pragmatism. They avoided political rhetoric, won what benefits they might, and opposed those Republican actions which threatened their self-interest. The IFU did not disdain to use the arbitration tribunals of the Republic, particularly in its negotiations with the ITGWU. In April 1920 its National Executive denounced the ITGWU for placing an embargo on exportation of certain foodstuffs, thus presuming 'to assume the functions of government'. Yet after a few weeks' bellicose mutterings concerning formation of the Farmers' Freedom Force, the IFU implicitly admitted the Dáil's fitness to exercise quasi-governmental functions by asking a Dáil tribunal to decide the issue. In April 1921 the Clare county executive turned over its accounts to the Republican National Land Bank (following the *Irish Farmer*'s warm congratulations to 'the promoters of this new national enterprise'); in October members of the National Executive expressed a 'sense of grievance' at the omission of IFU representatives from the Dáil's Education Commission, a grievance only palliated by the general secretary's belief that 'the action did not represent a deliberate policy on the part of Dáil Éireann, but was due to some other cause'; and in November O'Callaghan-Westropp backed proposals for a formal deputation to wait upon Mr de Valera, arguing that to ask the President of the alternative government to promote agricultural interests was 'both properly courteous and respectful, as well as safe'.[55]

But the Republican administration was to remember the Clare Farmers' Association more vividly for its campaign against payment of rates than for its tactful gestures of respect. In October 1921, with admirable even-handedness, the county executive threatened simultaneously to withhold land annuities from the British administration if Canadian store cattle were allowed the freedom of British abbatoirs, and to withhold rates if the Republican County Council did not regularise its collection procedures. Indignant at administrative extravagance, rising rates and alleged diversion of moneys collected to the IRA, Clare farmers 'were actually taking up arms to resist by force any attempt to collect the Rates' by early October. After negotiations between the association's executive and W. T. Cosgrave of the Dáil ministry, O'Callaghan and his supporters agreed to urge members to temper their defiance by paying the overdue first moiety for 1921–22 immediately, on the understanding that the second moiety would not be demanded until mid-1922. The executive divided, but O'Callaghan eventually triumphed (or, as the Dáil ministry's inspector unkindly put it, the association 'capitulated').[56] Long before the legal transfer of power, organised farmers busied themselves in the lobbies of the Dáil administration—now pleading respectfully, now protesting grimly—as they had done in the lobbies of Westminster and the Castle.

By 1921 the Irish Farmers' Union had become a fairly powerful lobby in Irish politics. A sign of its growing influence in Clare was O'Callaghan's appointment to the County Committee of Agriculture shortly before the Truce, after the Republican County Council had decided to eject various lazy Sinn Féiners including Bishop Fogarty himself. It is true that the farmers' movement never developed so efficient an organisation as the ITGWU, and that both bodies found it extremely difficult to arrange meetings, form branches, collect dues and lobby politicians during the terrible year before the Truce. Already in August 1920 the National Executive was receiving dispiriting reports from the counties: four county organising secretaries had proven dishonest or incompetent, one county organisation had suffered from 'the unwarrantable interference of demagogue politicians and other enemies of the movement', another had fallen out with the national headquarters, four had reported unsatisfactory progress, five had failed to carry out their obligations to the National Executive, and only ten were considered in satisfactory order. At the annual congress six months later seven counties were disfranchised for failing to send in their due contributions. As the *Irish Farmer* remarked, 'the stirring times' were 'beginning to affect in their own peculiar way the development of the Irish Farmers' Union movement'—not only by endangering the lives of prominent officials, but also by changing times of meeting from the convivial evening to the drab early afternoon. In Clare branch formations continued during the revolution, but whereas branch activity in sixteen districts was first reported in the first eight months of 1920, over the following year only thirteen further districts answered the call. One prominent Republican soldier and politician maintains, indeed, that the IFU 'didn't count' in Clare before the Truce. Yet the movement's organisational limitations should not conceal the crucial and enduring influence which the mass of farmers and men of property exerted upon Irish politics throughout the revolution. It was they who paid much of the cost of revolution, they who housed the men on the run, their sons who staffed the IRA and their daughters who staffed the Cumann na mBan. As Michael Brennan put it early in 1922:

> He was glad to say that if the farmers were not behind them in the war it was not treaties they would be discussing. If the farmers had not stood by them they would not have been able to carry on the war for one week. He knew the farmers' homes all over Clare, he knew they were always open to him, and whatever they had was his and freely given to the army. . . . In Dublin it was said that nothing troubled the farmers but pounds, shillings, and pence. This was an absolute lie.[57]

But in order to win the co-operation of farmers, both as individuals and as participants in an organised movement, the revolutionaries had to tame whatever impulses they felt towards social change. Labour, for all its organisational power, never succeeded in redirecting the mainstream of revolution towards the goals of social radicalism. The farmers, despite their organisational weaknesses, by sheer weight of numbers, wealth and social status, directed the course of revolution as though by right.

In their eagerness to harness every movement of popular protest to the 'national cause', Republican leaders spasmodically resorted to the language of radicalism, thrusting their rhetoric behind the small man's struggle for land in 1918 and 1920 and Labour's wage agitation in 1919. But whenever social protest began seriously to threaten the interests of men of substance, Republicanism ostentatiously dissociated itself from agitation and sprang, however ineffectively, to the defence of law and order. The more Republican institutions came to resemble an alternative administration, the less often were their organisers heard to mouth the gospel of social revolution, for their political triumph depended upon support from those opposed to social revolution. Sinn Féin, the Dáil's courts and councils and the Irish Republican Army were all too diffused and decentralised to permit any militant minority to infiltrate, conquer and make them its instruments. The Irish Revolution was directed not by conspirators, thinkers and politicians but by great surges of opinion from below, expressed by countless forgotten spokesmen in countless bars and churchyards. The strongest and most insistent surge from below was the conservative resurgence imperfectly manifested by the growth of the Irish Farmers' Union, and in that surge the few voices crying for a new social order were quickly, and it may be finally, submerged.

Epilogue

PERHAPS the last words of historians, like generals, would better be left unsaid. In a fair-minded world generals would be judged not according to the manner of their dying, but of their living; historians not according to their conclusions, but their explorations. This book has explored the political experience of many groups of Irishmen during the last years of British rule. My concerns have been to portray the multifariousness of Irish political behaviour, and also the frontiers of behaviour, over which the natives did not dare or did not care to cross. To write a conclusion is at best to provide the reader with a map. No map could substitute for the explorer's detailed report. This epilogue is therefore not a crib for those who have not read my book, but a mnemonic for those who have.

In the process of Ireland's political transformation between 1913 and 1921 every Irishman was to some extent both actor and observer. The roles of actor and observer are, of course, only formally distinct. A man's past actions (particularly those which betoken his affiliation to some group) colour his perception of the behaviour of others; his future actions will be influenced by changes which he perceives in the behaviour of others—in the manner of life and conduct of neighbours, friends, associates and public figures. The purpose of a great many political actions is to minimise the impact of external political and social change upon one's own life. To the extent that a man values his social status, he will act to protect it whenever he observes that the *status quo ante* is under challenge—by defending his property, life and liberty, by seeking to hold or regain the respect of his peers and deference of his presumed inferiors, by gesturing angrily against the challengers or by currying favour with them. Yet for every observer the fact of external change offers not only the threat of impoverishment, injury or humiliation, but also the promise of bettering oneself at the expense of others. Few men are so content with their lot that, seeing others improve theirs, they will not attempt to improve their own. Hence political behaviour in times of change should be interpreted as in part defensive, in part creative, the portions varying according to the extent of one's self-satisfaction. The frontiers of defensive behaviour are clearly marked, being determined once people's prior expectations as to their social status have been established. The frontiers of creative behaviour are always in flux, since people's expectations of conceivable self-improvement change as their perceptions of the status of others change. To use terms from the last chapter, both the 'radical urge' and the 'conservative resurgence' are endemic not only to revolutions but to all those who experience revolutionary change.

Ireland in 1913 was a country in which a remarkably large part of the people was apparently satisfied with its lot. The publicans and priests who organised the provincial Home Rule movement already monopolised local government and local political societies, and confidently expected that the internal government of the country would soon be in their hands (Chapter 3). Policemen looked down upon labourers, farmers looked down upon both, farm labourers were apparently content to serve benevolent masters and flattered at the government's novel interest in furnishing them with cottages and gardens (Chapters 1 and 7). The survivors of the Protestant Ascendancy, despite the loss of much of their land and political influence, still inspired daylight deference in their servants, tradesmen, labourers and former tenants (Chapter 2). Most Irishmen thought that there was a good deal in their lives worth defending.

Every Irishman, needless to say, had his grievances. Policemen were often demoralised by poor pay and harsh conditions of service, Protestants were widely subjected to nocturnal outrage, farmers and labourers were indignant at the slow pace of land purchase and wage improvement, priests were worried at the spread of secularism in political and social organisations, publicans at the ever-increasing burden of excise duty. Yet Irish society in 1913 seemed flexible enough to give each man a reasonable prospect of working his way up the social ladder without first finding it necessary to pull down the ladder and replace it with a new model. The labourer might hope to inherit land from farmer relatives, the small farmer to accumulate capital enough to augment his property, the policeman to win promotion. For most Irishmen the most rational strategy for improving one's lot seemed to be to conserve what one had already and play the game of social betterment according to the accepted rules.

An important agent in persuading pre-war Irishmen that their lot could best be improved 'within the system' was politics. Politics was a game which every Southern Irishman (except policemen or Unionists) could play with some hope of victory; political organisations were open to exploitation by any quick-witted Irishman, whatever his social status. Although publicans and priests had the easiest time of it, the dense network of sectional organisations, united only in their pious advocacy of Home Rule, gave farmers and labourers too a chance to launch themselves into local politics, with its promise of money, popularity and the increased respect of one's peers. The Home Rule movement had proven remarkably efficient in persuading Dublin Castle and the British government that Irish Nationalists were for once united in a single movement and that their struggle was consequently irresistible in the long run. Seeing the benefits of solidarity, local politicians were content to shelve possible divisive 'issues' and devote themselves to struggling for local influence under a single umbrella. The advantages of falling into line were so great, and the personal costs so small in the short run, that outside Dublin political heresy was almost unknown. Orthodoxy was practised because it seemed to have been successful, and the criteria for its success or failure were seldom questioned.

That Irish Nationalists repudiated the Home Rule programme in increasing numbers after 1916 did not indicate repudiation of the assumptions underlying the organisation of the Home Rule movement (Chapter 4). That the Home Rule umbrella became almost universally unwelcome was the result of spectacular political changes which affected the vast majority of Irishmen, yet were initiated by small numbers of conspirators (the 1916 Rising) and Westminster politicians (the post-Rising repression). In Chapters 3 and 4 I traced the complex process by which the slogans of Nationalism were rewritten and the ingenious course whereby the new 'Sinn Féin' movement was built up in the image of its precursor. Because the Home Rule organisations had worked, because their collapse was evidently caused not by internal rottenness but by a bizarre series of accidents, the architects of the new mass movement rebuilt those organisations under different names. Placemen from Home Rule days and youngsters without influence before 1916 combined to seek benefits for themselves according to the old attractive *quid pro quo*—the chance to win local influence in exchange for vague declarations of fidelity to the 'national cause'. The most common response to the unexpected change in national leadership and programme was to re-establish with all possible speed and efficiency the Old Order. Until 1918 little evidence may be found of radical or 'creative' behaviour in face of changing circumstances. When Dublin leaders dreamed that post-Rising Ireland was plastic in their hands, they were deceived. By 1918 the conservative resurgence seemed virtually complete; Sinn Féin seemed as tightly run at local level and as resistant to radical thrusts initiated at national level as the old Home Rule movement had been. The damage done after Easter 1916 seemed to have been expertly patched up.

Between 1918 and 1921 the circumstances of Irish political life changed with bewildering speed. The direction of change was determined less by far-sighted Nationalist planning than by successive blunders on the part of the British government. Each repressive government action provoked Irish political reaction, at the same time rendering the old organisational system developed in Home Rule days and perfected after 1916 less efficient. The increasing threat of imprisonment, death or economic impoverishment for Nationalists, together with the diminishing prospects of dispensing patronage and the increasing administrative intervention in local affairs of central government and the army, made the life of the traditionalist Nationalist orator ever more dangerous and less likely to end in self-betterment. Consequently many Irishmen lost interest in the old proven political system. Politics became the preserve of small, often clandestine bodies of a sort which had never before won such influence in the provinces: flying columns, rebellious county councils assembling in barns instead of courthouses, makeshift courts outside the traditional legal system (Chapters 5 and 6).

At the same time significant social changes associated with the European war encouraged for the first time noisy demands from once quiescent social groups (Chapter 7). The increasing flow of cash in the agricultural economy rendered farmers as well as shopkeepers and priests potentially substantial contributors to Nationalist funds, entitled therefore to expect greater influence in local politics. The collapse of policing in rural Ireland after 1918 (Chapter 1) encouraged smallholders to seize by force the land which they had once sought to purchase through the good offices of their local MPs. Labourers' economic expectations were immeasurably enhanced by the abnormal labour shortage of wartime, only to be seriously threatened in 1919 by the arrival home of hordes of former soldiers seeking jobs. These social changes undoubtedly opened up new means by which Irishmen might expect to better their lot, and increased the determination of labourers and farmers to win a stake in whatever new political order was to emerge out of chaos. Farmers and labourers would never again be content to give first place in local politics to publicans and priests.

Thus a great many Irishmen behaved during the revolutionary convulsion in a manner inconceivable in 1913. Nevertheless, the assumptions underlying their reactions to those extraordinary events had changed remarkably little. Smallholders still sought landownership; labourers still sought the means to acquire a plot of land and with it higher social status—status being assessed according to traditional standards. Farmers, although determined to buy political influence when times grew less troubled, were more intent during the revolutionary years upon seeking peace with their labourers and with the British government, so that their prosperity might not be spoiled by further economic dislocation. For their part, the Republican leaders did their best to placate the men of substance by ostentatiously repudiating the few truly radical demands voiced during the revolutionary period, such as Labour's insistent demand for higher wages (underlined by the threat of strike action) and for the division of grazing lands as well as small plots among the needy. The revolutionaries found that Volunteer companies and Republican courts and councils could no more be kept up without the monetary backing of men of substance than the local political organisations of earlier years. The Republican administration was innovatory only in so far as the courts and councils required adaptation to allow them to administer social control according to the traditional fashion. In form they aped the British institutions they sought to supersede; in practice they functioned in traditional manner if in unfamiliar surroundings. For those who participated in the Republican courts and councils, they provided instruments for carrying on ancient land disputes or securing patronage as before. Occasional hesitant attempts on the part of national leaders to purify local administration were contemptuously ignored in the provinces. The Irish revolution was guided from below, and few revolutionaries have been so conservative in their response to social and political cataclysm as those who gave their guidance during the Irish Troubles.

For those groups which had already lost much of their status before 1913, such as policemen and Protestant Unionists, there was little to conserve during the revolution but one's dignity. Unlike former Home Rulers, these unhappy groups could not fit easily into the New Order and influence its development. After 1916 two choices only remained open: to shrink into their shells of inherited belief and pray that the Troubled Times would pass, or to repudiate publicly their cherished beliefs and hope for toleration, as apostates from their own kind. In Chapters 1 and 2 I traced the divergent paths followed by diehards and pragmatists as the menace of revolution made choice increasingly urgent. Yet even among the pragmatists—the policemen who resigned or spied for the IRA, the Protestants who threw over their Unionism—old-established social expectations and self-images lingered. Even those whose behaviour changed most radically between 1913 and 1921 were intent upon preserving whatever they could salvage of their former social prestige—whether by keeping their Big Houses unburnt or by winning admission to the police force of the future Irish state.

Irishmen showed remarkable resilience in adapting themselves to revolutionary change without for the most part radically changing their outlook upon the world. Most of them, it may be, never lost that pre-war vision of a golden age with its promise of Home Rule, unlimited jobbery, ownership of land by its occupiers, ever-increasing prosperity and social peace. Once one had glimpsed water in the desert, why should one march off in some other direction—even if it were a mirage? Most Irish revolutionaries, like their opponents and victims, never escaped their roots. Through all the muddle and confusion of that ardent epoch a pattern may be discerned. The revolutionary muddle was nothing but the familiar muddle of Irish life—with all its evils, injustices, absurdities, palliatives and delights—expressed in a new language.

Appendix

Political Organisation and Participation in Clare 1913–21

THE following tables provide a synoptic account of my systematic analysis of political activity in Co. Clare, frequently referred to in the text. The many problems of interpreting these tables cannot be discussed at length in this appendix. The major source for all four tables is the body of reports of political meetings published by the *Clare Champion,* 1913–21, supplemented where necessary by reports in the *Saturday Record.* For each meeting date, place, names of participants and subjects of discussion were recorded.

Table A.1 measures the frequency with which organisations of twelve categories coexisted in the same localities. All told, 113 localities (villages or towns) are known to have had meetings of at least one organisation between 1913 and 1921. For each organisation the total number of localities from which activity was reported is given, together with the number of 'collocations' with each of the remaining eleven organisations (i.e. the number of localities in which each pair of organisations coincided). Trade unions, with the exception of the ITGWU, have been consolidated into the category 'Labour', since the political aims and functions of different unions at the same time were broadly uniform. To allow comparisons between pre-1916 and post-1916 politics, the three bodies which straddled 1916 have been cut in half. Although the Gaelic League, Labour and farmers' movements (RPA and CFA) were to some extent formally continuous, in each case 1916 was a watershed, a period of comparative inactivity followed by regeneration—sometimes under the same banners, but usually by different men, in different places, with different aims to those prevalent before the Easter Rising. Since local newspaper reporting of ITGWU and farming organisations was defective, ITGWU reports and records (Bibliography, F 17 and R 2) and reports in the *Irish Farmer* have also been analysed. Clare had several political organisations not analysed in this table, notably the IRA, for which data was too patchy to permit systematic study.

Table A.2 shows the geographical distribution of the same twelve organisations. Co. Clare has been arbitrarily divided into three convenient regions: East Clare (1911 population 25,830, comprising the Rural Districts of Limerick No. 2, Scariff and Tulla); Mid-Clare (44,539, Ballyvaughan, Corofin, Ennistymon and Ennis—Rural and Urban); and West Clare (33,863, Killadysert, Kilrush—Rural and Urban).

Table A.3 shows the number of priests and laymen known to have participated in political meetings of various categories at least once between 1913 and 1921. Priests are divided into senior clergy (parish priests and administrators in the Clare parishes of the dioceses of Killaloe and Kilfenora) and junior clergy (curates and members of religious orders). Laymen active in Ennis and Kilrush

Appendix 237

Table A.1: Collocations of Various Political Organisations

	1913–16									1917–21				
1913–16	Total	UIL	AOH	Lab.	GL	RPA	INV	IV	SF	ITGWU	Lab.	GL	CFA
UIL	33	—	8	7	15	6	22	2	28	6	8	12	21
AOH	27	8	—	9	12	9	21	3	22	13	11	12	19
Labour	19	7	9	—	8	8	14	2	15	10	9	7	14
Gaelic League	33	15	12	8	—	7	20	5	27	9	10	16	19
RPA	13	6	9	8	7	—	12	2	13	7	8	7	11
Irish National Volunteers	49	22	21	14	20	12	—	4	45	13	16	19	34
Irish Volunteers	8	2	3	2	5	2	4	—	6	2	2	5	3
1917–21													
Sinn Féin	76	28	22	15	27	13	45	6	—	14	18	24	43
ITGWU	22	6	13	10	9	7	13	2	14	—	9	9	11
Labour	20	8	11	9	10	8	16	2	18	9	—	12	15
Gaelic League	36	12	12	7	16	7	19	5	24	9	12	—	23
CFA	54	21	19	14	19	11	34	3	43	11	15	23	—
Total localities	113	33	27	19	33	13	49	8	76	22	20	36	54

Table A.2: Geographical Distributions of Various Political Organisations

Number of localities	1913–16							1917–21				
	UIL	AOH	Lab.	GL	RPA	INV	IV	SF	ITGWU	Lab.	GL	CFA	Total
East Clare	6	12	2	2	3	13	1	19	9	2	4	11	84
Mid-Clare	11	9	10	12	5	20	3	32	9	9	14	22	156
West Clare	16	6	7	19	5	16	4	25	4	9	18	21	150

Table A.3: Claremen Prominent in Politics, both Priests and Laymen

	Senior Clergy	Junior Clergy	Laymen	Senior Clergy	Junior Clergy	Laymen
Home Rulers	21	25	749			
UIL	5	6	170			
AOH	6	2	214			
INV	6	16	311			
UIL and AOH	1	—	9			
UIL and INV	—	3	21			
AOH and INV	1	1	25			
Home Rulers also prominent in:						
Farmers' movement	2	—	12			
Labour movement	—	2	18			
Gaelic movement	5	8	24			
Separatists				16 [1]	57 [3]	913 [41]
Separatists also prominent in:						
Farmers' movement				3 [–]	– [–]	19 [8]
Labour movement				1 [–]	5 [1]	16 [3]
Gaelic movement				8 [3]	17 [5]	47 [17]
Separatists once prominent in:						
Home Rule movement				9	12	116
UIL				4	2	22
AOH				2	1	24
INV				2	8	72
Total				34	85	1,546

Table A.4: Subjects of Discussion at Political Meetings

	UIL			AOH				Sinn Féin			
	1913	1914	1915–16	1913	1914	1915	1916–20	1917	1918	1919	1920–21
Pious gestures											
Condolence for dead	29	11	7	13	37	22	21	32	13	55	1
Praise for clergy	2	—	—	1	6	3	2	1	1	7	2
Versus outrages	7	1	—	3	5	4	1	—	—	—	—
Political gestures											
Praise for leaders	26	16	5	1	19	3	5	2	1	1	—
Peace and war	—	—	1	—	—	—	—	6	1	—	—
Issues											
Versus imprisonments	6	4	—	3	1	1	2	10	4	11	—
Versus government acts	—	3	1	—	2	1	7	7	3	—	1
Versus landlords	44	10	4	—	1	—	—	—	5	—	—
Local administration	5	—	—	—	2	1	—	2	—	6	—
Economic matters	—	—	—	—	—	—	—	11	5	1	1
Organisation											
Internal troubles	2	—	3	—	3	3	1	1	1	4	—
Praise for others	5	4	—	3	5	—	2	2	2	1	—
Versus others	2	1	—	—	—	—	—	12	—	—	—
Jobs for boys	2	—	—	1	12	3	1	2	3	13	1
Election campaign	—	—	—	—	—	—	—	49	4	—	—
Fund-raising	29	5	—	1	4	—	—	13	1	36	—
Number of meetings	147	45	12	43	132	57	34	245 [391]	58 [192]	140 [140]	6 [6]

have been omitted from analysis, since their identity was often impossible to establish. Otherwise virtually all known participants in political meetings have been analysed, provided their address could be established with tolerable certainty. I have assumed, where necessary, that two names with the same initials and surname, associated with a single locality, refer to the same person. 'Home Rulers' include those associated with the UIL, AOH, TTA or Irish National Volunteers; participants in pre-Rising 'Nationalist' meetings or meetings of tenants; and campaigners for Patrick Lynch, KC, in the 1917 East Clare by-election. 'Separatists' include Sinn Féiners, supporters of Count Plunkett or de Valera in 1917, militant critics of the Irish Party, agents of the Irish National Assurance Company, Republican justices and officers of the Irish Volunteers and Fianna Éireann (information unevenly supplemented from IRA and Fianna roll books, Dáil and RIC records), and those arrested for political offences, April 1916–1921. Those already reportedly active in the separatist, farmers', Labour and Gaelic movements before 1916 are distinguished by brackets but included in totals. 'Farmers' movement' includes RPA and CFA activists, 1913–21; 'Labour movement' includes prominent members of the ITGWU and other unions; 'Gaelic movement' includes Gaelic Leaguers and GAA administrators (not players). (Analysis of the last two organisations was not exhaustive, so that the figures given probably understate the correlations between Gaelicism and separatism or Home Rule activism.)

Table A.4 shows the number of meetings of Sinn Féin, the UIL and the AOH at which subjects of various categories are known to have been discussed. Not all subjects known to have been discussed are covered by these categories, and a great many subjects of discussion certainly failed to win press notice. All reported meetings of the AOH and UIL were analysed for subjects of discussion, but 280 of the 729 reported Sinn Féin meetings were excluded from analysis. The total number of Sinn Féin meetings reported during each period is given in brackets.

Abbreviations

AFIL	All for Ireland League	LGB(D)	Local Government Board (Department of Dáil)
AG	Adjutant-General		
AOH	Ancient Order of Hibernians	LLA	Land and Labour Association
APL	Anti-Partition League	M(C)R	Monthly (Confidential) Report
BG	Board of Guardians		
CC	Catholic Curate	MHA	Ministry for Home Affairs of Dáil
CDB	Congested Districts Board		
CFA	Co. Clare Farmers' Association	n.a.	not available
CI	County Inspector RIC	NLI	National Library of Ireland
COS	Chief of Staff	OC	Officer Commanding
CS(O)	Chief Secretary for Ireland (Office of)	PC	Press Censor
		PGA	Public General Acts
DATII	Department of Agriculture and Technical Instruction for Ireland	PP	Parish Priest
		PRO(D)	Public Record Office, London (Dublin)
DC	District Councillor (on UDC or RDC)	RDC	Rural District Council
		RIC	Royal Irish Constabulary
DI	District Inspector RIC	RM	Resident Magistrate
DMP	Dublin Metropolitan Police	ROIA(R)	Restoration of Order in Ireland Act (Regulations)
DORA(R)	Defence of the Realm Acts (Regulations)	RP	Registered Papers, CSO, in SPO (Bibliography, A 30, iv)
GAA	Gaelic Athletic Association		
GOC	General Officer Commanding Forces in Ireland	RPA	Ratepayers' Association
		SF	Sinn Féin
GPB	General Prisons Board	SPO	State Paper Office, Dublin
IFU	Irish Farmers' Union	TCD	Trinity College, Dublin
IG	Inspector-General	TD	Teachta Dála (member of Dáil Éireann)
ILPTUC	Irish Labour Party and Trades Union Congress (until 1918, ITUCLP)		
		TLA(U)	Trade and Labour Association (Union)
INL	Irish Nation League		
I(N)V	Irish (National) Volunteers	TLC	Trades and Labour Council
IRA(B)	Irish Republican Army (Brotherhood)	TTA(L)	Town Tenants' Association (League)
ITGWU	Irish Transport and General Workers' Union	UCD	University College, Dublin
		UDC	Urban District Council
IUA	Irish Unionist Alliance	UIL	United Irish League
LB	Letterbooks of O'Callaghan-Westropp (Bibliography, F 49)	ULA	United Labourers' Association
		US	Under-Secretary, CSO

Notes

PROLOGUE
(pp. xi–xiv)
1. Harry R. G. Inglis, *The 'Contour' Road Book of Ireland*, Edinburgh 1908–09, 148, 206; Census of Ireland, 1911 (H 1).
2. Hooton and Dupertuis, *Physical Anthropology*, I, 84, 145, 257; Arensberg, *The Irish Countryman*, 106. (Full information concerning these and all other sources summarily cited in these notes may be found in the bibliography, to which code references in parentheses after citations refer.)
3. 1911 Census; Supplement to Report of Registrar-General, 1910 (1914 xv, Cd 7528, 5); Quarterly Returns of Marriages (H 17), *passim*. Between 1901 and 1910, 54 per cent of all Clare marriages were contracted in the first quarter of the year, compared with 30 per cent for Ireland all told. Both proportions diminished significantly during the period of my study, being 45 per cent and 29 per cent respectively for the period 1914–18, and 42 per cent and 26 per cent for the period 1919–21.
4. Arthur Young, *Tour in Ireland*, ed. Arthur Wollaston Hutton, London 1892, I, 287; Agricultural Statistics, 1913 (H 5); 1911 Census; O'Mahony, 'In County Clare' (S 16), 36.
5. Hely Dutton, *Statistical Survey of the County of Clare, with observations on the means of improvement; drawn up for the consideration and by direction of the Dublin Society*, Dublin 1808, xii.

Chapter 1
FORCES OF THE CROWN
(pp. 3–39)
1. *Constabulary Gazette* (hereafter *Gazette*), 27 May 1916; autograph by J. Hassett, Co. Clare, O'Neill Papers (F 28). The 'Man in Blue' was presumably not of the RIC (dark green) but the DMP.
2. Appendix to 1914 Police Committee (H 20), Minutes 3873 and App. viii; *Gazette*, 4 Oct. 1919; Intelligence Notes (A 22, i), *passim*.
3. RMs' reports to US, 3 Jul. and 28 Jun. 1914, RPs 11012 and 10572/1914; *Clare Champion* (hereafter *Champion*), 25 Jan. 1913; Judicial Statistics, 1913 and 1914 (H 12); Bodkin, *Recollections*, 357.
4. A. M. Sullivan, *The Last Serjeant*, London 1952, 109; Appendix to 1914 Police Committee, Minutes 1795–1803, 387–409; RIC *Manual* (L 4), 19–20; O'Donoghue, *No Other Law*, 113.
5. Appendix to 1914 Police Committee, App. i, Minutes 1810–21, 4269–71, 4373, 3312, 1737–44; Report, pp. 8, 28. At 5.9 weekly the Irish resignation rate in 1913 was the highest since 1882, although well below the decadonal averages for the 1850s and 1860s (11.0, 9.6). (RIC Personnel Returns 1841–1919, HO 184/54 (A 23).)
6. *Clare Journal*, 5 May and 9 Jan. 1913; 1914 Police Committee Papers, SPO (A 30, iii), and Appendix, Minutes 3896–3900; *Gazette*, 14 Feb. 1920.
7. PGA 4 & 5 Geo. V, c. 54, 6 & 7 Geo. V, c. 59, 8 & 9 Geo. V, c. 53; Irish Convention Report (H 9), p. 127; Thomas Barrington in *Journal of the Statistical and Social Inquiry Society of Ireland*, XV (1925–26), 253.
8. *Commons Debates*, Vol. 100, col. 642; RIC Registers (A 23), *passim*; correspondence in RP 18742/1915, especially IG to US, 13 and 28 Oct. 1915, US to CS, 16 Oct. 1915.

Service statistics were taken from 1914 Police Committee, Appendix, p. 338 (Ireland, 31 Dec. 1913) and RIC Nominal Returns, HO 184/61 (Clare only, 1 Jan. 1920). For military enlistments see RIC *List* (L 3), Jan. 1919, and Rebellion Commission (H 16), Minutes 10194 for variant figure (745 enlistments before 1916). For Nathan's correspondence with Recruiting Department (Kelly to Nathan, 11 Nov. 1915, and reply, 13 Nov.) see SPO, Irish War Savings Committee Papers, parcel A.

9. *Gazette*, 24 Jun. and 1 Jul. 1916; *Saturday Record*, 6 May 1916; CI, MCRs, Sep. and Dec. 1916, Oct., Nov. and Dec. 1917, Jan. and Apr. 1918; IG, MCR, Sep. 1918; CI to RIC Office, 18 Jan. 1918, RP 5975/1918.
10. Returns of Outrages (A 22, vii) to 25 Apr. and 9 May 1920, 20 Mar. 1921, 27 Jun., 17 Dec. and 11 Apr. 1920; Maurice Headlam, *A Holiday Fisherman*, London 1934, 35.
11. RP 24711/1918; CI, MCRs, Jul. 1918, Nov. 1919; *Gazette*, 28 Aug. 1920; information from Michael Maher, formerly Lieutenant, Doolin Company, Irish Volunteers.
12. Return of Outrages to 10 Jul. 1921; F. Dinneen (*Freeman's Journal*) to John Redmond, 26 Oct. 1915, MS. Nathan 460 (A 5), ff. 113–14; IG, MCR, Mar. 1917 and Seán Burke, 'Some of the Activities of the 4th Battn Mid Clare Bde' (F 39), Chap. 1; Liam Haugh, 'History of the West Clare Brigade' (B 3). Haugh's account is hearsay, and the incident dated at 1917 may well be that referred to in CI, MCR, Jan. 1919.
13. CI, MCR, Feb. 1918; CI to RIC Office, 18 Jan. 1918, RP 5975/1918; Piaras Béaslaí, *Michael Collins and the Making of a New Ireland*, London 1926, II, 337; *Saturday Record*, 9 Aug. 1919; IG, MCR, Aug. 1919; CI, MCR, Aug. 1920; Return of Outrages to 3 Apr. 1921. The honour of having hosted the first military raid upon a police barracks might be disputed among several counties: Clare (Inch, unsuccessful raid, 16 Jan. 1918); Kerry (Ballybunion, shots fired by 'mob', 11 Jul. 1917 (IG and Kerry CI, MCRs)); and Cork (Eyeries, 17 Mar. 1918, arms removed, probably with police connivance (Cork West Riding CI, MCR)).
14. Many variant estimates of police casualties have been published. These figures were drawn from Outrage Returns (H 15); Street, *Ireland in 1921*, 7; CP 2782, 3151 and 3564 in Cab. 24/121, 126 and 138. Clare figures were culled from police reports and other sources.
15. *An tÓglach*, 31 Jan. and 19 Feb. 1919, 15 Apr. and 1 Oct. 1920; Home Secretary, Sinn Féin, to Clerk of Dáil, 22 Apr. 1919, and draft reply 23 Apr. 1919, SPO, DE 2/175; AG to OC (Acting), Mid-Clare, 8 May(?) 1920, Military Archives (B 3), p911. On 10 April 1919 de Valera proposed social ostracism of policemen as 'a first step' in self-defence of the Irish people. (Dáil *Minutes*, 67.)
16. *Champion*, 3 Jun. 1916, 12 Jun. 1920; Lynch-Robinson, *The Last of the Irish R.M.s*, 152–3; Crane, *Memories*, 256–7; C. Prescott Decie to IG, RIC, 26 Feb. 1921, RP 2337/1921; Major Johnston, MRs of non-attendance at petty sessions, RP 3126/1921.
17. Report of 29 Jul. 1921, RP 2369/7/1921; Capt. C. FitzGerald Blood to US, 5 Sep. and 10 Nov. 1921, with cutting from *Saturday Record*, 22 Oct. 1921, *ibid*. Blood himself had lately found difficulty in performing his functions as High Sheriff. At Ennis spring assizes he had been able to organise the ceremonial opening only at great expense, for '5 men had to be put into livery, as an inducement to attend on H. M. Judges, and they had to get a handsome tip from me.' Despite five applications for reimbursement, the captain lost his money, for the Castle had lost its pride. (RP 2901/18/1921.)
18. From Judicial Statistics (H 12), *passim*; CI, Report for County Clare for 1916, 24 Jan. 1917, CO 904/120 (A 22, v). In Table 1.1 'persons convicted' include those committed to higher courts.
19. IG, MCR, Mar. 1919; *Champion*, 25 Jan. 1919; McElroy to CSO, 23 Apr. 1918, 30 Jan. 1919, RPs 11790/1918 and 2923/1919.

20. Lynch-Robinson, *op. cit.*, 153–5; CI, MCR, Nov. 1917; *Gazette*, 9 Oct. 1920. In December 1919 Lord French sent the IG on leave after expressing 'very strong disapproval' of the 'supine attitude' of the RIC towards enforcement of the recent proclamation of Sinn Féin. (French, Journal (A 17), 9 Dec. 1919, p. 60.)
21. Cab. 23/4/283(18), 27 Nov. 1917; Privy Council Office, proclamation of 13 Jun. 1918, in Proclamation Book 1896–1920, SPO. The powers of courts martial and summary courts in regions where the machinery of the 'ordinary law' had been obstructed were extended under ROIA, 9 Aug. 1920. (PGA, 10 & 11 Geo. V, c. 31.)
22. 'Record of the Rebellion' (A 11), II, 4; Irish Convention Report, p. 129; MS. Nathan 478 (A 5), ff. 26–8. Tom Bowden's chapters in *Revolt to Revolution*, ed. Bowden *et al.*, Manchester 1974, and Townshend, *The British Campaign*, *passim*, examine the organisation and operation of police intelligence. The need to prevent policemen 'becoming marked men in any particular locality' caused increasingly frequent transfers and therefore diminishing accumulation of local knowledge after 1919. (See Macready, *Annals*, II, 482.)
23. RIC Lists (L 3), *passim*; *Gazette*, 7 Jul. 1917, 13 Sep. 1919.
24. *Champion*, 10 Jul. 1920; Tudor to Churchill, 27 Jun. 1920, Cab. 27/108; 'Willie' to *Gazette*, 18 May 1920. Sir Warren Fisher, in a report to the Chancellor of the Exchequer, 11 Feb. 1921 (Lloyd George Papers, F/17/1/9), criticised police in the martial law zone for keeping 'their own arrangements for "patrolling" the country—a shibboleth by which they mean that they are shewing themselves as on the top and which gunmen interpret as providing victims for ambushes'.
25. Anderson to Greenwood, 20 Jul. 1920, Anderson Papers (A 22, xv), B74; CI, MCR.
26. US to Commander of Forces in Ireland, Oct. 1912 (draft revision, Irish Command Defence Scheme), CO 904/174 (A 22, xii); interviews with police and military officials, MS. Nathan 467, ff. 141–3; IG to Irish Convention, Report, p. 128.
27. CI, MCRs, Sep. and Oct. 1919; Tudor to Conference of Ministers, 23 Jul. 1920, CP 1693, Cab. 24/109; circular to CIs, 14 Jun. 1921, CO 904/178; *Gazette*, 29 Jan. 1921.
28. Lyttelton, *Eighty Years: Soldiering, Politics, Games*, London [1927], 287; CI, MCR, May 1916; W. H. M. Lowe to Irish Command, 27 May 1916, in MS. Asquith 44 (A 2), ff. 20–1; *Gazette*, 24 Jun. and 1 Jul. 1916.
29. CI to IG, 26 Jun. 1917, and C. J. Perceval to US, 27 Jun. 1917: RPs 15662 and 15904/1917; CI, MCR, Dec. 1917; correspondence, etc., concerning use of military patrols, RP 5975/1918; Duke to Hankey, 25 Feb. 1918, GT 3736, Cab. 24/43; proclamations in RP 7921/1918.
30. Report by Lord French, 30 Aug. 1918, GT 5570, Cab. 24/62; 'Record of the Rebellion' (A 11), I, 33; 6th Division, Weekly Operational Strength Returns (A 27), 3 Feb. to 21 Jun. 1920.
31. 1914 Police Committee, Appendix, p. 340; Registers (A 23), *passim*; Irish Office Weekly Surveys, Cab. 24 and 27, *passim* (1920–21). Certain figures have been adjusted to account for constables registered but not enlisted.
32. IG to US, 4 Oct. 1919, Strathcarron Papers (A 6), c490, ff. 123–4; Brind to IG, 27 Aug. 1919, Shaw to CS, 19 Sep. 1919, and IG to US, 4 Oct. 1919: *ibid.*, ff. 105–8, 113–15, 123–4.
33. 1919 Police Commission, Report (H 18); PGA, 9 & 10 Geo. V, c. 68 (20 Nov. 1919); US to Irish Office, 30 Apr. 1920, CO 906/19; RIC Registers and Irish Office Weekly Surveys, *loc. cit.*; 'History of the 5th Division' (A 11), 33–4. Pay figures exclude war bonuses. The first batch of English-born recruits was appointed on 2 January 1920, although for some months a fair proportion of Irish-born recruits had been ex-soldiers. The Registers exclude some but not all temporary constables assigned to the Auxiliary Division. Cf. Townshend, *The British Campaign*, 46 and *passim*.

34. Cab. 23/21/29/20(App. II), Cab. 24/106, CP 1317 and Cab. 23/21/30/20(4); Wilson Diaries (A 13), 11 and 28 May 1920; Outline of Terms (H 19); Irish Office Weekly Surveys, *loc. cit.*; 'Order of Battle', 29 Jun. 1921, Hemming Papers (A 9), which for Clare lists one company (Killaloe) and two detachments (Corofin and Lisdoonvarna). The boundaries between the Auxiliary Division and the regular RIC were indistinct: many temporary constables were seconded to the division, many temporary cadets later became regular police officers (permanent cadets) or policemen (especially in the Transport Division), and a few ex-army officers joined the regular RIC as constables early in 1920.
35. RIC Officers' Registers; RMs, Record of Service Book, 1882–1921, SPO (no information concerning certain additional and temporary magistrates); Winter, *Winter's Tale*, 121. Winter had previously exercised his talents as Boundary Commissioner for Schleswig-Holstein for one week, after which he resigned to take the Irish job at a lower salary.
36. From RIC Registers, *passim*, excluding Auxiliaries but including former constables who re-enrolled. 'Clerks' includes shopkeepers, managers and others engaged in occupations other than skilled or unskilled labour or trade. Occupational percentages discount the few recruits without known previous occupation. 'Farmers' includes farmers' sons. Cf. Townshend, *op. cit.*, 209.
37. *Gazette*, 14 Feb., 9 Oct. and 21 Aug. 1920; Lynch-Robinson, *op. cit.*, 159–60; Bill Munro in Gleeson, *Bloody Sunday*, 56 ('messing about').
38. CI, MCRs, Dec. 1920, Mar. and Apr. 1921, Nov. 1920; Seán Edmonds, *The Law, the Gun and the Irish People*, Tralee 1971, 92–7 (RIC *v.* Auxiliaries); Cahir RIC to Burke, 902, Cork, 28 Nov. 1921, O'Donoghue Papers (A 18).
39. Cab. 23/14/390A(3), 12 Apr. 1918. On 5 Jul. 1921 Sir Henry Wilson noted that more and more Irish-born soldiers were seeking exemption from Irish service. (Callwell, *Wilson*, II, 299.)
40. 'History of the 5th Division' (A 11), 20, 31–2; C. Prescott Decie to Strickland, 20 Feb. 1921, CO 904/188/2 (A 22, xv). On 10 December 1920 Macready had written to Jeudwine: 'Strickland will have to watch the Police very carefully, because certainly Prescott-Decies [*sic*] will think that Martial Law means that he can kill anybody he sees walking along the road whose appearance may be distasteful to him.' (Jeudwine Papers (A 11).)
41. E.g. Military Intelligence Report from Limerick, 14 Aug. 1917, CO 904/157/1 (A 22, ix); Clare CI, MCR, Oct. 1919; IG to US, 4 Oct. 1919, Strathcarron Papers, c490, ff. 123–4; West Cork CI, MCRs, Dec. 1920 and Feb. 1921 (urging that 'the Riding should be flooded with troops stationed everywhere in strong detachments'); 'History of the 5th Division', 33; lecture by Major A. E. Percival (1923), Percival Papers (A 12), 4/1.
42. Limerick CI, MCRs, Aug. and Dec. 1920; cf. IG, MCR, May 1921 (few CIs 'pretend to see any improvement, the majority are plainly of opinion that matters are becoming worse').
43. *The Times*, 27 Sep. 1920; Munro in Gleeson, *op. cit.*, *passim*; West Cork CI, MCR, Oct. 1920.
44. Official figures (for sources see note 14) record 144 military deaths before the Truce, but 180 soldiers were commemorated at a memorial service in November 1922 of whom 18 were killed after the Truce. (Macready, *Annals*, II, 666.)
45. Wilfrid Ewart, *A Journey in Ireland, 1921*, London and New York 1922, 94–6; *Champion*, 17 Apr. and 19 Jun. 1920, and Return of Outrages to 17 Apr. 1920 (A 22, vii); Gaynor, 'Kilmihil Parish' (F 40), 486. A rough index of military success in this pursuit is the rate of occurrence of venereal disease, of which (5th Division only) 201 cases were reported from January to May 1920, 141 from June to December, 102 from January to July 1921 and 67 from August 1921 to January 1922. ('History of the 5th Division', *loc. cit.*, App. v.)

46. Montgomery to Percival, 14 Oct. 1923, Percival Papers, 4/1; 'Sinn Fein and the Irish Volunteers' (*c*. Oct. 1920), WO 32/4308 (A 26); 'Notes on Guerilla Warfare in Ireland' in 'History of the 5th Division', *loc. cit.*, App. xxvi; Clarke, 'Memoirs' (A 15), Chap. 6; enclosure in Macready to Stevenson, 20 Jul. 1921, Lloyd George Papers, F/36/2/19; Percival Papers, 4/3.
47. Percival lecture (1923), *loc. cit.*, referring specifically to Auxiliaries; 'Record of the Rebellion' (A 11), II, 24–9, and Tom Barry, *Guerilla Days in Ireland*, Dublin 1949, 105–12; Macready, *op. cit.*, II, 460–1; 'History of the 5th Division', 83–4.
48. *Ibid.*, 8, 134–5.
49. 'Record of the Rebellion', I, 33, 54–6; 'History of the 5th Division', 172–3.
50. Macready, *op. cit.*, II, 495, 500–2; Sturgis Diaries (A 25), Vol. 1, p. 27 (18 Aug. 1920); 'History of the 5th Division', 56; Macready to Wilson, early Oct. 1920, CO 904/188/1, B66; *Champion*, 23 Apr. 1921; 6th Division officer to 18th Infantry Brigade, 27 May 1921, PRO, WO 35/169. On 1 Oct. 1920 (Cab. 23/22/53/20(2–4)), a conference of ministers reached 'complete agreement' that reprisals by burning must be stopped, but 'confidence was expressed' that orders already issued by the Irish executive would suffice. As for reprisals 'in hot blood' after murders of policemen, such natural responses were 'hard to stop'—what more could one say or do?
51. Macready, *op. cit.*, II, 500–2; Sturgis Diaries, Vol. 3. pp. 39–41 (23 and 24 Dec. 1920) (cf. Crozier, *Ireland for Ever*, 177–80, who denounces his own Auxiliaries but adds that soldiers helped burn Cork); Ennistymon DI to Temporary CI, 30 Oct. 1920, reproduced in *Report of the Labour Commission to Ireland*, London [1921], 69. Cf. Townshend, *The British Campaign*, 95–6.
52. C. Prescott Decie to Assistant Under-Secretary, 1 Jun. 1920 (signed original), Crime Special Branch Records (A 30, ii), carton 23 (text also quoted in Breen, *My Fight*, 128); Sturgis Diaries, Vol. 1, p. 27 (18 Aug. and 4 Sep. 1920); RIC Circular, 28 Sep. and 12 Nov. 1920, Hemming Papers (A 9); Tudor to OC Auxiliaries, 19 Feb. 1921 (the date at which Crozier was 'permitted to resign' his command), and circulars of 18 Dec. 1920 and 6 Apr. 1921, Hemming Papers. The Listowel affair is re-examined in J. A. Gaughan, *Memoirs of Constable Jeremiah Mee, R.I.C.*, Dublin 1976; cf. Crozier, *op. cit.*, 286–7 and Commons *Debates*, Vol. 132, cols 1606–9, for variant accounts of Smyth's address of 19 Jun. 1920.
53. Sturgis Diaries, Vol. 2, p. 70 (24 Sep. 1920); *ibid.*, Vol. 1, p. 30 (19 Aug. 1920); *ibid.*, Vol 3, p. 91 (12 Feb. 1921); *Weekly Summary*, 8 Oct. 1920; CI, MCR, Oct. 1920; *Champion*, 23 Oct. 1920 (cf. Bodkin, *A Considered Judgement* (S 2) for details of compensation after Rineen). Soldiers are alleged to have participated in the reprisals at Miltown and Feakle. (Anthony Malone, Statement (F 45); *American Commission on Conditions in Ireland*, Evidence, Washington [1921], 366–76.) Macready, *op. cit.*, II, 495, admits that houses in Ennistymon were 'systematically burnt by orders of a senior [military] officer', presumably after the Rineen ambush.
54. Monthly Returns of Desertions, WO 35/173/5 (A 27); Military Intelligence Officer (Southern District), MR, Nov. 1917, and Clarecastle RIC report, 21 Nov. 1917: CO 904/157/1 and 122; Macready to Greenwood, 17 Jul. 1920, Anderson Papers, CO 904/188/1, B72 (A 22, xv).
55. Letter of 16 Feb. 1916, and CI to IG, 11 Mar. 1916: RPs 3297 and 4664/1916; CI, MCR, Nov. 1917; *An tÓglach*, 14 Sep. 1918.
56. Breathnach, *The Irish Police*, 74–8; *Gazette*, 30 Dec. 1916; Asquith to King, 2 Nov. 1916, Cab. 41/37/38, and Neligan, *The Spy in the Castle*, 53–5; Commons *Debates*, Vol. 113, col. 2210; Deputy IG to CIs, 4 Feb. 1919, in PC, MR, Feb. 1919, CO 904/167 (A 22, xi); PC to Chief Constable, DMP, 29 May 1919, and PC to IG, 7 Jul. 1919: SPO Press Censorship Records (A 33); Neligan, *op. cit.*, 54 *et seq.*; *Gazette*, 9 Aug. 1919. Cf.

Gaughan, *op. cit.*, for the history of police unionisation. The 1919 pay increases were harnessed with a clause (9 & 10 Geo. V, c. 68, 2 (1)) forbidding policemen to join anything remotely resembling a union, on pain of exclusion by all imperial police forces.
57. Fisher to Lloyd George, quoting Macready to Fisher, 21 Jul. 1920, Anderson Papers, CO 904/188/1, B75 (A 22, xv). In his MCR for July 1920 the CI was more circumspect: IRA activity had had a 'certain measure of success' in sapping police morale. One must read between the lines of bland police reports. Cf. Townshend, *op. cit.*, 97.
58. From Irish Office Weekly Surveys, *loc. cit.* Over this period 258 Auxiliaries and 867 RIC were dismissed or discharged without pension or gratuity (cf. 85 between 1917 and 1919 (Personnel Returns, HO 184/54 (A 23))). Officers are excluded. Figures include dismissals for misconduct or desertion, and discharges for ill-health, unfitness or unsuitability (not distinguished).
59. Breen, *op. cit.*, 106, *Saturday Record*, 20 Sep. 1919, and Brennan, 'Statement' (F 38); OC, East Clare Brigade IRA to COS, 22 Jun. 1921, Mulcahy Papers, P/7/A/19; Military Archives (B 3), p918, and Return of Outrages (A 22, vii) to 4 Dec. 1921. Cf. Winter, *op. cit.*, 295: 'Agents and informers were difficult to obtain, for the Irishman's appetite for gold had been replaced by a surfeit of terror.'
60. SF Standing Committee, Minutes, 23 May 1918, copy in PROD (B 6); IG, MCR, Apr. 1918; 'Resignations and Retirements from Irish Police Forces', embodying Dáil ministry decision of 11 Jun. 1920, SPO, DE 2/87, *Sinn Féin*, No. 1 (letter by P. O'Keeffe), Jul. 1920 (copy in NLI); Dáil *Minutes*, 232 (17 Sep. 1920); Report by J. Mee, General Employment Agency, sent by Labour Department to Clerk of Dáil, 28 Sep. 1920 (reply 1 Oct.), SPO, DE 2/87; Neligan, *op. cit.*, 80–1. Cf. Gaughan, *op. cit.*
61. Deputy IG, MCR, Aug. 1920; CP 1693, Cab. 24/109; Irish Office Weekly Surveys, *loc. cit.*, collated with figures in Return of Outrages to 25 Apr. 1920 (A 22, vii) and Commons *Debates*, Vol. 133, col. 24. Figures refer to applications to resign, some of which were later withdrawn. Officers are excluded. Figures for 1910–19 are drawn from RIC Personnel Returns, HO 184/54.
62. Return of Outrages to 25 Apr. 1920, *loc. cit.*; RIC Registers, *passim* (cf. Table 1.2 p.22). For the six batches of recruits analysed at Table 1.2 the proportions eventually resigning (dismissed or discharged) were 24 (14), 23 (23), 39 (15), 27 (13), 19 (9) and 14 (6) per cent. Cf. Townshend, *op. cit.*, 209.
63. 1914 Police Committee, Appendix, Apps iv and xiv (service of entire RIC on 31 Dec. 1913, and of all RIC resigning during 1913); RIC Nominal Returns, HO 184/61 (service of Clare RIC on 1 Jan. 1920); RIC *Lists* and Registers, *passim* (names and service of Clare RIC resigning between 1913 and 1919, and 1920 and Apr. 1921, excluding those recruited outside Ireland). The 31 Clare Black and Tans resigning in 1920–21 had all, of course, served for less than two years. The experience distributions upon which figures in the bottom two rows are calculated are those for all Ireland (31 Dec. 1913) and Clare (1 Jan. 1921). Officers are excluded.
64. RIC *Lists* and Registers, *passim*. See note 36 for interpretation of occupational categories.
65. Irish Office Weekly Surveys, *loc. cit.*; RIC Personnel Returns, HO 184/54; Greenwood's analysis of RIC experience, 10 Dec. 1921, CP 3542, Cab. 24/131. Retirements include discharges on gratuity as well as pension.
66. RIC *Lists* and Registers, *passim*. Causes of resignation analysed in Table 1.8 are those ascribed to resigning policemen by the compilers of the Registers, largely based on the applicants' stated motives for resignation. 'Conflict with RIC' embraces suspected Sinn Féinism (2 cases 1913–21), complaints as to conditions (9), disciplinary charges pending (8). 'Family reasons' embraces family circumstances (12), required at home (5),

intimidation (1). 'Bettering one's condition' embraces emigration (13), joining other police forces (3) and 17 others. 'Private reasons' includes ill-health (12).

67. *Gazette*, 3 Jul. 1920; Dáil *Debates*, Vol. 6, col. 3 (10 Jan. 1924). Officials found 'great difficulty . . . in forming conclusions as to the motives which appear to have actuated ex-members of the Royal Irish Constabulary in resigning'. (T. M. Healy to Duke of Devonshire, 7 Feb. 1923, Cabinet Secretariat Papers, S 1764, SPO.)
68. Local Centre (Limerick) to 'O' (Winter), 3 Nov. 1921, CO 904/151; T. J. Byrnes, Tulla, to Minister for Home Affairs, 13 Nov. 1921 (and reply 25 Nov.), PROD DE 10/4 (B 5); *Champion*, 9 Dec. 1922; Dáil *Debates*, Vol. 1, col. 1820; *ibid.*, Vol. 9, cols 747 *et seq.*; *ibid.*, Vol. 6, cols 815 *et seq.*; *ibid.*, Vol. 7, cols 238 *et seq.*; John O'Brien to Edward MacLysaght, 26 Aug. 1925, NLI, MS. 2650 (F 21).
69. GHQ War Diary, 29 Aug. 1921, WO 35/93/1/1 (A 27); Instructions by Chief of Police, 30 Oct. 1921, CO 904/178 (A 22, xiii); 'Record of the Rebellion', *loc. cit.*, I, 54; Mulcahy Papers (B 8), P/7/A/23, and CO 904/151 (listing allegations of Truce breaches made by the IRA and RIC respectively); Macready, *op. cit.*, *passim*; Greenwood, 'The Future of the RIC', 10 Dec. 1921, CP 3542, Cab. 24/131; RIC circulars of 24 and 25 Jan., 15 and 29 Mar. 1922, CO 904/178; RIC terms of disbandment, 31 Mar. and [May] 1922 (revised), tabled as 1922 xvii, Cd 1618A, 797 and Cd 1673, 807; Hemming to Troup, 13 Dec. 1923, in Hemming Papers.
70. Clarke, 'Memoirs' (A 15), Chap. 6; Deputy IG's circular, 31 Jan. 1922, CO 904/178; *Saturday Record*, 4 Feb. 1922; Burke, 'Some of the Activities of the 4th Battn Mid Clare Bde' (F 39), Chaps 23 and 24; *Gazette*, 28 Jan. 1922.

Chapter 2
PROTESTANTS AND UNIONISTS
(pp. 40–71)

1. Ross-Lewin, *Poems*, 68–9.
2. Census of Ireland, 1911 (H 1); Thomas Keane, 'Demographic Trends' in Hurley, *Irish Anglicanism*, 170; *Burke's Landed Gentry of Ireland*, London 1904, *passim*; Return of Owners of Land . . . in Ireland, 1876, lxxx, C. 1492, 61. Another guide to the Irishness of the Clare landowning class is its propensity to live there. The Return, for the Year 1870, of the Number of Landed Proprietors (HC, 1872 (167) xlvii) shows that absenteeism in Clare was relatively low: 51 per cent of Clare landowners lived on or near their property (cf. Munster, 41 per cent; Ireland, 41 per cent) and 23 per cent occasionally so (cf. Munster, 7 per cent; Ireland, 4 per cent). But the residence of only 1 per cent of Clare landowners was unascertainable (cf. Munster, 14 per cent; Ireland, 10 per cent).
3. Ross-Lewin, *op. cit.*, 87–8; Report of the Estates Commissioners to 31 Mar. 1915 (H 10); *Champion*, 7 Nov. 1914. The average rent reduction agreed by Clare landlords in preparation for land purchase was the largest for any Irish county, as was their net loss after deduction of compensatory bonuses (analysis confined to holdings with rents previously judicially agreed). (Irish Convention, Report (H 9), especially pp. 92–3, 105–7.)
4. These figures were laboriously collated from the annual reports of the CDB, Estates Commissioners and Land Commissioners (H 3, 10 and 11). Not all anomalies could be smoothed out, but in estimating total purchases I have taken account of demesne lands resold to their vendors, as well as of probable purchase rates in the six counties of Northern Ireland after 1920. Of all land sold by its owners under the Land Purchase Acts, 1870–1919, 72 per cent had been sold by 31 March 1915 and 81 per cent by 31 March 1920. For Clare corresponding figures were 57 per cent and 71 per cent. Of all land bought by its occupiers (often after long administrative delay), 58 per cent and 70 per cent had been bought by 1915 and 1920 respectively (cf. Clare, 46 per cent and 66 per cent).

5. Commons *Debates*, Vol. 50, col. 709 (17 Mar. 1913); Butler Papers (F 8); CDB Report to 1915, App. viii; Inchiquin Papers, NLI, MS. 14590; Reports of Estates Commissioners, *passim*. The Estates Commissioners executed all compulsory expropriations, but within the 'Congested Districts Counties' they acted only at the CDB's request. Private land sales are excluded from analysis.
6. Sources cited at note 4 allow rough estimation of the amount of untenanted land ('parcels') sold by owners and bought by migrants, estate employees and others (see Chapter 7) under the Land Purchase Acts, 1870–1919. Such estimates cannot take account of variations in the rate of distribution of untenanted land by the CDB, or the irritating inclusion among untenanted lands bought by purchasers after 1920 of formerly tenanted lands surrendered to migrants. Analysis for Clare shows that 87 per cent of all untenanted lands sold under these acts had been sold by 1915, and 96 per cent by 1920, whereas only 28 per cent of untenanted lands bought had been bought by 1915 and 55 per cent by 1920. As a proportion of all lands bought, untenanted purchases rose from 4.0 per cent before 1915 through 8.5 per cent, 1915–20, to 9.0 per cent after 1920, but as a proportion of all lands sold, untenanted sales dropped from 9.5 per cent before 1915 through 3.9 per cent, 1915–20, to 0.8 per cent after 1920. Partially comparable figures for sales and purchases under the later (Southern) Irish Land Purchase Acts, 1923–65, are given in the Reports of the Irish Land Commissioners (I 8), *passim*.
7. Nicolette Devas, *Two Flamboyant Fathers*, 18; Macnamara to Congestion Commission (H 4), First Appendix to Seventh Report, Minutes 39775, 39637 *et seq.*; O'Brien Account Book, MS. 5038 (F 35); Tottenham, 'Records of Mount Callan' (F 32). By keeping servants landowners did not necessarily benefit their neighbours: O'Callaghan recruited his servants from outside Clare, often from Ulster; Macnamara's seven indoor servants in 1911 were all strangers to the county (three of them Protestants). Tottenham's five servants, on the other hand, were all Catholics from Clare or Tipperary. (Census Returns (A 28).)
8. Macnamara to Congestion Commission, *loc. cit.*, Minutes 39787–88; *Notes from Ireland*, Jan. 1913; Inchiquin Papers, NLI, MS. 14591; O'Callaghan to solicitors, 9 May 1912, LB (F 49) i, pp. 210–12; *ibid.*, pp. 327–8, 338; *Saturday Record*, 11 Jul. 1914.
9. Plunkett, *Noblesse Oblige: An Irish Rendering*, Dublin 1908, 5, 26; *Champion*, 15 Mar. 1913; *Clare Journal*, 13 Nov. 1913. In the 1890s the Vandeleurs' Kilrush estate had been chosen by the government as one of six 'test estates' for which special assistance (such as battering rams) was given for eviction of tenants and suppression of the Plan of Campaign. (L. P. Curtis, jr, *Coercion and Conciliation in Ireland 1880–1892: A Study in Conservative Unionism*, Princeton and London 1963, 240 *et seq.*)
10. 1911 Census (H 1); Robertson, *Crowned Harp*, 37, 74–5; O'Callaghan to Midleton, 8 Sep. 1918, LB i, p. 962. In Clare Protestant women were well represented among civil servants, medical and teaching staffs.
11. *Clare Journal*, 9 Jan. 1913; Devas, *op. cit.*, 18 (but Mrs Joe Connole, Ennistymon, indignantly denies that poachers were welcomed at the rook shoot); Spanish Point, Church of Ireland Records (D 2); O'Callaghan to Dr K. Lund, LB i, p. 691; Robertson, *op. cit.*, 76; MacLysaght Papers (F 21), 'Master of None', Chap. vi; letter from Clare Club, Ennis, 26 Jul. 1915, MS. 2649. Small Protestant schools such as Kilmanaheen were for the poor, not the gentry. Of eleven landed gentlemen in Clare in our period for whom schooling is recorded (mainly in *Burke's Landed Gentry of Ireland*, London 1958), five went to British schools or universities, two to Irish, four to both, and none to Kilmanaheen.
12. In 1911 Clare had 1,709 Episcopalians, 166 Presbyterians, 38 Methodists, 19 other non-Catholics (and 102,300 Roman Catholics). More than half the Presbyterians lived in the two largest towns, compared with less than one in four Episcopalians.

13. Ross-Lewin, *op. cit.*, 94; Kilmanaheen Parish Preachers' Books, Spanish Point Records (D 2). Average Sunday morning attendance at another Church of Ireland (Tuamgraney) declined from 23.2 in 1912–13 through 20.1 in 1913–14 to 15.9 in 1914–15. Total general collections for each year were £14 19s 6d, £13 7s 3d and £9 17s 6½d. Average morning attendance at Tuamgraney dropped from 20 in October 1913 to 16 in October 1918 and 8 in October 1920. Corresponding figures for three other churches (Kiltinanlea, O'Brien's Bridge and Killaloe Cathedral) were 20, 15 and 11; 14, 8 and 7; 53, 50 and 96. The Church (albeit with the help of Auxiliary worshippers at Killaloe) proved resilient in adversity. See Preachers' Books (D 1, 3), *passim*.
14. O'Callaghan to Crozier, 5 Aug. 1918, to M. G. S. Welsh, 10 Mar. 1913, to *Daily Express*, 27 Jul. 1915, and to Bishop Berry, 10 Sep. 1918: LB i, pp. 957, 336, 627–8, 964.
15. Robertson, *op. cit.*, 80; O'Callaghan to solicitor, 23 Jan. 1919, LB ii, p. 17; Magistrates (Ireland) Returns for Nov. 1910–11, 1911–12 and 1912–13, HC 1911 (277) lxv, 431, *ibid.* 1912/13 (38) lxix, 693, and *ibid.* 1914 (461) lxvii, 1003; Gerald Arbuthnot in *Nineteenth Century*, LXI (1907), 1027; Kerry CI, MCR, Oct. 1914; *Champion*, 31 Jan. 1914; *Saturday Record*, 1 Feb. 1919; Clare County Council Records (C 1), *passim*; O'Grady, *Selected Essays and Passages*, Dublin [1918], 166.
16. O'Brien Journal, 16 Mar. 1913, and letter to Frances Arnold Forster, 31 Jul. 1914, MSS 5044, 5004–6 (F 35); Brooke, *The Brimming River*, 97 *et seq.* (cf. the Aberdeens'—predominantly Lady Aberdeen's—twee reminiscences '*We Twa*', London 1925, and *More Cracks with 'We Twa'*, London 1929); O'Callaghan to IUA Secretary, 17–18 Mar. 1914, LB i, p. 453; David Greene in Hurley, *Irish Anglicanism*, 117–18, and Patton (Archdeacon of Killaloe), *Fifty Years*, 287; *Champion*, 12 Jul. 1913 (cf. Chapter 7).
17. O'Callaghan to *Clare Journal*, 25 Feb. 1911, LB i, p. 101; J. MacK. Wilson to IUA, 23 Jan. 1916 (F 34), reporting Inchiquin's membership estimate. O'Callaghan to Midleton, 27 Sep. 1918, LB i, p. 971, estimated peak branch membership at only ninety. Clare had one branch of the IUA in 1893, but the reorganised club did not reaffiliate until 1913. (Buckland, *Documentary History* (M 7), 143–7; *Clare Journal*, 27 Oct. 1913.)
18. O'Callaghan to Inchiquin, 10 Dec. 1911, and to Midleton, 12 Sep. 1918: LB i, pp. 154, 965–6; Arthur Lynch, *Ireland*, 148–52 n; Macnamara to County Clare Unionist Club, *Clare Journal*, 3 Feb. 1913; *ibid.*, 20 Feb. 1913; *Irish News*, quoted in *Champion*, 24 Jan. 1914; *Champion*, 22 Feb. 1913. A Mr Patterson had denounced 'professional politicians' for being ready to 'plunge our country into the horrors of civil war' for the sake of Home Rule, and despite temperate noises from Col. Tottenham the club agreed. (*Clare Journal*, 3 Feb. 1913.)
19. Ross-Lewin, *op. cit.*, 7–9, 27–8; O'Callaghan to solicitors, 22 Jan. 1913, and to IUA Secretary, 26 Apr. 1914: LB i, pp. 305, 464; O'Brien Journal, 3 Jan. 1913 (F 35).
20. O'Callaghan to M.P. O'Callaghan, 5 Oct. 1913, LB i, pp. 400–1; *Champion*, 7 Feb. 1914.
21. O'Callaghan to Bedford, 30 Dec. 1913, and draft notes, probably Feb. 1914: LB i, pp. 421, 437–42; club resolution, 17 Apr. 1914, RP 6519/1913; *Clare Journal*, 3 Feb. 1913. O'Callaghan's wariness of piano-tuners was not without foundation, for one of that craft was Denis McCullough, Special War 'B' List Suspect and President of the Supreme Council of the IRB in 1916.
22. *Notes from Ireland*, Mar. 1914; Head, *No Great Shakes*, 145–6; 'Ulster 1912', quoted in A. T. Q. Stewart, *The Ulster Crisis*, London 1967, 56; O'Callaghan to IUA Secretary, 15 Sep. and 29 Oct. 1913, 8 Mar., 26 Apr. and 19 May 1914, and to daughter, 25 Mar. 1914: LB i, pp. 395, 409, 451, 464, 469, 459.
23. *Irish Times*, 5 Aug. 1914; James O. Hannay in *Nineteenth Century*, LXXVIII (1915), 396; O'Brien to Forster, 14 Jul. 1914, O'Brien Papers, MSS 5004–6; O'Callaghan to IUA Secretary, 6 Aug. 1914, LB i, p. 498; IUA Executive Committee resolution, 16 Sep. 1914, *Notes from Ireland*, Nov. 1914; *Irish Times*, 16 Sep. 1914.

24. *Ibid.*, 2, 10 and 5 Jun. 1914; O'Callaghan to J. MacK. Wilson, 7 Jun. 1914, and to P. J. Ford, 8 Jun. 1914: LB i, pp. 477, 480. The Tuamgraney rector, R. Twiss MacLaurin, was granted police protection in July 1914 after receiving 'unpleasant attentions from the local Volunteers'. (CI, MCR.) On 20 September he recorded in his Preacher's Book (D 1): 'On this even. Micheal MacMahon came and ordered me to stop ringing the bell as the Chapel bell was ringing in honour of Redmond and I was interfering with it. I did not stop.' And on 13 June 1915: 'The new Sexton was stoned this day while making the gas, and stated that Canon Macnamara P.P. had directed him to cease ringing the bell.'
25. O'Brien to Forster, 20 Jul. 1914, O'Brien Papers, MSS 5004–6; O'Callaghan to IUA Secretary, 6 Aug. 1914, to *Saturday Record*, 5 Aug. 1914, to Stacpoole, 14 Aug. 1914, to C. MacDonnell, 23 Aug. 1914, and to D. G. Astley, 17 Jan. 1915: LB i, pp. 498, 497, 501, 503, 567–71; *Saturday Record*, 15 Aug. 1914. In May 1914 the CI (MCR) had remarked that Hugh O'Brien was the only 'Person of Standing' yet interested in the Volunteers. But on 13 August (?) 1914 Ernest Brown, O'Callaghan's ex-agent, hoped that retired officers would help 'teach them proper discipline, and how to act in large bodies'. Several Protestants were offered the Clare inspectorship, including a Unionist who innocently suggested: 'Let us all join Lord Kitchener's army for the War' and a Home Ruler who could not think that 'red hot Unionists are quite the leaders for this job'. Another Clare worthy, Lieut.-Gen. Kelly-Kenny, was proposed for the national command by Casement; but as Denis Gwynn points out, the suggestion was 'impracticable' since 'he was already paralysed in both legs'. (Brown to W. Redmond(?), 13 Aug. 1914, W. G. Butler to Moore, 22 Sep. 1914, and Hickman to Moore, 13 Aug. 1914: Moore Papers (F 23), MS. 10547/5; Casement to J. Redmond, 9 Jun. 1914, quoted by Gwynn in *The Life of John Redmond*, London 1932, 320.)
26. Vestry Minutes, 25 Aug. 1915, Spanish Point Records (D 2); O'Callaghan to Fogarty, 16 Jan. 1915, to Stacpoole, 26 Mar. 1916, and to IUA Secretary, 9 Aug. 1915; LB i, pp. 566, 711, 633; *Notes from Ireland*, May 1915; Brothers Ross-Lewin, *In Britain's Need*, 7.
27. O'Callaghan to Ford, 15 Nov. 1917, 25 Aug. 1914, to Wallace, 28 Feb. 1915, to Director of Recruiting (Limerick), 21 Nov. 1915, to a cousin, 7 Dec. 1915, and to IUA Secretary, 15 Nov. 1915: LB i, pp. 885–8, 505, 588, 670, 677–8, 664; *Notes from Ireland*, Aug. 1915, Nov. 1916; Brothers Ross-Lewin, *op. cit.*; *Saturday Record*, 22 Jan. 1916, 17 Aug. 1918, 8 Feb. and 4 Oct. 1919.
28. Cf. H. Kingsmill Moore, Principal of the Church of Ireland Training College, referring to 1916–17: 'Absorbed as we were in the issues of the Great War, we Unionists took little note of lesser happenings, contenting ourselves with gasping from time to time at the supineness of the Government.' (*Reminiscences and Reflections*, London 1930, 269.)
29. O'Callaghan to Messrs Browne & Nolan, 24 Jul. 1916, to M. P. O'Callaghan, 6 Nov. 1916, to IUA Secretary, 13 Jul. 1916, and to Bonar Law, 11 Jun. 1916: LB i, pp. 756, 784, 752, 743–6; Archbishop Bernard in *National Review*, LXVIII (Oct. 1916), 217; *Irish Times*, 28 Apr.–1 May and 27 Jun. 1916; *Notes from Ireland*, Aug. 1916.
30. Buckland, *Irish Unionism* (M 6), *passim*; R. B. McDowell, *The Irish Convention 1917–18*, London and Toronto 1970; Robert H. Murray, *Archbishop Bernard*, London 1931, 323. The IUA split on 24 January 1919, almost a year after 'The Crisis in Ireland. Call to Unionists' had put forward the diehard Ulsterite view (*Irish Times*, 4 Mar. 1918).
31. Wilson's report (F 34), *loc. cit.*; O'Callaghan to Inchiquin, 22 Sep. 1918, to Midleton, 21 Jul. and 12 Sep. 1918, to P. J. Ford, 27 Jan. 1919, and to Lady Ashtown, 19 Dec. 1917: LB i, pp. 968–9, 949–54, 965–6, 896, and LB ii, pp. 20–1 (Ford). A list of APL subscribers includes four Claremen (two of them absent from O'Callaghan's list and excluding O'Callaghan). Although a Midletonite, O'Callaghan urged a still

more generous settlement including home control of customs: 'We Unionists cannot stand for ever with one foot in England, the other in Ireland, and both insecurely planted. With the rise of Labour and Bonar Law turned Bolshevic we ought to show our countrymen that it is as Irishmen we want to live amongst them.' (Midleton Papers, PRO 30/67/40, ff. 2366–7; O'Callaghan to Midleton, 14 Jan. 1918, LB i, p. 905.)

32. Butler Papers (F 8), figures referring to 1896–1914 and 1915–21, 'outlay' referring to the costs of buying beasts only; Inchiquin Papers (F 16), MSS 14591 *et seq*. See Chapter 7 for further study of economic change.
33. O'Callaghan to Duke, 19 Jan. 1917, to A. J. Parker, 26 Mar. 1917, and to G. P. Stewart (Irish Landowners' Convention), 9 Oct. 1917, and statement of stock, Sep. 1919: LB i, pp. 809–10, 839, 868, and LB ii, p. 76.
34. Cf. Chapter 7; *Champion*, 7 Jun. 1919, 12 Feb. and 22 Jan. 1921; *Saturday Record*, 25 Oct. 1919; O'Callaghan to W. Wilson Lynch, 25 Jul. 1919, LB ii, p. 58 (Kilkishen).
35. CS to US, 7 Oct. 1919, RP 32310/1919; O'Callaghan to CS, 1 Sep. 1919, to Lord French, Nov. 1919, to Ennis CI, 15 Sep. 1919, and to Stacpoole, 31 Oct. 1919: LB ii, pp. 65–6, 100, 73, 94; *Champion*, 13 Dec. 1919. On 11 December 1919 Lord French noted 'much divergence of opinion' within the executive over the ban, which was lifted in January 1920. But sporadic bans continued, and by June 1921 fairs and markets were outlawed in five Clare districts. Under martial law military permits were required even after the Truce. (*Champion*, 31 Jan. 1920, 23 and 30 Jul. 1921; CI, MCR, Jun. 1921 (Clare); French Journal (A 17), p. 61.)
36. CDB Report for 1915 (H 3), p. 8; list of estates where sale pending at 31 Mar. 1916, RP 3591/1916; cf. Chapter 7 and notes 4 and 6 above.
37. *Champion*, 30 Jan. 1915; O'Callaghan to Ennis CI, 22 Nov. 1916, LB i, p. 786.
38. Connolly to Magill, 21 Mar. 1917, CSO Official Papers (A 30, iii), parcel 5; IG, MCRs, Jan. 1917, Feb. 1918; *Champion*, 23 Mar. 1918; Ennistymon RDC Minutes (C 2), 19 Mar. 1918; Hibbert, 'Report on the West of Ireland', in Buckland, *Documentary History*, 380–1; CI, MCRs, Dec. 1920, Jul. 1921.
39. Lords *Debates*, Vol. 40, cols 421–2; Commons *Debates*, Vol. 117, cols 1269–72, and Vol. 126, col. 432. Bonar Law's promise was made without prior cabinet discussion, and on 11 March the CS complained that the cabinet had made no 'definite ruling' on his own proposals. On 19 May the Lord Chancellor looked forward to consideration of a new Land Purchase Bill 'not very much later than the Home Rule proposals', but the cabinet's 'final sanction' for the draft bill was still unforthcoming. It never came. (CP 849, Cab. 24/100; CP 624, Cab. 24/98; Lords *Debates*, Vol. 40, cols 421–2.)
40. O'Callaghan to CS, 24 May 1921, to OC Troops Ennis, 3 Feb. 1921, and to C. Quinn, 2 Feb. 1921: LB ii, pp. 242, 202, 201; CFA Resolution, 8 Jan. 1921, *ibid*., p. 206; O'Callaghan to IFU Secretary, 22 Dec. 1921, *ibid*., 303–4; Inchiquin Papers, MSS 14596–9. In September 1921 the CI reported (MCR) that Inchiquin's tenants had been ordered by notice to hold back their rents. Cf. Chapter 7.
41. CI, MCR, Jan. 1915 (Clare); *Champion*, 13 Feb. 1915; O'Callaghan to Secretary, Agricultural Wages Board, 21 Oct. 1917, LB i, p. 872; cf. Table 7.2; O'Brien Household Account, MS. 5026 (F 35).
42. E. K. Kearney to CS, 2 Mar. 1918, CSO Official Papers (A 30, iii), parcel 12; O'Callaghan to Secretary, Irish Landowners' Convention 27 Sep. 1918, LB i, p. 972; Anne, Lady Inchiquin's recollection; O'Brien to F. A. Forster, 31 May 1921, O'Brien Papers, MSS 5004–6; Tottenham Rainfall Book (F 54), 11 Nov. 1921, and documents on arbitration (F 32).

43. O'Callaghan to insurance firm, 16 Feb. 1918, and to Major Blackwood Price, 14 Jan. 1920: LB i, p. 914, and LB ii, p. 129; Hibbert to CS, 23 Feb. 1918, RP 5564/1918; entries in Tottenham Rainfall Book, *loc. cit.*, 21 Nov. 1919, 27 Jun. 1920, 27 Feb. 1921; Hibbert, 'Report on the West of Ireland', 23 Apr. 1920, in Buckland, *Documentary History*, 380–1; copy of report by P. A. Mulcahy on Mid-Clare Brigade, Military Archives (B 3), p. 915; *Champion*, 3 Jan. 1920; Macnamara's application for compensation, PROD, ID.34.28 (A 29).

44. OC Mid-Clare Brigade to COS, 6 Jun. 1921, enclosing letter (29 May) from Vice-Commandant, 1st Battalion, Mulcahy Papers (B 8), P/7/A/19; CI, MCR, Jul. 1920; Barry, *Guerilla Days*, 116; Hibbert, 'Report', *loc. cit.*; OC Mid-Clare Brigade to COS, 25 Jun. 1921, and reply, 5 Jul. 1921, Mulcahy Papers, P/7/A/20; Tottenham, 'Records of Mount Callan' (F 32). At least two of the six houses burned by the IRA were considered ripe for occupation by Crown forces. A seventh Big House was burned, according to O'Callaghan (to H. E. Yarley, 17 Feb. 1921, LB ii, p. 208), by persons 'Land Grabbing, not Sinn Fein'. By the end of May 1921 seventy country houses had been reported burned in the martial law region; in June and July 1921 twenty-seven were burned in the 5th Division region (not under martial law). ('Record of the Rebellion' (A 11), I, 31; 'History of the 5th Division' (A 11), 77.)

45. Kerry CI, MCR, May 1918; R. E. Parkinson, *History of the Grand Lodge of Free and Accepted Masons of Ireland*, Dublin 1957, II, 254; Webster in Phillips, *Church of Ireland* (M 20), III, 414–15; Lady FitzGerald to Twiss MacLaurin, [19 May] 1918, Spanish Point Records [D 2]; Vestry Minutes, 2 Sep. 1919, *ibid.*; Tottenham Rainfall Book, *loc. cit.*, Nov. 1919; *Champion*, 4 Jun. 1921; O'Callaghan to T. Edwards, 30 Mar. 1921, LB ii, pp. 223–4; O'Brien to Forster, 6 Jun. 1921, O'Brien Papers, MSS 5004–6. Head (*No Great Shakes*, 212), thought game-shooting 'a trusty barometer of the state of Irish affairs'.

46. O'Callaghan to Lord Mayo, 28 Jan. 1920, LB ii, p. 133; *Notes from Ireland*, Aug. 1919, May 1920, Mar. and Aug. 1921; 18th Infantry Brigade, Intelligence Summary, 20 Aug. 1921, captured copy in Mulcahy Papers, P/7/A/23; *Notes from Ireland*, Feb. 1922. At least three more houses (cf. note 44) were burned in Clare during the Civil War. (Irish Claims Compensation Association, *The Irish Free State. The Campaign of Fire*, London [1923].)

47. O'Callaghan to M. P. O'Callaghan, 16 Mar. 1920, and to T. Edwards, 26 Oct. 1921: LB ii, pp. 153–4, 277–8; 'Statement of Certain Happenings . . .' (F 49).

48. Wilson's Report (F 34); Devas, *op. cit.*, 20; Forster to O'Brien, 26 Jan. 1918 (quoting O'Brien to Forster, missing), O'Brien Papers, MSS 5004–6; O'Callaghan to M. P. O'Callaghan, 19 Jun. 1917, to *Irish Times*, 25 Jun. and 16 Jul. 1917, to Lord French, 11 Oct. 1918, and to Macpherson, 7 Oct. 1919: LB i, pp. 845, 847–8, 850–3, 979–80, and LB ii, p. 78; *Saturday Record*, 28 Jul. 1917; Lynch-Robinson, *The Last of the Irish R.M.s*, 122; cf. Jones, *Whitehall Diary*, III, 24–5 (Volunteer traffic wardens).

49. *Irish Times*, 4 Oct. 1921 (cf. *Champion*, 29 Oct. 1921, which at last welcomed Unionists back to Irish political life, praising 'Col O'Callaghan Westropp [sic] and many others giving incomparable and unselfish service to the country'); O'Callaghan to C. J. France, 23 Apr. 1921, to Figgis, 5 Feb. 1920, to Cosgrave, 23 Dec. 1921, and to a government official, 4 Dec. 1922: LB ii, pp. 235, 139–40, 305, 339.

50. Land Commission Report to 1971 (I 8); Notice, 23 Oct. 192(?), Listowel Papers (F 2); Diary of Ethel, Lady Inchiquin (F 16); Burke, 'Some of the Activities of the 4th Battn Mid Clare Bde' (F 39), Chap. 25; inscription in Tottenham Visitors' Book (F 54), 8 Jun. 1923. Happily, Col. Tottenham's descendants continue to occupy, farm and improve Mount Callan.

Chapter 3
HOME RULERS
(pp. 72–104)

1. Birmingham, *An Irishman Looks at His World*, 297.
2. Lyons, *The Irish Parliamentary Party*, 169, 176–80; *Thom's Official Directory . . . for the Year 1915*, Dublin 1915, 136–8, 224 *et seq*.
3. *Champion*, 23 Jun. 1917; *In Memoriam. MajorWillie Redmond*, Dublin 1918; Lynch, *My Life Story*, 50, 237 and *passim*; Harmsworth to lawyer, 26 Jan. 1903, printed copy in Redmond Papers (F 31), MS. 15202. Most of Lynch's many books, whatever their ostensible subjects, are primarily concerned with Lynch. Éamon de Valera was the other student of quaternions.
4. *Champion*, *passim* (its tabulations of voting figures were, alas, spasmodic). The Boards of Guardians comprised the local RDCs together with representatives elected from urban districts. By the Local Government (Ireland) Act, 1898 (61 & 62 Vic., c. 37), the archaic property franchise was replaced by the parliamentary franchise (which by 1911 covered 17 per cent of the Clare population and 56 per cent of its adult males), extended to peers and qualified women. Women could stand for UDCs and RDCs, and after 1911 for county councils also. (See especially John Collins, *Local Government*, Dublin 1954, 26–7; John J. Webb, *Municipal Government in Ireland Mediaeval and Modern*, Dublin 1918, 276–9; Brian Walker, 'The Irish Electorate, 1868–1915', *Irish Historical Studies*, XVIII (Mar. 1973), 359–406).
5. Arensberg and Kimball, *Family and Community* (revised ed.), 385; *Champion*, 11 Oct. and 1 Mar. 1913; 'Paddy the Cope' [Patrick Gallagher], *My Story*, Dungloe n.d., 139. Many shopkeepers were also farmers: in 1911 Clare had 540 adult male and 531 female grocers, shopkeepers and publicans, and 153 occupiers of land also engaged in these pursuits. It is uncertain whether or not all or some of the latter were counted among the former. (See 1911 Census.)
6. *Champion*, 25 Oct. and 28 Jun. 1913.
7. Patrick O'Farrell, *Ireland's English Question*, London 1971, 225, 252 *et seq*.; cf. Appendix. Parish priests, who comprised just under two-fifths of the secular clergy in 1914, were over-represented among Home Rule advocates (21 of 45), but not among Gaels (8 of 19), suggesting that the junior clergy was rather more inclined to support the less respectable cause.
8. *Champion*, 25 Jul. 1914; Memorial to Dr Fogarty [1908?], Diocesan Archive (E 1).
9. Military Intelligence Officer, MR to OC Southern District, Sep. 1916, CO 904/157/1; Basil Chubb, *The Government and Politics of Ireland*, London and Stanford 1970, 131 (1968 sample of persons aged over fifteen); O'Malley, *On Another Man's Wound*, 124.
10. This challenge appeared on the *Champion*'s letterhead (see letter no. 85, 6 Jun. 1916, in SPO (A 33)). The *Herald* appeared between 1877 and 1922, the *Champion* from 1903 onwards, the *Journal* from 1828 to 1917, and the *Record* between 1885 and 1936. Cf. Frank O'Dea's article in Thomas Dillon, ed., *The Banner* (S 33).
11. Analysis of advertisements was limited to one issue of each paper in January of each year, measurement being made in column centimetres. 225 *Champion* leaders between 1913 and 1916 and 248 between 1917 and 1921 were classified. Between 1917 and 1921, 54 per cent of these concerned the national struggle, 17 per cent the administration of Ireland, 8 per cent world affairs, 5 per cent local affairs and 13 per cent agrarian or labour matters (cf. 9 per cent 1913–16), reflecting the editor's growing absorption in specifically Irish issues.
12. *Champion*, 7 Jun. and 25 Oct. 1913 (leaders).

13. *Ibid.*, 20 Feb. 1915; Childers, *Framework of Home Rule*, xiii; Kettle, *Open Secret*, 64. Kettle predicted the collapse of the Irish Party and growing dominance of the Ulster Unionists (p. 159), yet induced John Redmond to write a preface.
14. *Westminster Gazette*, 11 Jul. 1913; *Champion*, 22 Nov. 1913. The next issue confessed that bad weather had forced cancellation of the monster meeting and that only five divisions of the AOH had taken part in the procession.
15. See Appendix for sources of these and similar figures throughout this chapter.
16. Returns of UIL strength and funds, CO 904/20 (A 22, ii); Lyons, *op. cit.*, especially pp. 149–54, 157; Redmond to Lynch, 15 Jul. 1907, Lynch to Redmond, 11 and 21 Jul. 1907, Redmond Papers, MS. 15202. In 1902 Lynch had been elected for North Galway, with the party's blessing, but was disqualified as a criminal and imprisoned for his actions in South Africa. After his release Redmond told Lynch that he had 'no power' to select party candidates and was 'hardly ever' asked for his recommendation. He added: 'Are you really serious in wanting to come back here, and are you wise in this?' Lynch, evidently with local UIL support, narrowly beat the officially favoured candidate at the West Clare electoral convention.
17. O'Callaghan to D. G. Astley, 17 Jan. 1915, LB i, pp. 567–71; *Champion*, 29 Jan. 1921 ('Side Lights of Life in Clare'), and 1 Nov. 1913; CI, MCR, May 1915 (Limerick).
18. AOH *General Rules* (N l); CI, MCR (Clare), Oct. 1913, Feb. and Mar. 1914, and MCR (Kerry), Jan. 1913. The rival 'Irish American Alliance' of the AOH, closely associated with Clan na Gael, had no branches in Clare.
19. CI, MCR (West Cork), Mar. 1914; David W. Miller, *Church, State and Nation in Ireland 1898–1921*, Dublin 1973, 210 *et seq*. The Church, at first alarmed by the popularity of this lay sectarian movement, sensibly decided to take it over once its initial admonitions had passed unheeded.
20. Between January 1913 and September 1914 the number of AOH divisions rose from 9 to 24 in Co. Clare. On 17 May 1913 Clare had 318 fully-fledged Hibernians and 1,057 insured members; by January 1916 it had 822 (presumably full) members. Meanwhile the Clare strength of the UIL had dropped from 3,246 members in 50 branches (March 1913) to 2,559 in 43 (September 1914) and 2,052 in 33 (March 1915). Analysis of branch distribution suggests, however, that the AOH grew strongest in regions where the UIL had been weakest. The AOH was most powerful in East Clare, the UIL in West Clare. (*Champion*, 17 May 1913; CI, MCRs, *passim*; UIL Returns, CO 904/20; cf. Appendix.)
21. *Champion*, 17 Jan. 1914, 9 Aug. 1913, 20 Mar. 1915.
22. *Saturday Record* and *Champion*, 4 Dec. 1915. 111 of the 749 Home Rulers analysed were associated either with two or more (non-separatist) Nationalist bodies, or one Nationalist and at least one ostensibly apolitical body (Gaelic League, GAA, returned soldiers', ratepayers', Labour or farmers' associations).
23. Hannay (when Vice-President of the Gaelic League) to 'a public man in the North', May 1907, quoted by R. B. D. French in *Hermathena*, CII (1966), 50.
24. *Champion*, 21 Mar. 1914; MacLysaght, Diaries (F 47), iv, 27 Jun. 1914.
25. *Champion*, 6 Jun. and 28 Nov. 1914; *Saturday Record*, 30 May 1914; P. J. MacNamara (Secretary, Ennis Volunteers) to IG's Office, 22 Sep. 1914 (and reply, 23 Sep.), Moore Papers, MS. 10547/5; *British Review* (Jul. 1914), 18–19. In May 1914 the RIC's IG, MCR, remarked that the Volunteers were no longer drawn from the 'extreme sections', but were 'spreading rapidly all over the country, taking in the Ancient Order of Hibernians, Gaelic Athletic Association, and all sections of Nationalists'.
26. Clare CI, MCR, Apr. 1914, and Limerick CI, MCRs, Nov. and Dec. 1913; *Champion*, 2 May 1914; J. D. Nugent's *'Private and Confidential'* circular, Ceannt Papers (F 9), NLI, MS. 13070; Maurice Moore's 'Appreciation' in *Major William Redmond* (S 18), 59–60.

27. *Saturday Record*, 23 May 1914; *Champion*, 30 May, 20, 27 and 6 Jun. 1914; Fr John O'Dea to Lysaght, 26 May 1914, in MacLysaght Papers, NLI, MS. 2650; CI, MCR, May 1914; IG, MCR, Jul. 1914. Before the party's takeover of the Provisional Committee its chairman, Eóin Mac Néill, had proposed that Willie Redmond join a new Chief Directory. Willie was willing, provided John agreed—which he did not. After the split with Mac Néill's followers, Willie Redmond became honorary treasurer of the new National Committee of the force. (Mac Néill to Devlin, 13 May 1914, W. Redmond to Mac Néill, 16 May 1914, and J. Redmond to Mac Néill, 16 May 1914: Redmond Papers, MS. 15204; Maurice Moore in *Irish Press*, 20 Jan. 1938; *National Volunteer*, 17 Oct. 1914.)

28. We should note that among the 21 INV companies formed in Clare before June 1914, 15 arose in localities with AOH divisions and only 7 in UIL localities; thereafter only 5 of the 28 formations occurred in AOH localities but 19 in UIL localities. So the party's stranglehold tightened.

29. Redmond to Asquith, 7 Jun. 1915, MS. Asquith 36 (A 2), f. 94; Fogarty to W. Redmond, 18 Oct. 1914, and W. Redmond to IG's Office, 21 Oct. (with reply from Moore, 23 Oct.): Moore Papers, MS. 10547/5. On the same visit Moore declined another priest's 'very insistent' lunch invitation: 'Our time table would not admit of such frivolities, but we brought him and the champagne along in the motor.' (*Irish Press*, 14 Feb. 1938.)

30. *Champion*, 18 Jul. and 19 Sep. 1914; Fr M. Gilligan, CC, to Moore, 21 Apr. 1915, Moore Papers, MS. 10547/5. Another priest told the Killaloe Volunteers that they 'were beyond reproach, but it had been said that in other parts of Ireland there is a temptation to go for a march for the purpose of getting drunk at public houses, and getting drunk and fighting'. (*Champion*, 15 Aug. 1914.)

31. Moore in *Irish Press*, 22 Jan. 1938; *Champion*, 20 Jun. 1914. The directive against participation in elections (cf. co-options) was dated 3 June 1914, the day *after* rural elections in Clare.

32. CI, MCR, Aug. 1914 (64 branches). In April 1915 the CI reported the existence of 59 companies but many were evidently unregistered with headquarters: a return dated 16 April 1915 lists only 24 Clare companies, of which eleven submitted returns of membership totalling only 819. (Moore Papers, MS. 10547/5.)

33. Martin, *The Irish Volunteers*, 145–6; Redmond to Mac Néill, 3 Aug. 1914, Redmond Papers, MS. 15204; *Memoirs of Desmond FitzGerald*, 46–7; W. Redmond to J. J. Horgan, 12 Sep. 1914, Horgan Papers (F 15); Martin, *op. cit.*, 148; Mac Giolla Choille, *Intelligence Notes* (L 16), *passim*. On 23 December 1914 Clare had 394 Irish (MacNeillite) Volunteers and 4,744 National Volunteers (*ibid.*, 109–12); but, as Col Moore recalled in the *Irish Press*, 15 Feb. 1938, 'I was told that politics were in a very uncertain state in Clare [late September], and very little would have changed the whole body of Volunteers from one side to the other.' FitzGerald's despondency over Redmond's declaration was not shared by Pádraic Pearse, who wrote to J. McGarrity on 3 August: 'We should be fools if we let slip an opportunity of taking over from the British Army the task of defending the soil of Ireland.' (Hobson Papers (F 14), MS. 13162.)

34. MacNamara to Barton, 1 Sep. 1914, D. Robinson to Moore, after 5 Sep. 1914, MacNamara to W. Redmond, 10 Sep. 1914, and J. de Courcy to IG's Office, 7 Oct. 1914: Moore Papers, MSS 10547/5 and 10544/4 (Robinson); *Champion*, 22 Jan. 1916. Despite rumours of gun-running in Clare and Hugh Vere O'Brien's distribution of rifles and bayonets sent to the Shannon estuary by the Limerickmen and Claremen of New York, arming of the Ennis Volunteers did not begin until 18 September. (*Saturday Record*, 26 Sep. 1914, and *Champion*, 1 and 8 Aug. 1914.) The Miltown Volunteers fared worse still, although Willie Redmond had promised to try to get them 'a fair share' of whatever rifles were available. (*Saturday Record*, 5 Sep. 1914.)

35. *Champion*, 8 and 29 Aug. 1914, 17 Jul. 1915. On 26 September 1914 the *Champion* merely pronounced it 'our duty to regard the Home Rule Bill as a treaty of peace'; finally on 24 October it referred to Redmond's statement of 20 September as an assurance that there would be no attempt 'to compel, or even to induce' anyone to join up against their will. The *Record*, although always coy in offering opinions, unmistakably backed Redmond's recruiting manifesto of the spring of 1916 (*Saturday Record*, 4 Mar. 1916).
36. Sir Bryan Mahon in William G. FitzGerald, ed., *The Voice of Ireland*, Dublin and London 1924, 125–6 (paraphrase of report to Kitchener, *c.* 4 Aug.); Mac Néill's undated memorandum on the abortive 'Paget Scheme' to give the Volunteers territorial status, Hobson Papers, MS. 13174. Redmond urged government and military leaders to allow Volunteers to enlist '*for home service only*', but predicted that 'the military spirit' would blossom and encourage them to volunteer for service abroad. Redmond did not denounce official intransigence in the Commons until November 1915, and as late as May 1916 his hopes may have been revived when Maxwell urged recognition of the Volunteers as 'part of the Forces of the Crown'. (Redmond to Asquith, 15 Feb. 1915, MS. Asquith 41, ff. 186–8; Redmond to Gen. Sclater, 8 Jul. 1915, Redmond Papers, MS. 15225; Commons *Debates*, Vol. 75, cols 537–50; Maxwell to French, 7 May 1916, MS. Asquith 44, ff. 1–3.)
37. IG, Clare and West Cork CIs, MCRs, Sep. 1914; Returns of army recruits, RP 21680/1916; Mac Giolla Choille, *Intelligence Notes*, 180–2. National returns of Volunteer recruits exclude metropolitan Dublin.
38. Clare figures culled from stray tables in RP 21680/1916 (showing that of 411 Claremen recruited between 15 October 1914(?) and 15 August 1915, 204 were recruited in Ennis and Kilrush districts); Mac Giolla Choille, *op. cit.*, 180–2; Men of Military Age (H 14). Figures for Ireland, Ulster and the four counties (Clare, Cork, Kerry and Limerick) served in 1918 by the recruiting offices in Cork and Tralee (covering Ennis, Limerick and Bandon), were culled from continuous tabulation of army, navy and air force recruits raised between 4 August 1914 and 9 November 1918. (PRO, Nat. Serv. 1/84 (A 24).) Many inconsistencies among published and unpublished returns inhibit analysis. My estimates show 949 Clare army recruits from 4 August 1914 to 15 October 1916, and 134,158 Irish recruits to all services throughout the war (excluding 17,804 reservists recalled in 1914, some 20,000 Irish regular soldiers, and an unknown number of Irishmen recruited in Britain). The estimate for men of military age in August 1914 (from H 14) is rough, being the number on the National Register, 15 August 1915 (except those medically unfit or indispensable to the economy) + recruits and reservists raised and recalled since outbreak of war (discounting deaths, emigration, age change). The table discounts naval reservists and army special reservists, for whom regional breakdowns were unavailable.
39. R. W. Needham to US, 11 Mar. 1916, RP 21679/1916 (cf. Minutes of Conference on Recruiting in Ireland, 15 Oct. 1915, Redmond Papers, MS. 15261/8); *Champion*, 4 and 25 Mar. 1916 (membership of West Clare Recruiting Committee).
40. *Champion*, 19 Sep. 1914 (next week the editor casually remarked that 'the intervention of the war may have the effect of delaying the opening of the Irish Parliament for six or eight months'); MacNamara to W. Redmond, 16 Sep. 1914, Moore Papers, MS. 10547/5; CI, MCR, Sep. 1914.
41. MS. Asquith 36, ff. 94 *et seq.*; *Champion*, 28 Aug., 4 and 25 Dec. 1915.
42. On 12 February 1914 Lynch had told the Commons: 'If England were now attacked by a foreign enemy I would fight for England. I go further, and say that all whom I could influence would also fight for her.' (Commons *Debates*, Vol. 58, col. 337.) On 23 May 1914 the *Champion* denounced the *Record*, which that same day called to its aid the *Kilrush Herald* ('there is no fault found in West Clare with the gallant gentleman'). But on 3 June

1914 Tom Clarke wrote to Devoy: 'We have Lynch nearly flattened out as it is. Tom Hayes, Ben Parsons and others here in Dublin have been going for his scalp, and Maguire, Editor of the *Clare Champion*, is after him. So between us we will do for the s— of a b—.' (*Devoy's Post-Bag* (O 7), II, 448.)

43. *Champion*, 3 Apr. and 20 Nov. 1915 and *passim*.
44. UIL, *The Irish Party* (N 15); *Champion*, 5 Jun. 1915; IG, MCR, 5 Jun. 1915. In times of decline newspaper reports provide a better index than police figures, with their lag in pronouncing death, of organisational vitality. Another measure of the UIL's decline, worsened by the suspension of elections and most land purchase during the European war, is the amount of funds collected quarterly by its Clare branches: 1913, £16, 110, 70, 74; 1914, 62, 4, 27, none; 1915, none, 6, none, 8; thereafter, none. (UIL Returns, CO 904/20.)
45. Lysaght to Hemphill (IG's Office), 14 Oct. 1914, P. J. MacNamara to IG's Office(?), 27 Jan. 1915, Bianconi to Moore, 16 Mar. 1916 (and reply, 23 Mar.), 21 Oct. 1915, 17 Apr. 1916, Eckersley to Moore, 23 Sep. 1915, and Bianconi to Hemphill, 25 Sep. 1915: Moore Papers, MS. 10547/5; *Champion*, 14 Aug. 1915 (advertisement). For the Raheen camp see correspondence and report in Moore Papers, MSS 10544/1, 10545/5.
46. O'Malley, *On Another Man's Wound*, 69.
47. *Ireland* (N.Y.), 6 May 1916; *Saturday Record*, 19 Aug. 1916; Commons *Debates*, Vol. 85, col. 2773 (23 Aug. 1916); *Champion*, 2 Dec. 1916; Stephen Gwynn, *John Redmond's Last Years*, 259. This proposal was not discussed at this time by the party, although renewed and rejected after the South Longford by-election defeat in May 1917.
48. Kerry CI, MCR, May 1916; Annie O'Brien to J. Redmond, 19 Jun. 1917, and T. Scanlan to J. Redmond, 19 Jun. 1917: Redmond Papers, MS. 15263/2; transcript of Lundon to Whitton, 7 Jul. 1917, with US's annotation, RP 16695/1917; Commons *Debates*, Vol. 104, col. 580 (14 Mar. 1918); *Saturday Record*, 28 Sep. 1918. Arthur Lynch's recruiting zeal was of long standing: in 1914 he had hoped for an Irish 'troop side by side with the brave French soldiers' (as in 1918 he urged Irishmen to fight 'side by side with the Irish-Americans' rather than the British); on 24 October 1916 Lloyd George had found it 'difficult to agree and difficult to refuse', upon one of his crusading offers; on 10 June 1918 the cabinet accepted his 'patriotic offer' since he was 'now thoroughly imbued with pro-Ally sentiment' and had, after all, shown such 'fine soldierly qualities' in South Africa. But on 2 September Lord French, his old Boer War antagonist, regretted that 'he ever was allowed to come over here for we have quite difficulties enough without men like him raising more for us'; and the government, according to Lynch, killed his crusade by turning down thirty-three of his proposals, refusing headlights for his touring car and so forth. Yet he was now a real colonel, had had his health proposed by Sir James Campbell, and had been promised six pipers in Irish kilts for his brigade. (*Saturday Record*, 12 Sep. 1914, 28 Sep. 1918; Cab. 42/22, no. 5; Cab. 23/6/429(18); French to Lloyd George, Lloyd George Papers, F/48/6/18; Lynch, *My Life Story*, 296–306; *The Times*, 19 Aug. 1918; Commons *Debates*, Vol. 110, col. 899 (24 Oct. 1918).)
49. Dillon's estimate to Scott, Trevor Wilson, ed., *The Political Diaries of C. P. Scott 1911–1928*, London 1970, 352. As Lyons shows in *John Dillon*, Redmond's successor had long been pessimistic about the party's chances of revival. On 26 September 1916 (p. 403) he had written to T. P. O'Connor that since the formation of the 1915 coalition ministry the party had been 'steadily and rather rapidly losing our hold on the people, and the rebellion and the negotiations only brought out in an aggravated form what had been beneath the surface for a year'.
50. CI, MCRs, Nov. 1916, Dec. 1917; *Saturday Record*, 21 Dec. 1918 (the councillor was re-elected in January 1920); *Champion*, 13 May 1916 (statement of George McElroy, RM).

The AOH's function as an approved benefit society helped it retain some vitality during the party's decline. Stephen Gwynn termed it 'the main support we had' after May 1917. Although by August 1919 the AOH had only two divisions and four other groups in Clare, the organisation had increased its Ulster membership by about 12 per cent between January 1916 and January 1919, and on 31 December 1918 still reported nearly 150,000 insured members (five-sixths the number five years earlier). (Gwynn, *op. cit.*, 259; AOH Agenda (N 2); CIs, MCRs, *passim* (nine counties of Ulster); Report by the Government Actuary, 1918, p. 50 (1922 ix, Cmd 1662, 485).)

51. F. J. Barrett to J. Redmond, 12 Oct. 1916, Redmond Papers, MS. 15262/8; Kerry CI, MCRs, Nov. 1918, Aug. 1919.
52. *Saturday Record*, 6 May 1916, 30 Jun. 1917, 9 Mar. 1918; *Champion*, 6 May and 11 Nov. 1916, 23 Jun. 1917, 5 and 19 Oct. and 2 Nov. 1918, 5 Apr. 1919.
53. Voluntary censorship, encouraged by threat of prosecution under DORA, was applied to proofs of newspapers and pamphlets and to telegrams sent by press correspondents in Ireland. Until the abolition of the British Press Bureau in April 1919, the Irish censor's authority was uncertain. The bureau, which limited its functions to protection of wartime security, controlled British papers with Irish circulation reporting Irish affairs, vied with the Irish censor in interfering with telegrams, and sometimes gave sanction by private wire to Irish dailies for articles condemned by the Irish censor. (A 22, xi; A 33.)
54. *Saturday Record* to PC, 19 Apr. and 2 May 1917, Correspondence, no. 211 (A 33); Sir Bryan Mahon to CS, 30 Nov. 1917, CO 904/122 (opposing seizure of the *Champion*'s plant); Sarsfield Maguire to PC, 24 Nov. 1917, Correspondence, no. 1° (A 33); DI Munro to IG, RIC, 2 Apr. 1918, RP 15041/1918; CI, MCR, Oct. 1919; chastened letters in Correspondence, no. 148ⁿ (A 33); lists of Sinn Féin and Irish Party papers, Aug. 1919 or earlier, in parcel (A 33). Major I. H. Price (minute, 6 Apr. 1918, RP 15041/1918) thought 'this paper [*Champion*] had a very bad local influence but was not nearly so pernicious as the Dublin Sinn Fein Press'; but the *Champion* (together with the *Catholic Bulletin, Irishman, Nationality, Young Ireland* and *New Ireland*) was one of six papers withheld from internees in Britain and from export from the UK. (Waller to Watt, 2 Sep. 1918; Decies (PC) to US, 2 Oct. 1918, Correspondence, nos 39 and 47ⁿ (A 33).)
55. The percentage of space devoted to advertisements in the first issues of the *Champion* for 1919–21 was 46, 45 and 33; for the *Record*, 31, 38 and 23.
56. *Champion*, 26 Jan. and 28 Sep. 1918; O'Brien Pocket Diary, 14 Sep. 1918 (O'Brien Papers (F 24), MS. 15705).
57. *Champion*, 10, 24 and 17 Jan., 7 Feb., 13 Mar. and 15 Apr. 1920. Late in 1920 many party men, including the deposed Ennis UDC Chairman, gave in to Republican pressure to resign their Commissions of the Peace. The *Watchword of Labour* unkindly headed its report of 515 resignations between 19 May and 31 August 1920 (nearly 10 per cent of all justices): 'RATS DESERT SINKING SHIP', the heading being printed upside down. (*Watchword*, 2 Oct. 1920; *Champion*, 28 Aug. 1920.)
58. *Champion*, 19 Aug., 26 Aug. and 22 Jul. 1916, 31 Mar., 7, 14 and 21 Apr. 1917; 'Analysis of Action on Circular by Public Boards' (from press reports), Plunkett Papers (F 30), MS. 11383. Plunkett's invitation was rejected outright by both UDCs and the Ballyvaughan Guardians.
59. *Champion*, 22 Sep. 1917, 14 Jun. 1919; *Record*, 15, 1 and 22 Jun. 1918. The re-elected vice-chairman was Sarsfield Maguire, editor of the suppressed *Champion*, whose canny political tergiversations we have already touched upon.
60. Maguire did not seek re-election in 1920, but P. J. O'Loghlen of Ballyvaughan, the publican who had been elected County Council chairman in 1918, was returned for Sinn

Féin. Only two other sitting councillors were re-elected (without opposition), both UIL veterans who (like O'Loghlen) had transferred their sympathies to separatism as early as 1917.

Chapter 4
SINN FÉINERS
(pp. 107–37)

1. Seán O'Faolain, *Vive Moi! An Autobiography*, London 1965, 146. I have followed contemporary informed usage in applying the term 'Sinn Féin' to (1) followers of Arthur Griffith, 1905–16; (2) the disorganised movement of opposition to the Irish Party, April 1916–summer 1917; (3) the organisation of local political clubs (distinct from the Irish Volunteers and from Dáil Éireann), summer 1917 onwards. Occasionally, especially in quotations, 'Sinn Féin' should be interpreted in its colloquial, abusive sense—embracing all organisations (political, military or administrative) advocating Nationalism but opposing the Irish Party.
2. Gaynor, *Faith and Morals*, 1; Clancy, *Failure of 'Parliamentarianism'*, 1, 10—both widely distributed lectures given in Ennis in the late summer or autumn of 1917 and on 13 December 1917 respectively.
3. Birrell, *Things Past Redress*, 212; 1916 Commission (H 16), Minutes, 520; IG, MCR, Sep. 1916.
4. MacLysaght, Diaries (F 47), iv, pp. 222 *et seq.*, 230, 232, 234 and 245; AE's 'Salutation', quoted in Richard J. Loftus, *Nationalism in Modern Anglo-Irish Poetry*, Madison and Milwaukee 1964, 101; 'The Irish Farmer's Awakening, May, 1916', in MacLysaght, *Poems*, Dublin and London 1928, 12–17; Diaries, *loc. cit.*, pp. 284, 300 *et seq.*, 335 *et seq.*
5. CI, MCRs, May, Aug. and Sep. 1916, Jan., Feb., Apr. and May 1917; IG, MCR, Jul. 1916; *Irish Book Lover*, VIII (Jul.–Aug. 1916).
6. The continuity of Nationalist iconography is suggested by the 'Catalogue of Gift Sale' held at Mansion House, Dublin, 20–21 April 1917, for the Irish National Aid and Volunteer Dependents' Fund (P. S. O'Hegarty's copy in NLI). 'Anon.' presented the 'block on which Robt Emmet was Beheaded', Miss Teresa Kelly surrendered 'Piece of outer Coffin which contained the Remains of Lord Edward Fitzgerald', W. B. Yeats presented *The King's Threshold* in a limited edition, and Mrs de Valera offered 'Pocket Flask, the Property of Edward de Valera, with his initials on case'.
7. *Studies*, IX (Dec. 1920), 517; *The Revival of Irish Literature*, London 1894, 161; *Champion*, 19 Jul. 1913 (message to Clare Feis), 25 Mar. 1916, 31 May 1913 (Nellie O'Brien to Thomond Feis); Brian Ó Cuív in Kevin B. Nowlan, ed., *The Making of 1916*, Dublin 1969, 25; Précis of CIs, MCRs, Sep. 1914; CI, MCR, Oct. 1914; McElroy to CSO, 14–15 Jul. 1917, RP 17396/1917; cf. Appendix. Advocacy of separatism was, of course, against the interests of the National Teachers, who organised most branches of the Gaelic League.
8. Nathan to Dillon, 30 Nov. 1914, quoted by Ó Broin, *Dublin Castle*, 41; table dated 7 Sep. 1915, CSO Official Papers (A 30, iii), parcel 17. Over half the edition of each paper except *The Spark* was sold in Dublin, the residue mainly being sold (in descending order of number) in Belfast, Cork, Limerick and Kerry.
9. A. Griffith to Sr Colomba B. Butler, 12 May 1921 (concerning her sister Mrs T. P. O'Nolan, née Mary Butler of Bunnahow, Co. Clare), Butler MS. 4577 (F 7); CI, MCRs, Jan. 1913, Jan. 1915; Ó Lochlainn's manifesto *To the Electors of the Lisdoonvarna County Division*, 22 May 1902, printed on 'Irish paper' with 'Irish ink', Markham Papers (F 53); *Champion*, 5 Apr., 28 Jun. and 23 Aug. 1913; Report by DI Marshall, 13 Dec. 1917, CO 904/122. According to Liam Haugh, 'History of the West Clare Brigade', Military

Archives (B 3), p915, 'The Sinn Féin movement was first launched in West Clare in the summer of 1909, on which occasion the Dublin Headquarters was represented by the late Seán MacDermott'—but no Sinn Féin activity was reported from West Clare between 1913 and 1916 in the local press.

10. Précis of CIs, MCRs, Dec. 1914; Brennan, 'Statement' (F 38); West Galway CI, MCR, Jul. 1916; Ceannt, Address Book (F 9): attributed to Ceannt, Director of Communications, by Dr Hayes, but with entries in several hands; Lynch, The I.R.B., 36; hearsay statement by Gus O'Loghlen, Tullagh; Ó Lochlainn to 'Seán' (John Joe Markham), 8 Jun. 1918 (F 53). On 4 November 1918 Michael Collins regretted the death 'from this damned plague' of 'an old friend of the Clare Election Tomás Ó Lochlainn'. (Collins to Stack, Collins Papers (F 10), MS. 5848.)

11. Earnán de Blaghd [Ernest Blythe], *Slán le hUltaibh*, Dublin 1970, 160–1 (kindly translated into English by Fr S. O'Dea); Younger, *Ireland's Civil War*, 60. Mr Blythe once described to me in withering terms the failure of most of his fellow-Brothers to help him organise Irish Volunteer companies—they were 'inclined to whisper'.

12. *Saturday Record*, 18 May 1918; cf. Appendix; H. J. Hunt to G. N. Plunkett, 13 May 1917, Plunkett Papers (F 30), MS. 11383/5. Of the first 21 Sinn Féin clubs founded in Clare (June to August 1917) 16 existed in localities with a recent tradition (1913–16) of UIL, AOH or National Volunteer organisation, 11 with a Gaelic League tradition and 2 with a MacNeillite Irish Volunteer tradition. For the 26 clubs founded in September 1917, corresponding figures were 22, 8 and 2; thereafter (29) corresponding figures were 15, 9 and 2. Thus the Home Rule influence seems to have been most evident in the month of Sinn Féin's fastest growth. (Cf. Chapter 3, note 28.)

13. CI Gelston to 1916 Commission (H 16), Minutes 1950–3; Art O'Donnell in Dillon, ed., *The Banner* (giving provenance of Culligan's speech); Gaynor, 'Kilmihil Parish' (F 40), 286–7 and *passim*; Clancy to Fogarty, 20 Mar. 1916, Diocesan Archive (E 1); Clancy to O'Brien, 3 Jul. 1916, O'Brien Papers (F 24), MS. 7998; *Champion*, 1 Dec. and 30 Jun. 1917. Culligan was one of three Clare priests reported by police for 'anti-recruiting and pro-German' speeches in 1914–15, and the only Clare priest among Fr O'Flanagan's forty-eight 'turbulent priests' likely early in 1917 to support Plunkett's Liberty Clubs. (Mac Giolla Choille, *Intelligence Notes*, 119, 172; 'Fr O F', list in Plunkett Papers (F 30), MS. 11383/1.) In November 1907 Clancy represented O'Brien's interests at an abortive 'Unity Conference' with Bishop O'Donnell (Redmondite). According to D. W. Miller, *Church, State and Nation in Ireland 1898–1921*, Dublin 1973, 206–8, Clancy was 'perhaps the highest-ranking ecclesiastic he [O'Brien] could command'.

14. John Tuohy (Gurrane, Feakle) to Plunkett, 9 Jun. 1917, Plunkett Papers, MS. 11383/5; report of Quin sermon, 14 May 1916, Barton Scrapbook, MS. 5650 (F 4); Gaynor, 'Kilmihil Parish', 341; East Cork CI, Report on County for 1916, CO 904/120; Mac Giolla Choille, *op. cit.*, 212–13; IG, MCR, Jan. 1917; Maxwell to Asquith, mid-May 1916, in Arthur, *Maxwell*, 261.

15. J. P. Mahaffy in *Blackwood's Magazine* (Oct. 1916), 553; Birmingham, *An Irishman Looks at his World*, London 1919, 65–6; John A. Murphy in *Christus Rex*, XXIII (1969), 257 (The revolution was virtually 'carried through without benefit of clergy. . . . It is a facet of the priest's ambivalent position in secular society that he should throw the revolutionary a rope only when the latter reaches dry land'); O'Farrell, *Ireland's English Question*, London 1971, 267, 279 *et seq.*; Fr J. Glynn (Kilmurry-Ibrickane) to Fogarty, 2 Nov. 1916, Diocesan Archive (E 1); Report by architects on state of Mullagh Church, 7 Jul. 1915, *ibid.*; *Champion*, 4 Aug. 1917; extract from Bishop's Visitation Book, 1917, St Flannan's Archive (E 2).

16. *Saturday Record* (Fr Slattery, Quin, on 'red ruin'), 7 Jul. 1917; Fr Molony to Kildysart meeting, 4 Oct. 1917, and Fr Flynn to Kilbane meeting, Aug. 1917: reports in CO 904/23/3. Slattery was one of eight parish priests who, with one curate, signed Lynch's nomination papers in 1917. Four PPs and three curates nominated de Valera, and twenty-eight priests are known to have taken part in de Valera's campaign. (Cf. Miller, *op. cit.*, 394, who counted just under twenty.) See *Champion*, 7 Jul. 1917 and *passim*. Fr Gaynor (*op. cit.*, 368), who organised the priestly campaign in East Clare, was on retreat during the poll but doubted 'if we profited by the lectures'.
17. MacLysaght, 'East Clare 1916–1921'; The *'Factionist'*, No. 22, 28 Jun. 1917, 'circulated privately, chiefly amongst Sinn Feiners, at Limerick': copy and DI's annotation in Press Censorship Records (A 33), Correspondence, no. 65; leaflets in Scrapbook, O'Brien Gift, NLI, P 116; CI, MCR, Jun. 1917; information from Con O'Donohue, Ballyvaughan district; Byrne to Duke, annotating report by McElroy, RM, 14–15 Jul. 1917, RP 17396/1917 (complaining that too much petrol had been made available during the campaign, allowing 'strangers including priests from all parts' to have 'a good time' in motors); CIs and IG, MCRs, Jun. 1917.
18. *Irish Nation*, 24 Jun. 1916 *et seq.*; Pim in *Nineteenth Century*, LXXXV (Jun. 1919), 1165–74, quoted passage in italics; O'Shiel, *The Rise of the Irish Nation League* (O 11), 8; Laffan in *Irish Historical Studies*, XVII (Mar. 1971), 353–79; Mary Clancy to Plunkett, 27 May 1917, and Owen Hegarty to Plunkett, 21 May 1917: Plunkett Papers, MS. 11383/5; CI, MCRs, *passim* (Cork, Kerry and Limerick likewise had no Liberty Clubs, and Limerick alone a single INL branch); *Champion*, 6 Oct. 1917.
19. West Cork CI, MCR, Aug. 1916; *Champion*, 4 Aug. and 3 Nov. 1917; Birmingham, *op. cit.*, 217; cf. Appendix; Hogan, *Four Glorious Years*, 7–8; CSO Judicial Division, MRs, especially Jun. 1918, CO 904/23/6 (summarising RIC reports of funds raised in rural Ireland); *How to Form Sinn Féin Clubs* (O 15); *Prospectus of the Sinn Fein Clubs*, undated, Plunkett Papers, MS. 11405; *Work for a Sinn Fein Branch*, Jun. 1917, CO 904/161/10. This leaflet urged formation of a club in every 'electoral district' (presumably District Electoral Division) rather than the more usual parish unit.
20. F. S. L. Lyons, *Ireland Since the Famine*, 2nd ed., London 1973, 384 (quoting Macardle quoting speech at Killaloe, 5 Jul. 1917); CI, MCR, Jul. 1917; Lysaght to H. Plunkett, 11 Nov. 1917, MacLysaght Papers (F 21), MS. 11381. Some separatists made a virtue of vagueness: thus Tadhg Barry felt that the Irish Volunteers, if unable to parade openly, should '"mark time", and adopt the negative policy of preventing others from stealing the energies begotten of their sacrifices'; and Fr Gaynor observed that 'A person can expound "Sinn Fein" to satisfy a Catholic Archbishop— he can also (if his mind be as elastic as the policy) expound it to satisfy a Marxian Socialist.' (*Irish Opinion*, 9 Sep. 1916, 9 Mar. 1918. The paper itself, however (14 Apr. 1917), claimed that Nationalists wanted 'something to do' other than pledging 'their allegiance to the cause of Ireland's Sovereign Independence', and sought 'the organising and disciplining of the Nationalist sentiment that is sweeping the country'.)
21. AE to Lysaght, received 19 Jul. 1916, MacLysaght Papers, MS. 2651; MacLysaght Diaries, v, 15 May 1917; annotation to letter from E. Mac Néill, 28 Jun. 1917, MacLysaght Papers, MS. 2650; Lysaght to Duke, 13 Jul. 1917, *ibid.*, MS. 2649; Lysaght to Mac Néill, 2 Jul. 1917, Diaries, v; Lysaght to Moore, 6 Jul. 1917, Moore Papers, MS. 10561/22 (dining habits); 'Master of None', 296–9, MacLysaght Papers, MS. 4750 (speech notes); MacLysaght to *The Leader* [1953], *ibid.*, MS. 2649; Fogarty to Lysaght, 31 Jan. 1918, *ibid.*; AE to Lysaght [Feb. 1918], *ibid.*, MS. 2651; cf. McDowell, *The Irish Convention*, *passim*.
22. Brennan, 'Statement' (F 38). On 8 October 1917, following Brennan's plan, the Director of Training ordered resumption of Irish Volunteer training as from 21 October (during

that month 140 cases of open drilling were reported by police, including 50 from Clare and 40 from Cork). On 13 March 1918 Michael Collins ordered Volunteers if arrested to deny the court's jurisdiction, give no bail and insist on special treatment. (IG, MCRs, Oct. 1917, Apr. 1918.)

23. US to CS, 19 Jul. 1917, CSO Official Papers (A 30, iii), parcel 17; IG to US, 26 Feb. 1918, CO 904/186/2; US, annotation to Military Intelligence Officer (Midlands and Connaught District), MR, Sep. 1917, CO 904/157/1; Austin Brennan in *Limerick Leader*, 16 Dec. 1972; 'Paddy' (Carriganinny, Macroom) to John Nolan (Cork), 9 Jan. 1917, CO 904/29/2; Francis Leary at Kilmurry McMahon, 18 Nov. 1917, CO 904/122 (Sergeant's Report); CI (Clare), MCR, Oct. 1917. On 28 November 1917 another policeman (CO 904/122) reported that one illegal driller 'wishes to be convicted by Court-Martial— knowing that such would secure him the position sought for'—viz mastership of the Corofin workhouse!

24. CS to GOC, 2 Nov. 1917; IG to US, 7 Nov. 1917; CS to US, 10 Nov. 1917, RP 19164/1918. On 20 October Duke had asked the cabinet for 'guidance' in dealing with the drillers; on 1 November he had admitted to the cabinet that 'considerable difference of opinion . . . as to the seriousness of the situation' existed within the Irish executive; on 3 December he confessed that his tactics had been upset by the hunger-strikers, against whom the prison authorities had shown 'no resource'. (GT 2353, Cab. 24/29; Cab. 23/4/262(4) and GT 2467, Cab. 24/30; GT 2845, Cab. 24/34.)

25. M. Brennan to Miss Oonagh O'Conor, *c.* 11 Oct. 1917 (intercepted by prison authorities), GPB, DORA Records (A 31), carton 1; *ibid.*, annotation by GPB Chairman, 25 Oct.; GPB Order, 29 Sep. 1917, Regulations, 19 Mar. 1918, and Order of 20 Aug. 1918, *ibid.*, cartons 1 and 2; Military Intelligence Officer (Southern District), MR, Dec. 1917, CO 904/157/1; captured Irish Volunteers' Order referred to by IG, MCR, Apr. 1918. By the regulations of 19 March 1918 ameliorations were limited to DORA convicts (excluding cattle-drivers and others guilty of acts 'criminal *per se*'). On 22 February 1918 the US formally told the GPB that forcible feeding must cease, likewise releases under the 'Cat and Mouse' Act (3 & 4 Geo. V, c. 4). By late 1918 it was generally thought cleverer to keep out of jail than get into it. The number of illegal drillings, processions and so forth reported by police to the military (CIs and IG, MCRs, *passim*) in the last three months of 1917 was 140, 334 and 293, and in the first half of 1918, 388, 386, 456, 507 (or 570), 340 and 93. Most of these reports came from Munster, sometimes over one-third of them from Co. Clare.

26. Commons *Debates*, Vol. 104, cols 586–93; Conor Clune to Lysaght, 31 Mar. 1918, MacLysaght Papers, MS. 2649; Permit Book, Parker-Hutchinson Papers (F 29), MS. 12052; Russell inquest findings, 28 Mar. 1918 (concerning killing in Carrigaholt), Crown and Peace Records (A 29), Co. Clare, 1D.39.113.

27. Figgis, *Recollections*, 192–4 (stating that de Valera and Griffith carried the day against Brugha's opposition, but agreed not to bind Sinn Féin to any commitments they might make at Mansion House); Proclamation, RP 7921/1918; *Saturday Record*, 27 Apr. 1918; Gaynor, 'Kilmihil Parish', 383–5; Brennan, *Allegiance*, 165; MacLysaght Diaries, v (28 Sep. 1918). In his sermon Dr Fogarty declared that 'they had their Bishops and their priests, and a country united as it never was before, standing together, under God, against this most horrible, inhuman, and atrocious Act of tyranny'. One lonely PP (Flagmount) who dared denounce the Anti-Conscription Pledge was punished by an attempt to burn down his church. (CI, MCR, Apr. 1918.)

28. The MCRs of various CIs show that in Clare, the only county under special military restrictions in the spring of 1918, Sinn Féin reached three-quarters of its maximum

recorded strength in February 1918 and increased by only 2 per cent between 31 March and 31 May 1918. Otherwise it seems fast growth was associated with late development: growth in Limerick (October 1917) was 4 per cent, in West Cork (February 1918) 18 per cent, in East Cork (April 1918) 52 per cent and in Kerry (April 1918) 44 per cent.

29. *Champion*, 12 Jan. 1918, 3 Nov. 1917; Michael McMahon interview with Matthew Bermingham (G); Clare CI, MCR, Dec. 1917 (cf. West Cork CI, Jan. 1917, reporting that some people 'openly profess to disapprove of Sinn Feinism, but secretly they admire the Sinn Feiners'); Programme, 22 Mar. 1919, suppressed by PC, CO 904/169/2; cf. Appendix. 165 laymen, 10 PPs and 14 curates were prominent either in several separatist bodies (e.g. Irish Volunteers and Sinn Féin) or in separatist bodies and some other organisation in which they had not achieved note between 1913 and the Rising (e.g. Gaelic League, GAA, Labour or farming movements).

30. *Champion*, 3 and 17 Nov. 1917, 4 Jan. 1919; cf. Appendix.

31. West Galway CI, MCR, Jul. 1916; O'Farrell to Duke, 8 Sep. 1916, Tudor to US, 21 Apr. 1921 (ban not lifted until 22 Jul. 1921, CSO to Midland and Great Western Railway), RP 3076/1921; undated DMP ruling quoted by DMP Chief Commissioner to US, 8 Apr. 1919 (original underlining), CO 904/169/2; Brendan Mac Lua, *The Steadfast Rule*, Dublin 1967, 52, and Terence Casey in *Capuchin Annual* (1960), 213; information from Austin Brennan, who was appointed convention secretary and instructed to summon its members. The ban on unauthorised meetings (under DORR 9AA, 4 Jul. 1918) had been opposed by the outgoing US, who felt it could not consistently be enforced and 'would not help the recruiting campaign'. (Byrne to French, 15 Jun. 1918, CO 904/169/2.) Police execution of the order varied: in Kerry outdoor meetings (unlike processions) were excluded from the ban, but in Limerick all GAA matches and Gaelic League Aeridheachtana were prohibited. I have no evidence to support Macardle's assertion that by secret instructions the order was extended to cover such events. (Kerry and Limerick CIs, MCRs, Jul. 1918; Dorothy Macardle, *The Irish Republic*, new ed., Dublin 1951, 257.)

32. Cf. Chapter 7. The intensity of agrarian agitation in 1918 is suggested by figures for cattle-drives and all indictable agrarian offences (excluding, oddly enough, many 'non-agrarian' cases of attacks upon cattle), for each year between 1913 and 1919. Cattle-drives: 55, 127, 36, 51, 64, 245 (1918), 92. All agrarian offences: 190, 235, 183, 158, 168, 355 (1918), 488 (and 1,114 in 1920, 216 in 1921 before 8 November). Clare cattle-drives only: 6, 13, 4, 1, 1, 57 (1918), 18. See Intelligence Notes, *passim*; Outrage Returns, 1920–21, CO 904/121/2 and 3.

33. IG, MCRs, Dec. 1917, Mar. 1918; Brennan, 'Statement' (F 38); *Champion*, 9 Mar. 1918, 30 Mar. 1918 (quoting captured order from Art O'Donnell to M. Tubridy, Ballykett); Circular from Sinn Féin Standing Committee to local secretaries, 23 Feb. 1918, PROD, 2B.82.116 (Minutes) (B 6), arising from discussion on 15 Feb. 1918 of letter from Tim Considine, Feakle, Co. Clare; Macardle, *op. cit.*, 241 (2 Mar. was the date of press publication, it seems). Bishop Fogarty claimed that cattle-driving had no 'political significance. . . . It is a social trouble, pure and simple.' (*Champion*, 16 Mar. 1918); but N. Marlowe, another of Lysaght's guests at Raheen, wrote that many young Claremen wished 'to use Sinn Fein for their own purposes, i.e. as a new instrument in the old agrarian campaign' (*Contemporary Review*, CXIII (Apr. 1918), 438). Who was using whom?

34. Intelligence Notes, 1919 and *passim*; IG, MCR, Feb. 1919 (enclosing Secretary's Report to Sinn Féin Árd-Chomhairle, 20 Feb., claiming 1,764 clubs); *Irish Catholic Directory*, Dublin 1913, 132; Mac Giolla Choille, *op. cit.*, 109–12 (National Volunteers); UIL Returns, CO 904/120; cf. Appendix and note 28. By the end of 1917 CIs, MCRs, show that Sinn Féin had reached some 46 per cent of its peak membership in Limerick, 52 per

cent in Cork, 53 per cent in Kerry, and a percentage unknown in the case of Clare owing to arithmetical ineptitude of police clerks.

35. McCracken, *Representative Government*, 20–1; Ó Tuile, *O'Higgins*, and 'Bean a' Tighe' in *Champion*, 14 Dec. 1918; *ibid.*, 19 Oct. and 9 and 23 Nov. 1918, Gaynor, 'Kilmihil Parish', 389, and Brennan, 'Statement', *loc. cit.* (for details of the struggle for nomination).

36. Draft article (published in much-mutilated form in *New Statesman*, 2 Mar. 1918), and entry for 25 Jan. 1919, MacLysaght Diaries, v; PC, MR, Sep. 1918, CO 904/167/1. Not until 5 Apr. 1919 (Diaries, vi) did Lysaght write: 'For a long time I suppose I have been really a Sinn Féiner: now at any rate I am definitely of that political party—I have always been of that political faith.'

37. *Champion*, 22 Feb. and 5 Jul. 1919; CI, MCR, Feb. 1919; IG, MCR (enclosure), Feb. 1919; Dáil Ministry, Minutes (B 7), DE 1/1, 11 Jul. 1919.

38. Brennan, 'Statement'; O'Hegarty, *Victory of Sinn Féin*, 29. Byron's *Opportunist Sinn Féiners* and MacNamara's *The Clanking of the Chains* express contemporary disgust at pollution of the pure stream of nationality. Byron contrasts ex-internee Paddy Joe Toole, that meandering 'melancholy monomaniac [sic]', with 'wilted and spineless' Sinn Féin youths terrified of conscription; MacNamara's visionary although ineffectual hero is hounded out of his parish by Irish Party-hearted 'officers' of the Irish Volunteers.

39. Two organisations represented ex-servicemen's interests, of which one (the Comrades of the Great War) accused the other (the Nationalist Veterans' Association) of being 'dominated by Sinn Féin'. Lord French's '*one great idea* [was] to keep these Soldiers' associations absolutely clear of any political colours'; and on 25 September 1919 he and Macpherson claimed that 'the Sinn Fein element have not succeeded in drawing any great number of them from the paths of loyalty and good-citizenship'. (French Journal (A 17), 16 Jul. 1919; GT 8227, Cab. 24/89. Cf. Chapters 3, 6 and 7.)

40. E.g. Limerick CI, MCR, Jan. 1920, and East Cork CI, MCR, Aug. 1919; Clare CI, MCR, May 1919, and *Champion*, 25 Oct. 1919; *ibid.*, 11 Jan. 1919. One veteran in Clare met a nastier fate in April 1921, being left dead with spy label attached (a killing for which IRA headquarters took responsibility). But then he was 'a well known loyalist' and a part-time employee of Lord Inchiquin's as well as Newmarket-on-Fergus secretary of the Comrades of the Great War, so what could he expect? (*Champion*, 4 Jun. 1921; Report of Military Court of Inquiry, CO 904/189; 'Running Diary', Mulcahy Papers (B 8), P7/A/16.)

41. CI, MCRs, Dec. 1918, Apr. 1919; James D. Kenny to G. N. Plunkett, 1 May 1917, Plunkett Papers, MS. 11383/5; *Champion*, 11 Jan. 1919.

42. Sinn Féin, Árd-Fheis, 16 Oct. 1919, 'Reports of Officers and Directors' (O 14); Michael Laffan in *Capuchin Annual* (1970), 234, showing drop in number of affiliated clubs from 1,009 (Aug. 1919) to 117 (1921)—although Secretary's Report to Oct. 1921 Árd-Fheis (O 14) lists 1,299 clubs not necessarily affiliated; *Instructions* (O 16); Dáil Ministry, Minutes, 9 Jan. 1921, DE 1/3 (presumably referring to Arthur Griffith who was, however, in Mountjoy at the time); Sinn Féin Honorary Secretaries to TDs, 25 Aug. 1921, Plunkett Papers, MS. 11405/5; de Valera to Sinn Féin local secretaries, 7 Sep. 1921, sent with Standing Committee's approval, PROD, 2B.82.117. The letter of 25 August asserted that Sinn Féin was 'largely the means by which further successes can be achieved, especially in the carrying out of the constructive work of Dáil Éireann'.

Chapter 5
REVOLUTIONARY ADMINISTRATORS
(pp. 138–64)

1. Quoted by 'O' (Deputy Chief of Police, Intelligence) to Clarke (CSO Public Information Branch), Jun. 1921, CO 904/168; O'Faolain, *Vive Moi!*, London 1965, 110, 147.

2. Declaration of Independence, approved by Dáil Éireann 21 Jan. 1919, Dáil *Minutes*, 16.
3. Mrs J. R. Green, *The Government of Ireland*, London 1921, 15; unsigned draft memorandum, annotated by Hobson, Hobson Papers (F 14), MS. 13174/13; Sinn Féin, Árd-Fheis, 25 Oct. 1917, *Notices of Motion* (NLI, P 1891). The Special Árd-Chomhairle, June 1918, provided a less fanciful departmental structure (five departments), of which one was dropped by the Árd-Fheis, October 1918. In February 1919 the Árd-Chomhairle was still discussing the provision of departments (still mostly imaginary), this time eleven of them. (Sinn Féin, Árd-Fheis (Oct. 1918, Apr. 1919), *Clár*; Agenda of 1919 meeting captured from Robert Barton, IG, MCR, Feb. 1919.)
4. Figgis, *Recollections*, 176–7; cf. files on food control grouped under RP 6813/1920 (concerning formation of committee, 1 Sep. 1917, resignation of five members, late Dec. 1917, and indignation at ministry's restrictions of activities, Jul. 1918); Circular on 'Prevention of Famine', Oct. 1917, Plunkett Papers (F 30), MS. 11405; IG, MCRs, Feb. 1918, Nov. 1917. Limerick and Kerry CIs, MCRs, Dec. 1917, scorned the census; but next month the Limerick CI wrote that the campaign for food control was 'not an exclusively Sinn Fein move', funds having been promised by the County Council.
5. IG, MCR, Feb. 1918; *Champion* leader, 19 Jan. 1918; *ibid.*, 5 Jan. 1918, Ennistymon RDC Minutes, 5 Feb. 1918 (C 2); Gaynor, 'Kilmihil Parish', 386; CI, MCR, Oct. 1919; DI Duffy's annotation to CSO anonymous letter received 5 Nov. 1919 from 'A Loyalist', RP 27279/1919 (reporting that 'only a few local people' had attended fairs arranged 'over most of the county' for 18 October). Gaynor, 'being a farmer's son', had opposed suggestions that farmers be asked to keep large stocks of food in case of conscription, and instead urged the immediate buying of produce and its sale virtually at cost price (half the ruling market price).
6. Local Government Committee, Reports, DE 2/243; Sinn Féin Árd-Chomhairle, Agenda of meeting, 20 Feb. 1919, in IG, MCR, Feb. 1919; Dáil *Minutes*, 38, 122, 140, 160 (4 Apr., 18 Jun., 19 Aug. and 27 Oct. 1919); Art O'Connor, 'A Brief Survey of the Work Done by the Department of Agriculture', Dáil *Report*, 59 (17 Aug. 1921); Laffan in *Capuchin Annual* (1970), 232; Griffith to Dáil, 23 Jan. 1919, in *Capuchin Annual* (1969), 332; *Saturday Record*, 15 Sep. 1917; C. Desmond Greaves, *Liam Mellows and the Irish Revolution*, London 1971, 138; [Childers], *Constructive Work of Dáil Éireann* (I 4), No. 1, 7 (cf. Hogan, *Four Glorious Years*, 72). During 1919 courts were reported from Galway and Limerick as well as Clare, perhaps without Dáil blessing.
7. *Champion*, 19 Apr. 1919 (court set up willy-nilly); Dáil Ministry, Minutes, 19 Dec. 1919, DE 1/2; Dáil *Minutes*, 151, 78 (20 Aug. 1919 and 12 Apr. 1919); Ryan in T. Desmond Williams, ed., *The Irish Struggle 1916–1926*, London 1966, 35 (referring specifically to Fine Arts Department and Resources and Industries Commission). IG, MCR, May 1919, reported that the Mansion House Conference had already received £21,000 and local Sinn Féin collectors had retrieved £15,000 of Anti-Conscription Funds offered back to subscribers after the crisis—twice the amount in the Dáil's hands three months later. The trustees still had £50,000 and £164,000 had been returned to subscribers or resubscribed to Church charities. In Ennistymon (*Champion*, 19 Jul. 1919) the £50 not reclaimed by subscribers was divided between the Dáil and Gaelic League.
8. Commons *Debates*, Vol. 138, col. 50.
9. Michael McMahon to M. Bermingham, Interview (G); 'Memo re Proposal to collect Income Tax', 28 Jun. 1920, and M. Collins to S. Moynihan, 15 Dec. 1920: Mulcahy Papers (B 8), P7/A/12; Dáil *Minutes*, 219, 223 (17 Sep. 1920); *Champion*, 15, 22 and 29 Nov. 1919 (threats by Kilrush, Ennistymon and Limerick No. 2 RDCs). Sinn Féin's Árd-Chomhairle considered a taxes and annuities strike on 20 February 1919, and a rates and

annuities strike after 23 October 1919; the Dáil, after unusually searching debate, approved Collins's memorandum on 29 June 1920. (IG, MCR, Feb. 1919; SF Standing Committee Minutes (B 6), 2B.82.117; Dáil *Minutes*, 181–2.) On 8 March 1921 the Dáil Ministry (Minutes) decided that income tax was 'impossible to collect in present circumstances'.

10. Reports of the Commissioners of His Majesty's Inland Revenue, 1920–23; Commons *Debates*, Vol. 130, col. 1427; Dáil *Minutes*, 204. Tax receipts analysed are net, including arrears; assessments comprise 'the total ultimate yield of the assessments made in [year] whether actually collected in that year or later'. Income tax arrears in Ireland, unlike arrears in annuities, were not chargeable to ratepayers of the district concerned (8 & 9 Geo. V, c. 40, s. 200).

11. The amount of Clare annuities outstanding on 31 March in 1916 was £2,744, in 1917 £105, in 1918 £529, in 1919 £831 and in 1920 £654; but virtually all these arrears were subsequently paid (for the entire decade 1903/4–13/14, only £1,407 was deducted from grants). The Agricultural and Estate Duty Grants for 1920/21 and 1921/22 were eventually paid in full to the Clare County Council, but between 1922 and June 1925 £19,682 and £10,986 respectively were withheld in lieu of arrears. (*Champion*, 3 May 1919, 17 Apr. 1920; *Saturday Record*, 9 May 1917; Commons *Debates*, Vol. 60, col. 1369 (2 Apr. 1914); 'Clare County Council. Statement of Rates to 30th June 1925', 23 Jul. 1925, O'Loghlen Papers (F 52).)

12. Dáil Éireann, Department of Finance, 'Statement of Receipts and Expenditure', Mulcahy Papers, P7/A/13. Estimates for 1 July 1920 to 30 June 1921 (adjusted) totalled £216,877, expenditure (from 1 May 1920) £180,672. (Dáil *Minutes*, 184, 259, 278.)

13. Monteagle quoted by Hogan, *op. cit.*, 75; Thomas Jones's unnamed friend, *Whitehall Diary*, III, 24–5; Brayden, *Republican Courts* (P 1), 4 (former editor, *Freeman's Journal*, and government press propaganda man). General Macready and his deputy Jeudwine both admitted that the Republicans tried to maintain law and order, and Macready wrote that 'good rather than harm would have resulted' had they confined their courts to arbitration. (Macready, *Annals*, II, 478, and memorandum, 25 May 1920, Lloyd George Papers, F36/2/14; 'History of the 5th Division' (A 11), 114.)

14. Brian Ó hUiginn, 'West Clare Courts . . . Rough Outline of Rules' (distributed within Dáil, 3 Mar. 1920), DE 2/38; *Champion*, 24 Jan. 1920; O'Shiel in *Irish Times* (P 14), 22 Nov. 1966, quoting report by Registrar, Roscommon courts, May 1920; *The Times*, 3 May 1920; MHA Report, Aug.(?) 1920, DE 2/51; O'Connor, 'A Brief Survey', *loc. cit.*, 57.

15. *Ibid.*; 'National Arbitration Courts. Report', 4 Mar. 1920(?), DE 2/38; Dáil Ministry, Minutes, 13 May, 10 and 26 Jun. 1920, DE 1/2; O'Connor, 'A Brief Survey', 60–1 (the consequent decree was approved by the Dáil, after some dispute, on 29 June 1920 (Dáil *Minutes*, 178–80)); *Champion*, 5 Jun. 1920; Dáil *Minutes*, 199–203, 224, 178 (6 Aug., 17 Sep. and 29 Jun. 1920); [Childers], *Constructive Work of Dáil Éireann* (I 4), No. 1, 23–4.

16. Ó Roideáin, 'Under the Terror' (P 5), 91. The new Irish legal code was current British law (21 Jan. 1919), unless 'clearly motivated by religious or political animosity'. Non-binding citations might be made to 'early Irish Law Codes' and commentaries on them, and Roman codes. Yet 'save as aforesaid, no legal text book published in Great Britain shall be cited in any Court'—a ridiculous rider which Land Commissioner Conor Maguire underlined and queried in his copy of *Judiciary. Rules and Forms* (NLI, LO).

17. Brehon D. H. McParland to MHA, 27 Jul. 1921, PROD, DE 10/4 (B 5); Davitt, 'Civil Jurisdiction' (P 9), 124 (Michael Davitt's son, Circuit Judge who visited West Clare between March and July 1921); O'Shiel in *Irish Times*, 14 Nov. 1966; McParland to MHA, 23 Aug. 1921, DE 10/4; information from Mr Seán MacNamara. The only rules of

procedure for Dáil Courts which accorded with practice were those of the Supreme Court. There were no rules of procedure for the Supreme Court. (Davitt, *op. cit.*, 119.)

18. Dáil *Minutes*, 140 (19 Aug. 1919); Dáil Ministry, Minutes, 16 Jun. 1920, DE 1/2; Stack, draft memorandum on 'Parish and District Courts', 16 Jun. 1920, DE 2/38; *Champion*, 24 Jul. 1920 (the Irish teacher Éamonn Waldron acted as the Dáil's 'representative' at the election). The five West Clare justices were a priest (top of the poll), three county councillors and one district councillor, and the first Registrar was Art O'Donnell, Volunteer brigade commandant. On 27 February 1922 the minister reported that some court officials were 'to say the least . . . not desirable', and urged that direct popular elections replace conventions, although these might 'have worked well as a War measure'. (*Ibid.*; Report in DE 25/1.)

19. AG, General Order No. 9 (N.S. 1920), NLI, MS. 739, and No. 12 (1 Nov. 1920), *ibid.*; Report of Police Officer to 3rd Brigade Council meeting, 1st Western Division, 2 Dec. 1921, Mulcahy Papers, P7/A/33. In some regions Volunteers acted as policemen long before the IRA staff so directed; in Kilmihil, for example, the local company appointed 'I. R. Police' before 24 January 1920 (report to 2nd Battalion Adjutant, West Clare Brigade, O'Donnell Papers (F 50)). They continued to do so long after General Order No. 31, 10 Nov. 1921, transferred nominal control over the police force to the Department of Home Affairs (NLI, MS. 739).

20. Gaynor, 'Kilmihil Parish', 465 *et seq.* By the time he took over brigade police work Gaynor 'had begun to wonder whether any man in the brigade could be trusted to forget family ties and family feuds and personal prejudices as Chief of Police and to uphold Sinn Féin law and justice without fear or favour' (p. 473).

21. Commons *Debates*, Vol. 138, col. 45 ('The organisation which was so perfect five or six months ago is now shattered'); *Weekly Summary*, 25 Feb. 1921 ('The "courts of justice" are as much a thing of the past as the medieval murder tribunals on which they were modelled'); O'Shiel in *Irish Times*, 14 Nov. 1966; D. H. McParland to MHA, 22 Jul. 1921, PROD, DE 10/4; Dáil *Report*, 22 (17 Aug. 1921) (Stack also complimented the West Clare District Court and others in Dublin, Cork, Limerick and Longford); Registrar's Report to MHA, 1 Jun. 1921, annotated by Kevin O'Higgins, Assistant Minister, DE 10/5; P. Kennedy (organiser) to Ministry, 27 Nov. 1921 (Ennistymon), *ibid.*; Register, Kilkee Parish Court, DE 15/21; Report of MHA, approved by Dáil 10 May 1921, DE 2/51 (SPO).

22. MHA Secretary to Registrar, West Clare Courts, 24 Sep. 1921, Organiser's Report, 27 Nov. 1921, list of cases signed by West Clare District Registrar, and C. Ó Faoláin (Registrar) to B. O'Higgins, *c.* 1 Jun. 1921: PROD, DE 10/5; Osborough, 'Law in Ireland', 49; Casey, 'Republican Courts', 337; *Champion*, 7 Aug. 1920, 6 Sep. 1919; Haugh, 'History of the West Clare Brigade' (B 3), p915. Casey claims that Republican courts exercised no jurisdiction in licensing matters, but numerous Munster CIs, MCRs, referred to enforcement of licensing regulations by Republican Police (e.g. Kerry, Oct. 1920; Limerick, Aug. 1921; East Cork, Sep. 1921). The Kilkee Parish Court dealt with four breaches of licensing regulations between September 1920 and September 1922, and Republican Police in East Clare bought whiskey from a publican they had just fined £10 for failing to close. (Kilkee Court Register, DE 15/21; information from Mr Austin Brennan.)

23. AG, General Order No. 9 (N.S. 1920), 19 Jun. 1920, NLI, MS. 739; O'Malley, *On Another Man's Wound*, 166, 319; O'Shiel in *Irish Times*, 18, 22 and 23 Nov. 1966; list of West Clare District Court cases, DE 10/5; Kilkee Parish Court Register, DE 15/21; Liam MacGowan in *Capuchin Annual* (1970), 306.

24. MHA Report to Dáil, probably submitted 6 Aug. 1920 ('the agitation was instantly quelled' after the Dáil's manifesto of 29 Jun. 1920(?): see Dáil *Minutes*, 178–80); [Childers], *Constructive Work of Dáil Éireann*, No. 1, 12; IG, MCR, Jun. 1920 ('The season for cattle-driving is past now that the May lettings are over'). In May 1921 Art O'Connor reported that 'there seems to be very little land agitation troubling the country at present', a judgment confirmed by the decline in number of indictable 'agrarian' offences known to the RIC—from 754 between February and May 1920 (68 per cent of the year's total) to 118 in the same part of 1921 (55 per cent of the year's total to 8 November). (SPO, DE 2/64; cf. Chapter 4, note 32.)
25. Meyler (6th Division) to Chief District Commissioner (Cork RIC), 22 Aug. 1921, CO 904/151; Deputy IG, Circular, 22 Aug. 1921, and Chief of Police, Instructions for RIC during Truce, 30 Oct. 1921: CO 904/178; MHA to Fr A. J. Moloney, Chairman, Ennis Parish Court, 16 Aug. 1921, and to P. Kennedy (organiser, Clare), 29 Nov. 1921: PROD, DE 10/5 and 11/180; Stack to district registrars, c. Aug. 1921, Plunkett Papers (B 4), MS. 11404; Reports of clerks, parish courts, supplemented where unavailable by those of district registrars (district courts excluded), *passim*, PROD, DE 16/5–6. The start of the period 'up to September 1921' is seldom known, but probably mid-1921 for most courts.
26. Rent agitation in 1921 is discussed in Chapter 7, Labour arbitration favourable to an employer (Tottenham) in Chapter 2. Volunteer participation in agrarian disputes was discussed by the 6th Battalion Council, Mid-Clare Brigade, on 15 December 1921, after farms of H. V. Macnamara had been taken over and a Republican Policeman shot; the staff decided 'that no Company Officers [should] have anything to do with land business'. (Report of Meeting (F 48).)
27. A. M. Sullivan, *Old Ireland*, London 1927, 219–20; Shortt to Lloyd George, 4 Jul. 1918, Lloyd George Papers, F45/6/6 ('I hope something has been done about the oath of allegiance to be taken by local bodies'); Dáil Ministry, Minutes, 31 Oct. 1919, DE 1/2; Agenda of Árd-Chomhairle meeting, IG, MCR, Feb. 1920; *Champion*, 8 and 15 Feb. 1919, 3 Jul. 1920; Interview with Michael McMahon by Matthew Bermingham (G); LGD Circular, 1 Jun. 1920, DF 2/243; Report, Clare Inspector to LGD [1921], SPO (C 5).
28. Under the Local Government (Ireland) Act, 1898 (61 & 62 Vic., c. 37) and Criminal Injuries (Ireland) Act, 1919 (9 Geo. V c. 14), local authorities were liable to pay awards against persons unknown responsible for personal injury to Crown servants and to victims 'of any combination of a seditious character or any unlawful association'. Payment was to be raised from rates, or (failing that) out of government moneys due to the authority concerned from the Local Taxation (Ireland) Account (a provision extended under ROIA, 10 & 11 Geo. V, c. 31, 9 Aug. 1920). Resistance by councils to these levies had been discussed from September 1919 onwards by Sinn Féin and the Dáil's LGD, with little effect. (Minutes of SF Standing Committee, 18 Sep. 1919, PROD, 2B.82.117; LGD Report, Oct. 1919 (indignant at Sinn Féin's prior discussion of the matter), SPO, DE 2/243; undated Dáil memorandum on legal position of bodies resisting levies, Plunkett Papers (B 4), MS. 11404.)
29. Sinn Féin Committee on Local Government, Report, 12 Feb. 1919, in IG, MCR, Feb. 1919; *Champion*, 8 Feb. 1919; Dáil Ministry, Minutes, 25 Mar. and 17 Jul. 1920, DE 1/2; O'Higgins to Ministry, Reports, early May and 2 Jun. 1920, DE 2/243; LGD, Report to Dáil, Aug. 1920, *ibid*. The minister noted 'a general desire expressed in communications for specific instructions' from the LGD.
30. Robinson, *Memories*, 307–9; LGB Secretary to local authorities, 29 Jul. 1921, RP 20971/1920. As early as 31 May 1920, immediately *before* the county council elections, a conference of ministers had discussed the possibility of winning over 'moderate public

opinion in Ireland' by intercepting grants to local authorities, thus increasing 'the pecuniary burdens of the Irish people'! (Cab. 23/21/33/20 (App. 111).)

31. Returns in RP 20971/1920, reporting responses until 23 Aug., 27 Aug. and 1 Sep. 1920; LGB Secretary to US, 27 Jan. 1921, and Orders for direct payments from Local Taxation (Ireland) Account to Boards of Guardians and RDCs, *passim: ibid.*; LGD Report, 3 May 1921, DE 2/243. By 6 August 1921 (CP 3230, Cab. 24/127), so Robinson told Greenwood, the LGB was recognised by 100 bodies in the six Northern counties, and 41 in the South (26 of them UDCs and two Towns' Commissioners). Fifty were doubtful or doubted, 320 had broken away. The Criminal Injuries (Ireland) Act of 23 December 1920 (10 & 11 Geo. V, c. 66) had alleviated the burden on obedient councils but worsened that on recalcitrant councils (by improving payment terms on the one hand, and extending local liability to injuries to property as well as person, on the other). By the end of 1921 the Clare County Council, for example, had become liable for decrees totalling £576,572 (of which £10,099 had been raised before inauguration of the new council and £47,569 deducted from grants), over ten times its annual receipts from government. (Returns of Decrees, RP 2900/1921.)

32. Dáil *Minutes*, 185 (29 Jun. 1920); Clare County Council, 'Memo of Scheme to deal with new Financial Situation' (Appendix A to Commission of Enquiry into Local Government, Interim Report, 6 Aug. 1920), and Commission's Final Report, 17 Sep. 1920: DE 2/243; Clare County Council Minutes (C 1), 24 Jul. and 26 Aug. 1920; LGD Directive, 10 Aug. 1920, DE 2/62; Dáil *Minutes*, 221 (17 Sep. 1920). The Commission circularised 294 bodies and elicited information of the finances of 209 of them.

33. Commission's Report, 17 Sep. 1920, DE 2/243; Art O'Connor, 'Memo on Suggested Policy for Councils of Agriculture', 15 Sep. 1920, and 'Report. Land Commission and Agricultural Department', 20 Jan. 1921: DE 2/64; Dáil Ministry, Minutes, DE 1/3 (11 Dec. 1920). In his Report of May 1921 (DE 2/64), O'Connor looked forward to the 'strong possibility' that Republicans might control the Council of Agriculture unless its constitution were changed. For its part the LGB kept moneys flowing to the committees, which it was agreed by a Castle conference in the autumn of 1920 'should be treated as separate entities and should have their State grants, provided they abstained from passing objectionable Resolutions and undertook to submit their accounts to audit'—a proviso which Robinson did his best to circumvent. (Anderson to Robinson, 1 Apr. 1921, CO 904/188/3.)

34. Brennan, 'Statement' (F 38); LGD Report to Dáil, Jul. 1921, DE 2/243. The grant to which Brennan refers (one of several) was possibly that for rebuilding sea walls at Lahinch and Kilkee. Before 24 May 1921 the Clare County Council applied for £43,000 to the Ministry of Labour's Unemployment Grants Committee (the largest Irish application); on 24 August, after tortuous interdepartmental negotiations, the committee approved a grant not exceeding £3,600 (still the largest Southern Irish grant approved). Since the LGB could not sanction grants to recalcitrant councils, the repair of sea walls was deemed, despite intermittent bureaucratic scepticism, to constitute a road work for which the Ministry of Transport could legally provide grants. (Correspondence in PRO, Lab. 4/146 and 151.)

35. *Champion*, 13 Aug. 1921 (Ennis UDC office raid, Nov. 1920); Ennistymon Guardians, Minutes, 9 Nov. 1920 (workhouse store ransacked), and Inspector to LGD, undated Report (raids on County Council, 22 Nov., 14 and 21 Dec. 1920), SPO (C 5); *Champion*, 20 Nov. 1920; Inspector to Chief of Inspection, LGD, 7 Apr. 1921, SPO (C 5); statistics from Minutes, *passim*, of Clare County Council and its finance committee (C 1), and Ennistymon Guardians (C 2).

36. Brennan, 'Statement' (F 38); *Champion*, 1 Jan. 1921 (Brennan's letter); information from Austin Brennan (Gearóid O'Sullivan, AG, congratulated him); Inspector's Report, undated, SPO (C 5); County Council Minutes, 18 May 1921 (C 1).
37. Statement of receipts by Local Authorities (1918–19), RP 20971/1920; *Champion*, 19 Mar. 1921 (letter from James D. Kenny).
38. LGB Circular, 11 Nov. 1920, DE 2/155; LGD to local officials, 19 Nov. 1920, *ibid.*; LGD Report, 20 Jan. 1921, DE 2/243 (referring to Dublin meeting of rate-collectors, Dec. 1920, which decided no rates should be collected for the time being); Dáil *Private Sessions*, 36 (22 Aug. 1921); Dáil *Minutes*, 270 (11 Mar. 1921).
39. Inspector to LGD, enclosure, 28 Oct. 1921, Inspector's undated Report from Ennis, Cosgrave to Brennan, 19 Sep. 1921, Brennan to Brugha, 11 Oct. 1921, and Inspector to LGD Chief of Inspection, 28 Oct. 1921: SPO (C 5); *Champion*, 5 Mar. 1921. By the end of 1921 collectors in Mid-Clare had reported collection of 51 per cent of their warrants on average, and one-third of the collectors had received and reported two-fifths or less. (F. N. Studdert to Frank Barrett, 13 Jan. 1922 (F 37).)
40. On 25 January 1921 the Dáil set aside £100,000 for loans to county councils which had collected three-quarters of the rates, a proviso set aside on 11 March to facilitate payment of arrears of salaries, wages and contracts, and provision of outdoor relief. Salaries amounting to £47,352 were said to be outstanding, yet by August 1921 only £10,000 had been distributed. (Dáil *Minutes*, 253–5, 276 (25 Jan. and 11 Mar. 1912); LGD Report, 9 Mar. 1921, DB 2/243; Dáil *Private Sessions*, 35 (22 Aug. 1921).)
41. Dáil *Minutes*, 23, 219 (21 Jan. 1919, 17 Sep. 1920); Minutes of various committees, Clare County Council, 18 Oct. 1920 (C 1); 'Abolition of the Poor Law System' (S 22); *Champion*, 23 Jul. 1921 (Brennan letter), 31 Oct. and 19 Nov. 1921; Secretary, Union and Rural District Clerks' Association of Ireland to Minister for Local Government, 9 Aug. 1921, and Cosgrave to Assistant Secretary, Clare County Council, 18 Oct. 1921: SPO (C 5). After Patrick Brennan had interviewed Cosgrave (probably on 21 July 1921) he declared himself 'absolutely dissatisfied with the running of the Local Government Department'. (Dáil *Private Sessions*, 37 (22 Aug. 1921).)
42. *Champion*, 12 Oct. 1918, 3 Sep. 1921; Minutes, Ennistymon RDC and Guardians, 26 Oct. 1920 and *passim* (C 2); Minutes, Ennistymon RDC, 11 Oct. 1921 (rents Oct. 1918–Mar. 1920, Apr. 1920–Jun. 1921), 20 May 1921 (letter from LGD), 14 Jun. 1921 (including Shannon to RDC, 27 May), and Report to LGD Chief of Inspection, 20 Jan. 1922 (C 5); Labourers (Ireland), Return, HC 1914/16 (280) liii, 73.
43. *Champion*, 18 Dec. 1920 (county surveyor), 12 Mar. 1921, 7 May 1921 (letter from J. J. Scanlon, explaining the finance committee's optimism); Clare County Council, Minutes, 1 Nov. 1920, and those of finance committee, 2 Apr. and 14 May 1921; CI, MCR, May 1921. Roadwork was intermittently undertaken from September 1921 onwards. (P. Ó Ruairc to LGD Chief of Inspection, 8 Mar. 1922 (C 5).)
44. Cf. Chapters 3 and 4. P. J. MacNamara, still a powerful man in Clare affairs, told the Ennis Guardians (whose chairman he was) on 23 July 1921: 'And I say, as a workman, that if things are carried out in the manner outlined by Mr Brennan on that occasion [proposal of the amalgamation scheme], the time has come when every working man's child will have a fair chance in a free country.' (*Champion*, 30 Jul. 1921.)

Chapter 6
GUERRILLA FIGHTERS
(pp. 165–91)

1. Dáil *Minutes*, 47, 152, 264, 278–9 (10 Apr. and 20 Aug. 1919, 11 Mar. 1920); Hogan, *Four Glorious Years*, 245 *et seq.* and 274; Piaras Béaslaí, *Michael Collins, Soldier and Statesman*, Dublin and Cork 1937, 142; Mulcahy's recollections, 28 Apr. 1922, in Dáil *Official Report*, 327–9; Notices of motion for proposed convention, Jan. 1920, annotated with fate of motions and the date 18 Mar. 1920, Plunkett Papers (F 30), MS. 11396. A police informant (IG, MCR, Aug. 1919) confirms that 'extremists' from the Volunteers and ICA met the Dáil 'Executive' on 25 August 1919, and that the Volunteers 'agreed to be guided by the advice of the Dáil until the return of de Valera [from America], on the assurance that the Dáil, if its methods failed, would fall back on the organized manhood of their organizations to rid the country of their enemies'. The Volunteers formally ordered administration of the oath (or declaration) of allegiance to the Republic and the Dáil by General Order No. 11 (N.S. 1920), 23 Jul. 1920, Plunkett Papers, *loc. cit.* Although Austin Brennan, who administered the oath to Volunteers in East Clare, assures me that it contained a specific reference to the 'IRA', this is not to be found either in the order of 23 July 1920 or in the generalised form of the oath given in Dáil *Minutes*, 151 (a form not related to the status of the declarant).

2. IG, MCR, Jul. 1917 (de Valera); Roll Book, Mid-Clare Brigade (F 36); CIs, MCRs, *passim*, and IG, MCR, Jan. 1918; Reports of Drilling, CO 904/122, *passim*; cf. Chapter 3 (post-Armistice demoralisation).

3. IG, MCR, Jun. 1918; CI, MCRs, and *Champion*, *passim*. The Cumann na mBan was founded early in 1914 to raise funds for the Volunteers, but was weak in the provinces before the Rising. See Fox, *Green Banners*, 285–7; Lil Conlon, *Cumann na mBan and the Women of Ireland 1913–25*, Kilkenny 1969, which 'does not purport to be a history—it is simply a pot-pourri of bitter-sweet memories culled in the garden of Yester-Year'. Clare papers reported 26 meetings in 1917, 17 in 1918 and 8 until April 1919 (despite the banning of the organisation in Clare in July 1918).

4. Reports of Drilling in Clare, Nov. and Dec. 1917, CO 904/122 (the *Champion* seldom carried Fianna reports); Lists of Fianna *sluaghta* (F 44); *Champion*, 8 Dec. 1917. A careful history of the Fianna by Bulmer Hobson, who founded the force in Belfast (1902) and Dublin (1909) is in Martin, *The Irish Volunteers*, 17–23. In one Clare town (Miltown Malbay), where no *sluagh* was formally established until January 1919, the RIC did report that eight boys had joined twenty-two adult drillers in December 1917. Their instructor held a whip in his right hand. (Report, 9 Dec. 1917, CO 904/122; Lists (F 44).)

5. *Champion*, 26 Feb. 1916; O'Malley, *On Another Man's Wound*, 118 (scheme evidently put forward *c.* 1919). Only four priests are known to have associated themselves with the Clare Volunteers between 1917 and 1921, two of whom held active office in the force (cf. Chapter 5).

6. MacLysaght, 'Master of None' (F 21), MS. 4750, pp. 315–17 (diary entry, 3 Jun. 1918); Shortt, Memorandum for War Cabinet 'on Demobilisation and Re-settlement', drafted 17 Nov. 1918, redrafted 19 Dec., Strathcarron Papers (A 6), c490, ff. 37, 44; O'Callaghan to *The Times*, 1 Dec. 1919, LB ii, pp. 107–8.

7. 'Officers' (term used loosely) comprises (1) drill leaders, Clare, Nov. and Dec. 1917; (2) Clare prisoners committed to Irish jails for DORR offences and the like, 1917–19; (3) company, battalion and brigade officers, 4th, 5th and 6th Battalions, Mid-Clare Brigade, *c.* Mar. 1919. 'Rank and file' comprises drillers (except 'Officers 1') reported by police, Nov. and Dec. 1917. CO 904/122; Record sheets and Returns, GPB (DORA Prisoners)

Files (A 31); Householders' Returns, 1911 Census, PROD (A 28), and Valuation Lists (A 14), using names from Roll Book, Mid-Clare Brigade (F 36). 'Age' refers to that given at the time of report (Officers 1, Rank and File), committal (Officers 2) and Mar. 1919 (Officers 3). 'Occupation' is that of the Volunteer, or that of the head of his household in 1911 (Officers 3).

8. Information from Art O'Donnell; IG, MCRs, Oct. and Nov. 1916; Mulcahy and O'Donoghue in *Capuchin Annual* (1967), 402, 381; O'Donnell in Dillon, ed., *The Banner*; Hobson, *Irish Volunteers*, 54–8; Martin, *The Irish Volunteers*, 170–83. On 8 April 1917, so Austin Brennan recalls, he represented Clare (in place of his brother Patrick, commander in Clare and staff officer even before the Rising) at a Dublin meeting to reorganise the Volunteers' executive.

9. O'Donoghue in *Capuchin Annual* (1967), 382; IG, MCR, Oct. 1917 (Volunteer pledge); Lynch, *The I.R.B.*, 33 ('there was a particular reason'—not specified—for the oath-ban); Brennan, *Allegiance*, 155. In September 1919 the IRB permitted its members to give their allegiance to the 'elected public authority', which they should 'loyally accept and obey'; but six months earlier it had acknowledged the Dáil's authority 'so long as it stands for complete Separation from England and the establishment of that republic'. (Revision of constitution with explanatory circular from IRB Supreme Council, Sep. 1919, in 'Record of the Rebellion' (A 11), II, 51 *et seq.*; Circular from Supreme Council to Divisional and County Centres, Mar. 1919, in IG, MCR, Aug. 1919.)

10. O'Donoghue and Mulcahy, *loc. cit.*, 381, 409; Mulcahy in *Capuchin Annual* (1968), 385–7 (a moribund 'Resident Executive' under the Minister for Defence retained formal control over the force); Commons *Debates*, Vol. 109, col. 111 (cf. *An tÓglach*, 15 Aug. 1918: 'Allowing for the blunder about "platoons", this compliment from an enemy is a very pretty one; but why does he confine our "complete military system" to the south and west of Ireland?'); O'Malley, *op. cit.*, especially pp. 118–19. Down-to-earth notes on organisation, widely studied, were contributed to *An tÓglach* by Michael Collins (e.g. 14 Sep. 1918: 'Forget the Company of the regular army'). British military opinions varied as to the thoroughness of the Volunteers' organisation, General Jeudwine coming nearest the truth (with the benefit of hindsight) in his 'History of the 5th Division' (A 11), 6–7, where he described the units of 1919 as 'paper organizations' rather than fighting units, taking their lead ('in *practical* form') from the turbulent south rather than the orderly Dublin headquarters.

11. Mulcahy in *Capuchin Annual* (1968), 387–8 (Eyeries raid; cf. Chapter 1); Mulcahy in *Capuchin Annual* (1969), 346–7; information from Paddy A. Mulcahy.

12. Collins to Stack, 28 Nov. 1918, Collins Papers (F 10), MS. 5848; O'Malley, *op. cit.*; 102–3; Mulcahy in *Capuchin Annual* (1969), 349; Malone, Statement (F 45). Austin's first spell in command was very brief (he does not recall having been appointed commandant), spanning the interval between elder brother Patrick's resignation (*c.* 28 Nov. 1918) and younger brother Michael's release from prison (24 Dec. 1918). The three brigades were organised just after Michael's return. Michael Brennan cites other reasons for Patrick's dismissal, including Dublin's failure to support him in a dispute over bank-raiding.

13. Collins to Barrett, 9 and 8 Aug. 1919, and Barrett to Collins, 1 Aug., 25 Jul. and 26 Aug. 1919: Military Archives (B 3), p915.

14. Brennan, 'Statement' (F 38); Mulcahy in *Capuchin Annual* (1969), 350–1. Terence MacSwiney, also irritated by headquarters which 'did not understand the country', proposed a similar plan for attacks on barracks in November 1919 which headquarters sanctioned in diminished form (*ibid.*, 351–2). After Austin's resumption of command Michael (like Patrick) was properly a private; but soon he became commander of the East

Clare flying column and early in 1921, with Austin's support, was appointed commander of the new 1st Western Division (see below).

15. Figgis, *Recollections*, 198–9 (concerning 1917); William Roche [Liam de Roiste], Diary, 18 and 21 Oct. and 18 Nov. 1917, O'Donoghue Papers (F 27); Collins to Stack, 21 Aug. 1918 (received), 17 and 18 May 1919, Collins Papers, MS. 5848; SF Standing Committee, Minutes, 31 Dec. 1918, PROD, 2B.82.116 (B 6).
16. Précis of Sinn Féin meetings, 1917, CO 904/23/3 (A 30, iii). The Volunteer revival in Clare was spurred on by the need to protect Sinn Féin electoral meetings: Clare Volunteers helped fight off Home Rulers in the East Clare and South Armagh by-elections, and the Waterford and East Mayo general election. Reports in the *Champion*, although uneven in coverage, strongly suggest that Sinn Féin clubs tended to be formed shortly before Volunteer companies in the same localities. During 1917–18 Volunteer activity was reported from 36 localities, 28 of which also hosted Sinn Féin clubs. In five cases first reported Volunteer activity preceded Sinn Féin's first reported meeting, in four cases followed it by less than a month, in seven cases by less than two months, in another seven by less than three months, and in five cases by a longer period.
17. O'Malley, *op. cit.*, 57; *Champion*, 3 Nov. 1917, 4 Jan. 1919; information from Patrick Hehir and Patrick Kerin (Kilshanny and Glendine companies). On 15 August 1918 *An tÓglach* reminded Volunteers that they were 'not politicians; they were not created for the purposes of parades, demonstrations, or political activities'; and on 14 September it urged that 'their political occupations shall not clash with their military activities' by making them obvious targets for 'the attention of the enemy'.
18. SF Standing Committee, Minutes, *passim*, PROD, 2B.82.116–17; Brennan, *Allegiance*, *passim*; Dáil *Minutes*, 173 (29 Jun. 1920).
19. Maxwell to French, 13 May 1916, in Ó Broin, *Dublin Castle*, 141; Brennan, 'Statement' (F 38). Variant versions of headquarters' 'plans' for Clare are offered by J. M. McCarthy, ed., *Limerick's Fighting Story*, Tralee n.d., 32–4; Lynch, *The I.R.B.*, 30; C. Desmond Greaves, *Liam Mellows and the Irish Revolution*, London 1971, 82. Clare police reported only minor incidents: three wire-cuttings, one arms raid and one agrarian outrage—messages from Clare RIC in MSS Nathan (A 5) 476, ff. 305, 435, 657, and *ibid.*, 477, f. 6; CI, MCR, May 1916.
20. Instruction of 22 May 1917, in O'Donoghue, *loc. cit.*, 382 (cf. *An tÓglach*, 15 Aug. 1918: 'The military lessons of Easter Week, 1916 . . . are a source of encouragement to us. . . . The surrender of Commandant Pearse was due, not to military reasons, but to political and humanitarian motives [*sic*!]'); Report in PC to US, 6 Jul. 1917, Press Censorship Records (A 33), Correspondence, no. 34; *Saturday Record*, 14 Jul. 1917; Brennan, *Allegiance*, 166; Mulcahy in *Capuchin Annual* (1968), 391–2 (meeting of 3 Apr. 1918).
21. Mac Giolla Choille, *Intelligence Notes*, 156–8; Regulations in CO 904/29; Table of Volunteer arms, 31 Mar. 1916, 1916 Commission, Appendix, p. 123 (giving 37 rifles for Clare); similar table, 28 Feb. 1917, CO 904/29. Arms regulations were further tightened in August and September 1920, when issue of further permits for sporting guns was forbidden and troops directed to collect all civilian arms. ('History of the 5th Division' (A 11), 59.)
22. Malone Statement (F 45); CI, MCR, Mar. 1918; Street, *Administration*, 72; first Outrages Return (H 15). Despite the withholding of rifles from soldiers on Irish furlough (IG, MCR, Jan. 1918), raids on police and military yielded a rich crop of weapons (27 were raided in 1919 and 60 beforehand). The Volunteers banned small-scale raiding on private houses, with little effect, on 25 February 1918, and again on 1 March 1920 (hoping 'that it will not be necessary to refer to this matter again'). (IG, MCR, Apr. 1918; *An tÓglach*, 1 Mar. 1920.)

23. *Champion*, 13 Oct. 1917; O'Malley, *op. cit.*, 105; information from Tom Burke (Lahinch company). Regular company drill was not, however, abandoned, instructions being carried in *An tÓglach*, 31 Jan. 1919; and in the Mid-Clare Brigade commandant's order to his battalion chiefs, 4 Dec. 1919, 'that every Coy in your Battn drills *openly* at least once a week', practising 'close and extended order, use of Rifle, Shot-gun, Revolvers, Hand grenade and Pike'. (Frank Barrett, Dispatch Book (F 36).)
24. P. S. O'Hegarty, *A History of Ireland Under the Union 1801 to 1922*, London 1952, 742; *An tÓglach*, 14 and 29 Oct. and 30 Nov. 1918, Feb., [Mar.], 15 Apr. and 15 Dec. 1919 (this was the first issue for seven months), Feb. and 1 Sep. 1920.
25. O'Hegarty, *op. cit.*, 742; cf. Chapter 4.
26. Record Sheets and Returns, GPB (DORA) Files (A 31) (figures exclude ten recommittals of prisoners let out to graze under the 'Cat and Mouse Act'); Brennan, 'Statement' (F 38); Peadar O'Loughlin (Tullagha, Kilfenora) to Dilly [Markham], 3 May 1918, Markham Papers (F 53). As early as 17 March 1916 Michael Brennan had told his men in Meelick to resist seizure of their arms by using not their butts, but 'the other ends of them and what is in them'. (CI Gelston to 1916 Commission, Minutes 1939–40.)
27. D. O'Hannigan in J. M. McCarthy, *op. cit.*, 88–9; Brennan, 'Statement' (amplified in discussion); Haugh, 'History of the West Clare Brigade' (B 3); Mid-Clare Brigade, Monthly Diary for Jan. 1921, Mulcahy Papers (B 8), P7/A/38; Frank Barrett to COS, 29 Apr. 1921, *ibid.*, P7/A/17. British authorities tended to ascribe formation of the columns to IRA headquarters: in July 1919 (IG, MCR) country units were reported to have been told to keep fifteen armed men ready to carry out any orders they might receive; in mid-October 1920 (according to 'Record of the Rebellion' (A 11), I, 24) 'the rebel leaders' initiated a scheme of 'flying columns'—rather rigidly distinguished from 'active service units' ('training establishments for "officers" I.R.A.'). *An tÓglach*, however, carried no reference to such bodies until 15 October 1920, no directives for their formation, and on 17 June 1921 used the terms 'flying column' and 'active service unit' indiscriminately, as do most Clare veterans whom I have questioned. There is evidence that bodies with both labels existed in Clare, both at brigade and battalion levels.
28. Brennan, 'Statement'; Roll Book, Kilfenora Company (F 56), accounts covering 1 Jun. to 16 Jul. 1921; Shaw Desmond, *The Drama of Sinn Fein*, London 1923, 203.
29. Roll Book, Kilfenora Company; Roll Book, Mid-Clare Brigade (F 36); Mid-Clare Brigade, Return of Strength at 11 Jul. 1921, signed by Frank Barrett, 30 May 1936 (F 36); Bermingham's interview with Michael McMahon (G); Barrett to COS 4 and 29 Apr. 1921, Mulcahy Papers (B 8), P7/A/17. The 1936 Return of Strength as at 11 July 1921 gives the strength of the Mid-Clare Brigade as 2,201. According to the Mid-Clare Brigade Roll Book, nominal strength on 1 May 1921 was 1,435 (together with 28 higher officers). A scribbled IRA muster captured in May 1921, which Macready conjectured might refer to flying columns and active service units only, recorded only 500 Republican soldiers in Clare with 46 rifles (cf. 3,386 and 344 for Munster, and 5,156 and 669 for Ireland). (Photocopy in Greenwood to Lloyd George, 11 May 1921, Lloyd George Papers (A 1), F19/4/10; Macready's Weekly Report to 17 May 1921, CP 2948, Cab. 24/123.)
30. Information from Miss Peg Barrett; lecture notes taken by Miss Aggie Marrinan, 1921 (F 46); Eóin O'Duffy's reports on Brigade Councils, 30 Sep. and 1 Oct. 1921, Mulcahy Papers, P7/A/25–26.
31. Barney Mellows, Circular to Fianna officers, Feb. 1921, Mellows Papers (F 22); Whyte, Autobiography (F 57); Fianna Records, 4th Battalion, Mid-Clare Brigade area (F 44), which list only four boys out of 150–200 enrolled before the Truce who were promoted to Volunteer companies; AG to Director of Organisation, 20 Aug. 1921, Mulcahy Papers,

P7/A/23. Naturally *sluaghta* not responding to the survey questionnaire were excluded. Brigade councils held at the end of September (see note 30) were told of eight *sluaghta* organised in East Clare, three in West Clare of which one had no contact with headquarters, and a number still 'being organised' in Mid-Clare. On 1 December another brigade council was told that 165 boys belonged to the Fianna in the 4th Battalion, Mid-Clare Brigade area (Mulcahy Papers, P7/A/33) (cf. lists of those enrolled up to 11 July 1921 showing variously 206 and 165 (Fianna Records, *loc. cit.*)).

32. Roll Book, Mid-Clare Brigade, supplemented by Roll of Officers as at 11 Jul. 1921, 2nd Battalion, Mid-Clare Brigade (F 36); officers as at Mar. 1919 and Jun. 1921, 4th, 5th and 6th Battalions, Mid-Clare Brigade, listed in Brigade Roll Book (cf. note 7 for definitions; note that number of officers for whom information concerning each characteristic is available usually falls short of full sample); Report on Mid-Clare Brigade, *c.* 1 Oct. 1921, Mulcahy Papers, P7/A/26; words of Seán MacNamara, 6th Battalion. Appointment of officers according to their efficiency rather than their social status was encouraged by the gradual abandonment of company elections. Organiser O'Malley, *op. cit.*, 130, eventually 'set the election system aside. I picked an eager boy and appointed him captain.' On 23 May 1921 Mulcahy wrote to Frank Barrett: 'In the case of organised Brigades and Battalions, we must now get away from the arrangement by which Officers were placed in command by election. We must see that the best man for the position is in every case appointed to it.' (Mulcahy Papers, P7/A/19.)

33. *Champion*, 31 Jan. 1920 (reporting *Daily News* reporting rumour); O'Duffy, Reports of Brigade Councils, *c.* 1 Oct. 1921, Mulcahy Papers, P7/A/25–26, and cf. note 29; words of Michael Maher (Doolin). The 1st Western Division, mainly Clare, was among the best-armed in Ireland, having more rifles late in 1921 than 14 of the 19 divisions. (Undated Return of Armaments, Mulcahy Papers, P7/A/28.)

34. Outrages Returns (H 15); Piaras Béaslaí, *Michael Collins and the Making of a New Ireland*, London 1926, I, 337; Statement of Operations, 2nd Battalion, Mid-Clare Brigade, concerning Ruan Barracks attack, 14 Oct. 1920 (F 36); Burke, 'Some of the Activities of the 4th Battn Mid Clare Bde' (F 39), Chap. 14; Michael Brennan to COS, 29 Apr. 1921, Mulcahy Papers, P7/A/38. The number of attempts to disarm soldiers and police in the four quarters of 1920 was 14, 46, 129 and 45. For 1921 figures are available for arms raids against civilians only: 91 between 1 January and 26 March, 134 between 27 March and 16 July, 17 between 17 July and 10 December. (Returns of Serious Outrages in CPs 2782, 3151 and 3564, Cab. 24/121, 126 and 138. Cf. note 22.)

35. Mid-Clare Brigade, Monthly Diaries for Apr., May and Jun. 1921 (Table 6.3), and Nov. 1920–Mar. 1921, Mulcahy Papers, P7/A/19–20, 38; CI, MCR, Nov. 1920; casualty figures from numerous police, newspaper and other reports. Table 6.3 refers to the number of days on which incidents occurred anywhere in the brigade area; subsequent statistics to the number of incidents (in effect the number of battalion-incident-days).

36. Mulcahy to Barrett, 23 May 1921, and Barrett to Mulcahy, 28 May and 11 Apr. 1921: Mulcahy Papers, P7/A/19 and 17. *An tÓglach* periodically lamented the regional unevenness of IRA activity: on 1 March 1921 it sharply criticised Volunteers who had left 'the gallant men of the South to bear all the brunt of the enemy's activities'. On 6 May it remarked 'the surprising increase in efficiency and effectiveness of our troops' and awakening of 'the backward districts . . . from their lethargy', but these heartening words were probably designed to alter reality, not to express it.

37. Barrett to Adjutant-General, May(?) 1920 (letter charred), Military Archives (B 3), p911; Michael Brennan to Mulcahy, 29 Apr. 1921, and Organisation Department, 'General Instructions to Divisional Commandants', *c.* Mar. 1921: Mulcahy Papers, P7/A/38, 17.

Notes to pages 189–96 277

Divisional commandants were held responsible for the dismissal and removal of officers of all ranks, and (subject to headquarters' sanction) for their appointment.
38. Brennan, 'Statement' (F 38). The division was constituted on paper in May 1921.
39. MacSwiney to Collins, 21 Oct. 1919, in Margery Forester, *Michael Collins, the Lost Leader*, London 1971, 110; Plunkett Papers (F 30), MS. 11396 (cf. note 1). The motion was evidently approved upon subsequent ballot.
40. Thoughts of Philip P. Lennon, New Ross, 14 May 1920 (F 3); Gaynor, 'Kilmihil Parish' (F 40), 432; cf. note 34 (for sources of national outrage figures); County tabulations of raids on mails, CO 904/158/1 (first 'quarter' of 1920 here covers January to April); *Champion*, 1 and 15 Jan. 1921; GPO Secretary to US, 14 Dec. 1920 (concerning Tipperary mail-car service), CO 904/158/1; Brennan to Mulcahy, 29 Apr. 1921, Barrett's Report to COS, after 30 Jun. 1921, and Barrett to Mulcahy 11 Apr. 1921: Mulcahy Papers, P7/A/38, 20 and 17; O'Callaghan to Tom Edwards, 30 Mar. 1921, LB ii, pp. 223–4; CI, MCR, May 1921. The same people were often drafted on successive nights and days, by Volunteers and Crown forces, to destroy and repair the same roads; the chairman of the Clare County Council (the 'injured person' in road trenching cases) was among the most indefatigable of organisers of road trenching. On 28 May 1921 Frank Barrett told Mulcahy (Mulcahy Papers, P7/A/19) that his men were not 'inclined' to fire on enemy road-repairing gangs, since on occasion 'the enemy had with him the fathers, brothers and friends of the men of the A.S. Unit'.
41. CI, MCR, Sep. 1921 (the inspector commented ironically that Volunteer recruiting for many young men was a form of conscription which they 'yielded to freely'); 'Summary of Attendance' at parades, 30 Nov. 1921, and Brennan's Report to Director of Organisation, 10 Nov. 1921: Mulcahy Papers, P7/A/28; information from Seán MacNamara (defeated motion).
42. Dáil Ministry, Minutes (B 7), 15 Sep. 1921 (cf. meetings of 4 November, instructing Brugha 'to take steps immediately to give effect' to that decision to review all officer commissions, and 25 November, accepting the status quo by terming the New Army the 'Re-Commissioned Army'—in effect, the Old Army); *Champion*, 26 Nov. 1921; Brennan to Mulcahy, 11 Nov. 1921, Mulcahy Papers, P7/A/29; *Champion*, 16 Jul. 1921. During the Truce *An tÓglach* did its best to tame the Volunteers' growing arrogance, reminding them that they were not 'a separate caste' or 'a band of men who delight in warfare for its own sake'. (*An tÓglach*, 18 Nov. and 22 Jul. 1921.)

Chapter 7
SEPARATISM AND SOCIAL CHANGE
(pp. 192–230)
1. *Champion*, 4 Jan. 1913, 3 Jan. 1914, 27 Sep. 1913.
2. DATII, *The Management of a Cottage Garden*, new ed., Dublin 1916; Labourers (Ireland) Return for 1914–15, HC 1914/16 (280) liii, 73; cf. Chapter 2, note 6. Under the Irish Land Act, 1903 (3 Edw. VII, c. 37), the scope of 'agricultural labourers' qualified to receive cottages and other benefits was extended to include all hired workers in rural districts (except domestic and menial servants) paid less than a specified wage and owning less than one quarter of an acre of land (Section 93). Under Section 2, untenanted parcels of land might be purchased by tenants of other holdings on the estates concerned (or their sons), by poor tenants or proprietors living nearby, or by former tenants (or their representatives). But by the act of 1909 (9 Edw. VII, c. 42), Section 17, eligibility was extended to those who had surrendered holdings to relieve congestion, and (once all others had been satisfied) to any other person to whom, in the Land Commission's opinion, 'an

advance ought to be made'. This provision encouraged landless labourers in their hopes of impropriation; but they were held to be ineligible for land distributed by the CDB under a curious interpretation of the ambiguous Section 53, which extended the specified categories to all tenants or proprietors in a congested district and to certain herdsmen, and was deemed to override the catch-all provision of Section 17. Cf. William L. Micks, *An Account . . . of the Congested Districts Board for Ireland . . .* Dublin 1925, 122. The number of outdoor agricultural workers aged twenty or more in 1911 (Census), including rural 'general labourers', was 4,709 in Clare and some 180,000 in all Ireland.

3. 1926 Census (I 3); 1911 Census. In compiling Table 7.1 I have assumed that 'assisting relatives', not listed separately in the 1926 Census for Northern Ireland, were counted among 'employees'. Those termed 'out of work' were normally occupied, and are included among 'employees' in the analyses which follow the table. 'Manual workers' are taken to include those employed or out of work in agricultural occupations, manufacture of food and clothing, building and contracting, wood and metal working, other industrial pursuits, and general labour (excluding domestic servants and transport workers). Study of change in the distribution of industrial status and occupation is impeded by changes in criteria for collection of statistics. Thus best estimates for the proportion (for example) of farm workers in Clare's agricultural population, using the 1926 Census, 1911 Census and DATII, *The Agricultural Output of Ireland. 1908*, London 1912, give 13, 28 and 21 per cent respectively!

4. DATII, Reports and Tables relating to Irish Agricultural Labourers (Command Papers, *passim*) (showing that Clare had virtually no seasonally migrating labourers); cf. Arensberg, *The Irish Countryman*; *Champion*, 26 Apr. 1913 (Ennistymon LLA); 'Return of Persons Claiming Reinstatement as Evicted Tenants, or Representatives of Evicted Tenants', covering Clare, 1879–1906, SPO, Official Papers 19630. 184 claimants were listed, for whom police knew of the circumstances of 162 (85 being 'poor') and the occupations of 157 (16 being dependent upon relatives and 7 upon the Poor Law Guardians).

5. Exceptions to this rule included the Direct Labour Association of local government road workers, with four branches noticed in Clare papers between 1913 and 1916, and the Town Tenants' League (seven branches) which catered, however, for publicans and shopkeepers as much as labourers.

6. 1926 Census; Limerick CI, MCR, Jul. 1914; O'Shannon, *Fifty Years*, 58–9; Kerry CI, MCR, Dec. 1915; *Champion*, 6 Sep. 1913, 25 Jul. 1914.

7. P. L. K. Dobbin, *Clare County. Report of the County Surveyor on Third Direct Labour Scheme*, Ennis 1912 (copy in F 52); Emigration Statistics (H 8); 1911 Census; Report of the Board of Trade on the State of Employment in the United Kingdom in February 1915, 1914/16 xxi, Cd 7850, 77; DATII, Reports and Tables relating to Irish Agricultural Labourers, 1914/16 lxxix, Cd 8036, 981, and 1916 xxxii, Cd 8386, 815.

8. IG, MCR, Mar. 1916 (passage underlined and marginated by some Castle official, to no known benefit to the labourer); Lysaght in *Irish Monthly* (Nov. 1919), 577, and Diaries, vi, 7 Apr. 1919 (F 47); Dobbin, *op. cit.*; *Saturday Record*, 5 Jun. 1915, 1 Jun. 1918.

9. Wage rates for 1907, 1913 and 1915 were the lowest commonly paid in summer to Clare's adult male farm labourers, without free house or board and lodging (and, for comparison, with board and lodging). Wage rates for 1918, 1919, 1920 and 1921 were those laid down by the Irish Agricultural Wages Board as minima for workers of the same category in rural Clare. Index figures for 1918 and 1919 refer to 60 hours' weekly labour, for 1920 and 1921 to 54. See DATII, Reports and Tables relating to Irish Agricultural Labourers, *passim*; Wages Board orders reproduced in DATII, *Journal*, XVIII (1917/18), 308–18, *Labour Gazette*, Jun. 1919, and *Dublin Gazette*, 13 Apr. 1920, 6 May 1921. Price

statistics (annual wholesale index figures) were adapted from Thomas Barrington's tabulation in *Journal of the Statistical and Social Inquiry Society of Ireland* (1925–26), 253.
10. Cf. Chapter 2, note 6 (Table 7.3 gives rough estimates only); *Champion* and *Saturday Record, passim*; Report by the Government Actuary (on societies approved for administering National Health Insurance), 1922 ix, Cmd 1662, 485; IG, MCR, Jul. 1919.
11. *Champion*, 28 Sep. 1918; 'List of Branches in Chronological Order' (F 17); *Voice of Labour*, 28 Sep. 1918, 1 Feb. 1919. According to O'Brien's Diary (F 24) and *Voice of Labour*, 28 Sep. 1918, O'Brien got under way a builders' workers' section of the ITGWU at Ennis during his visit five months before the official formation date of the Ennis branch of the union.
12. RIC figures for Clare are taken from CI, MCRs, and for Ireland from IG, MCRs, Jan. and May 1919, and returns for Apr. and Dec. 1920 in CO 904/158/5 (note irregularities in dates, due to incompleteness of returns). ITGWU figures are drawn from ITGWU, *Annual Reports* (figure under 'December 1919' in fact refers to 31 January 1920); registrations at ITGWU head office were recorded in 'List of Branches', *loc. cit.*; details of branches sending remittances (during the years ended December 1918, January 1920(?) and December 1920) are also given in *Annual Reports*. Using Clare newspapers in addition to these sources we find that twenty-two ITGWU branches were formed 1918–21.
13. Various RIC reports, cf. Chapter 5; MR on ITGWU, Dec. 1920, CO 904/158/5; cf. Appendix.
14. *Champion, passim*; list of Newmarket branch officials, O'Brien Papers (F 25), MS. 13948; ITGWU, *Annual Reports*, and ILPTUC, *Reports of the Annual Meetings, passim*; *Irish Opinion*, 3 Aug. 1918 (Provisional Committee, Irish Labour Press Co-operative Society); *Voice of Labour*, 28 Jun. 1919 (but cf. *ibid.*, 20 Sep. 1919: 'The Councils, if they are properly organised, efficiently conducted, and intelligently directed and developed, can become most effective instruments in the battle of Labour for the emancipation of the workers'). Early in 1922 the Ennis Trades Council renamed itself the Clare Workers' Council, and its new Vice-President, Paddy MacNamara of the United Labourers' Association, expressed regret that the Ennis ITGWU branch had seceded from the old council 'for political reasons', and declared that 'we are bound to help the Transport Union and vice versa in labour matters.' (*Champion*, 21 Jan. 1922).
15. Censuses of active membership at 30 Jun. 1918 and 31 Jan. 1920, O'Brien Papers, MS. 13948, and *Watchword of Labour*, 25 Sep. 1920; O'Brien, *Forth the Banners Go*, 110–11; *Irish Opinion*, 25 May 1918; *Voice of Labour*, 30 Aug. 1919 (Labour's Kildare victory, obtained through Dáil arbitration, was qualified by each side's undertaking not to raise 'the question of union and non union labour'); Kerry CI, MCRs, Mar. and Apr. 1919; East Cork CI, MCR, Jan. 1920; *Watchword of Labour*, 25 Sep. 1920 (the current statutory minimum was only 32s 6d weekly). Between mid-1918 and early 1920 the proportion of agricultural workers among active ITGWU members rose from 22 to 38 per cent.
16. Reports of disputes in Clare and Labour papers, *passim*; ITGWU, *Annual Reports, passim* (remittances). The RIC's MRs on the ITGWU, Feb. 1920 to Nov. 1921, CO 904/158/5, provide incomplete returns of 'strikes engineered' by the union, including four in Clare (one of them unreported in the press), 29 in Munster and 85 throughout non-metropolitan Ireland during 1920. Some 16 of those 85 strikes involved farm workers, and only three were stated to have been settled by Republican arbitration. Of the 28 Clare disputes analysed at least 13 gave rise to strikes, five of them in 1920.
17. CI, MCR, Jan. 1919; *Champion*, 22 Mar. and 8 Feb. 1919; 'List of Branches', *loc. cit.*; MacLysaght, Diaries, v and vi (19 Feb. and 7 Apr. 1919), and 'Master of None' (F 21), 322a; *Saturday Record*, 2 Aug. 1919; *Watchword of Labour*, 30 and 23 Oct. 1920.

18. ITGWU, *Annual Report* for 1918, 7; Boyle, 'Irish Labour' (R 5), 128; *Champion*, 17 Apr. 1920; *Workers' Republic*, 1 Jan. 1916.
19. *Champion*, 10 May 1919; West Cork CI, MCR, Mar. 1919; *Voice of Labour*, 12 Apr. 1919; *Watchword of Labour*, 9 Oct. 1920 (urging formation of 'Red Guards' where companies of the Irish Volunteers and Irish Citizen Army did not exist). For their part, the Comrades of the Great War had praised the ITGWU's 'comradeship and steadfastness' in the strike to free hunger-strikers, endorsing 'their proceedings to liberate our fellow countrymen from sufferings to which they have been condemned for the same crime as we have been guilty of in loving our country and fighting for its liberties'. (*Ibid.*, 1 May 1920.)
20. West Cork CI, MCR, Jan. 1919; East Cork CI, MCR, Feb. 1919; Clare CI, MCR, Mar. 1919 (cf. Table 7.4); *Champion, passim* (increases awarded in May 1920, Nov. and Mar. 1919), 29 May 1920, 22 Nov. 1919; Clare County Council, Minutes (C 1), 26 Aug. 1920; Dobbin, *op. cit.*; Quarterly Returns of average prices to farmer of agricultural produce, DATII, *Journal, passim*; Unemployment Returns for 31 Dec. 1920 and 28 Jan. 1921 in RP 2195/1921, and for 9 Dec. 1921 in Clarkson, *Labour and Nationalism*, 441; *Watchword of Labour*, 20 Nov. 1920 (Kilrush ITGWU); ITGWU, *Annual Report* for 1920, 8. Some two-fifths of those on the live register of employment in December 1920 were ex-servicemen, one-third a month later. The number unemployed in about three-quarters of Co. Clare on 31 December 1920 was 928 (including 269 veterans); on 28 February 1921, 1,720 (298); on 6 May 1921, 2,920 (435), the peak figure; and on 2 December 1921, 2,063 (349). (RP 2195/1921.)
21. Connolly, *Labour and Easter Week*, Dublin 1949, 136; *Workers' Republic*, 15 Apr. 1916 (the 1915 Congress had been abandoned for fear that 'the intense political feelings engendered by the war' might provoke arguments causing 'irreparable breaches in the ranks of Labour'); Mansergh, *The Irish Question*, 242 (quoting Thomas Johnson); O'Shannon, *Fifty Years*, 71–2, and Clarkson, *op. cit.*, 314–15; *Irish Opinion*, 23 Feb. 1918. Johnson's article was inspired by a meeting to acclaim the Bolshevik 'social revolution' at which William O'Brien had 'hoped that one day they in Ireland would be able to emulate Russia, and the Citizen Army [cf. IRA] would form the nucleus of the revolutionary army of the future'. (PC, MR, Feb. 1919, CO 904/166.)
22. The language of Bolshevism came to Ireland on two famous occasions during the revolutionary period. In April 1919 the Limerick TLC 'became' the Limerick Workers' and Soldiers' Council, and (with support from the IRA, the mayor and the bishop) called a general strike against imposition of military permits upon workers and others entering and leaving the city. Prices were regulated, food collected and distributed, 'Treasury notes' printed. On 26 April the *Voice of Labour* cried: 'All power to the Limerick Soviet,' but two days later the strike collapsed, the *Voice* grew muted (10 May), and *New Ireland* (3 May) complained of the 'dead weight of the old-style politicians' which had stifled it. Then on 29 May 1920 the *Watchword* heralded the 'Knocklong Soviet Creameries', which after five days' heroics were handed back by their worker-occupiers to their owners in exchange for a generous wage settlement. The Soviet movement resumed in the autumn of 1921 and spread in mid-1922, but its object was invariably to seek higher wages, not social revolution or even management reconstruction. See, e.g., C. Desmond Greaves, *Liam Mellows and the Irish Revolution*, London 1971, 317–18; reports of 'Soviet'-style strikes, 1921, CO 904/158/5.
23. Michael MacDonagh in *Contemporary Review*, CXIII (Apr. 1918), 433; *Irish Opinion*, 20 and 27 Apr., 11 May, 27 Jul. and 31 Aug. 1918; ITUCLP Circular, 24 Jun. 1918, Johnson Papers (F 19), MS. 17115/2; *New Ireland*, 4 Jan. 1919.
24. *Voice of Labour*, 31 Aug. 1918 (explicitly accusing Home Rulers and Unionists, and implicitly Sinn Féiners, of trying to put up 'bogus' Labour candidates), 5 Oct. and 28 Sep.

1918; ITUCLP, Draft Circular, 20 Sep. 1918, Johnson Papers, MS. 17249; Farrell, *The Founding of Dail Éireann*, 32 *et seq.*

25. Farrell, *op. cit.*, 44 and *passim; Voice of Labour*, 9 Nov. 1918, 9 Aug. 1919 and *passim.* O'Shannon of the *Voice* regretted Labour's withdrawal, rendering 'more difficult and less effective the influence of Irish Labour on the International in favour of self-determination'; but as Thomas Cassidy told the 1919 Congress, 'Under the then existing circumstances ... the result would indeed have been disastrous to the cause of Labour.' Thomas McPartlin, a leading advocate of withdrawal of Labour candidates at the November 1918 Congress, was equally strongly against Labour's identifying itself with Sinn Féin: 'If they had Sinn Féin becoming the dominant power they would have to fight them as they had to fight the rotten and corrupt party in 1914.' (ILPTUC, *Report of . . . the Special Congress*, 1918, 106.)
26. Clare CI, MCRs, Feb. and Jun. 1919; Limerick CI, MCR, Feb. 1919; ITGWU, *Annual Report* for 1919, 9.
27. Cf. Clarkson, *op. cit.*, 251 *et seq.*, and Mitchell, *Labour in Irish Politics*, 35–40; *Champion*, 17 Jan., 6 and 20 Jun. 1914, 28 Sep. 1918; IG, MCR, Feb. 1919 (enclosing Report of Sinn Féin Committee on Local Government); Circular by Thomas Foran in *Voice of Labour*, 8 Mar. 1919; *Irish Republic*, 20 Sep. 1919; *Watchword of Labour*, 25 Oct., 1 and 15 Nov., 6 Dec. 1919.
28. *Watchword of Labour*, 6 Mar. 1920 (final analysis by Proportional Representation Society of Ireland), 31 Jan. and 28 Feb. 1920 and *passim*; Mitchell, 'Labour and the National Struggle', 279–80. Labour's share of valid first preference votes in contested seats (1,735 seats out of 1,984) was 16 per cent in Leinster, 17 per cent in Munster and Connaught, and 20 per cent in Ulster, being two-thirds of Sinn Féin's share overall but well under half outside Ulster. Mitchell's analysis (*ibid.* and *Labour in Irish Politics*, 126), otherwise less complete than that given above, refers to 116 unaccredited trade union councillors (possibly including those elected in Cork under a pact agreed between thirty Sinn Féiners and ITGWU representatives, omitted from my analysis), a figure confirmed in ILPTUC, *Report of the Annual Meeting*, 1920, 9. This report admitted that in Cork, Limerick, Wexford, Dublin, Londonderry and Belfast Labour's campaign had been impeded by nomination of candidates independent of the Trades Councils, some of them 'running in alliance with another political party'.
29. *New Ireland*, 4 Jan. 1919 ('Lector' is said to have been A. J. O'Rahilly); cf. Appendix; James Kemmy in *Cuimhnionn Luimneach* (Casg 1966), 109; *Old Ireland*, 1 Nov. 1919. This paper, although a Sinn Féin rather than a Labour organ, was printed by the Socialist Labour Press in Glasgow.
30. *Workers' Republic*, 11 Mar. 1916; *Voice of Labour*, 24 Aug. 1918.
31. 'Summarised Statement' on help given to ex-servicemen, from Irish Office to Prime Minister's Office, 10 Oct. 1921, RP 3504/1921; e.g. *Voice of Labour*, 9 Aug. 1919 (Housing of the Working Class Act); Dáil Ministry, Minutes (B 7), 6 Nov. 1920. The ministry, having discussed the pending Unemployment Insurance (Temporary Provisions Amendment) Act (10 & 11 Geo. V, c. 82), which extended the range of those qualified for immediate benefits, concluded merely that 'It appears Labour are against interfering.'
32. *Irish Opinion*, 1 Dec. 1917, 16 Feb., 9 and 16 Mar. 1918. On 19 April 1919 *New Ireland* criticised the Sinn Féin Árd-Fheis for its coolness towards Labour's cause: 'It is no use saying we must wait to get England out first. . . . Men cannot eat Irish liberty, nor clothe and house their children with it.'
33. *Irish Opinion*, 5 Jan. 1918 (cf. Chapter 5); *Voice of Labour*, 25 Jan. 1919; *New Ireland*, 12 and 19 Apr. 1919; Dáil *Minutes*, 78. Curiously, Limerick had in effect been handed over to the Trades Council (or Soviet) six days before Lector's cutting rejoinder (doubtless written beforehand) was published.

34. *Watchword of Labour*, 4 and 25 Oct. 1919 (the anti-Brugha/Burgess/The Bourgeois sally had been instigated by the *Voice* in May 1919); Kerry CI, MCR, Jan. 1920; *Watchword*, 1 May 1920 (other passages of this article caused the editor to demur); *An tÓglach*, 1 May 1920; Clare CI, MCR, Jun. 1920. The IG, RIC, however, felt the likelihood of a split had recently diminished: 'The Union at present seems to be completely dominated by Sinn Fein and is working with it. Members of the Union are generally also members of the local Sinn Fein Club.' (MR on ITGWU for May 1920, but dated 1 Jul. 1920, CO 904/158/5.)
35. Cf. Chapters 2 and 5. In August 1920 the ILPTUC resolved without dissent that 'any attempt on the part of any Government to compel Trade Unionists to submit their disputes to arbitration must be vigorously resisted', but the Labour Party and ITGWU frequently submitted to voluntary Dáil arbitration. (ILPTUC, *Report of the Annual Meeting*, 1920, 38, 113.)
36. *Watchword of Labour*, 10 Apr. and 19 Jun. 1920; Mitchell, 'Labour and the National Struggle' (R 10), 281 (*Irish Bulletin* analysis); *Champion*, 1 Oct. 1921 and *passim*; O'Brien, *Forth the Banners Go*, 293–305. The April 1921 manifesto proposed a moratorium on rents and annuities, provision of tillage for labourers and promotion of industrial production, but explicitly postponed discussion concerning workers' control of industry. Only one (unaccredited) Labour candidate stood for the Southern parliament in May 1921 (Richard Corish), although in Clare both the ITGWU and Ennis Asylum Workers' Union had urged Labour's participation. (ILPTUC, *Official Report of . . . the Annual Meeting*, 1921, 18; *Champion*, 16 Apr. 1921.)
37. *Champion*, 17 Apr. and 19 Jun. 1920; *Watchword of Labour*, 15 May and 16 Oct. 1920; O'Shannon, *Fifty Years*, 77.
38. IG, MCR, Jan. 1920; *Watchword of Labour*, 16 Oct., 24 Jul. and 4 Dec. 1920; Limerick CI, MCR, Aug. 1920; *Champion* and *Saturday Record*, *passim*; O'Shannon quoted by Richard Bennett, *The Black and Tans*, London 1959, 199.
39. Cf. Chapters 4 and 5.
40. The Irish Landowners' Convention represented the former Ascendancy rather than the many low-born graziers who bought up bankrupted estates in the nineteenth century or grazed lands on the eleven-month leasehold system.
41. Donal Nevin, ed., *1913: Jim Larkin and the Dublin Lock-Out*, Dublin 1964, 42; *Champion*, 20 Nov. and 11 Dec. 1915, 5 Jul. and 9 Aug. 1913; cf. Appendix; *Champion*, 26 Apr. and 10 May 1913, 16 May 1914.
42. *Irish Farmer and Stockowner*, 24 Mar. 1917, 12 Jan. 1918, 25 Jul. and 20 Oct. 1917, 9 and 23 Feb., 13 Apr. and 26 Oct. 1918; *Champion*, 19 Jul. 1919, 27 Mar. 1920; O'Callaghan to M. F. O'Hanlon (IFU Secretary), 4 Sep. and 14 Oct. 1919, LB ii, pp. 67, 84. The IFU had been founded in 1911, but had few branches until 1918.
43. O'Callaghan to O'Hanlon, 14 Oct. 1919, LB ii, p. 84; Reports of branch meetings in *ibid.*, p. 206, *Irish Farmer* and *Champion*, *passim* (first report of each branch is taken to refer to its formation, whether explicitly stated or not).
44. *Irish Farmer and Stockowner*, 24 Mar. 1917; O'Callaghan to O'Hanlon, 23 Aug. 1921, LB iii, p. 29; Ennistymon RDC, Minutes (C 2), 28 Oct. 1919, and CI, MCRs, Nov. and Dec. 1919, Jan. 1920; CFA Resolutions in O'Callaghan Papers, LB ii, pp. 200, 206 (cf. Chapter 2); *Champion*, 12 Feb. 1921.
45. *Irish Farmer and Stockowner*, 12 Jan. and 2 Mar. 1918, 12 Apr. 1919 (letter from Secretary, Co. Meath Farmers' Association).
46. *Irish Farmer*, 24 Apr. 1920, 11 Jun. 1921, 15 May 1920 (Fermoy branch); *Irish Farming World*, 16 May 1919, 21 May 1920; Circular, Nov. 1921, in O'Callaghan Papers, LB ii, pp. 285–7.

47. *Irish Farmer and Stockowner*, 31 May 1919; *Irish Farmer*, 14 Aug., 29 May, 12 and 19 Jun. 1920. The *Irish Farmer* reported wage agreements with the ITGWU during 1920 in Kildare, Meath, Waterford, Louth and Carlow.
48. *Irish Farmer*, 22 and 29 May 1920.
49. *Ibid.*, 19 Jun. and 3 Jul. 1920 and *passim*. According to Mitchell, *Labour in Irish Politics*, 127, the Force put forward candidates in the June 1920 elections, especially in Wexford; but delegates from 50 branches to the Wexford County Executive, IFU, decided early in June 'that consideration of the "Farmers' Freedom Force" Scheme be postponed' (*Irish Farmer*, 12 Jun. 1920). Five provincial IFU branches discussed the Force but did not make their views explicit.
50. *Watchword of Labour*, 5 Jun. 1920; *Farmers' Gazette*, 29 May 1920, 12 Jul. 1919, 3 Apr. 1920.
51. *Ibid.*, 28 Jun. 1919; *Champion*, 23 Jul. 1921 (address on amalgamation scheme).
52. *Irish Farmer and Stockowner*, 25 Jul. 1917, 19 Oct. 1918; *Champion*, 27 Mar. 1915 (Resolution of General Meeting, Co. Clare RPA); *Irish Farmer*, 15 and 22 Jan. 1921, 17 Dec. 1921; O'Callaghan to O'Hanlon, 12 Jan. 1922, LB ii, p. 317. After some wavering the IFU selected at least 25 candidates for the 1922 general election in the twenty-six counties, but after intimidation combined with assurances that candidates adhering to the Collins–de Valera 'Pact' had the farmers' interests at heart, only 12 were nominated and seven elected (cf. Labour's 18 nominees and 17 TDs). In Clare the IFU's two candidates, like Labour's, were withdrawn on nomination day when informed that 'a contested election in Clare would lead to grave disorder and perhaps worse'. (*Irish Farmer*, *passim*; O'Callaghan to Quinn (Secretary, CFA), draft letter to press, 11 Jun. 1922, LB iii, pp. 95–9; McCracken, *Representative Government*, 73.)
53. Cf. Chapter 2; Analysis of meetings reported in local press only; *Farmers' Gazette*, 1 Nov. 1919 (reporting National Executive's approval of O'Callaghan's resolution); *Irish Farmer*, 20 Nov. 1920, 12 Mar. 1921; O'Callaghan to Midleton, 14 Jan. 1918, LB i, p. 905.
54. 'AE', *A Plea for Justice*, Dublin [1921]; Northern Division, East Cork CI, MCR, May 1921; *Irish Farmer*, 16 Jul. 1921; *Champion*, 19 Mar. 1921 (Ballymena IFU branch).
55. *Farmers' Gazette*, 24 Apr. 1920; Dáil *Minutes*, 191 (6 Aug. 1920); Dáil Official Report, p. 69 (retrospective account of Dáil arbitration involving the IFU); *Champion*, 9 Apr. 1921; *Irish Farmer*, 5 Mar. and 29 Oct. 1921; O'Callaghan to Quinn, 19 Nov. 1921, LB ii, p. 288.
56. *Champion*, 8 Oct. 1921; 'Poor Rates in Co. Clare. The Co. Clare Farmers' Association and Clare County Council', 18 Jan. 1923, O'Callaghan Papers (cf. Chapter 5); Inspector to Chief of Inspection, LGD, 24 Nov. 1921 (C 5). At a CFA referendum O'Callaghan's proposal had won only 229 votes, compared with 181 for a boycott until all arrears had been collected and 979 for payment of the first moiety at 1920 rates, but a 'prolonged and very stormy' meeting of the executive accepted O'Callaghan's advice that the last proposal would not be accepted by the Dáil's LGD.
57. County Council, Minutes (C 1), 30 Jun. 1920, and *Champion*, 6 Aug. 1921 (reporting implementation of decision); *Irish Farmer*, 21 Aug. 1920, 26 Feb. 1921, 23 Oct. 1920; Austin Brennan's judgment; *Champion*, 14 Jan. 1922.

Bibliography

> If Jupiter and Saturn meet,
> What a crop of mummy wheat!
> W. B. YEATS

BIBLIOGRAPHIES are, by nature, bundles of incongruous things. Bad, useful books jostle with good, useless books, and simply awful books, and, occasionally, splendid books ('Jupiters'). Four-page pamphlets rub shoulders with lifes' works of a thousand pages and all receive their allotted line of description. The lists which follow are not free from incongruities, but some attempt has been made to regulate them. Useful, scholarly books and extensive collections of unpublished papers relevant to this study are asterisked. Most books which are either awful or useless have been omitted. Sources pertinent to the subject of each chapter, which are either useful or good and which bear to some extent upon the period 1913 to 1921, are listed in classes L to R. Class K covers the British administration of Ireland, aspects of which are discussed throughout this book. Class S, material relating to Co. Clare, is somewhat less selective, although general parish histories and the like have been omitted. Primary sources (administrative records, private collections, spoken recollections, official publications and periodicals) have been collated for convenience in lists A to J, but extensive cross-references are provided in the subject lists. Where individuals hold the copyright on documentary collections, their names have been given in brackets.

PRIMARY SOURCES

UNPUBLISHED MATERIAL

A. British Administration of Ireland

Beaverbrook Library, London (at time of consultation)
A1. *Lloyd George Papers*. Wonderfully cross-indexed, including useful files of correspondence with Macready, Duke, French and Greenwood, and other files for Fisher (of the Treasury), Shortt, Macpherson, Wilson, Wimborne and FitzAlan. Almost exclusively incoming letters.

Bodleian Library, Oxford
A2. *Asquith*, especially MSS 36–37, correspondence concerning Ireland in chronological order (1909–May 1916; May 1916–Jun. 1918), including a few letters from Birrell and Wimborne; and MSS 41–45, Irish papers, including military reports of Easter Rising (42) which supplement the Nathan collection (A5). [M. Bonham Carter]

A3. *Birrell Collection*, especially Dep. c.299. Includes many letters from Nathan. [J. C. Smedley]
A4. *A. P. Magill* (MS. Eng. lett. c.213). Includes Birrell's letters to his private secretary, and a few from Duke, together with Magill's brief appraisal of the latter.
A5. **Nathan*. Splendidly sorted and presented, sure evidence of the Under-Secretary's punctiliousness. Diaries (MSS 49–51 for 1914–16) are in fact appointment books. Useful correspondence with Lords Lieutenant (448) and Birrell (449), and an outstanding file of papers relating to the Easter Rising (476–78).
A6. *Strathcarron* (formerly James Ian Macpherson), MS. Eng. hist. c.490–91. Duplicates of official CSO papers, drafts and originals of official letters and memoranda. Useful papers on demobilisation and proposals for recruiting policemen among British ex-servicemen.

British Museum, London
A7. *Birrell Collections*, especially Add. MSS 49372 and 49382.
A8. *Viscount Gladstone Papers*. Includes correspondence with Birrell (Add. MS. 46081 etc.) and Aberdeen (45995).

Corpus Christi College, Oxford
A9. *Francis Hemming* (a CSO and Irish official 1920–23). Includes useful RIC memoranda, and informative notes for speeches using documents not otherwise traced.

Imperial War Museum, London
A10. *Colonel F. O. Cave*, especially pocket diary for 1921 (FOC–1/6), describing life as an officer in Donegal.
A11. *Jeudwine* (commander of 5th Division, 1919–22, and acting Irish army commander in late 1921). Includes 'Record of the Rebellion in Ireland in 1920–21 and the part played by the Army in dealing with it' (1922—most useful); correspondence with Irish officials and Wilson; interesting 'Confidential. History of the 5th Division in Ireland' (1922) (file 72/82/2).
A12. *Percival* (intelligence officer in Co. Cork, 1920–21). Diverting relics of his Irish service, and two lectures on 'Guerilla Warfare—Ireland 1920–21' delivered in 1923, with Monty's criticisms (4/1). [Major A. J. MacG. Percival]
A13. *Sir Henry Wilson* (CIGS, 1918–21). Microfilms, unexpurgated, of his famous diaries (cf. K10), and correspondence with the Egyptian commander General Congreve (2 vols, 1919–22). Strong stuff. [Major C. J. Wilson]

Irish Valuation Office, Dublin
A14. *Valuation Lists* and Ordnance Survey maps annotated with boundaries of holdings referred to in the lists. Maps and lists have been constantly amended since the time of Griffith's Valuation with an ingenious sequence of coloured inks. Useful for supplementing census returns (A28) in analysing the social background of individuals. Lists arranged by townland and bound by electoral division.

King's College Centre for Military Archives, London
A15. *F. A. S. Clarke.* Typescript memoirs, 'The Memoirs of a Professional Soldier in Peace and War' (by 'Musketeer', 1968), covering service in Co. Cork, 1920–21.
A16. *R. Macleod.* Typed memoirs, 'An Artillery Officer in the First World War', including interesting account of service at Curragh, 1914.

National Library of Ireland, Dublin
A17. *French of Ypres.* Fragment of Journal (Jun. 1919–Mar. 1920), including occasionally detailed accounts of interviews amidst bare lists of official functions (MS. 2269).
A18. *Florence O'Donoghue.* Uncatalogued collection (see also F27). Includes transcripts of telephone and telegraph messages intercepted by Cork No. 1 Brigade, IRA (Aug. 1921–Mar. 1922, about 300 typed pp.)—useful for British army and police movements during the Truce.
A19. *RIC Orders* (MS. 10472), Mar. 1918–Aug. 1919, intercepted by IRA.

Nuffield College, Oxford
A20. *Edward Shortt* (CS, 1918–19). Very slim file of transcripts of parts of a few letters. [Mrs A. D. Ingrams]

Public Record Office, London
A21. **Cabinet Papers.* Much on Ireland in Cabinet Conclusions, occasionally reporting remarks by Irish officials (Cab. 23); Cabinet Memoranda (24, of which 24/28, 43, 20 and 93 are of Clare interest); Cabinet Committee on Ireland, reports, memoranda and minutes, 1919–20 (27/68–70); Irish Situation Committee papers, 1920–21 (27/107–08, last memoranda January 1921); Memoranda of Cabinets 1913–16 (37, less useful than 24); Asquith's letters to the King (41).
A22. *Colonial Office,* Dublin Castle Records (CO 903–906). Includes all CSO records believed in 1922 to be of possibly enduring importance (for the residue see A 30). A few collections are still for some reason suppressed, including CO 904/24/2 (Sinn Féin Arbitration Court, 1919), 24/4 (Sinn Féin clubs), 25 and 26/1–2 (Nationalist-inclined civil servants) and 193–216 (biographical files on leading Nationalists)—but the reports of lower ranking policemen to their County Inspectors (most of which I have been unable to trace) are not among the suppressed collections.

The following categories contain material of particular importance to my study:

i. *Intelligence Notes,* CO 903/19. Printed but confidential notes compiled annually for Chief Secretary (mainly from police reports cited in A22, v). Those for 1913–16 are edited and reproduced in L 16; those for 1917–19 are available only in this collection.

ii. *United Irish League,* CO 904/20/2. Returns by county, 1913–21.

iii. *Sinn Féin Meetings,* CO 904/23/2–3. Typed précis (112 pp.) of major meetings, 1917 (23/2); indexed report (80 pp.) of Sinn Féin convention, 1917, with press reports, and monthly reports on Sinn Féin funds, Jun. 1917–Jun. 1918 (23/3).

iv. *Volunteers*, CO 904/29/2. Includes list of Volunteer arms and membership in Cork, before 22 Feb. 1917 (document captured from John Nolan, Cork, and worth comparing with police return, 28 Feb. 1917, in same collection).

v. **Monthly Police Reports*, Crime Special Branch, RIC, CO 904/89–116, 119–20 (covering 1913–21). County Inspectors' Confidential Reports, handwritten and bound by months. Useful for assessments of a policeman's lot, for survey of crime and especially reports on political activities. From Jan. 1916 (99) tables of branches, membership and armament of all political organisations are provided. I checked all available reports for Counties Clare, Kerry, Limerick, Cork West and East Ridings (Nov. 1913–Dec. 1921). Reports for Limerick, and Clare until 1917 at least, are unusually full and rewarding. In 1917 some returns of offences under DORR are given, and in 1920–21 detailed returns of outrages (intermittently). Missing reports are those for Aug. 1917 (all), Mar.–May 1920 (all), Aug. 1920 (Kerry), Sep. 1920 (all) and Mar. 1921 (Kerry). Detailed précis of these reports (typed) are filed in 119–20 (1913–15, last available), 94 (Sep. 1914), 95 (Nov. and Dec. 1915), 96 (Jan.–Mar. 1915), and 97 (May–Aug. 1915). Those for Dec. 1913, Mar., May and Jul. 1914 are missing. The useful monthly reports of the Inspector-General are filed with the CIs' reports. More detailed reports on each county in 1916 (collected Jan. 1917) are in 120.

vi. *Illegal Drillings*, CO 904/122/1–2. Includes useful constables' reports of drillings, Nov. and Dec. 1917, many from Co. Clare. Also file of *Clare Champion* reports to which press censor objected.

vii. *Returns of Outrages*, CO 904/148–50. Biweekly, then weekly, 29 Mar. 1920–Dec. 1921 (by day, not county). Also some statistical summaries and transcribed barracks reports. More useful than returns in 123–47.

viii. *Alleged Truce Breaches* by IRA, Jul.–Nov. 1921, CO 904/151.

ix. *Military Intelligence Officers*, Monthly Reports, CO 904/157/1, Sep. 1916–Jul. 1918. Clare covered by reports from Southern, and Midlands and Connaught Districts. Much less detailed and useful than A22,v.

x. *Seditious Leaflets*. CO 904/161/3. Summary tables of tracings by county, 1914–Mar. 1916.

xi. *Press Censorship Files* (complementing A22, vi and A33), CO 904/166–67. See especially Censor's Monthly Reports (Aug. 1917–Mar. 1919, May and Nov. 1918 missing). These include extracts from deleted articles, and comments on them.

xii. *Wartime Mobilisation of RIC*, CO 904/174. Useful for police strengths and weaknesses.

xiii. *Circulars to RIC Officers*, CO 904/178. Two sequences covering Jun. 1921–May 1922, and Jan. 1921–May 1922.

xiv. *Reduction of Troops in Ireland*, CO 904/187/1. Three proposals and correspondence, 1917–19 (collate with A6).

xv. *Sir John Anderson* papers, CO 904/188. Includes important official and semi-official correspondence between the Joint Under-Secretary in 1920–21 and other Irish officials, civil and military.

A23. *Home Office Papers*, HO 184, records of the RIC. Includes the General Register of the RIC, which gives extensive biographical information on all recruits to the RIC, including temporary constables (Black and Tans) and temporary cadets (Auxiliaries). Information was abstracted on all those who resigned from the force after 1913 (list obtained from L3), involving study of the registers from 1892 onwards (/29–42). More details are given in the Officers' Registers (/46–48 studied, including all officers recruited from 1884 to 1921). The separate Auxiliary Division Register (/50) is scrappy and unenlightening. The nominal returns of policemen by county (/61 for 1920 examined) provide a useful indication of the number of men serving, but give no biographical information except their religion. The returns of personnel (/54 for 1884–1919) give convenient summaries of the strength of the RIC and wastage from it.

A24. *Department of National Service Papers*, Nat. Serv. 1/84–85. Various returns of military recruiting, 1914–18, disappointingly incomplete and unsystematic in treatment of recruitment in each provincial centre. Fuller information may be found in A30, iii, 1914–Dec. 1916; and A33, Jun.–Nov. 1918; with less detailed and complete returns for 1917 and early 1918 in A22, v (IG, MCRs) and A22, ix (for Southern District, Irish Command).

A25. *Mark Sturgis's Diaries*, PRO 30/59, 1–5. Covers the experiences of an alert Castle official, Jul. 1920–Jan. 1922—fascinating material, not apparently intended for publication. Whiffs of Wodehouse.

A26. *War Office Papers*, WO 32/4308. Includes two versions (May 1919 and Sep. 1920) of the booklet finally published under the title *Sinn Féin and the Irish Volunteers*—another army assessment of the war (cf. A11, A12 above) while it was actually happening.

A27. *War Office Papers*, WO 35. Includes the War Diary of General Staff GHQ Ireland, 1 Dec. 1920–Mar. 1923, typed and highly condensed, including some correspondence, reports of engagements and conferences, but disappointing source for military history (WO 35/93/1/1). /173/5 contains a monthly return of military desertions, by divisions, Jan. 1921–Apr. 1922. Of particular interest are the weekly returns of army strength, of which I summarised those for the 6th Division (covering Co. Clare). The periods covered are Feb.–Jun. 1920 (/179/1) and Jul. 1921–May 1922 (/179/2). Most of the other papers in WO 35 refer to the Dublin area, although war diaries exist for some other districts (excluding 6th Division).

Public Record Office, Dublin

A28. *Returns of 1911 Census*. The original householders' returns, as well as townland abstracts prepared by the census enumerators, are preserved in filthy brown paper parcels, parcelled by electoral divisions and grouped by townland. These have been used, in conjunction with A14, to elicit biographical information on Clare Volunteer officers.

A29. *Crown and Peace Records*, Co. Clare. The printed Register of Electors and Absent Voters' List for West Clare, 1 Oct. 1918 (1D.34.89), arranged by townland, was examined to give a notion of the number of soldiers (absent voters) from various parts of the county. Papers concerning coroners' inquests, 1916–20 and 1922–23 (1D.39.113) give useful précis of evidence and conclusions reached. This collection also includes numerous files on criminal injuries.

State Paper Office, Dublin

A30. *Chief Secretary's Office Papers*. What was left after papers described in A22 were sent to London. Organisation of these papers is chaotic, and particular papers can only be traced with great labour. The most useful among the collections consulted were the following:

i. *Convict Department Files*. The Convicts Reference Book 1912–20 (Room VIC), Criminal Index Book 1912–20 (Room VIE), the files of those indexed (Room V) and their penal records (Room VIIE) relate to disappointingly few 'political' prisoners. Those imprisoned for Defence of the Realm breaches are treated in files A31.

ii. *RIC, Crime Special Branch Records*. Includes (carton 5) reports on cattle-driving in Clare, and (carton 23) returns of youths fleeing the country for fear of conscription (1914–15), various reports on disloyal clergy (1914–15, 1917) and disloyal civil servants (1916) and an interesting report (1920) on Munster No. 1 Division by the Divisional Commissioner, RIC.

iii. *Miscellaneous and Official Papers*. Includes lists of prosecutions under the Defence of the Realm Act and reports of Mountjoy prisoners' conduct (1917, including Clare prisoners), in parcel 5; military recruiting returns, more notes on disloyal civil servants and biographical notes on disloyal leaders, including the Brennans, in parcel 17; material collected for the 1914 RIC Commission of Inquiry, in parcel 23; and reports on the Clare troubles of early 1918, in parcel 12.

iv. *Registered Papers*. Those consulted are too numerous to list, but many specific references appear in notes to most chapters. Pertinacious use of the original indices and registers makes possible consultation of a fair proportion of the papers listed, though many of the plums have been plucked by departmental archivists in London. Files include police and military reports and extensive archives of Castle committees and departments. Since no index exists for 1921, I examined all sixty-eight cartons and four parcels of papers, finding much important material, particularly on local government. A few important files relating to the transfer of administration from British to Irish hands have been renumbered and properly catalogued under the heading 'Rialtas Sealadach na hÉireann' (catalogue in State Paper Office).

A31. *General Prisons Board Papers* (Room II). Includes reports on condition of hunger-strikers (many of them from Clare), 1918–20; returns of unconvicted 'Sinn Féin' prisoners in custody in each Irish prison (daily returns of those received and discharged, Jul.–Nov. 1920 and Feb.–May 1921—too laborious to be systematically checked; weekly returns of those in custody, Nov. 1920–May 1921, checked for Claremen); virtually complete files of record sheets, etc., of prisoners imprisoned for breaches of the Defence of the Realm Act and Regulations, giving useful biographical information (early 1918–early 1920), with many intercepted letters from prisoners, and much correspondence on the proper treatment of 'political' prisoners. Despite the misleading manner in which the GPB indexed its files, particularly the last collection described, study of these cartons is well worth while for students of the pre-revolutionary period. Unfortunately the returns of unconvicted prisoners exclude internees in Britain or on Spike Island (that is, the vast majority).

A32. *Department of National Service Papers* (see also A24) (Room VIB). Another disappointing collection, though it contains a useful history of the department (file 2538) and inspectors' reports on the department's work from most counties—excluding Clare.

A33. *Press Censorship Records* (see also A22, xi) (Room VIIC). Extensive correspondence with local newspapers (much with the *Clare Champion* and other Clare papers), 1917–19, indexed on cards by subject and newspaper. Also includes a four-volume register of telegrams sent by pressmen in Ireland, with précis of contents and summary of deletions, allowing one to abstract a full list of pressmen in, say, Ennis and what they were not allowed to report. Serials sent out by the censor to the press (Jun. 1916–Jan. 1919, May–Aug. 1919) are also preserved and indexed.

A34. *Resident Magistrates' Papers* (Room IV). Record of Service Book, 1882–1921, gives biographical details of all RMs appointed. A set of routine circulars from CSO to RMs (one parcel, 1905–21) is available in Official Papers (A30, iii). The extensive monthly summaries of each RM's duties (Room VIIC) are less informative than the monthly reports on attendance at courts (RP 3126/1921).

University College Archives, Dublin

A35. The *Mulcahy Papers* (see B 8) include a few British military intelligence reports, captured by the IRA in 1921 (P7/A/23 and 37).

B. Republican Administration of Ireland

National Library of Ireland, Dublin

B1. Dáil Éireann, *Financial Documents*, MS. 8602. Includes several letters by Michael Collins (/4) and a scribbled pocket letterbook of an unnamed department (/2, 6 Oct.–2 Nov. 1921).

B2. *George Gavan Duffy Papers*, MS. 15440. Includes various proceedings and minutes of Dáil meetings, and departmental reports (1919–23). These largely duplicate the official file (B7).

B3. **The Military Archives*, Department of Defence, Dublin, reproduced on microfilm, p911–21. Rather disordered, many documents damaged. Elaborate but inadequate index. Includes captured British military documents, mainly relating to Cork (AO413, p918); correspondence of Adjutant-General Collins with provincial brigades, 1919 (West Clare, AO363, p915, including Liam Haugh, 'History of the West Clare Brigade' (typescript, c. 1934); Mid-Clare, AO362, p915 and p911, unnumbered); later correspondence with brigades, mainly 1920 (Mid-Clare, p911, unnumbered; East Clare, AO522, p919; West Clare, p911, AO523). Also many historical accounts by former Volunteers, mainly written in the 1930s, and certain rather unreliable lists of IRA executions and war casualties.

B4. *George Noble Plunkett Papers*, MS. 11404. Includes circulars and memoranda issued by many Dáil departments (1919–21).

Public Record Office, Dublin
B5. *Dáil Courts* (Winding Up) Commission Files. DE 10/4–5 includes some correspondence between the Dáil Ministry for Home Affairs and the Clare district court registrars (1921–22). DE 15/20–22 and 25 include the registers of three parish courts in Clare up to 1922 (mostly post-Truce). DE 16/5–6 comprises incomplete sets of reports on cases by parish court clerks, about Sep. 1921–Mar. 1922.
B6. *Sinn Féin Funds Case, Papers.* Typed copies of certain documents prepared to aid the courts in deciding which faction of Sinn Féin held the apostolic succession. The only useful pre-Civil War document is the set of minutes of the Standing Committee of Sinn Féin, Jan. 1918–Mar. 1922 (2B.82.116–17).

State Paper Office, Dublin
B7. *Dáil Records* 1919–22. A surprisingly small collection, for once beautifully catalogued. Much use was made of the ministry and cabinet minutes (four xeroxed volumes, DE 1/1–4, very cryptic statements of heads of discussion and conclusions); the reports, circulars and correspondence of the Departments of Agriculture (especially DE 2/64) and Home Affairs (DE 2/38 and 51). Sets of Dáil decrees (DE 2/8) are of little use, since they cover only a small proportion of the decisions reached by the ministry. The departmental reports are of considerable interest—'really rather good', according to Sturgis of Dublin Castle (cf. A25).

University College Archives, Dublin
B8. *Mulcahy Papers.* Now adequately catalogued, these include various papers of Michael Collins as Minister for Finance, among them various memoranda on income tax policy (P7/A/12) and home affairs and agriculture (P7/A/13). A large amount of correspondence (mainly 1921) between Mulcahy (Chief of Staff) and provincial IRA brigades is listed under P7/A/17–38 (detailed references appear in the notes to Chapter 6). The collection is still richer, however, in sources for Civil War history.

C. Local Administration of Ireland

Clare County Council, Ennis Courthouse
C1. *County Council Minute Books* (volumes cover 1911–16, 1916–Aug. 1920 and Nov. 1920–Sep. 1923); also minutes of finance committee (1917–Sep. 1920, Dec. 1920–1923) and various committees (1912–Oct. 1921, clearly incomplete). There is also a bound volume of correspondence between the Dáil Ministry for Local Government and the Ennis Board of Guardians and Rural District Council (Jun. 1921–1925).

Clare County Library Garage, Ennis
C2. *Boards of Guardians and Rural District Councils, Minute Books*. Those for Ennistymon only were analysed, but a catalogue was made of all books surviving for Clare for the period 1913–21. The missing volumes are as follows: Ennis BG, May–Oct. 1918 and Jan. 1920–Mar. 1921; Ennis RDC, Nov. 1917–Apr. 1918 and after Jul. 1921; Tulla BG, entire period; Tulla RDC, after Dec. 1920; Scariff BG, before Apr. 1921; Scariff RDC, before Apr. 1919 and Jun. 1920–May 1921; Limerick No. 2 RDC, before Feb. 1915 and after Feb. 1918; Killadysert BG and RDC, entire period; Ballyvaughan BG and RDC, Kilkee Town Commissioners and Kilrush UDC, entire period. The minutes of the Kilrush, Corofin and Ennistymon BGs and RDCs are complete, though some are damaged by damp. Records of the remaining local body, the Ennis UDC, are kept separately in the Ennis museum. Immense labour is needed both to obtain and to analyse these volumes, but only they contain the statistical secrets of how Irish local government worked in Clare.

Public Record Office, Dublin
C3. *Boards of Guardians, Minute Books*, 1916 only (173 volumes). These are duplicated in holdings throughout the country, but are conveniently consolidated in this collection.

State Paper Office, Dublin
C4. *Dáil Records*. Includes reports and memoranda of Department of Local Government, 1920–21 (DE 2/62, 155 and 243); files on recognition of Dáil by local bodies (/444) and local elections of 1920 (/81).
C5. *Dáil Local Government Records*. Files by county of correspondence between Dáil ministry and local bodies, and minutes sent in for vetting. I examined the files for the Clare County Council (few minutes, but many letters and some orders by the official Local Government Board, 1920–21); and the Ennistymon BG and RDC (duplicate minutes for period Aug. 1920–Feb. 1922, sometimes usefully annotated by ministry).

D. Church of Ireland

Deanery, Killaloe
D1. A collection of preachers' books (including size of congregation and collection at each service), vestry books and glebes committee and other minute books, for St Flannan's Cathedral, Killaloe and the churches of three nearby Clare parishes. Consulted as examples only (similar holdings probably exist in most parish churches). [Very Rev. Dr Bourke, Killaloe]

Church of Ireland, Spanish Point
D2. Similar books to those listed in D1, for the Ennistymon and Kilrush districts. Certain letters relating to the Kilmanaheen School, Ennistymon, of considerable social interest. [Rev. Mr Jenkins]

Representative Church Body Library, Rathgar (Dublin)
D3. Similar holdings for parishes on the Clare–Limerick border (O'Brien's Bridge and Kiltinanlea). These seem to be the only Clare Church of Ireland records to have been consolidated in a central collection (excluding parish registers).

E. Roman Catholic Church

Diocesan Archive, Ennis
E1. Includes a small collection of fairly political papers of Dr Michael Fogarty, Bishop of Killaloe (1904–55). Includes abstract of receipts from the Irish Relief Fund, and cryptic notes of disbursals. Fragmentary records arranged by parish give information on church maintenance, etc., in the twentieth century (only one letter of political interest was found, in the Kilballyowen file). Dr Fogarty evidently either did not answer his letters or kept no copies of his answers. [Most Rev. Dr Harty]

St Flannan's College, Ennis
E2. Materials on history of Killaloe parishes collected by Dermot Gleeson. Fragmentary, with little bearing on political or social history, but including some useful historical sketches by Co. Clare priests. Extracts are given from the bishop's visitation books to certain parishes.

F. Private Collections

Ennis Museum (now in Clare County Library, Ennis)
F1. Photographs, telegrams concerning the East Clare by-election (1917), poems composed in Derry Jail, 1921.

Kerry County Library, Tralee
F2. *Earl of Listowel.* Papers (unsorted), including rental books and auction notice.

Limerick City Library
F3. *James Ledden* (hunger-striker, May 1920). Diary, with autographed quips, poems, etc. by fifty-nine comrades, including Frank Barrett of Ennis, Thomas Wall of Scariff and at least four other Claremen.

National Library of Ireland, Dublin
F4. *Robert Barton* (Dáil Secretary for Agriculture). Scrapbooks, MSS 5637–38, 5650. Includes (5637) collection of propaganda from East Clare by-election campaign.
F5. *Mathias McDonnell Bodkin* (the County Court judge in Clare and once a leading Irish Party opponent of Parnell). Drafts of essays (mainly on political matters, for reviews, several from period of this study) (MS. 14261).
F6. *F. S. Bourke Collection.* A few letters to and from Bodkin (F5) (MS. 10702).
F7. [*Butler*]. Letter from Arthur Griffith concerning naming of Sinn Féin by Mrs O'Nolan, née Mary Helen Butler, Co. Clare (MS. 4577).

F8. *Butler Estate*, Castlecrine, Co. Clare. Estate records, including cattle book (1896–1938)—a few sheep strayed in with the cattle (MS. 4254).

F9. *Éamonn Ceannt*. Unsigned, undated address book, evidently of Ceannt's provincial Volunteer contacts, 1915 (MS. 4733); scrapbooks, love letters addressed both to women and the Irish language (MSS 13069–70).

F10. *Michael Collins* (see also F27, B3 and B8). Letters to Austin Stack, Jul. 1918–Aug. 1919, which show human qualities as well as facilitating study of military–political revolutionary relationships (MS. 5848); certain photostated letters (MS. 15723).

F11. *George Gavan Duffy* (see also B2). Includes letters concerning the Irish Nation League, 1916–17 (MS. 5581).

F12. *Thomas Farren* (Labour leader). Letters concerning Irish Food Control Committee, 1917 (MS. 7341).

F13. *T. P. Gill* (Secretary, Department of Agriculture and Technical Instruction (Ireland) and former Irish Party politician). Large collection, including interesting letters on inside Irish Party politics (MS. 13486).

F14. *Bulmer Hobson* (Fianna and Volunteer organiser till 1916). Much material on history of Irish Volunteers, some of which was published in O3 and O27. MSS 12178–79 are drafts of the unpublished chapters of his Volunteer history. MS. 13170 includes his statements to the Bureau of Military History (whose holdings are, notoriously, sealed). It is regrettable that MSS 13158–75 (of which I checked 13158, 59, 60, 68 and 73–75 thoroughly and the rest briefly) are uncatalogued.

F15. *J. J. Horgan* (Cork Irish Party man). Includes letters of William Redmond, MP for East Clare, 1891–1917—fairly intimate letters but little concerned with Clare (microfilm, p 4645).

F16. *Inchiquin Papers*. Rental and estate books, unusually informative (1914–22 in MSS 14591–99); sketch book of Lucius O'Brien, including three suggestive drawings from 1922 (MS. 14847); diary of Ethel, Lady Inchiquin, 1924 (MS. 14875).

F17. *Irish Transport and General Workers' Union*. Indexed list of branches 1909–22 (giving birth and death dates of branches, membership, and names and addresses of organisers and secretaries), with typed list of branch membership 1918 (MS. 7282).

F18. *Irish Volunteers*. Adjutant-General's General Orders (complete file of Nos 1–31, May 1920–Nov. 1921, mostly typed copies, in MS. 739; a few photostats of the same orders in MS. 8415); training memoranda (Nos 1–18, complete) and other odd orders, in MS. 739. Files of most of these orders are also kept in the Mulcahy Papers (B 8).

F19. *Thomas Johnson* (Labour leader). Useful correspondence, draft memoranda, etc., on Labour as a political movement (especially MSS 17112, 13, 15, and 47, and MS. 17249). Handlist of this large collection now available.

F20. *Diarmuid Lynch* (IRB organiser). Drafts of statement for Bureau of Military History, etc., mainly published in O 25. Various notes on historical accounts of the revolution (MSS 11128–29).

F21. *Edward MacLysaght* (formerly E. E. Lysaght, prominent Clare employer, writer, etc., etc.). Three bound, indexed volumes of correspondence, 1913–52

(MSS 2649–51); dossier on Bloody Sunday shooting of Clareman Conor Clune (MS. 5368); sharp-edged (hence unpublished) memoirs, 'Master of None', 1952 (MS. 4750).

F22. *Barney Mellows* (Fianna Adjutant-General, Liam's brother). Includes reports on provincial Fianna organisation, especially Clare, 1921–22 (MS. 13771/1).

F23. *Maurice Moore (Inspector-General, Irish National Volunteers). Immense collection of virtually all the correspondence between the Inspector-General and provincial companies (1914–17), as well as his colleagues in Dublin and political leaders. MSS 9703, 04, 08, 09, 10, 13, and 07 contain lists of provincial officers, secretaries and instructors of the Redmondite Volunteers. MSS 9700–02 are Moore's official letter books (Aug. 1914–Jun. 1916), the contents of which prove that Moore preserved all his letters. MS. 9239 is the bound Minute Book of the National Committee, Sep. 1914–Mar. 1917 (little reference to provincial organisation). Most valuable of all is the set of provincial correspondence, reports, etc., sorted but uncatalogued in MSS 10544–55. The 200-odd documents on Clare in MS. 10547/5, and other letters in the indexed folders of general correspondence in MS. 10561, were the basis of my study of the early Volunteer movement.

F24. *William O'Brien* (Labour leader). Another huge collection (MSS 13906–79 and 15650–712). Includes lists of branch officers of ITGWU, and census of membership, 1918 (MS. 13948); a few documents on the East Clare by-election (MS. 15692, complemented by O'Brien's extensive scrapbook collection of propaganda in LO P116—cf. F4); pocket diaries of engagements, 1913–19, with many references to engagements in Clare (MS. 15705—the 1921, but not 1920, diary is in MS. 15706).

F25. *William O'Brien* (Irish Party politician, deviant). Letters to (MS. 7998) and from (8506 and 11440/4) O'Brien, 1916–27. An interesting correspondence with Fr James Clancy, Kilballyowen, Co. Clare, on how to handle Irish Party devils.

F26. *Seán T. Ó Ceallaigh* (Dáil emissary and bishop-cultivator). Material on preliminary meetings of Dáil, Jan. 1919 (MS. 8385/3).

F27. **Florence O'Donoghue* (IRA leader, historian and collector; see also A18). A vast, uncatalogued and unsorted archive of twenty-three boxes, of which I have examined seven fully and the rest cursorily. Part, but not all, of the collection is sorted into unindexed, numbered folders. Includes much material on the Bureau of Military History, which O'Donoghue helped set up: bound revolutionary chronologies (five volumes, covering 1909–21), 'not available for publication'; copy of Collins's cryptic diary, Jan. 1918–Jan. 1921 and Oct. 1921–Aug. 1922, pp. 11–296 (noting appointments, deaths, election results, petty cash movements, receipts, some interviews); 'strictly confidential' reports by BMH Director on accessions, etc. (Nos 4, 6, 7–13, 15–27, 1947–56, excluding, alas, the final report). Extensive files on the Cork brigades, and smaller ones on the Limerick Brigade (1918, including Brigade Council Minutes and Orders) are also preserved, as are three interesting volumes of diaries by William Roche [Liam de Roiste], Cork Sinn Féin leader (Aug. 1917–May 1918). A typed roll of IRA officers of battalion rank and above throughout Ireland, receiving or entitled to receive military pensions (folder 22, 125 pp.) was also consulted.

F28. *P. J. O'Neill* (Co. Kerry). Spike Island autograph album, Sep. 1921 (microfilm p 5485). Includes entries by many friends, including Claremen.

F29. *Standish Parker-Hutchinson* (Nenagh, Co. Tipperary). Permit book allowing him to enter Clare, May 1918 (MS. 12052).

F30. **George Noble Plunkett* (father of Easter rebels, Liberty Club organiser; see also B4). Interesting files include those on Liberty Clubs, 1917 (several letters from Clare, May–Jul. 1917, in MS. 11383/5; lists of men of influence approached, MS. 11383/1; circulars, /3); on Irish Volunteers including aborted 1920 Convention (MS. 11396); on Sinn Féin organisation, 1917–21 (MS. 11405); on IRA Courtmartials, 1920 (MS. 11406). MS. 11374 is a collection of letters received (1886–1939), including a few of interest regarding politics and Co. Clare.

F31. *John Redmond Papers*. Extensive, thoroughly catalogued collection. Of Clare interest is his correspondence with Arthur Lynch, MP (MS. 15202, covering period 1900–17); with Dr Fogarty, Bishop of Killaloe (MS. 15188); concerning James Halpin, Newmarket-on-Fergus, Co. Clare (May 1916, MS. 15262/5).

F32. *Robert Garnier Tottenham* (Mount Callan, Co. Clare). 'Records of Mount Callan', history of the estate, 1837–1923 (microfilm p 4910). (See also F54.)

Plunkett Foundation for Co-operative Studies, Oxford

F33. Includes a little correspondence between Plunkett and Edward Lysaght (cf. F21) (Lys. 1–8/2).

Public Record Office of Northern Ireland, Belfast

F34. Extensive holdings on Southern Unionism (cf. M6, 7), of which I have examined J. M. Wilson's report on local feeling in Clare, Jan. 1916, with an appended opinion about Claremen's feelings 'on the Present War' (D989A/9/7).

Trinity College Library, Dublin

F35. *Florence Vere O'Brien Papers* (Ballyalla, Co. Clare). Includes interesting correspondence with her sister (MSS 5004–06, mostly sorted chronologically), with intermittent but revealing comments on the life of a philanthropic Protestant Home Ruler during the revolution; household accounts and cottage industry accounts (MSS 5026, 5038); journal to Jun. 1913 only, giving some insight into local government in Clare (MS. 5044/b).

The following papers have kindly been made available to me by those named at the end of each entry:

F36. *Barrett Family* (Darragh, Co. Clare). Roll Book of the Mid-Clare Brigade, in handwriting of its commandant, Frank Barrett, listing officers as at about 1 Mar. 1919, and companies and officers as at Jun. 1921, with statistical return as at 1 May 1921 (clearly a contemporary document). Miscellaneous accounts of size, leadership and activities of brigade, especially the 2nd Battalion, prepared by Bernard and Joe Barrett mainly in the 1930s. Frank Barrett's Dispatch Book (Dec. 1919–May 1921) including copies of some of the Brigade Monthly Reports also found in the Mulcahy Papers (B 8). [Mr Bernard Barrett, Manus, Co. Clare]

F37. *Barrett Family*. Rolls of the Cumann na mBan, Mid-Clare Brigade, compiled in the 1930s by Miss Peg Barrett and other officers (names and numbers). Frank Barrett's memo book (1921) of certain expenses (mainly on arms) and receipts (of local government rates). Fr O'Kennedy's receipt book as trustee of the county rates, and original stubs, with explanatory letter. Correspondence between Frank Barrett and his subordinates, and the County Council, regarding collection of rates. [Miss Peg Barrett, Ennis]

F38. *Michael Brennan. 'Statement of Lieut.-General Michael Brennan, Simonscourt House, Simonscourt Road, Ballsbridge, Dublin' (typed, 120 pp.). A vital source for the history of the revolution, both military and civic, in Clare.

F39. *Seán Burke* (Adjutant of 4th Battalion, Mid-Clare Brigade). 'Some of the Activities of the 4th Battn Mid Clare Bde' (typed, 31 chapters). Provides both information and anecdotes about the military movement (1918 to early 1922). Partly published in the *Connacht Tribune* (1973, *passim*). [The late Mr Seán Burke, Limerick]

F40. *Fr Patrick Gaynor, PP*. 'Kilmihil Parish. Its origin and scraps of its history' (handwritten, 652 pp., 1946). Fascinating fourth part of 402 pp., entitled 'Sinn Féin Days (personal memories)', giving acid account of mismanagement of Volunteers and Republican courts in West Clare. Also interesting accounts of Sinn Féin in Tipperary, and headquarters (Fr Gaynor was a member of the Standing Committee after 1917). Ruthless appraisals of his own motives and those of others (including priests). [Fr Éamonn Gaynor, Quin]

F41. *Michael Guthrie* (Volunteer officer, Liscannor). Roll Call of Liscannor Company, 1920–21, and other statements about the company's history. Roll Book includes number attending each parade, Nov. 1921–Feb. 1922. [Mr John Guthrie, Lisdoonvarna]

F42. *Patrick Hehir* (Volunteer officer, Kilshanny). List of members and activities of Kilshanny Company, compiled in the 1930s. [Mr Patrick Hehir]

F43. *O'Brien Family* (Dromoland House, Co. Clare). Visitors' Book from 1896. [The late Anne, Lady Inchiquin]

F44. *Michael Kilmartin* (Commandant of Fianna, 4th Battalion, Mid-Clare Brigade). Lists of members, and certain biographical notes about them, of Fianna troops (*sluaghta*), carefully and scrupulously prepared for Pensions Department. Brief, unscrupulous statement by Thomas J. Keane of alleged strength of Fianna, 1st Battalion, Mid-Clare. [Mr Michael Kilmartin, Dublin]

F45. *Anthony Malone* (Volunteer officer, Glandine, and Battalion Vice-Commandant, 4th Battalion, Mid-Clare Brigade). Statement for Bureau of Military History (16 pp.), and another account (12 pp.) of battalion activities. [The late Mr Anthony Malone, Miltown Malbay]

F46. *Aggie Marrinan* (Cumann na mBan officer, Lahinch). Notes taken from Cumann na mBan lectures (1921), and statement on Miltown Malbay branch. [Miss Aggie Marrinan, Lahinch]

F47. **Edward MacLysaght*. MS. Diaries. Most useful and interesting reflections, of which three large bound volumes cover the period (Jul. 1913–Feb. 1917, Mar. 1917–Feb. 1919, Mar. 1919–Dec. 1923: volumes cited in notes as Diaries, iv, v and vi). Each volume had about 200 pp., of which some have been removed. Important source for history of Clare economy, Irish Convention (1917–18) and Republican movement (1916 onwards), but disappointingly little on Lysaght's literary enterprises. [Dr E. MacLysaght, Dublin]

F48. *Seán MacNamara* (Volunteer officer, Commandant, 6th Battalion, Mid-Clare Brigade, Ballyvaughan). Report of GHQ inspector on 6th Battalion, Oct. 1921; lists of officers and attendance at parades, late 1921; report of battalion council meeting, Dec. 1921. [Mr Seán MacNamara, Muckinish, Co. Clare]

F49. *Colonel George O'Callaghan-Westropp. Letterbooks, of which the following volumes were immensely useful: Sep. 1909–Dec. 1918 (1,005 pp. of O'Callaghan's letters out); Dec. 1918–Dec. 1927 (999 pp.); Jun. 1921–Jun. 1922 (100 pp., pencilled copies): volumes cited in notes as LB i, ii and iii. The vast majority of these letters touch either on politics or the lot of Protestants in an unfriendly world. Various other papers are preserved, including a useful statement on local government rates. [Mr Conor O'Callaghan-Westropp, formerly of Lismehane]

F50. *Arthur O'Donnell* (first Commandant, West Clare Brigade). A few documents buried in 1920 and lately uncovered, including reports by various subordinate officers, 1920, and signature book of those with him at Richmond Barracks and Lewes Prison, 1916. [The late Mr Art O'Donnell]

F51. *Peadar O'Loghlen*. Field Book of Martin Devitt (Vice-Commandant, Mid-Clare Brigade till his death in Feb. 1920), with copies of his dispatches to Feb. 1920; Field Book of Peadar O'Loghlen (who later held the same position), Aug.–Dec. 1921, enclosed in covers of a British Army Field Message Book. [Mr Gus O'Loghlen, Tullagha, Kilfenora]

F52. *Peter J. O'Loghlen* (Ballyvaughan, County Council chairman in 1918–19, etc.). A few documents on local government rates, amalgamation scheme, Clare, 1921, and three original rate books. Various papers of the Ballyvaughan RDC, of which O'Loghlen was chairman from 1912–20. [Mr Edward O'Loghlen, Ballyvaughan]

F53. *John Joe Markham* and *Dilly Markham* (later Mrs Shannon). Letters from Tomás Ó Lochlainn and Peadar O'Loghlen, and a few other documents on the Republican movement in Mid-Clare (1917–19). [Mr Michael Shannon, Corofin]

F54. *Tottenham Family* (Mount Callan; see also F32). Visitors' Book, elegantly illustrated, 1893–1923; Rainfall Book interspersed with diary entries on all subjects, 1913–28; correspondence concerning strike of staff and Republican arbitration, Nov.–Dec. 1921. [Mr Robert E. Tottenham, Mount Callan]

F55. *Éamonn Waldron* (Irish teacher and Volunteer officer, Ennistymon and Ennis). Biographical newspaper cuttings, and copy of a 'Testimonial to Éamonn Waldron', 11 Mar. 1919 (also a copy in F53). [Mrs Harriet Waldron, Galway]

F56. *Patrick Ward* (Volunteer officer, Kilfenora). Roll Book of company, including parade rolls for about 1918 and for 1920, with jottings concerning flying column expenses in 1921. Also notes of lectures taken at Volunteer training camp, Kilfenora, Aug. 1921. [Mr Patrick Ward, Lisdoonvarna]

F57. *Martin Whyte* (Fianna member after about 1918, Lisdoonvarna area). Untitled autobiography (hand-written), with a few interesting pages on what it felt like to be a boy Republican. [Mrs T. Carroll, Lisdoonvarna district]

G. Spoken Recollections

Recollections of participants in and observers of the movements analysed in this book have been used to supplement written testimony and (more crucially) to aid its interpretation by sorting out riddles, distinguishing between different persons of the same name doing much the same things (a common trap in inbred rural Ireland) and revealing the contexts in which written records were compiled. The following survivors were kind enough to guide me through many interpretative tangles: Mr Bernard Barrett (Manus), Miss Peg Barrett (Ennis), the late Mr Ernest Blythe, Messrs Austin and Michael Brennan (Dublin), Messrs Ned Burke (Ennistymon), the late Messrs Seán and Tom Burke, Tom Carroll (Lisdoonvarna), Séamus Conneely (Clouna), Tone Cotter (Ballyea), Patrick Hehir (Kilshanny), the late Anne, Lady Inchiquin, Messrs Seán Kelly (Ennis), Pako Kerin (Ennis), Michael Kilmartin (Dublin), Dr Edward MacLysaght (Dublin), Messrs Seán MacNamara (Muckinish), Michael Maher (near Doolin), the late Mr Anthony Malone, Miss Aggie Marrinan (Lahinch), Messrs Paddy A. Mulcahy (Dublin), the late Mr Art O'Donnell, Andy O'Donoghue (Lickeen) and Con O'Donohue (below Corkscrew Hill), Messrs Gus O'Loghlen (Tullagha), Martin S. O'Loghlen (Ennis), Paddy Queally (near Lahinch), Michael Shannon (Corofin), Mick Sheedy (Lisdoonvarna), Michael Tubridy (Kilrush), Patrick Ward (Tullagha), the late Mr Martin Whyte, Mrs Joe Connole (Ennistymon), Mrs Bill Haugh (Kilkee) and Rev. Mother Lelia McKenna (Ennis). Fr Séamus O'Dea (Cross) and Mr Matthew Bermingham (Dublin) kindly gave me access to their recorded conversations with the late Mr Michael McMahon and Mr Michael Honan (near Kilrush).

OFFICIAL PUBLICATIONS

H. British Administration

Command Papers, House of Commons
H1. Census of Ireland, 1911. Province of Munster. County of Clare; Summary Tables (1912/13 cxv, Cd 6050).
H2. Reports of the Commissioners of His Majesty's Inland Revenue. For the Years ended 31st March, 1921, 1922 and 1923 (1921 xiv, Cmd 1436, 439; 1922 Session 2 ii, Cmd 1780, 665; 1923 xii Pt 2, Cmd 1934, 403). County breakdowns of income tax collections are not provided.
H3. Congested Districts Board for Ireland. Reports, 1913–20 (1914 xvi, Cd 7312, 1097; 1914/16 xxiv, Cd 7867 and 8076, 621 and 693; 1916 vi, Cd 8356, 525; 1917/18 xv, Cd 8853, 199; 1918 vii, Cd 9139, 769; 1920 xix, Cmd 759, 889; 1921 xiv, Cmd 1409, 613). (See also H10, H11 and I8.)
H4. Royal Commission on Congestion in Ireland. First Appendix to the Seventh Report. Minutes of Evidence (1908 xl, Cd 3785, 5). Much of interest on Clare land tenure.
H5. DATII. Agricultural Statistics of Ireland, with detailed reports for the years 1913–17 (1914 xcviii, Cd 7429, 591; 1916 xxxii, Cd 8266, 621; 1917/18 xxxvi, Cd 8563, 539; 1919 li, Cmd 112, 97; 1921 xli, Cmd 1316, 135).

H6. DATII. The Departmental Committee on Food Production. Report; Minutes and Appendix (1914/16 v, Cd 8046 and 8158, 799 and 827). Incorporates Census of Production, 1912.

H7. Documents Relative to the Sinn Féin Movement (1921 xxix, Cmd 1108, 428). Documents dated May 1918 and earlier, edited without scruples.

H8. Emigration Statistics of Ireland for the years 1913–20 (1914 lxix, Cd 7313, 1001; 1914/16 lxxx, Cd 7883, 319; 1916 xxxii, Cd 8230, 915; 1917/18 xxxvii, Cd 8520, 269; 1918 xxv, Cd 9013, 17; 1919 li, Cmd 77, 401; 1920, 1, Cmd 721, 439; 1921 xli, Cmd 1414, 401). County figures. National figures for 1921 may be obtained from the non-parliamentary official paper, Emigration Statistics. Ireland. Return of the Number of Emigrants . . . during the Month of December, 1921.

H9. Irish Convention. Report of the Proceedings (1918 x, Cd 9019, 697). Includes useful tables and information on Land Purchase and the state of the RIC.

H10. Irish Land Acts, 1903–9. Reports of the Estates Commissioners for the years 1912–13 to 1919–20 (1914 xxxvi, Cd 7145, 485; 1914/16 xxiv, Cd 7663 and 8083, 379 and 499; 1917/18 xv, Cd 8456 and 8766, 253 and 337; 1919 xxiv, Cmd 29, 137; 1920 xix, Cmd 577, 965; 1921 xiv, Cmd 1150, 661).

H11. Reports of the Irish Land Commissioners for the periods 1912–13 to 1919–20 (1913 xxx, Cd 6979, 253; 1914 lxv, Cd 7575, 581; 1914/16 xxiv, Cd 8042, 225; 1917/18 xv, Cd 8481 and 8742, 421 and 533; 1919 xxiv, Cmd 19, 219; 1920 xix, Cmd 572 and 1064, 1045 and 1149).

H12. Judicial Statistics, Ireland, 1913 and 1914, 2 parts each (1914 c, Cd 7600 and 7536, 519 and 689; 1914/16 lxxxii, Cd 8077 and 8066, 451 and 621); briefer Judicial Statistics, 1915–19 (1917/18 xxxvii, Cd 8636, 283; 1918 xxv, Cd 9066, 29; 1919 lii, Cmd 43, 1 and Cmd 438, 101; 1921 xli, Cmd 1431, 591).

H13. Local Government Board for Ireland. Annual Reports . . . for the years ended 31st March, 1913–20 (1913 xxxii, Cd 6978, 457; 1914 xxxix, Cd 7561, 595; 1914/16 xxv, Cd 8016, 341; 1916 xiii, Cd 8365, 199; 1917/18 xvi, Cd 8765, 257; 1919 xxv, Cmd 65, 1; 1920 xxi, Cmd 578, 1; 1921 xiv, Cmd 1432, 781). (No county tabulations after 1915–16.)

H14. Statement giving Particulars regarding Men of Military Age in Ireland (1916 xvii, Cd 8390, 581).

H15. Outrages (Ireland). Return showing . . . the Number of Political Outrages on Persons and Property in Ireland from the 1st day of January, 1919, to the 30th April, 1920 (1920 xl, Cmd 709, 803). Returns showing the Number of Serious Outrages reported by the Royal Irish Constabulary and the Dublin Metropolitan Police during the months of May and June, 1920; July, August and September, 1920; October, November and December, 1920 (1921 xl, Cmd 859 and 1025, 805 and 807; xxix, Cmd 1165, 397). The later returns, slapdash and carelessly bundled together, refer to Ireland only but give weekly figures. Cf. returns of Sinn Féin and other serious outrages (A22, vii), 1920–21.

H16. Royal Commission on the Rebellion in Ireland. Report; Minutes of Evidence and Appendix of Documents (1916 xi, Cd 8279 and 8311, 171 and 185). Includes testimony from Clare police and much on growth of Irish Volunteers.

H17. Detailed Annual Reports of the Registrar-General for Ireland, 1913–20 (1914 xv, Cd 7528, 127; 1914/16 ix, Cd 7991, 687; 1916 vi, Cd 8416, 1; 1917/18 vi, Cd 8647, 585; 1918 vi, Cd 9123, 357; 1919 x, Cmd 450, 849; 1920 xi, Cmd 997, 629; 1921 ix, Cmd 1532, 47). Give county breakdowns of marriages, which for 1921–22 may be supplemented by the Quarterly Returns of the Marriages . . . in Ireland (non-parliamentary).

H18. Vice-Regal Commission. Reorganisation and Pay of the Irish Police Forces. Report (1920 xxii, Cmd 603, 1125). No minutes of evidence published or traced.

H19. Royal Irish Constabulary. Auxiliary Division. Outline of Terms on which Cadets were engaged . . . (1922 xvii, Cmd 1618, 785); Revised Terms of Disbandment (1922 xvii, Cmd 1673, 807); and Terms of Disbandment (1922 xvii, Cmd 1618A, 797).

H20. Royal Irish Constabulary and Dublin Metropolitan Police. Committee of Inquiry. Report; Appendix to the Report (1914 xliv, Cd 7421, 247; 1914/16 xxxii, Cd 7637, 359). Includes much evidence (in Appendix) from Clare police. Cf. A30, iii.

Other Official Publications

H21. DATII, *Journal* (quarterly, checked from 1913–23). Contains useful tables of farm prices by province, and lists of government orders, etc.

H22. *Dublin Gazette* (twice weekly, checked from 1918–21). Chaotically presented, inadequately indexed, incomplete even in publication of government orders.

H23. Return, for the Year 1870, of the Number of Landed Proprietors in each county and province [of Ireland], HC 1872 (167) xlvii. Useful tabulation not kept up to date thereafter.

H24. Land Owners in Ireland. Return of Owners of Land of one acre and upwards . . . in Ireland, HC 1876 lxxx, C. 1492, 61—names of immediate lessors from Valuation Books.

H25. The Parliamentary Debates (Official Report), House of Commons (5th Series). Cited as Commons *Debates*. Examined with particular regard to Clare for period 1913–21.

H26. The Public General Acts. Examined for the period 1913–21 and other relevant years.

H27. Restoration of Order in Ireland. Regulations (August 1920). Cf. collection of orders amending DORR, 1914–20, with explanatory notes, in RP 25934–35/1920.

I. Dáil Administration

I1. Saorstát Éireann. Acts, 1922 *et seq*. Numbered chronologically by year.

I2. Saorstát Éireann. The Agricultural Output of Saorstát Éireann, 1926/27 (1930). May be partially collated with statistics in H6, and in DATII, The Agricultural Output of Ireland. 1908 (1912), non-parliamentary British official paper.

I3. Saorstát Éireann. Census of Population 1926 (10 volumes, 1928). Fewer county breakdowns than 1911 Census (H1), and arranged differently. May be partially supplemented by Government of Northern Ireland. Census of Population of Northern Ireland 1926. General Report (1929), despite many irritating anomalies of presentation.

14. [Erskine Childers], Dáil Éireann, *The Constructive Work of Dáil Éireann*, Dublin 1921. Only Nos 1 and 2 of 3 have been traced (NLI), summarising the Dáil's work in justice and agriculture.

15. Dáil Éireann. *Minutes of Proceedings* of the First Parliament of the Republic of Ireland. 1919–1921. Official Record.

16. Dáil Éireann. *Tuairisg Oifigiuil (Official Report)*. For Periods 16th August, 1921, to 26th August, 1921, and 28th February, 1922, to 8th June, 1922. This and the preceding volume have lately been reprinted (Dublin n.d.).

17. Dáil Éireann. *Private Sessions of Second Dáil*. Minutes of Proceedings 18 August 1921 to 14 September 1921 and Report of Debates 14 December 1921 to 6 January 1922. Private sessions for earlier months are reported in 15.

18. Saorstát Éireann. Report of the Irish Land Commissioners for the period from 1st April, 1923, to 31st March, 1928 (. . . 1971). Used to complement land purchase statistics culled from H3, H10 and H11.

19. Saorstát na hÉireann (Department of Home Affairs), *Judiciary. Rules and Forms, Parish and District Courts* (1920). Copy in NLI (LO) has Conor Maguire's annotations.

J. Newspapers and Periodicals

The following periodicals of the period 1913–21 proved worth close scrutiny: *Blackwood's Magazine*; *The Catholic Bulletin and Book Review* (heavily martyrolatrous in politics as well as religion); *The Constabulary Gazette*; *The Contemporary Review*; *Dublin Review*; *The Farmers' Gazette*; *The Irish Farmer*; *The Irish Farmer and Stockowner*; *Irish Opinion*; *The Irish Times*; *The National Hibernian* (Irish-American Alliance organ); *New Ireland*; *The Nineteenth Century*; *Notes from Ireland*; *An tÓglach*; *Old Ireland*; *The Royal Irish Constabulary Magazine*; *Journal of the Statistical and Social Inquiry Society of Ireland*; *The Times*; *The Voice of Labour*; *The Weekly Summary*; *The Watchword of Labour*. Files of these journals may be found either in the British Museum, or the National Library of Ireland. Fuller details are given in subject lists. See list S for Co. Clare local newspapers, a major source for this study.

SUBJECT LISTS

K. British Administration of Ireland

CONTEMPORARY PUBLICATIONS

K1. 'Periscope' [G. C. Duggan], 'The Last Days of Dublin Castle', *Blackwood's Magazine*, CCXII (Aug. 1922), 137–90. Intimate though opinionated account of the Castle under Greenwood and Anderson.

K2. J. G. Swift MacNeill, 'The Breakdown of the Dublin Castle Regime', *Contemporary Review*, CX (Jul. 1916), 22–31.

K3. J. H. Morgan, 'How Ireland is Governed', *Nineteenth Century*, LXXIV (Sep. 1913), 568–79. Mainly concerns lord lieutenancy.
K4. R. Barry O'Brien, *Dublin Castle and the Irish People*, 2nd ed., London 1912. Massive compendium based partly on interviews with officials.
K5. 'I.O.' [C. J. C. Street], *The Administration of Ireland, 1920*, London 1921. Another compendium, using some confidential police reports, by a minor Castle official, also author of the less useful *Ireland in 1921*, London 1922.

LATER PUBLICATIONS
K6. Marquess and Marchioness of Aberdeen, *'We Twa'*, *Reminiscences*, London 1925. As if this were not enough, the Marchioness (and, of course, the Marquess) produced *More Cracks with 'We Twa'*, London 1929.
K7. Sir George Arthur, *General Sir John Maxwell*, London 1932.
K8. Augustine Birrell, *Things Past Redress*, London 1937.
K9. D. G. Boyce, *Englishmen and Irish Troubles*, London 1972. Concerns public rather than politicians' opinion, categorising attitudes towards Irish affairs (1918–22) rather than analysing their genesis.
K10. Sir C. E. Callwell, *Field-Marshal Sir Henry Wilson, Bart*, London 1927. Mainly edited extracts from his diaries (see A13), with some of the ill-natured epithets excised—but not all.
K11. L. P. Curtis, *Anglo-Saxons and Celts*, Connecticut 1967. An attempt, conducted with some sleight of hand, to establish that 'the English governing class' shared a stereotypical view of the Irish.
K12. Gerald French, *The Life of Field-Marshal Sir John French, 1st Earl of Ypres*, London 1931. Much on French's period as Viceroy.
K13. Maurice Headlam, *Irish Reminiscences*, London 1947. The angler and Treasury Remembrancer at the Castle (1912–20).
K14. Thomas Jones, *Whitehall Diary*, Vol. III, ed. Keith Middlemas, London 1971. Whole volume on Irish affairs (1918–25) as reported by the cabinet secretary.
K15. Sir Bryan Mahon, 'The Irish Welter as I Found It: An Indictment of British Methods', in William G. FitzGerald, ed., *The Voice of Ireland*, Dublin 1924, 125–8. Assessment by an army commander (1916–18) who became a Senator in the Free State in 1922.
K16. R. B. McDowell, *The Irish Administration 1801–1914*, London and Toronto 1964. A painstaking and systematic descriptive account.
K17. R. B. McDowell, *The Irish Convention 1917–18*, London and Toronto 1970. Account of the last serious attempt by the Castle to understand what Irishmen were asking for.
K18. Nevil Macready, *Annals of an Active Life*, 2 vols, London 1924. Most of the second volume relates to his command in Ireland (1920–22), and it is fascinating.
K19. Leon Ó Broin, *The Chief Secretary: Augustine Birrell in Ireland*, London 1969. An elegant presentation of the case for Birrell's bad luck, embedded in the voluminous Nathan and Birrell papers (see list A).
K20. Leon Ó Broin, *Dublin Castle and the 1916 Rising*, revised ed., London 1970. Vastly inferior in range and presentation to K19. Focuses upon Nathan, 1914–16.

K21. W. A. Phillips, *The Revolution in Ireland*, 1906–1923, revised ed., London 1926. The only general account to concentrate on how the revolution looked from the Castle, based on a sketchy survey of police reports.

K22. Sir Henry Robinson, *Memories: Wise and Otherwise*, London 1924. Delightful anecdotes and vignettes by the head of the Irish Local Government Board. Less useful is *Further Memories of Irish Life*, London 1924, which, as the author warned, has 'no historic value whatever'.

K23. John W. Wheeler-Bennett, *John Anderson, Viscount Waverley*, London 1962. Useful on Anderson's period as Joint Under-Secretary for Ireland.

L. Forces of the Crown

PRIMARY SOURCES

The police journals—*R.I.C. Magazine* (to 1916), *Constabulary Gazette* (to 1922) and *The Weekly Summary* (1920–21, incomplete file in NLI)—are all of interest. Extensive collections of police reports are held by PRO and SPO, and the most useful sources for military history are those in the PRO (War Office papers and cabinet memoranda and conclusions). For details see:

A1, 2, 5, 6, 9, 10, 11, 12, 13, 15–19, 21, 22 (especially i, v, ix, xii, xiii, xiv), 23, 26, 27, 30 (ii, iii, iv), 35.

H12, 15, 18–20, 27–29.

CONTEMPORARY PUBLICATIONS

L1. R. C. Grey, *The Auxiliary Police*, London [1920/21]. Account of the Auxiliaries at Killaloe, Co. Clare, written for the Peace with Ireland Council.

L2. 'A Woman of No Importance' [Mrs Stuart Menzies], *As Others See Us*, London 1924. Small hagiologies of policemen and Castle diehards who would never surrender.

L3. Royal Irish Constabulary *List and Directory* (biannual to 1921). Includes lists of police and law officers, and of police resignations, dismissals and so forth.

L4. *The Royal Irish Constabulary Manual; or, Guide to the Discharge of Police Duties*, 5th ed., Dublin 1898. Amusing introduction.

LATER PUBLICATIONS

(see also list K, for memoirs of military leaders)

L5. Richard Bennett, *The Black and Tans*, London 1959. Very little about Black and Tans, despite its title.

L6. Conor Brady, *Guardians of the Peace*, Dublin and London 1974. Includes account of breakdown of civil order in 1920–21.

L7. Séamus Breathnach, *The Irish Police*, Dublin 1974. Disappointingly little on revolutionary period.

L8. C. P. Crane, *Memories of a Resident Magistrate 1880–1920*, Edinburgh 1938.

L9. F. P. Crozier, *Impressions and Recollections*, London 1930, and *Ireland For Ever*, London 1932. Memoirs of an adventurer turned pacifist, and Auxiliary commander turned campaigner against 'reprisals'.

L10. Sir William Y. Darling, *So It Looks to Me*, London 1952. On staff of Chief of Police, 1920–21, but little to say about it.

L11. Douglas V. Duff, *Sword for Hire*, London 1934, and several other versions of autobiography by a Black and Tan who, it appears, butchered many Shinners.

L12. G. C. Duggan, 'The Royal Irish Constabulary', in O. Dudley Edwards and Fergus Pyle, ed., *1916: The Easter Rising*, London 1968, 91–9.

L13. Vere R. T. Gregory, *The House of Gregory*, Dublin 1943. Includes his reminiscences as RIC County Inspector during the Troubles.

L14. Richard Hawkins, 'Dublin Castle and the R.I.C. (1916–1922)', in T. Desmond Williams, ed., *The Irish Struggle 1916–1926*, London 1966, 167–82.

L15. Sir Christopher Lynch-Robinson, *The Last of the Irish R.M.s*, London 1951.

L16. Breandán Mac Giolla Choille, ed., *Intelligence Notes 1913–16*, Dublin 1966. Supplements holdings in PRO (see A 22, i).

L17. Hervey de Montmorency. *Sword and Stirrup*, London 1936. Former Irish Volunteers inspector of 1914 who became Dublin Castle intelligence man after Bloody Sunday (1920).

L18. Bill Munro's reminiscences in James Gleeson, *Bloody Sunday*, London 1962, 56–78. A Scottish Auxiliary stationed at Macroom and Dublin.

L19. David Neligan, *The Spy in the Castle*, London 1968. Factually unreliable.

L20. Sir Ormonde Winter, *Winter's Tale*, London 1955. Sinister recollections of many odd jobs, among them Deputy Chief of Police (Intelligence), Ireland, 1920–21.

L21. Charles Townshend, *The British Campaign in Ireland 1919–21*, Oxford 1975. Painstaking analysis published after this chapter had been written.

M. Protestants and Unionists

PRIMARY SOURCES

The foundation of my study were the Letterbooks of Colonel O'Callaghan-Westropp (F49). Also useful were the *Irish Times* and *Notes from Ireland* (studded with self-pitying reports from abandoned provincial Unionists). Other relevant sources include:

D1, 2, 3.
F2, 8, 16, 32, 34, 35, 43, 54.
H3, 4, 9, 10, 11, 23, 24.
I8.

CONTEMPORARY PUBLICATIONS

M1. George A. Birmingham [Rev. J. O. Hannay], *An Irishman Looks at His World*, London 1919. Generalised survey by an enlightened Protestant clergyman.

M2. James Winter Good, *Irish Unionism*, Dublin and London 1920. Purports to cover period 1801–1920, but virtually nothing on post-1913 years.

M3. 'An Irishman', *Intolerance in Ireland*, London 1913. One of many virulent denunciations of RC intolerance, by a Munster Protestant.

LATER PUBLICATIONS

M4. Mark Bence-Jones, 'The Changing Picture of the Irish Landed Gentry', in *Burke's Landed Gentry of Ireland*, 4th ed., London 1958, xviii–xxi.

M5. Raymond F. Brooke, *The Brimming River*, Dublin 1961. Mercantile Kildare Streeter.

M6. Patrick Buckland, *Irish Unionism 1: The Anglo-Irish and the New Ireland 1885–1922*, Dublin and New York 1972. Mainly concerned with revolutionary period, unfortunately mainly confined to the development of the Southern Unionist political movement rather than the curious mentalities which lay behind it.

M7. Patrick Buckland, *Irish Unionism 1885–1923. A Documentary History*, Belfast 1973. Documents taken exclusively from the PRO of Northern Ireland.

M8. Ian d'Alton. 'Southern Irish Unionism: A Study of Cork Unionists, 1884–1914', *Transactions of the Royal Historical Society*, V, Vol. XXIII (1973). Interesting essay in, for once, social rather than aridly party-political history.

M9. L. P. Curtis, 'The Anglo-Irish Predicament', *Twentieth-Century Studies* (Nov. 1970).

M10. Lt-Col. Charles O. Head, *No Great Shakes*, London 1943.

M11. Brian Inglis, *West Briton*, London 1962. One of the best autobiographies in the field.

M12. Michael Hurley, SJ, ed., *Irish Anglicanism 1869–1969*, Dublin 1970. Several interesting essays on Church's social enterprises.

M13. Rev. Thomas J. Johnston, Ven. John L. Robinson and Very Rev. Robert Wyse Jackson, *A History of the Church of Ireland*, Dublin 1953.

M14. H. Cameron Lyster, *An Irish Parish in Changing Days*, London 1933. Enniscorthy, 1895–1930.

M15. 1st Earl of Midleton (W. St J. F. Brodrick), *Ireland—Dupe or Heroine*, London 1932. Oddly mild.

M16. 1st Earl of Midleton (W. St J. F. Brodrick), *Records and Reactions 1856–1939*, London 1939.

M17. R. P. McDermott, 'The Church of Ireland since Disestablishment', *Theology*, LXXIII (1970), 208–13.

M18. Henry E. Patton, *Fifty Years of Disestablishment: A Sketch*, Dublin 1922.

M19. Nora Robertson, *Crowned Harp: Memories of the Last Years of the Crown in Ireland*, Dublin 1960. Daughter of Cork army commander.

M20. Very Rev. C. A. Webster, 'The Church since Disestablishment', in W. A. Phillips, ed., *History of the Church of Ireland*, III, London 1933, 387–424.

M21. Terence de Vere White, *The Anglo-Irish*, London 1972. Soothing vignettes.

N. Home Rulers

PRIMARY SOURCES

No outstanding collection was found to help unravel the workings of the Irish Party and its organisations in the provinces, but the party line was followed week by week through the *Saturday Record* and (until 1916) the *Clare Champion*, which

published the regular syndicated columns of party opinions. Relevant primary sources are:
A22 (ii).
F5, 6, 13,15, 23, 25, 31, 35, 49.
H9, 25.

CONTEMPORARY PUBLICATIONS
N1. Ancient Order of Hibernians (Board of Erin) Friendly Society, *General Rules (All previous rules rescinded)*, Dublin 1917 [in fact 1918].
N2. Ancient Order of Hibernians, National Convention, *Agenda*, Dublin 1919.
N3. James J. Bergin, *History of the Ancient Order of Hibernians*, Dublin [1910].
N4. Erskine Childers, *The Framework of Home Rule*, London 1911.
N5. John Dillon, *The Irish Electors, 1921*, Dublin [May 1921].
N6. William J. Flynn, *Ireland and Political Calumny. How Irish Co Councils Work*, Dublin 1907. Denies Irish Party monopoly of local boss-ships.
N7. Stephen Gwynn, *John Redmond's Last Years*, London 1919.
N8. John J. Horgan, 'Precepts and Practice in Ireland, 1914–1919', *Studies*, VIII (Jun. 1919), 210–26.
N9. Irish National Volunteers, *Constitution and Rules 1915*, Dublin 1916.
N10. T. M. Kettle, *The Open Secret of Ireland*, London 1912. Preface by John Redmond.
N11. Felix Lavery (compiler), *Irish Heroes in the War*, London 1917. Another Redmond preface.
N12. William O'Brien, *The Downfall of Parliamentarianism*, Dublin and London 1918.
N13. William O'Brien, *The Irish Revolution and How It Came About*, London 1923.
N14. William O'Brien, *'The Party': Who They Are and What They Have Done*, Dublin and London 1917.
N15. United Irish League, Standing Committee, *The Irish Party: What It Has Done for Ireland . . . Magnificent Record . . .* [1915]. Joe Devlin's 1915 report.

LATER PUBLICATIONS
N16. John J. Horgan, *Parnell to Pearse: Some Recollections and Reflections*, Dublin 1948.
N17. *F. S. L. Lyons, *The Irish Parliamentary Party 1890–1910*, London 1951. Useful analysis of strength, distribution and personnel of the party, but little inquiry into the workings of its vaguely affiliated provincial organs.
N18. F. S. L. Lyons, *John Dillon: A Biography*, London 1968.
N19. R. B. McDowell, *The Irish Convention 1917–18*, London and Toronto 1970.

O. Sinn Féiners

PRIMARY SOURCES
Edward Lysaght's Diaries (F47) give a valuable sequential account of the Sinn Féin mentality forming. The endlessly bickering Sinn Féin papers of 1916–17

were of remarkably little value in that regard. The following primary sources clarified aspects of Sinn Féin history:
A22 (iii, x), 30 (iv), 31.
B6.
F1, 4, 7, 9, 11, 14, 15, 19, 21, 24, 27, 30, 33, 38, 40, 49.
H7.

CONTEMPORARY PUBLICATIONS

O1. 'Lesley Byron', *Opportunist Sinn Féiners*, London [1921].
O2. Darrell Figgis, *Recollections of the Irish War*, London 1927.
O3. Bulmer Hobson, *A Short History of the Irish Volunteers, 1913–1916*, Dublin 1918. Marked '1st Volume', but in fact draft continuation (for which see F14) was never published.
O4. Thomas Johnson (compiler), *A Handbook for Rebels*, Dublin 1918. 'Hints on the science of Bloodless Revolution' culled from Unionist speeches by a Nationalist.
O5. M. J. Judge, 'The Inner History of the Volunteers', *Irish Nation*, I (22 Jul. 1916–19 May 1917). Disappointing anti-conspiratorial interpretation.
O6. Brinsley MacNamara [John Weldon], *The Clanking of Chains*, Dublin and London 1920.
O7. William O'Brien and Desmond Ryan, ed., *Devoy's Post-Bag*, II (1880–1928), Dublin 1953. Useful conspiratorial letters to elderly Fenian.
O8. P. S. O'Hegarty, *Sinn Féin: An Illumination*, Dublin 1919. Written 1917.
O9. P. S. O'Hegarty, *The Victory of Sinn Féin*, Dublin 1924.
O10. The O'Rahilly, *The Secret History of the Irish Volunteers*, 3rd ed. Dublin [1915], 20 pp.
O11. Kevin O'Shiel, *The Rise of the Irish Nation League* (no provenance [1916]).
O12. Herbert Moore Pim, 'Sinn Féin: Past, Present, and Future', *Nineteenth Century*, LXXXV (1919), 1165–74. Disillusioned Griffithist journalist.
O13. Capt. H. B. C. Pollard, *The Secret Societies of Ireland: Their Rise and Progress*, London 1922. Rebel documents surprisingly accurately transcribed by a Castle publicist, apart from misdating of IRB constitution. (Cf. O25, p. 33.)
O14. Sinn Féin, Agenda and other documents relating to Árd-Fheiseanna of Oct. 1917, Oct. 1918, Apr. 1919, Oct. 1919 and Oct. 1921 are preserved in the pamphlet and Irish collections, NLI.
O15. Sinn Féin, *How to Form Sinn Féin Clubs* (no provenance [1917]).
O16. Sinn Féin, *Instructions to Sinn Féin Cumainn regarding Programme of Work, 1920–1921* (no provenance).
O17. Weekly Irish Times, Dublin (compiler), *Sinn Féin Rebellion Handbook. Easter 1916*, 2nd ed., Dublin 1917. Extracts from official papers and press handouts.

LATER PUBLICATIONS

O18. Earnán de Blaghd [Ernest Blythe], 'The Change of Attitude', *Easter Commemoration Digest*, VIII (1966), 33–41.
O19. Earnán de Blaghd [Ernest Blythe], *Slán le hUltaibh*, Dublin 1970. Second volume of memoirs, dealing with early organisation (1914–15) of MacNeillite Volunteers. Passages kindly translated for me by Fr Séamus O'Dea.

O20. Thomas Dillon, 'Birth of the New Sinn Féin and the Árd-Fheis 1917', *Capuchin Annual*, XXXIV (1967), 394–9. By the Hon. Secretary of the Mansion House Committee, 1917.
O21. Various FitzGeralds, ed., *The Memoirs of Desmond FitzGerald, 1913–1916*, London 1968. Interesting on early Volunteer organisation in Kerry.
O22. Michael Laffan, 'The Sinn Féin Party 1916–1921', *Capuchin Annual*, XXXVII (1970), 227–35.
O23. Michael Laffan, 'The Unification of Sinn Féin in 1917', *Irish Historical Studies*, XVII (Mar. 1971), 353–79. Careful tracing of who organised what when, but little attempt to explain how, why or wherefore.
O24. M. J. Lennon, 'The Easter Rising from the Inside', *Irish Times*, 18–23 Apr. 1949. Includes Seán Fitzgibbon's rather disappointing recollections.
O25. Diarmuid Lynch (ed. Florence O'Donoghue), *The I.R.B. and the 1916 Insurrection*, Cork 1957. (Cf. F20.)
O26. F. X. Martin, 'Eoin MacNeill on the 1916 Rising', *Irish Historical Studies*, XII (Mar. 1961), 226–71.
O27. F. X. Martin, ed., *The Irish Volunteers 1913–1915: Recollections and Documents*, Dublin 1963. Largely selected from Hobson Papers (F14).
O28. Capt. Robert Monteith, *Casement's Last Adventure*, Dublin 1953. Despite title, includes interesting reminiscences of a Volunteer drill instructor.
O29. Col. Maurice Moore, 'History of the Irish Volunteers'. Evidently written 1917, but published in *Irish Press*, 4 Jan.–2 Mar. 1938, and deposited in bound volume in NLI (ILB 94109).
O30. Desmond Ryan, *The Rising*, Dublin 1949.
O31. Maureen Wall, 'The Plans and the Countermand: the Country and Dublin', in Kevin B. Nowlan, ed., *The Making of 1916*, Dublin 1969, 201–54.

P. Revolutionary Administrators

PRIMARY SOURCES

The most wide-ranging collection on the Dáil administration is the official deposit of Dáil records (B7 and B5), though these are deficient in correspondence. Other sources of interest are:
A30 (iv).
B1, 2, 4, 8.
C1–5.
E1.
F26, 37, 38, 40, 49, 52.
H2.
I4–7, 9.

CONTEMPORARY PUBLICATIONS

P1. W. H. Brayden, *Republican Courts in Ireland*, Chicago [1920].
P2. 'Dalta' [C. Llewelyn-Davies], *National Land Policy*, Dublin 1920. Henry Georgian ideas for reconciling holders and present owners of land.

P3. Labhrás Mag Fhionnghail [Lawrence Ginnell], *The Land Question*, Dublin [1917–18].
P4. National Land Bank Ltd, *Report of the Directors* (for half-years ending December 1920 to December 1922, except June 1922—file in NLI).
P5. Cionnaith Ó Roideáin, 'Under the Terror, 1: In a Sinn Féin Court', *The Belvederian*, VI (1922), 89–91.

LATER PUBLICATIONS
P6. Robert Brennan, *Allegiance*, Dublin 1950. Reminiscences of Dáil publicist, almost too detailed to be convincing (a rare fault).
P7. James Casey, 'Republican Courts in Ireland, 1919–1922', *Irish Jurist*, N.S., V (1970), 321–42. One of the few to consult B5.
P8. Geraldine Counahan, 'The People Backed the Movement 1920', *Capuchin Annual*, XXXVII (1970), 250–4. By the discoverer of C5.
P9. Cahir Davitt, 'The Civil Jurisdiction of the Courts of Justice of the Irish Republic, 1920–1922', *Irish Jurist*, N.S., III (1968), 112–30. Very few personal recollections, though Davitt was a circuit judge.
P10. Brian Farrell, *The Founding of Dáil Éireann*, Dublin and London 1971.
P11. J. L. McCracken, *Representative Government in Ireland, 1919–48*, London 1958.
P12. Conor A. Maguire, 'The Republican Courts', *Capuchin Annual*, XXXVI (1969), 378–88. Rather patchy reminiscences of a land settlement commissioner.
P13. W. N. Osborough, 'Law in Ireland 1916–26', *Northern Ireland Legal Quarterly*, XXIII (1972), 48–81. Little specifically on Dáil Courts.
P14. Kevin O'Shiel, 'Memories of My Lifetime', *Irish Times*, 7–23 Nov. 1966. Most interesting of the Dáil Court reminiscences, quoting a few documents of interest.

Q. Guerrilla Fighters

PRIMARY SOURCES
An tÓglach (the Irish Volunteers' clandestine organ, Aug. 1918 to 1922) was a valuable source. The Military Archives and the Mulcahy Papers (B3 and B8) were consistently useful. The continued closure of the Bureau of Military History, which collected many reminiscences and some documents, is irritating; but the duplicate copies of statements can often be elicited from their writers, and Florence O'Donoghue preserved many valuable items which would otherwise have been lost to the bureaucrats in F27. See also:
A14, 22 (iv, vi, vii, viii), 28, 31, 35.
F2, 10, 18, 20, 22, 28, 30, 36–39, 41, 42, 44–46, 48, 50, 51, 53, 56, 57.
H15, 16.

CONTEMPORARY PUBLICATIONS
Q1. W. J. Brennan-Whitmore, *With the Irish in Frongoch*, Dublin 1917.
Q2. Michael Collins, *The Path to Freedom*, new ed., Cork 1968.

LATER PUBLICATIONS

Q3. Tom Barry, *Guerilla Days in Ireland*, Dublin 1949.

Q4. J. Bowyer Bell, *The Secret Army: A History of the IRA 1916–1970*, London 1970. Chatty, disappointing study, with little material on the revolutionary years.

Q5. Tom Bowden, 'The Irish Underground and the War of Independence 1919–21', *Journal of Contemporary History*, VIII, 2 (1973), 3–23.

Q6. Dan Breen, *My Fight for Irish Freedom*, Dublin 1924, enlarged ed., Tralee 1970.

Q7. Tim Pat Coogan, *The I.R.A.*, London 1971.

Q8. Giovanni Costigan, 'The Anglo-Irish Conflict, 1919–1922: A War of Independence or Systematic Murder?', *University Review*, I (1968), 64–86. Decides it was no more murderous than other wars.

Q9. David Hogan [Frank Gallagher], *The Four Glorious Years*, Dublin 1953. Covers 1917–21.

Q10. General Richard Mulcahy, 'Conscription and the General Headquarters' Staff', *Capuchin Annual*, XXXV (1968), 382–95.

Q11. General Richard Mulcahy, 'Chief of Staff—1919', *Capuchin Annual*, XXXVI (1969), 340–52.

Q12. General Richard Mulcahy, 'The Irish Volunteer Convention, 27 October, 1917', *Capuchin Annual*, XXXIV (1967), 400–10. These three items by Mulcahy all provide interesting information.

Q13. Kevin B. Nowlan, 'Dáil Éireann and the Army: Unity and Division', in T. Desmond Williams, ed., *The Irish Struggle 1916–1926*, London 1966, 67–77. See also G. A. Hayes-McCoy, 'The Conduct of the Anglo-Irish War . . .' (pp. 55–66).

Q14. Florence O'Donoghue, *No Other Law: The Story of Liam Lynch and the Irish Republican Army, 1916–1923*, Dublin 1954. Very detailed but rather an official history-biography.

Q15. Florence O'Donoghue, 'Reorganisation of the Irish Volunteers 1916–1917', *Capuchin Annual*, XXXIV (1967), 380–5.

Q16. Florence O'Donoghue, 'Volunteer "Actions" in 1918', *Capuchin Annual*, XXXV (1968), 340–4.

Q17. Ernie O'Malley, *On Another Man's Wound*, London and Dublin 1936.

Q18. Calton Younger, *Ireland's Civil War*, London 1968. Much on pre-Treaty period.

R. Separatism and Social Change

PRIMARY SOURCES

For the history of Labour and the farmers' movement various weekly newspapers were particularly useful. Labour papers after the Rising include *Irish Opinion* (Dec. 1917–Apr. 1918); *The Voice of Labour* (Apr. 1918–Sep. 1919, organ first of the Irish Labour Party, then (from Mar. 1919) of the ITGWU); *The Watchword of Labour* (Sep. 1919–Dec. 1920). Farmers' journals include *The Farmers' Gazette, The Irish Farmer and Stockowner* (to Sep. 1919), *The Irish Farmer* (Sep. 1919–Aug. 1922,

NLI), the IFU's official organ, and *Irish Farming World* (to Sep. 1920). Other sources for this chapter were:
A21, 22 (v).
B7, 8.
F12, 17, 19, 24, 47, 49.
H1, 3, 4, 5, 6, 8, 10, 11, 17, 21.
I2, 8.

CONTEMPORARY PUBLICATIONS

R1. Irish Labour Party and Trades Union Congress (until Nov. 1918, ITUCLP), *Reports of the Annual Meetings* (1918 et seq. in NLI).
R2. ITGWU, *Annual Reports* (1918 et seq. in NLI). Include detailed information on the ITGWU in the provinces.
R3. Michael MacDonagh, 'Sinn Fein and Labour in Ireland', *Contemporary Review*, CXIII (Apr. 1918), 424–33.
R4. J. R. White, *The Significance of Sinn Féin*, Dublin [1919]. Sinn Féin's socialist destiny.

LATER PUBLICATIONS

R5. John W. Boyle, 'Irish Labour and the Rising', *Éire-Ireland*, II (1967), 122–31.
R6. J. Dunsmore Clarkson, *Labour and Nationalism in Ireland*, New York 1925.
R7. Raymond D. Crotty, *Irish Agricultural Production: Its Volume and Structure*, Cork 1966. Interesting account of the imaginative deficiencies of Irish peasants.
R8. R. M. Fox, *Green Banners*, London 1938; and *Labour in the National Struggle*, Dublin 1947.
R9. Nicholas Mansergh, *The Irish Question 1840–1921*, London 1965. Includes useful account of Irish Nationalism in its social and economic context. Regrettably, has 'modified, or altogether removed, exuberances of style which now appear to me no longer tolerable' (cf. 1st ed., 1940).
R10. Arthur Mitchell, 'Labour and the National Struggle 1919–1921', *Capuchin Annual*, XXXVIII (1971), 261–88, and *Labour in Irish Politics*, Dublin 1974.
R11. R. J. P. Mortished, 'Trade Union Organisation in Ireland', *Journal of the Statistical and Social Inquiry Society of Ireland* (1925–26), 213–28.
R12. William O'Brien, *Forth the Banners Go*, Dublin 1969. Labour leader's reminiscences as told to Edward MacLysaght; most revealing, especially for period before 1919.
R13. [Cathal O'Shannon, ed.], *Fifty Years of Liberty Hall*, Dublin 1959.
R14. J. E. Pomfret, *The Struggle for Land in Ireland 1880–1923*, Princeton 1930.

S. County Clare

PRIMARY SOURCES

The county newspapers were a major source on almost all subjects, and were systematically analysed for various purposes (see Chapter 4 and Appendix). The *Clare Champion* was particularly useful for its reports of political meetings, covering virtually every village in the county (at this period it was usual for secretaries to submit reports of virtually every meeting held). The Ennis *Saturday Record* offered an almost identical coverage to its rival until 1917, after which the two papers diverged in their treatment of Sinn Féin. I skimmed the entire series of the *Record*, and carefully analysed the issues from March to September 1918 (when the *Champion* was suppressed). *The Clare Journal and Ennis Advertiser* (to April 1917) used the same matrices as the *Record* but appeared twice weekly. *The Kilrush Herald and Kilkee Gazette* was an almost illiterate but touchingly humble paper, largely set up in England. *The Irish Poultry Weekly* (published in Sixmilebridge between August 1918 and July 1919, then Castleconnell, Co. Limerick, until June 1920) is of strictly specialised interest.

Documentary collections with extensive reference to Clare include:
A14, 21, 22 (iii, v, vi, ix), 28, 29, 30 (ii, iii, iv), 31, 33, 34.
B3, 5, 8.
C1, 2, 5.
D1, 2, 3.
E1, 2.
F1, 4–8, 15,16, 21–25, 29–57.
H1, 3, 4, 8, 10–13, 16, 20, 24.

CONTEMPORARY PUBLICATIONS

S1. M. McD. Bodkin, *Recollections of an Irish Judge: Press, Bar and Parliament*, London 1914.
S2. M. McD. Bodkin, *A Considered Judgement*, Dublin 1921. Concerning Bodkin's awards of compensation to Clare victims of 'reprisals'.
S3. Rev. J. Clancy, *The Failure of 'Parliamentarianism'*, 2nd ed., Ennis 1917–18. Lecture by Sinn Féin leader in West Clare, lightly censored (according to press censorship records in SPO, see A33).
S4. 'Dun Cairin' [Dr Michael Fogarty?], 'The Argument from Irish History', *Studies*, VII (Dec. 1918), 545–52.
S5. Rev. P. Gaynor, *The 'Faith and Morals' of Sinn Féin*, Ennis [1917]
S6. Charles E. Glynn, *List of Kilrush Men Who Served with the Colours during the Great War, 1914–1918*, Waterford 1918. Copy in PRO, CO 904/151.
S7. *In Memoriam. Major Willie Redmond*, Dublin 1918.
S8. Edward E. Lysaght, *The Gael*, Dublin and London 1919. Interesting novel redolent of Clare, taking the enlightenment of a young Nationalist up to the Easter Rising.
S9. Edward MacLysaght, *Poems*, Dublin and London 1928. Including the contents of *Irish Eclogues*, an earlier (and even slimmer) volume.
S10. Edward MacLysaght, *The Small Fields of Carrig*, London 1929. Novel translated from Irish; free from politics except for ungenerous treatment of that curious breed, the Clare landlord.
S11. Francis Macnamara, *Marionettes*, London 1909. More verses by a Clareman.
S12. N. Marlowe, 'A Week in Clare', *Contemporary Review*, CXIII (Apr. 1918), 434–9.

S13. Georgina O'Brien, ed., *The Reminiscences of the Right Hon. Lord O'Brien*, London 1916. Chief Justice of Ireland to 1913, from Kilfenora district.

S14. Arthur Lynch, *Ireland: Vital Hour*, London 1915.

S15. Arthur Lynch, *My Life Story*, London 1924.

S16. Nora Tynan O'Mahony, 'In County Clare', *Irish Monthly*, XLII (1914), 36–9.

S17. William Redmond, 'After Thirty Years: An Irish MP's Recollections of the House', *Westminster Gazette*, 11 Jul. 1913.

S18. *Major William Redmond*, London 1918. Saccharine tributes; includes an 'Appreciation' (pp. 59–60) by Col. Maurice Moore.

S19. [Richard Ross-Lewin], *Poems by a County of Clare West Briton*, Limerick 1907.

S20. The Brothers Ross-Lewin, *In Britain's Need*, Dublin and London 1917.

S21. 'A Holiday in Ireland', *Round Table*, XIV (1924), 310–22.

S22. Co. of Clare, 'Scheme for the Abolition of the Poor Law System' (Jun. 1921). Copy annotated by William T. Cosgrave in SPO (see C5).

S23. *Seoid Cuimhne (Souvenir) of President de Valera's Visit to Ennis August 15, 1924*, Ennis 1924. Includes list and some photographs of Claremen killed during the revolution and Civil War.

LATER PUBLICATIONS

S24. *Conrad M. Arensberg, *The Irish Countryman: An Anthropological Study*, London 1937. Famous study of villages in north-west Clare.

S25. Conrad M. Arensberg and Solon T. Kimball, *Family and Community in Ireland*, Cambridge, Mass. 1940; revised ed., 1968. More detailed but less successful than S24. Revised edition includes unsatisfactory account of Ennis, the county town.

S26. Austin Brennan, 'Forcibly Fed, at Five Bob a Head', *Limerick Leader*, 16 Dec. 1972. Memories of 1917 hunger-striking.

S27. Hugh Brody, *Inishkillane: Change and Decline in the West of Ireland*, London 1973. Study of communal life in coastal Clare.

S28. Kevin J. Browne, 'A Man and a County', *Clare Champion*, Oct. 1971–Jan. 1972. Illustrated extracts from revolutionary *Champions*. (The man is de Valera, the county Clare.)

S29. 'Chief of Staff Retires', *An Cosantóir*, XX (1960), 4–5. (P. A. Mulcahy.)

S30. Robert Cresswell, *Une Communauté Rurale de l'Irlande*, Paris 1969. Portentous sociology of Kinvarra, Co. Galway, near Clare border.

S31. Rafaël Debevere, *William Redmond, 1861–1917*, Rekkem 1967. With brief English résumé of brief Dutch text.

S32. Nicolette Devas, *Two Flamboyant Fathers*, London 1966. One of the fathers was Francis Macnamara of Ennistymon House (cf. S11).

S33. Thomas Dillon, ed., *The Banner*, New York 1963. Anthology of articles on Clare, including Arthur O'Donnell's 'The I.R.A. in Clare', a useful little piece.

S34. James Frost, *County of Clare: Irish Local Names Explained*, Limerick 1906. Essential for historical tourists. Also author of standard history of Clare to 1700.

S35. Ernest A. Hooton and C. Wesley Dupertuis, *The Physical Anthropology of Ireland*, Cambridge, Mass. 1955. Solidest study was done in Co. Clare, though this fascinating book covers all Ireland.

S36. Denis I. F. Lucey and Donald R. Kaldor, *Rural Industrialization*, London, etc., 1969. Heavy study of two communities including Scariff, Co. Clare.
S37. Patrick Lynch, *Some Memories of the Munster Circuit*, Cork 1946; and duplicated but published *Reminiscences*, Cork 1946. Disappointing jottings by de Valera's victim in East Clare, 1917.
S38. J. M. MacCarthy, ed., *Limerick's Fighting Story*, Tralee 1948. Clare references.
S39. E. MacLysaght, *East Clare 1916–1921*, Ennis 1954.
S40. E. MacLysaght, 'The East Clare By-election, July 1917', *Irish Times*, 28 and 29 Nov. 1966.
S41. E. MacLysaght, 'Some Memories of the Irish Convention 1917–1918', *Capuchin Annual*, XXXV (1968), 345–50.
S42. Mgr John T. McMahon, '"The Cream of their Race": Irish Truce Negotiations, 1920–1921', *Clare Champion* (Jun. 1972 *et seq.*). Includes recollections of Dr Fogarty in the revolution. Some chapters shown me in typescript by Mr Patrick Arkins, Galway.
S43. An tAthair Séamus Ó Dea, 'Clare 1920', *Capuchin Annual*, XXXVII (1970), 276–86. A rare attempt to deal with the social rather than military history of the revolution.
S44. Aodh Ó Haichir, *A Rebel Churchman: Very Rev. Canon William O'Kennedy, B.D., St Flannan's, Ennis*, Tralee 1962.
S45. Ernie O'Malley, 'I.R.A. Raids', *Sunday Press*, *passim*. Articles relating to Clare appeared on 23 and 30 Oct., 6 and 13 Nov. 1955. Cf. Q17.
S46. Pádraig Ó Tuile, *Life and Times of Brian O'Higgins*, Navan n.d. Fat title for a slim volume.
S47. Sisters of Mercy, Ennistymon, *Centenary Souvenir, 1872–1972*, Ennistymon 1972.
S48. Very Rev. P. White, *History of Clare and the Dalcassian Clans of Tipperary, Limerick, and Galway*, Dublin 1893. Includes disappointing sketch of nineteenth century in Clare, in which White played a prominent part as a Nationalist.
S49. *With the I.R.A. in the Fight for Freedom 1919 to the Truce*, Tralee n.d. Includes article on Clare by Joe Barrett and Patrick Lynch (not de Valera's opponent).

Index

Reference is made to persons active in Irish life between 1913 and 1921 (with titles and biographical information appropriate to that period), to Irish place-names (by locality in the case of Clare but by county otherwise), to all contemporary societies and institutions mentioned (except for sections of the Irish administration named merely in passing) and to sundry other matters. Little sub-classification has been feasible, but the consequent inconvenience to the user should be reduced by the thematic arrangement of the chapters. Only the seven chapters of text have been analysed.

Aberdeen and Temair, 1st M (1847–1934, Lord Lieutenant 1906–15): 51; Marchioness (1857–1939): 48
active service units, IRA: *see* flying columns
'AE': *see* Russell
agrarian unrest: 4, 18, 41, 43, 61–3, 65, 69, 81, 126, 130–2, 146, 152, 193, 208, 217–18, 220, 229; *see also* boycott, cattle-driving, land purchase, evictions
Agricultural Wages Board (Ireland): 64, 200, 223; *see also* wages
AFIL: 121
AOH (Board of Erin): 32, 73, 74, 80, 82, 83 (map), 84, 86–9, 92, 95–6, 98–9, 103, 115, 121, 146, 216
Anderson, Sir John (1882–1958, Joint US 1920–22): 16
Anti-Partition League, 1916: *see* Irish Nation League; 1918: 57; *see also* IUA
Anti-Sinn Féin Society, Gang or League: 28, 31, 69
arms supply, controls: 91, 177; *see also* DORA
army in Ireland, British: 1, 16–18, 20–1, 23–31, 38, 68, 101, 124, 126, 153, 187, 219; desertions: 31, 168; *see also* Military Areas (Special), martial law
army, Irishmen in British, recruiting: Table 3.1; 7, 55–6, 63, 92–3, 108, 126–7, 199; conscription threats: 32, 34, 56, 98, 108, 126–8, 135, 167, 171, 176–8, 210–12; *see also* National Defence Fund, Mansion House Conference;

ex-servicemen: 8, 19, 64, 86, 101, 135–6, 158, 168–9, 207–8, 215; *see also* RIC
arrests and imprisonment: 1, 15–16, 17, 23, 120, 124–6, 128, 138, 141, 169–70, 174, 180, 184, 219; *see also* RIC, justice
Ashe, Thomas (1884–1917, Easter rebel): 125
Asquith, Herbert Henry (1852–1928): 51, 56, 94
Auxiliaries: *see* RIC

Ballyalla: 43, 48
Ballyvaughan: 162
Barrett, Frank (1891–1931, Master of Ennis Workhouse, Volunteer leader): 172, 183, 187–8, 190–1
Barton, Robert Childers (1881–1975, TD and minister): 91
Béaslaí, Piaras (1881–1965, TD, journalist): 186
Bedford, 11th D (1858–1940): 51
Belfast: 4, 15, 20, 32, 52, 198
Belgian Refugees' Fund: 85
Bianconi, John (born O'Connell, National Volunteers' organiser, Kildysart): 96
Birmingham, George A.: *see* Hannay
Birrell Augustine (1850–1933 CS 1907–16): 108
'Black and Tans': *see* RIC
Blythe, Ernest (1889–1975, TD and minister): 115, 178

316

Bodkin, Mathias McDonnell (1850–1933, Clare County Court judge 1907–22): 4, 11, 13–14, 67
Bodyke: 44
boycott: 8–11, 35, 50, 81, 127, 141, 146, 168, 189, 193, 206; 'Belfast boycott': 143, 215
Brennan, Austin (b. 1894, Meelick, Volunteer leader): 124–5, 156, 172–3
Brennan, Michael (b. 1896, Meelick Volunteer leader): 114, 115, 124–6, 130, 135, 155, 158–9, 161–2, 164, 172, 176, 179–81, 186, 188–91, 226, 229
Brennan, Patrick (b. 1892, Meelick TD for Clare 1921–22, Volunteer leader): 124, 126, 162, 172, 174, 191
Brennan, Robert (b. 1881, Wexford journalist, Sinn Féin and Dáil official): 176
Brugha, Cathal (1874–1922, TD and minister): 165–6, 170, 171, 173, 217
Bunratty Castle: 17
Butler, Misses (of Castlecrine): 42, 58–9

Cappa (near Kilrush): 183
Carrigaholt: 9, 49; *see also* O'Curry Irish College
Carrigoran (near Newmarket): 44, 67
Carron: 113–14
Carson, Sir Edward Henry (1854–1935): 52, 54, 88, 120
Casey, Jack (Newmarket Labour leader): 206
Castlecrine (near Sixmilebridge): 42, 58
casualty figures (Anglo-Irish War): 10, 26, 187
cattle-driving: 51, 62, 65, 130–2, 146, 150, 151, 153
Cavan, Co.: 141
Ceannt, Éamonn (1881–1916, Easter rebel): 107, 114
Childers, Robert Erskine (1870–1922, TD): 78
Churchill, Winston Spencer (1871–1965): 20, 52
Church of Ireland: 40, 46–7, 49, 54–5, 56–7, 66–7, 134
civil dislocation, due to Anglo-Irish War: Table 6.3; 12, 67, 143, 159–60, 181, 187, 189–90, 227

civil restrictions, imposed by British army or administration: 18, 68, 124, 127, 129–30, 163–4, 219, 227; *see also* martial law, Military Areas (Special), DORA, fairs and markets
Civil War (1922–3): 34, 68, 71, 164, 184, 188, 191, 192
Clancy, Rev. James (PP, Kilballyowen, near Carrigaholt): 108, 117
Clare County Club (Ennis): 46, 109, 219
Clifden (near Corofin): 50, 51
Collins, Michael (1890–1922, Volunteer leader, TD and minister): 32, 38, 143–4, 172–4, 175, 176, 178, 189
Committee for Relief of Distress in Ireland, American: 70
Comrades of the Great War, Association of: 102, 208, 214
CDB: 42, 61, 158, 201
Connolly, James (1868–1916, Easter rebel, Labour leader): 199, 207, 210, 211–12, 218
conscription: *see* army
Conyngham, 5th M (1883–1918): 44
co-operation, agricultural: 74–5, 109, 124, 210, 212, 217, 225, 227
Cooraclare: 150
Corcomroe (abbey, near Ballyvaughan): 111
Cork, City and Co.: Table 4.1; 4, 16, 23–7, 29, 39, 46, 47, 64, 71, 80, 82, 93, 99, 110, 117, 120, 125, 167, 171, 173–4, 187, 189, 205, 208, 212, 213, 217, 224, 227
Corkery, Daniel (1878–1964, TD and writer): 111
Corofin: 39, 88, 102, 116
Cosgrave, William Thomas (1880–1965, TD and minister): 70–1, 159, 162, 228
CFA: Chapter 7, part 3; 59–60, 63–4, 162; *see also* IFU
Co. Clare Unionist Club: 49–50, 51, 57–8, 95
Craig, Sir James, 1st Bt (1871–1940, Ulster Unionist leader): 120
Crowe, Rev. Michael (CC, Doora near Ennis): 142
Culligan, Rev. Charles (CC, Carrigaholt): 116
Cumann na mBan: 122, 128, 167, 173, 178, 183, 191, 229

Dáil Éireann (1919–22): Chapter 5; 10, 71, 134, 137, 165–6, 173, 175, 178, 189, 192–3, 216–17, 218, 228; ministry and ministers: Chapter 5; 34, 38, 137, 144–8, 150, 159, 165–6, 175, 189, 228; *see also* local government, justice; internal and external loans: 144, 189

Daly, Constable (RIC): 31

Daly, John (d. 1916, Limerick IRB organiser): 114

Darragh: 170

de Blacam, Aodh (1890–1951): 217

DORA, DORR: 99–100, 113, 177

DATII: 195, 227–8

de Valera, Éamon (1882–1975 Easter rebel, TD for East Clare and Clare, 1917–22, Dáil President): 69, 98–100, 102, 114, 118–22, 123, 128, 130, 133, 136, 139, 142–3, 166–7, 176, 178, 191, 201, 216–17, 228

Devlin, Joseph (1871–1934, MP, AOH organiser): 82, 98, 107

Devoy, John (1842–1928, Irish-American leader): 95

Dillon, John (1851–1927, MP, Nationalist leader): 55, 98, 102, 108, 113, 123, 135

Direct Labour Association: 204, 221

District Clerks' Association: 162

District Cottiers' Association (Newmarket): 204

Doolin: 9, 69

Doonbeg (near Kilkee): 112

Down, Co.: 50

drink: 4, 18, 31, 44, 71, 79, 89–90, 121, 151, 155, 181, 221; *see also* shop-keepers

Dromoland Castle: 55, 64, 67

Dublin City and Co.: 32, 46, 49, 52, 64, 70, 86, 88, 109, 120, 125, 134, 142, 145, 148, 163, 172–3, 174, 176, 198, 204, 212, 213, 221

Dublin Farmers' Association: 221

DMP: 16, 32

Duke, Henry Edward (1855–1939, CS 1916–18): 126, 128

Dunboyne, 17th B (1874–1945, Knoppogue Castle): 159–60

Easter Rising (1916): 7–8, 56, 65, 97, 99, 102, 107–11, 113–20, 121, 139, 166, 169, 175–7, 201, 210, 212

elections (House of Commons): general elections, 1910: 72–3; 1918: 98, 122, 133, 135, 140, 211–12, 226; by-elections, East Clare (July 1917): 17–18, 98–100, 102, 117, 118–20, 122, 124, 129, 130, 141, 167, 176; other: 98, 119, 120

elections (local government bodies), 1902: 113; 1906: 48; 1914: 74, 84, 90, 213; 1920: 101–3, 141, 154, 213–4, 218, 226

emigration: 39, 41, 61, 67, 68, 199

employment: Table 7.1; 19, 42–3, 53, 64, 82, 158–9, 162–4, 196–200, 207, 208, 215, 217, 219, 220–1

Ennis 4, 11, 23, 29, 31, 38–9, 49, 54, 60, 74, 78, 87, 89, 90, 93, 96–8, 101–2, 115, 120–1, 125, 136, 139–40, 147, 151, 159, 162, 172, 183, 194–5, 198, 202, 204, 206, 207–8, 211, 213–4, 216

Ennistymon: 9, 31, 39, 43, 47, 71 (House), 74, 84, 102, 112, 121, 140, 151, 155, 159, 163, 167, 197, 219

Evicted Tenants' Association, Committees: 80, 128

evictions, and victims of: 42, 43, 81, 147, 150, 196, 197–8, 218

ex-servicemen: *see* army

fairs and markets: 18, 59, 60, 122, 140, 143, 152, 216, 223, 227

Falvey, Thomas (Doonaha CFA organiser): 226–7

Farmers' Freedom Force: 224–5, 228; *see also* IFU

Feakle: 31, 76

Fergus, River: 7

Fianna Éireann: 128, 167–8, 178, 183–4, 191

Figgis, Darrell (1882–1925, writer and Sinn Féin organiser): 15, 70–1, 140

FitzGerald, Lady Clara (widow of Sir Augustine FitzGerald, Bt, of Carrigoran): 46, 67

Fitzgerald, Maurice (JP, Cahirciveen, Kerry): 48

FitzGerald, William Walter Augustine (second husband of Lady Clara): 44, 67

flying columns: 34, 70, 180–1, 183–6, 188, 190–1

Fogarty, Most Rev. Michael (1859–1955, Roman Catholic Bishop of Killaloe from 1904): 55, 89, 94, 117, 124, 127, 229
French, Sir John Denton Pinkstone (1852–1925, Lord Lieutenant 1918–21): 67
Friends of Irish Freedom (American): 144

GAA: 79–80, 84, 85–6, 90, 111–12, 128–30
Gaelic League: 49, 75, 79, 85, 86, 88, 109, 111–12, 115, 129–30, 174
Gallagher, Patrick (1873–1966, 'Paddy the Cope'): 75
Galway, City and Co.: 4, 110, 114, 129, 149, 176, 214
Gárda Síochána: 38; *see also* Police, Republican
Gaynor, Rev. Patrick (1887–1949, CC, Kilmurry-Ibrickane or Mullagh, Sinn Féin organiser): 107–8, 127, 140, 150, 162, 189, 216
GPB: 126; *see also* arrests
Glynn, Rev. John (PP, Kilmurry-Ibrickane): 118
Gonne-MacBride, Maud (1866–1953): 48
Government of Ireland legislation, 1914: 49, 50–1, 53, 68, 78, 91, 93, 97, 108–9; 1920: 39, 63, 68
Grand Lodge of Ireland (Masonic): 67, 225
Green, Alice Stopford (1847–1929, historian): 86, 139
Greenwood, Sir Hamar (1870–1948, CS 1920–22): 29
Griffith, Arthur (1872–1922, TD and minister, founder of Sinn Féin): 97, 113, 122, 137, 139, 141, 142
Griffy, Nicholas (Clerk of Ennistymon Union): 85

Hales, Seán (d. 1922, TD and Volunteer leader, Cork): 27
Hannay, James Owen (1865–1950, 'George A. Birmingham'): 53, 72, 85, 118, 121
Healy, Timothy Michael (1855–1931, MP, Cork, Nationalist leader): 98
Hibbert, Capt. Robert F. (of Woodpark, Scariff): 62, 65–6
Hickman, Mrs: 63

Hobson, Bulmer (1882–1969, Belfast IRB organiser, INV founder): 175
Home Rule legislation: *see* Government of Ireland legislation
Honan, Thomas Vincent (c. 1875–1954, Ennis Sinn Féin organiser): 29
hunger-strikes: 125, 219
Hunt, Hubert J. (Corofin politician): 116, 142, 172
Hyde, Douglas (1860–1949, founder of Gaelic League): 111

imprisonments: *see* arrests
income tax: 143–4
Inchiquin, Anne, Lady (d. 1975, widow of 16th B): 47
Inchiquin, Ethel, Lady (d. 1940, wife of 15th B): 6, 71
Inchiquin, 15th B (1864–1929, of Dromoland Castle): 42, 43, 49, 57, 59–60
Irish administration: *boards and departments separately indexed*
Irish Citizen Army: 128
Irish Convention (1917–18): 57, 69, 123–4, 226
Irish Dominion League: 70
IFU: Chapter 7, part 3; 43, 60, 63, 70, 194, 218; *see also* CFA, Dublin Farmers' Association
Irish Food Control Committee: 140
ILPTUC (until 1918, ITUCLP): Chapter 7, parts 1–2; 64; *see also* Trades and Labour Councils
Irish Land Commission (and Estates Commissioners): 42, 61, 148, 158; *see also* Land Commission (established by the Dáil)
Irish Landowners' Convention: 52, 59, 222
Irish Nation League: 100, 120–1, 171
Irish National Foresters: 73, 80, 128
Irish National Volunteers (Nov. 1913 to Oct. 1914 split): Table 4.1; 53–4, 79, 85–6, 87 (map) 88–91, 112, 114, 168, 170; *see also* Irish Volunteers, National Volunteers
Irish Parliamentary Party: Chapter 3; 53–4, 56, 70, 107–9, 111, 120, 122–3, 127, 128, 133, 135, 139, 192–3, 209, 211–12

Irish Peace Conference (1920 Dublin): 70
IRA: *see* Irish Volunteers
IRB: 114–15, 142, 170–1, 201
ITUCLP: *see* ILPTUC
ITGWU: Table 7.4; Chapter 7; 34, 101, 136
IUA: 45, 49, 52, 55–7, 62, 225; *see also* Anti-Partition League
Irish Volunteers (Oct. 1914–1916, including MacNeillite sections of INV): 54, 76, 96, 112, 114–15, 116, 168, 170, 177
Irish Volunteers (1916–22): Tables 6.1, 6.2, 6.3; Chapter 6; 9–10, 15, 18, 27, 31–2, 34, 38–9, 62–7, 70, 76, 110, 119–20, 122, 124–30, 135, 137, 141–3, 146, 147, 149–51, 153–5, 158–9, 161, 164, 182 (map), 192–3, 208, 210, 214, 218–21, 227–9

Johnson, Thomas (1872–1963, Labour leader): 210
justice, 'British' administration: Table 1.1, 4–5, 11–14, 48, 141, 148, 153; *see also* martial law, RIC; Republican administration: Table 5.1; Chapter 5, part 2; 12, 141–2, 148–9, 218, 225, 230; *see also* Police, Republican

Keane, Thomas J. (of Ennis): 125
Kerry, Co.: Table 4.1; 11, 25, 30, 38, 48, 67, 82, 91, 93, 97–8, 99, 117, 152, 156, 167, 174, 176, 198, 205, 217
Kettle, Thomas J. (1880–1916, publicist): 78
Kilbaha (near Carrigaholt): 114
Kildare, Co.: 18, 20, 28, 205, 223
Kildysart (Killadysert): 206
Kilfearagh (near Kilkee): 10
Kilkee: 4–5, 9, 44, 86, 151, 152
Kilkenny, City and Co.: 117, 141, 224
Killaloe: 23
Kilkishen (near Tulla): 60
Kilmurry (near Sixmilebridge): 40
Kilnamona (near Inagh): 195
Kilnasoolagh (parish including Dromoland): 55
Kilrush: 44, 55, 67, 77, 93, 94, 98, 101–2, 128, 140, 146, 155, 157, 159, 178, 183, 198, 204, 206, 208–9, 214

Kipling, Joseph Rudyard (1865–1936): 52
Kitchener of Khartoum, 1st E (1850–1916): 92
Knoppogue Castle (near Quin): 159–61

Labourers' and Farmers' Association: 198
Lahinch: 31, 46, 88, 183
Land and Labour Association: 73, 80, 84, 198, 200–2, 221, 223
land annuities: 143–4, 158, 228; *see also* rental, land purchase
Land Commission (established by Dáil): 148; *see also* Irish Land Commission
land purchase: Table 7.3; 41–2, 61–3, 65, 71, 80, 146, 196, 200–1, 215, 217–18, 227–8; *see also* land annuities, rental, evictions, CDB, Irish Land Commission
Larkin, James J. (1876–1947, Labour leader): 199
Law, Andrew Bonar (1858–1923): 53, 63, 156, 227
Ledden, James (b. *c*. 1865, Limerick IRB organiser): 189
Leix (Queen's Co.): 109
Liberty League: 116, 117, 120–1, 171
Limerick, City and Co.: Table 4.1; 6, 12, 15, 25, 26, 29, 32, 40, 43, 80, 88, 93, 96, 114, 119–20, 145, 167, 173, 176, 189, 198, 211, 212, 214, 219, 222, 224
Limerick and Clare Farmers' Association: 222, 224; *see also* CFA
Linnane, P. J. (Ennis politician): 49
Lismehane: 43, 55–6, 66
Listowel, 3rd E (1883–1924): 71
Lloyd George, David (1863–1945): 20, 56–7, 59, 70, 108–9, 123–4, 142, 150
Local Government Board (Ireland): 70, 156–7, 161, 192; local bodies: Table 5.2; Chapter 5, part 3; 5, 48, 62, 74, 77, 84–5, 94, 101–3, 121, 140, 191, 208, 213–14; Republican administration: Chapter 5, part 3; 141–3, 191, 192, 215, 220, 230
London Metropolitan Police: 32
Long, Walter Hume (1854–1924, CS 1905): 145
Longford, Co.: 147
Louth, Co.: 11

Lynch, Arthur Alfred (1861–1934, Australian-born MP for West Clare, 1909–18): 44, 73, 81, 95, 97, 98, 102–3
Lynch, Diarmuid (Jeremiah Christopher, 1878–1950, Cork IRB organiser): 114
Lynch, Fionán (TD, Kerry): 174
Lynch, Patrick (d. 1947, lawyer, de Valera's opponent in East Clare 1917): 98–100, 119, 128
Lysaght, Edward: *see* MacLysaght
Lyttelton, Sir Neville Gerald (1845–1931, army commander in Ireland 1908–12): 17

MacCurtain, Tomás (1884–1920 Lord Mayor of Cork): 125, 173
MacDermott, Seán (1883–1916, Easter rebel): 107, 115
MacDonagh, Thomas (1878–1916, Easter rebel): 108, 111
McElroy, George (b. 1869, Ennis RM 1910–20): 4, 14, 63–4, 112, 151
McKenna, Rev. Michael (CC, Kilmurry-Ibrickane, Volunteer leader): 150
MacLysaght, Edward Edgeworth Anthony (b. 1887, named Lysaght until 1920, Raheen employer, writer, National Volunteer organiser): 46, 86, 88–9, 96, 109–10, 119, 122, 123–4, 127, 134, 168, 195, 200, 206
Macnamara, Henry Valentine (1861–1925, of Ennistymon House): 43, 46, 48–50, 58, 62, 66, 69, 95
MacNamara, Patrick J. (Ennis Labour leader): 89, 91, 93, 96, 101, 164, 202
Mac Néill, Eóin (1867–1945, founder of Gaelic League and INV): 69, 96, 123, 139–40, 174–5; MacNeillite Volunteers: *see* Irish Volunteers
Macready, Sir Cecil Frederick Nevil (1862–1946, GOC in Ireland 1920–23): 28–32, 38
MacSwiney, Terence James (1879–1920, Lord Mayor of Cork): 125, 189
Mahaffy, Sir John Pentland (1839–1919, historian): 118
Mahon, Sir Bryan Thomas (1862–1930, army commander in Ireland 1916–18): 92

Mannix, Most Rev. Daniel (1864–1963, Cork-born Archbishop of Melbourne from 1917): 117
Mansion House Conference (1918): 210–11; *see also* army (conscription)
markets: *see* fairs
Markievicz, Constance Georgina (1868–1927, Labour leader, sister of Gore-Booth gazelle): 48
martial law: 17–18, 25, 28, 117, 141; *see also* Military Areas (Special)
Maxwell, Sir John Grenfell (1859–1929, army commander in Ireland 1916): 56, 110, 117, 175
Mayo, Co.: 147
Meath, Co.: 133, 172, 205, 223
Meelick: 114, 170
Mellows, Liam (1892–1922, Easter rebel, IRB organiser): 176
Midleton, 9th V (1856–1942, IUA leader): 57–8
Mid-Ulster Farmers' Union: 225
Military Areas, Special: 8, 18, 62, 126, 133, 220
military engagements, Anglo-Irish War: Table 6.3; Chapter 6; 9–10 26, 32, 65–6, 69; *see also* casualty figures, Easter Rising, Rineen, Ruan, Shessamore, 'reprisals'
Miltown Malbay: 31, 91, 219
Monteagle of Brandon, 2nd B (1849–1926): 57
Montgomery, Capt. Bernard Law (1887–1976): 26
Moore, Col. Maurice George (1854–1939, INV organiser): 46, 68, 86, 89, 91, 96, 99
Mount Callan: 43, 64–5, 67, 71
Mulcahy, Patrick A. (b. 1897, Richard's brother, Ennis Volunteer officer 1919): 172
Mulcahy, Richard James (1886–1971, TD and minister, Volunteer organiser): 171–3, 176, 178, 187–8
Mullagh: 88, 150
Murphy, William Martin (1844–1921, Cork and Dublin businessman): 221
Mutton Island (near Miltown): 150

Nathan, Sir Matthew (1862–1939, US 1914–16): 108
National Defence Fund, Committee (against conscription): 34, 115, 127, 142
National Land Bank, Ltd (Republican): 144, 228
National Union of Railwaymen: 219
National Volunteers (from Oct. 1914): 54, 73, 84, 87 (map), 92–7, 99, 101, 109, 114–16; *see also* Irish National Volunteers
Neligan, David (b. 1899, DMP): 34
Newmarket-on-Fergus: 128, 204, 206

O'Brien, Hon. Edward Donough (1867–1943, of Roslevan): 66
O'Brien, Florence Vere (d. 1936, of Ballyalla House): 43, 48–9, 51, 53–4, 64, 67, 69; Hugh Murrough Vere (1887–1955, her son, INV organiser): 54; Robert Vere (1842–1913, her husband): 51
O'Brien William (1852–1928, MP, founder of UIL and AFIL): 72, 98, 107; his political supporters: 76, 117, 120
O'Callaghan-Westropp, Col. George (1864–1944, O'Callaghan until 1885, of Lismehane; organiser of IFU, CFA and IUA): 42–71, 81, 162, 164, 169, 190, 222–3, 226–8
O'Connor, Arthur John (1888–1950, TD and minister): 146–8, 158
O'Connell Club (Ennis): 73
O'Curry Irish College (Carrigaholt): 49, 112, 133
Oddfellows, Society of: 73
O'Donnell, Arthur (1890–1974, Volunteer organiser from Tullycrine): 170, 172
O'Duffy, Eóin (1892–1945, TD and Volunteer organiser): 185
Offaly (King's Co.): 127, 172
O'Grady, Standish James (1846–1928, Irish scholar): 48
O'Hegarty, Patrick Sarsfield (1879–1955, Sinn Féin publicist): 135, 178–9
O'Higgins, Brian (b. 1882, TD for West Clare and Clare, 1918–22): 133, 146
O'Higgins, Kevin Christopher (1892–1927, TD and minister): 150–1, 156, 158

O'Kelly, Seán T. (1883–1966, organiser of Gaelic League and Sinn Féin): 217
O'Kennedy, Rev. William (1881–1932, President of St Flannan's College from 1919): 129, 132, 134, 142
Ó Lochlainn, Tomás (d. 1918, Carron organiser of IRB and Sinn Féin): 113–15
O'Loghlen, Sir Michael, 4th Bt (1866–1934, of Drumconora near Ennis): 60
O'Loghlen, Peter Joseph (d. 1972 of Ballyvaughan, local politician): 162
O'Malley, Earnán (1898–1957, Volunteer organiser): 76, 171, 174, 178
O'Mara, Stephen Mary (1885–1926, Mayor of Limerick): 120
O'Neill, Major the Hon. Robert William Hugh (b. 1883, Ulster Unionist MP): 63
Orange Order: 82
O'Shannon, Cathal (1889–1969, TD and Labour leader): 204, 208, 210, 216, 219
O'Shea, Constable Michael (RIC, Kilrush): 6, 21
O'Shiel, Kevin R. (Dáil Land Commissioner): 147–8, 150, 152

Paris Peace Conference (1918–19, and Versailles Treaty): 19, 119, 134, 136, 145
Parsons, Sir Lawrence Worthington (1850–1923, army commander at Cork 1906–9): 45; Nora (his daughter): 45, 47
Pearse, Pádraic (1879–1916, Easter rebel): 55, 107, 110, 165, 170, 175–6,
pensions: 7, 34, 36, 38–9, 161, 173, 183, 190, 215; *see also* wages
Pim, Herbert Moore (b. 1883, Belfast publicist): 120
Plunkett, George Noble (1851–1948, Papal Count, TD and minister, poet): 102, 116, 117, 119, 120, 136; *see also* Liberty League
Plunkett, Sir Horace Curzon (1854–1932, agriculturist): 44, 57, 123; *see also* co-operation (agricultural)
Police, Republican: 9, 34, 38, 142, 149–50, 151–2, 161; other police forces: *see* Anti-Sinn Féin Society, DMP, Gárda Síochána, London Metropolitan Police, RIC

Police and Prison Officials' Union (Dublin): 32
Police Employment Bureau (Republican): 34
Presbyterian Church: 47
press: 74, 76–7, 92, 95, 99–101, 113, 120, 134, 178–9
prices and profits: Table 7.2; 6, 58–9, 62, 63–5, 69, 118, 140, 199, 209, 215, 227–8

Raheen (HQ, East Clare Brigade, Volunteers): 96, 110, 195, 206
Ratecollectors' Association: 221
Ratepayers' Protective Associations: 49, 79, 84, 221–2, 226 (Clare), 214 (Galway)
rates, local government: 71, 113, 143, 156, 157–8, 160–2, 164, 193, 221–2, 228
Red Guards: 205, 224; see also ITGWU
Redmond, John Edward (1856–1918, MP, Nationalist leader): 54, 57, 72–3, 77, 78, 81, 88–92, 94–100, 102, 108–9, 112, 119, 123, 201
Redmond, William Hoey Kearney (1861–1917, MP for East Clare 1891–1917): 69, 73, 78, 88–9, 91, 93, 97–8, 128, 130
rental: 12, 41–2, 43–4, 48, 59, 143, 153, 163, 223; see also land annuities, land purchase
Repeal League (1916): 120
'reprisals': 28–9, 68–9, 186–7, 219, 227; see also army, RIC, military engagements, Anti-Sinn Féin Society, Ennistymon, Lahinch, Miltown Malbay, Ennis
Rineen (ambush): 31, 45, 186, 219
Roberts, Albert Augustine (b. 1861, Ennis CI, RIC, 1910–13): 6
Robinson, Sir Henry Augustus, 1st Bt (1856–1927, head of LGB(I), 1898–1922): 192
Roman Catholic Church: 8, 30, 54, 75–7, 82, 89, 95, 107–8, 112, 116–18, 121, 127–9, 132, 140, 149–50, 152, 168, 209, 216
Roscommon, Co.: 119, 120, 146
Roslevan House (near Ennis): 66
Ross-Lewin, Rev. Richard Sargint Sadleir (1848–1921, Rector of Kilmurry): 40–1, 46, 50, 55 (and his reverend brother)

RIC: Tables 1.2, 1.3, 1.4, 1.5, 1.6, 1.7, 1.8, 7.4; Chapter 1; 62, 66, 81, 91, 96, 101, 111–13, 115, 118, 124–5, 127, 129–30, 134, 136, 141, 143, 145–6, 150–1, 152–3, 167, 171, 172, 177, 183, 186–7, 190; 'Black and Tans': 16, 20–3, 25, 26, 35, 37, 155, 183–4, 206; Auxiliary Division (1921–2): Tables 1.4, 1.5; 20, 23–7, 29–30, 34, 39; resignations and dismissals: Tables 1.4–1.8; 31, 34–9; recruiting: Tables 1.2, 1.3; 7–8, 19–21
Ruan: 34
Russell, George William (1867–1935, 'AE', writer and agriculturalist): 110, 123–4

St Flannan's Training College (Ennis): 117–18
St Vincent de Paul Society (Kilrush): 140
Scariff: 62, 122
Self-Determination Fund: 144
Senate, of Southern Ireland (1921): 70; of Irish Free State (1922, Seanad Éireann): 71
Shalee (near Ennis): 195
Shannon, River: 54, 208
Shessamore (ambush, near Doolin): 66, 69
shopkeepers and publicans: 74–5, 89, 116, 132, 134, 146, 168, 185, 198–9, 207, 209, 220–1; see also boycott, drink, prices
Sinn Féin: Table 4.1; Chapters 4 and 7, part 2; 10, 31–4, 37, 68–9, 72, 98, 101–4, 131 (map), 139–42, 145–6, 149, 154, 156, 165, 167, 169, 171, 173–5, 177, 192–3, 201–2, 204, 207–8, 220–1, 227, 230
Smyth, Lt-Col. Brice Ferguson (1885–1920, RIC Divisional Commissioner at Cork): 30
Stack, Austin (1880–1929, TD and minister): 146–7, 149, 151, 153, 172–4
Stacpoole, Richard John (1870–1959, of Edenvale House near Ennis): 50, 59–60, 63
strikes: 32, 64, 153, 202, 205–6, 208, 219, 224; see also hunger-strikes
Strong, Anna Louise: 48
Sturgis, Mark Beresford Russell (1884–1949, Joint Assistant US 1920–22): 30

teachers: 75, 80, 112, 114, 127, 136
tillage, controls upon: 59, 62, 130, 199, 227
Tipperary, Co.: 8, 10, 23, 26, 109, 171, 180, 205
Tottenham, Lt-Col. Frederick St Leger (1850–1933, of Mount Callan): 59, 64–5, 67, 71; Mabel (d. 1914, his wife): 43
Town Tenants' Association: 80, 84
Trade and Labour Association (Union): 80, 198, 201–2, 204, 206
Trades and Labour Council, Ennis United: 101–2, 198, 202, 204–5, 211, 213; others: 194, 211, 217, 223; *see also* ILPTUC
trade unions: *see* ILPTUC, ITGWU, National Union of Railwaymen, Direct Labour Association, IFU, Police and Prison Officials' Union, United Labourers' Association, Trade and Labour Association
Treacy, Seán (1895–1920, Tipperary Volunteer leader): 180
'Treaty' (December 1921, Articles of Agreement for a): 68, 71, 226
'Truce' (July 1921, cessation of hostilities in Ireland): 38, 68, 152–3, 161, 190
Tuamgraney: 54, 88
Tudor, Brig.-Gen. Henry Hugh (b. 1871, Police Adviser, 1920–22): 29–30
Tulla: 9, 47, 60, 127
Tullycrine: 170, 180

Ulster Farmers' Union: 225
Ulster Provisional Government (1914): 52

Ulster Unionist Party: 56, 108
Ulster Volunteers: 52, 85
unemployment: *see* employment
UIL: Table 4; 1, 61, 75–6, 80–4, 83 (map), 86, 88–9, 96, 98–9, 113, 115, 121, 129, 201, 220
United Labourers' Association (Ennis): 101, 194, 202, 207

Vandeleur, Alexander Moore (1885–1914, of Kilrush): 44
Volunteers: *see* Ulster Volunteers, Irish Volunteers, Irish National Volunteers, National Volunteers

wages: Table 7.2; 6–7, 16, 19–20, 32, 43, 60, 63–4, 157, 160, 164, 195–6, 198–200, 205–9, 210, 215–16, 217–18, 220, 223, 227, 230; *see also* pensions, prices, employment
Waldron, Éamonn (d. 1966, Mayo-born organiser of Ennistymon Gaelic League, Volunteers): 114
Waterford, City and Co.: 211–12
Wexford, Co.: 73, 110, 212, 224–5
Wicklow, Co.: 73, 89, 91
Wilson, Woodrow (1856–1924): 136
Wimborne, 2nd B (1873–1939, Lord Lieutenant 1915–18): 55
Woodpark (near Mountshannon): 65–6

Yeats, William Butler (1865–1939, prophet): 44, 111, 134, 165, 192